CHURCH HISTORY

BOARD OF EDITORS

EDITOR IN CHIEF

Daniel H. Ludlow
Brigham Young University

SENIOR EDITORS

Robert J. Matthews
Brigham Young University

Charles D. Tate, Jr.
Brigham Young University

Robert K. Thomas
Brigham Young University

EDITORS

Stan L. Albrecht
Brigham Young University

S. Kent Brown
Brigham Young University

Richard L. Bushman
Columbia University

Ronald K. Esplin
Brigham Young University

Addie Fuhriman
University of Utah

Jeanne B. Inouye
Provo, Utah

Truman G. Madsen
Brigham Young University

Terrance D. Olson
Brigham Young University

Larry C. Porter
Brigham Young University

Noel B. Reynolds
Brigham Young University

John W. Welch
Brigham Young University

PROJECT COORDINATOR

Doris Bayly Brower

CHURCH HISTORY

SELECTIONS FROM THE

ENCYCLOPEDIA OF MORMONISM

EDITED BY

DANIEL H. LUDLOW

DESERET BOOK COMPANY
SALT LAKE CITY, UTAH

© 1992 by Macmillan Publishing Company, a division of Macmillan, Inc.

This collection of articles from the *Encyclopedia of Mormonism* is published by Deseret Book Company under license from Macmillan Publishing Company.

© 1995 by Deseret Book Company

All rights reserved. No part of this book may be reproduced or transmitted in any form or by any means, electronic or mechanical, including photocopying, recording, or by any information storage and retrieval system, without permission in writing from Macmillan Publishing Company, 866 Third Avenue, New York, NY 10022 or Maxwell Macmillan Canada, Inc., 1200 Eglinton Avenue East, Suite 200, Don Mills, Ontario M3C 3N1.

Deseret Book is a registered trademark of Deseret Book Company.

Library of Congress Cataloging-in-Publication Data

Encyclopedia of Mormonism. Selections.
Church History : selections from the Encyclopedia of Mormonism / edited by Daniel H. Ludlow.
p. cm.
Includes bibliographical references and index.
ISBN 0-87579-924-8
1. Church of Jesus Christ of Latter-day Saints—Encyclopedias. 2. Mormon Church—Encyclopedias. 3. Mormons—Encyclopedias. I. Ludlow, Daniel H. II. Title.
BX8605.5.E62 1995
289.3'03—dc20 94-44792
CIP

Printed in the United States of America

10 9 8 7 6 5 4 3 2 1

CONTENTS

LIST OF ARTICLES

LIST OF CONTRIBUTORS

Douglas D. Alder
Dixie College, St. George, UT
Comprehensive History of the Church

Thomas G. Alexander
Brigham Young University
Salt Lake City, UT

James B. Allen
Brigham Young University
History of the Church: c. 1945–1990
McKay, David O.

A. Gary Anderson
Brigham Young University
Smith, Joseph, Sr.
Smith Family Ancestors

Karl Ricks Anderson
Business Consultant, Lyndhurst, OH
Consecration: Consecration in Ohio and Missouri
Hiram, Ohio

Paul L. Anderson
Museum of Church History and Art, Salt Lake City
Tabernacle, Salt Lake City

Richard Lloyd Anderson
Brigham Young University
Cowdery, Oliver
Smith, Lucy Mack

Harriet Horne Arrington
Historian, Salt Lake City
Smith, Bathsheba Bigler

Leonard J. Arrington
Brigham Young University
Economic History of the Church
History of the Church: c. 1844–1877
Pioneer Economy
Young, Brigham: Brigham Young

Danel W. Bachman
Church Educational System, Salt Lake City
Plural Marriage

Milton V. Backman, Jr.
Brigham Young University
History of the Church: c. 1831–1844
First Vision
Kirtland, Ohio

Howard H. Barron
Brigham Young University
Hyde, Orson

Alexander L. Baugh
Church Educational System, Columbia, SC
Patten, David W.

Maureen Ursenbach Beecher
Brigham Young University
Biography and Autobiography
Snow, Eliza R.
Snow, Lorenzo

Evalyn Darger Bennett
Writer, Lecturer, Salt Lake City
Williams, Clarissa

Richard E. Bennett
University of Manitoba, Winnipeg, Manitoba
Canada, The Church in
Council Bluffs (Kanesville), Iowa
Winter Quarters

Reed A. Benson
Brigham Young University
Benson, Ezra Taft

Joseph Ivins Bentley
Attorney, Newport Beach, CA
Martyrdom of Joseph and Hyrum Smith
Smith, Joseph: Legal Trials of Joseph Smith

LaMar C. Berrett
Brigham Young University
Adam-ondi-Ahman
Independence, Missouri
Salt Lake Valley

Jack M. Bethards
Schoenstein Organ Co., San Francisco
Tabernacle Organ

Alma R. Blair
Graceland College, Lamoni, IA
Haun's Mill Massacre

David F. Boone
Brigham Young University
Perpetual Emigrating Fund (PEF)

Edward J. Brandt
Church Correlation Dept., Salt Lake City
Wentworth Letter

R. Lanier Britsch
Brigham Young University
Asia, The Church in: Asia, East
Asia, The Church in: Asia, South and Southeast
Hawaii, The Church in
Oceania, The Church in

Richard L. Bushman
Columbia University
History of the Church: c. 1820–1831
Smith, Joseph: The Prophet

D. James Cannon
Consultant, Salt Lake City
Pioneer Day

Donald Q. Cannon
Brigham Young University
Kane, Thomas L.
King Follett Discourse

Janath Russell Cannon
Church Temple Matron, Frankfurt, Germany
Robison, Louise Yates

Michael C. Cannon
Church News, Salt Lake City
Deseret Industries

Shirley A. Cazier
Writer, Logan, UT
Rogers, Aurelia Spencer

Lance D. Chase
Brigham Young University—Hawaii
Zion's Camp

Horace H. Christensen
IBM, Endwell, NY
Harmony, Pennsylvania

Howard A. Christy
Brigham Young University
Handcart Companies
Richmond Jail

Don F. Colvin
Church Educational System, Ogden, UT
Nauvoo Temple

Richard O. Cowan
Brigham Young University
History of the Church: c. 1945–1990

Julio E. Dávila
General Authority, Salt Lake City
South America, The Church in: South America, North

Ray Jay Davis
Brigham Young University
Antipolygamy Legislation

Sheri L. Dew
Deseret Book Co., Salt Lake City
Benson, Ezra Taft

Reed C. Durham, Jr.
Church Educational System, Logan, UT
Nauvoo Expositor
Westward Migration, Planning and Prophecy

William G. Eggington
Brigham Young University
Australia, The Church in

S. George Ellsworth
Utah State University, Logan, UT
History, Significance to Latter-day Saints
Smith, George Albert

Jessie L. Embry
Brigham Young University
Parmley, LaVern Watts

Donald L. Enders
Museum of Church History and Art, Salt Lake City
Carthage Jail
Sacred Grove

Amy Lyman Engar
Writer, Salt Lake City
Lyman, Amy Brown

Ann Willardson Engar
University of Utah
Lyman, Amy Brown

Flavia Garcia Erbolato
Church Area Historian, São Paulo, Brazil
South America, The Church in: Brazil

Ronald K. Esplin
Brigham Young University
History of the Church: c. 1831–1844
Mountain Meadows Massacre
Plural Marriage

Max J. Evans
Utah State Historical Society, Salt Lake City
Forgeries of Historical Documents

Lawrence R. Flake
Church Educational System, Missoula, MT
Liberty Jail

Philip M. Flammer
Brigham Young University
Nauvoo Legion

Robert B. Flanders
Southwest Missouri State University, Springfield, MO
Nauvoo Economy

Lamar E. Garrard
Brigham Young University
Colesville, New York
Fayette, New York

Leland H. Gentry
Church Educational System, Salt Lake City
Missouri: LDS Communities in Caldwell and Daviess Counties

L. Brent Goates
LDS Hospital, Salt Lake City
Lee, Harold B.

Kenneth W. Godfrey
Church Educational System, Logan, Utah
Council of Fifty

Bryan J. Grant
Church Public Communications, Nuneaton, Warks, England
British Isles, The Church in the

Richard F. Haglund, Jr.
Vanderbilt University
Intellectual History

Elizabeth Huntington Hall
Writer, Orem, UT
Silk Culture

Annette P. Hampshire
Writer, Upminster, Essex, England
Nauvoo Politics

Marion D. Hanks
General Authority, Salt Lake City
Salt Lake Temple

Edwin O. Haroldsen
Brigham Young University
West Indies, The Church in the

William G. Hartley
Brigham Young University
History of the Church: c. 1878–1898
Immigration and Emigration

Lisa Bolin Hawkins
Brigham Young University
Persecution

Harvard S. Heath
Brigham Young University
Smoot Hearings

Frank W. Hirschi
Church Educational System, Centerville, UT
Consecration: Law of Consecration

Helene Holt
Brigham Young University
Nauvoo House

Richard P. Howard
Reorganized Church of Jesus Christ of Latter Day Saints, Independence, MO
Reorganized Church of Jesus Christ of Latter Day Saints (RLDS Church)

L. Dwight Israelsen
Utah State University, Logan, UT
United Orders

Richard H. Jackson
Brigham Young University
City Planning
Historical Sites

Florence Smith Jacobsen
Formerly with Church Arts and Sites, Salt Lake City
Taylor, Elmina Shepard

Rhett Stephens James
Church Educational System, Logan, UT
Harris, Martin

Richard L. Jensen
Brigham Young University
Colonization
Colorado, Pioneer Settlements in
Immigration and Emigration
New Mexico, Pioneer Settlements in

Dean C. Jessee
Brigham Young University
Smith, Joseph: The Prophet
Smith, Joseph: Writings of Joseph Smith
Woodruff, Wilford

Clark V. Johnson
Brigham Young University
Missouri: LDS Communities in Jackson and Clay Counties

Jeffery Ogden Johnson
Utah State Archives, Salt Lake City
Deseret, State of

R. Val Johnson
International Magazines, Salt Lake City, Utah
Hunter, Howard W.

Edward L. Kimball
Brigham Young University
Kimball, Heber C.
Kimball, Spencer W.

James L. Kimball, Jr.
Church Historical Dept., Salt Lake City
Nauvoo Charter
"This Is the Place" Monument

Stanley B. Kimball
Southern Illinois University, Edwardsville, IL
Kinderhook Plates
Mormon Pioneer Trail

John Langeland
Zions First National Bank, Salt Lake City
Scandinavia, The Church in

E. Dale LeBaron
Brigham Young University
Africa, The Church in

Glen M. Leonard
Museum of Church History and Art, Salt Lake City
Nauvoo

Tomás Frederico Lindheimer
Writer, Buenos Aires, Argentina
South America, The Church in: South America, South

Edward Leo Lyman
Victor Valley College and California State University, San Bernardino
Utah Statehood

Carol Cornwall Madsen
Brigham Young University
Smith, Emma Hale
Wells, Emmeline B.

Gordon A. Madsen
Attorney, Salt Lake City
South Bainbridge (Afton), New York

Susan Arrington Madsen
Author, Hyde Park, UT
Horne, Mary Isabella
Smith, Mary Fielding

Truman G. Madsen
Brigham Young University Center for Near Eastern Studies, Jerusalem, Israel
Smith, Joseph: Teachings of Joseph Smith

Robert D. Marcum
Church Educational System, Rexburg, ID
Idaho, Pioneer Settlement in

Robert L. Marrott
Church Educational System, Bloomington, IN
Testator

Dean L. May
University of Utah
History of the Church: c. 1844–1877

Amelia S. McConkie
Writer, Salt Lake City
Smith, Joseph Fielding

Mark L. McConkie
University of Colorado at Colorado Springs
Smith, Joseph Fielding

Charles L. Metten
Brigham Young University
Salt Lake Theatre

Samuel C. Monson
Brigham Young University
Deseret Alphabet

James R. Moss [deceased]
Former Utah State Superintendent of Education, Salt Lake City
Missions of the Twelve to the British Isles

Maren M. Mouritsen
Brigham Young University
Spafford, Belle Smith

Hugh W. Nibley
Brigham Young University
Young, Brigham: Teachings of Brigham Young

Richard G. Oman
Museum of Church History and Art, Salt Lake City
Beehive Symbol

Howard Palmer [deceased]
University of Calgary
Canada, LDS Pioneer Settlements in

Scott Parker
Intermountain Health Care, Inc., Salt Lake City
Deseret Hospital

Stephen Parker
Doctoral Candidate, University of Chicago
Deseret

Max H Parkin
Church Educational System, Salt Lake City
Lamanite Mission of 1830–1831
Missouri Conflict

Keith W. Perkins
Brigham Young University
Kirtland Temple
Whitmer, David
Whitney Store

Charles S. Peterson
Utah State University, Logan, UT
Arizona, Pioneer Settlements in

Paul H. Peterson
Brigham Young University
Manifesto of 1890
Reformation (LDS) of 1856–1857

Louise Plummer
Brigham Young University
Gates, Susa Young

Richard D. Poll
Western Illinois University, Macomb, IL
Utah Expedition

Larry C. Porter
Brigham Young University
Far West, Missouri
History of the Church: c. 1820–1831
Palmyra/Manchester, New York
Pratt, Parley Parker
Visions of Joseph Smith

Allan Kent Powell
Utah State Historical Society, Salt Lake City
Utah Territory

Carolyn J. Rasmus
Brigham Young University
Temple Square

Sydney Smith Reynolds
Author, Orem, UT
Smith Family

Mary Stovall Richards
Brigham Young University
Kimball, Sarah Granger
Wells, Emmeline B.

Eldin Ricks [deceased]
Brigham Young University
Moroni, Visitations of

Robert E. Riggs
Brigham Young University
Legal and Judicial History of the Church
Reynolds v. United States

Shirley Taylor Robinson
Writer, Chihuahua, Mexico
Mexico, Pioneer Settlements in

Maxine Lewis Rowley
Brigham Young University
Home Industries

Boanerges Rubalcava
Medical Research, Barcelona, Spain
Mexico and Central America, The Church in

Richard W. Sadler
Weber State University, Ogden, UT
History of the Church: c. 1898–1945
Seagulls, Miracle of

Howard C. Searle
Church Educational System, Salt Lake City
Historians, Church
History of the Church (History of Joseph Smith)

Gene A. Sessions
Weber State University, Ogden, UT
History of the Church: c. 1878–1898

Robert L. Simpson
General Authority, Salt Lake City
New Zealand, The Church in

Paul Thomas Smith
Church Educational System, Salt Lake City
Snow, Lorenzo
Taylor, John
Wells, Junius F.

Steven R. Sorensen
Church Historical Dept., Salt Lake City
Schools of the Prophets

Martin S. Tanner
Attorney, Salt Lake City
Schismatic Groups

Linda Thatcher
Utah Historical Society, Salt Lake City
Fox, Ruth May

Douglas F. Tobler
Brigham Young University
Europe, The Church in
History, Significance to Latter-day Saints

James A. Toronto
Brigham Young University
Middle East, The Church in the

Richard E. Turley, Jr.
Church Historical Dept., Salt Lake City
Mountain Meadows Massacre

Bruce A. Van Orden
Brigham Young University
Rigdon, Sidney
Smith, Hyrum
Smith, Joseph F.

Ronald W. Walker
Brigham Young University
Grant, Heber J.
History of the Church: c. 1898–1945
Pioneer Life and Worship

Ted J. Warner
Brigham Young University
California, Pioneer Settlements in
Nevada, Pioneer Settlements in
Wyoming, Pioneer Settlements in

Dale A. Whitman
University of Missouri, Columbia, MO
Extermination Order

David J. Whittaker
Brigham Young University
Danites
Intellectual History
Missions of the Twelve to the British Isles
Pratt, Orson

Ted L. Wilson
University of Utah
Salt Lake City, Utah

Larry T. Wimmer
Brigham Young University
Kirtland Economy

Mary Firmage Woodward
Writer, Provo, UT
Young, Zina D. H.

John F. Yurtinus
University of Nevada, Carson City
Mormon Battalion

PREFACE

This preface appears in volume 1 of the Encyclopedia of Mormonism. *Its spirit applies to all the volumes containing selections from the* Encyclopedia.

According to a standard definition, an encyclopedia is to "treat comprehensively all the various branches of knowledge" pertaining to a particular subject. The subject of this *Encyclopedia* is The Church of Jesus Christ of Latter-day Saints, widely known as the Mormon church. This is the first major encyclopedia published about the Mormons. It presents the work of hundreds of Latter-day Saint (LDS) lay scholars and others from throughout the world and provides a comprehensive reporting of Mormon history, scripture, doctrines, life, and knowledge, intended for both the non-Mormon and the LDS reader. Readers will find an article on almost any topic conceivably related to the general topic of Mormonism, and yet no article is exhaustive because of space limitations. Most articles include bibliographic references; cross-references to other articles in the *Encyclopedia* are indicated by small capital letters.

When Macmillan Publishing Company asked authorities at Brigham Young University whether they would be interested in developing an encyclopedia about The Church of Jesus Christ of Latter-day Saints, President Jeffrey R. Holland took the query to his Board of Trustees. They instructed him to proceed. Working closely with Church authorities and Macmillan, President Holland chose an editor in chief and a board of editors. Discussion of possible titles concluded that the work should be called the *Encyclopedia of Mormonism* since that is the term by which the Church is most widely known, though unofficially.

The contract called for a work of one million words in about 1,500 articles in four volumes including pictures, maps, charts, appendices, indices, and a glossary. It soon became apparent that references to what the Church calls the standard works—the Bible, the Book of Mormon, the Doctrine and Covenants, and the Pearl of Great Price—would be so frequent that readers who did not have ready access to those works would be at a serious disadvantage in using the *Encyclopedia.* A fifth volume was decided upon to include all the LDS standard works except the Bible, which is readily available everywhere.

The Church does not have a paid clergy or a battery of theologians to write the articles. It functions with a lay ministry, and all members are encouraged to become scholars of the gospel. Over 730 men and women were asked to write articles on topics assigned because of previous interest and study.

Six major articles unfold the history of the Church: (1) the background and founding period in New York; (2) the Ohio, Missouri, and Illinois period ending with the martyrdom of Joseph Smith; (3) the exodus west and the early pioneer period under Brigham Young; (4) the late pioneer Utah period ending at the turn of the century and statehood; (5) a transitional period during the early twentieth century; and (6) the post–World War II period of international growth. The history of the Church has been dramatic and moving, considering its brief span of just over 160 years. Compared to Catholicism, Judaism, ancient Far East religions, and many Protestant churches, the Church has a very short history. Nearly 250 articles explain the doctrines of the Church, with special emphasis on basic principles and ordinances of the gospel of Jesus Christ. Twenty-four articles are clustered under the title "Jesus Christ," and another sixteen include his name in the title or relate directly to his divine mission and atonement.

Over 150 articles relate the details on such topics as the First Vision, Zion's Camp, Handcart Companies, Plural Marriage, the Salt Lake Temple, Temple Square, and the Church throughout the world. Biographies cover men and women contemporary in the life of Joseph Smith, Presidents of the Church, and auxiliary founders and past presidents. The only biography of a person living at the time of publication is on the present prophet and President of the Church, Ezra Taft Benson. [Since the publication of the *Encyclopedia of Mormonism,* Howard W. Hunter was sustained as President of the Church.]

And finally, there are over a hundred articles primarily concerned with how Latter-day Saints relate to their families, the Church, and to society in general. It is said there is a "Mormon culture," and several articles explore Mormon lifestyle, folklore, folk art, artists, literature, and other facets that distinguish Latter-day Saints.

It may be that the growth of the Church in the last decades has mandated the encyclopedic account that is presented here. Yet, even as the most recent programs were set down and the latest figures listed, there is an acute awareness that the basic tenet of the Church is that its canon is open-ended. The contemporary President of the Church is sustained as a "prophet, seer, and revelator." While this makes some theological discussion moot, the basic beliefs of the Latter-day Saints, summarized in the Articles of Faith, do not change.

In several areas, the Church shares beliefs held by other Christians, and a number of scholars from other faiths were asked to present articles. However, the most distinctive tenets of the Church—those regarding the premortal and postmortal life, living prophets who receive continuous and current revelation from God, sacred ordinances for deceased ancestors, moral and health codes that provide increasingly well-documented benefits, and the potential within man for progression into an infinite future—are all treated primarily by writers selected from among Latter-day Saints.

Lest the role of the *Encyclopedia* be given more weight than it deserves, the editors make it clear that those who have written and edited have only tried to explain their understanding of Church history, doctrines, and procedures; their statements and opinions remain their own. The *Encyclopedia of Mormonism* is a joint product of Brigham Young University and Macmillan Publishing Company, and the contents do not necessarily represent the official position of The Church of Jesus Christ of Latter-day Saints. In no sense does the *Encyclopedia* have the force and authority of scripture.

ACKNOWLEDGMENTS*

The support and assistance of many persons and groups are necessary to produce a work as extensive as an encyclopedia. Special thanks are extended to the executives of Macmillan Publishing Company who introduced the idea of the the *Encyclopedia of Mormonism* to Brigham Young University. Charles E. Smith made initial contacts on the project, while Philip Friedman, President and Publisher of Macmillan Reference Division, and Elly Dickason, Editor in Chief of Macmillan Reference Division, have followed through on the multitudinous details, demonstrating skill and patience in working with us in the preparation of this five-volume work.

The editors also wish to thank the General Authorities of the Church for designating Brigham Young University as the contractual Author of the *Encyclopedia.* Two members of the Board of Trustees of the university, who are also members of the Quorum of the Twelve Apostles, were appointed by the First Presidency to serve as advisers to the project: Elder Neal A. Maxwell and Elder Dallin H. Oaks. Other General Authorities who accepted special assignments related to the project include four members of the Quorum of Seventy: Elders Dean L. Larsen, Carlos E. Asay, Marlin K. Jensen, and Jeffrey R. Holland.

Special support also came from the Administration of BYU. Jeffrey R. Holland, president of BYU at the time the project was initiated, was instrumental in appointing the Board of Editors and in developing early guidelines. Rex E. Lee, current president of BYU, has continued this support.

* The major parts of the acknowledgments appear in volume 1 of the *Encyclopedia of Mormonism.* The statement has been modified here by (1) deleting credits to individuals and institutions providing general help, illustrations, and photographs for the *Encyclopedia* and (2) adding the names of those giving special assistance to the preparation of this particular publication.

The efforts of the Board of Editors and the Project Coordinator, whose names are listed at the front of each volume, have shaped and fashioned every aspect of the project. We offer special thanks to them, and to companions and family members for graciously supporting our efforts over many months. Others who shared in final editing include Bruce B. Clark, Soren F. Cox, Marshall R. Craig, and Ellis T. Rasmussen.

Many others have provided assistance in specialized areas, including Larry E. Dahl, Michelle Eckersley, Gary R. Gillespie, Devan Jensen, Luene Ludlow, Jack M. Lyon, Robert J. Matthews, Frank O. May, Charlotte McDermott, Robert L. Millet, Don E. Norton, Monte S. Nyman, Patricia J. Parkinson, Charlotte A. Pollard, Larry C. Porter, Merle Romer, Evelyn E. Schiess, Judith Skousen, Charles D. Tate, Jr., Jay M. Todd, and John Sutton Welch. Special thanks also to Ronald Millett and Sheri Dew at Deseret Book Company for their help with this volume.

Finally, we express appreciation to the 738 authors who contributed their knowledge and insights. The hopes of all who were involved with this project will be realized if the *Encyclopedia* assists readers to come to a greater understanding and appreciation of the history, scriptures, doctrines, practices, and procedures of The Church of Jesus Christ of Latter-day Saints.

TOPICAL OUTLINE

The topical outline is designed to help the reader discover all the articles in this volume related to a particular subject. The title of every article in this volume is listed in the topical outline at least once.

The volume *Church History* contains the major articles from the *Encyclopedia of Mormonism* concerned with the history of the Church, including bibliographies of leaders and articles relating to the growth and distribution of the Church.

A. **Major persons associated with the organization and development of the Church.**

1. *Joseph Smith, his forebears, and immediate family members:* Smith, Emma Hale; Smith Family; Smith Family Ancestors; Smith, Hyrum; Smith, Joseph* (*see also* Prophet Joseph Smith); Smith, Joseph, Sr.; Smith, Lucy Mack.

2. *Close associates and supporters of the Prophet Joseph Smith:* Cowdery, Oliver; Harris, Martin; Hyde, Orson; Kane, Thomas L.; Kimball, Heber C.; Patten, David W.; Pratt, Orson; Pratt, Parley P.; Rigdon, Sidney; Smith, Mary Fielding; Snow, Eliza R.; Snow, Lorenzo; Taylor, John; Whitmer, David; Woodruff, Wilford; Young, Brigham*.

3. *Subsequent Presidents of the Church* (listed alphabetically): Benson, Ezra Taft; Grant, Heber J.; Hunter, Howard W.; Kimball, Spencer W.; Lee, Harold B.; McKay, David O.; Smith, George Albert; Smith, Joseph F.; Smith, Joseph Fielding; Snow, Lorenzo; Taylor, John; Woodruff, Wilford; Young, Brigham*.

* Indicates additional related articles are clustered under that entry title.

4. *Biographies of other leaders and of friends of the Church,* including some founders and presidents of auxiliary organizations: Fox, Ruth May; Gates, Susa Young; Horne, Mary Isabella; Kimball, Sarah Granger; Lyman, Amy Brown; Parmley, LaVern Watts; Robison, Louise Yates; Rogers, Aurelia Spencer; Smith, Bathsheba Bigler; Spafford, Belle Smith; Taylor, Elmina Shepard; Wells, Emmeline B.; Wells, Junius F.; Williams, Clarissa; Young, Zina D. H..

B. Major events and places associated with the establishment and development of the Church.

1. *Entries associated with events and places in the western New York area around Palmyra:* Colesville, New York; Fayette, New York; First Vision; Harmony, Pennsylvania; Harris, Martin; Historical Sites; History of the Church*; New York, Early LDS Sites in; Palmyra/Manchester, New York; Prophet Joseph Smith; Sacred Grove; South Bainbridge (Afton), New York; Visions of Joseph Smith.

2. *Entries associated with the Ohio area around Kirtland:* Consecration*; Hiram, Ohio; Historical Sites; History of the Church*; Kirtland, Ohio; Kirtland Economy; Kirtland Temple; Lamanite Mission; Ohio, LDS Communities in; Schools of the Prophets; Whitney Store.

3. *Entries associated with the Missouri area around Independence, Jackson County:* Adam-ondi-Ahman; Book of Commandments; Consecration*; Danites; Extermination Order; Far West, Missouri; Haun's Mill Massacre; Historical Sites; History of the Church*; Independence, Missouri; Lamanite Mission; Liberty Jail; Missouri*; Missouri Conflict; Patten, David W.; Reorganized Church of Jesus Christ of Latter Day Saints (RLDS); Richmond Jail; Zion's Camp.

4. *Entries associated with the Illinois area around Nauvoo:* Carthage Jail; City Planning; Council of Fifty; Historical Sites; History of the Church*; Illinois, LDS Communities in; Iowa, LDS Communities in; King Follett Discourse;

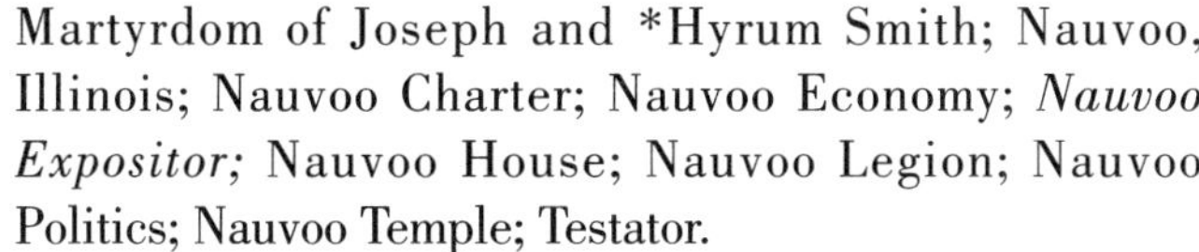

Martyrdom of Joseph and *Hyrum Smith; Nauvoo, Illinois; Nauvoo Charter; Nauvoo Economy; *Nauvoo Expositor;* Nauvoo House; Nauvoo Legion; Nauvoo Politics; Nauvoo Temple; Testator.

5. *Entries associated with the exodus from Nauvoo, Illinois, and the migration to the Great Basin:* Council Bluffs (Kanesville), Iowa; Council of Fifty; Handcart Companies; Historical Sites; History of the Church*; Immigration and Emigration; Iowa, LDS Communities in; Kane, Thomas L.; Mormon Battalion; Mormon Pioneer Trail; Perpetual Emigrating Fund (PEF); "This Is the Place" Monument; Westward Migration, Planning and Prophecy; Winter Quarters.

6. *Entries associated with the pioneering efforts of Brigham Young and with the Territory of Deseret:* Arizona, Pioneer Settlements in; California, Pioneer Settlements in; Canada, Pioneer Settlements in; Colonization; Colorado, Pioneer Settlements in; Danites; Deseret Alphabet; Deseret, State of; Historical Sites; History of the Church*; Home Industries; Idaho, Pioneer Settlements in; Mexico, Pioneer Settlements in; Mountain Meadows Massacre; Nevada, Pioneer Settlements in; New Mexico, Pioneer Settlements in; Pioneer Day; Pioneer Economy; Pioneer Life and Worship; Plural Marriage; Polygamy; Reformation (LDS) of 1856-1857; Salt Lake City, Utah; Salt Lake Temple; Salt Lake Theatre; Salt Lake Valley; Seagulls, Miracle of; Silk Culture; Tabernacle Organ; Tabernacle, Salt Lake City; United Orders; University of Deseret; Utah Expedition; Utah Territory; Wyoming, Pioneer Settlements in; Young, Brigham*.

7. *Entries associated with the establishment of the state of Utah:* Beehive Symbol; Historical Sites; History of the Church*; Manifesto of 1890; Salt Lake City, Utah; Temple Square; Utah Statehood.

8. *Entries associated with the growth and dispersion of the Church in the twentieth century:* Africa, The Church in;

Asia, The Church in*; Australia, The Church in; British Isles, The Church in the; Canada, The Church in; Europe, The Church in; Hawaii, The Church in; Historical Sites; History of the Church*; Mexico and Central America, The Church in; Middle East, The Church in the; New Zealand, The Church in; Oceania, The Church in; Scandinavia, The Church in; South America, The Church in*; West Indies, The Church in the.

9. *General items pertaining to the history of the Church:* Biography and Autobiography; Council of Fifty; Economic History of the Church; Forgeries of Historical Documents; Historians, Church; Historical Sites; History of the Church*; *History of the Church* (History of Joseph Smith); History, Significance to Latter-day Saints; Intellectual History; Kinderhook Plates; Legal and Judicial History; Missions of the Twelve to the British Isles; Persecution; Pioneer Economy; Pioneer Life and Worship; *Reynolds v. United States;* Schismatic Groups; Schools of the Prophets; Smoot Hearings; Temple Square; United Orders; Wentworth Letter.

KEY TO ABBREVIATIONS

AF	Talmage, James E. *Articles of Faith.* Salt Lake City, 1890. (All references are to pagination in printings before 1960.)
BOM	The Book of Mormon: Another Testament of Jesus Christ. Salt Lake City, 1981.
CHC	*Comprehensive History of the Church,* 6 vols., ed. B. H. Roberts. Salt Lake City, 1930.
CR	*Conference Reports.* Salt Lake City, 1898–.
CWHN	*Collected Works of Hugh Nibley,* ed. S. Ricks, J. Welch, et al. Salt Lake City, 1985–.
Dialogue	*Dialogue: A Journal of Mormon Thought,* 1965–.
D&C	The Doctrine and Covenants of The Church of Jesus Christ of Latter-day Saints. Salt Lake City, 1981.
DS	Smith, Joseph Fielding. *Doctrines of Salvation,* 3 vols. Salt Lake City, 1954–1956.
ER	*Encyclopedia of Religion,* 16 vols., ed. M. Eliade. New York, 1987.
F.A.R.M.S.	Foundation for Ancient Research and Mormon Studies. Provo, Utah.
HC	*History of the Church,* 7 vols., ed. B. H. Roberts. Salt Lake City, 1st ed., 1902; 2nd ed., 1950. (All references are to pagination in the 2nd edition.)
HDC	Historical Department of the Church, Salt Lake City.
IE	*Improvement Era,* 1897–1970.
JC	Talmage, James E. *Jesus the Christ.* Salt Lake City, 1915.
JD	*Journal of Discourses,* 26 vols., ed. J. Watt. Liverpool, 1854–1886.
JST	*Joseph Smith Translation of the Bible.*
MD	McConkie, Bruce R. *Mormon Doctrine,* 2nd ed. Salt Lake City, 1966.
MFP	*Messages of the First Presidency,* 6 vols., ed. J. Clark. Salt Lake City, 1965–1975.
PGP	The Pearl of Great Price. Salt Lake City, 1981.
PJS	*Papers of Joseph Smith,* ed. D. Jessee. Salt Lake City, 1989.
PWJS	*The Personal Writings of Joseph Smith,* ed. D. Jessee. Salt Lake City, 1984.
T&S	*Times and Seasons,* 1839–1846.
TPJS	*Teachings of the Prophet Joseph Smith,* comp. Joseph Fielding Smith. Salt Lake City, 1938.
WJS	*Words of Joseph Smith,* ed. A. Ehat and L. Cook. Provo, Utah, 1980.

A

ADAM-ONDI-AHMAN

Adam-ondi-Ahman, a settlement in Daviess County, Missouri, received its unusual name from the Prophet Joseph SMITH in 1838 when Latter-day Saints were moving into the area. Members of the Church had been forced out of Jackson County, Missouri, in 1833 after three years of temporary asylum, and were subsequently asked to leave Clay County. When they appealed to the state legislature to make a new county "for Mormons," Caldwell and Daviess counties were organized. The Saints immediately moved into Caldwell County with Far West as the county seat, and soon also began settling in adjoining Daviess County. In May 1838 Joseph Smith led surveyors to a horseshoe bend of the Grand River, seventy miles north of present-day Kansas City, and proclaimed a new community, which he named Adam-ondi-Ahman because, said he, "it is the place where Adam shall come to visit his people, or the Ancient of Days shall sit, as spoken of by Daniel the Prophet" (*HC* 3:35; D&C 116). Orson Pratt interpreted the name to mean "Valley of God, where Adam dwelt" (*JD* 18:343).

The Prophet's revelations indicated several things about the area: (1) the Garden of Eden was located in Jackson County, Missouri, and after Adam was expelled from the garden, he went north to Adam-ondi-Ahman; (2) three years before Adam's death, he gathered the righteous of his posterity to Adam-ondi-Ahman and bestowed upon them his last blessing; (3) this site would be the location of a future meeting of the Lord with Adam and the Saints, as spoken of by the prophet Daniel (Dan. 7:9–14, 21–27; 12:1–3).

When Joseph Smith arrived in the valley with the survey team, he found three or four Latter-day Saint families already living there and made the log cabin of Lyman Wight his headquarters. From June to October 1838, the population of the two-mile-square Adam-ondi-Ahman increased to about 400 people. Another 600 scattered throughout Daviess County viewed Adam-ondi-Ahman as their capital city.

Approximately 90 percent of the Saints in Daviess County settled on land under "preemption rights," which meant that the government had not yet made the land available for purchase. Believing that they would eventually own the land, the Latter-day Saints worked hard to develop their farms. In June 1838, when the third stake of the Church was organized at Adam-ondi-Ahman, with John Smith as stake president, a peaceful atmosphere seemed to prevail. However, in July the settlers were served public notice to leave Daviess County or face serious consequences. The Saints placed their militia in a state of readiness to defend themselves. When hostilities erupted in August, the militia from Church headquarters at Far West went to Adam-ondi-Ahman, but no battle ensued. Similar action occurred in September.

On October 11, mobs forced the Latter-day Saints from DeWitt in Carroll County and then turned to Daviess County, intent on driving them all out of the state. They burned cabins, stole animals, and harassed families. When the Far West militia arrived for the third time, in October 1838, Church members throughout Daviess County gathered to Adam-ondi-Ahman for safety, and the community's population swelled to more than a thousand. Confinement in tents and wagons and a sudden snowstorm added to their miseries.

While Joseph Smith and the Far West militia were in Adam-ondi-Ahman during October, the Church members assembled to witness the dedication of the public square by Brigham YOUNG. At this time, Joseph Smith pointed out a location where Adam had once built an altar. In May the Prophet had identified this same site as one that had also been used by early American Indians.

After the October plundering and burnings by the mobs and

retaliatory actions by the Latter-day Saints, who were intent on defending themselves, the state militia forced them to surrender their arms on November 7, 1838, and gave them ten days to move to Far West. Adam-ondi-Ahman was abandoned and fell into the hands of non-Mormon settlers. Church families from Daviess County spent the winter at Far West before being expelled from the state in the spring of 1839.

The Missourians who were responsible for expelling Church members from Daviess County knew that in four days their land would be offered for sale by the U.S. government. With the Mormons gone, these residents purchased the improved land and reaped the benefits of the Saints' labor.

John Cravens purchased most of the central area of the city of Adam-ondi-Ahman and renamed it Cravensville. The town existed for thirty-two years and had enough residents to vie with Gallatin for the county seat of Daviess County, but after 1871 the land was returned to farming and grazing.

In 1944 Wilford C. Wood purchased thirty-eight acres at Adam-ondi-Ahman for the Church, and an additional 3,000 acres have since been purchased. Archival research and archaeological excavation have helped to determine the location, size, nature, and history of the city.

BIBLIOGRAPHY

McConkie, Bruce R. *The Millennial Messiah*, pp. 575–88. Salt Lake City, 1982.

LAMAR C. BERRETT

AFRICA, THE CHURCH IN

The Church of Jesus Christ of Latter-day Saints has been a presence in Africa since 1853, but for the first 125 years it was established only in southern Africa. Applications by the Church for admittance into central Africa in the 1960s were denied, but those in 1978 were approved, and growth of the Church there has been impressive.

From 1853 until 1978 most of the work of the Church in Africa was with European immigrants and their descendants in South Africa and in Northern and Southern Rhodesia (now Zambia and Zimbabwe, respectively). In June 1978, when the First Presidency announced the revelation extending the priesthood to all worthy male members of the Church, the way was opened for the Church to extend its full program to all the nations of Africa (see D&C, Official Declaration—2). Missionaries were sent to Nigeria and Ghana at the request of many local people who had already studied the Church scriptures and literature and had organized themselves into units that they unofficially called The Church of Jesus Christ of Latter-day Saints. Church missions were later organized in Zaire, Sierra Leone, Liberia, the Ivory Coast, and Mauritius and Reunion islands.

The establishment of the Church in Africa began at a special Church conference in Salt Lake City in August 1852, when President Brigham YOUNG called 106 men to leave their wives in charge of their families, homes, farms, and businesses and go on missions to various lands of the world to proclaim the restored gospel. Three were called to go to South Africa: Jesse Haven, William H. Walker, and Leonard I. Smith, with Elder Haven assigned to preside. Leaving their families in the care of God, they arrived at the Cape of Good Hope on April 18, 1853, and set about to establish the Church in South Africa, encouraging the converts to "gather to Zion" in Utah. The missionaries faced heavy opposition from the local clergy and indifference to their message among the people generally; fewer than 200 people accepted baptism in the two and a half years they served.

One of the first converts in South Africa in 1853 was Nicholas Paul, a thirty-year-old builder who aided and protected missionaries and let them use his home for meetings. He became the president of the first branch of the Church in Africa, which was organized in his home in Mowbray (Cape Town area). The 1853 missionaries also organized a branch of the Church in Port Elizabeth. When they returned to their families in America in 1855, other missionaries from America and South Africa were called to replace them. Between 1855 and 1865, 278 converts to the Church emigrated from South Africa to Utah.

No LDS missionaries served in South Africa from 1866 to 1903, and the Church grew slowly. Missionaries returned in 1903 and served until 1940, when they were withdrawn because of World War II. During those years 230 missionaries had worked in South Africa. Since the return of LDS missionaries to South Africa in 1944, the

Church has grown steadily there and also expanded to other areas of Africa.

In addition to the efforts of foreign missionaries, much of the growth of the Church in Africa has resulted from the service of local members. Johanna Fourie instituted the Primary program for teaching the children in 1932 and spent the rest of her life (thirty-eight years) guiding and building this program throughout South Africa.

In 1954 President David O. MCKAY became the first General Authority of the Church to visit South Africa. The first LDS Church stake in South Africa was organized in Johannesburg in 1970, with Louis P. Hefer as stake president. That stake was divided into two stakes in 1978. In 1972 Church seminaries and institutes of religion were introduced into southern Africa. All African countries in which the Church is established now have these programs. The added weekday religious training of the youth has increased local missionary participation. In 1973 President Spencer W. KIMBALL pronounced a dedicatory prayer upon the land of South Africa which included the promise that wards and stakes would dot the land and a temple would be built there. New stakes were created in Durban (1981) and Cape Town (1984). The first black African stake was organized in 1988 in Aba, Nigeria, with David W. Eka as its president.

Church growth in Africa since 1978 has been much higher in percentage than in the rest of the world. The major challenge is no longer to gain converts but to prepare local priesthood leadership. And as the Church continues to expand into sub-Saharan Africa, it must face the challenges of poverty and illiteracy. In addition to contributing to famine relief programs, the Church is helping its members in Africa to learn and implement the principles of self-reliance and independence.

The Church has always tried to teach the gospel in the language of the people. As Afrikaans is an official language in South Africa, many missionaries sent there have learned to speak it. The Book of Mormon was published in Afrikaans in 1973, and the Doctrine and Covenants and the Pearl of Great Price in 1981. The Book of Mormon has also been translated into several African languages: Efik (Nigeria, 1983), Kissi (Kenya, 1983), Malagasy (Madagascar, 1986), Akan (Ghana, 1987), Zulu (South Africa, 1978), and Shona (Zimbabwe, 1988). Local members have helped make these translations possible, such as Pricilla Sampson-Davis, a retired schoolteacher from Cape Coast, Ghana, who translated the Book of Mormon, LDS Hymns, and other Church publications into Akan. Translations into additional African languages continue in process.

One of the most significant events in the history of the Church in Africa was the dedication of the temple in Johannesburg in 1985, which has made it possible for the members to receive locally all the ordinances of the Church and to perform them in proxy for their deceased ancestors. The first temple president and matron of this temple were Harlan W. and Geraldine Merkley Clark. Although the work of the Church in Africa was slow and localized from 1853 until the 1980s, Elder Alexander B. Morrison of the Seventy stated in 1987: "The gleaning and gathering of the children of God in Africa is just beginning. In the words of the Prophet Joseph, it will go forward 'boldly, nobly, and independent, till . . . [the truth of God has] swept every country, and sounded in every ear, till the purposes of God shall be accomplished, and the Great Jehovah shall say the work is done'" (p. 26).

BIBLIOGRAPHY

Brigham, Janet. "Nigeria and Ghana: A Miracle Precedes the Messengers." *Ensign* 10 (Feb. 1980):73–76.

LeBaron, E. Dale. "Gospel Pioneers in Africa." *Ensign* 20 (Aug. 1990):40–43.

———. *All Are Alike unto God.* Salt Lake City, 1990.

Lye, William. "From Burundi to Zaire: Taking the Gospel to Africa." *Ensign* 10 (Mar. 1980):10–15.

Mabey, Rendell N., and Gordon T. Allred. *Brother to Brother: The Story of Latter-day Saint Missionaries Who Took the Gospel to Black Africa.* Salt Lake City, 1984.

Morrison, Alexander B. "The Dawning of a New Day in Africa." *Ensign* 17 (Nov. 1987):25–26.

E. DALE LEBARON

ANTIPOLYGAMY LEGISLATION

Bigamy is the crime of marrying while an undivorced spouse from a valid prior marriage is living. Because many prominent nineteenth-century Mormon men became polygamists under Church mandate, both their vulnerability to prosecution for bigamy and the legal attacks on the Church and its members for supporting PLURAL MARRIAGE created a crisis for Mormonism during the 1870s and 1880s.

Bigamy was recognized as an offense by the early English ecclesiastical courts, which considered it an affront to the marriage sacrament. Parliament enacted a statute in 1604 that made bigamy a felony cognizable in the English common law courts. After American independence, the states adopted antibigamy laws, but they received little attention until the nineteenth century in Utah.

The United States government has constitutional power to enact laws governing territories, and under that authority Congress enacted the Morrill Act (1862), making bigamy in a territory a crime punishable by a fine and five years in prison. The statute was upheld in REYNOLDS V. UNITED STATES (1879), although the defendant argued that the law violated the First Amendment guarantee of the free exercise of religion.

Few Mormons were prosecuted for bigamy because the government had difficulty obtaining testimony about plural wedding ceremonies. Rather, they were charged with bigamous cohabitation, a misdemeanor created by the Edmunds Act (1882). Proving cohabitation was easy enough, and over 1,300 Latter-day Saints were jailed as "cohabs" in the 1880s.

Antipolygamy legislation also put pressure on the Church by threatening members' civil rights and Church property rights. The Edmunds Act barred persons living in POLYGAMY from jury service, public office, and voting. The Edmunds-Tucker Act (1887) disincorporated both the Church and the PERPETUAL EMIGRATING FUND on the ground that they fostered polygamy. Furthermore, it authorized seizure of Church real estate not directly used for religious purposes, and acquired in excess of a $50,000 limitation imposed by the Morrill Act. In the Idaho Territory a test oath adopted in 1885 was used to ban all Mormons (and former Mormons) from voting because of the Church's position on polygamy.

In 1890 after the U.S. Supreme Court upheld the seizure of Church property under the Edmunds-Tucker Act in *The Late Corporation of the Mormon Church v. United States* and the Idaho test oath in *Davis v. Beason*, it became clear that plural marriage was leading toward the economic and political destruction of the Church.

Shortly after these decisions, a revelation was received by President Wilford WOODRUFF, who then withdrew the requirement for worthy males to take plural wives and announced the MANIFESTO, formally stating his counsel to Latter-day Saints to abide by antibigamy laws (see D&C Official Declaration—1). The Manifesto ended the legal confrontation between the U.S. government and the Church.

Congress passed a final federal antibigamy provision in 1892, which excluded polygamists from immigration into the United States. This exclusion remains part of the U.S. Immigration and Naturalization Code.

Utah, Oklahoma, New Mexico, and Arizona incorporated antibigamy provisions into their turn-of-the-century state constitutions as required by Congress for admission to the Union. Idaho's constitution not only outlaws bigamy but also bars polygamists and persons "celestially married" from public office and voting. However, that was interpreted in *Budge v. Toncray* by the Idaho court not to include monogamous Mormons married in an LDS temple.

During the twentieth century, federal and state governments have prosecuted other polygamists under a variety of general statutes. For example, federal officials have filed cases against polygamists, charging unlawful use of the mails to proselytize for polygamy and alleging that moving plural wives across state boundaries violates laws against interstate kidnapping and interstate transportation of women for immoral purposes. Because of their practice of plural marriage, polygamists have also had legal troubles with state laws about adoption, inheritance, and government employment. Changing social attitudes about unconventional personal relationships may undermine the use of legislation in this way. For example, in 1988 an Arizona court held that it was illegal to deny a law enforcement security bond to an admitted polygamist merely because of his marital status.

Laws against plural marriage and its practitioners were enacted with reforming zeal. Congress and party platforms considered Mormon polygamy and southern slavery the "twin relics of barbarism." However, the lawmakers were not so forthcoming about their own religious bigotry: their aim was to destroy the Church's economic and political power, and bigamy was their tool. The Church's temporal position was eroded, but it survived the crisis.

BIBLIOGRAPHY
American Law Institute. *Model Penal Code and Commentaries*, Sec. 230.1. Philadelphia, 1980.
Davis, Ray Jay. "The Polygamous Prelude." *American Journal of Legal History* 6 (1962):1–27.
Driggs, Ken. "The Prosecutions Begin." *Dialogue* 21 (1988):109–125.

RAY JAY DAVIS

ARIZONA, PIONEER SETTLEMENTS IN

Mormon pioneering in Arizona began in the mid-1800s and continued until well after 1900, and was especially active from 1873 until 1890. Latter-day Saints first came to Arizona in 1846, with the march of the MORMON BATTALION from Santa Fe to southern California. Later missionaries such as Alfred Billings, Jacob Hamblin, Ira Hatch, and Thales Haskell explored the territory in the 1850s and 1860s. By 1870 interest in transportation on the Colorado River, in grazing, in border control, and in the desert as a refuge led to the establishment of Callsville and Lees Ferry on the Colorado River and Pipe Spring on the Arizona Strip.

In 1873 COLONIZATION began in earnest. Brigham YOUNG, with Thomas L. KANE, planned a colonizing thrust that would eventually extend from Salt Lake City to a Mormon seaport at Guaymas, Mexico. A party of scouts under Lorenzo Roundy examined the San Francisco Mountains and the Little Colorado River drainages for town sites. Brigham Young called 200 colonizing and Indian missionaries who, without adequate preparation, hurried south in the winter and spring of 1873. This mission foundered in the desert country north of the Little Colorado, and the missionaries retreated to Utah. Only John D. Lee and a few others held on at Lees Ferry and Moenkopi.

The southward movement lay dormant for two years. When it revived, plans focused on UNITED ORDER settlements and Indian missions. Missionaries James S. Brown and Daniel W. Jones led expeditions south, and four colonizing companies were dispatched under Lot Smith, a tough Mormon Battalion veteran known for his exploits against the UTAH EXPEDITION. During 1876 these colonists established united order towns at Sunset, Brigham City, Obed, and Joseph City on the lower Little Colorado. By 1878 Latter-day Saints had settled farther upstream, at Snowflake, Taylor, St. Johns, Concho, and Eagar, as well as at several sites in western New Mexico. Colonists also moved farther south into the Salt River Valley, where several towns were established, including Mesa and Lehi. Others settled at Pima, Thatcher, and Safford in the Gila River country, and at St. David on the San Pedro River.

The intense united order impulse of the earliest companies soon diminished, and towns established after 1877 were organized on a less communal basis. Even the strongest orders at Sunset and Joseph City gave up communal organization by 1886. The proselytization of Indians also lapsed as economic competition created tensions between Native Americans and whites. Although irrigation was a continuing struggle, prosperous agricultural villages soon flourished in all the Mormon districts. Led by John W. Young, Arizona Latter-day Saints became a major force in building the Santa Fe railroad and in ranching on the Arizona Strip and near Flagstaff. Establishing a branch of Zion's Cooperative Mercantile Institution (ZCMI), they also engaged in commerce, freighting, and banking.

At first Latter-day Saints found political life in Arizona difficult. In Apache County, friction among Mexicans, ranchers, and traders escalated into fierce struggles by 1880. In 1884 David K. Udall and a few others were imprisoned for practicing PLURAL MARRIAGE; many fled to Mexico. But after the MANIFESTO was issued in 1890, two-party politics were embraced and Church members found a place in Arizona's political institutions.

The 1890 federal census counted 6,500 Latter-day Saints in Arizona. Although Church settlement continued well into the twentieth century, the pioneer period ended by 1900. By that time Latter-day Saints, firmly established Arizonans both in their own minds and in the eyes of others, comprised a distinctive cultural element in Arizona.

The erection of a temple at Mesa, dedicated in 1927, reflected the significance of Arizona to the Church, and provided Native American members and other Church members in Mexico with closer access to temple ordinances. Among twentieth-century Church leaders with Arizona roots was Spencer W. KIMBALL, President of the Church from 1973 to 1985. By 1990 there were 236,000 Latter-day Saints in Arizona, most of them residing in urban areas.

BIBLIOGRAPHY

Fish, Joseph. *The Life and Times of Joseph Fish, Mormon Pioneer.* Danville, Ill., 1970.

McClintock, James H. *Mormon Settlement in Arizona: Record of Peaceful Conquest of the Desert.* Phoenix, Ariz., 1921.

Peterson, Charles S. *Take Up Your Mission: Mormon Colonizing Along the Little Colorado River 1870–1900.* Tucson, Ariz., 1973.

Smith, Jesse N. *Journal of Jesse Nathaniel Smith.* Salt Lake City, 1953.

CHARLES S. PETERSON

ASIA, THE CHURCH IN

[*This entry is made up of two articles:*

Asia, East
Asia, South and Southeast

Asia, East *discusses the growth and development of the Church in China, Japan, South Korea, Hong Kong, and Taiwan.* Asia, South and Southeast *discusses Church growth in the Philippines, Thailand, Singapore, Indonesia, Vietnam, India, and Sri Lanka.]*

ASIA, EAST

EARLY LDS MISSIONARY ATTEMPTS IN CHINA AND JAPAN. President Brigham YOUNG sent Hosea Stout, James Lewis, and Chapman Duncan to China in August 1852. They reached Hong Kong on April 28, 1853. Although they preached the gospel to the people, they could not gain a foothold and sailed home after fifty-six days. On January 9, 1921, David O. MCKAY, an apostle, visited Beijing and dedicated the Chinese realm to missionary work, but the Church did not attempt to go to China until 1949.

Efforts to establish the Church in Japan came almost fifty years after the unsuccessful first Chinese attempt. In February 1901, President Lorenzo SNOW announced plans to open a mission in Japan, with Heber J. GRANT, an apostle, as president and Louis A. Kelsch, Horace S. Ensign, and eighteen-year-old Alma O. Taylor also to serve. Elder Grant dedicated Japan to the preaching of the gospel on September 1, 1901, at Yokohama. Learning the language, customs, and traditions was so difficult, however, that the new missionaries spent eighteen months studying before they ventured out among the

Japanese people. The slow start was symptomatic of the entire mission until its closure in August 1924. Although they had baptized only 166 people in 23 years, they did publish a Japanese translation of the Book of Mormon (1909), several tracts, and a hymnal.

THE CHURCH IN JAPAN SINCE WORLD WAR II. In the spring of 1947, the First Presidency assigned Edward L. Clissold to reopen the Japanese mission, and missionary work was resumed in Japan in 1948. President Clissold had served in the U.S. occupation forces in Japan and was acquainted with government offices and procedures. The first group of missionaries arrived on June 26, 1948. They were helped by LDS service personnel, who contributed much to the success of the postwar mission. For example, Sato Tatsuo, the first Japanese to join the Church after World War II, was taught the gospel by Boyd K. Packer, later an apostle, and three of his fellow servicemen. Sato organized the first Sunday School in Nagoya in 1946. He later translated the Doctrine and Covenants and the Pearl of Great Price, and retranslated the Book of Mormon into contemporary Japanese. By August 1949, missionaries were proselytizing in at least ten major cities and Japanese members numbered 211.

The Church has grown steadily in Japan, and native Japanese serve in all levels of leadership in the Church. When the Tokyo stake was organized on March 15, 1970, the president was Tanaka Kenji, and all the stake officers were Japanese. Most of the mission presidents have been either native Japanese or Americans of Japanese ancestry, and by 1990 almost one-third of the more than two thousand LDS missionaries in Japan were local Japanese. In 1977, Yoshihiko Kikuchi became the first Japanese and Asian called as a General Authority of the Church.

Members of the Church in Japan have access to the full program of the Church: for example, seminaries and institutes (started in 1972); a translation services department to provide Church written materials in the Japanese language; and genealogy services through the microfilming of registers at civic and Buddhist repositories. At an area conference held in Tokyo in August 1975, President Spencer W. KIMBALL announced to the 12,300 participants plans to build a temple in Tokyo. He returned to dedicate the completed structure on October 27–29, 1980.

By 1955, the Japanese mission included South Korea and

Okinawa, and the name of the mission was changed to the Northern Far East Mission. At the same time, the Church organized the Southern Far East Mission with H. Grant Heaton as its first president. That mission included Hong Kong, Taiwan, the Philippines, and Guam. For several years during the Korean conflict, the successive Japan mission presidents, Vinal G. Mauss and Hilton A. Robertson, supervised proselytizing as well as Church organizations for military people throughout East Asia, Guam, and the Philippines. With the truce in Korea, it became possible to establish missionary work there.

CHURCH GROWTH IN SOUTH KOREA. Although the Church did not officially move into Korea until 1955, LDS military personnel had taught and baptized some twenty Koreans by May 1953. Kim Ho Jik, a Korean who had studied for a doctorate at Cornell University, joined the Church in New York in 1951. On returning home he became an influential member of the Church and of the Korean government. Until his death in 1959, Kim facilitated the founding of the Church in South Korea. As in Japan, the Church in Korea is in the hands of local leaders.

The newly appointed mission president, Paul Andrus, sent the first two elders from Japan to Seoul in April 1956. By the summer of 1962, when Korea became a separate mission with Gail E. Carr as president, there were over 1,600 members. In 1968, the Church was established in every major city and all provincial capitals. Unlike most other areas of the world, the majority of Koreans baptized were men, and even in the late 1970s, 55 percent of converts were male. Korea has remained the most fruitful Asian mission other than the Christian Philippines.

The second and third mission presidents, Spencer J. Palmer and Robert H. Slover, did much to enlarge the Church in Korea. Both men emphasized public relations, translation work (the Book of Mormon was published in Korean in 1967 and the Doctrine and Covenants and Pearl of Great Price in 1968), leadership training, the purchase of property for chapels and other uses, and preparation for stakes. President Edward Brown later supervised the beginning of the seminary and institute program. In March 1973, Rhee Ho Nam was sustained as president of the first Korean stake. Two years later, in 1975, the Korea Seoul Mission was divided and a new mission was organized in Pusan with Han In Sang as president. On December 14–15, 1985, President Gordon B. Hinckley dedicated the Seoul Korea Temple.

CHURCH DEVELOPMENT IN THE CHINESE REALM. The Chinese-speaking area of Asia has over a billion inhabitants, but the Church has had access only to Taiwan (twenty million), Hong Kong (five million), and Macao. Political conditions in the People's Republic of China have not allowed proselytizing. Church growth in Hong Kong and Taiwan has, however, been significant.

In 1949, the Church briefly opened missionary work in Hong Kong, but because of the Chinese civil war between the Nationalists and the Communists (which ended in October 1949) and the Korean conflict, the Hong Kong colony had many problems. Although nine missionaries served and fourteen Chinese joined the Church, the Hong Kong Mission was closed on February 6, 1951. After the end of the Korean conflict, when missionary numbers had increased, Church leaders reopened the Chinese area mission in August 1955. It was comprised of Hong Kong, Taiwan, Guam, the Philippines and other parts of Southeast Asia, and the People's Republic of China, even though the latter was still closed to missionary work. By June 1956, there were forty missionaries in Hong Kong and three hundred Chinese had been baptized.

On June 4, 1956, four elders flew from Hong Kong to Taipei, Taiwan, to commence missionary work in the Mandarin Chinese language. LDS military people gave considerable support during the founding stages in Taiwan. By mid-1958 there were 286 Chinese members there. On June 1, 1959, Mark E. Petersen, an apostle, dedicated Taiwan to the preaching of the gospel, reinvoking Elder McKay's 1921 dedication of the entire Chinese realm.

The founding of LDS missionary work in the Philippines and other parts of Southeast Asia was directed by the presidents of the Southern Far East Mission during the 1960s. Because various countries were broken off to form new missions, the name and scope of the Southern Far East Mission were changed to the Hong Kong-Taiwan Mission on November 1, 1969. Fourteen months later, on January 11, 1971, a separate mission was established in Taiwan.

Since then, development has been separate but quite parallel. On April 22, 1976, Chang I-Ch'ing was sustained as president of the

Taiwan Taipei Stake. Three days later, Poon Shiu-Tat (Sheldon) was sustained as Hong Kong's first stake president. The founding of seminaries and institutes in 1975 and the development of translation work were also parallel. In 1990 each region had multiple missions and stakes. The Taipei Taiwan Temple was dedicated November 17–18, 1984, by Gordon B. Hinckley of the First Presidency.

MAINLAND CHINA. Formal missionary work has not been undertaken in the People's Republic of China. Three branches of the Church were organized on the Chinese mainland in 1990, but they were restricted to expatriates. Since 1979, a number of Brigham Young University performance groups have toured the People's Republic of China, garnering high praise and great popularity.

ASIA, SOUTH AND SOUTHEAST

EARLY HISTORY. The first two Latter-day Saints to reach India were George Barber and Benjamin Richey, British sailors who in 1849 visited Calcutta and made friends who asked for missionaries. In June 1851, Elder Joseph Richards arrived. He baptized eight people, ordained Maurice White an elder, and appointed him branch president of the "Wanderer's Branch," the first unit of the Church in Asia. That December, William Willes, a second missionary, arrived in Calcutta. By mid-May, when he counted 19 Europeans and 170 Indian farmers as Church members, he wrote to Utah for more missionaries. However, his branch withered quickly when the Indian farmers learned that there would be no immediate, direct material gain from joining the Church. Meanwhile, President Brigham Young dispatched nine additional missionaries from Utah to India and four to Siam (Thailand) in August 1852. After a difficult trip, they arrived in Calcutta on April 23, 1853.

Although they and some of their converts traversed thousands of miles of dusty or muddy Indian and Burmese roads, preached in notable and humble surroundings, published tracts in five languages (and had the Book of Mormon translated into Urdu), and bore a witness to the peoples of India, Burma, and Siam that the gospel had been restored, they had little success, and the Church was not established in India or Southeast Asia until after World War II.

THE CHURCH IN THE PHILIPPINES. Joseph Fielding SMITH, an apostle, dedicated the Philippines for the preaching of the gospel on August 21, 1955, and the first four missionaries arrived from Hong Kong in June 1961. Establishing the Church in the Philippines progressed more smoothly than in any other part of Asia because over 90 percent of the population were Christian, almost 50 percent used English to some degree, and Americans who were teaching a religion with American origins were generally popular. By 1967, the Philippines was made a separate mission with Paul Rose as president, and by 1973, over 13,000 Filipinos had been baptized. On May 20, 1973, Ezra Taft BENSON, an apostle, organized the Manila Philippines Stake with Augusto A. Lim as president. Four years later the Manila stake was divided into three stakes. The developing of experienced leadership and building of adequate meetinghouses have been a challenge, but members have had the full program of the Church, including seminaries and institutes, since 1972. Selections from the Book of Mormon were published in Tagalog (1987); a missionary training center was established in Manila (1986); and on September 25–27, 1984, President Gordon B. Hinckley dedicated the Manila Philippines Temple. In 1988 the First Presidency made Manila the headquarters for the Philippines/Micronesia area of the Church and assigned an area president to live there. Church growth in the Philippines has been the most rapid of all Asian countries, and over 80 percent of the missionaries in 1990 were local Filipinos.

THE CHURCH IN THAILAND. Church growth in Thailand has progressed slowly because the Thais' devotion to king, country, the Buddhist religion (94 percent), and tradition appears to form a seamless whole. The Church entered Thailand when Latter-day Saints were part of the U.S. military personnel sent there in 1961. In July 1966, an LDS servicemen's branch was organized with two hundred members. On November 2, 1966, Gordon B. Hinckley, then an apostle, dedicated Thailand for the preaching of the gospel. By late 1967, the first six elders were sent to Bangkok from Hong Kong. In July 1973, the Thailand Bangkok Mission was organized, and the Book of Mormon was published in Thai in 1976.

THE SINGAPORE MISSION AREA. Missionary activity began in Singapore in 1968, the first branch of the Church being organized on October 13. Earlier that year, on March 19, two missionaries had been assigned there from Hong Kong. Elder Ezra Taft Benson dedicated Singapore for the preaching of the gospel on April 14, 1969, and on November 1, it became the headquarters for the Southeast Asia Mission with G. Carlos Smith, Jr., as president. He was responsible for missionary work in all the nations of South and Southeast Asia except the Philippines.

LDS expansion in Singapore has not been easy because the government banned all foreign missionaries from Singapore and prohibited open proselytizing in 1970. The Church is allowed only a limited number of visas, including those of the mission president and his wife, at any one time, but through the efforts of young local missionaries the growth of the Church has been steady.

INDONESIAN CHURCH GROWTH. Since 1980, virtually all LDS missionary work in Indonesia has been performed by local members. Indonesia is the only Muslim country where Church proselytizing has succeeded. The Church officially entered Indonesia when Elder Ezra Taft Benson dedicated that country for the teaching of the gospel on October 26, 1969. G. Carlos Smith, Jr., the newly called president of the Southeast Asia Mission, sent six elders from Singapore on January 5, 1970. But on April 11, the Indonesian government halted door-to-door proselytizing and church meetings until the Church obtained official recognition. Although government recognition came nine days later, relations between the Church and various departments of the Indonesian government have not been smooth.

In April 1975, the First Presidency organized the Indonesia Jakarta Mission with Hendrik Gout as president. He had the Book of Mormon translated and published in Bahasa Indonesian (1977), fostered the work of welfare services missionaries, and facilitated the establishment of an elementary school in Jakarta in 1976. (It closed in 1988.)

In 1978, government regulations required that Indonesian nationals hold all missionary (and ministerial) positions, and by late 1980 all non-Indonesian LDS missionaries were removed from the country. It was necessary to recombine the Indonesia Jakarta Mission with the Singapore Mission until 1985, when Effian Kadarusman, an Indonesian, was appointed president over the reestablished mission. By 1988, close to one hundred Indonesians were serving full-time missions in their country. In 1989 the Indonesia Jakarta Mission was again made a part of the Singapore Mission.

THE CHURCH'S BRIEF ENCOUNTER WITH VIETNAM. The first Latter-day Saints in Vietnam were military advisers in the early 1960s, and by 1968 more than five thousand LDS servicemen were assigned there. The first servicemen's group was organized in Saigon on June 30, 1963. In December 1965, Vietnam became a district of the Southern Far East Mission with headquarters in Hong Kong. At the same time, six servicemen were called to serve as part-time missionaries. By February 1966, several U.S. servicemen and thirty Vietnamese had been baptized. On October 30, 1966, Elder Gordon B. Hinckley dedicated Vietnam for the preaching of the gospel.

On April 6, 1973, four full-time missionaries were transferred to Saigon from Hong Kong. The Vietnamese Book of Mormon was distributed to members in photocopy form in May 1974. By March 1975, the Church had fifteen missionaries and more than three thousand Vietnamese members. At that point the missionaries were withdrawn, and a month later, Saigon fell. Almost all of the LDS members eventually left Vietnam and migrated to the United States.

CHURCH GROWTH IN INDIA AND SRI LANKA. India and Sri Lanka have laws prohibiting proselytizing by foreigners, and the Church respects those laws. Most of the growth within India and Sri Lanka has been the result of efforts of local members who have conveyed the gospel message to their friends. For example, in 1965, S. Paul Thiruthuvadoss was baptized after an individual search for the gospel of Jesus Christ. He was briefly assisted by foreign missionaries, and his efforts resulted in the baptism of more than two hundred Tamil-speaking South Indians.

In December 1978, Edwin Dharmaraju and his wife, both of whom had been baptized in Western Samoa, served a short mission in their home city of Hyderabad, India. Before returning to Samoa, Dharmaraju baptized twenty-two family members, ordained four men to the Aaronic Priesthood, and organized a group of the Church. Also, Sister Dharmaraju's father, a Baptist minister, had found such interest in the Book of Mormon that he translated it into the Telugu language (48 million speakers). It was published in 1982, as was the complete Hindi (175 million speakers) version and selections in Tamil (42 million speakers). Bengali (48 million speakers) selections of the Book of Mormon were published in 1985.

Another important Indian missionary was Raj Kumar, who

strengthened new members and branches as they were established. By 1986 local missionaries were serving full-time missions for the Church in India and Sri Lanka, assisted by North American friendship-missionary couples sent from the Singapore Mission to make friends for the Church in various cities. They and other expatriates, such as business and government personnel stationed in India, did not proselytize, but answered questions and taught the gospel to those who sought them out.

CHURCH IN ASIA as of December 31, 1989

Area	*Members*	*Missions*	*Stakes/Districts*	*Wards and Branches*
China	NA	0	0/0	3
Hong Kong	17,000	1	4/0	26
India	800	0	0/3	9
Indonesia	4,100	0	0/3	18
Japan	91,000	9	23/15	264
Korea, Republic	50,000	4	14/4	146
Macao	200	0	0/0	1
Malaysia	300	0	0/1	3
Pakistan	NA	0	0/0	2
Papua New Guinea	2,100	0	0/1	13
Philippines	213,000	9	38/39	638
Singapore	1,400	1	0/1	5
Sri Lanka	100	0	0/0	1
Taiwan	17,000	2	3/2	47
Thailand	3,600	1	0/3	16
Asia Total:	400,600	27	82/72	1,192

BIBLIOGRAPHY

Britsch, R. Lanier. "The Latter-day Saint Mission to India: 1851–1856." *BYU Studies* 12 (Spring 1972):262–78.

———. "The Closing of the Early Japan Mission." *BYU Studies* 15 (Winter 1975):171–90.

———. "From Bhutan to Wangts'ang: Taking the Gospel to Asia." *Ensign* 10 (June 1980):6–10.

———. "The Church's Years in Vietnam." *Ensign* 10 (Aug. 1980):25–30.

Moss, James R.; R. Lanier Britsch; James R. Christianson; and Richard O. Cowan. *The International Church*. Provo, Utah, 1982.

Palmer, Spencer J. *The Church Encounters Asia*. Salt Lake City, 1970.

R. LANIER BRITSCH

AUSTRALIA, THE CHURCH IN

The Church of Jesus Christ of Latter-day Saints was introduced into Australia when a seventeen-year-old British convert, William James Barratt, emigrated from England to Adelaide in November 1840. He had been ordained an elder by George A. Smith, a member of the Quorum of the Twelve Apostles, who instructed him to share the gospel whenever he could. Barratt, whose descendants still live in the Adelaide area, eventually drifted away from the Church, but not until after he had baptized Robert Beauchamp, probably the first Australian convert. Beauchamp later became president of the Australian Mission. Andrew and Elizabeth Anderson, also British converts, immigrated to Wellington, near Dubbo, New South Wales, with their three children in 1841. Anderson baptized several converts and in 1844 organized the first Australian branch of the Church, in Wellington.

Official LDS missionary work did not begin in Australia until John Murdock and Charles W. Wandell arrived in Sydney from Utah on October 30, 1851. Thereafter, the Church grew slowly in Australia until President David O. MCKAY visited the area in 1955 and authorized construction of meetinghouses for the branches. The first Australian stakes were organized in 1960 in Sydney, Brisbane, and Melbourne. Significant growth has continued since then, leading to the building of a temple in Sydney. It was dedicated in September 1984. By 1990 the Church was strong throughout Australia, with the Pacific Area presidency based in Sydney, and with a temple, 5 missions, 18 stakes, and 205 wards and branches serving 73,200 members in the country as a whole. Australian members of the Church appear to have successfully blended their cultural values of ruggedness and individualism with gospel teachings, creating a uniquely Australian Church culture.

The early days of the Church in Australia were difficult. Prompted by the public preaching of the LDS missionaries, newspapers published articles attacking the Church's doctrines. The missionaries countered with articles, tracts, and spirited defenses of the Church and its teachings in public meetings, many of which were held at the Sydney racecourse. Many of the early converts immigrated to Utah in the spirit of gathering to Zion, some dying en route in the wreck of the *Julia Ann* in 1852 (Devitry-Smith, 1989). This spirit of migration also brought to Australia a significant number of British Saints who were hoping to find gold in the newly discovered goldfields in order to fund their further travel to Utah. Most were unsuccessful in reaching their monetary goal. After 1900, Church leaders encouraged members to stay in their own nations to strengthen the local membership.

When the American missionaries were called home during the UTAH EXPEDITION in 1857, the Church branches in Australia were left to the few members who had not emigrated. When the missionaries returned to the region a few years later, much of their effort was directed toward New Zealand, where many Maoris were joining the Church. During the 1880s the Sydney Branch was discontinued, but the Melbourne Branch remained strong. In 1896, the Sydney Branch was reestablished, and in 1898 the Australian Mission, which then also included New Zealand, was divided, making New Zealand a separate mission. In 1904, with Church assistance in funding, the Brisbane Saints built the first LDS meetinghouse in Australia at Wooloongabba.

Most members of the Church in Australia live in large cities and towns, but many branches also thrive in small rural towns and communities throughout the Australian bush and outback. A small meetinghouse to accommodate aboriginal members of the Church was erected in 1984 at Elliott, about 450 miles south of Darwin. Many Australian members travel considerable distances to attend Church meetings; for example, members of the Alice Springs Branch travel more than 900 miles to attend district conferences in Darwin. Other members live in outback communities totally isolated from personal contact with organized branches. In 1929, recognizing the need for better communication among members scattered over such a large area as Australia, mission president Clarence Tingey began publication of *Austral Star*, which provided members with local and international news of the Church and messages and instructions from Church leaders.

Among prominent Church members with Australian connections are Joseph Ridges, the designer of the original Mormon Tabernacle organ; William Fowler, author of the LDS hymn "We Thank Thee, O God, for a Prophet"; and Robert E. Sackley of the Quorums of the

Seventy. Both Marion G. Romney and Bruce R. McConkie, later of the Council of the Twelve, served missions in Australia.

BIBLIOGRAPHY

Britsch, R. Lanier. *Unto the Islands of the Sea: A History of the Latter-day Saints in the Pacific.* Salt Lake City, 1986.

Devitry-Smith, John. "William James Barratt: The First Mormon Down Under." *BYU Studies* 28 (Summer 1988):53–66.

———. "The Wreck of the *Julia Ann.*" *BYU Studies* 29 (Spring 1989):5–29.

Newton, Marjorie. "The Gathering of the Australian Saints in the 1850s." *BYU Studies* 27 (Spring 1987):67–78.

WILLIAM G. EGGINGTON

B

BEEHIVE SYMBOL

Nineteenth-century leaders of The Church of Jesus Christ of Latter-day Saints consciously created symbols to buttress their community. The most persistent of these pioneer symbols was the beehive.

Its origin may relate to the statement in the Book of Mormon that the Jaredites carried "with them deseret, which, by interpretation, is a honey bee" (Ether 2:3). The *Deseret News* (Oct. 11, 1881) described the symbol of the beehive in this way: "The hive and honey bees form our communal coat of arms. . . . It is a significant representation of the industry, harmony, order and frugality of the people, and of the sweet results of their toil, union and intelligent cooperation."

Working together during this early period, individuals contributed specialized talents and skills for building an integrated and well-planned community in a hostile environment. Community, not individuality, created this persistent symbol. The beehive has appeared on public and private Mormon buildings (such as temples, tabernacles, meetinghouses, Brigham Young's Beehive House, and the mercantile institution ZCMI) as well as in folk art and on furniture.

Today it appears as a logo of some Church-related organizations, on the seals of the state of Utah and of two universities, on Church welfare products, and on some commercial signs in Utah. It links the

Mormon community across time while symbolizing the Mormon pioneer past.

BIBLIOGRAPHY

Cannon, Hal. *The Grand Beehive*. Salt Lake City, 1980.

Oman, Richard, and Susan Oman. "Mormon Iconography." In *Utah Folk Art: A Catalog of Material Culture*, ed. H. Cannon. Provo, Utah, 1980.

RICHARD G. OMAN

BENSON, EZRA TAFT

Ezra Taft Benson (1899–1994), thirteenth President of The Church of Jesus Christ of Latter-day Saints, was noted for his extensive Church service and his distinguished career in government. He served forty-two years as a member of the Quorum of the Twelve Apostles and was U.S. secretary of agriculture for eight years in the administration of President Dwight D. Eisenhower. As President of the Church, he repeatedly bore witness that the Book of Mormon is the major instrument to bring the members of the Church and the world to Christ, and he admonished the Saints to strengthen their families and to preserve their God-given freedoms.

President Benson was born August 4, 1899, in the small rural community of Whitney, Idaho, the oldest of eleven children born to George Taft Benson, Jr., and Sarah Dunkley. He was named after his great-grandfather, Ezra T. (Taft) Benson, an apostle, who entered the Salt Lake Valley with the first Mormon pioneer company in July 1847. The pioneer Ezra T. was the son of John Benson, Jr., and Chloe Taft of Mendon, Massachusetts. John Benson, Sr., was an officer during the American Revolution.

Ezra Taft Benson was reared on the family farm in Whitney, driving a team of horses at the age of five, milking cows, and thinning sugar beets. He entered grade school at the age of eight. "Be as careful of the books you read as of the company you keep" was the counsel that governed his reading habits (Dew, p. 24). In addition to the scriptures, he read Bunyan's *Pilgrim's Progress*; biographies of George Washington, Benjamin Franklin, and Abraham Lincoln; and success stories by Horatio Alger. His grandparents gave him a two-volume set by Orison S. Marden, *Little Visits with Great Americans* (1905), which he devoured.

Increased responsibility was thrust on him as a youth when his father was called as a missionary to the Northern States Mission, leaving behind his wife and seven children; the eighth was born while he was in the mission field. A spirit of missionary work enveloped the home, and all eleven children eventually served at least one full-time mission.

In 1914, Ezra entered the Church-sponsored Oneida Academy in Preston, Idaho, graduating in 1918. That year as Scoutmaster, he led his Scouts into choral competition and won the Cache Valley chorus championship. Also during that year he enlisted in the military service just before the close of World War I.

As a young man, he developed a love for the land and for the Lord, two fundamental influences in his ensuing life. He felt that the basic ingredient for successful farming was intelligent, hard work. To increase his agricultural skills, he took correspondence courses and began attending the Utah State Agricultural College (now Utah State University). He accepted a mission call to England in 1921, where he served as Newcastle Conference clerk, Sunderland Branch president, and president of the Newcastle Conference, which included all of northern England. Upon his return, he soon enrolled at Brigham Young University, where he was president of the Agriculture Club and Men's Glee Club and was named the most popular man on campus. He graduated with honors, majoring in animal husbandry with a minor in agronomy.

He married Flora Smith Amussen in the Salt Lake Temple on September 10, 1926. She was the youngest child of Carl Christian Amussen, a Danish convert who crossed the plains and became a prominent Utah jeweler, and Barbara McIsaac Smith. Flora attended Utah State Agricultural College, where she served as vice-president of the student body, took the lead in a Shakespearean play, and won the women's singles tennis championship. She served a mission in the Hawaiian Islands.

Of his wife, President Benson said, "She had more faith in me than I had in myself" (Dew, p. 96). One Church leader commented that if there were more women in the Church like Sister Benson, there would be more men in the Church like Brother Benson. They became the parents of six children—Reed, Mark, Barbara, Beverly, Bonnie, and Beth.

Ezra Benson received a research scholarship to Iowa State College, where he obtained his master's degree in agricultural economics on June 13, 1927. He returned to the family farm, which he and his brother Orval had purchased from their father, and on March 4, 1929, was appointed Franklin County agricultural agent. He helped farmers solve their problems by setting up demonstration farms, inviting in specialists, teaching crop rotation, and introducing improved varieties of grains.

In 1930, he was promoted to agricultural economist and marketing specialist for the University of Idaho, with offices in the state capitol in Boise. Traveling throughout Idaho, he encouraged farmers to work cooperatively in producing and marketing their goods. For five years, he served as the executive secretary of the Idaho Cooperative Council. He took a leave in 1936 for additional graduate study, attending the University of California in Berkeley on a fellowship awarded by the Giannini Foundation for Agricultural Economics. Soon after his return to Boise, he was called by the Church in November 1938 to serve as stake president. In April 1939, he became executive secretary of the National Council of Farmer Cooperatives at its headquarters in Washington, D.C. The council represented some 4,000 cooperative purchasing and marketing organizations involving almost 1.6 million farmers. Ezra Benson represented cooperatives before committees of Congress and served on a four-man national agriculture advisory committee to President Franklin D. Roosevelt during World War II.

On June 30, 1940, the Church called him as the first president of the Washington, D.C., stake, and on July 26, 1943, he was called to the Quorum of the Twelve Apostles. He was sustained in that position at the October general conference and was ordained an apostle by President Heber J. GRANT on October 7, 1943.

In December 1945, following the devastation of World War II, President George Albert SMITH called Elder Benson to be the European Mission president. His faith in the Lord, administrative skills, and experience in dealing with government helped him accomplish the four-point charge given to him by the First Presidency: "First, to attend to the spiritual affairs of the Church in

Europe; second, to work to make available food, clothing, and bedding to our suffering Saints in all parts of Europe; third, to direct the reorganization of the missions of Europe; and, fourth, to prepare for the return of missionaries to those countries" (*IE* 50 [May 1947]:293). He was among the first American civilians to administer relief in many of the devastated areas. During his first five months in Europe, he visited over one hundred cities in thirteen countries. Within ten months, he completed his mission, having distributed ninety-two boxcar loads of food, clothing, bedding, and medical supplies; reopened missions with new mission presidents and full-time missionaries; and given the Latter-day Saints in Europe a renewed spirit of hope.

In 1952, following the counsel of President David O. MCKAY, Ezra Taft Benson accepted the Cabinet position of secretary of agriculture in the Eisenhower administration. His selection was greeted with widespread approval. In his "General Statement on Agricultural Policy," he said, "The supreme test of any government policy, agricultural or other, should be 'How will it affect the character, morale, and well-being of our people?'. . . A completely planned and subsidized economy weakens initiative, discourages industry, destroys character, and demoralizes the people" (Benson, 1962, p. 602).

He assumed office when farm income was declining and wartime legislation was piling up surpluses in government warehouses, inviting increased government controls of agriculture. He worked to reverse that course, winning significant legislative victories in spite of intense political opposition.

He became known for his integrity, and friend and foe alike acknowledged that he was a man of religious principles who stood by his convictions despite political pressures. He traveled hundreds of thousands of miles, carrying his farm message throughout the nation and the world, and aggressively encouraged consumption of U.S. farm products. He authored three books, *Farmers at the Crossroads* (1956), *Freedom to Farm* (1960), and *Crossfire: The Eight Years with Eisenhower* (1962).

He served eight years in the Cabinet, meeting with heads of state and agriculture leaders and farmers in over forty nations. He had discussions with such leaders as Chiang Kai-shek, Nehru, Khrushchev, King Hussein, and David Ben-Gurion. During this time, his example and activities brought positive and widespread attention to the Church. President David O. McKay said that Secretary Benson's work in the Cabinet would "stand for all time as a credit to the Church and the nation" (Benson, 1962, p. 519).

With the encouragement of President David O. McKay, a major thrust of Elder Benson's many Church and civic addresses pertained to freedom and the threats to it. The substance of those messages is found in his books *The Red Carpet* (1962), *Title of Liberty* (1964), and *An Enemy Hath Done This* (1969). In Church general conference in April 1965, he warned, "To have been on the wrong side of the freedom issue during the war in heaven meant eternal damnation. How then can Latter-day Saints expect to be on the wrong side in this life and escape the eternal consequences?" (*IE* 68 [June 1965]:537).

President Benson's international stature helped to facilitate the acceptance and growth of the Church throughout the world. He dedicated several nations to the preaching of the gospel, established the first stakes in many countries, and supervised various areas of the world. He served as chairman of Quorum of the Twelve committees and sat on numerous boards.

In December 1973, Ezra Taft Benson became president of the Quorum of the Twelve Apostles. His executive abilities were again demonstrated in this calling. A great spirit of unity was manifest, and he measured proposed policies or procedures by the yardstick "What is best for the kingdom?" (Petersen, p. 3).

Brigham Young University honored him by establishing the Ezra Taft Benson Agriculture and Food Institute in 1975 to help relieve world food problems and raise the quality of global life through improved nutrition and enlightened agriculture practices.

Many national and international citations and awards, including a number of honorary doctorate degrees, were bestowed on him. From the Boy Scouts of America he received the Silver Beaver, Silver Antelope, and Silver Buffalo; he served on their National Executive Board. On April 1, 1989, he was presented world Scouting's highest award, the Bronze Wolf. During his ninetieth birthday celebration, the President of the United States conferred upon him the Presidential Citizens Medal, naming him "one of the most distinguished Americans of his time" (*Church News*, Aug. 5, 1989, p. 4).

Upon the death of President Spencer W. KIMBALL, Ezra Taft

Benson became President of the Church on November 10, 1985, at the age of eighty-six. At that time he delivered a statement reiterating the mission of the Church—to preach the gospel, perfect the Saints, and redeem the dead—and reaffirming that the Church is led by the Lord Jesus Christ. He selected as his counselors in the First Presidency Gordon B. Hinckley and Thomas S. Monson. The new First Presidency soon issued a special invitation to those members who had ceased activity or become critical of the Church to "come back" (*Church News*, Dec. 22, 1985, p. 3), and they opened the temples to worthy members married to unendowed spouses.

In a solemn assembly at general conference April 6, 1986, he was sustained by Church members as the prophet, seer, and revelator, and President of the Church. In his opening address at that conference, President Benson stressed the need to "cleanse the inner vessel (see Alma 60:23), beginning first with ourselves, then with our families, and finally with the Church" (*Ensign* 16 [May 1986]:4). In commencing that cleansing, he declared, "The Book of Mormon has not been, nor is it yet, the center of our personal study, family teaching, preaching, and missionary work. Of this we must repent" (*Ensign* 16 [May 1986]:5–6).

In his concluding address of the conference, he said, "The Lord inspired His servant Lorenzo Snow to reemphasize the principle of tithing to redeem the Church from financial bondage. . . . Now, in our day, the Lord has revealed the need to reemphasize the Book of Mormon to get the Church and all the children of Zion out from under condemnation—the scourge and judgment" (*Ensign* 16 [May 1986]:78; see D&C 84:54–58). To that end, his address "The Book of Mormon Is the Word of God" was repeated in regional conferences throughout the Church. This emphasis greatly accelerated the distribution and reading of the Book of Mormon and "brought more souls to Christ, both within and without the Church, than ever before" (*Ensign* 18 [Nov. 1988]:4).

Continuing to help set the Church in order and perfect the Saints, he delivered another landmark address entitled "Beware of Pride" and gave separate messages to the children, young men, young women, single adult brethren, single adult sisters, fathers, mothers, and the elderly.

Throughout the years, the home and family were the center of many of President Benson's conference messages, such as his widely broadcast address "Our Homes—Divinely Ordained" (*IE* 52 [May 1949]:278–79, 332–33) and his frequent reference to his goal that there be "no empty chairs" in the family circle in the next life (Dew, p. 363). He has manifested a great love for the children and youth of the Church.

He was President during the Bicentennial of the U.S. Constitution and, as one of its greatest defenders, he delivered messages honoring this divine document and its inspired framers (*The Constitution: A Heavenly Banner*, Salt Lake City, 1986).

During his presidency, new temples were announced and several were dedicated, and missionary work expanded around the world with special opportunities being afforded, particularly in Eastern Europe, in countries previously closed.

For nearly fifty years his thousands of speeches stressed mankind's three great loyalties—loyalty to God, loyalty to family, and loyalty to country. His life was exemplary in striving to live those loyalties as a prophet, a patriarch, and a patriot.

BIBLIOGRAPHY

Benson, Ezra Taft. *A Witness and a Warning*. Salt Lake City, 1988.
———. *Come, Listen to a Prophet's Voice*. Salt Lake City, 1990.
———. *Crossfire: The Eight Years With Eisenhower*. New York, 1962.
———. *God, Family, Country*. Salt Lake City, 1974.
———. *The Teachings of Ezra Taft Benson*. Salt Lake City, 1988.
Dew, Sheri L. *Ezra Taft Benson: A Biography*. Salt Lake City, 1987.
Petersen, Mark E. "President Ezra Taft Benson." *Ensign* 16 [Jan. 1986]:2–4.

REED A. BENSON
SHERI L. DEW

BIOGRAPHY AND AUTOBIOGRAPHY

From the earliest decades members of the Church have adhered to the Puritan tradition of writing spiritual autobiographies, often for reasons similar to those of their forebears, namely, to express their faith and to justify their actions in the light of that faith. New models and counsel also influenced the Latter-day Saints in this regard: the Book of Mormon, one of the first documents of the Church, begins autobiographically—"I, Nephi, having been born of goodly parents . . ." (1 Ne. 1:1)—and it contains long sections of both biography and autobiography. A version of Joseph Smith's autobiography is canonized in the Pearl of Great Price, and the Doctrine and Covenants injunction that "a record [be] kept among you" (D&C 21:1) has been interpreted in practice to apply to Latter-day Saints individually as well as institutionally.

In 1977 the annotated *Guide to Mormon Diaries and Autobiographies* listed nearly 3,000 such documents published or available in various libraries and archives. About half are retrospective autobiographies, as distinguished from journals of daily entries. As a result of the general LDS interest in family history, encouraged especially by President Spencer W. KIMBALL, that number multiplied in the 1980s. In addition, countless personal accounts and family histories remain in family possession throughout the Church.

The variety of Mormon autobiographies is vast, ranging "from conscious virtuosity to self-conscious artifice, from unconscious brilliance to dull-minded monotony" (Lambert, p. 69). In the classic *Autobiography of Parley Parker Pratt* (1874), Pratt artistically portrays himself variously as mystic, recluse, proselyte, jokester, preacher, acolyte, and apostle, each presented in form and language suited to the posture. In contrast, the equally well-known *A Mormon Mother: An Autobiography*, by Annie Clark Tanner, is less artful but more introspective, revealing a complexity of unresolved questions in its author. Mary Goble Pay's short autobiography (in Cracroft and Lambert, pp. 145–53) well represents the life-writing of a comparatively unlettered Latter-day Saint. In stark simplicity and with convincing sincerity, it tells her story as if to a child.

Biography is likewise a frequent LDS literary form. Drawing on the literary tradition of the previous three centuries, early LDS biographers took as models the "life and times" forms, depicting the public achievements of Church leaders. Usually the works reflected the double value placed on Latter-day Saint individuality and community by merging the life of the individual with the history of the movement. Often didactic, these works were defensive in tone, tending to conceal as much as they revealed about the character and experience of the subject. Sensitive facts were either omitted or passed over lightly: a man's excommunication, his plural wives, an altercation with a fellow churchman, or an unsuccessful venture. Sometimes, of course, such facts were already known; in that case, the biographer's role often became one of explaining them away.

A half-century after Lytton Strachey, the eminent Victorian biography writer, altered the fashion of biography by insisting on telling the whole truth about his subjects, Latter-day Saint writers began to include more in their accounts about the private lives of Church leaders. Marion G. Romney's much-quoted directive, printed in the foreword of a jointly authored biography of J. Reuben Clark, Jr. (Fox, 1980; Quinn, 1983), states that "any biographer of President Clark must write the truth about him; to tell more than or less than the truth would violate a governing principle of his life." Romney, a counselor in the First Presidency, advised the authors not to produce "a mere collection of uplifting experiences" or "a detailed defense of his beliefs." He required of them "a biography of the man himself, as he was, written with the same kind of courage, honesty, and frankness that J. Reuben Clark himself would have shown," including "his decisions and indecisions, sorrows and joys, regrets and aspirations, reverses and accomplishments" (Fox, p. xi). That statement, exemplified in the biography of Spencer W. Kimball (Kimball and Kimball, 1977), indicates a turn of tide in Mormon biography, wherein the bland, impeccably moral, and defensive biographies were replaced by studies reflecting flesh-and-blood reality.

Many have attempted to write the life of the Prophet Joseph Smith. His mother, Lucy Mack SMITH, dictated the first serious study, *Biographical Sketches of Joseph Smith the Prophet* (1853), but it was as much her own autobiography as her son's biography. On both counts, the book has held up as accurate source material, though not as a finished prose study. Subsequent Joseph Smith biographies by George Q. Cannon (1888), John Henry Evans (1933), Preston Nibley (1944), Leon Hartshorn (1970), and Francis M. Gibbons (1977), while appropriate to LDS audiences of the time, do not satisfy the recent taste for a complete embodiment of the subject.

In a more scholarly mode, though less than thorough or accurate in its use of sources, was Fawn M. Brodie's *No Man Knows My History* (1945). Its appearance caused a furor among Latter-day Saints and issued a challenge to answering scholars, which contributed to historians paying increased attention to serious research in their writing of Church history. An alternative to Brodie is Donna

Hill's *Joseph Smith, the First Mormon* (1977), and her brother Marvin's review "Secular or Sectarian History? A Critique of *No Man Knows My History*" (1974) in *Church History*.

None, however, has totally succeeded in vivifying Mormonism's founder. Richard L. Bushman's *Joseph Smith and the Beginnings of Mormonism* comes close, but it deals only with the first years of the Prophet's life. Nevertheless, it is a promising re-creation, striving to see people and events as the participants would have understood them. With the commencement of Dean Jessee's publication of the *Papers of Joseph Smith* in 1989, it became possible for biographers to be even more rigorous and complete in their presentation of the full man in all his complexity.

With the growing interest in social history has come an increase in biographies of members of the Church other than General Authorities. People such as those covered in Leonard Arrington and Davis Bitton's *Saints Without Halos: The Human Side of Mormon History* and Donald Q. Cannon and David J. Whittaker's *Supporting Saints: Life Stories of Nineteenth-Century Mormons* are being featured in separate biographical volumes. Juanita Brooks's *John D. Lee* (rev. ed., 1972), for many years the exemplar of Mormon biography, and Leonard Arrington's *From Quaker to Latter-day Saint: Bishop Edwin D. Woolley* (1976) demonstrate how universally interesting the drama of life can be when it is well written.

Latter-day Saint women have seldom been subjects of full-length biographies. The 1984 Newell-Avery study of Emma Hale SMITH stands alone as a full-length treatment of a woman leader, but biographies of Eliza R. SNOW and Emmeline B. WELLS are in progress. Of a lay Mormon woman, one biography of significance has been published, that of historian Juanita Brooks by Levi Peterson (1988).

A few autobiographical accounts of Latter-day Saint women are already available. Besides *A Mormon Mother*, there are the self-told lives of such people as Ellis R. Shipp, Mary Jane Mount Tanner, Sarah Studevant Leavitt, and Aurelia Spencer ROGERS, though it must be recognized that few of these accounts were written for distribution beyond the author's family. Another nineteenth-century woman, Fanny Stenhouse, used the autobiographical mode to produce her *Exposé of Polygamy in Utah* (1872), later revised and widely published as *Tell It All* (1874).

Modern female novelists such as Virginia Sorenson, author of *Where Nothing Is Long Ago* (1963), and Rodello Hunter, author of *Daughter of Zion* (1972), have published autobiographical material combined with some of the trappings of fiction. Several handwritten lives, such as that of Martha Cragun Cox, and others published to limited audiences, such as that of Louisa Barnes Pratt and Mary Ann Weston Maughan, remain largely untapped in obscure archives.

To encourage the writing of Latter-day Saint biographies, the David Woolley and Beatrice Cannon Evans family endowed a prize that has been awarded annually since 1983. It is now administered by the Mountain West Center for Regional Studies at Utah State University. Winners of that award are marked with an asterisk in the following selected main LDS biographies: Allen, James B. *Trials of Discipleship: The Story of William Clayton, A Mormon*. Urbana, Ill., 1987*; Arrington, Leonard J. *Brigham Young: American Moses*. New York, 1985*; Brodie, Fawn M. *No Man Knows My History: The Life of Joseph Smith, the Mormon Prophet*, 2nd rev. ed. New York, 1971; Brooks, Juanita. *John D. Lee: Zealot, Pioneer Builder, Scapegoat*, rev. ed. Glendale, Calif., 1985; Bushman, Richard. *Joseph Smith and the Beginnings of Mormonism*. Urbana, Ill., 1984*; Fox, Frank W. *J. Reuben Clark: The Public Years*. Provo, Utah, 1980; Hill, Donna. *Joseph Smith: The First Mormon*. New York, 1977; Hoopes, David S., and Roy H. Hoopes. *The Making of a Mormon Apostle: The Story of Rudger Clawson*. Lanham, Maryland, 1990; Kimball, Edward L., and Andrew E. Kimball, Jr. *Spencer W. Kimball: Twelfth President of the Church of Jesus Christ of Latter-day Saints*. Salt Lake City, 1977; Kimball, Stanley B. *Heber C. Kimball: Mormon Patriarch and Pioneer*. Urbana, Ill., 1981; Larson, Andrew Karl. *Erastus Snow: The Life of a Missionary and Pioneer for the Early Mormon Church*. Salt Lake City, 1971; Launius, Roger D. *Joseph Smith III: Pragmatic Prophet*. Urbana, Ill., 1988*; Lyon, T. Edgar, Jr. *John Lyon: The Life of a Pioneer Poet*. Provo, Utah, 1989; Madsen, Truman G. *Defender of the Faith: The B. H. Roberts Story*. Salt Lake City, 1980; Merrill, Milton R. *Reed Smoot: Apostle in Politics*. Logan, Utah, 1989; Newell, Linda King, and Valeen Tippetts Avery. *Mormon Enigma: Emma Hale Smith*. New York, 1984*; Peterson, Levi S. *Juanita Brooks: Mormon Woman Historian*. Salt Lake City, 1988*; Quinn, D. Michael. *J. Reuben Clark: The Church Years*. Provo, Utah, 1983;

Schindler, Harold. *Orrin Porter Rockwell: Man of God, Son of Thunder*, 2nd ed. Salt Lake City, 1966; Yarn, David H. *Young Reuben*. Provo, Utah, 1973.

BIBLIOGRAPHY

Allen, James B. "Writing Mormon Biographies." In *World Conference on Records: Preserving Our Heritage*, ser. 116, pp. 1–15. Salt Lake City, 1980.

Bitton, Davis. *Guide to Mormon Diaries and Autobiographies*. Provo, Utah, 1977.

———. "Mormon Biography." *Biography: An Interdisciplinary Quarterly* 4 (Winter 1981):1–16.

Cracroft, Richard, and Neal Lambert, eds. *A Believing People*, pp. 145–53. Provo, Utah, 1974.

Lambert, Neal. "The Representation of Reality in Nineteenth-Century Mormon Autobiography." *Dialogue* 11 (Summer 1978):63–74.

Sondrup, Steven P. "Literary Dimensions of Mormon Autobiography." *Dialogue* 11 (Summer 1978):75–80.

Walker, Ronald W. "The Challenge and Craft of Mormon Biography." *BYU Studies* 22 (Spring 1982):179–92.

Whittaker, David J. "The Heritage and Tasks of Mormon Biography." In *Supporting Saints*, ed. D. Cannon and D. Whittaker, pp. 1–16. Salt Lake City, 1985.

MAUREEN URSENBACH BEECHER

BRITISH ISLES, THE CHURCH IN THE

The Church of Jesus Christ of Latter-day Saints came to the British Isles when seven LDS missionaries landed at Liverpool, England, on July 19, 1837. The success of this first mission (more than 1,500 converts by April 1839) set the stage for the even more successful apostolic mission of 1839–1841, which saw nine of the eleven apostles (the twelfth place was vacant at the time) serving as missionaries in England under the direction of Brigham YOUNG. The Church grew rapidly in Great Britain among the working classes of the Northwest, the Midlands, and especially Wales. Membership counts at the end of 1851 showed 33,000 members of the Church in the United Kingdom and Ireland and 12,000 in Utah. Although total membership in the British Isles declined after the mid-1850s due to emigration and attrition, substantial additions through baptisms continued through the 1860s. From 1870 to the mid-1950s, the Church did not experience sustained growth in the United Kingdom and Ireland. But the dedication of the London Temple (in Lingfield, Surrey) in September

1958 and the creation of the Manchester England Stake on March 27, 1960, initiated a second growth phase of membership; by 1990 the Church had more than 160,000 members in 9 missions, 40 stakes, and more than 330 wards and branches in the British Isles. The strength of the Church in the United Kingdom and Ireland in 1990 is indicated by the number of stakes: thirty-two in England, five in Scotland, two in Wales, and one in Northern Ireland. Branches (congregations) in the Republic of Ireland, whose members are not as numerous as in other areas, are under the jurisdiction of mission districts rather than a stake.

When the missionaries first arrived in the British Isles, they went to Preston, England, where Joseph Fielding's brother, Rev. James Fielding, had invited him and his missionary companions to preach at his Vauxhall Chapel. James's enthusiasm waned when it became apparent that he risked losing his congregation, and he promptly closed the chapel to the missionaries. They then taught in private homes, and a week later baptized the first nine British converts in the river Ribble, at Preston. By Sunday, August 6, there were nearly fifty converts in Preston, and Elder Heber C. KIMBALL organized the Preston Branch. In two months, membership had reached 140, and the original branch was divided into five separate branches in October. Missionary work was extended to Bedford, and to Alston, near the Scottish border, where the missionaries had relatives. Elder Kimball preached in the villages of the Ribble Valley.

On Christmas Day of 1837, the members met for the first conference in Britain, and on Sunday, April 8, 1838, another conference held in the Cockpit, Preston, drew down the curtain on the first phase of Mormon missionary work in Britain. There were 1,500–2,000 British members of the Church, and the leadership was transferred to Joseph Fielding as elders Kimball and Orson HYDE set sail for America.

APOSTOLIC MISSION, 1838–1841. The second major LDS missionary thrust in the British Isles began on July 8, 1838, at Far West, Missouri, when the Prophet Joseph SMITH received a revelation instructing the Twelve Apostles to prepare to serve a mission in Great Britain. Brigham Young and six other apostles left from New York for Britain between December 1839 and March 1840. Willard Richards, who had remained there after the 1837 mission, was ordained an apostle in Britain on April 14, 1840, by Brigham Young. The missionaries baptized thousands of converts (Wilford WOODRUFF personally baptized more than a thousand), organized branches and conferences, and directed the work of the Church, including printing scriptures and tracts, and began publishing the *Millennial Star,* the British Church periodical that would have a continuous run from 1840 through 1970. In 1841, shortly before he returned to America, Brigham Young arranged for richly bound copies of the Book of Mormon to be presented to Queen Victoria and Prince Albert. The volume presented to the queen was located in the Royal Library at Windsor in 1986.

The Britain of those days was ripe for a message of hope, and the preaching of a restored gospel of Jesus Christ was timely. By June 1842 there were 8,245 members of the Church in the United Kingdom and Ireland. Six years later there were 18,000, and by the end of 1851 England had 24,199 Latter-day Saints, Wales had 5,244, Scotland had 3,291, and Ireland had 160—a total of almost 33,000—and an additional 11,000 had already emigrated to America. In 1851 there were more members of the Church in the United Kingdom and Ireland than there were in Utah (12,000).

EMIGRATION. Emigration to the United States to help build the main body of the Church was the recommended pattern for the members during the first century of the Church in the British Isles. The PERPETUAL EMIGRATING FUND was established in September 1849 to assist. Those who emigrated with the help of this revolving fund were to pay back the money as they could, so that others might be helped. The fund was formally discontinued in 1887, after thousands had benefited from it. Additional thousands were assisted by friends and relatives who had already emigrated. From 1847 to 1869, more than 32,000 British and Irish converts to the Church left their homelands for a new life in pioneer America. When the novelist Charles Dickens visited the *Amazon* before it set sail from London on June 4, 1863, to see what the Mormon emigrants were like, he noted: "I . . . had come aboard this Emigrant Ship to see what eight hundred Latter-day Saints were like. . . . Nobody is in an ill-temper, nobody is the worse for drink, nobody swears an oath or uses a coarse word, nobody appears depressed, nobody is weeping, and down upon the deck in every corner where it is possible to find a few square feet to kneel, crouch or lie in, people, in every suitable attitude for writing, are writing letters. Now, I have seen emigrants ships before this day in June. And these people are strikingly different from all other people in like circumstances whom I have ever seen, and I wonder aloud, 'What *would* a stranger suppose these emigrants to be!' . . . I should have said they were in their degree, the pick and flower of England" (Dickens, pp. 223–25).

Dickens set down his impressions of Mormon emigrants in one of a series of essays that appeared at intervals between 1860 and 1869 in his weekly magazine, *All the Year Round*. He later published them in the chapter "Bound for the Great Salt Lake" in *The Uncommercial Traveller*. He concluded with:

> I afterwards learned that a dispatch was sent home by the captain before he struck out into the wide Atlantic, highly extolling the behaviour of these emigrants, and the perfect order and propriety of all their social arrangements. . . . I went on board their ship to bear testimony against them if they deserved it, as I fully believed they would; to my great astonishment they did not deserve it; and my predispositions and tendencies must not affect me as an honest witness. I went over the *Amazon's* side, feeling it impossible to deny that, so far, some remarkable influence had produced a remarkable result, which better known influences have often missed [Dickens, p. 232].

The 895 LDS emigrants under the direction of Elder William Bramall were well organized. The ship's captain explained:

> The most of these came aboard yesterday evening. They came from various parts of England in small parties that had never seen one another before. Yet they had not been a couple of hours on board, when they established their own police, made their own regulations, and set their own watches at all the hatchways. Before nine o'clock, the ship was as orderly and quiet as a man-of-war [Dickens, p. 223].

THE CHURCH IN BRITAIN IN THE TWENTIETH CENTURY. The early years of the twentieth century were troubled times for the Church in the United Kingdom and Ireland. Much of its strength had been drawn away through emigration; between 1870 and 1892 Church membership declined from 9,000 to barely 2,600. Then, against the backdrop of the polygamy issue, and fanned by newspaper exposés and by novels from writers such as Sir Arthur Conan Doyle and Winifred Graham, an "anti-Mormon crusade" reached a peak in 1911. Persecution was rife, violence was threatened, and missionaries were occasionally tarred and feathered, as in Nuneaton, Warwickshire. Nevertheless, the Church grew in this time of trials, more than doubling in membership between 1897 and 1910, and averaging more than 8,000 members in Great Britain from then until after the end of World War I. But with missionary work disrupted by two world wars, a modest decline kept membership at an average of about 6,000 through 1950.

In the mid-1950s, membership in the United Kingdom and Ireland stood at 9,000, when the second major phase of the growth and development of the Church in the British Isles began. Emphasis was given to "staying and building," and steps were taken to ensure that Church members in the United Kingdom did not need to emigrate to enjoy all the blessings of the Church membership.

President David O. MCKAY dedicated the London Temple, at Lingfield, Surrey, on September 7–9, 1958. The first European stake was created March 27, 1960, in Manchester, and others followed in rapid succession. Where only a handful of LDS chapels existed in Britain before 1960, with most congregations worshiping in rented rooms or halls, by 1970 more than 100 chapels had been completed, and this number rose to around 250 by the end of the 1980s. These manifestations of a permanent presence led to a dramatic reawakening in the British Isles, and an era of increased baptisms and Church growth.

The Public Communications Department was established in 1975 to disseminate information about the Church. The Church Educational System began its work with youth, and missionary and temple work increased. More genealogical records were obtained for microfilming, and a network of family history centers was inaugurated. The Church Welfare Services program, with its support to the needy based on the principle of work, commenced in 1980 with the purchase of a 305-acre farm at Kington, Worcestershire. In January 1985 the London Missionary Training Center, located near the temple, opened its doors.

THE 150TH ANNIVERSARY. Media attention peaked in 1987, when the Church celebrated its 150th anniversary in the British Isles.

Broadcaster and writer Ian Bradley produced a thirty-minute BBC documentary on the Church that aired twice on radio in Britain, and also on the World Service.

At the anniversary dinner at the Savoy Hotel in London, on July 24, and in the presence of distinguished guests from both sides of the Atlantic, the British contribution to the colonizing of the American Far West was formally recognized in a videotaped message from U.S. President Ronald Reagan: "The Mormon contribution to American life is beyond measuring, and the contribution of the British Isles to the Mormon Church is also immense. They are the contributions of love and joy; of faith and family; of work and community. They are a dedication to the values that are at the heart of free nations—and good ones—and they are a faith in the promise of tomorrow."

THE CHURCH IN THE BRITISH ISLES IN 1990. Britain, like many other parts of Europe, has experienced a decline in religious observance since World War II. Many British churches now have congregations that are predominantly middle-aged to elderly, and largely female. Latter-day Saints in the United Kingdom and Ireland, in contrast, are experiencing the second flowering of the Church there. About 37 percent of British LDS baptisms came between 1837 and 1869, and nearly 50 percent have come since 1950. During the 1970s and 1980s, a new LDS congregation was established in the United Kingdom and Ireland almost every two weeks, and a new chapel was dedicated almost every month.

DEMOGRAPHICS. In demographic terms, the LDS Church in the British Isles at the end of 1989 had a young membership profile. While 43 percent of the British population that year were under thirty, the Church figure was 53 percent. Primary children (ages three to eleven) made up 20 percent of the British Latter-day Saints; 10 percent were teenagers (ages twelve to eighteen); and 25 percent were young adults (ages eighteen to thirty).

EDUCATION. The majority of LDS British youth attended state schools in 1989. Studies showed 13 percent of members of the Church had some form of higher education. Among recent converts this figure was 18 percent.

EMPLOYMENT. In 1989 unemployment was a major social problem

in the British Isles, and the rate for LDS men was similar to the national figure of 13 percent. When they were employed, Church males generally showed a higher percentage in white-collar occupations compared with the figure for all British men; fewer LDS women were in the labor force than British women generally.

THE CHALLENGE OF A LAY CLERGY. The recent increased growth of the Church in the United Kingdom and Ireland meant that the majority of local Church leaders in 1989 were still first-generation members. This created great need for effective leadership training of its lay clergy.

BRITISH CONTRIBUTIONS TO THE CHURCH. British contributions to the Church have taken two main forms: providing a training ground for many early Church leaders, and helping to build and sustain the fledgling Church through the influx of British immigrants. Of the 1839 apostolic mission, in particular, it is important to note that that group of missionaries contained the next four Presidents of the Church: Brigham Young, John TAYLOR, Wilford Woodruff, and Lorenzo SNOW. They received vital training and experience in the British Isles, and forged a strong unity within the Quorum of the Twelve that sustained the Church through the testing times that followed the martyrdom of the Prophet Joseph Smith in 1844. These men would lead and direct the Church into the twentieth century.

All of the men who have served as President of the Church, from Joseph Smith to Ezra Taft Benson, trace their ancestry back to the British Isles. The ancestors of President Benson, for example, came from Caversham, Oxfordshire. All of the Church Presidents except Joseph SMITH, Harold B. LEE, and Spencer W. KIMBALL labored as missionaries in Great Britain.

CHURCH LEADERS BORN IN BRITAIN. John Taylor, the third President of the Church, was born in Milnthorpe, Westmoreland, and joined the Church in Upper Canada. George Q. Cannon and Charles W. Penrose, both of whom became members of the Quorum of the Twelve and later counselors in the First Presidency, came from Liverpool and Camberwell, London, respectively. George Teasdale and James E. Talmage, also apostles, were from London and from Hungerford, Berkshire. John Rex Winder, from Biddenden, Kent, was a counselor in the First Presidency (1887–1910), and George Reynolds, from

London, and B. H. Roberts, from Warrington, were presidents of the Seventy.

Other British General Authorities were John Longden, from Oldham, Lancashire, and John Wells, from Carolton, Nottinghamshire. In 1990, Nottingham-born Derek A. Cuthbert was serving in the First Quorum of the Seventy. Ruth May Fox, born in Westbury, Wiltshire, in 1853, was the General President of the Young Women from 1929–1937. May Anderson of Liverpool was editor of the Church's *Children's Friend* magazine from 1902 to 1940, first counselor in the General Presidency of the Primary from 1905 to 1925, and its President from 1925 to 1939. She was also the moving force behind the establishment of the Primary Children's Hospital in Salt Lake City. May Green Hinckley, of Brampton, Derbyshire, was General President of the Primary and editor of the *Children's Friend* from 1940 to 1943. The Church's Sunday School organization was founded in 1849 by Scotsman Richard Ballantyne.

Life was not all work. The Saints carried with them a love of music. As the first pioneer party crossed the plains, they did so to the strains of William Pitt's Brass Band, from the English Midlands. One of the best-remembered British converts is William Clayton, from Penwortham, Lancashire. He founded the branch of the Church in Manchester before emigrating, and went on to serve as a clerk to Joseph Smith. While crossing the plains, he kept a meticulous record, and wrote the rallying song "Come, Come, Ye Saints," which is one of the best-known hymns of the Church.

THE MORMON TABERNACLE CHOIR. The renowned Mormon Tabernacle Choir owes its existence, in no small measure, to British emigrants. It is said that Brigham Young, hearing a group of Welsh converts singing four-part harmony in their native tongue, commented, "I don't understand the words, but you should become the nucleus of a great church choir." The first conductor of the Mormon Tabernacle Choir was John Parry, born in Newmarket, Flintshire, and its first organist was a sixteen-year-old native of Norwich, Joseph Daynes. Other early conductors also came from Britain, including George Careless, from London; Ebenezer Beesley, from Oxfordshire; and Evan Stephens, from Pencader, Carmarthenshire. In fact, seven of the first eight directors of the choir were born in the British Isles.

The first Tabernacle pipe organ was designed by an Englishman, Joseph Ridges, who built it in Australia.

In June 1982 the British contribution to the choir—indeed, to the Church itself—was graphically demonstrated at the conclusion of a concert in the Royal Albert Hall, London, when the presenter asked all members of the choir with British ancestry to stand. All but four of the 350-voice choir stood.

At a time when a number of the mainstream churches in the United Kingdom and Ireland are wrestling with some of the fundamental doctrines and practices of Christianity—the nature of resurrection, the virgin birth, ecumenism, and the ordination of women—the unchanging nature of LDS beliefs appeals to many who come into contact with the Church. Mormons seem to have found a way to hold on to the fundamentals of the faith yet be receptive to the pressures of the present. In his cover story for the November 15, 1987, issue of the Sunday *Times Magazine*, journalist Keith Wheatley wrote: "The phenomenal growth of the Latter-day Saints in recent times shows that they have no need to dilute their doctrines. . . . They seem to be a church whose hour has come."

BIBLIOGRAPHY

Allen, James B., and Thomas G. Alexander, eds. *Manchester Mormons*. Santa Barbara, Calif., 1974.

Bloxham, Ben; James R. Moss; and Larry C. Porter, eds. *Truth Will Prevail: The Rise of The Church of Jesus Christ of Latter-day Saints in the British Isles, 1837–1987*. Solihull, U.K., 1987.

Cannon, Donald Q., and Larry C. Porter, eds. *Mormonism in the British Isles 1837–1987. BYU Studies* 27 (Winter and Spring 1987):3–131; 3–135 (two whole issues on the topic).

Cowley, Matthias F., ed. *Wilford Woodruff: History of His Life and Labors, as Recorded in His Daily Journals*. Salt Lake City, 1964.

Cuthbert, Derek A. *The Second Century: Latter-day Saints in Great Britain,* Vol. 1, *1937–1987*. Salt Lake City, 1987.

Dickens, Charles. *The Uncommercial Traveller* and *Reprinted Pieces, Etc.* London, 1958.

Evans, Richard L. *A Century of "Mormonism" in Great Britain*. Salt Lake City, 1937.

Jensen, Richard L., and Malcolm R. Thorp, eds. *Mormons in Early Victorian Britain*. Salt Lake City, 1989.

Kimball, Stanley B. *Heber C. Kimball: Mormon Patriarch and Pioneer*. Urbana, Ill., 1986.

Taylor, P. A. M. *Expectations Westward: The Mormons and the Emigration of Their British Converts in the Nineteenth Century*. Edinburgh and London, 1965.

BRYAN J. GRANT

C

CALIFORNIA, PIONEER SETTLEMENTS IN

Spaniards founded missions, presidios, pueblos, and ranchos in California seventy-seven years before the arrival of the Mormons, but Latter-day Saints were among the first Anglo-Americans to establish settlements there. Brigham YOUNG believed that a seaport on the West Coast was essential to the landlocked community in Utah. He may have thought early of San Francisco as a Mormon seaport, and the ports of San Diego and San Pedro (Los Angeles area) ultimately were included within the boundaries of the proposed state of Deseret (*see* DESERET, STATE OF).

The first Latter-day Saint settlers in California located at Yerba Buena, a port connected with the mission and presidio San Francisco de Asís. Founded in 1776, the Catholic mission had fewer than one hundred people living in the area. After Elder Sam Brannan and 238 Saints arrived there on the ship *Brooklyn* on July 31, 1846, Latter-day Saints for a time predominated in Yerba Buena. About twelve families of the *Brooklyn* Saints founded the first Mormon colony in California, the short-lived agricultural community of New Hope (1846–1848), on the Stanislaus River in central California. Another of the *Brooklyn* Saints, John M. Horner, became a wealthy farmer at the southern end of San Francisco Bay. He helped found eight towns in the area and made substantial financial contributions to the Church's missionary work in the 1850s.

Recognizing the rich potential of California, Brannan journeyed east to meet Brigham Young, then traveling west with the original pioneers of 1847. At their meeting on the Green River in western Wyoming, Brannan tried to persuade Brigham Young to continue on to California rather than stop in the Great Basin. Failing in this effort, Brannan returned to Yerba Buena, where he headed a prosperous LDS community until the gold rush of 1848–1849 and internal difficulties led to its dissolution. In 1847 Yerba Buena was renamed San Francisco.

Some 340 men of the MORMON BATTALION reached southern California in January 1847. Though they arrived shortly after the California War for Independence, or Bear Flag Revolt, ended, battalion veterans nevertheless had a significant impact on California history. When the battalion came to San Diego, their one-year enlistment was nearly completed. Fifteen men left California on an escort assignment, and the rest (about 245) were later discharged. Eighty-one men reenlisted. Though some of the discharged immediately joined their families in the SALT LAKE VALLEY, others remained in California to obtain funds before traveling to Utah. Some worked in the San Diego and Los Angeles areas, while others moved north to seek employment in San Francisco or at Sutter's Fort, on the American River near present-day Sacramento.

Six recently discharged members of the battalion were at Sutter's Mill when the initial discovery of gold was made on January 24, 1848. Indeed, it is the journal of Mormon Battalion veteran Henry W. Bigler that historians use to set the date for the initial discovery of gold in California. Other battalion veterans were involved in the early 1848 search for gold, and one particularly rich region was called "Mormon Diggings." Probably the most successful Mormon gold miner was Thomas Rhoads, who had taken his large family overland from Missouri to California in 1846. Some of the Mormon miners took an estimated $25,000–$30,000 in gold to Salt Lake City, providing a substantial boost to the infant economy. Brigham Young called a limited number of Latter-day Saints on missions to mine gold in California in 1849 and 1850. Others who were disillusioned with the Great Basin or infected with "gold fever" gravitated to California against his advice.

In 1851, under the direction of Charles C. Rich, an apostle, 437 colonists from Utah were sent to found a settlement near the Cajon Pass. The result was San Bernardino, the principal LDS settlement in California along the "Mormon Corridor" connecting Utah settlements and the West Coast. It was intended to be a gathering place for immigrants from the Pacific as well as a way station to assist LDS immigration via the Pacific. Latter-day Saints from the gold fields also gathered there. By 1856 about 3,000 settlers lived in San Bernardino, but the colony was plagued by dissension. In 1857, as the U.S. Army approached Utah (*see* UTAH EXPEDITION), Brigham Young instructed the San Bernardino Saints, along with other outlying settlers, to return to Utah. Only a little more than half complied, and many of those who remained drifted from the Church. After the 1857 evacuation, as before, California attracted some Latter-day Saints who were dissatisfied with Brigham Young's relatively authoritarian style of leadership, or with the practice of polygamy, or with the Great Basin itself.

After its official withdrawal from California in 1857–1858, the Church sponsored no further COLONIZATION in the state. Latter-day Saints subsequently moved to California as individuals rather than at the request of the Church. Many migrated there in the 1920s during the southern California land promotion boom. Thousands moved there during World War II for employment opportunities in war industries such as shipping and aircraft. Today California has perhaps the greatest density of Latter-day Saints outside the states of Utah and Idaho. Two LDS temples are located there, in Los Angeles and Oakland, with another under construction in San Diego in 1990.

BIBLIOGRAPHY

Arrington, Leonard J. *Great Basin Kingdom*. Cambridge, Mass., 1958.

———. *Charles C. Rich: Mormon General and Western Frontiersman*, pp. 137–213. Provo, Utah, 1974.

Bailey, Paul. *Sam Brannan and the California Mormons*. Los Angeles, 1943.

Campbell, Eugene E. "The Mormon Gold Mining Mission of 1849." *BYU Studies* 1–2 (Autumn 1959–Winter 1960):19–31.

———. "Brigham Young's Outer Cordon: A Reappraisal." *Utah Historical Quarterly* 41 (Summer 1973):221–53.

Davies, J. Kenneth. *Mormon Gold: The Story of California's Mormon Argonauts*. Salt Lake City, 1984.

Hunter, Milton R. *Brigham Young the Colonizer*. Salt Lake City, 1940.

Orton, Chad M. *More Faith Than Fear: The Los Angeles Stake Story*. Salt Lake City, 1987.

TED J. WARNER

CANADA, THE CHURCH IN

By October 1830, converts to the Church were teaching the gospel to family and friends in Canadian cities and towns less than 200 miles from Palmyra, New York. Between 1830 and 1845, LDS missionaries labored in Upper Canada (now Ontario) and the more easterly Maritime Provinces of British North America. Lower Canada (Quebec), with its Roman Catholic heritage and traditions, was then largely impervious to competing religious influences. Brigham YOUNG, Parley P. PRATT and Orson PRATT, John E. Page, and even the Prophet Joseph Smith visited and preached in Upper Canada during these early years. Some 2,500 Canadians joined the Church in Kingston, Earnestown, Toronto, Brantford, Mount Pleasant, North and South Crosby, and elsewhere. Yet so many Latter-day Saint Canadian converts migrated to the centers of the Church or fell away that the 1861 census counted only seventy-four Mormons in all of Upper Canada.

The second LDS penetration into Canada came some fifty years later and 2,500 miles farther west, when Church President John TAYLOR, a British-born Canadian convert, sent Charles Ora Card to Canada to find a place of refuge for the Saints from the U.S. government's campaign against PLURAL MARRIAGE. Card's small 1887 settlement on Lee's Creek in southern Alberta became Cardston. The Canadian government also outlawed plural marriage, but most public opposition to the Church declined with the 1890 MANIFESTO, which officially ended the practice.

Taking full advantage of the Canadian government's "National Policy," which encouraged immigration, several thousand skilled and seasoned Latter-day Saints moved north, and soon several other Mormon towns sprang up around Cardston: Raymond (1890), and Stirling and Magrath (1898). The Alberta Stake was organized on June 9, 1895, the first LDS stake outside the United States. Charles O. Card was its president. Skilled in farming, particularly sugar beets, and in irrigating large land acreages, LDS farmers soon earned the admiration of friend and foe. By 1914, more than 10,000 Latter-day Saints were settled in a score of communities in southern Alberta. In 1923 the Church dedicated the Cardston Temple, the first temple outside the United States and its territories.

Gradually the LDS populations in Canada have shifted northward to the larger urban centers of Lethbridge, Calgary, Red Deer, and Edmonton. In the process, many members of the Church have shifted from agricultural to professional careers. Since 1950, Latter-day Saints have been known for their involvement in the oil and gas industry, railroad construction, provincial politics, education, and in many other pursuits. In 1990, more than 50,000 members of the Church lived in Alberta, 12,000 in Calgary alone.

From the Latter-day Saint communities in Alberta, members have pursued educational and vocational careers in Canadian communities from coast to coast. The ranks of Church members all across Canada have grown steadily, though not spectacularly. The story has often been the same—a few local converts, some Alberta move-ins, a steady stream of missionaries, some more local converts and leaders, rented halls giving way to Church-built meetinghouses, branches becoming wards, districts becoming stakes. The first Canadian stakes outside Alberta were organized in Toronto, Ontario, and Vancouver in 1960. Since then stakes have been organized in Manitoba, Saskatchewan, Nova Scotia, and New Brunswick, characteristically encompassing large land areas. Quebec, once hostile, had two stakes, one English- and one French-speaking, in 1990.

Hugh B. Brown and Nathan Eldon Tanner, who had been successful business, military, and education leaders in Alberta, came to serve as counselors in the First Presidency of the Church in 1961–1970 and 1963–1982, respectively.

In 1990 more than half the Canadian LDS population of approximately 125,000 lived outside of Alberta, in sixteen of the country's thirty-four stakes. The dedication and opening of the Toronto Temple in 1990 symbolized more than 150 years of achievements by the Church in Canada.

BIBLIOGRAPHY

Bennett, Richard E. "A Study of The Church of Jesus Christ of Latter-day Saints in Upper Canada, 1830–1850." M.A. thesis, Brigham Young University, 1975.

Card, Brigham Young. *The Canadian Mormon Communities in Southwestern Alberta, Canada: Origins, Persistence, and Transformation of an Ethnic Identity.* Canada, 1988.

——— et al., eds. *The Mormon Presence in Canada.* Logan, Utah, 1990.

Tagg, Melvin S. *A History of the Mormon Church in Canada.* Lethbridge, Alta., 1968.

RICHARD E. BENNETT

CANADA, LDS PIONEER SETTLEMENTS IN

LDS experience in Canada provides an important comparison to the study of the Church in the United States. Though the Church settlements of southern Alberta, begun in the late nineteenth century, were an extension of the LDS cultural region in the Great Basin, they gradually developed a unique character because they lay at the frontier intersection of two commonwealths, the Canadian and the Mormon—and as a hinterland of each. Constantly influenced by the exchange of people, ideas, and culture with the Great Basin, LDS settlements in Alberta contributed to the Church several General Authorities, including Hugh B. Brown and N. Eldon Tanner, both of whom served in the First Presidency.

Since most early Church converts from eastern Canada in the 1830s and 1840s soon joined the Saints in the United States, the LDS presence in Canada was fleeting until the late 1880s. The first permanent Church settlements in Canada were built in Alberta by Latter-day Saints from Utah seeking refuge from PERSECUTION that followed increasingly harsh ANTIPOLYGAMY LEGISLATION. Led by Charles Ora Card, they established farms in 1887 around present-day Cardston.

Card, a prominent community and Church leader in Cache Valley, Utah, had been arrested in July 1886 for practicing polygamy. After escaping from custody, he visited Church President John TAYLOR, a British-born resident of Canada at the time of his conversion, who directed Card to go to Canada to seek "British justice." President Taylor's son, John W., an apostle, entrepreneur, and visionary, joined Card in leading the early development of Canadian LDS settlements.

In the fall of 1886, Card and two companions selected southwestern Alberta—a region with good land, water for irrigation, accessible timber and coal, and close to the Blood Indian reservation—where they hoped to proselytize. Cardston was established on April 26, 1887, and the Cardston ward of the Cache stake was organized in 1888. By 1891 there were 359 Saints in the area.

Influenced by prolonged conflict between the U.S. government and the Mormons, the press and politicians elsewhere in Canada opposed LDS settlement. But local boosters and Canadian government officials welcomed the arrival of farmers skilled in irrigation in an area known for its aridity. However, official opposition to polygamy was clear. When, in November 1888, Church leaders sought permission to bring existing plural families to Canada, the government quickly outlawed polygamy. Most opposition to the Church in Canada declined after the 1890 MANIFESTO announced the official end of plural marriage.

Previous experience helped the new settlers meet the challenges of pioneering in Canada. The Cardston Company, a joint-stock venture, mobilized capital for community projects, including a flour mill, cheese factory, steam threshing outfit, sawmill, and other enterprises. Some of the capital came from Card's wife, Zina, a daughter of Brigham YOUNG, who was a former college professor and a suffragette who served as a role model for other Canadian LDS women. The economic success of the Saints broke down barriers that separated them from local society. A series of drought years in the early 1890s showed the necessity of irrigation and highlighted LDS achievements with small-scale irrigation projects.

Beginning in the late 1890s, a second wave of LDS immigrants came primarily for economic reasons. The Galt coal mining interests in Lethbridge, hoping irrigation would allow them to sell sizable tracts of land to agricultural interests, formed a partnership with Card, who saw the potential for a major colonization program for LDS farmers from the United States. The 1898 contract between the Galt Company and the Church attracted LDS subcontractors, laborers, and teamsters to Alberta to build an irrigation system. Most were farmers intent on settling. By 1900 the canal was completed, and Lord Minto, the Canadian governor general, and George Q. Cannon and Joseph F. SMITH of the First Presidency attended the opening.

These new LDS settlers founded several new towns, including Magrath and Stirling. During the late 1890s and early 1900s, population growth in the Cardston area and a continuing influx from the United States prompted Latter-day Saints to settle in Beazer, Kimball, Leavitt, Taylorville, Woolford, Jefferson, and Del Bonita.

A new surge of settlement began in 1902–1903 when wealthy Utah mine owner Jesse Knight established a sugar factory in Raymond. Latter-day Saints played a key role both as growers and as managers of the sugar company in establishing the sugar beet industry, which remains an important part of southern Alberta's economy.

In 1906, E. J. Wood, successor to Charles O. Card as president of the Alberta Stake, bought a large ranch, opening 35,000 acres to colonization and laying out the towns of Glenwood (1908) and Hillspring (1910). Church settlements also developed outside the southwest Alberta core area, at Barnwell, Taber, Orton, and Frankburg. Irrigation, the village settlement pattern (*see* CITY PLANNING), cooperative economic enterprise, and an active cultural, social, and religious life were transferred from the American Great Basin to southern Alberta. By 1911 Latter-day Saints had established eighteen new communities in southern Alberta, and 10,000 Saints, mostly farmers and their families, lived in the area of southwest Alberta alone.

With the outbreak of World War I, many young Canadian Latter-day Saints showed their loyalty to their homeland by joining the Canadian armed forces. Before the war, in order to offset questions about their patriotism, Church leaders had asked several young men, including Hugh B. Brown, to take officer training and to recruit others. By 1915 more than 200 LDS youth from the Cardston area had been recruited.

Pioneering, wartime nationalism, and the passage of time all contributed to the growing identification of Latter-day Saints with Alberta and Canada. This identity was solidified with the dedication of the temple in Cardston in 1923 by President Heber J. GRANT. A new Alberta-born and educated LDS generation emerged in small towns full of vitality. Cars, roads, and the telephone broke down rural isolation. Amateur sports, music, drama, school fairs, picnics, and rodeos reached their zenith. Alberta Latter-day Saints came into increasing contact with a wide variety of other ethnic and religious groups, including the communal Hutterites and Japanese and eastern Europeans, brought in to labor in the sugar industry.

Intense sports rivalries between the neighboring towns cemented hometown loyalties. The small LDS communities in southern Alberta dominated men's basketball in the province for decades and served as training grounds for several provincial and national basketball championship teams.

While they had an active cultural life, LDS towns did not thrive financially in an era of agricultural boom and bust. Magrath and Raymond grew quickly after their founding: by 1906 Magrath had a population of 884 and Raymond a population of 1,568. But with limited agricultural hinterlands, their growth quickly leveled off, and they grew little after 1911. Both towns developed a small industrial base that lasted until the 1960s: Raymond with its sugar factory and Magrath with a woolen mill and canning factory. With a bigger agricultural hinterland and the temple, Cardston remained the largest predominantly LDS town. Its population grew gradually from 1,000 in 1906 to about 2,000 by the 1920s.

During the 1920s many of the Canadian-born generation began looking for other opportunities. Some left for urban areas in Alberta or elsewhere in Canada, or for the United States. Church growth in other parts of Canada has often depended on leadership provided by Latter-day Saints who had pioneer roots in southern Alberta but migrated elsewhere.

Hard hit by the Great Depression of the 1930s, many Latter-day Saints rallied to the Social Credit party, which swept into power in Alberta in 1935 and retained power until 1971. Several LDS community leaders supported the monetary-reform movement, including Cardston high school principal N. Eldon Tanner, a cabinet minister from the late 1930s until the early 1950s, and schoolteachers John Blackmore and Solon Low, who both became national leaders of the party. Several other Church members were elected to the provincial legislature. The three largest cities in Alberta have each elected LDS mayors.

Since 1947 immense oil and gas discoveries have transformed Alberta. With oil-induced prosperity and farm mechanization, many Latter-day Saints moved to the cities, gradually making them the focal point of LDS life. Eventually Latter-day Saints in Calgary numbered more than in all the other Mormon towns of southern Alberta. From a tight-knit, rural, geographically compact group consisting mostly of farmers, Latter-day Saints in Canada have become increasingly urban, middle class, and geographically dispersed. Those in Alberta, however, retain their strong cultural, religious, and kinship links with American Latter-day Saints while serving as full-fledged members of Canadian society.

BIBLIOGRAPHY
Card, Brigham Y., et al., eds. *The Mormon Presence in Canada.* Edmonton and Logan, 1989.
Lethbridge Stake Historical Committee and Melvin S. Tagg. *A History of the Mormon Church in Canada.* Lethbridge, Alberta, 1968.

HOWARD PALMER

CARTHAGE JAIL

The old jail in the town of Carthage, Illinois, seat of Hancock County, was the site of the MARTYRDOM OF JOSEPH AND HYRUM SMITH on June 27, 1844, by a mob of approximately 150 men. Today it is a historical site of the Church and serves as a memorial to prophets of God who suffered martyrs' deaths.

The jail was built in 1839. Constructed of native red limestone, the two-story rectangular gable-front building measures twenty-nine by thirty-five feet. Like other county jails in Illinois, Carthage Jail was built to incarcerate petty thieves and debtors and to serve as a temporary holding place for violent criminals. It housed a debtor's room in the northwest corner of the first floor, and a dungeon, or "criminal cell" on the second floor, north side. There was also a living area for the jailer's family that included a kitchen, a dining room, and bedrooms. The cells were dark and generally foul-smelling and had only meager makeshift furnishings.

Joseph SMITH, Hyrum SMITH, and several other LDS leaders were incarcerated in Carthage Jail on June 25, 1844, to answer charges stemming from the destruction of the press used to print the anti-Mormon newspaper *Nauvoo Expositor*. During their three-day confinement they sought, through letters and personal appeals—even to the governor, then in Carthage—for an impartial resolution of the charges and for protection from people openly threatening their lives.

They were first placed in "close confinement" in the dungeon. Later they were moved to the debtors' cell and then to the jailer's upstairs bedroom in the southeast corner. By midday of June 27, only the Smiths and John TAYLOR and Willard Richards of the Quorum of the Twelve Apostles remained confined in the jail. The governor had disbanded the militia, left the prisoners under guard of the Carthage

Greys (known enemies of the Latter-day Saints), and gone to NAUVOO with a detachment of troops.

Shortly after 5:00 P.M. a large force of armed men with blackened faces rushed the jail. Overcoming token resistance by the Greys, some of the mob entered the building, ascended the stairs to the landing just outside the upstairs bedroom, and commenced shooting into the room through the closed door. Hyrum Smith, Patriarch to the Church and associate President in the Church's First Presidency, was gunned down. John Taylor was critically wounded, but Willard Richards miraculously escaped injury (*HC* 6:561–622). The Prophet, shot from both inside and outside the jail as he prepared to leap from an upstairs window, fell to the ground dead, near a well.

Carthage Jail served Hancock County until 1866. It was then a private residence, until the Church purchased it in 1903. Assisted by the Illinois Department of Public Works and Buildings, the Church completed a partial restoration of the jail in 1935.

In 1989, on the 145th anniversary of the martyrdom, the Church completed a major renovation of the whole Carthage Jail block. The jail proper was restored to its 1844 condition, and the block was fenced, landscaped, and dressed with walks, monuments, and sculpture. The adjacent visitors center, enlarged to accommodate 150 people, now holds exhibits and a theater showing a film that portrays Joseph Smith's religious and spiritual experiences.

BIBLIOGRAPHY

Baker, LeGrand L. "On to Carthage to Die." *IE* 72 (June 1969):10–13, 15.

McRae, Joseph A., and Eunice McRae. "Carthage Jail: A Physical Description of an Historical Structure." *IE* 45 (June 1942):372–73, 391.

DONALD L. ENDERS

CITY PLANNING

For Latter-day Saints, city planning began with the Prophet Joseph SMITH, who emphasized the advantages of living in compact communities rather than on isolated farms. Many of his ideas were adopted in modified form in LDS settlements in Missouri, Illinois, and the Great Basin of the American West. These communities always provided opportunities for education, cooperation, fine arts, and worship.

Joseph Smith's ideas about city planning are contained in a document known as the City of Zion plan, which he prepared in 1833. The characteristics of this Zion plan include a regular grid pattern with square blocks, wide streets (132 feet), alternating half-acre lots so that houses face alternate streets on each block, uniform brick or stone construction, homes set back 25 feet from the street, frontyard landscaping, gardens in the backyard, the location of farms outside of town, and the designation of central blocks as a site for temples, schools, and other public buildings.

Though Joseph Smith did not identify the sources behind the plan, perhaps he was influenced by the biblical pattern of Moses arranging the tribes around the tabernacle (Num. 2), as well as by towns in his own experience. Clearly his goal was to design communities that enhanced the cooperation and religious unity envisioned in the revelations about Zion.

LDS portions of KIRTLAND, OHIO, which was surveyed shortly after this plan was presented, followed it closely. Other cities influenced by Joseph Smith were somewhat different. The Saints at Far West, Missouri (1836–1839), surveyed their city into square blocks of four acres with only four one-acre lots on each. Four 132-feet-wide streets bounded a central square, but other streets were narrower. NAUVOO, Illinois (1839–1846), was similar to Far West, but only the two main streets were wider than 50 feet.

Immediately after the pioneers arrived in the SALT LAKE VALLEY in 1847, President Brigham YOUNG issued instructions for establishing SALT LAKE CITY. His plan reflected elements of the City of Zion plan, with blocks the same size, but instead of twenty half-acre lots in each block, each contained eight lots, 1.25 acres in size. As in Joseph Smith's plan, all streets were 132 feet wide and the houses on each block faced alternate streets, with each set 20 feet back from the sidewalk. The most important difference was that the lots were much larger. Each city lot became a minifarm with animals, barns, and gardens. The rapid influx of settlers into Salt Lake City led to the early subdivision of the large lots.

Other settlements (*see* COLONIZATION) followed the same general pattern as Salt Lake City, but the actual lot, block, and street sizes varied from community to community. While most communities adhered to the rigid grid pattern oriented to the cardinal directions, street widths ranged from 66 to 172 feet, block sizes from four to ten acres, and lot sizes from one-half to more than one acre. Though differing in details, Mormon towns were characterized by large lots, wide streets, and large blocks, features that still distinguish these communities of America's Intermountain West. This expansive pattern later enhanced urbanization, providing space for four lanes of traffic and for large-scale downtown development.

The emphasis on large scale has also created a distinctive landscape in the small Mormon agricultural communities of the Intermountain West. Typically, the wide streets have only a narrow two-lane strip of pavement, flanked by twenty- to thirty-foot unimproved shoulders of weeds or gravel. Most residents of these villages use the large lots only for small gardens; barns, corrals, and outbuildings of the nineteenth century often remain as landscape relics. Where population growth has led to subdivision of the street frontage of the large lots, the center of the blocks has often remained open. The interior of these large blocks may be devoted to household gardens or simply allowed to remain vacant until land prices justify higher density apartment buildings or other uses for the space.

City planning in the Mormon culture region incorporates the experiences of the Mormons in their migration across the American frontier. Joseph Smith's plan combined his New England village background with the rectangular blocks and lots typical of Philadelphia. Brigham Young adopted this rectangular pattern and added to it an emphasis on subsistence agriculture, which led to large blocks and lots for minifarms within the community. Joseph Smith's requirement to build of brick or stone was paralleled by Brigham Young's encouragement to build of adobe (unfired clay bricks). Old Mormon villages are currently dominated by adobe, brick, and stone homes, and even the modern suburbs in Mormon communities have a high concentration of brick construction. The large scale of both Joseph Smith's and Brigham Young's visions of the ideal city and the emphasis on uniform setback, landscaping, and brick or stone construction combine to make the Mormon village a distinctive pattern of city planning in America.

BIBLIOGRAPHY

Jackson, Richard H. "The Mormon Village: Genesis and Antecedents of the City of Zion Plan." *BYU Studies* 17 (Winter 1977):223–40.

Nelson, Lowry. *The Mormon Village: A Pattern and Techniques of Land Settlement.* Salt Lake City, 1954.

Ricks, Joel Edward. *Forms and Methods of Early Mormon Settlement in Utah and Surrounding Regions, 1847–1877.* Logan, Utah, 1964.

RICHARD H. JACKSON

COLESVILLE, NEW YORK

Colesville, New York, is a township located in Broome County, in the south central part of the state, where one of the earliest branches of the Church was organized in 1830. The central part of the township lies approximately ten miles northeast of the present city of Binghamton. In October 1825 Joseph SMITH went to the area to work intermittently for Josiah Stowell for a little over a year. Stowell lived just south of the village of South Bainbridge in adjoining Bainbridge Township, Chenango County (since 1857 the village of Afton, Afton Township). Sometime during 1826 Joseph Smith also worked for Joseph Knight, Sr., who with his family resided on a farm located on Pickerel Pond, immediately east of Nineveh, a village in Colesville Township on the Susquehanna River.

Joseph Smith maintained a friendly relationship with the Knight family and others in the Colesville area. In 1829, when Joseph and Oliver COWDERY were translating the Book of Mormon in HARMONY, PENNSYLVANIA, Joseph Knight, Sr., came from Colesville to visit and to give them food and writing materials. At other times, Joseph traveled the thirty miles from Harmony to Colesville for supplies. Joseph Smith related that the Melchizedek Priesthood was bestowed upon him and Oliver Cowdery by Peter, James, and John along the banks of the Susquehanna River between Colesville and Harmony (D&C 128:20).

After the Church was organized on April 6, 1830, in FAYETTE, NEW YORK, Joseph made several visits to the Knight family in Colesville to preach the gospel. On one of these visits, he cast an evil spirit out of Newel Knight, a son of Joseph Knight, Sr. This was the first miracle performed in the Church after its organization (*HC* 1:82–83). Numerous converts were baptized in the area, despite strong opposition from enemies of the Church. Joseph was brought to

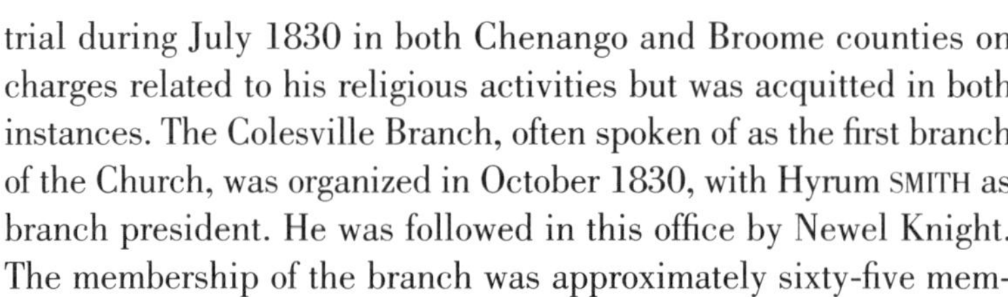

trial during July 1830 in both Chenango and Broome counties on charges related to his religious activities but was acquitted in both instances. The Colesville Branch, often spoken of as the first branch of the Church, was organized in October 1830, with Hyrum SMITH as branch president. He was followed in this office by Newel Knight. The membership of the branch was approximately sixty-five members.

The Saints in the Colesville area, following instruction of the Prophet (D&C 38), migrated to KIRTLAND and then Thompson, Ohio, in April–May 1831, and subsequently on to Kaw Township, Jackson County, Missouri, during June–July 1831. Through all their moves they stayed together and were known as the Colesville Branch.

BIBLIOGRAPHY

Porter, Larry C. "A Study of the Origins of The Church of Jesus Christ of Latter-day Saints in the States of New York and Pennsylvania, 1816–1831." Ph.D. diss., Brigham Young University, 1971.

LAMAR E. GARRARD

COLONIZATION

[*This entry is an overview of Latter-day Saint colonization in the Great Basin. Articles on* City Planning *and* Immigration and Emigration *discuss principles guiding colonization decisions. For further discussion of colonization outside Utah, see entries on LDS pioneer settlements in* Arizona; California; Canada; Colorado; Idaho; Mexico; Nevada; New Mexico; *and* Wyoming. *Related articles are* Economic History of the Church *and* Young, Brigham.]

Latter-day Saints were industrious colonizers of the American West. During the Brigham YOUNG administration alone, they founded nearly four hundred settlements, with three hundred more thereafter. Though some were distant from SALT LAKE CITY, they were not isolated villages but maintained close communication with adjacent settlements and Church headquarters. Following a pattern that emerged in the Church's first decade, each was founded to provide protection and promote unity and shared values.

Between 1830 and 1846, Latter-day Saints settled in or near a series of Church headquarters. After conflict and persecution in New York, Ohio, Missouri, and Illinois, they sought refuge in a virtual no-man's-land in the West. After establishing a new headquarters in the heretofore largely uninhabited SALT LAKE VALLEY, Latter-day Saints sought to ensure self-rule by establishing a dominant influence over a vast territory including present-day Utah and Nevada and parts of Idaho, Wyoming, and California. Immigrant converts, first from the United States and the British Isles and after 1852 from continental Europe, swelled the ranks of colonists. Under the direction of President Brigham Young, exploring parties were sent out and settlements were established in a corridor extending from the Salt Lake Valley southwest to Las Vegas, Nevada, and San Bernardino, California. Missions to Native Americans prompted the establishment of several settlements around the perimeter of the Mormon sphere of influence: Fort Limhi, Idaho, on the Salmon River to the northwest; the Elk Mountain Mission to the southeast (near present-day Moab, Utah); and Harmony and Santa Clara, Utah, and Las Vegas to the southwest. Settlements in Carson Valley, Nevada, on the west were an outgrowth of individual LDS enterprise along the route of gold-seekers traveling to California, reinforced at the direction of Church leaders. To the northeast, Fort Bridger and Fort Supply, Wyoming, were to anchor a series of way stations between Salt Lake City and the Missouri River along the MORMON TRAIL to facilitate immigration and trade. San Bernardino was to be a temporary gathering place for Saints from the Pacific Coast.

For various reasons, most of these outer colonies proved less than successful and were discontinued by 1858. The march of the UTAH EXPEDITION toward Utah and hostility provoked by the MOUNTAIN MEADOWS MASSACRE prompted a withdrawal from most distant outposts. After the conclusion of the so-called Utah War, colonization resumed, but within a more compact territory. St. George, Utah, the focal point of the 1861 Cotton Mission, became a key settlement in the Southwest. With President Young's persistent support, that settlement survived the demise of its cotton industry after America's Civil War and the abandonment of LDS efforts to establish a route for trade and immigration via the Gulf of California and the lower Colorado River. With the addition of settlements in northern Utah and southern

Idaho, the population came to be most heavily concentrated in the territory's northern region.

Meanwhile, the extension of settlement beyond the Salt Lake Valley deprived Native Americans of prime hunting and fishing lands. After initial conflicts, President Young established a policy of feeding the Indians rather than fighting them, but still advised villages to build fortifications against possible attack. Latter-day Saints sought to convert the Indians both to their religion and to the pursuit of agriculture. Even with the assistance of federally sponsored farms, however, few Indians made successful transitions. The continued influx of LDS immigrants and the failure of Church and government efforts to reverse the gradual impoverishment of the Native American population led to the Walker War of the 1850s and to the Black Hawk War of the 1860s. The subsequent resettlement of the surviving Indians to reservations removed one of the major obstacles to further colonization.

Before Brigham Young's death in 1877, additional settlements were planted along the Little Colorado River in Arizona, followed by more in Colorado, New Mexico, Canada, and Mexico. Elsewhere, the Palawai Valley on the island of Lanai and, later, Laie on Oahu became gathering places for Saints in Hawaii, the first such settlements outside western North America.

Colonization was generally directed and coordinated from Church headquarters. Church leaders selected key sites and handpicked leaders to direct the founding of new villages. Some settlers volunteered, while others received a calling to relocate. When LDS families established new locations on their own initiative, Church leaders usually visited soon afterward to ensure that the settlement was properly organized. Thus, each settlement was effectively a colony of the mother settlement in Salt Lake City. From initial sites, Latter-day Saints spread out to occupy most of the arable land nearby and founded new towns.

Beginning in 1880, Mormon villages spread along the route of the Utah and Northern Railway and the Upper Snake River Valley in Idaho. Many of these were settled through individual initiative rather than Church direction, and Church leaders labored with some difficulty to encourage the location of homes in the customary compact

Mormon villages rather than scattered throughout the surrounding farmland.

Colonies in Alberta, Canada, and in Chihuahua, Mexico, largely resulted from the Church's attempts to find refuge for polygamists under threat of prosecution during the 1880s (*see* ANTIPOLYGAMY LEGISLATION). Later efforts included the Big Horn Basin of Wyoming by 1900 and Kelsey, Texas, in 1901. Though Kelsey was one of only a handful of LDS settlements established outside the larger sphere of Latter-day Saint influence, the town still exhibited many of the characteristics of a planned Mormon village.

Early in the twentieth century, new colonization ceased and emphasis was placed on strengthening congregations throughout the world rather than on gathering to already predominantly LDS communities.

BIBLIOGRAPHY

Arrington, Leonard J. *Great Basin Kingdom.* Cambridge, Mass., 1958.

Campbell, Eugene E. "Brigham Young's Outer Cordon—A Reappraisal." *Utah Historical Quarterly* 41 (Summer 1973):220–53.

Hunter, Milton R. *Brigham Young the Colonizer.* Santa Barbara, Calif., 1973.

Sherlock, Richard. "Mormon Migration and Settlement After 1875." *Journal of Mormon History* 2 (1975):53–68.

RICHARD L. JENSEN

COLORADO, PIONEER SETTLEMENTS IN

The first Latter-day Saints in Colorado were predominantly from the American South. In 1846, converts from Mississippi, expecting to join Brigham YOUNG and the pioneer company en route to the Great Basin, wintered at the site of present-day Pueblo after learning that the first company of NAUVOO emigrants would not leave the Missouri River until the next spring. A group of sick members of the MORMON BATTALION, including women and children, joined these Mississippi Saints, and all left Pueblo in time to reach the Great Salt Lake Valley in July 1847.

Southern converts also formed the nucleus of permanent LDS colonization in Colorado, wintering in Pueblo in 1877–1878 and settling in 1878 in the San Luis Valley. Joined by settlers from Sanpete

County and elsewhere in Utah and by two families from New Mexico, they founded several settlements in the following decade. The San Luis Stake, with headquarters at Manassa, was organized in 1883 and consisted of LDS colonists in Conejos County. Jack Dempsey, a son of expatriate southern Latter-day Saints, was born in Manassa and, as world heavyweight boxing champion, bore the nickname "Manassa Mauler."

Beginning as early as 1880, LDS settlers began to establish farms along the Mancos River in southwest Colorado. In 1901, after land in the nearby Fort Lewis Indian Reservation was made available for settlement, Latter-day Saints began to establish farms on the Fort Lewis Mesa. They constituted a majority of the settlers in that area, though Mancos itself was not a predominantly Mormon town. The Young Stake, organized in 1912, consisted of Latter-day Saints in Mancos, the Fort Lewis Mesa, and northwestern New Mexico.

Early growth of the Church along the eastern slope of the Rocky Mountains came largely through the proselytizing of the Western States Mission, long headquartered in Denver; branches of the Church were established there and in Englewood, Fort Collins, and Pueblo by 1930. Farther west, additional growth came in Alamosa and Grand Junction in the first third of the twentieth century. By 1990, after continued proselytizing and in-migration, there were 87,000 Latter-day Saints in Colorado.

BIBLIOGRAPHY

Anderson, Carleton Q.; Betty Shawcroft; and Robert Compton. *The Mormons: 100 Years in the San Luis Valley of Colorado 1883–1983*. La Jara, Colo., 1982.

Jenson, Andrew. *Encyclopedic History of The Church of Jesus Christ of Latter-day Saints.* Salt Lake City, 1941.

The Stone Rolls Forth: A History of The Church of Jesus Christ of Latter-day Saints in Southeastern Colorado 1846–1986. Compiled by the Colorado Springs, Colorado North Stake, 1988.

RICHARD L. JENSEN

COMPREHENSIVE HISTORY OF THE CHURCH

Intended as a centennial history of the LDS Church (1830–1930), Elder B. H. Roberts's six-volume *Comprehensive History of the*

Church stands as a high point in the publication of Church history to that time. Most earlier works were either attacks upon or defenses of the Church. Although Roberts's study was a kind of defense, he set a more even tone, a degree of uncommon objectivity.

Like several historians preceding him (Bancroft, Whitney, Tullidge), Roberts set out to produce a multivolume work. Originally a periodical series prepared for the *Americana* magazine, Roberts's articles appeared in forty-two-page installments between July 1909 and July 1915 (*CHC* 1:v–vi). As the centennial year of 1930 approached, Elder George Albert SMITH suggested that Roberts bring his work up to date and that the Church publish it for the centennial.

Published in handsome bindings with numerous illustrations, the work was impressive. But to the reader of today its importance lies beyond its format. Roberts was pointing the way to a new approach; he wanted Church history to avoid apology and undiscriminating defense of the faith. For example, he was skeptical of including any myths parading as history: "I find my own heart strengthened in the truth by getting rid of the untruth, the spectacular, the bizarre, as soon as I learn that it is based on worthless testimony" (Madsen, p. 363). He treated the difficulties of the Saints in Missouri objectively, assigning some elements of blame to both sides.

Roberts was willing to deal with sensitive topics. His analysis of the MOUNTAIN MEADOWS MASSACRE was fairly exacting. He was also willing to press his editors to get what he felt was fairness; he insisted on including Joseph Smith's KING FOLLETT DISCOURSE despite urgings to the contrary by some members. In some ways Roberts's *Comprehensive History* was an act of courage; certainly it was his magnum opus.

Though not trained as a historian, Roberts was well known as an orator and as a theologian. He read widely and was a vibrant politician, a noted missionary, and a popular Church leader. His theological writings continue to attract attention. All of this energy, even charisma, flows into his writing, producing rhapsodic prose that sometimes overshoots the mark. He wrote in the Romantic style, accepting Prescott and Parkman as his models.

The *Comprehensive History* is the high-water mark of studies produced before academic scholars undertook the writing of Church history after 1950. Roberts shows a faithfulness to documentary sources and rules of evidence. The six-volume set is a worthy monument to the Church's first century and still attracts serious attention.

BIBLIOGRAPHY

Bitton, Davis. "B. H. Roberts as Historian." *Dialogue* 4 (Winter 1968):25–44.

———, and Leonard Arrington. *Mormons and Their Historians*, pp. 69–86. Salt Lake City, 1988.

Madsen, Truman G. *Defender of the Faith: The B. H. Roberts Story*, pp. 357–66. Salt Lake City, 1980.

DOUGLAS D. ALDER

CONSECRATION

[*The following two articles deal with the LDS concept of consecration.* Law of Consecration *offers an overview of the origin and extended practice of the principles of consecration among Latter-day Saints. The article* Consecration in Ohio and Missouri *specifically addresses both LDS efforts to live such principles and the resulting economic impact on LDS communities that flourished in these states between 1832 and 1846.*]

LAW OF CONSECRATION

The law of consecration was introduced through revelations given to the Prophet Joseph SMITH. As early as 1829, he was directed by the Lord to "seek to bring forth and establish the cause of Zion" (D&C 6:6; 11:6; 12:6; 14:6). Anciently, the Zion of Enoch was made up of people who "were of one heart and one mind, and dwelt in righteousness; and there was no poor among them" (Moses 7:18). These features have characterized the Lord's people who have accepted and applied the fulness of the gospel in their lives, such as the people of the city of Enoch (Moses 7:17–18) and the Nephite golden era (4 Ne. 1:2–3, 15–17) and some of the early Christians (Acts 4:32–37). Latter-day Saints have also been given the law of consecration as an ideal and a challenge and promise for the future (D&C 42:32–39).

The level of dedication required to live the law of consecration has many ancient echoes. The Bible records acts of consecration expressly connected with instituting covenants with God (e.g., Gen. 9:8–17; Num. 6). The willingness to sacrifice Isaac signified the complete dedication of Abraham to God's commands (Gen. 22:1–18).

Exodus and Leviticus also disclose various sacrificial acts involving consecration to God, principally by Aaron and his sons (cf. Ex. 40:12–16; Lev. 1–7). The New Testament records that early Christians were called upon to set their hearts first on the kingdom of God and to have "all things in common" (Acts 2, 4, 5).

After the risen Jesus established his Church in the Western Hemisphere about A.D. 34, the Book of Mormon people followed the practice of consecration for nearly 200 years. "The people were all converted unto the Lord, upon all the face of the land, both Nephites and Lamanites, and there were no contentions and disputations among them, and every man did deal justly one with another. And they had all things common among them; therefore there were not rich and poor, bond and free, but they were all made free, and partakers of the heavenly gift" (4 Ne. 1:2–3).

On January 2, 1831, the Lord revealed to the Prophet Joseph Smith in FAYETTE, NEW YORK, that anciently he had taken the Zion of Enoch to himself and then commanded him to go to Ohio to receive the law (D&C 38:4, 32; cf. Moses 7:21). When Joseph Smith arrived at KIRTLAND, OHIO, in February, he found the Saints organized in a communal society called "the family." He persuaded them to abandon this practice for "the more perfect law of the Lord." On February 9, while in the presence of twelve elders, he received the revelation that embraced "the law of the Church" (*HC* 1:146–48; D&C 42). This revelation presented the laws of Church government and of moral conduct for members and established the basic principles of consecration (D&C 42:32–39).

The key principles given in the revelations are consistent with those required for celestial living: all things belong to God, and his people are stewards (D&C 38:17; 104:11–14); individuals are to esteem others as themselves (D&C 38:24–27; 51:3, 9; 70:14; 78:6; 82:17); mankind must retain free agency (D&C 104:17); men and women are made equal according to their wants, needs, and family situations (D&C 51:3); and there must be accountability (D&C 72:3; 104:13–18). Although the implementation of the law of consecration of property as revealed in the early 1830s was temporarily suspended (cf. *HC* 4:93), the principles themselves were not discontinued.

THE COVENANTS OF CONSECRATION TODAY. The Lord revealed several purposes for the law of consecration: to bring the Church to stand independent of all other institutions (D&C 78:14); to strengthen Zion, adorning her in beautiful garments, as a bride prepared and worthy of the bridegroom (D&C 33:17; 58:11; 65:3; 82:14, 18; etc.); and to prepare the Saints for a place in the celestial kingdom (D&C 78:7).

Commenting on this subject, President John TAYLOR stated that consecration is a celestial law and, when observed, its adherents become a celestial people (*JD* 17:177–81). Thus, men and women today can become like as those of Enoch's day, "of one heart and one mind, . . . with no poor among them" (Moses 7:18). Orson PRATT, an early apostle, observed that if the Lord's people aspire to the celestial kingdom, they must begin to learn the order of life that is there (*JD* 2:102–103).

IMPLEMENTATION OF THE LAW OF CONSECRATION. The law of consecration requires dedicating all of one's time, talents, and possessions to the Church and its purposes (D&C 82:19; 64:34; 88:67–68; 98:12–14). John A. Widtsoe, an apostle, noted that its operation was quite simple. Those who joined such an order were to place all their possessions in a common treasury—the rich their wealth, the poor their pittance. Then each member was to receive a sufficient portion—called an "inheritance"—from the common treasury to enable that person to continue in trade, business, or profession as desired. The farmer would receive land and implements; the tradesman, tools and materials; the merchant, necessary capital; the professional person, instruments, books, and the like. Members working for others would receive proportionate interests in the enterprises they served. No one would be without property. All would have an inheritance (Widtsoe, pp. 302–303).

A person's inheritance was to consist of personal property, to be operated permanently and freely for the benefit of the person and the family. Should the person withdraw from the order, the inheritance could be taken with him, but the person would have no claim upon surplus donations or possessions initially placed in the common treasury (D&C 51:3–6). At the end of a year or set period, the member who had earned more than needed for his family would voluntarily place the surplus in the common treasury. Substantial profits were to be administered by the group rather than by one individual. Men and women who, despite diligence, had a loss from their operations would have the loss made up by the general treasury for another start, or they might—with consent—be placed in some activity better suited to their gifts. In short, the general treasury was to establish every person in a preferred field and was to care for those unable to profit from their inheritance. The general treasury, holding members' surpluses, would also finance public works and make possible all community enterprises decided upon by the group (D&C 104:60–77).

President J. Reuben Clark, Jr., counselor in the First Presidency, explained that the law of consecration as practiced was not a fully communal life. There was no common table. Each family lived as a unit. Property that was not turned back to the donor by mutual consent of the donor and the bishop became the property of the Church and was placed in the storehouse. Every member of the Church had equal access to the contents of the storehouse according to personal needs, circumstances, and needs of the family (Clark, p. 3).

EFFORTS TO LIVE THE LAW OF CONSECRATION. An early effort to live the law of consecration was first tried at Thompson, Ohio, in May 1831 by the members from the Colesville Branch who had moved there from New York. Complications arose when one of the participants withdrew his land and some of the members left for Missouri to help establish the center place of Zion before the practice could take root (Stewart, p. 125). Continued efforts to make necessary refinements in practicing the law in Ohio ultimately failed. A similar attempt was also made at this same time to institute the law of consecration and stewardship in Missouri, but intolerance and bickering among some of the Saints and the lack of any surplus to consecrate rendered the attempt unsuccessful (*see* CONSECRATION IN OHIO AND MISSOURI below).

After these early failures, the Lord adapted the requirements of the law of consecration to the capacities of the Saints and revealed the law of tithing as a practice to follow (*HC* 3:44; D&C 119). Although tithing does not require the giving of everything to the Lord, it teaches the fundamental elements upon which the character of a Zion people rests: self-control, generosity, love of fellow humans, love for God, and a desire to build the kingdom of God. Giving tithing for over a century, as the Saints proved their ability to live this commandment, prepared them to accept also the welfare program, introduced in 1936 by Church President Heber J. GRANT (*CR* [Oct. 1936]:3). Five years later, President J. Reuben Clark, Jr., observed that the practices of tithing, fast offerings, and Church welfare had brought Church members closer to the original principles of the UNITED ORDER and law of consecration (*CR* [Oct. 1942]:57).

Concerning the future, Zion can be redeemed only by obedience to the law of consecration. At the proper time, the Lord's leaders will implement the program. While it is not clear what procedures will be revealed, Latter-day Saints anticipate that the principles of stewardship, equality, agency, and accountability will eventually be subscribed to by all participants and that the goals originally envisioned will be reached (D&C 78:7, 14; 82:14).

BIBLIOGRAPHY

Clark, J. Reuben, Jr. "Testimony of Divine Origin of Welfare Plan." *Deseret News*, Church Section, Aug. 8, 1951, p. 3.

Cook, Lyndon W. *Joseph Smith and the Law of Consecration*. Provo, Utah, 1985.

Nelson, William O. "To Prepare a People." *Ensign* 9 (Jan. 1979):18–23.

Stewart, George, et al. *Priesthood and Church Welfare*. Salt Lake City, 1939.

Widtsoe, John A. *Evidences and Reconciliations*. Salt Lake City, 1943.

FRANK W. HIRSCHI

CONSECRATION IN OHIO AND MISSOURI

The principles of consecration were implemented in various forms in Ohio and Missouri in the 1830s to provide for the needs of the poor and of a financially struggling Church (*see* KIRTLAND, OHIO; KIRTLAND ECONOMY). Many of the Latter-day Saints migrating to Ohio and Missouri lacked the means to support themselves, and the Church had few resources to construct buildings such as the temple or to finance publications. The various implementations of the law of consecration helped to meet these practical needs as well as to teach participants to live a celestial law.

The law of consecration was never fully practiced in Ohio but was implemented in Missouri in several forms between 1831 and 1839. In its 1831 form, the law of consecration required all participants, or "stewards," to consecrate or convey their possessions to the Church storehouse. The bishop would then give back to each individual or family a "stewardship" of land, money, and other possessions according to just wants and needs. Surplus profits generated from these stewardships were contributed to the storehouse to assist the poor and serve other general purposes. To administer the system, separate bishops and storehouses were established in the two Church centers of Kirtland and Missouri.

In 1833, the practice of consecration was modified to provide for private ownership of stewardships, and in 1838, the principle of tithing introduced another change. The law of tithing required the Saints to give "all their surplus property" to the bishop, and subsequently "one-tenth of all their interest [increase] annually" (D&C 119:1, 4).

Implementation of consecration was difficult for the early Latter-day Saints and occurred only intermittently. The impoverished Missouri Saints were driven and persecuted by mobs and repeatedly lost personal possessions, lands, and crops. Church property was often taken or destroyed (*see* MISSOURI CONFLICT). Under such circumstances, most members required more for their stewardships than they could contribute to the pool of resources. Others were reluctant to donate their surpluses, and some who left the Church pursued legal means to recover consecrated properties. In the face of such obstacles, the sincere efforts of some faithful Saints to implement the law are all the more remarkable.

The United Firm, more commonly known as the UNITED ORDER, a corporate enterprise based on consecration principles, was a second and more limited implementation of consecration, which operated in Kirtland with a branch in Missouri from March 1832 to April 1834. About twelve men consecrated their possessions and received stewardships in this business venture. Surpluses were to go into the storehouse for printing the revelations and for meeting other Church needs. The firm dissolved when loan payments could not be made.

The Literary Firm, a third implementation of consecration principles, continued longer than the other two. Established in November 1831 to print the revelations and other publications for the Church, it operated in several forms until August 1837. Following the 1833 Missouri mob actions, printing operations were moved from Independence to Kirtland. Up to eight men were made stewards over the revelations and consecrated their efforts to manage publication. Although constantly beset by problems, the firm published the Doctrine and Covenants (1st ed.), the Book of Mormon (2nd ed.), and other Church books and periodicals.

BIBLIOGRAPHY

Arrington, Leonard J.; Feramorz Y. Fox; and Dean L. May. *Building the City of God: Community and Cooperation Among the Mormons*. Salt Lake City, 1976.

Cook, Lyndon W. *Joseph Smith and the Law of Consecration*. Salt Lake City, 1985.

KARL RICKS ANDERSON

COUNCIL BLUFFS (KANESVILLE), IOWA

Between 1846 and 1852, Council Bluffs, then known as Kanesville, was the headquarters for a substantial LDS presence in western Iowa. During the exodus from Illinois to the Rocky Mountains in the late 1840s, thousands of Latter-day Saints wintered at the Missouri River. After many proceeded westward, WINTER QUARTERS, their original headquarters on the western bank, was abandoned in early 1848 in response to governmental pressure to leave Indian lands. Latter-day Saints who had not gone west relocated on the east bank of the river, in Iowa.

The new townsite was laid out in December 1847, on what originally had been Henry W. Miller's encampment on Indian Creek, in a hollow below the east bluffs of the Missouri River. That same month, Brigham YOUNG was sustained as President of the Church in a reorganization of the First Presidency in Kanesville. The new town of Kanesville took its name from a non-Mormon emissary of U.S. President James K. Polk, Colonel Thomas L. KANE, who had proven himself a friend of the Latter-day Saints.

President Brigham Young assigned Orson HYDE of the Quorum of the Twelve Apostles to remain in Kanesville to supervise the movement of Latter-day Saints to the West as quickly as possible. The town's location on the Missouri River was particularly advantageous for several thousand British converts who had postponed their migration to America until a new gathering place and headquarters in the West had been established. By sailing to New Orleans, steamboating to St. Louis, and then upriver to Kanesville, these immigrants were spared the rigors of overland travel at least that far.

At one time, as many as thirty-one small encampments were clustered in and about Kanesville. At its height, Kanesville consisted of 350 log cabins, two log tabernacles, a post office, and numerous shops, stores, and other business establishments. Wheat, corn, and many vegetables thrived then, as they do today, in the rich riverbed soil near the bluffs. The town's most pressing problem, to provide adequate food, shelter, employment, and wagon outfits for large numbers of poor immigrants "passing through," was made easier by the California Gold Rush of 1849–1851, which resulted in a boom for Kanesville and other outfitting towns. The gold rush greatly expedited LDS migration while transforming Kanesville from a Mormon into a "Gentile" town.

By the summer of 1852, more than 12,000 Latter-day Saints—6,100 from Great Britain alone—had traveled west via Kanesville, ending the period of concentrated LDS presence in the area. In December 1853, non-LDS residents incorporated Kanesville and renamed it Council Bluffs, in memory of Lewis and Clark's council with the Indians in 1804 on or near the city site.

Kanesville is also remembered as the place where Oliver COWDERY was rebaptized by Orson Hyde in November 1848, ending years of estrangement from the Church he had helped organize in 1830.

BIBLIOGRAPHY

Aitchison, Clyde B. "The Mormon Settlements in the Missouri Valley." *The Quarterly of the Oregon Historical Society* 8 (1907):276–89.

Bennett, Richard E. *Mormons at the Missouri 1846–1852*. Norman, Okla., 1987.

Webb, Lynn Robert. "The Contributions of the Temporary Settlements Garden Grove, Mount Pisgah and Kanesville, Iowa, to Mormon Emigration, 1846–1852." Master's thesis, Brigham Young University, 1954.

Wyman, Walker D. "Council Bluffs and the Westward Movement." *Iowa Journal of History* 47 (Apr. 1949):99–118.

RICHARD E. BENNETT

COUNCIL OF FIFTY

The Council of Fifty, a council formed in NAUVOO in 1844, provided a pattern of political government under priesthood and revelation. It was, to its members, the nucleus or focus of God's latter-day kingdom.

Old Testament prophecy speaks of a stone "cut out of the mountain without hands" that will roll forth to fill the whole earth (Dan.

2:44–45). Joseph SMITH and his associates believed that the "little stone" represented in part a political kingdom similar to the other kingdoms referred to by Daniel. Joseph Smith taught that in this, the dispensation of the fulness of times, "all things" would be set in place for Christ's return, including the basic principles and organization for a system that would govern the earth during the Millennium (*JD* 1:202–203; 2:189; 17:156–57).

On April 7, 1842, Joseph Smith received a revelation giving the formal name of the "Living Constitution"—or, as it came to be known by the number of its members, the Council of Fifty—and indicating that the nucleus of a government of God would be organized. Two years later, in the spring of 1844, after a small group of faithful Church leaders and members had received their temple endowment, the Prophet formally established the Council of Fifty.

Members of the council understood its principles to be consistent with the ethics of scripture and with the protections and responsibilities of the Constitution of the United States. Non-Latter-day Saints could be members (three were among the founding members), but all were to follow God's law and seek to know his will. The President of the Church sat as council president, with others seated according to age, beginning with the oldest. Revealed rules governed proceedings, including one that required that decisions be unanimous.

The council had some practical responsibilities for organizing Joseph Smith's presidential campaign in 1844, the exodus from Nauvoo in 1845–1846 (*see* WESTWARD MIGRATION, PLANNING AND PROPHECY), and early government in the Great Basin. But what interested council members most was not their specific duties but the expectation that the council represented something much larger: it was a working demonstration of the principles and pattern for a future kingdom of God on earth. The Church already had a well-developed apocalyptic outlook, including belief in the latter-day collapse of existing governments before Christ's return. In this framework, the Council of Fifty was viewed as the seed of a new political order that would rule, under Christ, following the prophesied cataclysmic events of the last days.

The council, therefore, did not challenge existing systems of law and government (even in Nauvoo), but functioned more as a private organization learning to operate in a pluralistic society. Its exercise of actual political power was modest, but provided a symbol of the future theocratic kingdom of God. Always, the Fifty functioned under the First Presidency and the Quorum of the Twelve Apostles, who were also members of the council.

After the westward migration and the early pioneer period, the Council of Fifty largely disappeared as a functioning body, except for a brief resurgence during John TAYLOR's presidency when the Church again faced intense political challenges. Still, the Saints found consolation in the belief that one day, when the Savior returned, the Council of Fifty, or a council based on its principles, would rise again to govern the world under the King of Kings.

BIBLIOGRAPHY

Andrus, Hyrum L. *Joseph Smith and World Government*. Salt Lake City, 1958.

Ehat, Andrew F. "It Seems Like Heaven Began on Earth: Joseph Smith and the Constitution of the Kingdom of God." *BYU Studies* 20 (Spring 1980):253–79.

Hansen, Klaus J. *Quest for Empire*. East Lansing, Mich., 1967.

Quinn, D. Michael. "The Council of Fifty and Its Members, 1844 to 1945." *BYU Studies* 20 (Winter 1980):163–97.

KENNETH W. GODFREY

COWDERY, OLIVER

Oliver Cowdery (1806–1850) was next in authority to Joseph SMITH in 1830 (D&C 21:10–12), and was a second witness of many critical events in the restoration of the gospel. As one of the three Book of Mormon witnesses, Oliver Cowdery testified that an angel displayed the gold plates and that the voice of God proclaimed them correctly translated. He was with Joseph Smith when John the Baptist restored to them the Aaronic Priesthood and when Peter, James, and John ordained them to the Melchizedek Priesthood and the apostleship, and again during the momentous KIRTLAND TEMPLE visions (D&C 110).

Oliver came from a New England family with strong traditions of patriotism, individuality, learning, and religion. He was born at Wells, Vermont, on October 3, 1806. His younger sister gave the only reliable information about his youth: "Oliver was brought up in

Poultney, Rutland County, Vermont, and when he arrived at the age of twenty, he went to the state of New York, where his older brothers were married and settled. . . . Oliver's occupation was clerking in a store until 1829, when he taught the district school in the town of Manchester" (Lucy Cowdery Young to Andrew Jenson, March 7, 1887, Church Archives).

While boarding with Joseph Smith's parents, he learned of their convictions about the ancient record that their son was again translating after Martin HARRIS had lost the manuscript in 1828. The young teacher prayed and received answers that Joseph Smith mentioned in a revelation (D&C 6:14–24). The Prophet's first history states the "Lord appeared unto . . . Oliver Cowdery and shewed unto him the plates in a vision and . . . what the Lord was about to do through me, his unworthy servant. Therefore he was desirous to come and write for me to translate" (*PJS* 1:10).

From April 7 through the end of June 1829, when they finished the translation, Joseph dictated while Oliver wrote, with "utmost gratitude" for the privilege (*Messenger and Advocate* 1:14). Oliver penned a letter then, expressing deep love for Christ, a lifetime theme. He later told how he and Joseph interrupted their work as they were translating the record of the Savior's post-resurrection American ministry, and how, as they prayed about baptism, they heard the "voice of the Redeemer" and were ministered to by John the Baptist, who gave them authority to baptize (JS—H 1:71, note).

In 1835 Oliver helped Joseph Smith correct and publish the revelations for the Doctrine and Covenants. Section 27 lists the major priesthood messengers of the restoration: John the Baptist, whom "I have sent unto you, my servants, Joseph Smith, Jr., and Oliver Cowdery, to ordain you unto this first priesthood" (D&C 27:8); and "Peter, James, and John, whom I have sent unto you, by whom I have ordained you and confirmed you to be apostles and especial witnesses of my name, and bear the keys of your ministry" (D&C 27:12).

The lesser priesthood was restored on May 15, 1829, two weeks before the Prophet and Cowdery moved to the Whitmers' in New York to complete the translation of the Book of Mormon (*HC* 1:39–41, 48–49). The higher priesthood also came before this move; David WHITMER remembered he was ordained as an elder only weeks after their first arrival at his upstate farm (Whitmer, p. 32). The ancient apostles appeared with priesthood keys as Joseph and Oliver traveled between their Pennsylvania home and Colesville, New York (D&C 128:20), where Joseph Knight, Sr., lived. Knight remembered their seeking help to sustain them while translating in April or May (Jessee, p. 36).

After the move to the Whitmer farm, the angel showed the plates to Joseph Smith and the Three Witnesses in June 1829. Oliver supervised the printing of the Book of Mormon that fall and winter. After the publication of the book on March 26, the Church was organized on April 6, 1830. Oliver spoke in meeting the next Sunday, which was "the first public discourse that was delivered by any of our number" (*HC* 1:81).

Few exceeded Cowdery in logical argument and elevated style. Moreover, his speeches and writings carry the tone of personal knowledge. Generally serving as editor or associate editor in the first publications of the Church, Oliver wrote with unusual consistency through two decades of published writings and personal letters. He insisted that a relationship with God required constant contact: "Whenever [God] has had a people on earth, he always has revealed himself to them by the Holy Ghost, the ministering of angels, or his own voice" (*Messenger and Advocate* 1:2). Oliver Cowdery led the LAMANITE MISSION, the first major mission of the Church (D&C 28:8; 30:5), which doubled Church membership and took the Book of Mormon to Native Americans. After the temple site was designated in Jackson County in 1831, he traveled there with copies of the revelations for their first printing. Because publishing was vital for spreading the gospel and instructing members, Oliver was called to work with William W. Phelps, an experienced editor (D&C 55:4; 57:11–13). After Missouri ruffians destroyed the press, Cowdery returned to Ohio to counsel with Church leaders, who assigned him to relocate Church publications there. Because of the importance of accurate information, he and Sidney RIGDON remained in Ohio in 1834 when many faithful men marched to Missouri with ZION'S CAMP to assist the Saints in returning to their homes and land in Jackson County.

In 1830–1831, Oliver Cowdery served as the first Church Recorder, a calling he again resumed between 1835 and 1837 (*see* HISTORIANS, CHURCH). Even in other years, he often kept the official minutes of meetings, and was often editor and contributor for the first Church newspapers. He wrote articles for the *Messenger and Advocate* that help document early LDS history. From June to October 1830, Oliver served as scribe while the Prophet completed important portions of the Joseph Smith Translation of the Bible.

An 1830 revelation named Oliver Cowdery next only to Joseph Smith in priesthood leadership (D&C 20:2–3), a status formalized in December 1834, when he was ranked above Sidney Rigdon, who had long served as Joseph's first counselor. Each would "officiate in the absence of the President, according to his rank and appointment, viz.: President Cowdery first; President Rigdon second, and President Williams third" (*PJS* 1:21). Cowdery wrote that this calling was foretold in the first heavenly ordination, though Missouri printing duties had intervened: "This promise was made by the angel while in company with President Smith, at the time they received the office of the lesser priesthood" (*PJS* 1:21; cf. *HC* 1:40–41). His office next to the Prophet—sometimes called "associate president"—was given to Hyrum SMITH in 1841 (D&C 124: 194–6), after Cowdery's excommunication.

Oliver's Church career peaked from 1834 to 1836. Minutes and letters picture him as a highly effective preacher, writer, and administrator. His 1836 journal survives, showing his devotion to religion and family, his political activities, his study of Hebrew, and the spiritual power he shared at the completion of the Kirtland Temple. Cowdery's last entry in this journal, penned the day of the temple dedication, says of the evening meeting: "I saw the glory of God, like a great cloud, come down and rest upon the house. . . . I also saw cloven tongues like as of fire rest upon many . . . while they spake with other tongues and prophesied" (Arrington, p. 426).

Oliver also alluded to more. A year later he penned an editorial "Valedictory." After mentioning "my mission from the holy messenger" prior to the organization of the Church, he wrote that such manifestations were to be expected, since the Old Testament promised that God would "reveal his glorious arm" in the latter days "and talk with his people *face to face*" (*Messenger and Advocate* 3:548). The words he italicized matched his recent temple vision of Christ on April 3, 1836, which he experienced in company with the Prophet (D&C 110:1–10). This was also the time that these first priesthood leaders received special priesthood keys from Moses, Elias, and Elijah, completing restoration of the "keys of the kingdom" (D&C 27:6–13) and completing Cowdery's mission as "second witness" to such restoration. Oliver had deep confidence in divine appearances. In 1835 he charged the newly appointed Twelve: "Never cease striving until you have seen God face to face" (*HC* 2:195).

Despite these profound spiritual experiences, Oliver's letters reveal a crisis of personal and family estrangement from Joseph Smith by early 1838. The Three Witnesses had seen an angel with Joseph Smith, but later they tended to compete rather than cooperate with his leadership. Cowdery disagreed with the Prophet's economic and political program and sought a personal financial independence that ran counter to the cooperative economics essential to the Zion society that Joseph Smith envisioned. Nonetheless, when Oliver was tried for his membership, he sent a resignation letter in which he insisted that the truth of modern revelation was not at issue: "Take no view of the foregoing remarks, other than my belief on the outward government of this Church" (*Far West Record*, pp. 165–66).

This trial was related to the excommunications of Oliver's brothers-in-law John Whitmer and David Whitmer, also at this time; this paralleled Oliver's earlier support of the Whitmer family in the matter of Hiram Page's competing revelations (D&C 28:11–13). The Church court considered five charges against Cowdery: inactivity, accusing the Prophet of adultery, and three charges of beginning law practice and seeking to collect debts after the Kirtland bank failure (*see* KIRTLAND ECONOMY).

Oliver's charge of adultery against the Prophet was simplistic, for Oliver already knew about the principle of PLURAL MARRIAGE. Rather than deny the charge, the Prophet testified that because Oliver had been his "bosom friend," he had "intrusted him with many things" (*Far West Record*, p. 168). Brigham YOUNG later said that the doctrine was revealed to Joseph and Oliver during the Book of Mormon translation (cf. Jacob 2:30); clearly a fuller understanding of the principle of plural marriage came by 1832, in connection with Joseph Smith's translation of Genesis (cf. D&C 130:1–2). Brigham Young added that Oliver impetuously proceeded without Joseph's permission, not knowing "the order and pattern and the

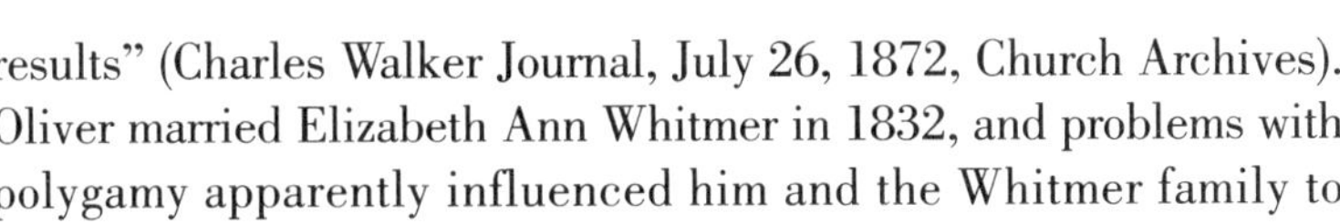

results" (Charles Walker Journal, July 26, 1872, Church Archives). Oliver married Elizabeth Ann Whitmer in 1832, and problems with polygamy apparently influenced him and the Whitmer family to oppose the principle later.

In 1838, following his excommunication, Oliver returned to Ohio, though he did not, as a fictitious deed states, then pay Bishop Edward Partridge $1,000 for the temple lot in Independence on behalf of his children, John, Jane, and Joseph Cowdery. Such children never existed; Oliver had no such money and showed no interest in Jackson County then or later. In fact, he continued law study and practiced in Kirtland, but in 1840 he moved to Tiffin, Ohio, where he became a prominent civic leader as an ardent Democrat. His law notices and public service regularly appeared in local newspapers, and he was personally sketched in the warm recollections of the prominent Ohio lawyer William Lang, who apprenticed under Cowdery and described him as being of slight build, about five and a half feet tall, clean, and courteous. Professionally, Cowdery was characterized as "an able lawyer," well informed, with "brilliant" speaking ability; yet "he was modest and reserved, never spoke ill of anyone, never complained" (Anderson, 1981, p. 41).

In 1847 Oliver moved to Wisconsin, where he continued his law practice and was almost elected to the first state legislature, in spite of newspaper accounts ridiculing his published declaration of seeing the angel and the plates. In his ten years outside the Church, Cowdery never succumbed to the considerable pressure to deny his Book of Mormon testimony. Indeed, letters to his LDS relatives show that he was hurt at the Church's rejection but remained a deep believer. Feeling that his character had been slandered, he asked for public exoneration, explaining that anyone would be sensitive about reputation "had you stood in the presence of John with our departed Brother Joseph, to receive the Lesser Priesthood, and in the presence of Peter, to receive the Greater" (Gunn, pp. 250–51).

These statements contradict a pamphlet that Oliver was alleged to have published in 1839 as a "Defense" for leaving the Church (*see* FORGERIES OF HISTORICAL DOCUMENTS). Surfacing in 1906, it portrays Oliver as confused about seeing John the Baptist. But no original exists, nor does any reference to it in Cowdery's century. Its style borrows published Cowdery phrases but rearranges his conclusions. A clumsier forgery is the "Confession of Oliver Overstreet," claims that the author was bribed to impersonate Cowdery and to the Church. Abundant documents show that Oliver retur Council Bluffs, Iowa, in 1848 with his wife and young daught

Diaries and official minutes record Oliver Cowdery's wo rejoining the Church. He sought only rebaptism and fellowsh office. He publicly declared that he had seen and handled the of Mormon plates, and that he was present with Joseph Smith occasions when "holy angels" restored the two priest (Anderson, *BYU Studies*, 1968, p. 278). The High Council tioned him closely about his published letter (to David Whit which Oliver claimed that he retained the keys of priesthood le ship after Joseph Smith's death. That was his opinion, Oliver said, before seeing the Nauvoo revelation giving all powers to Hyrum Smith "that once were put upon him that was my servant Oliver Cowdery" (D&C 124:95). "It was that revelation which changed my views on this subject" (Anderson, *IE*, Nov. 1968, p. 19).

Because they had started for Council Bluffs late in the season, the Cowdery family were forced to winter in Richmond, Missouri, where most of the Whitmer family lived. Letters throughout 1849 repeat Oliver's hope to move west and also disclose his lack of means. They speak of his coughing up blood, a long-term respiratory condition that finally took his life March 3, 1850. The circuit court recorded a resolution of fellow lawyers that in the death of "Oliver Cowdery, his profession has lost an accomplished member, and the community a valuable and worthy citizen" (Anderson, 1981, p. 46).

David Whitmer and other relatives living near Oliver Cowdery in his final year later claimed that he disagreed with many Kirtland and Nauvoo doctrines, but Oliver's documented criticisms at this time concern only intolerance and a continuing concern about polygamy. Although David Whitmer considered Joseph a fallen prophet, in 1848 Cowdery said publicly and privately "that Joseph Smith had fulfilled his mission faithfully before God until death" (Geo. A. Smith to Orson Pratt, *MS* 11 [Oct. 20, 1848]:14), and "that the priesthood was with this people, and the 'Twelve' were the only men that could lead the Church after the death of Joseph" (Anderson, *IE*, Nov. 1968, p. 18). In his last known letter, Oliver accepted an assignment from the Twelve to lobby in Washington, and acknowledged the leadership of the "good brethren of the [Salt Lake] valley" (Gunn, p. 261).

Oliver's wife, Elizabeth Ann Whitmer Cowdery (1815–1892), had known him when he was taking dictation during the translation of the Book of Mormon, before their marriage. Said she of his lifelong commitment: "He always without one doubt . . . affirmed the divinity and truth of the Book of Mormon" (Anderson, 1981, p. 63). This confidence stood the test of persecution, poverty, loss of status, failing health, and the tragic deaths of five of his six children. Dying at forty-three, Oliver was surrounded by family members who told how he reaffirmed the divinity of the Book of Mormon and the restored priesthood and voiced total trust in Christ. Just before rejoining the Church, he penned his inner hopes to fellow witness David Whitmer: "Let the Lord vindicate our characters, and cause our testimony to shine, and then will men be saved in his kingdom" (Oliver Cowdery to David Whitmer, July 28, 1847, *Ensign of Liberty*, 1:92).

BIBLIOGRAPHY

Anderson, Richard L. "Reuben Miller, Recorder of Oliver Cowdery's Reaffirmations." *BYU Studies* 8 (Spring 1968):277–93.

———. "The Second Witness of Priesthood Restoration." *IE* 71 (Sept. 1968):15–24; and 71 (Nov. 1968):14–20.

———. *Investigating the Book of Mormon Witnesses*. Salt Lake City, 1981.

Arrington, Leonard J. "Oliver Cowdery's Kirtland, Ohio, 'Sketch Book.'" *BYU Studies* 12 (Summer 1972):410–26.

Cannon, Donald Q., and Lyndon W. Cook. *Far West Record*. Salt Lake City, 1983.

Gunn, Stanley R. *Oliver Cowdery, Second Elder and Scribe*. Salt Lake City, 1962.

Jessee, Dean C. "Joseph Knight's Recollection of Early Mormon History." *BYU Studies* 17 [1976]:36.

Porter, Larry C. "Dating the Restoration of the Melchizedek Priesthood." *Ensign* 9 (June 1979):5–10.

Whitmer, David. *Address to All Believers in Christ*. Richmond, Mo., 1887.

RICHARD LLOYD ANDERSON

D

DANITES

Following the violence in northwestern Missouri in 1838, the Mormon dissident Sampson Avard, star witness in a court of inquiry weighing evidence against LDS leaders, charged that the Church had organized a band of armed men bound by secret oaths who had engaged in illegal activities against non-Mormon neighbors (*Document*, pp. 97–108). With the 1841 publication of the court proceedings, Avard's account became the foundation for all subsequent non-Mormon "Danite" accounts. Thus was born the legend of the Danites.

Though no Danite organization was known in NAUVOO or in Utah, the stereotype persisted, becoming a part of national discussion about Utah and the Latter-day Saints and for decades a staple of dime novels. By 1900 at least fifty novels had been published in English using the Avard-type Danite to develop story lines of murder, pillage, and conspiracy against common citizens. Arthur Conan Doyle (*A Study in Scarlet*) created Sherlock Holmes to solve a murder committed by Danites. Zane Grey (*Riders of the Purple Sage*) and Robert Louis Stevenson (*The Dynamiter*) were among the authors who found the image of the evil Danites well suited for popular reading audiences who delighted in sensationalism (Cornwall and Arrington). The image became so pervasive that few readers were willing to question the accuracy of such portrayals.

The reality of Danites in Missouri in 1838 is both less and more than the stereotype. Contemporary records suggest something fundamentally different. In October 1838, Albert Perry Rockwood, an LDS resident of Far West, Missouri, wrote in his journal of a *public* Danite organization that involved the whole Latter-day Saint community. He described in biblical terms companies of tens, fifties, and hundreds (cf. Ex. 18:13–26)—similar to the organization the pioneers later used during the migration to the Great Basin. Here the Danite organization encompassed the full range of activities of a covenant community that viewed itself as a restoration of ancient Israel. Working in groups, with some assigned to defense, others to securing provisions, and still others to constructing dwellings, these Danites served the interests of the whole. This was not the secret organization Avard spoke of; in fact, Rockwood's letters to friends and family were even more descriptive than his journal (Jessee and Whittaker).

In the fall of 1838, with old settlers in Missouri swearing to drive the Mormons out rather than permit them to become a political majority and with LDS leaders declaring that they would fight before again seeing their rights trampled, northwestern Missouri was in a state of war (*see* MISSOURI CONFLICT). Sparked by an effort to prevent LDS voting, violence erupted in August and soon spread. On both sides, skirmishes involved members of state-authorized militias. Evidence suggests that during this time of fear, clashes, and confusion, Sampson Avard, probably a captain within the public Danite structure and a militia officer, subverted the ideals of both by persuading his men to undertake the criminal activities he later argued were the authorized actions of the whole community. Encouraged perhaps by the firmly stated intentions of leaders to meet force with force but apparently without their approval, Avard used his Danite and military positions to mold a covert renegade band to avenge anti-Mormon outrages. He succeeded because after weeks of responding to violence with strictly defensive measures, Avard was not alone in feeling that the time for forbearance had passed. Others of the time in late reminiscences recalled that clandestine meetings were held, which were subsequently reported to Joseph SMITH, who then denounced Avard, removed him from his official command, and disbanded the maverick body. Though short-lived and unauthorized, this covert organization, thanks to Avard's distorted and widely publicized testimony, usurped the former usage of "Danites," and the once honorable appellation became a synonym for officially sanctioned secret lawlessness.

In contrast, when five hundred men in the Caldwell County (Mormon) militia later took the offensive in response to two months of unrelenting violence and depredations, there was nothing secretive about it. In mid-October, with supplies running low, they left defensive positions to forage and to punish enemies—a very public effort to improve security by preemptive forays. Two weeks later, facing increasing numbers of volunteers and a militia emboldened by the governor's EXTERMINATION ORDER, they surrendered their arms in defeat.

The reality, then, behind the supposed secretive, lawless Danites of legend was this renegade band formed briefly in 1838 in the midst of war. There is no evidence of any such band later, and even in 1838, the Latter-day Saint community as a whole did not deserve blame for the unauthorized actions of a few. As Parley P. PRATT, an apostle, wrote to his family after hearing Avard's court testimony, "They accuse us of things that never entered into our hearts." From LIBERTY JAIL on December 16, 1838, Joseph Smith summarized the situation as he then understood it: "We have learned also since we have been in prison that many false and pernicious things which were calculated to lead the saints far astray and to do great injury have been taught by Dr. Avard as coming from the Presidency . . . which the presidency never knew of being taught in the church by any body untill after they were made prisoners . . . the presidency were ignorant as well as innocent of these things" (*PWJS*, p. 380).

Unfortunately, in an age when Latter-day Saints were hated and persecuted, Avard's story provided a ready explanation for anyone who wanted to believe the worst. The reality was far less sensational.

BIBLIOGRAPHY

Cornwall, Rebecca Foster, and Leonard J. Arrington. "Perpetuation of a Myth: Mormon Danites in Five Western Novels, 1840–90." *BYU Studies* 23 (Spring 1983):147–65.

Document Containing the Correspondence, Orders, Etc. in Relation to the Disturbances with the Mormons; and the Evidence Given before the Hon. Austin A. King. Fayette, Mo., 1841.

Gentry, Leland H. "The Danite Band of 1838." *BYU Studies* 14 (Summer 1974):421–50.

Jessee, Dean C., and David J. Whittaker, eds. "The Last Months of Mormonism in

Missouri: The Albert Perry Rockwood Journal." *BYU Studies* 28 (Winter 1988):5–41.

Whittaker, David J. "The Book of Daniel in Early Mormon Thought." In *By Study and Also by Faith: Essays in Honor of Hugh W. Nibley on the Occasion of His Eightieth Birthday*, Vol. 1, pp. 155–201. Salt Lake City, 1990.

DAVID J. WHITTAKER

DESERET

The word *deseret* is found in the most ancient book in the Book of Mormon, "And they did also carry with them deseret, which, by interpretation, is a honey bee" (Ether 2:3).

Because the Book of Mormon was written in "reformed Egyptian" (Morm. 9:32), Hugh Nibley has suggested that the etymology of the word *deseret* is related to the ancient Egyptian word *dšrt*, read by Egyptologists as desheret. In Egyptian, *dšrt* means the red crown (of the king of Lower Egypt). The Egyptian word for bee is *b't*. In the discussion of the sign *dšrt*, Alan Gardiner, in *Egyptian Grammar*, states that was used to replace in two Egyptian titles where was used to mean the *b'ty* King of Lower Egypt. Thus, the title *n-sw-b't* was sometimes written as *n-sw-b't*, which literally means "He who belongs to the sedge plant (of Upper Egypt) and to the bee (of Lower Egypt)," normally translated "The King of Upper and Lower Egypt." This substitution of for has led Nibley to associate the Egyptian word *dšrt* and the Book of Mormon word *deseret*.

The beehive and the word *deseret* have been used variously throughout the history of the Church. The territory settled by the Mormon pioneers was called the State of Deseret. The emblem of the beehive is used in the seal of the State of Utah and is a common decoration in Utah architecture, symbolizing industriousness. Brigham YOUNG's house in Salt Lake City is called the Beehive House. Early Sunday schools were part of the Deseret Sunday School Union. A vital part of the Church welfare program carries the name Deseret Industries.

BIBLIOGRAPHY

Gardiner, Alan. *Egyptian Grammar*, 3rd ed., pp. 73–74, and signs L2 and S3. Oxford, 1982.

Nibley, Hugh. *Abraham in Egypt*, pp. 225–45. Salt Lake City, 1981.

———. *Lehi in the Desert / The World of the Jaredites / There Were Jaredites*. *CWHN* 5:189–94, 319–22.

STEPHEN PARKER

DESERET, STATE OF

On February 2, 1848, by the Treaty of Guadalupe Hidalgo, Mexico ceded to the United States an extensive area that included the Great Basin, where Mormon pioneers had begun settlement six months earlier. Even before the treaty was signed, Church leaders began discussing petitioning the U.S. government for recognition as a state or asking for territorial privileges. In July 1849 a committee wrote a constitution. It used as models the U.S. Constitution and the Iowa Constitution of 1846, from which the committee took fifty-seven of the sixty-seven sections of the new constitution. The committee requested that the state be named DESERET and that the boundaries be Oregon on the north, the Green River on the east, Mexico on the south, and the Sierra Nevada on the west, including a portion of the Southern California seacoast. "Deseret," a word from the Book of Mormon, means "honeybee" (Ether 2:3) and is symbolic of work and industry. A slate of officers was approved, with Brigham YOUNG as governor. Almon W. Babbitt, appointed representative to Congress, was instructed to carry the plea for statehood to Washington, D.C.

This effort by Latter-day Saint settlers to organize themselves into a provisional government was much like the attempt made in the 1780s by settlers in Tennessee, who organized the state of Franklin when they felt neglected by North Carolina, and the settlers of Oregon, who established a local government that functioned without recognition from the U.S. government until they were given territorial status in 1848.

The State of Deseret General Assembly met in regular session from December 1849 to March 1850. After special sessions during the summer, the members assembled for their second regular session in December 1850. Earlier, on September 9, U.S. President Millard Fillmore had signed an act to create a much smaller UTAH TERRITORY and appointed Brigham Young the first territorial governor. After word of the creation of the territory reached Utah, the tentative state of Deseret was dissolved on March 28, 1851. The provisional government had lasted only about a year and a half.

The territorial status did not provide the self-government Latter-day Saints desired, and even though Brigham Young was appointed first governor, Church leaders and the territorial legislature continued efforts to obtain statehood. In 1856, delegates met to again write a constitution and propose the state of Deseret, an effort rejected by Congress. As a part of a third effort in 1862, Brigham Young called the State of Deseret General Assembly into session for the first time since 1851. Thereafter it met each year until 1870, each session lasting only a few days and focusing on winning statehood on the basis of the proposed constitution of 1849 with only minor changes.

In the meantime, Brigham Young had been replaced as territorial governor by a series of outside appointees, who became progressively more hostile to the meetings of the General Assembly and complained about this "ghost government," as they called it. In 1872 a constitutional convention drew up a new constitution and dropped the name Deseret from the petition. This petition also failed, and hope for the state of Deseret came to an end.

[*See also* History of the Church: c. 1844–1877; Utah Statehood.]

BIBLIOGRAPHY

Constitution of the State of Deseret. Kanesville, Iowa, 1849.

Crawley, Peter. "The Constitution of the State of Deseret." *BYU Studies* 29 (Fall 1989):7–22.

Morgan, Dale L. "The State of Deseret." *Utah Historical Quarterly* 8 (1940):65–251. Reprinted as *The State of Deseret*. Logan, Utah, 1987.

JEFFERY OGDEN JOHNSON

DESERET ALPHABET

On April 8, 1852, Brigham YOUNG announced that the Board of Regents of the University of Deseret was preparing a new method of writing English. The idea was to develop a sort of universal system, especially so that foreign-language-speaking converts could learn to read English more easily.

The final version of the Deseret Alphabet utilized thirty-eight characters corresponding to sounds of English. Like Noah Webster and other early Americans who studied language, Brigham Young objected to sounding the letter *a* differently in the spellings of mate, father, fall, man, and many. In this, he was apparently influenced by studying shorthand with his secretary George D. Watt, who had studied systems of shorthand and spelling reform based on phonemes, the significant sounds of English, under Isaac Pitman.

The Regents discussed letter forms and sounds to be represented. The forms finally adopted were unfamiliar and unadaptable to cursive writing. The range of basic English sounds was close to present-day analyses, but the schwa (the unaccented, reduced vowel in ideA, tradEd, ratIfy, biolOgy, Upon) was omitted, leading to respellings based upon traditional spelling.

Learning the Deseret phonetic system was easy. A previously illiterate missionary wrote letters home after only six lessons. Hosea Stout, Thales Haskell, and others kept diaries in Deseret. However, since pronunciation, which varies, determined spelling, many words might appear more than one way in the same individual's usage, resulting in some confusion.

Scriptural passages written in the Deseret Alphabet appeared in the *Deseret News* in 1859. Orson PRATT transcribed further materials that were published in New York City, printed with type designed and cast there, at a total cost of $18,500. These included first and second school readers in 1868 and the Book of Mormon and a third reader of excerpts from it in 1869. Although few of these books were sold, some Sunday Schools as well as territorial schools used them.

In 1873 Pratt estimated the cost of printing a meager library of 1,000 titles at $5 million—prohibitively expensive for a sparse population in a subsistence economy. Those already literate had little incentive to learn the Deseret Alphabet, while illiterates would have had very little to read. The death of President Young in 1877 marked the end of efforts on its behalf.

BIBLIOGRAPHY

Ivins, Stanley S. "The Deseret Alphabet." *Utah Humanities Review* 1 (1947):223–39.

Monson, Samuel C. "The Deseret Alphabet." Master's thesis, Columbia University, 1948.

SAMUEL C. MONSON

DESERET HOSPITAL

With increasing evidence that home care of the sick and injured was no longer adequate, the women of the Relief Society, with the support of the First Presidency, opened Deseret Hospital in Salt Lake City on July 17, 1882. Though Roman Catholics and Episcopalians already sponsored hospitals in Utah, this was the first official endorsement of allopathic medicine by The Church of Jesus Christ of Latter-day Saints. A desire to have a place where spiritual ministrations could accompany medical treatment was among the motivations for the institution, and staff members were blessed and set apart by Church leaders for their tasks. The hospital also specialized in obstetrics, both in providing care and in training midwives and others.

Deseret Hospital was originally located in downtown Salt Lake City in a building vacated when the Catholics moved their hospital to larger quarters. In July 1884, Deseret Hospital moved to a larger building that could accommodate forty to fifty patients, though it seldom had more than sixteen at a time.

Deseret Hospital featured a homelike atmosphere, the latest surgical equipment from New York, and a staff of dedicated, well-trained, mostly female physicians, including Ellen B. Ferguson, Ellis R. Shipp, and Romania B. Pratt. Long before its doors opened, the women of the Church, led by Eliza R. SNOW, raised funds for the hospital. Though these efforts continued, support was never adequate to pay for the treatment of the many "free" patients, and the hospital was forced to close in 1894. The hospital kept its nursing and midwifery schools operating until the opening of the Groves Latter-day Saints Hospital in 1905.

BIBLIOGRAPHY

Arrington, Leonard J. "The Economic Role of Pioneer Mormon Women." *Western Humanities Review* 9 (Spring 1955):161–63.

Noall, Claire Wilcox. "Utah's Pioneer Women Doctors: The Story of the Deseret Hospital." *IE* 42 (May 1939):274–75, 308–309.

SCOTT PARKER

DESERET INDUSTRIES

Toward the end of the Great Depression, in August 1938, Deseret Industries was established "to help Church members help themselves" through a program of donated household items, volunteer labor, and vocational training.

In a letter to LDS congregations in Utah's SALT LAKE VALLEY dated August 11, 1938, the First Presidency and Presiding Bishopric called for "contributions of clothing, papers, magazines, articles of furniture, electrical fixtures, metal and glassware" from each household. The letter explained that the project would be known as Deseret Industries, and that the organization would make "periodic collections of these materials from homes . . . and employ men and women to sort, process, and repair the articles collected for sale and distribution among those who desire to obtain usable articles . . . at a minimum cost."

Since then, goods have been sold at thrift stores bearing the Deseret Industries name. Local Church congregations continue donation drives, during which volunteer workers collect goods from the homes of members. Anyone can donate items at any Deseret Industries store as well.

The Deseret Industries program was implemented specifically for the benefit of members who could not obtain employment elsewhere, and its initial work force consisted primarily of the unemployed and elderly. It was operated under the umbrella of the Church Security Plan—now Church Welfare Services—and continues as an integral part of the Church welfare system. Church leaders use Deseret Industries not only for employment training but as a resource for clothing and household items for needy members.

There were more than a dozen Deseret Industries stores in Salt Lake County and five in the Los Angeles area before World War II. Most of those were closed during the war, and operations were consolidated. By 1948 there were six stores, and growth continued slowly but steadily into the 1950s.

Deseret Industries started a rug-making operation in 1954 and acquired a woolen mill in 1957. The plants not only provided additional jobs but also goods to be distributed to needy Church members through the welfare program. Many elderly and handicapped members found work at Deseret Industries, and those who were sufficiently able were trained and moved into private industry.

As the program moved through the 1960s and into the 1970s, the emphasis on rehabilitation increased. Preparing people to enter the private workplace became a forte of Deseret Industries. Stores and equipment were upgraded through the mid-1970s and early 1980s to compare favorably with any of their kind.

Deseret Industries outlets have followed large concentrations of Church members. At the beginning of the 1990s there were forty-six Deseret Industries retail stores in cities of the western United States.

The Deseret Industries program still focuses on those with disabilities and those who have other social, employment, and economic challenges and obstacles to overcome. An estimated 60–70 percent of the people in the program are somewhat limited physically, mentally, emotionally, or socially. In 1980, Deseret Industries placed about 240 people into jobs with private companies. In 1989, it placed more than 700.

People needing training are usually referred to Deseret Industries by a Church leader. A program for each person is written with the individual's supervisors and rehabilitation workers. It incorporates personal and work-related goals and is closely monitored. Local Church members sometimes receive callings to help with training and rehabilitation.

Most Deseret Industries programs are more closely related to work adjustment than to skills training. Trainees get the experience of entering the workplace every day, being on time, learning to get along with coworkers, and taking directions from supervisors. Deseret Industries is not set up to train people to be journeymen plumbers or electricians, for example, though people may get experience doing these types of things.

Employment or career development is one of six standards of personal and family emergency preparedness outlined by the Church, the others being literacy and education, financial and resource management, home production and storage, physical health, and social-emotional and spiritual strength.

The mission of Deseret Industries parallels the mission of Church Welfare Services. A 1936 statement by the Church's First Presidency explains the philosophy of the welfare program:

> Our primary purpose was to set up, in so far as it might be possible, a system under which the curse of idleness would be done away with, the evils of a dole abolished, and independence, industry, thrift and self-respect be once more established amongst our people. The aim of the Church is to help the people help themselves. Work is to be re-enthroned as the ruling principle of the lives of our Church membership [*CR*, Oct. 1936].

BIBLIOGRAPHY

Searle, Don. "Deseret Industries at 50." *Ensign* 18 (July 1988):32–37.

Cannon, Michael. "Deseret Industries Commemorates 50 Years." *Church News*, Aug. 13, 1988, pp. 8–9, 12.

Lloyd, R. Scott. "Finding Dignity Through Work." *Church News*, Sept. 23, 1989, pp. 8–9.

MICHAEL C. CANNON

E

ECONOMIC HISTORY OF THE CHURCH

From their beginnings Latter-day Saints have regarded economic welfare as an indispensable part of religion. An 1830 revelation received by Joseph SMITH stated, "Verily I say unto you, that all things unto me are spiritual, and not at any time have I given unto you a law which was temporal" (D&C 29:34–35). Accepted as part of the revealed word of God, this principle implied that every aspect of life had to do with spirituality and things eternal. For President Brigham YOUNG, who led the Church in the West for thirty years, this revelation meant that "in the mind of God there is no such a thing as dividing spiritual from temporal, or temporal from spiritual; for they are one in the Lord" (*JD* 11:18).

> We cannot talk about spiritual things without connecting with them temporal things, neither can we talk about temporal things without connecting spiritual things with them. . . . We, as Latter-day Saints, really expect, look for and we will not be satisfied with anything short of being governed and controled by the word of the Lord in all of our acts, both spiritual and temporal. If we do not live for this, we do not live to be one with Christ [*JD* 10:329].

Emphasis on economics was strengthened and supported by the social and economic experiences of the early Saints. Two early decisions were extremely important. The first was to move the headquarters and body of the Church from New York to KIRTLAND, OHIO, and to MISSOURI. This meant that leaders had to devise ways of helping poor members move westward. The move also involved Church leaders in buying land and formulating plans for community development (*see* CITY PLANNING), and in initiating financial enterprises and industries to provide employment. As the germ of the kingdom of God, the Church was to gather and organize its members, settle them, and assist them in creating an advanced society. Ultimately, according to LDS belief, the Church must establish Zion, the literal and earthly kingdom of God over which Christ will one day rule in person.

The second decision came as a reaction to PERSECUTION. Church leaders assumed responsibility for coping with persecution and looking after the welfare of its persecuted members. Persecutions thus created cohesiveness and community identity. They also necessitated frequent removals, forcing the Church to organize for the migrations and, in a new home, again purchase land and initiate industries. Above all, persecution prevented the rise of individualism and class distinction and diminished the surplus wealth that would have created a barrier between the rich and the less fortunate.

These experiences, and the social, intellectual, and religious origins of the Church, led to the development of a set of economic ideals and institutions that became a more or less permanent aspect of Latter-day Saint belief and practice, and made the LDS community a unique group in frontier America. The intimate association of religion with economic activity produced a planning and community concern that made possible a more just and permanent society than existed elsewhere in the West. These early LDS economic goals can be summarized under four headings: (1) ecclesiastical promotion of economic growth and development, often called "building the kingdom of God"; (2) ecclesiastical sponsorship of group economic independence and self-sufficiency; (3) cooperation and organized group activity for attaining these goals; and (4) achievement and maintenance of economic equality.

PROMOTION OF ECONOMIC GROWTH. An early revelation called for the gathering "of mine elect" and declared that "the decree hath gone forth from the Father that they shall be gathered in unto one place upon the face of this land" (D&C 29:7–8). Thus gathered, they could build the kingdom of God and prepare for the Millennium to come.

This policy of "accumulating people" as a prerequisite to building the kingdom was implemented, beginning in the 1830s, by the development of a large and effective missionary system and an overseas emigration service (*see* IMMIGRATION AND EMIGRATION), and by the establishment of a series of Zions or gathering places. This emigration system assisted 5,000 European converts in migrating to NAUVOO, ILLINOIS, and, beginning in 1846, organized 16,000 persons in and around Nauvoo to make the great trek to WINTER QUARTERS, Nebraska, and later to the SALT LAKE VALLEY. The PERPETUAL EMIGRATING FUND company alone assisted in transporting some 26,000 immigrants to the West between 1852 and 1887, when Congress dissolved it (*see* ANTIPOLYGAMY LEGISLATION). By 1890 Church agents had directed the migration of 83,000 European members to the Salt Lake Valley. The system efficiently converted donations of cattle, grain, and other produce into passenger fares, covered wagons, and oxen. Scholars have regarded the Church's arrangements as perhaps the best system of regulated immigration in U.S. history.

Often immigrants newly arrived in Salt Lake City were first put to work building the kingdom by means of a public works system. Centered on TEMPLE SQUARE in Salt Lake City, the Church Department of Public Works provided employment for immigrants during their first winter in the Salt Lake Valley. They added such useful structures to the commonwealth as roads, walls, meetinghouses, railroads, telegraph lines, canals, the SALT LAKE THEATRE, and the famous SALT LAKE TEMPLE and TABERNACLE.

New arrivals were soon dispatched in organized companies to settle in outlying agricultural villages (*see* COLONIZATION). Rights and property in these villages were allocated and regulated to ensure the highest possible development of resources. The governing principle, one of stewardship, was consistent with the heavenly instruction of 1830 that declared: "Every man shall be made accountable unto me, a steward over his own property" (D&C 42:32). Each was to have property sufficient to support his family, while any surplus belonged to the Lord's storehouse. Property rights were granted conditionally and were not protected if the owner refused to utilize or develop the property. Indeed, the first pronouncement of President Brigham

Young regarding government of the infant pioneer colony in the Salt Lake Valley included the following stipulation:

> No man will be suffered to cut up his lot and sell a part to speculate out of his brethren. Each man must keep his lot whole, for the Lord has given it to us without price. . . . Every man should have his land measured off to him for city and farming purposes, what he could till. He might till as he pleased, but he should be industrious and take care of it [Arrington, 1958, p. 46].

This policy seems to have been adhered to. The speculative withholding of land from use was prohibited, and the purchase or appropriation of town lots simply for the sake of the increase in value was prevented. Hoarding money was also against Church rules.

After the settlement of villages and the determination of property rights, the Saints were to proceed with the orderly development of local resources. Making the waste places blossom as the rose and the earth yield abundantly was more than an economic necessity: It was a form of religious activity. One early leader noted that the LDS religion consisted of digging water ditches as well as undergoing water baptism; religious duty encompassed both the redemption of man's home (the earth) and of his soul. The earth, as the future abiding place of God's people, was to be made productive and fruitful, transformed into a virtual Garden of Eden. "The Lord has done his share of the work," Brigham Young told them. "He has surrounded us with the elements containing wheat, meat, flax, wool, silk, fruit, and everything with which to build up, beautify and glorify the Zion of the last days." "It is now our business," he concluded, "to mould these elements to our wants and necessities, according to the knowledge we now have and the wisdom we can obtain from the heavens through our faithfulness." Only in this way "will the Lord bring again Zion upon the earth, and in no other" (*JD* 9:283–84).

The acceptance of this stewardship principle of resource development explains the passionate and devoted efforts of Latter-day Saints to develop the resources of the Great Basin to their fullest extent.

ECONOMIC INDEPENDENCE. The goal of LDS colonization and resource development, and of the Mormon village, was economic independence: The LDS commonwealth was to be financially and economically self-sufficient. A revealed "law" of the Church established this principle in 1831: "Let all thy garments be plain, and their beauty the beauty of the work of thine own hands" (D&C 42:40). Another revelation directed that they were to "contract no debts with the world" (D&C 64:27).

The principles of this revelation were applied often and broadly. In the Great Basin, the Latter-day Saints were asked to manufacture their own iron, produce their own cotton, spin their own silk, and grind their own grain—all without borrowing from "outsiders." It was reasoned that self-sufficiency was a practical policy because God had blessed each region with the resources necessary for the use of the people and the development of that region. As a result of the application of this principle, the Great Basin was the only major region of the United States whose early development was largely accomplished without outside capital.

Officially sponsored projects for self-sufficiency included an iron mission, consisting of about 200 families called by the Church who devoted strenuous efforts to develop the iron and coal resources near Cedar City; a sugar mission, in which several hundred people were united in the 1850s in an effort to establish the sugar-beet industry in Utah; a lead mission, in which some fifty men were called to work lead mines near Las Vegas, Nevada, to provide lead for paint and bullets; a cotton mission, which sent more than a thousand families to southern Utah to raise cotton, olives, grapes, indigo, grain sorghum, and figs; silk missions, which involved the growing of mulberry trees and establishment of a silk industry in every suitable community; and a flax mission, a wool mission, and even a winery to provide wine for the holy sacrament.

UNITY AND COOPERATION. Qualities required to execute successfully the economic program of the Church were unity of its members and the ability to organize for the pursuit of economic goals. This meant Churchwide cooperation. The seminal revelation enjoining unity was received in January 1831: "I say unto you, be one; and if ye are not one, ye are not mine" (D&C 38:27). This group spirit was induced both by the belief that unity was a Christian virtue and by the trying times that LDS pioneers experienced in their efforts to establish an independent commonwealth. Group solidarity and a strong central organization symbolized this effort. Whether they were migrating, building forts, digging ditches, or constructing mills, participants in the sublime task of building the kingdom were to submit themselves to the direction of God's leaders and display a spirit of willing cooperation.

As is well known, Brigham Young developed unified action and combined endeavor. He instituted cooperative arrangements for migration, colonization, construction, agriculture, mining, manufacturing, merchandising and, in fact, for every realm of economic activity.

EQUALITY. In "working out the temporal salvation of Zion," to use a common expression of the day, the formulators of Church policy focused primary attention on production and on the better management of available human and natural resources. Nevertheless, influenced by Christian principles, by its own necessities, and by the democratic concepts of Jacksonian America, early Mormonism was distinctly egalitarian in theology and economics. This had significant influences on Church policies and practices in the Great Basin.

The LDS doctrine of equality was formulated early. "If ye are not equal in earthly things, ye cannot be equal in obtaining heavenly things," read one March 1832 revelation (D&C 78:6), and, from the beginning, there was an earnest attempt to conduct business in this spirit of equality. When New York converts to the young Church began to arrive at the newly established gathering place of Kirtland, Ohio, in May 1831, the governing principle for the allotment of land and other properties was that every man receive "equal according to his family, according to their circumstances," and that all "receive alike, that ye may be one" (D&C 51:3, 9). Similarly, a revelation in Ohio instructed the Saints that "in your temporal things you shall be equal, and this not grudgingly, otherwise the abundance of the manifestations of the Spirit shall be withheld" (D&C 70:14). Similar instructions accompanied the stewardship system tried in Jackson County, Missouri: "And you are to be equal, or in other words, you are to have equal claims on the properties, for the benefit of managing . . . your stewardships, every man according to his wants and his needs, inasmuch as his wants are just" (D&C 82:17).

The core of the policy was reflected in the system of immigration (the more well-to-do were encouraged to donate means to assist in the immigration of poorer converts), the construction of public works (those with a surplus were expected to contribute), the allotment of land and water (parceled out equally to all by means of community drawings), and the initiation of many cooperative village stores and industries. But the influence of the ideal of equality was still wider. It led to several attempts to completely reorganize society and put economic affairs on a more egalitarian basis. Communities holding to these ideals were attempted by the Latter-day Saints in Ohio and Missouri (*see* CONSECRATION) and in more than 150 communities in the Far West, from Paris, Idaho, on the north, to Bunkerville, Nevada, and Joseph City, Arizona, on the south (*see* UNITED ORDERS). These cooperative communities were characterized by a high degree of economic equality and, although most of them lasted only a short time, their influence on LDS thought and self-conception is evident still.

It is fair to say that the Church could have gone much further in achieving its economic goals if the federal government had not intervened to prevent it. The UTAH EXPEDITION of 1857–1858, the Anti-Bigamy Act of 1862, the antipolygamy legislation of the late 1860s and the 1870s, and, even more, the hostile Edmunds Act, passed in 1882, and the Edmunds-Tucker Act of 1887—all of these undercut new Church economic activity, and forced the Church to withdraw from many existing activities.

By a strange coincidence of history, however, the Panic of 1891, ushering in the more severe Panic of 1893 and depression of the 1890s, helped reverse this trend. Utah, whose agriculture and mining industries were marginal, suffered more severely than many states; unemployment and low farm incomes were disturbing realities. In this crisis, Church leaders used all the resources at their command—including assets confiscated earlier by the federal government but now returned—to expand and improve the Great Basin economy. Their concerted efforts helped launch many new and successful industries. With an investment of about $500,000, the manufacture of sugar was reinitiated; another $500,000 financed the beginnings of the hydroelectric power industry in the West; some $250,000 was expended on the development of a salt industry on the shores of Great Salt Lake. To provide employment, the Saltair recreation resort was constructed. Railroads were projected, canals built, new colonies started—in short, Church leaders did everything possible to expand the economic base of the Great Basin and surrounding regions.

This expansion of economic activity was disturbing to national political and business leaders, who used the SMOOT HEARINGS of 1903–1907 to force the Church to sell most of its business interests. Holdings in the sugar and salt industries, in railroad and hydroelectric power, in coal and iron lands, in the telegraph system—these and others were sold to eastern capitalists. For the next decade and more, Utah's economy came to resemble that of other states in the Rocky Mountain region.

By mid-twentieth century, national sentiment was more sympathetic to Church-sponsored endeavors. Since the Great Depression of the 1930s, and especially since World War II, through the welfare services plan and other enterprises, the economic ideals of the founding generation have again been more actively pursued. Nonetheless, growing needs, especially outside North America, have required refocusing on areas central to the mission of the Church. As in the past, tithing and other donations remain the key to the Church's active economic involvement. In the last half of the twentieth century, increasing emphasis has been placed on extending the full program of the Church, including temples, to members throughout the world. As "building the kingdom" has become increasingly international, the construction and maintenance of meetinghouses and temples in many lands have dominated Church finances. While the Church has invested in media facilities, including a satellite communications system, and expanded international microfilming of genealogical records (and a network of family history libraries to make the records available throughout the world), it has divested itself of many holdings that primarily benefited only Latter-day Saints in America's Mountain West.

At the end of the 1980s, the Church began implementing new budgeting arrangements that move toward greater equality. Divorcing funding levels from levels of contributions, these arrangements guarantee the funding of facilities and activities at a modest level for all Church members while limiting the amount the more affluent local units may spend. Also, with a growing worldwide membership, efforts at economic independence have increasingly focused on individual (family) self-sufficiency, and on aiding members everywhere to improve their economic situation and prepare for emergencies.

Nonetheless, efforts to expand the reach and impact of the Church's Welfare Services and disaster relief programs also continue.

Though the present-day Church plays a direct role in economic development less often than it did in the pioneer economy, the fundamental ideals of self-sufficiency, unity and cooperation, and equality still characterize LDS economic goals. Latter-day Saints look forward to a more prosperous and just world even as they continue their efforts to establish institutions capable of blessing the lives of men and women as one essential preparation for the second coming of Christ.

[*See also* Kirtland Economy; Nauvoo Economy; Pioneer Economy.]

BIBLIOGRAPHY

Arrington, Leonard J. *Great Basin Kingdom: An Economic History of the Latter-day Saints, 1830–1900*. Cambridge, Mass., 1958.

———. "Religion and Economics in Mormon History." *BYU Studies* 3 (Spring-Summer 1961):15–33.

Arrington, Leonard J.; Feramorz Y. Fox; and Dean L. May. *Building the City of God: Community and Cooperation Among the Mormons*. Salt Lake City, 1976.

LEONARD J. ARRINGTON

EUROPE, THE CHURCH IN

[*This article discusses the establishment and growth of the Church in continental Europe. See separate articles on the Church in the* British Isles, *the* Middle East, *and* Scandinavia.]

The Protestant countries of Western Europe—Scandinavia, Switzerland, Germany, and the Netherlands—played a major role in the growth and success of the Church from the beginnings in the 1830s until well into the twentieth century. Along with the United States, Canada, and Great Britain, continental Europe provided most of the early LDS converts until around 1960, when successes in Latin America and Asia began to overshadow it as a source of new converts. Without the waves of European converts, many of whom emigrated to fill up the pioneer settlements of the Great Basin Kingdom (*see* COLONIZATION), the Church would, at best, have grown more slowly, been more insular and provincial.

That success in Europe was, however, geographically uneven. Early converts came overwhelmingly from the countries of the Protestant Reformation. Attempts were made as early as the 1850s to gain converts in France, Italy, Ireland, and Austria-Hungary, but results were meager and missionaries became discouraged. Real success in these and other Catholic countries would have to wait for the more open societies and attitudes of the twentieth century. LDS missionaries also found virtually no access to the Orthodox populations of Eastern Europe, whether in Russia, Greece, or the Balkans, and there were only a very few conversions of European Jews.

LDS converts came from many different Protestant denominations and sects, but most of them were religious "seekers" of one kind or another, sometimes already united in congregations like Timothy Mets's "New Lighters" in Holland in the early 1860s. Most of the seekers had studied the Bible and were looking for a church with apostles, prophets, and the spiritual gifts they had read about in the New Testament. They also tended to be discouraged with traditional doctrines and the behavior of churches and pastors, and longed for the assurance of communion with the spirit of God in preparation for Christ's imminent return.

Most European converts came from the middle, lower middle, and especially the working classes. One study which surveyed LDS immigrants to the United States between 1840 and 1869 found that only 11 percent were middle class, mostly artisans; the rest came overwhelmingly from the working classes. Early attempts were made by missionaries to interest such dignitaries as the queens and kings of various countries, but these appeals fell on deaf ears and sometimes even led to the missionaries' banishment. Their preaching also had little resonance with the traditional nobility, the moneyed aristocracy, and an increasingly secular and powerful intelligentsia. Thus, cut off from "respectable" society, they went "to the poor like their Captain of old" (*Hymns*, 1985, No. 319), among whom they found believers. Only in the later twentieth century, as they had done in America, did European Latter-day Saints as a group begin to be part of the growing middle class as they received greater opportunities for higher education and financial success.

The new European Saints of the nineteenth century came from

both rural and urban societies. Farmers, agricultural workers, and artisans joined with industrial workers and townspeople leaving the depressed countrysides and the slums of industrializing Europe for the kingdom of the Saints in what they and thousands of other emigrants believed was the promised land, the land of unlimited opportunity.

Some three years after the Church was established in Europe, it introduced the doctrine of the gathering, which encouraged the new members to gather to Zion. Before 1900 more than 91,600 heeded the call, and although after the turn of the century Church authorities began to discourage emigration, thousands more joined the ever-broadening stream of European immigrants to America. They scrimped and saved, sometimes for years—the average wait was ten years—to get the eighty to one hundred dollars needed to get from Liverpool to Salt Lake City. Saints from the Continent went to Liverpool, where, with British converts, they booked passage on large emigrant ships, such as the *Amazon, Nevada*, or *Monarch of the Sea*. They first landed in New Orleans for the trip upstream to Nauvoo, later they landed at New York, Philadelphia, or Boston, traveled by train to Omaha, and then journeyed by covered wagon or handcart the remaining 1,100 miles to Utah. For some the trip was better than tolerable; for many others, it was an ordeal endured only through faith and determination.

Seeing that most new converts were so poor that they could not emigrate without help, the Church, in 1849, set up the PERPETUAL EMIGRATING FUND which allowed thousands of Saints to borrow the money to emigrate and then repay the fund after they were settled in the American West. After the completion of the transcontinental railroad in 1869, the journey was not so arduous because the railroad brought emigrants directly to Zion.

European LDS emigration peaked in the 1850s and 1860s, although a fairly constant stream, especially of Germans, continued after the turmoil of both world wars. They all became part of the "melting pot," with few Saints returning to their native lands.

The European members turned out to be exceptionally good pioneers. Most brought with them solid religious conviction and faith, an unusually strong work ethic, usable and practiced skills derived from the quality artisanship of Europe, and a desire to blend into their new society and surroundings. They also brought a deep respect for Church leaders as God's chosen servants, a willingness to settle where they were called, and a desire to help promote the missionary cause, especially in their native lands. They were persuasive recruiters of their fellow countrymen to the new LDS settlements. Many met incoming emigrant trains to take settlers to their new paradise.

Besides laborers and skilled craftsmen, there were also businessmen and entrepreneurs and teachers; there were women trained as midwives and a few as doctors. Europe also produced poets, journalists, artists, architects, photographers, musicians, and also dramatists. From their ranks arose a range of great leaders from General Authorities to missionaries—who usually labored in their homelands. Devout women and children who supported the Church, often at great sacrifice, carried out their own daily and Church duties. Most important, however, were the tens of thousands of less-known European Saints; Zion could not have done without them. Census figures give us some idea of their numbers. In 1880, out of a total Utah population of 143,863, almost 43,000, or 30 percent, were foreign-born. If children born in America to foreign-born members are included, the figure would exceed 60 percent.

Not all European converts to the Church immigrated to America, even in the peak years of the gathering. Some had families they could not and would not leave; others lacked faith and funds. Some drifted from the faith or could not find suitable marriage partners in it. Others succumbed to the extraordinary anti-Mormon pressures and persecutions that arose simultaneously almost everywhere with the arrival of the missionaries. Throughout Europe in the nineteenth and early twentieth centuries, Latter-day Saints, and especially missionaries, were at one time or another harassed, abused, vilified, stoned, jailed, and expelled; yet these same missionaries were simultaneously fed, clothed, housed, protected, and warned by generations of grateful and admiring members. In the nineteenth century, the Church was taken seriously, perhaps too seriously, by those in power. Many Europeans regarded the Church as a non-Christian American sect. Throughout Europe, where the marriage of church and state had been sanctified by tradition, political authority often took its cues on religious matters from a clergy made more vocal by declining influence.

Prominent Europeans visited Utah to get a firsthand view of this unusual and exotic LDS society. They admired the way the Saints had made the "desert . . . blossom as the rose" (Isa. 35:1) but found the people fanatical and their theology incomprehensible. Polygamy was considered especially uncivilized by Europeans, who viewed their own culture, especially near the end of the nineteenth century, as the apogee of civilization. For the European intelligentsia, the LDS Church was purely and distinctly an aberrational American phenomenon.

In spite of all this, the Church took hold in Europe, at least enough to strengthen the Church in America when strengthening was needed most, and also to lay a foundation for its own existence later on. Following their great successes in Great Britain in the 1830s and 1840s, the missionaries crossed the English Channel to work on the European mainland. The responses in Switzerland and Hamburg, Germany, were generally positive, with a foothold established in each of these areas. Less successful were the missions of Lorenzo SNOW in Italy and John TAYLOR in France, but even in those nations a few converts were made, from whom significant LDS posterities have grown. There was a slow but steady growth of the Church in Switzerland and Germany, especially after German unification in 1870. A mission was established in the Netherlands in the 1860s, and over the years thousands became Latter-day Saints and immigrated to Zion.

Results were not so encouraging in the huge Austro-Hungarian Empire of more than fifty million that sprawled over most of the map of East Central Europe. In 1865 President Brigham YOUNG sent one of the apostles, Orson Pratt, to open that empire to missionary work. Elder Pratt and his companion, William Riter, had little success, spending most of their time in jail. A later missionary, Thomas Biesinger, made scattered converts in Vienna and Prague; and a Hungarian convert, Misha Markow, traveled throughout most of the Balkan states and Russia, beginning in 1903, performing isolated baptisms and encountering ubiquitous opposition.

At the same time, attempts were made to breach the edges of the Islamic world in neighboring Turkey. A Swiss convert, Jacob Spori, established a mission there in 1884 with limited success (*see* MIDDLE

EAST, THE CHURCH IN). After Spori baptized some Russians, Elder Francis M. Lyman, an apostle, and Joseph Cannon dedicated imperial Russia to preaching the gospel in 1903.

TWENTIETH CENTURY. For Europeans, Church members included, the dawning twentieth century would bring historic and cataclysmic changes. These included two devastating world wars with literally millions of casualties and a debilitating depression in between, fascism and communism, the Cold War and Americanization, prosperity and the rebirth of Europe, and finally, by 1990, the extension of freedom and democracy to most of the people of the continent.

There were also significant changes in European LDS life. Emigration gradually declined, allowing the European population to grow and more permanent LDS congregations to emerge. New countries, first in the West, then later in the East, were opened to missionary work; and some, such as France, Belgium, and Italy, that had been opened but later closed, reopened and became more fruitful. Freedom of religion and the end of religious persecution spread as democracy overcame a variety of tyrannies. The discontinuance of polygamy and the accommodation to the broader palette of political realities in the world emphasizing the spiritual mission of the Church opened doors.

The defeat of Germany and the Central Powers in World War I, though viewed as a disaster for the people, did have a bit of a silver lining for the Church, especially in Central Europe. The coming of democracy to Germany and Austria permitted the return of missionaries. A vigorous branch was established in Vienna that would serve as a strong foundation for the Church in Austria. The rigors of war and defeat had produced a poverty and humility among the people that helped make them more receptive to the gospel message. Missionaries streamed into post–World War I Germany and, especially in the first years of the Weimar Republic, baptisms were at an all-time high. By 1930 there were more Latter-day Saints in Germany than in any other country outside the United States of America, and expectations ran high for continued growth.

The coming of Hitler to power changed life for the Church and its members, not only in Germany but eventually in the rest of Europe as well. Soon the omnipresent police state was making life in Germany more difficult for the Saints, especially the missionaries;

many anticipated the Church would be closed down, but it never was. Both members and missionaries made every effort to get along with the regime while rejecting its excesses. What was important to them was to be able to continue to preach the gospel, to stay in the country, and to keep the branches together and prospering after so many years of struggle. Moreover, their numbers were small and they had little leverage with the regime. The Church grew slowly throughout Europe in the 1930s, and the growing tension in society made missionary work progressively more difficult.

In the fall of 1938, at the time of the Munich conference, missionaries were taken out of Germany temporarily; this became a valuable dress rehearsal for the situation a year later, when the Church was forced overnight to withdraw all missionaries from Germany and eventually from all of Europe. After European Mission President Thomas E. McKay left in April 1940, the local leaders of the Church units on the Continent were on their own throughout the war.

The cataclysm of World War II prompted Church leaders to send Elder Ezra Taft BENSON to Europe in 1946 to survey the damage, find the Saints, arrange for temporal help, and, most important, let them know that the Church cared about them. Elder Benson found decimated but devout congregations of Saints wherever he went, from England to Austria. He lamented over their circumstances and was inspired by their devotion. He also arranged for them to meet, and he set in motion the wheels that would bring the welfare supplies that had been accumulating in America to the needy in Europe. Years later, members vividly and gratefully remembered this mission of mercy and found in it hope and encouragement to face a difficult future; one non-Mormon German professor recalled having received his first pair of shoes after the war from the Mormons. Soon help began to pour in as CARE packages of relief supplies arrived from friends and fellow Saints in America. The Saints in the Netherlands, which had been invaded and occupied by Germany, sent potatoes. Trainloads of welfare supplies were sent from Utah to needy Mormons and non-Mormons alike. It was a great expression of Christianity in action, and the image of the Church in Europe began to change for the better as a result of its participation in this collective humanitarian effort.

Missionaries began to return to Europe as early as 1946. Soon missions were reestablished and some mission presidents had to locate scattered Saints, but others found things intact. Members met where they could, sometimes in bombed-out quarters, sometimes in members' apartments, and sometimes out in the open. A new mission was also established in Finland in 1947. During the first decade after the war, efforts focused again on the traditional interests of strengthening the Saints and gaining new ones.

Prior to the war, European members had never been able to attend a local Church temple. Many had been diligent in doing genealogical research, but unless they had immigrated to the United States or had been able to visit there, they had not had the opportunity to attend a temple and receive the blessings given only therein.

But all this was to change dramatically. Members in post-World War II Europe soon acquired all of the blessings and responsibilities of Saints in America. In 1952, a year after he became President of the Church, David O. MCKAY announced plans to build the first temple in Europe just outside of Bern, Switzerland. This temple was dedicated in September 1955; a second one was completed and opened near London in 1958. The building of these temples symbolized the inauguration of the new age for the Church in Europe. In the 1980s, the Church dedicated a temple in 1984 at Västerhaninge (near Stockholm), Sweden; in 1985 at Freiberg, then the German Democratic Republic (GDR); and in 1987 at Friedrichsdorf (near Frankfurt), then the Federal Republic of Germany.

Some other important changes were the creation of new missions and the establishment of Europe's first stake in 1961. In addition, the progress of secularization, with its emphasis on freedom of religion, the ecumenical spirit of Vatican II in the Roman Catholic Church, and the presence of American LDS service personnel helped to break down the traditional prejudices and make it possible for the Church to gain a real foothold in Italy, and later in Spain and Portugal. New vigor was experienced in France as baptisms increased; membership in France grew from 1,509 in 1960 to 8,606 in 1970. Most significant was the conviction that it was now possible to do missionary work among the Catholics of Western Europe in the same way, and with as encouraging results, as among Protestants.

The Saints became not only more numerous but also more prosperous and better educated; Europeans such as F. Enzio Busche

(Germany), Charles A. Didier (Belgium), Derek A. Cuthbert (England), Jacob de Jager (the Netherlands), and Hans B. Ringger (Switzerland) were called as General Authorities. Stakes, wards, and new missions were organized with leadership essentially in local hands; European LDS youth were better educated in Church doctrine through the establishment of seminary and institute classes; a new and larger wave of missionaries from Europe joined the worldwide force; and Central and Eastern Europe were, especially after the political revolutions of 1989, opening their doors to the Church.

In Europe the image of the Latter-day Saints and the Church was changing. The coming of real democracy, with its basic human rights, including the freedom of religion; the pervasive influence of the United States as the primary defender of an exposed Europe in the Cold War; the mobility and growing prosperity that came to Europe; and the continuing growth of the Church generally gave it a more favorable press.

At the same time, the deepening Cold War made life progressively more difficult for some seven thousand Saints in the GDR. Strong anticommunist rhetoric from America, plus Russian influence and strong communist prejudices against churches and people of religious conviction, brought Latter-day Saints behind the Iron Curtain continued surveillance and harassment. The erection of the Berlin Wall in 1961 left them largely to their own devices, with only occasional visits by Church authorities from the West. Some, in order to make their peace with the new order, withdrew from Church fellowship, but a majority banded together to form a strong, cohesive LDS community.

In the 1960s, the Church began a vigorous program of building chapels for European congregations that helped to meet the needs of the Saints as well as to gain some respectability in society. By 1970 chapels dotted the Western European landscape; they attracted some positive outside attention and gave members a new sense of accomplishment. They also helped Saints begin to shed the "sect" image and mentality and to move more confidently into their various national societies after years of persecution and disrespect.

In an attempt to strengthen the LDS European youth, the seminary and institute programs of the Church were established in the early 1970s. These would help LDS families teach their children the gospel and prepare them for missions and lifetimes of service. Gradually, an increasing number of young men and women did serve missions. The 1970s also brought area conferences at which the European Saints were able to see how many of them there actually were and to be counseled anew by Church leaders to remain where they were and help strengthen the Church in their own areas.

EASTERN EUROPE. Prior to the 1960s, LDS success in Europe had been confined largely to the Protestant countries of Western Europe. A few converts, such as Janos Denndorfer, had been made in Hungary around the turn of the century, and a few others later in Czechoslovakia, but the turmoil of the first half of the twentieth century and the dropping of the Iron Curtain around Eastern Europe effectively precluded the early introduction of the gospel and Church into those countries.

In the 1960s, attempts were made to begin missionary work in Yugoslavia, but it was not until Kresimir Cosic came to Brigham Young University, became a convert to the Church, and later was a basketball hero in his native country, that the Church could take hold there. A few missionaries were allowed to enter, but their opportunities to teach the people were circumscribed.

Vienna became the center of attempts by the Church to push into Central and Eastern Europe, much as it had been the capital of the polyglot Austro-Hungarian Empire of the nineteenth century. In the 1970s a few missionary couples were called to serve in Budapest, Hungary, and by the early 1980s they had established a branch comprised of more than one hundred capable, educated Hungarians. This gradual breakthrough almost exactly mirrored the gradual turning of Hungarian society and government away from the strict subservience to the Communist masters and toward the West.

For President Spencer W. Kimball, the need to preach the gospel everywhere in the world, especially in the large areas from which the Church had heretofore been excluded was a consuming passion. He had no political agenda. A major breakthrough came with the work of Ambassador David M. Kennedy in gaining official recognition of the Church in various areas and in the dedication of Poland for the preaching of the gospel by President Kimball in 1977. This represented a major change in Church policy toward communist governments and paved the way for even more significant opportunities in the late 1980s. It became the basis for a policy that allowed contacts with scattered Saints in Czechoslovakia and brought the Church recognition and respect from the communist leadership of the GDR, in all a breakthrough in that part of Europe. The most dramatic results of this changed relationship were the 1985 erection of the temple at Freiberg, GDR, wherein for the first time hundreds of lifelong Latter-day Saints were able to fulfill their dreams of temple worship, and the subsequent admission of LDS missionaries into the country for the first time in nearly forty years. In 1989 the first missionaries allowed to leave the GDR arrived in Salt Lake City to be sent throughout the world.

The nearly bloodless revolutions of 1989 presented the Church with an opportunity to begin a new epoch in Central and Eastern Europe. As the communist order crumbled and more democratic regimes were established in one country after another, one common demand was for freedom of religion. As a result, by the end of 1990 the Church in these countries existed under virtually the same conditions as in Western Europe and the United States. The reunification of Germany applied all of the rules of the Bonn Constitution to what had been the GDR. Missions have been established in Poland, Hungary, and Greece, and reestablished in Czechoslovakia. Leaders of these nations have welcomed Latter-day Saints because of their strong Judeo-Christian values and their wholesome families. Missionaries are currently proselytizing on a limited basis. Congregations of the Church have been officially recognized in the Soviet Union, and it has good prospects there, and in Yugoslavia, for the immediate future. Missionaries have been permitted into Romania and Bulgaria, the first significant breakthroughs in those countries. Thus, at the beginning of the 1990s, The Church of Jesus Christ of Latter-day Saints in Europe stands on a new threshold. Its major challenge, in both East and West, is to become better known and respected. Europeans are generally unaware of its dynamic worldwide growth, the nature of its teachings, or the quality of life it offers.

In Western Europe, the Church is growing slowly, with the exception of its clear success in Portugal, but a process of consolidation appears to be taking place. Strong second-, third-, and even fourth-generation LDS families are appearing everywhere. Church members are taking advantage of expanded opportunities for education, especially higher education, and are thus better able to contribute to and benefit from the prosperity of Western Europe. European Latter-day Saints are sending out more of their own as missionaries than ever before, and two and three generations of indigenous leaders are heading the Church in Europe.

Finally, from an LDS point of view, Europe is still divided. The Western countries are awash in secularism, prosperity, and religious apathy that pose a major challenge for the Church to find new ways to gain the interest and respect of these secular societies. For Central and Eastern Europe, the new decade and the coming new century will undoubtedly see thousands of new LDS converts and congregations. Perhaps even as the people in these countries have brought a new inspiration of freedom and human rights to the West, they will also bring a new spirit of religious desire that will benefit the Church.

BIBLIOGRAPHY

Babbel, Frederick W. *On Wings of Faith*. Salt Lake City, 1972.

"Encore of the Spirit," *Ensign* 21 (Oct. 1991): 32–53.

Sharffs, Gilbert W. *Mormonism in Germany*. Salt Lake City, 1970.

DOUGLAS F. TOBLER

EXTERMINATION ORDER

A military order signed by Missouri Governor Lilburn W. Boggs on October 27, 1838, directed that the Mormons be driven from the state or exterminated (*see* MISSOURI CONFLICT). Boggs's action was based on information brought to him that day by two citizens of Richmond, Missouri, concerning the Mormon–Missourian conflicts in northwest Missouri and on reports of the Battle of Crooked River, in which armed Mormons had clashed with a company of state militia on October 25.

Boggs, acting in his capacity as commander-in-chief of the Missouri militia, ordered General John B. Clark to march to Ray County with a division of militia to carry out operations against armed Mormons. The order described the Mormons as being in "open and avowed defiance of the laws, and of having made war upon the people of this State." It stated that "the Mormons must be treated as enemies, and must be exterminated or driven from the State if necessary for the public peace—their outrages are beyond all description."

A copy of the order reached General Samuel D. Lucas of the state militia by the time he encamped outside the LDS town of Far West, in Caldwell County, on October 31. Lucas gave a copy to the LDS Colonel George M. Hinkle and other Church representatives, to whom he dictated terms of surrender, and they showed it to Joseph SMITH. It was probably a significant factor in the Prophet's decision to surrender to Lucas.

Following Joseph Smith's surrender, arrest, and imprisonment, the governor's order was carried out by a combination of militia troops and vigilantes. It culminated in the forcible removal from Missouri of virtually all members of the Church during the winter and early spring of 1838–1839.

The legality and propriety of Boggs's order were vigorously debated in the Missouri legislature during its 1839 session. The order was supported by most northwest Missouri citizens but was questioned or denounced by others. However, no determination of the order's legality was ever made.

On June 25, 1976, Governor Christopher S. Bond issued an executive order rescinding the Extermination Order, recognizing its legal invalidity and formally apologizing in behalf of the state of Missouri for the suffering it had caused the Latter-day Saints.

BIBLIOGRAPHY

"Document Containing the Correspondence, Orders, etc. in Relation to the Disturbances with the Mormons; and the Evidence Given before the Hon. Austin A. King." Office of the Boon's Lick Democrat, Fayette, Mo., 1841, p. 61 (contains full text of the order).

Gentry, Leland H. "A History of the Latter-day Saints in Northern Missouri from 1836 to 1839." Ph.D. diss., Brigham Young University, 1965.

LeSueur, Stephen C. *The 1838 Mormon War in Missouri.* Columbia, Mo., 1987.

DALE A. WHITMAN

F

FAR WEST, MISSOURI

Far West, Caldwell County, Missouri, was settled in 1836 as Latter-day Saints sought a home and refuge from persecution in Clay County. It became the county seat, with an estimated 3,000 to 5,000 inhabitants. Far West is important to LDS history because that is where the following happened: (1) a temple site was dedicated and the cornerstones laid; (2) seven revelations now published in the Doctrine and Covenants (113, 114, 115, 117, 118, 119, 120) were received; (3) Joseph F. SMITH, sixth president of the Church, was born (November 13, 1838); (4) the Quorum of the Twelve Apostles officially left from for a mission to Great Britain; (5) a stake of Zion was organized; (6) Joseph SMITH and his family lived (beginning March 14, 1838); (7) and for a short time the headquarters of the Church was located.

Among the notable revelations in the Doctrine and Covenants received at Far West and vicinity are: the proper name of the church was given (115:4); four new members of the Twelve Apostles were named and the Twelve as a quorum were called to serve an overseas mission (118:1–6); and the law of tithing was explained (119, 120).

Joseph Smith and other Church leaders were arrested in Far West on October 31, 1838, by the state militia and taken to Independence, then to Richmond, and from there to Liberty, Missouri, where they were imprisoned. While the Prophet was in prison during the winter and spring of 1838–1839, the Latter-day Saints were driven from Far West and other Missouri sites under Governor Boggs's EXTERMINATION ORDER and relocated in Illinois.

The Church still has interest in Far West and has erected appropriate monuments at the temple site.

[*See also* History of the Church: c. 1831–1844; Missions of the Twelve to the British Isles; Missouri.]

BIBLIOGRAPHY

Cannon, Donald Q., and Lyndon W. Cook. *Far West Record*. Salt Lake City, 1983.

Gentry, Leland H. "A History of the Latter-day Saints in Northern Missouri from 1836 to 1839." Ph.D. diss., Brigham Young University, 1965.

LARRY C. PORTER

FAYETTE, NEW YORK

The township of Fayette, New York, is located in Seneca County between Seneca and Cayuga lakes. The Church of Jesus Christ of Latter-day Saints was organized in the log cabin of Peter Whitmer, Sr., approximately 4.7 miles northwest of the village of Fayette and 3 miles southwest of modern Waterloo, New York.

Joseph SMITH first came to Fayette in the spring of 1829, when David WHITMER, who knew Oliver COWDERY, invited him and the Prophet to come to his father's house from HARMONY, PENNSYLVANIA, to complete the translation of the Book of Mormon. They arrived in Fayette the first week of June and completed the translation by the end of June. They also preached occasionally in the area, baptizing many converts. Joseph Smith received five revelations in Fayette during that month (D&C 14–18). Soon after the translation was completed, Whitmer, Cowdery, and Martin HARRIS testified that they were shown the plates by a heavenly messenger near the Whitmer home.

In April 1830, the Prophet received a revelation instructing him to organize the Church on April 6, which was accomplished in the home of Peter Whitmer, Sr. (D&C 20–21). In the days and months that followed, many meetings were held in the general area of Fayette and more converts were baptized. The first general conference of the Church was held in Fayette on June 9, 1830.

Because of renewed opposition in Harmony, Pennsylvania, where Joseph and his wife, Emma, had returned after the Church was organized, they moved again to the Whitmer home in Fayette, living there from August 1830 to January 1831. In those months, Joseph continued the work of his inspired translation of the Bible, part of which was later published as the book of Moses; he also received thirteen additional revelations (D&C 28–40). The second general conference was held in Fayette on September 26, 1830.

In December 1830 and January 1831, revelations were received instructing the Latter-day Saints to move to Ohio to a more friendly environment (D&C 37:1–3; 38:31–32), where LDS missionaries had made many converts. Joseph and Emma Smith left Fayette in the latter part of January 1831, and most of the remaining members left later that spring and summer.

Today the Church has built a visitors center, a chapel, and a replica of the Whitmer log cabin on the old Whitmer farm.

BIBLIOGRAPHY

Porter, Larry C. "A Study of the Origins of The Church of Jesus Christ of Latter-day Saints in the States of New York and Pennsylvania, 1816–1831." Ph.D. diss., Brigham Young University, 1971.

LAMAR E. GARRARD

FIRST VISION

The first vision of the Prophet Joseph Smith is the beginning point, the fountainhead, of the restoration of the gospel in this dispensation. This theophany occurred in a grove near Palmyra, New York, in the spring of 1820.

Joseph's narratives record that when he was in his twelfth year he began to sense the need for redemption and investigated several religious groups. A short time after his family moved to Manchester, New York, he witnessed unusual religious excitement in the area, bringing divisions of allegiance in his community and family. As converts began filing off to one faith and another, he observed that their professed good feelings for each other were lost in "a strife of words and a contest about opinions" (JS—H 1:5–8). Confused and concerned, he asked himself, "If any one of them be right which is it?

And how shall I know it?" (Backman, pp. 156, 162, 168; Jessee, p. 198).

Searching the scriptures, Joseph was influenced by an admonition to prayer in the epistle of James. "If any of you lack wisdom, let him ask of God" (James 1:5). "Never," he later recalled, "did any passage of scripture come with more power to the heart of man than this did at this time to mine" (JS—H 1:12). He retired to a secluded grove near his father's log-cabin farmhouse and knelt in prayer (Backman, p. 156).

A struggle with a satanic influence followed, but with divine help he survived it. As he continued to call upon God, he records, "I saw a pillar of light exactly over my head, above the brightness of the sun, which descended gradually until it fell upon me." Immediately he was delivered from oppressive darkness (JS—H 1:16). Within the light, he saw two personages "whose brightness and glory defy all description" and who "exactly resembled each other in features and likeness" (JS—H 1:17; WENTWORTH LETTER; Backman, p. 169). One of them spoke his name, pointed to the other, and said, "This is My Beloved Son. Hear Him!" (JS—H 1:17). In what followed, Joseph learned that through Christ, who had taken upon himself the sins of mankind, he was forgiven of his sins. "Behold I am the Lord of glory. I was crucified for the world that all those who believe on my name may have eternal life" (Backman, p. 157). He was also assured of the reality and imminence of Christ's second coming "to bring to pass that which [hath] been spoken by the mouth of the prophets and apostles" (Backman, pp. 157, 167, 169; Jessee, p. 6). When he recovered, Joseph asked which church he should join and was told to join none because they all taught "incorrect doctrines"; they had a form of godliness, but "denied the power thereof" (cf. 2 Tim. 3:5). Further, he was told "that the fulness of the gospel should at some future time be made known unto me" (JS—H 1:17–20; Backman, pp. 163, 169; Jessee, p. 213). As he left the grove, he recalled, "My soul was filled with love," and for many days "I could rejoice with great joy and the Lord was with me" (Backman, p. 157).

Joseph's tranquillity was short-lived. At first, except from his family, he met only contempt from those who learned of his experience. He had not anticipated the bitter denunciations that this event would call forth.

On several occasions between 1832 and 1842, the young Prophet wrote or dictated accounts of the vision, each in a different setting, the last two for publication. Each record omits or adds some details. In 1832, for example, Joseph Smith wrote that prior to his first vision he searched the scriptures and concluded that no society taught New Testament Christianity (Backman, p. 156; Jessee, p. 5). In the 1838 account he notes that he often said to himself, "Who of all these parties are right; or, are they all wrong together?" Later in this same account he parenthetically adds "(for at this time it had never entered into my heart that all were wrong)" (JS—H 1:10, 18; Jessee, pp. 198, 200).

Latter-day Saints regard this vision as authentic and revelatory of the nature of God. In the biblical and scriptural context, they see it as parallel to the visions of Moses or the theophanies recorded in the Book of Mormon. Joseph himself compared his experiences in and after the vision to those of Paul (JS—H 1:24; *TPJS*, p. 151).

LDS teaching is, in the words of Stephen L Richards (a former counselor in the First Presidency), "steeped in the verity of the First Vision." It undergirds the doctrine of an anthropomorphic God and theomorphic man, of the relationships of the persons of the Godhead, and of continual revelation. Mormon prayers, hymns, forms of worship, and eschatology are all rooted in this understanding. It renews the witness of the Hebrew prophets that visions are not the least but the most reliable mortal access to the divine; that the majesty, glory, and power of God are "beyond description"; that the biblical record of face-to-face communion with God is more than a strained metaphor. It confirms the New Testament testimony of the apostles (1) that God the Father and Jesus Christ are separate persons who manifest themselves as they are to the sons and daughters of God and (2) that the Son is in the similitude of the Father, and the Father in the similitude of the Son.

[*See also* Visions of Joseph Smith.]

BIBLIOGRAPHY

Backman, Milton V., Jr. *Joseph Smith's First Vision*. Salt Lake City, 1980.

Smith, Joseph. *The Personal Writings of Joseph Smith*, comp. and ed. Dean C. Jessee. Salt Lake City, 1984.

MILTON V. BACKMAN, JR.

FORGERIES OF HISTORICAL DOCUMENTS

The possibility of forgery must be considered by all historians as they ponder their evidence and by archivists as they build their collections. Forged Dutch colonial documents have been found in New York, and forgeries of Lone Star Republic documents have been identified in Texas.

One of the most famous forgeries in LDS history is the alleged "Joseph Smith Revelation" appointing James J. Strang his successor. It was created in the 1840s, probably by Strang, and is now located at the Beinecke Library at Yale University. The motives of Strang, who hoped to succeed Joseph Smith, were clear. Equally apparent were the reasons for the forgery of a pamphlet attributed to Joseph Smith's early associate, Oliver COWDERY. *Defense in a Rehearsal of My Grounds for Separating Myself from the Latter Day Saints*, supposedly written in Ohio in 1839, first appeared in an anti-Mormon publication in 1906 (Anderson, pp. 20–21). Others have attempted forgeries for money, ego, or the desire to influence or alter history.

The Hofmann forgeries of the 1980s have raised questions about some historical documents related to early Latter-day Saint history. In their search for new sources for information about the Church's formative period, historians were fascinated by the seemingly endless cache of historical documents supposedly located by Mark Hofmann. These documents purported to illuminate such topics as Joseph Smith's reception and translation of the records known as the Book of Mormon and the selection of his successor in Church leadership. Many, if not most, "Hofmann documents" turned out to be skillful forgeries. Hofmann had built a paper fortune from document dealing and duplicity, but when he was unable to produce additional promised documents for clients, he murdered a Salt Lake City businessman and the wife of an acquaintance in 1985. The subsequent investigation led to his arrest, confession of murder and forgery, and life sentence in the Utah State Prison.

The story of the Hofmann forgeries is the subject of several books and numerous articles. The case has deeply embarrassed both historians and the dealers and collectors who handled his documents. It has also prompted greater caution and healthy skepticism about the validity of purported historical documents of unknown background or provenance.

Documents that have been maintained in the official custody of a church or government agency throughout their life cycle should be considered more reliable than "newly found" documents. Scholars and archivists should be especially wary of those documents whose provenance is unclear. In all cases new and startling evidence must be critically evaluated against the standard of known and reliable documents.

BIBLIOGRAPHY

Anderson, Richard L. "The Second Witness of Priesthood." *IE* 71 [Sept. 1968]:15–16, 18, 20–22, 24.

Jessee, Dean C. "New Documents and Mormon Beginnings." *BYU Studies* 24 (Fall 1984):392–428.

Sillitoe, Linda, and Allen Roberts. *Salamander: The Story of the Mormon Forgery Murders.* Salt Lake City, 1988.

Whittaker, David J. "The Hofmann Maze: A Book Review Essay with a Chronology and Bibliography of the Hofmann Case." *BYU Studies* 29 (Winter 1989):67–124.

MAX J. EVANS

FOX, RUTH MAY

Ruth May Fox (1853–1958) devoted many years to the Young Ladies' Mutual Improvement Association (YWMIA; in 1977 Young Women), serving as president from 1929 to 1937, following her tenure as first counselor to President Martha Horne Tingey from 1905 to 1929. Vibrant and spirited, Ruth May Fox was a woman of great strength and refined features. A poet and songwriter, she wrote the text to "Carry On," a hymn traditionally associated with the Mutual Improvement Association; it was introduced and featured at that association's June conference in 1930. She was an advocate of woman suffrage and education, evidenced in part by her sponsorship of the Traveling Library Program and her focus on self-education.

Ruth May Fox was born November 16, 1853, in Westbury, Wiltshire, England, the daughter of Mary Ann Harding and James May. Five months later, her parents joined the LDS Church. After her mother's death in 1855, her father was called to be a traveling elder for the Church, causing her to live with various LDS families and relatives until she was approximately eight years old, when her father took her to Yorkshire, where he was employed. Around 1865 he emigrated to America, where Ruth joined him a few months later, and soon after, he remarried. The family lived in the Philadelphia area for two years, during which time she worked in factories to earn enough money to help finance their journey to Utah.

In July 1867 the Mays started for Utah, first traveling to North Platte, Nebraska. After securing supplies for their journey, they had only enough money to buy one yoke of cattle, so they shared a wagon with another family and walked most of the way to Utah.

Ruth worked in the Deseret (Salt Lake City) and Ogden Woolen Mills, where her father was a carder, and used her earnings to help purchase the family home. She then attended John Morgan's College in Salt Lake City for four months, which ended her formal education. When her father returned to Salt Lake City and started his own mill, she helped him operate the heavy equipment.

On May 8, 1873, when she was nineteen and he was twenty, she married Jesse Williams Fox, Jr.; they were blessed with twelve children. Ruth and Jesse prospered in the early years of their marriage but met financial difficulties around 1888. Soon after, Jesse took a second wife, without any forewarning to Ruth. He eventually lost his business, accumulated large debts, and lost the family home. The two families lived separately, and as Jesse lived with the other household, Ruth was largely left to her own resources to survive. In 1900 she and her children ran the Saint Omer Boarding House to supplement their income; in 1914 she began work as a typist for the YWMIA. She lived with her children from 1914 until her death in 1958, resuming housekeeping only to nurse her husband through illnesses in 1921 and from 1927 until his death in 1928.

Among Ruth May Fox's lifelong beliefs was a strong commitment to suffrage for women. She was active in the Utah Woman Suffrage Association and the Republican party and helped draft the suffrage clause of the Utah Constitution. She served as president of the Utah Woman's Press Club, treasurer of the Utah Woman Suffrage Association, chairman of the Salt Lake County Second Precinct Ladies' Republican Club, and board member of the Deseret Agricultural and Manufacturing Society and of Traveler's Aid Society. She died on April 12, 1958, in Salt Lake City at the age of 104.

BIBLIOGRAPHY
"Ruth May Fox (1853–1967 [*sic*])." In Kenneth W. Godfrey, Audrey M. Godfrey, and Jill Mulvay-Derr, eds., *Women's Voices: An Untold History of the Latter-day Saints, 1830–1900*. Salt Lake City, 1982.
Thatcher, Linda. "'I Care Nothing for Politics': Ruth May Fox, Forgotten Suffragist." *Utah Historical Quarterly* 49 (Summer 1981):239–53.

LINDA THATCHER

G

GATES, SUSA YOUNG

Susa (Susan, Susannah) Gates was born on March 18, 1856, in Salt Lake City. A writer, publisher, advocate for women's achievements, educator, missionary, genealogist, temple worker, wife, and mother of thirteen children, she was fond of saying, "Keep busy in the face of discouragement" (Person, p. 208).

The second daughter of Brigham Young's twenty-second wife, Lucy Bigelow Young, Susa Young has been called "the most versatile and prolific LDS writer ever to take up the pen in defense of her religion" (Cracroft, p. 73). Following private education that included music and ballet, she entered the University of Deseret at age thirteen. The next year she became co-editor of the *College Lantern*, possibly the first western college newspaper.

In 1872, at age sixteen, she married Dr. Alma Bailey Dunford; they had two children, Leah Eudora Dunford and Alma Bailey Dunford. The marriage ended in divorce in 1877. The next year, Susa entered Brigham Young Academy in Provo and, while a student, founded the department of music and conducted a choir. During a trip to the Sandwich Islands (Hawaii), she renewed her acquaintance with Jacob F. Gates, whom she married on January 5, 1880. The success of their marriage has been attributed to their mutual respect for, and support of, one another's work. Only four of the eleven children born to this marriage survived to adulthood: Emma Lucy Gates

Bowen, Brigham Cecil Gates, Harvey Harris (Hal) Gates, and Franklin Young Gates.

During the 1880s and 1890s, Susa Gates focused her energy on childbearing and child-rearing, missionary work, education, writing, and women's concerns. After completing a Church mission with her husband to the Sandwich Islands in 1889, she founded the *Young Woman's Journal*. It was adopted as the official magazine for the Young Ladies' Mutual Improvement Association in 1897. She founded the Utah Woman's Press Club, became press chairman of the National Council of Women, and founded the *Relief Society Magazine*, which she edited until 1922. She wrote biographies of Lydia Knight and of her father, Brigham Young, novels including *John Stevens' Courtship* and *The Prince of Ur*, a pamphlet entitled the "Teachings of Brigham Young," and a history of women in the Church, on which she was still working at the time of her death.

Concern for women's achievements was a prominent force in Susa Gates's life. During the 1890s, while she was most occupied with raising her own children, she became a charter member of the National Household Economic Association and was a representative to women's congresses in Denver, Washington, D.C., Toronto, and London, where she was invited to speak on the topic "Equal Moral Standards for Men and Women" and where she joined other women of the International Council, including Susan B. Anthony, for tea with Queen Victoria.

At the turn of the century, Susa suffered a nervous and physical breakdown. Ill for three years, she was forced to terminate a mission that she and her husband had begun in 1902. A priesthood blessing that promised her she would live to do temple work marked the beginning of her recovery. She underwent a year of intense spiritual introspection and later wrote of that period, "I disciplined my taste, my desires and my impulses—severely disciplining my appetite, my tongue, my acts . . . and how I prayed!" (Person, p. 212). While maintaining her commitments to family and women's advancement, she focused her energy on genealogy and temple work.

In 1906, Susa Young Gates organized genealogical departments in two newspapers, the *Inter Mountain Republican* and the *Deseret News*, and wrote columns for both papers over the next ten years. She produced instructional manuals for genealogists, devised a systematic index of names for the Church, and published the *Surname Book and Racial History*. In 1915, she introduced genealogical class work at the International Genealogy Conference in San Francisco and became head of the Research Department and Library of the Genealogical Society of Utah in 1923. She personally cataloged more than 16,000 names of the Young family. She spent much time in the last years of her life doing ordinance work in the Salt Lake Temple with her husband. She died on May 27, 1933.

BIBLIOGRAPHY

Arrington, Leonard J. "Blessed Damozels: Women in Mormon History." *Dialogue* 6 (Summer 1971):22–31.

Cracroft, R. Paul. "Susa Young Gates: Her Life and Literary Work." Master's thesis, University of Utah, 1951.

Person, Carolyn W. D. "Susa Young Gates." In *Mormon Sisters: Women in Early Utah*, ed. Claudia L. Bushman, pp. 198–223. Cambridge, Mass., 1976.

LOUISE PLUMMER

GRANT, HEBER J.

Heber J. Grant (1856–1945), seventh President of The Church of Jesus Christ of Latter-day Saints, was a business leader and a devoted follower of the gospel of Jesus Christ who used his talents in the service of his Church. As an apostle, he was instrumental in preserving Mormonism's credit and reputation after the economic devastation of the Panic of 1893. As President, he was a model of strong character and an ambassador of goodwill to a world often hostile to the Latter-day Saints.

Born November 22, 1856, in Salt Lake City to Jedediah M. and Rachel Ridgeway Ivins Grant, Heber associated from a young age with Church and territorial leaders. His father served as Brigham YOUNG's counselor in the First Presidency and as mayor of the city, and his mother enjoyed the society of the leading women of the LDS community.

Heber did not benefit from the association of his father directly. Jedediah Grant died nine days after Heber was born, the victim of "lung disease," and Rachel became the paramount influence in Heber's life. Prim and reserved, she came from a New Jersey family of merchants and devoted practitioners of religion. She joined the Church just prior to her twentieth birthday, in part because of the labors of the fiery missionary who later became her husband. In 1855, Rachel became one of Jedediah's plural wives.

After Jedediah's death, diminished means eventually forced Rachel and her son to move from the substantial Grant home on Main Street to a "widow's cabin" several blocks away. The change was wrenching. Declining the proffer of Church aid, Rachel supported the family by sewing and taking in boarders. Young Heber sat on the floor many an evening and pumped the sewing machine treadle to relieve his weary mother.

The location of the Grants' new home placed them within the Salt Lake Thirteenth Ward, one of the largest and most culturally diverse LDS congregations in the territory, and so Heber enjoyed the best of frontier Mormonism. He was one of the few youths of the city to serve as a "block teacher," and at the unusually young age of fifteen he was ordained to the office of seventy in the priesthood.

In the absence of public schools, Rachel found the means to enroll her son in good private schools, beginning with Brigham Young's school at State and South Temple streets. Grant remembered himself as being good at mathematics, memorization, and recitation, but less gifted in grammar, spelling, and especially foreign languages. Following frontier practice, his class experience was limited; he left school at the age of sixteen.

When the Thirteenth Ward organized the first Young Men's Mutual Improvement Association (YMMIA) in 1875, Grant was called as a counselor to its president at age nineteen. The YMMIA's weekly sessions gave him a chance for study, self-improvement, and speech-making. On his own he read LDS and Protestant devotional literature, Samuel Smiles's chatbooks idealizing the self-made man, and books of readings filled with firm and traditional values. As a young man, he was an active member of the "Wasatch Literary Association," a high-spirited local group that met each Wednesday evening for cultural exercises. These might include declamations, lectures, debates, readings, musical renditions, and even small-scale theatrical productions. In later years he often acknowledged his debt to the "Wasatchers" for much of his cultural and intellectual training.

For several years business became Grant's preoccupation. In addition to selling insurance, he peddled books, found Utah retailers for a Chicago grocery house, performed tasks for the Deseret National Bank, and taught penmanship. With Brigham Young's support, he was appointed assistant cashier of the Church-owned Zion's Savings and Trust Company. Hard work began to pay dividends. A typical Utah wage earner might make $500 annually; in his early twenties, Grant earned ten times that amount. Soon he opened another insurance agency in Ogden and began to fulfill his hope of developing "home industry." With a partner, he purchased the Ogden Vinegar Works.

On October 30, 1880, Grant was called as president of the Tooele Stake, about twenty-five miles west of Salt Lake City. Not yet twenty-four years old, he presided over more than a half-dozen congregations, dispensing spiritual and temporal counsel to frontier-hardened and not always pliant settlers. Moreover, the area presented one special difficulty: with the opening of western Utah mines, non-Mormons had settled in the county and for a time wrested local political control from the Church.

To Grant's new challenges were added personal difficulties. He had married a longtime acquaintance from the Thirteenth Ward, Lucy Stringham, on November 1, 1877, three weeks before his twenty-first birthday. Shortly after the couple moved to Tooele, she developed a lingering stomach illness and related problems that twelve years later claimed her life. Not long after, his Salt Lake City businesses began to suffer from lack of attention. His Ogden vinegar factory burned, and he was underinsured.

Although he enjoyed ministering to his Tooele flock, his personal difficulties weighed heavily on him. He later admitted that during these years he felt so "blue" that he did not know what to "do or where to turn" (Grant to B. F. Grant, July 21, 1896, Grant Papers, LDS Archives). Under this burden, his six-foot, 140-pound frame almost gave way. The attending doctor pronounced a diagnosis of "nervous convulsions" and warned the young man that if he did not slow his pace he would certainly experience a "softening of the brain" (Grant typed diary, Nov. 1, 1887; Francis M. Lyman diary, Jan. 7, 15, 16, 23, 1882, Church Archives).

In 1882, less than two years after his arrival in Tooele and ten months after his nervous collapse, Grant was asked to attend a council meeting in Church President John Taylor's office, where President Taylor announced a revelation filling two vacancies in the Quorum of the Twelve Apostles. As the document was read, Grant learned of his appointment to the quorum. He felt unprepared to serve in what he believed was such a high and important calling. He also wondered whether his relish for commerce properly mixed with religion. Grant's troubled "long night of the soul" was resolved during one of his first preaching tours. While traveling in Arizona, he had a spiritual manifestation that confirmed his call and put an end to his self-doubts. The epiphany also affirmed several blessings that Grant had received while a youth. On several occasions, Church leaders had prophesied his eventual high Church service.

During Grant's early service as an apostle, he concluded that wealth and money-making were honorable when dedicated to the common good, by which he meant two things: almsgiving and the founding of businesses to aid the Church and community. During his years as a young apostle, he did both. His gifts to friends and worthy purposes often took a third of his income. At a time when apostles commonly engaged in private activities, he was tireless in founding and developing "home institutions" to benefit the community. The enterprises included a Utah retail and wholesale business, a livery stable, two "home" insurance companies, a bank, a Salt Lake newspaper, the famed Salt Lake Theatre, the Utah Sugar Company, and a series of less prominent enterprises.

He was equally busy with Church assignments as a member of the Church Salary Committee, the Sunday School Board, and the Mutual Improvement superintendency. Twice he proselytized among the dangerous Yaqui Indians in Mexico, and his many tours to the Southwest earned him the title "the Arizona Apostle."

Grant eventually married three wives, who bore him twelve children. In addition to Lucy Stringham, he entered into plural marriage with Huldah Augusta Winters and Emily Wells. The three Grant wives were similar in many ways. Well educated for the times, all had taught school, and each descended from old pioneer families. "One's wealth consists in those whom he loves and serves and who love and serve him in return," he often said. Incessant travel took him away from the family, an absence he bridged by his long and sensitive personal letters. More than 50,000 letters are preserved in the Church archives, many of them to his children and grandchildren.

The Panic of 1893 caught both Grant and the Church overextended and eventually caused him to go to New York City to negotiate credit for himself and the Church. His loan brokering allowed him and the Church to remain solvent during the hard times of the 1890s, but the effects of the panic were severe for him personally; he lost his fortune and never fully recovered it.

As Utah and the Church entered the twentieth century, Grant's ministry changed. The growing Church required more and more of his time. He filled two foreign assignments, opening the Japanese Mission (1901–1903) and later presiding over the European Mission (1903–1905). On returning to the United States, he was assigned to supervise Church education, the Genealogical Society, and the Church magazine, the *Improvement Era*. He also still found time for community service, including assisting the cause of prohibition and directing World War I Liberty Bond drives.

In 1916 his seniority brought him to the presidency of the Quorum of Twelve Apostles. Two years later, Church President Joseph F. SMITH, on his deathbed, took Grant's hand and said, "The Lord bless you, my boy, the Lord bless you. You have got a great responsibility. Always remember that this is the Lord's work and not man's. The Lord is greater than any man. He knows whom he wants to lead his Church and never makes any mistake. The Lord bless you" (*CR*, Apr. 1941). On November 23, 1918, Heber J. Grant was sustained as President of the Church.

During his twenty-six-and-a-half-year administration—the Church's second longest—Church members grew familiar with the hardy, pioneer themes of President Grant's leadership. He repeatedly spoke of the need for charity, duty, honor, service, and work, and admonished the Saints to live modestly and to observe the prohibitions of the Church's health code, the Word of Wisdom. For Saints disoriented by the century's rapid social and cultural changes, President Grant's firm voice, ramrod-straight posture, and forceful—and sometimes sharp-tongued—delivery conveyed strength and resolution. He personified time-tested values.

After years of adverse Church publicity and misunderstanding, President Grant gladly accepted invitations to speak to non-Mormon groups throughout the United States, often traveling with his sole surviving wife, Augusta, in the hope of improving the image of the Church. He usually mixed personal reminiscence, business homilies, and a message about the Church. His influence was not limited to formal addresses. He cultivated personal contacts with business, cinema, media, and political leaders in the hope of presenting the Church in a more sympathetic light to the public at large. The production of such pro-LDS Hollywood films as *Union Pacific* and *Brigham Young* was partly due to his quiet influence. He promoted national tours by the Mormon Tabernacle Choir and supported the political activity of Utah senator and LDS apostle Reed Smoot, whose growing national influence brought favorable comment to Utah and the Church.

Faced with regional and then national economic depression during the late 1920s and the 1930s, the Grant administration had to cope with hard times. In keeping with the lessons learned during the depressed 1890s, President Grant trimmed Church expenses wherever he could; also his business experience, and particularly his eastern contacts, repeatedly helped to stabilize the Church financially. He advised a number of local businesses—both Mormon and non-Mormon concerns—without compensation, helping to pull them through the difficult times. Moreover, in 1936 the Church under his leadership sought to assist impoverished Latter-day Saints by establishing the Church Security Program, later renamed the Church Welfare Program, one of the major accomplishments of his administration. To help get it established, President Grant gave the program his large dry farm in western Utah, in which he had invested more than $80,000.

During his time as president, he dedicated three new temples: Laie, Hawaii (1919), Cardston, Canada (1923), and Mesa, Arizona (1927). Several hundred chapels were constructed, many in areas outside the Utah heartland. The Washington, D.C., chapel, dedicated in 1933, symbolized Church growth nationally.

Many of the characteristics of the Church in the twentieth century came into focus during President Grant's administration. Religious education received new emphasis with the establishment of an extensive seminary and institute program to provide a spiritual dimension in the education of the youth. Under his direction, Church leaders stressed sacrament meeting attendance, temple activity, observance of the Word of Wisdom, family-history research, and monthly visits to Church members in their homes. To cope with the expansion of the Church, he called a new group of General Authorities, Assistants to the Twelve Apostles.

Near the end of his life and under his direction, the First Presidency addressed the moral perplexities of war. A statement issued at the beginning of World War II said, "The Church . . . cannot regard war as a righteous means of settling international disputes." Yet the statement urged allegiance to "constitutional law" and acceptance of national military service, whatever the nationality of Church members (*IE* 45 [May 1942]:348–49). The scrupulously neutral statement reflected President Grant's own reservations about American entrance into the conflict and his growing personal pacifism.

Members came to love President Grant's expansive ways. Until mounting burdens and declining health intervened, his office door was open to General Authorities, stake and local leaders, and even to members troubled with problems. He traveled widely throughout America and in 1937 heralded the Church's European centennial by touring the missions of Great Britain and western Europe, the second LDS President to venture across the Atlantic Ocean while in office. Seeking to personalize his presidency, he distributed thousands of homiletic books, personally autographing each and sometimes marking passages for emphasis. Recalling his mother's struggles, he freely gave of his personal means, particularly to widows, and established a missionary fund for his increasing progeny.

In 1940, while visiting Southern California, he suffered a series of strokes that slowed his pace and forced him to delegate active administration of the Church, relying primarily on J. Reuben Clark, Jr., his first counselor. President Grant died on May 14, 1945, at Salt Lake City.

During President Grant's administration Church membership doubled. He traveled more than 400,000 miles, filled 1,500 appointments, gave 1,250 sermons, and made 28 major addresses to state, national, civic, and professional groups. His greatest achievements, however, cannot be measured statistically. During almost sixty-five years of Church service, he helped transform the Church from a sequestered, misunderstood, pioneer faith to an accepted, vibrant religion of twentieth-century America.

BIBLIOGRAPHY

No modern, full-scale biography of Heber J. Grant exists. For admiring surveys, see Bryant S. Hinckley, *Heber J. Grant: Highlights in the Life of a Great Leader* (Salt Lake City, 1951); Francis M. Gibbons, *Heber J. Grant: Man of Steel, Prophet of God* (Salt Lake City, 1979); and Ronald W. Walker, "Heber J. Grant," in *The Presidents of the Church*, ed. Leonard J. Arrington (Salt Lake City, 1986).

For accounts of various events of Grant's life, see Ronald W. Walker, "Crisis in Zion: Heber J. Grant and the Panic of 1893," *Arizona and the West* 21 (Autumn 1979):257–78, reprinted in *Sunstone* 5 (Jan.–Feb. 1980):26–34; "Heber J. Grant and the Utah Loan and Trust Company," *Journal of Mormon History* 8 (1981):21–36; "Young Heber J. Grant: Entrepreneur Extraordinary," *The Twentieth Century American West*, Charles Redd Monographs in Western History, (1983):85–119; and "Young Heber J. Grant's Years of Passage," *BYU Studies* 24 (Spring 1984):131–49.

For his role in stabilizing Church finances in the early twentieth century, see Thomas G. Alexander, *Mormonism in Transition* (Urbana, Ill., 1986).

RONALD W. WALKER

H

HANDCART COMPANIES

The large backlog of needy LDS converts awaiting passage from Europe and reduced tithing receipts at home persuaded Brigham YOUNG in 1855 to instruct that the "poor saints" sailing from Liverpool to New York and taking the train to Iowa City should thence "walk and draw their luggage" overland to Utah. In 1856 five such handcart companies were organized to make the 1,300-mile trip on foot from the western railroad terminus at Iowa City to Salt Lake City (*see* IMMIGRATION AND EMIGRATION; MORMON PIONEER TRAIL).

Success seemed assured when the first two companies, totaling 486 immigrants pulling 96 handcarts, arrived safely in Salt Lake City on September 26, 1856. They accomplished the trek in under sixteen weeks. The third company, and presumably the last of the season, made up of 320 persons pulling 64 handcarts, arrived on October 2. But at that point the two remaining companies, totaling 980 people and 233 handcarts, were still on the way, having started dangerously late. One of these companies, under James G. Willie, left Iowa City on July 15, crossed Iowa to Florence (Omaha), Nebraska, then, after a week in Florence, headed out onto the plains. The last company, under Edward Martin, departed Florence on August 25. Three independent wagon companies, carrying 390 more immigrants, also started late.

A week after the departure of the Martin Company, Franklin D.

Richards, an apostle who had organized the handcart effort as president of the European Mission, also departed Florence with sixteen other returning missionaries. This party, on horseback and in fast carriages, passed the Martin Company on September 7, the Willie Company on September 12, and arrived in Salt Lake City on October 4.

Richards's report that many more immigrants were coming was a shock: the late-starting immigrants would not be adequately clothed for the cold weather they would surely experience; they, like those in all previous lightly supplied handcart companies, would be perilously short of food; and, as they were unexpected, the last resupply wagons, which were routinely dispatched into the mountains to meet immigrant companies, had already returned.

Anticipating the worst, President Young mobilized men and women gathered for general conference and immediately ordered a massive rescue effort. A party of twenty-seven men, led by George D. Grant, left on October 7 with the first sixteen of what ultimately amounted to 200 wagons and teams. Several of the rescue party, including Grant, had been among the missionaries who had ridden in from the East five days before.

Two weeks later, one of the earliest blizzards on record struck just as both the handcart companies and the independent wagon companies were entering the Rocky Mountains in central Wyoming. After several days of being lashed by the fierce blizzard, people in the exposed handcart companies began to die.

Grant's rescue party found the Willie Company on October 21—in a blinding snowstorm one day after they had run out of food. But the worst still lay ahead, when, after a day of rest and replenishment, the company had to struggle over the long and steep eastern approach to South Pass in the teeth of a northerly gale. Beyond the pass, the company, now amply fed and free to climb aboard empty supply wagons as they became available, moved quickly, arriving in Salt Lake City on November 9. Of the 404 members of the company, 68 died and many others suffered from severe frostbite and near starvation.

Those of the Martin Company, three-fourths of them women, children, and the elderly, suffered even more. When the storm hit on October 19, they made camp and spent nine days on reduced rations waiting out the storm. Grant's party, after leaving men and supplies with the Willie Company, plunged farther east through the snow with eight wagons in search of the Martin Company. A scouting party sent out ahead of the wagons found them 150 miles east of South Pass.

The company, already in a desperate condition, was ordered to break camp immediately. The supply wagons met them on the trail, but the provisions were not nearly enough and, after struggling 55 miles farther, the company once again went into camp near Devil's Gate to await the arrival of supplies.

In the meantime, the rescue effort began to disintegrate. Rescue teams held up several days by the raging storm turned back, fearing to go on and rationalizing that the immigrant trains and Grant's advance party had either decided to winter over or had perished in the storm.

The Martin Company remained in camp for five days. When no supplies came, the company, now deplorably weakened, was again forced out on the trail. It had suffered fifty-six dead before being found, and it was now losing people at an appalling rate.

Relief came barely in time. A messenger ordered back west by Grant reached and turned around some of the teams that had abandoned the rescue. At least thirty wagons reached the Martin Company just as it was about to attempt the same climb to South Pass that had so sorely tested the Willie Company. Starved, frozen, spent, their spirits crushed, and many unable to walk, the people had reached the breaking point.

But now warmed and fed, with those unable to walk riding in the wagons, the company moved rapidly on. The Martin Company, in a train of 104 wagons, finally arrived in Salt Lake City on November 30. Out of 576, at least 145 had died and, like the Willie Company, many were severely afflicted by frostbite and starvation.

Elements of the three independent wagon companies and the rescue effort straggled into Salt Lake City until mid-December—except for twenty men, under Daniel W. Jones, who remained for the winter at Devil's Gate to guard freight unloaded there by the independent wagon companies, in part to make room for exhausted members of the Martin Company. The Jones party suffered misery and starvation at Devil's Gate. At one point they were reduced to eating rawhide until friendly Indians gave them some buffalo meat.

The decision to send out the Willie and Martin companies so late in the season was extremely reckless. In mid-November President Brigham Young angrily reproved those who had authorized the late start or who had not ordered the several parties back to Florence when they still had the opportunity, charging "ignorance," "mismanagement," and "misconduct." Though terrible, the suffering could have been far worse. Had the rescue effort not been launched immediately—well before the storm struck—the handcart companies would probably have been totally destroyed.

Six more handcart companies crossed the plains after 1856. To demonstrate that the idea was still viable, seventy missionaries made the trip in the opposite direction in the spring of 1857. Five companies, totaling 1,076 immigrants with 223 handcarts, crossed west with little difficulty: two in 1857, one in 1859, and two in 1860. In all, 2,962 immigrants walked to Utah with handcarts. About 250 died along the way—all but about 30 of those in the Willie and Martin companies.

For Latter-day Saints, the handcart story, particularly the account of the Willie and Martin companies, has darkened the collective memory of the westering saga. But that episode is also remembered for the unparalleled gallantry exhibited by so many, immigrants and rescuers alike. Of particular note is the superb performance of the women; their courage and mettle contributed enormously to the eventual survival of both companies. It was at once the most ill-advised and tragic, the most heroic, and arguably the proudest single event in the Mormon pioneer experience.

BIBLIOGRAPHY

Cornwall, Rebecca, and Leonard J. Arrington. *Rescue of the 1856 Handcart Companies.* Vol. 11 of the Charles Redd Monographs in Western History. Provo, Utah, 1981.

Hafen, LeRoy R., and Ann W. Hafen. *Handcarts to Zion: The Story of a Unique Western Migration, 1856–1860.* Vol. 14 of the Far West and the Rockies Historical Series. Glendale, Calif., 1960.

Stegner, Wallace. *The Gathering of Zion: The Story of the Mormon Trail.* New York, 1964.

HOWARD A. CHRISTY

HARMONY, PENNSYLVANIA

Harmony, Pennsylvania, is an important HISTORICAL SITE of The Church of Jesus Christ of Latter-day Saints on the Susquehanna River in northeastern Pennsylvania. Significant events occurred there during the periodic residence of the Prophet Joseph SMITH from 1825 to 1830. Harmony was the home of Isaac Hale, father of Joseph Smith's wife, Emma Hale. Joseph Smith and his father boarded with Isaac Hale in 1825 while working on Josiah Stowell's mining project. In December 1827, Joseph and Emma moved to Harmony from Manchester, New York, to work on the translation of the plates of the Book of Mormon. Eventually they bought a small farm and house, where most of the Book of Mormon was translated between April 7 and early June 1829. Nearby, on May 15, 1829, Joseph Smith and Oliver COWDERY received the Aaronic Priesthood from John the Baptist and were authorized to baptize each other. The first convert baptism, that of Samuel H. Smith, took place there ten days later. Somewhere between Harmony and COLESVILLE, NEW YORK, Peter, James, and John restored the Melchizedek Priesthood. After the Church was organized in 1830, Joseph and Emma returned to Harmony and lived there through that summer. Fifteen revelations now found in the Doctrine and Covenants were received in Harmony.

The Harmony in Church history refers to a township rather than the village of Harmony. The township boundary was changed in 1853, placing the Church site in present-day Oakland Township. The site of the Hale residence lies about a mile and a half west of present-day Oakland, Pennsylvania, in Susquehanna County, along the north side of Route 171.

Today the Church owns about 288 acres at the Harmony location. On a small landscaped triangular plot located between the highway and a railroad right-of-way, a granite and bronze monument dedicated in 1960 commemorates the restoration of the Aaronic Priesthood. The exact location of the restoration is not known.

The house owned by Joseph and Emma Smith burned in 1919. The buried foundation is just west of the monument. The graves of Isaac and Elizabeth Hale and of an infant son born to Joseph and Emma are close to Route 171, in a public cemetery located east of the Church property.

BIBLIOGRAPHY
Porter, Larry C. "A Study of the Origins of The Church of Jesus Christ of Latter-day Saints in the States of New York and Pennsylvania, 1816–1831." Ph.D. diss., Brigham Young University, 1971.

HORACE H. CHRISTENSEN

HARRIS, MARTIN

Martin Harris (1783–1875), a New York farmer, was one of the Three Witnesses to the divine origin of the Book of Mormon. He also financed the first publication of the Book of Mormon in 1830 at a cost of $3,000 and later helped finance publication of the Book of Commandments.

Martin Harris was born May 18, 1783, in Easton (now Saratoga), Washington County, New York, and died July 10, 1875, in Clarkston, Cache County, Utah. On March 27, 1808, he married his first cousin, Lucy Harris. At least six children were born to the couple. In the War of 1812, Private Harris was a teamster in the Battle of Buffalo. By May 1814, at the Battle of Puttneyville, he was first sergeant in the Thirty-ninth New York Militia. He returned home an honored war veteran. He inherited 150 acres and by 1828 owned a total of 320 acres. His wife characterized him as industrious, attentive to domestic concerns, and an excellent provider and father.

Harris stood about five feet, eight inches tall; had a light complexion, blue eyes, and brown hair; and wore a Greek-style beard off the edge of his jaw and chin. When formally dressed, he wore a favorite gray suit and a large, stiff hat. Non-Mormon contemporaries extolled Harris's sincerity, honesty, memory, generosity, neighborliness, shrewd business practices, and civic spirit.

Harris promoted construction of the Erie Canal through Palmyra along a route that passed not far from his house. Palmyra's citizens elected him road overseer for seven years, and he was a member of Palmyra's vigilance committee. A Jeffersonian-Jacksonian Democrat, he was a believer in the value of homespun common sense. He favored gold and silver money and rejected paper currency. He distrusted banks, Federalists, and authoritarians. A Christian democratic activist, he admired ancient Greek culture and raised money for Greek Christians to fight the Turks.

Looking on himself as an unchurched Christian, Harris chose to follow God on his own. As a "restorationist," he looked for the return of biblical Christianity. He stated that "in the year 1818 . . . I was inspired of the Lord and taught of the Spirit that I should not join any church" (interview by Edward Stevenson, Sept. 4, 1870, Stevenson Microfilm Collection, Vol. 32, *HDC*).

Martin Harris met Joseph SMITH some time after 1816, when the Smith family moved to Palmyra. By 1824, Joseph Smith, Sr., had told him about the angel Moroni's appearances and the golden plates, and in the fall of 1827, Martin consented to help publish the translation. He helped Joseph Smith protect the plates from thieves and financed the Prophet's move from Manchester to Harmony, Pennsylvania, when persecution intensified.

In February 1828, Harris visited Joseph Smith in Harmony and obtained a transcription and translation of characters from the plates. He took the two documents to "learned men" in Utica, Albany, and New York City, where Samuel Latham Mitchill and Charles Anthon examined the texts. Harris and Smith believed that these visits fulfilled a prophecy in Isaiah 29:11–14 concerning a book to be translated by an unlearned man. Harris hoped that the scholars' comments would help win financial and religious support for the Book of Mormon in the community.

From April 12 to June 14, 1828, Martin Harris served as Joseph Smith's scribe, producing 116 manuscript pages. To gain family support, he persuaded Joseph to let him take the pages to Palmyra to show his family, and during a three-week period when he visited relatives, attended to business, and served jury duty, the 116 pages were stolen. It is reported that Lucy Harris said that she burned them. Ill and suffering the insecurity of progressive deafness, she reportedly feared that Palmyra's boycott of the Book of Mormon would lead to her and her husband's financial ruin. After the loss of the manuscript, Harris ceased his work as scribe.

In June 1829, Martin Harris, along with Joseph Smith, Oliver COWDERY, and David Whitmer, prayed and received no answer. Harris blamed himself for the failure and withdrew. The Prophet, Cowdery, and Whitmer prayed again and were shown the gold plates of the Book of Mormon by the angel Moroni. Subsequently, the angel appeared to Harris and Joseph Smith. In this vision, Harris heard the voice of God say that Joseph's translation was correct, and Jesus Christ commanded Harris to testify of what he had seen and heard. The testimony of the Three Witnesses is printed in the Book of Mormon.

When translation of the book was completed, Joseph Smith had trouble finding a printer who would undertake publication. The printers feared that local opposition would hurt sales. A Palmyra printer, Egbert B. Grandin, finally agreed to print the Book of Mormon after Harris agreed to mortgage some of his farm for $3,000 as security. On April 7, 1831, Harris sold part of his farm to pay the printing bill, though he may have had other reasons to part with this acreage than just to satisfy Grandin.

Martin Harris was present at the organization of the Church on April 6, 1830, and was baptized that day by Oliver Cowdery. In May 1831 he led fifty converts from Palmyra to Kirtland, Ohio. Lucy and their children remained in Palmyra, resulting in two households and periodic trips for Harris between the two locations.

In the summer of 1831, Harris accompanied Joseph Smith and others to Missouri to purchase property and designate the site for Zion, where the Saints were to gather. He was one of the first to be asked to live the "law of consecration," a divinely revealed plan for equalizing the distribution of property and providing for the poor. That year, he also helped supervise and finance Church publications.

Returning east in 1832, Harris and his brother Emer served a mission together, baptizing one hundred persons at Chenango Point (now Binghamton), New York. In January 1833, Martin Harris was imprisoned briefly in Springville, Pennsylvania, in an attempt to stop him from preaching.

Returning to Kirtland in January 1834, Harris became a member of the first high council of the Church. Later that year, he volunteered to go to Jackson County, Missouri, with ZION'S CAMP to assist persecuted Mormons. On February 14, 1835, in accord with an earlier revelation (D&C 18:37–38), "the three witnesses" selected the first Quorum of Twelve Apostles.

In 1836, Harris attended the dedication of the Kirtland Temple. Later that summer Lucy Harris died. Harris married Caroline YOUNG,

Brigham Young's niece, on November 1, 1836. The couple had seven children.

During 1837, a time of intense conflict within the Church, Harris clashed with Sidney Rigdon and refused to join the Church-sponsored Kirtland Safety Society, which was issuing paper money. Harris was released from the high council on September 3, 1837, and was excommunicated during the last week of December 1837. Although evidence exists that Harris's excommunication was never official, he accepted the action and subsequently applied for and was baptized on November 7, 1842.

When Brigham Young led the body of Latter-day Saints west, Harris went to England to bear witness of the Book of Mormon. The Strangites, a splinter group formed after Joseph Smith's death (*see* SCHISMATIC GROUPS), paid his expenses, though he did not believe or preach Strangite doctrine. In 1829, Harris had prophesied that the Book of Mormon would be preached in England, and he was eager to preach there himself. Returning to Kirtland, he prospered and acted as a self-appointed guide-caretaker of the deserted Kirtland Temple, listing himself in the 1860 census as "Mormon preacher."

Prior to 1856, LDS missionaries, some of whom had already gone to Utah, the Harris family, and Brigham Young invited Martin and Caroline Harris to join the Saints in Utah. In the spring of 1856, Caroline and the children journeyed to Utah, but Harris remained in Kirtland until 1870. In 1860 he lived with George Harris, his son by Lucy. From 1865 to 1870, he supported himself by leasing ninety acres of land in Kirtland.

In 1869, efforts were renewed to bring Martin Harris to Utah. William H. Homer, Edward Stevenson, Brigham Young, and many other Latter-day Saints helped him financially to make the journey. Still active and vigorous at age eighty-seven, Martin Harris, accompanied by Edward Stevenson, arrived by train in Salt Lake City on August 30, 1870. He accepted rebaptism as evidence of his reaffirmation of faith on September 17, 1870, and, at Brigham Young's invitation, publicly testified of the Book of Mormon. He moved to Harrisville, then to Smithfield, Utah (where he saw Caroline and their son Martin Harris, Jr.), and in 1874 to Clarkston, Utah, where he died on July 10, 1875, after once more bearing testimony of the Book of Mormon.

Martin Harris inspired a folk-hero tradition that has lasted down to the present. In 1983 the Church's musical play *Martin Harris: The Man Who Knew* was produced in Clarkston. The play marked a fourth generation's rehearsal of Martin Harris's witness: "Yes, I did see the plates on which the Book of Mormon was written. I did see the angel, I did hear the voice of God, and I do know that Joseph Smith is a true Prophet of God, holding the keys of the Holy Priesthood" ("The Last Testimony of Martin Harris," recorded by William H. Homer in a statement sworn before J. W. Robinson, Apr. 9, 1927, *HDC*).

BIBLIOGRAPHY

Anderson, Richard Lloyd. *Investigating the Book of Mormon Witnesses.* Salt Lake City, 1981.

Gunnell, Wayne Cutler. "Martin Harris—Witness and Benefactor to the Book of Mormon." Master's thesis, Brigham Young University, 1955.

James, Rhett Stephens. *The Man Who Knew: The Early Years—A Play About Martin Harris, 1824–1830, and Annotated History of Martin Harris.* Salt Lake City, 1983.

Shelton, Scott R. "Martin Harris in Cache Valley—Events and Influences." Master's thesis, Utah State University, 1986.

Tuckett, Madge Harris, and Belle Harris Wilson. *The Martin Harris Story.* Provo, Utah, 1983.

RHETT STEPHENS JAMES

HAUN'S MILL MASSACRE

On October 30, 1838, segments of the Missouri militia attacked a settlement of Latter-day Saints at Jacob Haun's mill, located on Shoal Creek in eastern Caldwell County, Missouri. Because the attack was unprovoked in a time of truce, had no specific authorization, and was made by a vastly superior force with unusual brutality, it has come to be known as "The Haun's Mill Massacre." It was one incident in the conflict between the Missourians and the Latter-day Saints that resulted in the LDS expulsion from the state in 1839 (*see* MISSOURI CONFLICT).

Tensions had been building up ever since the Latter-day Saints began moving into Caldwell and Daviess counties in central Missouri in 1836. From August to October 1838, incidents of overt conflict had grown dramatically. Rumors abounded that the Mormons planned to "despoil" the Missourians and take their land. Specifically, some believed that the Haun's Mill's population threatened to spill over into non-Mormon Livingston County. Outbursts of violence led Governor Lilburn W. Boggs on October 27 to issue an "Extermination Order," demanding that the Latter-day Saints leave the state or be exterminated. It is uncertain whether this order was a catalyst for the attack, but it is clear that both the Latter-day Saints and the Missourians believed that their rights had been violated and their existence threatened.

Thirty to forty LDS families were at Haun's Mill when some 200 to 250 militia from Livingston, Daviess, and Carroll counties, acting under Colonel Thomas Jennings, marched against the village. Assuming that an earlier truce still held, the residents were surprised by the late afternoon attack. Church leader David Evans's call for "quarter" was ignored, and the villagers were forced to flee for safety. The Mormon women and children fled south across a stream into the woods, while the men gathered in the blacksmith shop, but found it a poor place for defense because the Missourians were able to fire through the widely spaced logs directly into the group huddled inside.

Seventeen Latter-day Saints and one friendly non-Mormon were killed. Another thirteen were wounded, including one woman and a seven-year-old boy. No Missouri militiamen were killed, though three were wounded. Certain deaths were particularly offensive to the Saints. Seventy-eight-year-old Thomas McBride surrendered his musket to militiaman Jacob Rogers, who shot him, then hacked his body with a corn knife. William Reynolds discovered ten-year-old Sardius Smith hiding under the bellows and blew the top of the child's head off.

While women cared for the wounded, the men remained in hiding during the night. The dead were thrown into an unfinished well and lightly covered with dirt and straw. A few Missourians returned the next day, took plunder, and warned the remaining Saints to leave Missouri.

The 1838–39 Missouri judicial proceedings investigating the "Mormon War" largely ignored the events at Haun's Mill, but Latter-day Saints wrote numerous, bitter accounts. The Haun's Mill

Massacre became embedded in the LDS psyche as an epitome of the cruel persecutions that they had endured.

BIBLIOGRAPHY

Blair, Alma R. "The Haun's Mill Massacre." *BYU Studies* 13 (Autumn 1972):62–67.

History of Caldwell and Livingston Counties, Missouri. St. Louis, 1886.

Johnson, Clark V. "Missouri Persecutions: The Petition of Isaac Leary." *BYU Studies* 23 (Winter 1983):94–103.

LeSueur, Stephen C. *The 1838 Mormon War in Missouri*. Columbia, Mo., 1987.

Times and Seasons 1 (1840):145–50.

ALMA R. BLAIR

HAWAII, THE CHURCH IN

The Church of Jesus Christ of Latter-day Saints has been in Hawaii since 1850, when Elder Charles C. Rich, an apostle, called ten LDS men from the gold mines of northern California to open missionary work in the Sandwich Islands, now Hawaii. Within several months five of the elders left the mission, but George Quayle Cannon, Henry William Bigler, James Keeler, William Farrer, and James Hawkins remained. Initial conversions came on the island of Maui, where the first branch was organized in the Kula District, near Pulehu, on August 6, 1851. The Church made remarkable headway, with more than 4,000 Hawaiian convert members in fifty-three branches by late 1854. By this time, several small schools were under way, meetinghouses were constructed, and the Book of Mormon had been translated into the Hawaiian language by Elders Cannon and Farrer and Jonatana H. Napela, a local member. It was printed in 1855. In 1990, the 49,000 members of the Church in Hawaii, both native Hawaiian and others were found in thirteen stakes, constituting more than a hundred wards and branches. A temple has served members in Hawaii since November 1919.

Following the pattern established elsewhere, an attempt was made to gather the Hawaiian Saints to a local Zion. A village, called the City of Joseph, was established on the island of Lanai in 1854. However, the project failed, at least partly because of environmental conditions. In addition, with the most devoted Hawaiian members having moved to Lanai, the branches on other islands were weakened, and the Church fell into decline. This trend became severe when the Mainland missionary leaders were called back to Utah in 1858 because of the UTAH EXPEDITION.

This leadership vacuum opened the way for the adventurer Walter Murray Gibson to run the Church on Lanai and elsewhere as his personal political kingdom from September 1861 until 1864. He was excommunicated from the Church in April 1864 for introducing many false doctrines, including selling offices in the priesthood.

Shortly thereafter, President Brigham YOUNG sent Francis Asbury Hammond and George Nebeker to Hawaii to buy property for a new gathering place. On January 26, 1865, the Church purchased for $14,000, a 6,000-acre plantation at Laie on Oahu island for the spiritual and temporal welfare of the members. Laie remains the focal point of LDS activities in Hawaii though strong stakes have also developed in Honolulu and in other areas.

Since 1865, there have been five major developments in the history of the Church in Hawaii:

First, on June 1, 1915, President Joseph F. SMITH dedicated a site at Laie for the Hawaii Temple. Four and a half years later, on November 27, 1919, his successor, President Heber J. GRANT, dedicated the completed structure, the first LDS temple outside the North American continent.

Second, President Grant organized the Oahu Stake on June 30, 1935, with Ralph E. Woolley as president.

Third, for the benefit of the Japanese people in Hawaii, President Grant formed the Japanese Mission in Hawaii in 1937, with Hilton A. Robertson as president. Its name was changed to the Central Pacific Mission in 1942. By 1949 missionaries of the Japanese/Central Pacific Mission had baptized 671 Americans of Japanese ancestry into the Church, and thousands of others have joined the Church since then. Many of these converts and their children have held important positions in the Church. Adney Yoshio Komatsu was the first of that group to be called as a General Authority.

Fourth, in September 1955 the Church College of Hawaii was founded under the direction of President David O. MCKAY. Initially a junior college, it was made a four-year school in 1959 and was renamed Brigham Young University—Hawaii Campus in 1974. Two thousand students, mostly from the Pacific and the Asian Rim, attend.

Finally, the Church founded the Polynesian Cultural Center at Laie in November 1963 to preserve and present the cultures of Polynesia and to provide employment for the college students. The center has grown to become Hawaii's number-one paid attraction, drawing nearly a million visitors a year.

BIBLIOGRAPHY

Britsch, R. Lanier. *Unto the Islands of the Sea: A History of the Latter-day Saints in the Pacific.* Salt Lake City, 1986.

———. *Mormona: The Mormons in Hawaii.* Laie, Hawaii, 1989.

R. LANIER BRITSCH

HIRAM, OHIO

Hiram, Ohio, a small town twenty-five miles south and slightly east of KIRTLAND, OHIO, was the site of a large branch of The Church of Jesus Christ of Latter-day Saints in the 1830s and served for one year as home to the Prophet Joseph SMITH. John and Elsa Johnson, a prosperous farmer and his wife, residents in Hiram Township, welcomed Joseph, Emma, and their adopted twins to live with them in September 1831. Joseph had healed Elsa's arthritic arm several months earlier.

During the Smiths' stay, Joseph received an outpouring of fifteen of the revelations now published in the Doctrine and Covenants. Section 1, known as the Preface, was given at one of many Church conferences held there. On February 16, 1832, Joseph and his scribe at this time, Sidney RIGDON, beheld a divine vision of the eternal worlds that forms the basis of Latter-day Saint understanding of life after death. In this vision they reported seeing both God the Father and his Son Jesus Christ and bore witness of Jesus Christ: "He lives! For we saw him, even on the right hand of God" (D&C 76:22–23). A Hiram conference in November 1831 voted to print all revelations received up to that date as the Book of Commandments.

On the cold night of March 24, 1832, a mob dragged Joseph and Sidney from their beds into a nearby meadow, beat them, and poured tar and feathers on their bodies (*HC* 1:261–65). Joseph and Sidney bore the marks of that night for the rest of their lives. Another consequence was the death of Joseph and Emma's adopted eleven-month-old son. Ill with the measles at the time, he was exposed to the cold and died five days later.

While living in Hiram, Joseph accomplished a significant portion of his translation of the Bible. He left the area only once for a trip to Missouri and for several nearby preaching missions.

The Johnson home is now owned by the Church and is open as a visitors center. The Hiram Ward meetinghouse stands nearby.

BIBLIOGRAPHY

Backman, Milton V., Jr. *The Heavens Resound.* Salt Lake City, 1983.

KARL RICKS ANDERSON

HISTORIANS, CHURCH

From its beginnings, the Church has considered record keeping and history writing an imperative duty (D&C 123:1–7). The Book of Mormon, published in 1830, is a product of ancient records kept by command of God (1 Ne. 9:3, 5; Jacob 1:2; 3 Ne. 23:4, 11–13). Record keeping is also commanded by modern revelation (D&C 21:1; 47:3; 69:3; 72:5–6). Latter-day Saints write history not only to obey divine injunctions but also to combat false reports and to convert and edify future generations (*HC* 1:1; 2:199; 6:409).

Although most of the early commandments pertained to the keeping of "official" Church records, Latter-day Saints also apply them to individuals. Joseph SMITH and other prominent leaders set the example by keeping journals. Clerks and scribes recorded revelations, minutes of meetings, speeches, correspondence, blessings, and ordinances.

EARLY CHURCH HISTORIANS, 1830–1842. Record keeping and history writing were institutionalized with the appointment of Oliver COWDERY as the first Church Recorder when the Church was organized on April 6, 1830 (D&C 21:1). That the Prophet's closest associate and most capable scribe, who also served as second elder in the Church, should be called as Church recorder is an indication of the importance attached to the position. According to his successor,

Cowdery wrote the history of the Church up to mid-1831, when he was released; that early history has never been located. During his second term in office (1835–1837), Cowdery completed a series of eight historical letters that he had started publishing in the *Messenger and Advocate* in October 1834.

John Whitmer, one of the eight Book of Mormon Witnesses, served officially as Church recorder between 1831 and 1834 and, after his release, wrote unofficially until his excommunication in 1838. His history for 1831–1838 was published in 1908.

George W. Robinson, a son-in-law of Sidney RIGDON, became general recorder in 1837 (*HC* 2:513). He accompanied Joseph Smith in visiting Church settlements in northern Missouri and kept a brief record captioned "The Scriptory Book of Joseph Smith, Jr." Robinson was released in 1840 when he moved across the river from Nauvoo.

From 1838 to 1843 there was considerable overlapping in the service of Church recorders and historians. Little progress had been made on the Church annals, which, in part, were being written to help combat highly visible anti-Mormon publications. In a flurry of activity to correct the situation, Joseph Smith had earlier minutes copied into the Far West Record, renewed efforts on his own history with the assistance of Sidney Rigdon, and called John Corrill and Elias Higbee as Church historians to work with Robinson.

Soon after his appointment, John Corrill chafed at criticism by the Prophet and chose to testify against his former associates in several legal proceedings, leading to his excommunication. To justify his break with the Church, he quickly wrote and published in 1839 the history that he never wrote as Church historian.

As a Church historian, Elias Higbee helped collect affidavits regarding the Saints' losses in Missouri, and in October 1839 he accompanied Joseph Smith and Sidney Rigdon to Washington, D.C., to present them to U.S. officials. After President Van Buren rebuffed them in February 1840, Higbee stayed on, trying unsuccessfully for a hearing before the Senate Judiciary Committee. His documents relating to this Washington mission, later incorporated in the "History of Joseph Smith," were his main contribution to Church history.

In 1840, twenty-eight-year-old Robert B. Thompson replaced Robinson as Church historian, but he had little time for history. He wrote in Joseph Smith's letter book, recorded patriarchal blessings, and served as city treasurer, clerk of the high council, and associate editor of the *Times and Seasons.* After Thompson died in 1841, James Sloan, an experienced clerk, served as historian, but within a year he was called on a mission to his native Ireland.

PIONEER CHURCH HISTORIANS, 1842–1900. After fluctuating changes in titles and personnel, the offices of Church recorder and Church historian merged and became stable with the appointment of Willard Richards in late 1842. He came to his literary duties singularly qualified and immediately brought new impetus and dignity to the position. Richards kept the Prophet's diary for him, wrote correspondence, compiled most of the "History of Joseph Smith" (*see* HISTORY OF THE CHURCH [HISTORY OF JOSEPH SMITH]), and either recorded or supervised the recording of the Prophet's sermons, minutes of meetings, and ordinances performed in the Nauvoo Temple.

Richards's efforts provided continuity during the unsettled years of pioneer travel. With the help of his assistant, Thomas Bullock, he packed Church records in sturdy boxes for removal to the West. At Winter Quarters he set up a temporary Church Historian's Office in an octagonal cabin that also served as Church headquarters. In Utah he maintained the Historian's Office in his own home in Salt Lake City until his death on March 11, 1854.

No one seemed more qualified to complete the "History of Joseph Smith" than Joseph Smith's cousin George A. Smith, who was appointed as Church historian and general Church recorder on April 7, 1854. He had a modest building constructed across the street from Brigham YOUNG's office that served as the Historian's Office from 1856 to 1917. His main contributions were completing the "History of Joseph Smith" and directing the compilation of the "History of Brigham Young."

Albert Carrington, a graduate of Dartmouth College, Brigham Young's secretary, and editor of the *Deseret News*, was ordained an apostle and appointed historian in 1870. During Carrington's four-year term, work continued on the Manuscript History of Brigham Young. Orson PRATT, an apostle, was sixty-three years old when he was appointed Church historian in 1874 and never involved himself personally in writing Church history. He died in 1881.

Although Wilford WOODRUFF served as Church historian from

1883 to 1889, he made his greatest contributions to Church history as assistant Church historian from 1856 to 1883. He was the prime motivator behind a project to publish a biography of each man who had served in the Quorum of the Twelve Apostles, and was instrumental in preparing the sermons of Joseph Smith for publication in the *History of the Church.* Woodruff's journals, which he kept with diligence from the time he joined the Church until a few weeks before his death, proved invaluable in compiling the histories of Joseph Smith and Brigham Young.

Franklin D. Richards, an apostle, served as an assistant Church historian for five years before becoming Church historian in 1889. He traveled to San Francisco to provide information for Hubert H. Bancroft, who was then preparing his histories of western states and territories. The resulting *History of Utah* (1890) was considered the most balanced and scholarly account of Church pioneer history to that time. Elder Richards energetically collected historical sources and authorized his assistant, Andrew Jenson, to travel extensively to gather materials. On his own initiative, Jenson had already undertaken historical projects beneficial to the Church before he was sustained as an assistant Church historian in 1897.

EARLY-TWENTIETH-CENTURY CHURCH HISTORIANS. Anthon H. Lund served from 1900 to 1921. An able and considerate administrator, he supervised significant projects, including moving the office and records in 1917 to the new Church Office Building. Andrew Jenson continued traveling to stakes and missions, gathering materials to compile a "manuscript history" of each; he also published thousands of biographical sketches. In 1906, when he was assigned responsibility for the "Journal History," Jenson began a retroactive compilation of sources in the form of annals extending back to 1830, a history that by 1932 had grown to 518 volumes. He also continued work on several private historical projects until his death in 1941.

Elder B. H. Roberts of the Seventy established himself as a historian with the publication of *The Life of John Taylor* (1892), *Outlines of Ecclesiastical History* (1893), *The Missouri Persecutions* (1900), and *The Rise and Fall of Nauvoo* (1900). In 1902 he was appointed assistant Church historian and assigned to edit and republish the *History of the Church.* He had completed six volumes by 1912, and a seventh in 1932, about a year before his death. While editing the

History of the Church, Roberts also wrote "A History of the Mormon Church," which first appeared in monthly installments in the *Americana* magazine, 1909–1915. Later revised, these were published in 1930 as Roberts' COMPREHENSIVE HISTORY OF THE CHURCH.

Joseph Fielding SMITH began a sixty-nine-year association with the Historian's Office in 1901, when he was employed as an assistant to Andrew Jenson. As an assistant Church historian (1906–1921), he wrote several historical pamphlets and booklets, and as Church historian (1921–1970), he continued writing. His *Essentials in Church History* (1922) remained a standard until the 1980s. His two-volume *Church History and Modern Revelation* (1953) provided explanations about the antecedents and historical setting of many revelations published in the Doctrine and Covenants. An apologist in the classical tradition, Elder Smith's philosophy of history has been widely influential within the Church.

RECENT CHURCH HISTORIANS. Joseph Fielding Smith worked to modernize operations of the Historian's Office. He improved standards for preserving, classifying, and managing archival materials; hired professional librarians and archivists; and helped plan a new four-story facility. As President of the Church, he appointed Elder Howard W. Hunter, an apostle, as Church historian (1970–1972). After consulting with professional historians and archivists, in 1972 Elder Hunter recommended a reorganization of the Historian's Office into a Historical Department with three divisions: a library for published materials, archives for manuscripts, and a division for research and writing.

Since Willard Richards, each Church historian and general Church recorder had been a member of the Quorum of the Twelve or First Presidency. That long-standing tradition was changed in 1972 when Leonard J. Arrington, a nationally prominent professional historian, was sustained in general conference as Church historian (1972–1977). His duties were also different from those of his predecessors: His main task was to produce scholarly works for publication. Earl E. Olson, Church archivist, was charged with gathering and preserving the materials of history; Donald T. Schmidt became librarian; and later Florence Jacobson headed an Arts and Sites Division. They all served under Managing Director Alvin R. Dyer, an Assistant to the Twelve. The Historical Department moved to enlarged quarters in November 1972. On May 17, 1976, Joseph Anderson, an Assistant to the Twelve, succeeded Elder Dyer as managing director.

With a corps of professional historians, Arrington promoted and directed the writing and publication of LDS history at an unprecedented rate. The division also assisted with acquisitions and conducted a dynamic oral history program.

The appointment of G. Homer Durham of the First Quorum of the Seventy as Managing Director in 1977 signaled a retrenchment in the Church's direct sponsorship of professional history writing. Several history writing projects were curtailed or abandoned. On June 26, 1980, the Church announced the establishment of the Joseph Fielding Smith Institute for Church History, which would be affiliated with Brigham Young University. Arrington directed the new institute, and most of the professional historians associated with him transferred to the university. This placed the writing of history in a university setting, leaving the Historical Department to manage materials in its archives in support of scholarship without the responsibility of monitoring a genre of "official" Church history.

Elder G. Homer Durham was appointed as Church historian on February 8, 1982. During his administration Florence Jacobsen became a prime motivator in the establishment of a new Museum of Church History and Art, which opened its doors in April 1984. The three divisions in the Historical Department were now the Archives, Library, and Museum. Following Durham, Elder Dean L. Larsen, of the Presidency of the Seventy, was sustained as Church historian and recorder (1985–1989). In 1989 John K. Carmack of the First Quorum of the Seventy, who had been serving under Elder Larsen since 1986, became the department's executive director.

BIBLIOGRAPHY

Bitton, Davis, and Leonard Arrington. *Mormons and Their Historians.* Salt Lake City, 1988.

Jenson, Andrew. *L.D.S. Biographical Encyclopedia,* 4 vols. Salt Lake City, 1901–1936.

Searle, Howard C. "Early Mormon Historiography." Ph.D. diss., University of California at Los Angeles, 1979.

HOWARD C. SEARLE

HISTORICAL SITES

The sites of historical importance to Latter-day Saints include those associated with Christianity in general (the Holy Land, Jerusalem, Bethlehem, Jordan River, Mount of Olives, etc.), as well as those directly related to LDS beliefs. The latter mainly include places in the United States associated with the founding and organization of The Church of Jesus Christ of Latter-day Saints and its subsequent migrations west. LDS historical sites are important to individual members because of the Church's emphasis on its history and cultural roots rather than as formal pilgrimage destinations (*see* HISTORY, SIGNIFICANCE TO LATTER-DAY SAINTS). Church members commonly visit these sites as tourists and, in the process, gain greater personal understanding of the history of the Church and its beliefs.

Many historical sites in the United States were obtained through the efforts of such individuals or entities as Joseph F. SMITH, Heber J. GRANT, Willard W. Bean, Wilford C. Wood, and the Corporation of the Presiding Bishopric of the LDS Church. Most of these sites have been restored to the time of the historical events and are staffed by local unpaid volunteers or missionaries.

Visitors centers are located at several sites, and are free and open to the public. Each location includes displays and literature explaining the site and its significance in Church history. One such site is the Joseph Smith Memorial in Sharon, Windsor County, Vermont. Joseph SMITH was born here on December 23, 1805. In 1905 the Church erected a 38.5-foot-high granite monument to commemorate the 38.5 years of his life. A full-time missionary couple live at the home.

Near the village of Palmyra, New York, in the township of Palmyra, is located the site of the log house in which the Smiths resided from 1817 to the early or mid-1820s and again intermittently until late 1830. In the adjacent township of Manchester is the Smith family farm, existing frame home, SACRED GROVE, and also the hill Cumorah only a few miles southeast of the home. The Sacred Grove is where the boy Joseph received his FIRST VISION, the initial event in the restoration of the Church. Latter-day Saints believe that the young Joseph Smith was directed by the angel Moroni to retrieve from the hill Cumorah the gold plates from which the Book of

Mormon was translated. The first edition of the Book of Mormon was printed in the Grandin Press Building in Palmyra. A mile and one-half north of Palmyra is the farm of Martin Harris, a portion of which was sold to finance the publication of the Book of Mormon. Thirty miles to the southeast is the Peter Whitmer farm in FAYETTE, NEW YORK, where the Church was formally organized in 1830. Yet another hundred miles southeast from Fayette is HARMONY, PENNSYLVANIA, where the majority of the Book of Mormon was translated by Joseph Smith and written down by Oliver Cowdery.

Joseph Smith moved his family to KIRTLAND, OHIO, in early 1831. They remained there until January 1838, when they fled to MISSOURI to escape mob violence. Events of importance in the life of Joseph Smith that occurred in Kirtland include receiving many revelations now found in the Doctrine and Covenants and the construction of the first Latter-day Saint temple. The WHITNEY STORE was the location of many of these events and has been restored. The KIRTLAND TEMPLE was dedicated on March 27, 1836. It is owned today by the REORGANIZED CHURCH OF JESUS CHRIST OF LATTER DAY SAINTS (RLDS).

At Independence, Jackson County, Missouri, an LDS visitors center is situated on a portion of the temple lot dedicated by Joseph Smith in 1831. Twelve miles to the north is LIBERTY JAIL in Clay County, Missouri, where Joseph was imprisoned from December 1, 1838, to April 6, 1839. Here he received sections 121–123 of the Doctrine and Covenants. The reconstructed remnant of the jail stands today as a reminder of the trials experienced by the Prophet for his beliefs, of the faithfulness of his followers (some of whom shared the jail with him), and of the suffering of his wife, Emma SMITH, and his children during the harsh winter while he was imprisoned. Northeast of Liberty are the historic sites of FAR WEST, in Caldwell County, Missouri, and ADAM-ONDI-AHMAN, in Daviess County, Missouri.

After TEMPLE SQUARE in Salt Lake City, NAUVOO is the second most visited historic location in the Church. Joseph Smith moved to the village of Commerce in Hancock County, Illinois, on May 10, 1839. Purchased by the Church, Commerce was renamed Nauvoo and became a major destination for converts to the Church, reaching a population in excess of 11,000 in 1845, and some 20,000 in the greater area. The Church has obtained a number of the buildings and sites owned by early members in Nauvoo and has restored or reconstructed them to show what life was like for the Saints in Nauvoo.

Near Nauvoo is the town of Carthage, the county seat for Hancock County. Here Joseph Smith was imprisoned on June 25, 1844, and murdered by a mob on June 27. Nauvoo and CARTHAGE JAIL are supervised by the Illinois Peoria Mission, and full-time missionaries staff them.

Following the martyrdom, the Saints, under the direction of Brigham YOUNG, left Nauvoo in the winter of 1846, founding a number of temporary settlements en route to the West. WINTER QUARTERS, NEBRASKA (now Florence, a suburb of Omaha), on the west bank of the Missouri River, and Kanesville, Iowa (now COUNCIL BLUFFS), on the east bank, were the locations of a large settlement in the fall and winter of 1846–1847, remaining there until 1852. The Winter Quarters cemetery is all that remains of this historical site today.

The MORMON TRAIL to Utah has a number of monuments and historic sites. Salt Lake City has numerous historical sites. Temple Square with the temple, tabernacle, assembly hall, and visitors center is the most visited site in the Church. Other sites include "THIS IS THE PLACE" MONUMENT, the Beehive and Lion houses built and occupied by Brigham Young, and the nearby cemetery with his grave.

The Church also maintains three historic sites in St. George, Utah: the Brigham Young winter home, representing the LDS expansion southward along the valleys of the Intermountain West; the St. George Tabernacle, an epitome of the construction of large assembly halls in the major communities settled by Latter-day Saints; and the St. George Temple, the first temple completed in Utah. The temple's dedication in 1877 demonstrated the commitment of the Latter-day Saints to temple work and to establishing permanent communities in the Intermountain West. It is an important example of LDS architecture of the period. And in nearby Santa Clara stands the home of Jacob Hamblin, one of the earliest missionaries to the Indians in southern Utah.

These and other historic sites serve as reminders of the humble yet extraordinary beginnings of the Church and of the sacrifices made by those individuals who committed their lives to follow its teachings.

LDS HISTORICAL SITES WITH FULL-TIME STAFF

Main Historic Dates	*Place*	*Location*
1805	Joseph Smith Memorial	Sharon, Vt.
1817–1818	Joseph Smith Farm	Manchester, N.Y.
1820	Sacred Grove	Manchester, N.Y.
1823–1827	Hill Cumorah	Manchester, N.Y.
1827–1831	Martin Harris Farm	Palmyra, N.Y.
1829–1830	Grandin Press Building	Palmyra, N.Y.
1829–1831	Peter Whitmer, Sr., Farm	Fayette, N.Y.
1831–1833	John Johnson Home	Hiram, Ohio
1831–1833	Independence Temple Site	Independence, Mo.
1831–1838	Newel K. Whitney Store	Kirtland, Ohio
1831–1838	Newel K. Whitney Home	Kirtland, Ohio
1836–1838	Kirtland Temple (RLDS owned and staffed)	Kirtland, Ohio
1838–1839	Liberty Jail	Liberty, Mo.
1839–1846	Nauvoo (LDS and RLDS sites)	Nauvoo, Ill.
1844	Carthage Jail	Carthage, Ill.
1846–1848	Winter Quarters	Omaha (Florence), Nebr.
1847	Temple Square	Salt Lake City, Utah
1847–1848	Mormon Battalion Duty Station	San Diego, Calif.
1854	Beehive House	Salt Lake City, Utah
1863–1869	Jacob Hamblin Home	Santa Clara, Utah
1867	Cove Fort	Cove Fort, Utah
1869–1877	Brigham Young Winter Home	St. George, Utah
1875 (Ded.)	St. George Tabernacle	St. George, Utah
1878 (Est.)	Thomas L. Kane Memorial Chapel	Kane, Pa.

BIBLIOGRAPHY

Burton, Alma P. *Mormon Trail from Vermont to Utah: A Guide to Historical Places of The Church of Jesus Christ of Latter-day Saints*. Salt Lake City, 1966.

Kimball, Stanley B. *Historic Sites and Markers Along the Mormon and Other Great Western Trails*. Urbana, Ill., 1988.

Oscarson, R. Don, and Stanley B. Kimball. *The Travellers' Guide to Historic Mormon America*. Salt Lake City, 1990, revised.

RICHARD H. JACKSON

HISTORY, SIGNIFICANCE TO LATTER-DAY SAINTS

History plays a vital role in LDS thought, where it joins with theology and practical religion to answer many of life's questions and to make daily life meaningful, intelligible, and worthwhile. God is seen as actively achieving his ultimate purposes through events that make up history, while simultaneously allowing individuals the choice of working for or against his purposes.

Although Latter-day Saints do not have an officially stated philosophy of history, several basic ideas in LDS theology establish the significance of history.

1. First is the nature of mankind. As God's literal spirit offspring, humans partake of divine attributes and destiny; they have the potential to attain godhood. On the other hand, humanity is fallen and has become "carnal, sensual, and devilish" (Moses 5:13), with capacities for evil and degradation comparable with those of the devil himself. Hence, there is dramatic interest among Latter-day Saints in the broadest spectrum of human thoughts, words, and deeds.
2. Second is an unequivocally positive commitment to life in this world. In LDS thought, a seamless web of individual being extends back in time to a self-conscious pre-earth life, and forward to the possibility and hope of eternal life in the presence of God. Prior choices and God's purposes have determined one's presence and place in this life; and, to a large extent, present choices will determine one's eternal future. In axioms such as "Men are, that they might have joy" (2 Ne. 2:25), LDS doctrine emphasizes the significance and goodness of the historical experience.
3. Human freedom is required. In order to preserve human agency, God does not break "across the line of history through the instrumentality of unmerited love," but he participates "in the historical process by inspiring men and co-operating with them in their efforts to improve the world's conditions" (Boyd, pp. 450, 453). Thus, God "directs and influences" the historical process, but he also respects the "centrality of freedom" for his children, something to which he is committed "partly by his nature and partly by his will" (Poll, pp. 33, 35).

4. History itself is part of eternal truth. "Truth is knowledge of things as they are, and as they were, and as they are to come" (D&C 93:24; cf. 88:79). Thus, written records (including sacred histories) can encompass only a small portion of eternal reality, and even under optimum circumstances are incomplete and imperfect.

The LDS idea of history has much in common with that of Jews and Christians who believe in the living God-who-acts-in-history. Latter-day Saints view human history as the unfolding of God's plan of salvation for mankind (*Heilsgeschichte*), a view that dominated Western civilization until the eighteenth century. They generally agree with the traditional linear concept of history laid down in Augustine's *City of God*, although they place the eventual divine society on this earth (in a glorified and eternal physical state), not in an otherworldly dimension.

LDS faith is intertwined with historical events. Latter-day Saints essentially believe the literal biblical account of God's direct role in the Creation and of the fall of Adam and Eve—the proof of human freedom. A series of gospel dispensations then unfolded. In each dispensation God's plan for mankind was revealed, only to be rejected eventually by chosen, but backsliding, human beings. The supreme set of events in history is the birth, ministry, death, and resurrection of Jesus Christ. This quintessentially Christian philosophy reaches its culmination in a hope, confidence, and preparation for Jesus' literal second coming, marking the end of this phase of the world's history. Latter-day Saints believe in a Christ-centered history and find power and reassurance in the fact that Jesus Christ became a real, historic person who endured mortality and its trials (Heb. 4:15–16). They add other elements to the Savior's historical reality. They believe that the resurrected Jesus appeared among the people of the Book of Mormon, and that God the Father and Jesus Christ appeared to Joseph SMITH in 1820 to open the last dispensation when the fulness of the gospel will be taught to all of the nations and people.

The foundations of the Church are grounded in a series of historic events, without which the Restoration would be incomprehensible and impotent. Joseph Smith recorded many visions and he received the gold plates from the angel Moroni, from which he translated the Book of Mormon. There followed many revelations to Joseph Smith and to the prophets who have succeeded him, revealing doctrines and applying eternal principles to existing historical and individual situations. That living prophets receive revelation from God, who is vitally interested in human needs in changing conditions, underscores the LDS view of God's continuing place in history.

That view is that God has played a role throughout ancient and modern history by foreordaining religious, political, scientific, and other leaders (e.g., Cyrus; see Isa. 44:28; Jer. 1:5). The great reformers (Luther, Calvin, Knox), discoverers such as Columbus, and the authors of the Constitution of the United States of America were foreordained to prepare the way for the Restoration and to establish a new nation "conceived in liberty" that, like ancient Israel, was not chosen for special privilege but was to be a blessing to all mankind (Petersen, pp. 69–72; Backman, p. 724). This view was summarized by President Ezra Taft BENSON: "God, the Father of us all, uses the men of the earth, especially good men, to accomplish his purposes" (*Ensign* 2 [July 1972]:59).

God's role in the mundane details of history may be less obvious but more frequent than thought. Elder Bruce R. McConkie declared that the real history of the world "will show God's dealings with men, [and] the place the gospel has played in the rise and fall of nations" (*MD*, 1958, p. 327). Still, the record is incomplete; many important issues about historical injustices and catastrophes are yet to be explained by the God who acts in history, and what is not yet fully known in the macrocosmic realm is often explained in the meaningful experiences of individual people. God knows and cares about each human being. As with the larger world, God intervenes in individual lives at decisive moments, but also recognizes human autonomy and leaves the majority of life's decisions to individual choice.

God's role in human history should not, however, be taken to the extreme. His foreknowledge does not require predestination. Foreordination means that in his wisdom and foreknowledge God has called an individual to a role in the human drama if that person chooses to fill it. To Latter-day Saints, history is a combination of God's direction (which is neither "coercive [n]or continuous" [Poll, p. 33]) and divine intervention when that is indispensable to his purposes, with broad freedom of choice for humans within God's expansive framework. In this large realm of human freedom, the panorama of history has taken place. Here, political, social, economic, psychological, and other such forces largely hold sway, and thus are essential in explaining human choices and actions.

This historical view became an integral part of early LDS theology, of Joseph Smith's personal mission, of his vision of the Church's mission throughout the world, and of the anticipated second coming of Jesus Christ. All of this may also account in part for the meticulous attention given to record keeping in the Church and by the prophets (*see* HISTORIANS, CHURCH; HISTORY OF THE CHURCH). All members of the Church are encouraged to write personal journals and family histories, and to make them a part of their extended families' sacred possessions.

In recent years the recognition of the Church by historians and sociologists as a distinctive new religion has generated broader interest in the writing and understanding of its history. But the writing of general history, especially religious history, has always had its difficulties. Surviving documents are limited and often inconsistent. Spiritual experiences are often kept private, and primarily lend themselves only to spiritual verification. Memories and lore are selective and fallible. Purposes, needs, audiences, historical fashions, and professional methods change from one decade to the next.

Traditional LDS historians, following their Jewish and early Christian predecessors, have tended to focus heavily on the hand of God in writing about Church and world history. Their histories are generally descriptive and declarative, sympathetic to the historical figures, and written mainly to inspire and build faith. According to William Mulder, "No where in Mormon record-keeping can [one] escape the teleological, the didactic, the eschatological" (p. 17).

This view is countered by other historians, such as Fawn M. Brodie, who explicitly rejected the prophetic truth claims of the LDS faith and interpreted Joseph Smith and the Restoration wholly on the basis of modern naturalistic, historicist, and psychoanalytic methods. Their objective is typically to provide causal explanations by emphasizing the human aspects while rejecting divine involvement.

Most recent LDS historical scholarship represents a wide and changing spectrum. There is, as Henry Bawden advised, room for a number of perspectives and purposes. On the one hand, there is "faithful history," as expressed by Richard L. Bushman and others, in which the historian has a responsibility not only to consider the divine role but also to lead the kind of life that will permit the discernment of God's influence. For others, strictly empirical social-scientific and historicist methods suffice. Most historians of "Mormonism," however, LDS and non-LDS alike, recognize that both secular factors and spiritual claims can be taken seriously, while at the same time adhering to traditional canons of historical scholarship and addressing historical questions raised by contemporary issues.

[*See also* Biography and Autobiography.]

BIBLIOGRAPHY

Backman, Milton V., Jr. "Preliminaries to the Restoration." *IE* 61 (Oct.–Nov. 1958):722–24, 769–71, 773, 846–54.

Boyd, George T. "God in History." *IE* 64 (June 1961):380–81, 449–57.

Bushman, Richard L. "Faithful History." *Dialogue* 4 (Winter 1969):11–25.

Mulder, William. "Mormon Angles of Historical Vision: Some Maverick Reflections." *Journal of Mormon History* 3 (1976):13–22.

Petersen, Mark E. *The Great Prologue*. Salt Lake City, 1975.

Poll, Richard D. *History and Faith*. Salt Lake City, 1989.

DOUGLAS F. TOBLER
S. GEORGE ELLSWORTH

HISTORY OF THE CHURCH

[*This entry discusses the history of the Church in the following six periods:*

c. 1820–1831, Background, Founding, New York Period
c. 1831–1844, Ohio, Missouri, and Nauvoo Periods
c. 1844–1877, Exodus and Early Utah Periods
c. 1878–1898, Late Pioneer Utah Period
c. 1898–1945, Transitions: Early-Twentieth-Century Period
c. 1945–1990, Post–World War II International Era Period

In addition, several other articles cover the history of the Church in the light of specific historical disciplines or approaches: see Economic History; Intellectual History; *and* Legal and Judicial History.

Bibliographic sources relevant to all of these periods are: James B. Allen and Glen M. Leonard, The Story of the Latter-day Saints, *Salt Lake City, 1976; Leonard J. Arrington and Davis Bitton,* The Mormon Experience, *New York, 1979; Church Educational System,* Church

History in the Fulness of Times, *Salt Lake City, 1989; and Joseph Fielding Smith,* Essentials in Church History, *Salt Lake City, 1950.*]

C. 1820–1831, BACKGROUND, FOUNDING, NEW YORK PERIOD

[*For other articles pertaining to events in the first period of Church history, see also* First Vision *and* Moroni, Visitations of.

Early biographical information can be found in articles on the Smith Family Ancestors, Joseph Smith, Emma Smith, *and several other members of the* Smith Family, *in addition to* Martin Harris, Oliver Cowdery, David Whitmer, *and* Sidney Rigdon. *For a listing of Mormon sites and communities of this period, see* New York, Early LDS Sites in.]

The establishment of The Church of Jesus Christ of Latter-day Saints began in the 1820s with events that occurred primarily in New York State. The Prophet Joseph SMITH received his FIRST VISION in 1820, obtained the gold plates of the Book of Mormon from the hill Cumorah in 1827, received priesthood authority in 1829, and officially organized the Church on April 6, 1830. By the time the Church left New York for Ohio early in 1831, it was organized and its basic direction was clearly established.

In its formative years, the infant Church learned above all to depend on revelation for direction. Joseph Smith, young and relatively unschooled, did not pretend to work out the doctrines of the new Church by himself. Direct revelations from God led him step by step. Perhaps the most revolutionary idea in the Church is its belief in Christian revelation beyond the Bible. Latter-day Saints have never doubted the inspiration of the Bible; it has been an essential standard from the beginning. Their experience led them to realize, however, that God also spoke to prophets who were not included in that conventional canon of scripture: the Book of Mormon showed them this (2 Ne. 29:10–14), and they heard Joseph Smith speak with the same authority as biblical apostles and prophets. Consequently, Latter-day Saints began to think of revelation in a new way, and the principle of continuing revelation greatly disturbed their fellow Christians, but from the beginning nothing was more basic to the Church.

The history of the Church begins with the family of Joseph SMITH, Sr., and Lucy Mack SMITH, the Prophet's parents (*see* SMITH FAMILY), who, with thousands of other New Englanders, flooded into New York in the early nineteenth century looking for better land. They brought with them their Calvinist religious intensity, but with a zeal modified by the new conditions of life in republican and pluralistic America. They had long searched without success for a faith on which they could rely. The increasing number of Christian denominations and a host of new intellectual influences from the Enlightenment made it more difficult to embrace religious faith than when Congregationalism had predominated in New England. Joseph Smith's quest for salvation began with the question of which Church is true. This question was possibly thrust upon him by his parents' uncertainties and by the plurality of churches—Presbyterian, Baptist, Methodist, Quaker—in his own village.

Moved by evangelical revivals, Joseph Smith asked for direction from God about the true religion in the early spring of 1820. Although only fourteen, he had confidence in the biblical promise that he could get an answer (James 1:5). He went into the woods near his home, kneeled down, and prayed. In his accounts of the event, he testifies that the answer he received astonished him. Both God the Father and Jesus Christ appeared and told him to join none of the existing churches. He was assured that he was in good standing with God, told many things he could not write about, and then the vision closed, leaving him overcome. This revelation of the Father and the Son is considered by Latter-day Saints to be the opening event in the restoration of the gospel.

For three and a half years Joseph received no further communication from the heavens. Wondering if he had disqualified himself through unworthiness, Joseph was praying on the evening of September 21, 1823, when to his astonishment, an angel appeared in the room and announced that he was Moroni and had come with instructions from God. He told Joseph about a record written on gold plates giving a history of the former inhabitants of the western continents. The resurrected Savior, Jesus Christ, had appeared to these people and had given them the fulness of the gospel. The angel said the plates were buried in a hill near Joseph's home. In the course of the night, the angel came three times, delivering the same basic message and adding a little more information each time. Although exhausted, Joseph went to the hill the next day and found the plates encased in a stone box just below the surface of the earth; but he was not allowed to remove them. The angel appeared again and told him he must come back again the following year on the same day, September 22. For the next four years, Joseph faithfully returned to that place in the same manner. Finally, on September 22, 1827, he was allowed to take the plates into his possession (*see* MORONI, VISITATIONS OF).

The events of the four-year interval between 1823 and 1827 doubtless helped Joseph Smith to mature in preparation for the responsibilities and challenges that subsequently came to him. There is some evidence that his father was involved in treasure hunting, a common activity among poor New England farmers who hoped through the use of magic to discover buried money, and it was necessary for Joseph to extricate himself from the mistaken notions of that superstition. The angel told Joseph that one of the reasons for the delay in giving him the gold plates was that he had dwelt on their monetary worth (*PWJS*, p. 7). In November 1825, Joseph and his father worked briefly with a man named Josiah Stowell of SOUTH BAINBRIDGE (AFTON), NEW YORK, who believed a Spanish treasure was located in HARMONY, PENNSYLVANIA, near the Susquehannah River. The project failed, and the Smiths gradually separated themselves from the money-digging activities of their neighbors to concentrate on the religious mission described by the angel. As a happy outgrowth of the Harmony project, while working there Joseph met Emma Hale (*see* SMITH, EMMA HALE), whom he married on January 18, 1827. In the meantime, his older brother Alvin died; Joseph was arrested in 1826 as a "glass looker" under a New York law that made it a crime "to tell fortunes, or where lost or stolen goods may be found" (see the legal definition of "Disorderly Persons," *The Justice's Manual*, Albany, New York, 1829, p. 144; *see also* SMITH, JOSEPH: LEGAL TRIALS OF); and his parents lost their farm through their inability to make the last mortgage payment. These misfortunes, along with other experiences, deepened and strengthened the young man as he learned to discern between good and evil and to endure opposition.

After Joseph obtained the plates in 1827, curious and sometimes malicious neighbors in Manchester and Palmyra, New York, made it impossible to begin work on the translation. They ransacked the Smith house and barn, and only by constantly moving and concealing the plates could he keep them safe. He had been strictly warned not to show them to anyone, but that did not satisfy the curiosity seekers. Emma's brother, Alva, offered to help; he transported the pair with their belongings and the plates—hidden in a barrel of beans—125 miles to Harmony, Pennsylvania, where Emma's father lived. Joseph procured some acreage from his father-in-law, Isaac Hale, and a small house was provided. It was here that the translation began.

A sympathetic neighbor from Palmyra, Martin HARRIS, took enough interest in the plates to visit Joseph in Harmony. With the plates, Joseph had received an instrument called interpreters, or a Urim and Thummim, that enabled him to translate the characters engraved on the metal tablets. Joseph made copies of a few characters for Martin to take to language experts in Albany and New York City to verify Joseph's work. There is some confusion about what happened in these interviews, but Martin Harris was unequivocally satisfied. When he returned to Harmony, he offered to take the dictation as Joseph translated. Between April 12 and June 14, 1828, the two of them completed 116 pages of manuscript. At this point, Harris, who suffered from his wife's doubts about the existence of the plates, asked permission to show the manuscript to her and four other family members. With great reluctance Joseph Smith agreed. After hearing nothing from Martin for a number of weeks, Joseph went to his parents' home in Manchester, New York, to confront him. Martin despairingly confessed that he could not find the manuscript. He had succumbed to pressure, shown the manuscript to neighbors beyond his agreement, and someone had stolen it.

On the occasion of the crisis, Joseph received a revelation through the Urim and Thummim in which the Lord severely rebuked him. He more than Martin was held responsible for the loss of the manuscript. "Behold, you should not have feared man more than God," he was told (D&C 3:7). Martin did no more transcribing for Joseph, and from that time until the spring of 1829, Joseph accomplished little on the translation. In April, Oliver COWDERY, a young schoolteacher who had boarded with the Smith family in Manchester, came to learn more about the Book of Mormon. Having himself received a vision of the Lord and the plates, he was persuaded that the work was divine and offered to serve as scribe (*PWJS*, p. 8). Beginning on April 7, 1829, the two, Joseph and Oliver, worked together almost constantly until the translation was completed in June, a little more than two months later.

In the course of translating a portion of 3 Nephi that described the manner of baptism, Joseph and Oliver wondered about their own need for baptism. As had become customary with Joseph, he sought instruction from God. On May 15, 1829, while he and Oliver prayed, a heavenly messenger appeared to them. Identifying himself as John the Baptist, he conferred on them the Aaronic Priesthood, which gave them the authority to baptize. With that newly received authority and under the direction of the angel, the two men baptized each other in the Susquehannah River. This revelation established an important principle in the Church: that divine ordinances such as baptism can be performed only by persons who have received priesthood authority by ordination. John the Baptist told Joseph and Oliver they would later receive a second and higher priesthood called the Melchizedek Priesthood. Subsequently Peter, James, and John appeared to them on the banks of the Susquehannah River some place between Harmony and Colesville, New York, and ordained them apostles.

By late May 1829, religious opposition against Joseph was growing in Harmony, and he and Oliver needed a calmer place to work. Oliver wrote to a friend, David WHITMER, who agreed to move them to his family's farm in FAYETTE, NEW YORK. Emma joined them in Fayette shortly afterward. A copyright was obtained for the Book of Mormon on June 11, 1829, and the translation soon was completed. As they completed the book, Joseph Smith learned through revelation that others would be allowed to see the golden plates. Witnesses were promised in the Book of Mormon itself, and Joseph's associates were eager to know who would have the privilege. Martin Harris, David Whitmer, and Oliver Cowdery were chosen, shown the plates by the angel Moroni, and heard the voice of God declaring to them that the work had been translated by the power of God. A few days later at Manchester, Joseph Smith was permitted to show the plates to eight other men. They examined the plates closely and lifted them with their hands. The statements of these two sets of witnesses were printed in the back pages of the 1830 edition of the Book of Mormon and appear in the front pages of all recent editions.

Finding a printer to publish the Book of Mormon proved to be difficult. Palmyra people who were suspicious of Joseph Smith banded together to intimidate the local printer, Egbert B. Grandin, by threatening not to purchase copies. Others, like Martin's wife, Lucy Harris, challenged Joseph's financial motives. After contacting printers as far away as Rochester, Joseph persuaded Grandin to accept the job. Martin Harris's guarantee made the difference in Grandin's decision. On August 25, 1829, Harris mortgaged his farm, pledging to pay $3,000 for 5,000 copies. Joseph and Martin hoped to sell enough copies to raise at least $3,000, but in the end Martin had to sell 151 acres to fulfill his agreement. Typesetting began in August 1829, and finished copies were available March 26, 1830.

Publication of the Book of Mormon brought to a close the endeavor that had occupied Joseph Smith since receiving the plates in 1827. Meanwhile, the revelations he was receiving made clear that translating the Book of Mormon was not the end of his divine mission. He was also to organize a church. Samuel Smith had been baptized in Harmony in late May 1829; Hyrum SMITH, David and Peter Whitmer, Jr., and others were baptized in June in Seneca Lake. They had begun meeting together, and they had taught and tried to persuade all who requested information. On April 6, 1830, in the house of Peter Whitmer, Sr., in Fayette, New York, Joseph Smith organized the Church of Jesus Christ. Six men subscribed as members, and over fifty people were present. The group sustained two officers as leaders of the Church, Joseph Smith as first elder and Oliver Cowdery as second elder. Joseph was also given the titles of seer, translator, and prophet. In addition, a revelation made provision for ordaining elders, priests, teachers, and deacons as a lay priesthood. Some of the lay persons present at the organization were ordained that day, and from the start, the Church made no provision for a special clerical order.

Three clusters of believers were organized into branches of the fledgling Church soon after its organization—one in Fayette; another in Manchester at the old Smith home; and a third in COLESVILLE in southern New York, which was near the farm of Josiah Stowell (in Bainbridge Township, Chenango County), Joseph's onetime employer and a loyal supporter. Members of the Joseph Knight family, who had provided Joseph and his assistants food and clothing during the translation, lived in Colesville and were the nucleus of the branch there. Joseph and Emma moved back to their house in Harmony, but met with all three branches at prescribed quarterly conferences held at the Peter Whitmer farm in June and September 1830.

In the summer of 1830, troubles began to arise. Twice Joseph was put on trial as a "disorderly person." Both times he was acquitted. More disturbing to Joseph, some of his own followers questioned his authority and claimed revelations and prerogatives of their own. Hiram Page, ordained a teacher in June 1830 and a husband of Catherine Whitmer, wrote out a sheaf of revelations he claimed came from God. Although still young and inexperienced, Joseph sensed the confusion and danger of many voices trying to speak authoritatively. At the September conference in Fayette, Joseph received a revelation that established that only one person approved by common consent was to receive commandments and revelations for the entire Church (D&C 20:65; 28:1–3, 11–13). Hiram Page lacked that authorization. After hearing Joseph, the conference confirmed him as sole revelator for the Church (D&C 28:2; D. Cannon and L. Cook, eds., *Far West Record*, Salt Lake City, 1983, p. 3). This principle of revelation for the whole Church coming through the man sustained as the Prophet remains a practice of the Church to this day.

In the six months after the organization of the Church, converts were added in small numbers. Joseph Smith's brother Samuel went out with copies of the Book of Mormon to share with anyone interested. Joseph Smith, Sr., visited his brothers, sisters, and parents in St. Lawrence County, New York, where most of them lived, to tell them what had happened. Later conversions resulted from these expeditions, but very few at the time. Parley P. PRATT, a farmer from Ohio, believed that God led him to the house of Hyrum Smith, Joseph's brother, to find out about the Book of Mormon.

The most successful early missionary venture was launched in September and October 1830, when Oliver Cowdery, Peter Whitmer, Jr., Parley Pratt, and Ziba Peterson were called to teach the Indians (*see* LAMANITE MISSION). The Book of Mormon had special relevance for Native Americans because it was a religious record from ancient America, and the four were charged to take this message to the Indians who were assembling in the territory west of Missouri. The mission was notable as much for what was accomplished en route, however, as for the preaching to the Indians. After leaving New York, the missionaries stopped in the Mentor-Kirtland area of northeast

Ohio near Pratt's former farm. Before joining the Church, Pratt had been associated with the Campbellite movement, which was forming into the Disciples of Christ church. This group believed in rigorously adhering to the teachings and practices of the New Testament church, sloughing off all later additions. The teachings of Joseph Smith appealed to many of them because his doctrines embodied for them a pure restoration of true Christianity. About 130 persons were converted, including the leading Campbellite preacher in the area, Sidney RIGDON. In a few weeks, the four missionaries nearly doubled the membership of the Church. They continued on to Indian country that winter, enduring severe hardships on their long trek on foot from St. Louis across Missouri. They found a land in western Missouri into which the Church would soon begin settling. They also taught among the Delaware and Shawnee Indians until government officials told them to stop because of a prohibition against proselytizing among the tribes.

Soon after the missionaries left Ohio for the West in December 1830, Sidney Rigdon left for New York, accompanied by Edward Partridge. They brought news of the conversions in Ohio and urged Joseph Smith and the membership to move there. Joseph was prepared to take the suggestion seriously because of revelations he received concerning the gathering of the Church (D&C 37:1–4; 38:31–33). Indeed, for the remainder of the century, converts to the Church would assemble at a central gathering place, first in Ohio, then in Missouri, in Illinois, and finally in Utah. Another revelation focused on the second coming of Jesus Christ and on the destructions to be visited upon the world before that event occurred. It said that before those tribulations, the people of God were to "be gathered in unto one place upon the face of this land" (D&C 29:8). A further revelation spoke of a city of Zion to be built somewhere in the West (D&C 28:9). These hints led Church members to realize that they would not remain long in New York.

When a revelation came in December 1830 (D&C 37) telling them to move to Ohio, it was accepted by most. At a conference on January 2, 1831, directions and an additional revelation (D&C 38) were given for the move. The Prophet, Emma, and a few others went ahead and arrived in KIRTLAND on February 1, 1831, to prepare for the arrival of others. The Colesville Branch, under Newel Knight; the

Fayette Branch, under the Prophet's mother and Thomas Marsh; and the Manchester Branch, under Martin Harris, traveled to Ohio in separate companies during April and May 1831. By mid-May virtually all of the New York Mormons from the named branches were in Kirtland.

BIBLIOGRAPHY

Backman, Milton V., Jr. *Eyewitness Accounts of the Restoration*, rev. ed. Salt Lake City, 1986.

Bushman, Richard L. *Joseph Smith and the Beginnings of Mormonism*. Urbana, Ill., 1984.

Madsen, Truman G., guest ed. *BYU Studies* 9 (Spring 1969):235–404 (entire issue devoted to LDS origins in New York).

Porter, Larry C. "A Study of the Origins of The Church of Jesus Christ of Latter-day Saints in the States of New York and Pennsylvania, 1816–1831." Ph.D. diss., Brigham Young University, 1971.

Smith, Lucy Mack. *History of Joseph Smith*, ed. Preston Nibley. Salt Lake City, 1958.

Whittaker, David J. "Sources on Mormon Origins in New York and Pennsylvania." *Mormon History Association Newsletter* no. 43 (Mar. 1980):8–12.

RICHARD L. BUSHMAN
LARRY C. PORTER

C. 1831–1844, OHIO, MISSOURI, AND NAUVOO PERIODS

[*This article focuses first on the Church in northeastern* Ohio, *where* Kirtland *served as Church headquarters, and in western* Missouri. *By 1839 the focus shifts to western* Illinois, *with* Nauvoo *the new headquarters city. For discussion of the difficulties that led to violence and finally expulsion from Missouri, see* Missouri Conflict.

This article outlines organizational and doctrinal developments and examines tensions and conflicts between the Saints and their neighbors, and within the Church itself. Many of these resulted from the attempt to build a tightly unified, sacral community that responded to continuing revelation within a larger society often hostile to these goals. The Prophet Joseph Smith, whose martyrdom ends this period, was a dominant figure; see articles under Smith, Joseph, *and* Visions of Joseph Smith. *The gathering and temples were central concerns; see* Kirtland Temple *and* Nauvoo Temple.]

In October 1830 four LDS missionaries on their way to preach to the Indians west of Missouri (*see* LAMANITE MISSION) introduced the restored gospel to the communities of northeastern Ohio. Before they resumed their journey, the missionaries baptized approximately 130 converts, organized the new members into small "branches," and appointed leaders over each group. Approximately thirty-five of these members lived in Kirtland, Ohio, a community directly east of what is today metropolitan Cleveland.

Sidney RIGDON, a restorationist preacher in that vicinity, joined the Church in November 1830 and notified Joseph Smith of the missionaries' success. As a result, the Prophet inquired of the Lord and recorded revelations (D&C 37:3; 38:32) calling the converts of the recently organized Church in New York to "assemble together at the Ohio." He and his family moved to Kirtland by early February 1831, and about two hundred New York Saints followed by summer, making northeastern Ohio the first LDS gathering place.

Most of the New York Saints and many of the earliest Ohio converts did not remain in Ohio. In the summer of 1831, Joseph Smith traveled to the Missouri frontier and identified Independence, Jackson County, Missouri, as a second gathering place. Latter-day Saints anticipated that a holy city, a New Jerusalem, would be established in a new North American Zion, a city of refuge from tribulations that would afflict the wicked in the last days (D&C 29:7–9; 45:65–71; 57:1–3). Sidney Rigdon dedicated the land for gathering, and Joseph Smith designated the specific site where a temple would be built, and, after appointing others to supervise the gathering to Zion, returned to Ohio.

In HIRAM, OHIO, a rural farming community about thirty miles south of Kirtland, Joseph Smith worked on his inspired translation of the Bible, a project that served him as a school. Prayerfully seeking enlightenment about particular passages and doctrines frequently brought new revelation and understanding. After the Prophet and Sidney Rigdon, who was serving as his scribe, were beaten and tarred and feathered by a mob in March 1832, they and their families moved to Kirtland.

The two gathering places of the early 1830s each had a different purpose. Although Latter-day Saints migrated to the Missouri frontier to lay the foundations of a new Zion, the administrative headquarters of the Church, responsible for directing the missionary program and building the first temple, remained in Ohio. There was some competition between the two centers, with both needing resources and members and both wanting the presence of the Prophet Joseph Smith. But, as revelation made clear, the goals of the two were complementary: the promised "endowment from on high" associated with the KIRTLAND TEMPLE was a prerequisite for success in Zion (D&C 105:9–13, 33). Joseph Smith resided in Kirtland until 1838, keeping in touch with Missouri members by mail and messenger, and traveling there five times to instruct Church members on policies, programs, and beliefs.

In Jackson County, Latter-day Saints published two periodicals, the *Evening and the Morning Star* and the *Upper Missouri Advertiser*, and attempted to establish a unique economic order based on CONSECRATION with assigned stewardship of property and other assets, as directed by revelations to Joseph Smith (*see* MISSOURI: LDS COMMUNITIES IN JACKSON AND CLAY COUNTIES). Disagreements about legal requirements and individual selfishness hampered implementation, but the basic impediment was that the Saints had too little capital and very little to consecrate. Still, some participants were inspired by the concepts involved, and the ideals behind the effort left a significant legacy (*see* UNITED ORDERS).

Although the Latter-day Saints migrated to western Missouri to build a city of peace and refuge, they encountered major hostility. Older settlers considered these newcomers a threat to their own patterns of living. Missourians complained that Mormons sought to influence slaves, that their "eastern" lifestyle was incompatible with the Missouri frontier, that they were an economic and political threat, that their friendship for the Indians threatened the region's security, and that they held unusual religious beliefs. These charges indicate a significant cultural clash between the LDS immigrants and older settlers. Rapid immigration of Latter-day Saints into Jackson County intensified the tensions, resulting in confrontation.

After violence erupted in the summer of 1833, Governor Daniel Dunklin sent a local militia into the area to establish peace. Assuming that the militia would protect all settlers, Latter-day Saints surrendered their arms to this military force. But other Missourians were not disarmed, leaving Church members defenseless. In early November 1833, mobs drove more than a thousand Latter-day Saints from Jackson County, forcing them to abandon their homes and farms. Most of them escaped across the Missouri River to Clay County.

Between November 1833 and the summer of 1836, Clay County was the major gathering place for Latter-day Saints in Missouri. During these years, Church members tried but failed to secure redress for the loss of property in Jackson County. They also sought government protection for an attempt to return to their lands. In 1834, believing that Governor Dunklin had agreed to extend the assistance of state militia to reinforce their own efforts, Church members assembled a small paramilitary force from Ohio and elsewhere to accompany the Missouri refugees back to Jackson County. ZION'S CAMP, as the expedition was called, failed to obtain gubernatorial support and disbanded in June rather than initiate armed conflict.

Though it failed in its primary aim, Zion's Camp profoundly affected many participants and had lasting significance. For most, the hurried march from Ohio to Missouri, more than 800 miles in humid heat, was the most difficult physical challenge of their lives. Some had even greater difficulty with the realization that in spite of that ordeal, they had not assisted the Missouri Saints to return to their lands. They found fault with Joseph Smith's leadership, and the experience contributed to their later dissent. But for many participants, Zion's Camp was an unparalleled opportunity to live day and night with the Lord's prophet—reminiscent of ancient Israel under Moses. The experience bonded them to Joseph and to each other, and out of the crucible of Zion's Camp came many future LDS leaders. The two reactions reflected differing views about prophetic leadership and about how a society based on revelation and priesthood should be organized—differences that became more pronounced in later Kirtland.

The revelation disbanding Zion's Camp refocused attention on Ohio and on the necessity of completing the Kirtland Temple without delay (D&C 105). Before returning to Ohio, Joseph Smith organized a Missouri stake and appointed a presidency and high council, matching what he had done in Kirtland the February before. Soon, several Missouri Church leaders left for Kirtland to assist with temple construction.

All parties concerned had viewed the Saints' stay in Clay County, Missouri, as temporary. With a return to Jackson County now unlikely, pressures mounted for them to find another location. Urged by community leaders to leave before violence erupted, most Latter-day Saints migrated northward, establishing a new western headquarters at Far West, Missouri. Responding to this movement of thousands of Latter-day Saints into unsettled northwestern Missouri, the state legislature in late 1836 created two new counties, Caldwell and Daviess (*see* MISSOURI: LDS COMMUNITIES IN CALDWELL AND DAVIESS COUNTIES). Since most Latter-day Saints settled in Caldwell, it became known as the Mormon County.

Joseph Smith later taught that a primary purpose for the gathering of the faithful in any age was to build a house of the Lord wherein could be revealed the ordinances of his temple. As temple construction progressed, the LDS population in Kirtland multiplied from about 100 in 1832 to over 1,500 in 1836. Latter-day Saints migrated there from New England, New York, and elsewhere to assist in building the Lord's house, in which, they had been promised as early as January 1831, they would be "endowed with power from on high" (D&C 38:32).

In March 1836 the Kirtland Temple was completed and dedicated, and during the months before and after the dedication, the Saints enjoyed an unusual pentecostal season. In the temple, a week after its dedication, keys of the priesthood were conferred on Joseph Smith and Oliver COWDERY in visitations by Moses, Elias, and Elijah. Blessings and instructions received in the temple were particularly significant for missionaries, whose proselytizing travels from Kirtland during the 1830s ranged from Canada to the American South and, in 1837, to the British Isles, with extensive missionary work within Ohio.

While its headquarters remained in Kirtland, the Church experienced major doctrinal and administrative development. A number of the most significant revelations in the Doctrine and Covenants were received in the Kirtland and Hiram areas, including the vision of the Resurrection and the three degrees of glory (D&C 76); the law of consecration and stewardship (D&C 42); the Word of Wisdom, sometimes called the Lord's law of health (D&C 89); revelations on the priesthood and its organization (D&C 84, 107); and the coming of the Millennium (D&C 1, 29, 88, 133). Many of these revelations came in response to questions raised by Joseph Smith's translation of the Bible. Joseph

Smith also received a revelation relating to PLURAL MARRIAGE (D&C 132), but it was not recorded until 1843. The book of Abraham, not published until 1842, resulted from the Prophet's acquisition in 1835 of a collection of mummies and papyri from Egypt.

As growth required organizational development, a series of revelations directed the establishment of both local and general Church officers. These included the office of bishop in 1831, the First Presidency of the Church in 1832, and a permanent high council in 1834. In February 1835 the Quorum of the Twelve Apostles and the Quorum of the Seventy were organized, selected principally from Zion's Camp veterans. Both quorums had responsibility for proselytizing. Though the Twelve were spoken of as second to the Presidency, their immediate assignments were to supervise the labors of the Seventy and to oversee the Church outside its organized stakes.

Revelation also directed officers of the Church to study widely in many fields of knowledge in preparation for their ministries and directed that a SCHOOL OF THE PROPHETS be organized for that purpose (D&C 88:77–80, 118–41). The attitudes and imperatives expressed in the revelation became influential not only in instituting that first Church-sponsored school but also in the Church's approach to learning and education throughout its subsequent history.

Publication of the *Evening and the Morning Star*, disrupted in Missouri by the expulsion from Jackson County, was resumed for nearly a year in Kirtland. The *Latter Day Saints' Messenger and Advocate*, successor to the *Star*, was the first Church periodical to publish some of Oliver Cowdery's letters dealing with the history of Joseph Smith. The Doctrine and Covenants, containing many of the revelations given to Joseph Smith, was published in Kirtland in 1835.

The promulgation of new doctrine and the establishment of a church hierarchy offended some Latter-day Saints who preferred the less complicated faith they had embraced in the Church's infancy. Those who did not share the Prophet Joseph Smith's vision of a new society organized under priesthood were also disturbed by the increased direction Church leaders gave members in temporal matters and by the Prophet's extensive involvement in economic affairs. The collapse of an unchartered Kirtland Safety Society that had been sponsored by Church leaders helped bring discontent to a head (*see* KIRTLAND ECONOMY). Lawsuits were filed against Joseph Smith, threats were made against his life, and against the lives of his most vigorous supporters, and a number of prominent Church members apostatized. In the midst of this turmoil, the Prophet sent some of his staunchest supporters as missionaries to the British Isles. There, in less than a year, they gained more than 1,500 converts and laid the groundwork for thousands more to follow (*see* MISSIONS OF THE TWELVE TO THE BRITISH ISLES).

By 1837, Latter-day Saints outnumbered other residents of Kirtland Township. That year, LDS candidates were elected to all major town offices except that of constable. Many Church members in Kirtland were relatively poor and lived in clusters of small temporary homes. Some non-Mormons became resentful of this influx of the poor and of Church leadership that seemed undemocratic and thus un-American. Economic and political rivalries developed, accompanied by threats and some mob violence. Outside pressure mounted for the removal of the Mormons from Kirtland at the same time as bitter internal dissension plagued the Church. In January 1838, Joseph Smith, Sidney Rigdon, and other Church leaders whose lives had been threatened fled to western Missouri, followed gradually by most of the Latter-day Saint residents of Kirtland and vicinity.

In 1837–1838, LDS migration into western Missouri increased rapidly. This growth sparked increased agitation among neighbors who feared Mormon economic and political domination and who saw the influx as a threat to their way of life. Grievances that had been expressed by Jackson County citizens in 1833 were repeated and enlarged. Rumors and accusations became the basis for intolerant actions. Some insisted that since Caldwell County had been created for Mormons, Latter-day Saints were not to settle outside the borders of that county.

The decisive confrontation was sparked by a fight that erupted when ruffians attempted to prevent LDS voting at Gallatin, Daviess County. Exaggerated reports of this melee unloosed agitation that had been mounting and led to the formation of mobs determined to drive all Mormons from Daviess County. Mobs also threatened Latter-day Saints living in DeWitt, Carroll County, until, on October 11, 1838, they were forced to leave their homes and farms. As the refugees traveled to the LDS stronghold at Far West, they were continually harassed and several died.

After Governor Lilburn Boggs refused pleas to protect the DeWitt Saints, Church leaders mobilized the Caldwell County militia and prepared to protect themselves. Some members of the DANITES, originally organized to assist with Latter-day Saint community development, engaged in paramilitary activity, including burning the headquarters of mobbers at Gallatin and Millport who had threatened their destruction. Meanwhile, a local militia forced Latter-day Saints to leave their farms in Ray County and threatened to shoot Church members accused of being spies. Trying to prevent the threatened executions, a unit of the LDS Caldwell County militia engaged the Ray militia on October 25 at Crooked River. Men were killed on both sides, and wildly exaggerated rumors of marauding Mormons enflamed the countryside. On October 27, without investigating the charges and countercharges, Governor Boggs accused Church members of initiating hostilities and ordered the state militia to exterminate the Mormons or drive them from the state (*see* EXTERMINATION ORDER). Three days later, the HAUN'S MILL MASSACRE, in which more than two hundred militiamen attacked a tiny LDS settlement and brutally killed seventeen, underscored the likelihood that Boggs's order would be carried out literally.

Confronted by overwhelming militia forces, the Latter-day Saints surrendered at Far West and agreed to leave the state. Approximately 10,000 Church members were forced to leave Missouri, most in winter and amid intense hostility. Traveling eastward, they crossed the Mississippi River into Illinois. After suffering immense losses of property and some loss of life, in early 1839 most reached Quincy and other western Illinois communities whose residents offered aid and refuge.

Meanwhile, Church leaders in Missouri were arrested and charged with treason. Most were promptly released, but ten were imprisoned without trial during the winter of 1838–1839, some in RICHMOND JAIL and others in LIBERTY JAIL. During the Prophet Joseph's half-year stay in Liberty Jail, he wrote some of the most insightful and eloquent inspired writings of his career (D&C 121–23), and he emerged in April 1839 with a clear understanding of what must be done to complete his mission satisfactorily and a firm determination to do so.

The Saints arranged to purchase land for a new gathering place on both sides of a bend in the Mississippi River north of Quincy. Nauvoo, Illinois, superseded the fledgling community of Commerce and became Church headquarters. Many members also settled across the river in Lee County, Iowa.

Plagued by malaria, Nauvoo-area Saints sought to confront larger issues while still struggling to establish a viable community after the Missouri disaster. Attempting to obtain redress for Missouri losses, President Joseph Smith visited national political leaders in Washington, D.C., but the prevailing emphasis on states' rights precluded federal assistance. Despite illness and poverty, nine members of the Quorum of the Twelve Apostles fulfilled an assignment to proselytize in the British Isles. They arrived in England in early 1840 and during the next fifteen months saw nearly 5,000 converts join the approximately 1,500 they found on arrival. The following year, Orson Hyde, an apostle, visited Jerusalem and dedicated Palestine for the gathering of the Jews.

In England the Twelve launched the *Latter Day Saints' Millennial Star* and published a hymnal and a second edition of the Book of Mormon, founding in the process what became a major LDS publication center for the next half century. The Twelve initiated the emigration of LDS British converts to America in 1840, and during the next six years nearly 5,000 migrated to Nauvoo (*see* IMMIGRATION AND EMIGRATION). Under the leadership of Brigham Young, the Quorum of the Twelve became an effective administrative force during this mission. When they returned to Nauvoo, they were given new responsibilities. In August 1841, Joseph Smith announced that the Twelve now stood "next to the First Presidency," and their jurisdiction was expanded to include supervision of the Church's stakes as well as mission areas.

Draining the swamps and welcoming a growing number of settlers, the Saints in Nauvoo created a thriving community that eventually numbered nearly 12,000, rivaling Chicago as the largest city in Illinois. Construction and growth fueled the economy, cultural life thrived, and the Saints developed the most important religious community of their short history. Having learned from experience that they could not rely on the goodwill of others for protection, they sought institutional guarantees. In the NAUVOO CHARTERS the Illinois state legislature provided the protections of home rule, a municipal judiciary, and a city militia. Determined never again to be defenseless as they had been in Missouri, they built their chartered NAUVOO LEGION into the largest militia in Illinois.

To an unusual degree, Joseph Smith occupied a position of political as well as ecclesiastical power, serving at various times as city councilman, mayor, commanding general of the Nauvoo Legion, and editor of the leading local newspaper, the *Times and Seasons*. These positions gave him wide latitude to build a sacral society and to accomplish the things he felt most central to his mission.

After receiving additional priesthood keys in the Kirtland Temple in 1836, Joseph Smith looked to the day when he could complete his temple-related responsibilities and convey additional teachings and ordinances to the Saints. He emerged from Liberty Jail convinced that his time to do so was short and that Nauvoo would be his last opportunity. As soon as the Saints had regrouped and were secure in their new home, he began unfolding a set of additional teachings, ordinances, and organizational patterns—many of them temple-related—that further distanced the Saints from their own earlier notions and from the beliefs of their neighbors. This process began with an important revelation of January 1841 (D&C 124) that, among other things, launched the construction of the NAUVOO TEMPLE, and continued for more than three years. By April 1844, just three months before his death, the process was complete.

In Nauvoo Joseph Smith expounded on the nature of the Godhead and the origin and destiny of the human race, stressing the concept of eternal progression in conjunction with the plan of salvation (*see* KING FOLLETT DISCOURSE). Teaching the universal availability of salvation, he introduced vicarious ordinances for deceased individuals, including baptism for the dead. Experiencing resistance to new doctrines and practices, yet driven by personal forebodings to avoid delay, the Prophet began in 1841–1842 to introduce PLURAL MARRIAGE and sacred temple ordinances privately to a limited number of trusted associates, including members of the Quorum of the Twelve, who were later to deliver them to worthy members of the Church once the temple was complete.

Among the most important Nauvoo organizational developments was the March 1842 founding of the Relief Society, a benevolent, social, and religious organization for women. The Relief Society provided women a structure to facilitate charitable work and sisterhood. More important, it brought women into close contact with priesthood organization and helped to prepare them for temple experiences to come. The Church's first wards, or basic congregational units, were founded in Nauvoo, and additional responsibilities for bishops were defined. The COUNCIL OF FIFTY was the last organizational element set up by Joseph Smith. Though it played a useful practical role for several years after its March 1844 organization, its greatest importance was in providing a governmental model for the future kingdom of God on earth.

From the temple to the Council of Fifty, members of the Quorum of the Twelve Apostles stood by the Prophet as his closest advisers and assistants. Foreseeing the day when the Saints might need a more secure haven in the isolated West, in February 1844 Joseph Smith assigned the Twelve to lead an expedition to find such a location (*see* WESTWARD MIGRATION), but shortly put the project on hold. First, he wanted them to travel to the East on a more political mission. When inquiries to the presidential candidates in the approaching national election produced no one willing to defend Mormon rights, the Prophet Joseph Smith launched his own presidential campaign, providing a platform for making his views known and speaking out on behalf of his people. During their usual summer proselytizing, the Twelve and other supporters would travel in the East, combining preaching with electioneering. Before they left, about March 26, 1844, Joseph Smith made his "last charge" to the Twelve. He declared that he had now given them every priesthood key that he possessed and that it was their responsibility to shoulder the burden of the kingdom while he rested. Before they returned from the East, he was murdered.

Although Nauvoo grew rapidly, progress on its most ambitious construction projects, the NAUVOO TEMPLE and the NAUVOO HOUSE hotel, lagged, in part because of a shortage of capital. Hopes to make Nauvoo a manufacturing center failed to materialize for the same reason (*see* NAUVOO ECONOMY). But the continued success of LDS proselytizing and the influx of immigrants, combined with LDS solidarity and industriousness, transformed Nauvoo into a formidable economic and political competitor to the other towns in Hancock County.

Neighbors unsympathetic to Nauvoo also had other complaints. The theocratic organization of the LDS community, with its apparent unity of purpose and its local autonomy, aroused resentment. The tendency for Latter-day Saints to vote as a bloc for local and state candidates who were most likely to benefit them alienated both Whigs and Democrats (*see* NAUVOO POLITICS). Nauvoo's strong militia aroused envy and distrust. The fact that the city's judicial system shielded Joseph Smith from prosecution provoked charges that he had placed himself beyond the law.

As these things increased the hostility of adversaries of the Church, Thomas Sharp, editor of a newspaper in nearby Warsaw, made his *Warsaw Signal* a voice for these concerns and took up a sustained crusade against Joseph Smith and Nauvoo. In the spring of 1844 several disgruntled former associates combined forces with anti-Mormons to mount an offensive against the Prophet from within Nauvoo itself. They published the *Nauvoo Expositor* newspaper, which attacked the Church and made inflammatory charges against Joseph Smith. The Nauvoo City Council declared the paper a public nuisance and ordered the sheriff to destroy it, an action that aroused the Prophet's enemies and provided the basis for his arrest. On June 27, 1844, Joseph and his brother Hyrum were murdered in the jail at the county seat, Carthage, while awaiting trial (*see* CARTHAGE JAIL; MARTYRDOM OF JOSEPH AND HYRUM SMITH).

The Prophet Joseph Smith established the doctrinal and organizational foundation of the modern Church and prepared Brigham Young and the Quorum of the Twelve Apostles to build on the foundation he had laid. His ministry and his mission were complete.

BIBLIOGRAPHY

Allen, James B., and Glen M. Leonard. *The Story of the Latter-day Saints*. Salt Lake City, 1976.

Backman, Milton V., Jr. *The Heavens Resound*. Salt Lake City, 1983.

Flanders, Robert Bruce. *Nauvoo: Kingdom on the Mississippi*. Urbana, Ill., 1965.

Gentry, Leland H. "A History of the Latter-day Saints in Northern Missouri from 1836 to 1839." Ph.D. diss., Brigham Young University, 1965.

Hill, Marvin S. *Quest for Refuge*. Salt Lake City, 1989.

LeSueur, Stephen C. *The 1838 Mormon War in Missouri*. Columbia, Mo., 1987.

Pratt, Parley P. *Autobiography of Parley P. Pratt*. Salt Lake City, 1985.

Underwood, Grant. "Millenarianism and the Early Mormon Mind." *Journal of Mormon History* 9 (1982):41–51.

MILTON V. BACKMAN, JR.
RONALD K. ESPLIN

C. 1844–1877, EXODUS AND EARLY UTAH PERIODS

[*After outlining developments in Nauvoo, Illinois, following the martyrdom of Joseph Smith, this article traces the exodus from Nauvoo to the West. It then focuses primarily on the political and economic developments associated with establishing a new commonwealth in the Great Basin under Brigham Young's direction. It also reviews Church organization, plural marriage, and the building of temples.*

To understand daily life and what it meant to be a Latter-day Saint during this period, see Pioneer Life and Worship. *For more on the Exodus, see* Westward Migration; Mormon Pioneer Trail; Historical Sites; Council Bluffs; Iowa, LDS Communities in; "This Is the Place" Monument. *For the development of the Mormon commonwealth, consult* Economic History; Pioneer Economy; Immigration and Emigration; Handcart Companies; City Planning; Deseret Alphabet; *and articles on pioneer settlements in* Arizona, California, Colorado, Idaho, Nevada, New Mexico, *and* Wyoming.]

The MARTYRDOM OF JOSEPH AND HYRUM SMITH on June 27, 1844, precipitated a major crisis. In the immediate aftermath and emotional shock of losing their founding prophet, many Latter-day Saints suffered a crisis of faith: Could *anyone* take his place? Would the Lord still be with the Church? Nor was it immediately clear to everyone *who* should lead: Would it be Sidney RIGDON, Joseph Smith's counselor in the First Presidency? The Quorum of the Twelve Apostles, led by Brigham YOUNG? Someone else? Whoever succeeded to leadership would face the challenge of resolving tensions within the Church and facing powerful adversaries without.

At the time of the assassination, most members of the Quorum of the Twelve were in the East on missions. Sidney Rigdon, who had left Nauvoo for Pittsburgh just before the martyrdom, returned August 3 and asserted a claim to lead as "Guardian." Three days later several of the Twelve, including Brigham Young, arrived just in time for an August 8 meeting already called to decide guardianship. Rigdon spoke first for his claims. He was followed by Brigham Young, who asserted the responsibility of the Twelve to lead the Church in Joseph's absence and to build on the foundation he had laid. The great majority voted to sustain the Twelve. Many claimed that Brigham Young was transfigured before them, speaking with the voice of the deceased prophet and appearing like him in person and manner.

The August 8 vote effectively settled the question of succession: no one else could make a persuasive claim of having either the authority or the full confidence of the Prophet. The vote sustained the Quorum of the Twelve, with Brigham Young at their head, as the leaders of the Church, but it did not immediately result in a new First Presidency; that would come later, after the Twelve had completed the Nauvoo Temple and located a new home for the Church in the West, responsibilities they felt an obligation to accomplish *as a quorum*. Nor did the vote satisfy those who longed for a way to be Latter-day Saints but without the Nauvoo innovations that they viewed as problematic and that the Twelve would continue—such things as the emphasis on temple, new doctrines including PLURAL MARRIAGE, and the unity of temporal and ecclesiastical concerns under the priesthood. Some of these briefly followed others who set themselves up as leaders, but many simply drifted away. Years later, some banded together as the REORGANIZED CHURCH OF JESUS CHRIST OF LATTER DAY SAINTS with emphasis and direction quite different from Joseph Smith in Nauvoo or the Twelve in the Great Basin (*see* SCHISMATIC GROUPS).

The first priorities of the Twelve were to complete the NAUVOO TEMPLE while privately preparing for the exodus to the West (*see* WESTWARD MIGRATION, PLANNING AND PROPHECY)—which they were committed to delay until the Saints received temple ordinances. The Saints so rallied behind the temple that the capstone was in place by May 1845, and the edifice was ready for ordinance work by December. Eventually nearly 6,000 men and women received temple ordinances before leaving for the West. In the spring of 1845, with the temple nearing completion, Church leaders began preparations for the move West. In September, shortly after mob violence erupted against the outlying settlements around Nauvoo, the Twelve publicly announced that the Saints would all depart.

Brigham Young was supported in these endeavors by eight of the Twelve—the same who had served abroad under his direction in 1840–1841—and by members of the COUNCIL OF FIFTY. Organized in March 1844 by Joseph Smith, the Council of Fifty had been involved in two major activities prior to his death: secretly negotiating with the Republic of Texas for possible settlements there, and publicly campaigning to support Joseph Smith's candidacy for the U.S. presidency. More than seventy-five percent of the surviving members of the original Council of Fifty supported Brigham Young, but William Smith, John E. Page, Lyman Wight, all apostles, and Nauvoo Stake President William Marks dissented and were never reconciled either to the temple or to the Great Basin exodus and its implications. The Council of Fifty helped organize the exodus from Nauvoo and, in early Utah, helped establish an economic and political theocracy.

The exodus began in February 1846, before renewed hostilities erupted. All during the spring and summer, a flow of wagons moved out across the Iowa prairies. The Latter-day Saints were still unsettled in Iowa when a U.S. military officer arrived on June 26 with a requisition for 500 volunteers to serve in the campaign against Mexico. Though sometimes regarded as an oppressive trial imposed upon the refugee Mormons by the U.S. government, the call actually resulted from secret negotiations with U.S. President James Polk (*see* MORMON BATTALION). Though the battalion took 500 able-bodied men from their midst, it brought a much-needed $70,000, which was used to aid the families of the men and fund the general program of the exodus.

Because the evacuation of Nauvoo and the trek across Iowa had largely exhausted the travel season, the Saints prepared to winter on the Missouri River. They built temporary settlements at WINTER QUARTERS on the river's west bank, now Florence, Nebraska, a suburb of Omaha, and on the east bank at Kanesville, later COUNCIL BLUFFS, IOWA. There preparations continued for the great migration to the interior basins of North America. On January 14, 1847, Brigham Young announced a revelation that the Saints should be "organized into companies [of hundreds, fifties, and tens], with a covenant and promise to keep all the commandments . . . of the Lord our God" (D&C 136:2–3). On April 5, 1847, he led the first pioneer company, departing from Winter Quarters.

After a three-month journey, advance scouts entered the valley of the Great Salt Lake. Three days later, on July 24, 1847 (*see* PIONEER DAY), Brigham Young entered the valley. On July 28 he designated a temple site and announced to the 157 pioneers that "this is the right spot," making it clear that he and the Saints intended a long stay in the vicinity of the Great Salt Lake.

After his return from Utah to Winter Quarters in October 1847, Brigham Young presented to the apostles the question of reorganizing the First Presidency. Although no written revelation explicitly authorized the Twelve to reorganize the presidency, many considered that right implicit in the 1835 revelation concerning the authority of that quorum in relation to the First Presidency (D&C 107:21–24). The Twelve sustained Brigham Young as President of the Church, with Heber C. Kimball and Willard Richards as his counselors, an action ratified by Church members later that month at a special conference at Kanesville, Iowa, and the following year in Salt Lake City.

In Utah, Brigham Young set out to fulfill Joseph Smith's dream of establishing a permanent refuge for the Saints. This included creating a political state in which the Church would play a dominant role. The theocratic nature of this government was indicated by the fact that a Church high council, presided over by Joseph Smith's uncle John Smith, conducted both religious and civil affairs in the SALT LAKE VALLEY from the fall of 1847 until the return of Brigham Young to the valley in September 1848, when the Twelve and the Council of Fifty assumed direction.

In the closing months of 1848, the Council of Fifty began deliberations toward establishing a more permanent government. Anticipating that the Great Basin would become United States territory, the Council debated the relative merits of petitioning Congress for territorial or statehood status. It opted first for a territory but soon after, in July 1849, following precedents in Texas and California, petitioned for statehood and began to organize the provisional State of Deseret (*see* DESERET, STATE OF). Brigham Young was elected Governor and other Church authorities comprised its executive and judicial branches and much of its legislative branch. The legislature convened in December 1849, and the State of Deseret functioned as an autonomous state within the national domain until March 28, 1851, when it was formally dissolved and superseded by UTAH TERRITORY, which had already been created as part of the national Compromise of 1850 (*see also* UTAH STATEHOOD).

The boundaries of the State of Deseret were vast, encompassing all of present Utah, most of Nevada and Arizona, more than one-third of California, and parts of Oregon, Idaho, Wyoming, Colorado, and New Mexico. To establish control of this domain, Brigham Young began a vigorous COLONIZATION program, which, before his death in 1877, founded nearly 400 settlements. An energetic system of proselytizing, particularly in the BRITISH ISLES and SCANDINAVIA, with thousands converted, of whom nearly 90,000 immigrated to Utah by the end of the century. The Church promoted, organized, and conducted this immigration. For the benefit of those who could not otherwise afford travel costs, the Church organized the PERPETUAL EMIGRATING FUND. Chartered in 1850 by the State of Deseret, for the next thirty-seven years the Perpetual Emigrating Fund Company raised funds and utilized Church resources to assist approximately 26,000 emigrants from Europe to the mountain West.

The State of Deseret was the closest the Church ever came to realizing the theocratic model previously outlined by Joseph Smith. Church authorities served in important civil positions. After federally appointed judges left the territory in 1851, probate courts, with bishops as judges, were given jurisdiction over both civil and criminal cases. The intention was that LDS influence over the political life of the territory would eliminate the PERSECUTION that had repeatedly occurred. In later years the very success of this theocratic society would create less violent but ultimately more dangerous conflicts with American society.

Inseparable from the prolonged conflict with the federal government was the LDS practice of PLURAL MARRIAGE. Although polygamy had been practiced privately prior to the exodus, Church leaders delayed public acknowledgment of its practice until 1852. In August of that year, at a special conference of the Church at Salt Lake City, Elder Orson Pratt, an apostle, officially announced plural marriage as a doctrine and practice of the Church. A lengthy revelation on marriage for eternity and on the plurality of wives, dictated by Joseph Smith on July 12, 1843, was published following this announcement (D&C 132). Viewing it as a religious obligation for faithful brethren to marry more wives than one, Latter-day Saints believed that polygamy was protected by constitutional guarantees of religious freedom. There were no federal laws against polygamy, and the territorial incorporation of the Church allowed it "to solemnize marriages compatible with the revelations of Jesus Christ" (Arrington and Quinn, p. 261). In some communities as much as twenty to twenty-five percent of the LDS population eventually lived in polygamous households, with most men who practiced polygamy having one to four plural wives.

For the first several years, life in their new western refuge seemed tenuous. A mild winter in 1847–1848 was followed by spring frosts and a discouraging summer. Then drought damaged and plagues of crickets devoured a good portion of the crops. Many believed that they saved a remnant of their crops only because of the miraculous intervention of great numbers of gulls that descended on the fields and devoured the crickets (*see* SEAGULLS, MIRACLE OF). After the lean winter of 1848–1849, however, the pioneers were able to raise enough in most years to see them through the winter. An unexpected bonanza came in 1849 when hundreds of travelers bound for the California gold fields came through Utah, eagerly trading scarce manufactured goods, exhausted animals, and even flour for local produce. The initial settlements by this time were well-enough established to begin colonization throughout the Rocky Mountain area.

The Saints founded dozens of colonies, at first primarily within the confines of present Utah. First settled was a core area extending north and south from the headquarters at Salt Lake City along the western edge of thc mountains. The next colonies were in the higher mountain valleys of the region, such as the Cache and Heber valleys. Almost at the same time, other colonies were established in more distant areas, in response to particular needs, such as the founding of an iron industry (Parowan, Jan. 1851; Cedar City, Nov. 1851); establishing stations along immigration routes (San Bernardino, 1851; purchase of Fort Bridger, 1855); undertaking missions to the Indians (Fort Lemhi in present Idaho; Las Vegas, Nevada; Fort Supply in 1853 in present Wyoming; and the Elk Mountain Mission in east-central Utah, all in 1855); producing warm-climate crops, such as cotton and sugar (St. George, 1861); or, later, searching for a refuge for polygamous families.

The most common motive for colonization was the need to find land for a growing population of farmers, a need leading to settlement of most suitable sites in Utah by 1880 as well as others in northern Arizona, southwestern Colorado, northwestern New Mexico, western Wyoming, and southeastern Idaho. Often new areas were opened with a "mission" call, wherein established settlers were asked to undertake a Church-sponsored mission to found a colony. Once the mother colony was established, nearby areas were settled spontaneously as young people coming of age sought land to farm.

The founding of a commonwealth in the West was not accomplished without conflicts and difficulties. A prolonged drought in 1855 was followed by a severe grasshopper infestation. The insecurities thus created may have helped feed the fire of the REFORMATION OF 1856–1857, a period of intense soul-searching and recommitment. The fiery and at times intemperate sermons of the Reformation had heightened pioneer anxieties when, early in 1857, believing exaggerated reports that the Mormons were in a state of rebellion, U.S. President James Buchanan secretly ordered 2,500 federal troops to Utah. Acting without the benefit of an investigation, Buchanan relieved Brigham Young as governor, a position to which Young had been reappointed even after the 1852 announcement of polygamy. Unfortunately, Buchanan did everything in secrecy, even stopping the mails to Utah to give the troops the advantage of surprise.

After receiving private confirmation of the government action, Brigham Young instructed all missionaries to return to Utah and ordered missions closed and the more isolated colonies abandoned. Accustomed to persecutions involving state militia, Latter-day Saints saw the advance of armed forces toward Utah as a prelude to plunder, rape, and slaughter. As they prepared for armed resistance, war hysteria swept the territory.

As advanced units of the UTAH EXPEDITION approached Fort Bridger, they encountered the Saints implementing a "scorched earth" policy of resistance. Mormon raiders seized and burned federal supply trains and destroyed the forage in front of the advancing troops. The timely arrival of heavy snows mired the army for the winter, allowing mediators, especially Thomas L. KANE, time to seek reconciliation. Meanwhile, President Young ordered northern Utah settlements abandoned and organized the "Move South." If the Latter-day Saints had to leave their refuge, they would leave the Great Basin as much a wilderness as they had found it. Negotiations succeeded by spring, just as the army started to move. Alfred Cumming was installed as governor, and on June 12, 1858, Brigham Young accepted a pardon for his supposed rebellion. Two weeks later, General Albert Sidney Johnston led his troops through a deserted Salt Lake City and established an isolated Camp Floyd forty miles to the southwest. The Utah War became fittingly known as Buchanan's Blunder.

A disastrous consequence of the war hysteria was the MOUNTAIN MEADOWS MASSACRE of September 1857, in which local officials in southern Utah joined with Indians to massacre a company of settlers en route to California. It is well documented that Brigham Young's command was to let the travelers pass through in peace, but his advice arrived too late to prevent the killing, and a locally orchestrated cover-up portrayed the crime as solely an Indian depredation. Responding to charges that whites were involved, President Young urged the new governor to investigate, but Governor Cumming maintained that if whites were involved they would be pardoned under the general amnesty granted in 1858. Eventually, as more information came to light, some of the principal participants were excommunicated from the Church and one, John D. Lee, was convicted in federal court and executed.

Though preoccupied by the Civil War, the federal government nonetheless demonstrated interest in Utah Territory. In 1862 Fort Douglas was established on the eastern edge of Salt Lake City, under the leadership of a dedicated anti-Mormon, Patrick Edward Connor. Connor and his troops were charged with guarding transportation routes, but they also published the aggressively anti-Mormon *Union Vedette*, encouraged mining, and promoted non-Mormon immigration to the territory. In 1863 Connor's troops attacked a group of Northern Shoshone Indians on the Bear River in the northern Cache Valley, killing some 250 men, women, and children.

The decade following the Utah War was one of general expansion for the Church. In 1862 Congress enacted a law prohibiting polygamy in the territories and disincorporating the Church, but the law went unenforced until after REYNOLDS V. UNITED STATES in 1879. Church immigrants continued to arrive by the thousands, and Brigham Young continued planting colonies to house them. The steady influx of non-Mormons to Utah and the construction of a transcontinental railroad, however, pointed toward future challenges to LDS domination of their Great Basin commonwealth.

The completion of the transcontinental railroad brought opportunities as well as challenges. Brigham Young had long anticipated the end of physical isolation and in some ways encouraged it. In

1852 and in 1854, the Saints petitioned Congress for a transcontinental railroad to pass through Utah. Such a railroad would simplify immigration and permit Church leaders to establish rail links connecting many distant colonies with Salt Lake City. When the Pacific Railroad Act was passed on July 1, 1862, President Young subscribed for $10,000 worth of stock in the newly organized Union Pacific Railroad Company, of which he became a director in 1865.

Though the railroad made it easier for Church immigrants to reach Utah, it also encouraged non-Mormon immigration. The end of isolation likewise threatened Utah's economic and political independence. In order to build the local economy and postpone the establishment of a powerful non-Mormon business community, Church officials had long struggled to discourage the importation of eastern manufactured goods. They now launched a determined campaign to discourage the purchase of imported luxuries, including tea, coffee, alcohol, and tobacco, and Joseph Smith's 1833 revelation discouraging the use of these products was given added emphasis.

Despite Brigham Young's long opposition to the development of precious metal-mining in Utah, the approach of the railroad revived enthusiasm for harvesting Utah's mineral wealth. Under the direction of several prominent Church businessmen and intellectuals such as William Godbe, Edward W. Tullidge, and Eli B. Kelsey, a "New Movement" developed within the Church against what they referred to as "Priesthood Autocracy." These men wrote persuasive articles in the *Utah Magazine* urging the exploitation of Utah's mineral resources in order to keep the industry in local (and therefore LDS) control. Envisioning a different result, Brigham Young denounced the "Godbeites" for inviting "Gentile" domination of Utah. Eventually, Godbe, whose doctrinal unorthodoxy posed an additional challenge, was excommunicated. Although Brigham Young rejected the Godbeite solution, he recognized the realities of the new economic situation and inaugurated a series of programs to reinforce spiritual solidarity and economic independence.

One part of Brigham Young's program involved the organization of the SCHOOL OF THE PROPHETS in 1867. The original School of the Prophets had been established by Joseph Smith in 1833 to provide adult education and prepare for the temple. In the Utah organization, adoption of an economic program accompanied discussions of theology. The Schools of the Prophets instructed landowners in methods of securing property titles, solicited contributions of labor and funds to finance branch railroads, established locally owned cooperative merchandising and manufacturing enterprises, urged the reduction of wages to allow greater exportation of Utah goods, organized boycotts of hostile Gentile establishments, and required that members pledge to observe the Word of Wisdom. The Schools also contracted with the Union Pacific and Central Pacific railroads to grade the transcontinental line in Utah, thus limiting the influx of non-Mormon laborers and providing cash revenue to Latter-day Saints. Within a few years, as economic conditions changed, these organizations gradually disappeared.

More permanent than the Schools of the Prophets were the organizations that Brigham Young established for the women and youth of the Church. Between the rebirth of the Relief Society in 1867 and Brigham Young's death a decade later, with General President Eliza R. SNOW assisting bishops in forming local organizations, the society spread to every Church settlement in the Great Basin. In addition to its charitable purposes, the Relief Society worked with the Schools of the Prophets in encouraging HOME INDUSTRY and discouraging the purchase of imports. Major achievements of the Relief Society included the beginning of a grain storage program, launching SILK CULTURE, founding the *Woman's Exponent,* building Relief Society halls in most settlements, starting a commission store for home industries, and impressive support of women's medical training. Relief Society leaders were also active in woman suffrage, and in 1870 Utah women were second to Wyoming women to receive the franchise.

In 1869 Brigham Young established an organization for young women with the unwieldy name "Young Ladies' Department of the Cooperative Retrenchment Association." He urged the girls to avoid all extravagances, and to "cease to build up the merchant who sends your money out of the Territory for fine clothes made in the East" (Susa Young Gates, *History of the Young Ladies Mutual Improvement Association of the Church*, p. 9 [Salt Lake City, 1911]). The Young Ladies' Mutual Improvement Association, as it was later named, became an organization primarily concerned with cultural, social, and religious activity.

After the completion of the transcontinental railroad in 1869, both Union Pacific and Central Pacific defaulted on their grading contracts. The losses to the Mormon economy were staggering: $500,000 in cash, and even greater aggregate losses to subcontractors, merchants, and laborers. In an effort to compensate for these losses, Church leaders sponsored railroads within the territory, using the half million dollars' worth of iron, construction equipment, and rolling stock that the bankrupt Union Pacific had used as a substitute payment on its obligations. Although these railroads brought benefits to Utah, their success did not completely assuage the bitterness the Saints felt toward the initial setbacks with the transcontinental railroad.

In addition to intensifying his call for home manufacture and boycotts of non-Mormon merchants as the rails approached Utah, Brigham Young established a cooperative system of merchandising. In October 1868 he organized Zion's Cooperative Mercantile Institution (ZCMI) to "bring goods here and sell them as low as they can possibly be sold and let the profits be divided with the people at large" (Arden Olsen, *History of the Mormon Mercantile Cooperation in Utah*, p. 80 [Ph.D. diss., University of California, Berkeley, 1935]). With widespread support, the new department store became a profitable enterprise that continues as Salt Lake City's largest retailer. Branch stores were established in many communities, as were cooperative tanneries, gristmills, dairies, butcher shops, banks, iron works, sawmills, woolen mills, and cotton factories. These helped the Saints forestall for another decade the "outside" control that the arrival of the railroad presaged.

The remarkable success of the Cooperative Movement suggested to Brigham Young that a revival of "The United Order of Enoch," long his goal, might now be feasible. Inaugurated by Brigham Young during the winter of 1873–1874, the Order Movement had been inspired by a desire to emulate attempts to live the law of CONSECRATION in the 1830s and by the success of the Brigham City Cooperative. Under the direction of Elder Lorenzo SNOW, Brigham City had become eighty-five percent self-sufficient, conducting virtually all agriculture, construction, manufacturing, and trade in the surrounding area. Almost the entire population was employed in the various departments of the cooperative, and received their remuneration in products rather than cash. So successful was the Brigham City Cooperative that it was hardly affected by the financial Panic of 1873.

After Brigham Young launched the UNITED ORDER movement, more than 200 orders were established throughout Utah, southern Idaho, northern Arizona, and Nevada. Because he left the operation of these orders in local hands, several different types emerged. Some, like Orderville in southern Utah, were almost totally communal. In the larger cities, where tightly organized communal orders were impossible, separate ward congregations financed individual cooperative enterprises, such as farms or factories, and then exchanged products. The manifestations of the United Order of Enoch varied, but they represented a genuine effort of the people to become "one," as the early revelations had commanded. As with nearly all voluntary enterprises of this nature, these orders eventually disbanded due to internal strains and external pressures. The movement itself ended by 1877, although some orders, such as that at Orderville, continued for another decade.

Prior to his death in 1877, Brigham Young was able to see the fulfillment of one of his most sacred aspirations—the completion of a temple in Utah. The full significance of temples and their ordinances dated back to the Nauvoo period, when Joseph Smith introduced baptism for the dead, marriage for eternity, and a set of religious instructions and covenants called the endowment. Since abandoning the Nauvoo Temple in 1846, Brigham Young dreamed of a temple in the West. Upon arriving in the valley he dedicated ground in Salt Lake City for such a temple, but the imposing structure took forty years to complete. In the meantime, a temporary endowment house, constructed in 1855, provided a place for sacred ordinances. After deciding to build a less imposing structure in the south, Brigham Young dedicated the completed St. George Temple on April 6, 1877. In the decade following his death, two additional temples were built in Utah (Logan and Manti) before the Salt Lake Temple was finally dedicated in 1893.

After the St. George Temple dedication, Brigham Young initiated a massive reorganization of the Church, primarily at the local level, clarifying and redefining priesthood responsibilities in the process.

Every ward and stake was affected and most received new leadership.

By the time of his death on August 29, 1877, Brigham Young had brought the Latter-day Saints to an apex of growth in their mountain retreat and kingdom. His dying words, "Joseph! Joseph! Joseph!" were appropriate for one who had lived his life, as he frequently said, as an apostle of Jesus Christ and of Joseph Smith. In his sometimes unbending manner, Brigham Young had worked for more than forty years to attain the goals of Joseph Smith. The Saints had achieved a unified economic and political power, though they would soon be forced to bend in the face of unrelenting federal pressure. More important, by courageously facing their challenges and pursuing their dreams in the desert, they had become a strong and cohesive people of faith. Committed to gospel ideals regardless of the costs, they left a heritage that continues to inspire Latter-day Saints throughout the world.

BIBLIOGRAPHY

General works focusing on this period include Leonard J. Arrington, *Brigham Young, American Moses,* New York, 1985; and *Great Basin Kingdom,* Cambridge, Mass., 1958; Eugene E. Campbell, *Establishing Zion: The Mormon Church in the American West, 1847–1869,* Salt Lake City, 1988; Dean L. May, *Utah: A People's History,* Salt Lake City, 1987; and a brief account in Leonard J. Arrington and D. Michael Quinn, "The Latter-day Saints in the Far West, 1847–1900," in F. Mark McKiernan, Alma R. Blair, and Paul M. Edwards, eds., *The Restoration Movement: Essays in Mormon History,* Lawrence, Kans., 1973, pp. 257–70.

In addition to numerous relevant articles in the *Journal of Mormon History, BYU Studies, Dialogue, Sunstone,* and the *Utah Historical Quarterly,* see: Richard E. Bennett, *Mormons at the Missouri 1846–1852,* Norman, Okla., 1987, for the period leading to Utah settlement; Wallace Stegner's *The Gathering of Zion,* New York, 1964, a classic account of migration to Utah; Leonard J. Arrington, Feramorz Y. Fox, and Dean L. May, *Building the City of God: Community and Cooperation Among the Mormons,* Salt Lake City, 1976, which focuses on communitarianism; and Norman F. Furniss's *The Mormon Conflict, 1850–59,* New Haven, Conn., 1960, the best book-length study of the Utah War.

LEONARD J. ARRINGTON
DEAN L. MAY

C. 1878–1898, LATE PIONEER UTAH PERIOD

[This article discusses a period of stress and adaptation following the death of Brigham Young as the Church confronted great pressures to conform to contemporary American mores. After presenting an overview

of the period, the article considers organizational changes, economic programs, establishment of new LDS settlements, and missionary work, then focuses on the struggle over Polygamy, *culminating in the* Manifesto of 1890 *announcing the official end of* Plural Marriage. *In the wake of the Manifesto came home rule for Utah (see* Utah Statehood*), expanded proselytizing, attempts to shore up religious education, and more limited Church economic involvement (see* Pioneer Economy*).*

To understand daily life and what it meant to be a Latter-day Saint during this period, see Pioneer Life and Worship. *For additional information on continued Church* Colonization *into new areas, see entries on pioneer settlements in* Mexico *and* Canada, *and in* Arizona, Colorado, Idaho, Nevada, New Mexico, *and* Wyoming. *On developments related to plural marriage, see* Legal and Judicial History; Antipolygamy Legislation; Reynolds v. United States; *and* Manifesto of 1890.]

During the 1878–1898 period of growth, severe problems, and pronounced changes, the Church met many challenges under Church Presidents John TAYLOR and Wilford WOODRUFF. The 1879 Supreme Court ruling upholding ANTIPOLYGAMY LEGISLATION introduced a decade of ever harsher enforcement of ever harsher laws. Facing governmental persecution and seeking "home rule" through statehood, the Church moved to end the practice of plural marriage and surrender its once firm control of UTAH TERRITORY's politics and economics. In the 1890s Utah Territory and its LDS residents embarked on the road to "Americanization."

Though this period was noted for its prolonged confrontation with the federal government, growth was also a striking characteristic. Church membership doubled (from 115,065 to 229,428), as did the number of stakes (20 to 40) and wards (252 to 516). LDS settlements extended into Mexico and Canada. As proselytizing efforts expanded, the number of missions increased (from 8 to 20). Priesthood quorum work became more orderly and standardized. General Authorities regularly visited quarterly stake conferences and ward conferences. Auxiliary organizations became widely established in stakes and wards, and general-level auxiliary presidencies and boards were appointed. The Church also finished three new temples, bringing the total in Utah to four.

After President Young's death in August 1877, the Quorum of the Twelve Apostles did not immediately organize a new First Presidency. John Taylor presided over the Church as president of the Twelve until October 1880. Under his leadership the Twelve completed the reorganization of wards and stakes that President Young had begun.

They also expanded auxiliary organizations. By 1880 the Twelve selected three of their own (Elders Wilford Woodruff, Joseph F. SMITH, and Moses Thatcher) to form a general superintendency of the Young Men's Mutual Improvement Association (YMMIA) and to supervise new central YMMIA boards or committees created first for counties and later for stakes. The Young Ladies' Retrenchment Association became the Young Ladies' Mutual Improvement Association (YLMIA) in 1878, with boards established in the stakes beginning that year and a Churchwide organization beginning in 1880 with Elmina S. TAYLOR as president. The Primary Association, a new organization to benefit children, was started in 1878 in Farmington, Utah. After other wards copied the program, a Churchwide primary organization was created in 1880, headed by Louie B. Felt. Relief Society President Eliza R. SNOW continued to supervise all women's work in the Church, which now included YLMIA and Primary. Elder George Q. Cannon of the First Presidency continued as general superintendent of the Sunday Schools throughout this period. The Sunday Schools, Relief Society, and MIA were organized in the British Isles and Scandinavia beginning in the late 1870s and early 1880s.

Legal tangles surrounding the settlement of Brigham Young's estate became a bothersome problem for the Twelve. After federal legislation severely limited Church holdings, President Young had controlled a complicated mix of personal and Church property. His heirs and the Church finally settled the matter by compromise out of court in 1879.

In 1880, its fiftieth birthday, the Church proclaimed a Year of Jubilee, modeled on an ancient Hebrew custom, to give relief to the poor. It erased from the books an indebtedness of $802,000 to the PERPETUAL EMIGRATING FUND—half of the outstanding total. In addition to distributing cattle and sheep to the needy, authorities forgave the worthy poor half their unpaid tithing. The Relief Society also lent nearly 35,000 bushels of wheat from its storage bins to help drought-stricken farmers.

After directing the Church for three years, in October 1880 John Taylor and the Twelve again organized a First Presidency: John Taylor, President of the Church, and George Q. Cannon and Joseph F. Smith, who had previously served in the First Presidency under Brigham Young, as counselors.

Revelations to President Taylor in 1882 and 1883 prompted a reorganization of the Seventy. For the first time the seventy-six local quorums were organized on a geographic basis, enrolling all seventies within their respective boundaries. In addition, between 1884 and 1888, twenty-five new quorums were created. This reorganization revitalized the Seventy, and the number of seventies filling full-time missions increased as soon as the change was implemented.

This period also saw a growth in Church-related publications. Two new magazines served the youth: the *Contributor* (1879–1896) for young men and the *Young Woman's Journal* (1889–1929) for young ladies. The *Morgenstjernen* (1882–1885), a historical publication in Danish, continued in English as *The Historical Record* (1886–1890). The Sunday School published its first music book (1884), and the Book of Mormon first appeared in a Swedish translation (1878). In 1880 the Church accepted by vote the Pearl of Great Price as scripture, giving the Church the fourth of its standard works. It also published, in 1879, editions of the Book of Mormon and Doctrine and Covenants, with Elder Orson Pratt's chapter and verse divisions, cross-references, and notes.

President Taylor also implemented a new economic program. Less rigidly structured than the earlier UNITED ORDERS, it struck a balance between private enterprise and group economic planning. Zion's Central Board of Trade fostered cooperative economic activity by promoting business, seeking new markets, providing information to farmers and manufacturers, preventing competition harmful to home industry, and sometimes regulating wages and prices. Stake boards of trade coordinated with the central agency. Unfortunately, by 1885 anti-Mormon crusades forced these boards of trade to disband. Pioneer and presiding bishop Edward Hunter, who had served since the 1850s, died in 1883 and was replaced in 1884 by William B. Preston.

During the 1880s the Relief Society further developed programs that had begun in the 1870s: storing grain, maintaining ward Relief Society halls and commission stores, sponsoring nursing and midwifery education programs, overseeing the organizations for children and young women, watching over the spiritual well-being of LDS women, and improving the ongoing care of the poor. New developments included the 1882 opening of the DESERET HOSPITAL, Utah's second hospital and the first operated by the Church. The death of Eliza R. Snow in 1887 marked the end of an era for the Relief Society; in 1888 Zina Diantha H. YOUNG replaced her as president.

Despite severe problems, Church leaders remained committed to providing the blessings of temples to more of the Saints. To supplement the one functioning temple in St. George, President John Taylor dedicated Utah's second temple, at Logan, on May 17, 1884. Built primarily with donated money, materials, and labor, it cost an estimated $800,000. A third temple, in Manti, Utah, built at a cost close to $1 million, was dedicated in 1888 by Elder Lorenzo SNOW, a member of the Quorum of the Twelve. Work also continued on the larger Salt Lake Temple, begun in 1853, but not completed until 1893.

Colonization continued. Between 1876 and 1879, no fewer than 100 new LDS settlements were established outside Utah and more than 20 within the territory. LDS settlements in Arizona expanded rapidly. Stakes, formed in the vicinity of the Little Colorado River in 1878 and 1879, were absorbed into the newly created St. Johns and Snowflake stakes in 1887. Meanwhile, along the Gila and Salt rivers, the St. Joseph and Maricopa stakes were formed in 1883. New LDS settlements appeared in Nevada; in eastern Utah, where the Emery Stake was created in 1882; and in southeastern Utah and nearby parts of Colorado and New Mexico, where the San Juan Stake was formed in 1883. Many LDS converts from the southern states settled in the San Luis Valley in south-central Colorado, and in 1883 their settlements became the San Luis Stake.

Antipolygamy prosecution caused Church leaders to found colonies in Mexico and Canada, beyond the reach of U.S. laws. After President Taylor's 1885 visit to Mexico, hundreds of Saints poured into Chihuahua and established villages in a region that is still identified as Mexico's "Mormon Colonies" (*see* MEXICO, PIONEER

SETTLEMENTS IN). These settlements at first were part of the Mexican Mission. Within a decade more than 3,000 Saints had moved in, more settlements were established, and in December 1895 the Juárez Stake was created to direct Saints in the Mexican colonies.

Under instructions from President Taylor, Cache Stake President Charles Ora Card located a place of refuge in southern Alberta in 1886 for Latter-day Saint colonists (*see* CANADA, LDS PIONEER SETTLEMENTS IN). The next spring, arrivals from Utah founded Cardston, fourteen miles north of the United States border. Settlements sprang up nearby in Aetna (1888) and Mountain View (1893). In June 1895 the Alberta Stake became the first stake organized outside the United States (the Salt Lake Stake excepted, then in Mexican territory).

Missionary work produced impressive successes and brought frustrating problems. Between 1879 and 1889 the Church operated a small mission in Mexico that had about 242 converts. In New Zealand a branch was organized among the Maoris in 1883. In 1884 Jacob Spori opened the Turkish Mission, which included Palestine. Numbers of missionaries bound for Europe increased. The gathering to Utah of European converts continued, despite anti-Mormon publicity that prompted U.S. officials to ask European governments to stop Mormons from emigrating. That request was not granted.

After a Southern States Mission was organized in 1875, conversions occasionally provoked violence. Missionaries were driven from some communities, and in 1879 a Georgia mob shot and killed Elder Joseph Standing. At Cane Creek, Tennessee, in 1884, a mob murdered two missionaries and two residents who had shown an interest in the Church.

Wanting to see their history told fairly, Church leaders provided extensive information to California-based historian Hubert Howe Bancroft. Bancroft's *History of Utah* (1889) was one of the first non-LDS scholarly histories to treat the Church in a fair light.

In 1879 the Supreme Court upheld as constitutional the Anti-Bigamy Act of 1862, affirming the illegality of plural marriage (*see* REYNOLDS V. UNITED STATES). As new legislation was passed and prosecutions became more severe, polygamous husbands and fathers had four choices—give up their families, hide from the law, face prosecution, or leave the United States. Despite this crisis, President Taylor, declaring that when the laws of man and God conflict he would obey God, refused to desert his own plural families or to tell the other brethren to abandon theirs. Attacks on polygamy, often led by religious organizations, came from every direction. When national women's groups urged President Rutherford B. Hayes to prosecute Utah polygamists, 2,000 LDS women signed a resolution affirming that plural marriage was a religious practice protected under the Constitution.

Bitterness between the Saints and the Gentiles brewed nationally and within Utah. Public pressure led Congress to pass the Edmunds Act in 1882, which mandated up to five years' imprisonment and $500 fines for polygamy, and up to six months and $300 fines for unlawful cohabitation (*see* ANTIPOLYGAMY LEGISLATION). Persons practicing polygamy or unlawful cohabitation lost their civil rights to serve on juries, hold public office, and vote. The law created a board of five commissioners to handle voter registration and elections. It declared children born of polygamists before January 1, 1883, legitimate, and it gave the president power to grant amnesties at his discretion.

The Utah Commission began its work in 1882 by declaring that anyone who had ever practiced plural marriage, even before the 1862 anti-bigamy law, could not vote. Since the commission required voters to take a "test oath," swearing that they were not in violation of the law, within one year the law disfranchised more than 12,000 Latter-day Saints. In 1885, however, the U.S. Supreme Court ruled that this test oath was unconstitutional.

The judicial crusade against polygamists severely disrupted Church society in Utah, Idaho, and Arizona. Polygamous men and their families suffered greatly, as did the Church as an organization. Otherwise law-abiding husbands and fathers—and some wives and children—became fugitives in a Mormon "underground," frequently moving from place to place to escape federal marshals hunting "cohabs." Saints developed secret hiding places in homes, barns, and fields, codes to warn one another, and spotters to watch for the marshals. Federal "deps" (deputy marshals) adopted disguises as peddlers or census takers and hired their own spotters to question children and neighbors and to invade the privacy of homes. Bounties were offered for every cohab captured. Families suffered, particularly wives left to tend farms while their husbands were in hiding. Wives who refused to testify against their husbands were sent to prison. Men, women, and children suffered long periods of deprivation and fear.

In Utah between 1884 and 1893, 939 Saints went to prison for polygamy-related charges. In Idaho and Arizona the Saints suffered from similarly harsh prosecution. When Arizona prisons became crowded, cohabs were sent to a Detroit penitentiary. One Utahan, Edward M. Dalton, was killed by a pursuing deputy, which embittered the Saints against the government. So did a U.S. Supreme Court ruling that a man who stopped living with his wife but who provided her food and shelter was guilty of cohabitation.

The crusade disrupted normal Church activities significantly. President Taylor avoided arrest by traveling. In the last public sermon he preached, he criticized what he called a judicial outrage, then went into hiding. Several apostles went into exile, taking special missions to remote areas in the West, Mexico, Canada, and Hawaii. Several others filled European missions and missions to Native Americans. Many stake presidents and bishops likewise tried to avoid arrest.

Between 1884 and 1887 general conferences were held in Provo, Logan, and Coalville, rather than in Salt Lake City, to help attenders avoid arrest. Few General Authorities attended. Elder Franklin D. Richards, an apostle who was immune from arrest because his plural wife had died, presided over some of the conferences. General epistles from President Taylor and President Cannon gave guidance to the conferences.

President Taylor directed the Church by letters. For more than two years President Taylor remained "underground," separated from most of his family and friends. He died in hiding in Kaysville, Utah, on July 25, 1887, after serving as a General Authority nearly forty-nine years. By the time of his death, nearly every settlement in Utah had been raided by federal marshals, hundreds of Saints had become refugees in Mexico or Canada, and nearly all the leaders were in hiding. At his funeral in Salt Lake City, he was honored for being a double martyr whose blood was shed in Carthage Jail with Joseph and Hyrum Smith and who then died in exile because of government persecution.

Once again the Council of the Twelve, led by senior apostle

Wilford Woodruff, took the helm of the Church and steered the course, largely from the "underground," until they again established a First Presidency at general conference in April 1889. Elder Woodruff became Church President, and George Q. Cannon and Joseph F. Smith were his counselors. This would be the last time that the Twelve delayed reorganizing the First Presidency upon the death of the President. In December 1892, President Woodruff, indicating that prolonged delay was not pleasing to the Lord, instructed senior apostle Lorenzo Snow to reorganize immediately upon his death.

By 1887 national political leaders saw that the Church was not bending to the law, so Congress framed a tougher measure, the Edmunds-Tucker Act, designed to destroy the Church as a political and economic entity in order to force the Saints to abandon plural marriage. The law dissolved the Church as a legal corporation, required the forfeiture of all property in excess of $50,000, dissolved the Perpetual Emigrating Fund Company and claimed its property, and disbanded the NAUVOO LEGION (territorial militia). To aid prosecutions, the law required compulsory attendance of witnesses at trials and confirmed the legality of forcing wives to testify against husbands. County probate judges, who helped impanel juries, had to be appointed by the President of the United States. Federally appointed officers took control of schools. Probate courts certified all marriages. The act disinherited all children born of plural marriages one year or more after the act was passed. Woman suffrage was abolished and a new test oath was designed. No one could vote, serve on a jury, or hold public office without signing an oath pledging support of antipolygamy laws.

Federal lawmen zealously tried to arrest and imprison Church leaders. President Woodruff stayed in the underground, near St. George, Utah, directing the Church by letter and private meetings. George Q. Cannon, President Woodruff's first counselor, was arrested in February 1886, posted bail, and then escaped into hiding until 1888 when, with a more lenient judge on the bench, he gave himself up. He served 175 days in prison and paid a $450 fine. Allowed visitors in prison, he was able to conduct much Church and personal business. He supervised the Sunday Schools and finished writing a biography of Joseph Smith. His presence buoyed up the spirits of his fellow cohabs in the prison. Latter-day Saints regarded these prisoners as martyrs and gave them gala receptions when they were released.

Arrests were a problem, but most damaging to the Church were its inability to acquire and use funds to further its work and the loss of political rights. To protect $3 million worth of real and personal property from confiscation, the Church asked prominent members to assume ownership of certain properties as trustees. Nonprofit associations were created to hold property, including the three Utah temples. Ward and stake associations took over local meetinghouses, tithing houses, and Church livestock. Many stakes established academies with the use of tithing that was returned to them by the Church.

Federal receivers confiscated about $800,000 worth of property not turned over to private parties or associations, then rented back certain properties to the Church, such as the Temple Block in Salt Lake City. Church leaders tested the constitutionality of the confiscations, but in 1890 the Supreme Court upheld the new law by a 5–4 vote. The economic destruction of the Church seemed certain.

Matching this economic crusade was a political assault. With all women, thousands of LDS men, and all convert-immigrants disfranchised, anti-Mormon politicians won control of the Ogden and Salt Lake City governments. In Idaho practically all Church members were disfranchised by a test oath requiring them to state under oath that they did not believe in or belong to a church that believed in plural marriage. When the Supreme Court in 1890 upheld the Idaho test oath, anti-Mormons pushed the Cullom-Struble Bill in Congress that would disfranchise all Latter-day Saints everywhere (*see* LEGAL AND JUDICIAL HISTORY).

Economically crippled and with its members denied political rights, the Church faced a ruinous future unless its practice of plural marriage was stopped. President Woodruff consulted with leaders and prayed earnestly to know what to do. After receiving divine revelation, he issued the MANIFESTO on September 24, 1890, announcing an official end to plural marriage. "The Lord showed me by vision and revelation exactly what would take place if we did not stop this practice," President Woodruff later said. "He has told me exactly what to do, and what the result would be if we did not do it" (*Deseret Evening News,* Nov. 14, 1891). The Manifesto said that the Church had halted the teaching of plural marriage and was not allowing new plural marriages. President Woodruff said he would submit himself to the laws of the land and urged Church members to do the same. At general conference on October 6, 1890, the Church accepted the Manifesto. It was incorporated into the Doctrine and Covenants in 1908.

Speaking for the First Presidency, George Q. Cannon explained that a revelation from 1841 applied in 1890; it had instructed the Church that when "enemies come upon them and hinder them from performing that work, behold, it behooveth me to require that work no more at the hands of those . . . men, but to accept of their offerings" (D&C 124:49). Most Saints accepted the new direction, but not easily and not all. Indeed, a limited number of new plural marriages occurred in the next decade before Church leaders made it clear that all who persisted in the practice faced excommunication.

With the issuance of the Manifesto, hostilities ebbed and the Church entered a new era of cooperation. It was generally understood that husbands would not be required to reject their plural wives and their children, and local prosecutors became very lenient in punishing those charged with polygamy. U.S. President Benjamin Harrison, who in 1891 had visited Utah and shaken hands with President Woodruff, granted a limited amnesty to the Saints in 1893, followed by a general amnesty granted by U.S. President Grover Cleveland in 1894. After the Manifesto and the amnesties, General Authorities resumed their normal administrative duties.

Seeking statehood for Utah, Church leaders instructed Utah Saints to join the national political parties and become Democrats or Republicans. A Republican Congress passed an enabling act in 1894 that Democratic President Grover Cleveland signed. Utah wrote a new constitution that prohibited plural marriage and ensured the separation of church and state. On January 4, 1896, Utah became a state, nearly fifty years after President Brigham Young first sought that status (*see* UTAH STATEHOOD).

In 1896 General Authorities accepted a "political manifesto" stipulating that none of them would run for elected office without prior approval of their presiding Church authorities. When Elder Moses Thatcher, an apostle, refused to sign the document, he was dropped from the Quorum of the Twelve.

During the 1890s the Church missionary force nearly tripled. In the Pacific region, missionary work penetrated into Samoa in 1888 and Tonga in 1891. In 1898 the Australasian Mission was split into the Australian and the New Zealand missions. Some Hawaiian Saints immigrated to Utah and created a settlement at Iosepa in western Utah. Missionary work was resumed in California in 1892 and in the eastern United States in 1893. Proselytizing continued in Europe, though emigration from there declined by 50 percent in the 1890s compared with the 1880s. By the 1890s the Church, with its base in America secured and most good land in the West occupied, discouraged immigration and asked overseas converts to build up stakes in their homelands rather than gather to Zion.

The Edmunds-Tucker Act strengthened public schools, which excluded religious education. In response, the Church began holding afterschool religion classes in meetinghouses and established academies or high schools in larger settlements. Between 1888 and 1891 thirty-one LDS academies were opened in Utah, Idaho, Arizona, Canada, and Mexico.

The 1890s saw Church women extending their reach and demonstrating their political rights. Continuing their affiliation with eastern women's movements, they became charter members of the National Council of Women and found their eastern associates to be important allies in their fight against disfranchisement. Relief Society-sponsored suffrage activities led to the inclusion of guaranteed woman suffrage in the 1895 Utah State Constitution.

After forty years, construction of the Salt Lake Temple was completed and dedicated in April 1893. Following a brief open house on April 5, the first opportunity for nonmembers to tour a temple, the sacred edifice was dedicated on April 6, forty years after the laying of the cornerstone. The dedicatory services were repeated between April 6 and May 18, and included five sessions reserved for children under the age for baptism; about 75,000 Latter-day Saints attended. Thereafter members of the Church entered the temple only to perform ordinances for the living and the dead. The following year President Woodruff announced by revelation that LDS family groups no longer needed to be sealed to prominent priesthood leaders by adoption but that they should be sealed by lineage as far back in time as possible. As a result, members began pursuing genealogy and performed sealing ordinances for ancestors several generations back. The Church created the Genealogical Society of Utah to assist researchers.

In 1893 the Salt Lake Tabernacle Choir, while on a major tour, sang at the Chicago World's Fair, winning second prize in an important contest. The entire First Presidency traveled with the choir, marking the first time a Church President had traveled east since the migration to the West nearly fifty years before. This performance was indicative of a new public image for the Church, though that same year the Church was denied representation in the World's Parliament of Religions, which also met in Chicago.

There were other significant developments under Wilford Woodruff's direction: in November 1896, the Church's monthly Fast Day was changed from the first Thursday to the first Sunday of each month, a practice that continues; in 1897, the custom of rebaptism was ended. In the same year, Wilford Woodruff, himself a pioneer of 1847, presided over a Churchwide commemoration of the first entrance into the Salt Lake Valley fifty years before. Salt Lake City celebrated with parades, programs, and the unveiling of a Brigham Young Monument.

During the 1890s the Church and Utah joined the American mainstream economically as well as politically. Many cooperative ventures became private, and most Church-controlled businesses were sold or started to compete as income-producing enterprises. But integration into the national economy was not painless. The earlier confiscation of properties and decrease in the payment of tithing caused by the antipolygamy crusade hurt the Church severely, as did the national depression of 1893. Leaders were forced to borrow heavily from eastern financiers to pay debts and meet obligations, and by 1898 the Church's debts exceeded $1,250,000. However, despite debt and a national depression, the Church promoted and invested in such basic industries as beet sugar manufacturing, hydroelectric power, and selected mining and transportation ventures to help expand the economic base of the Great Basin and benefit Latter-day Saint communities (*see* ECONOMIC HISTORY).

With the ending of plural marriages, the achievement of statehood for Utah, and entrance into the American mainstream in terms of politics and finances, Latter-day Saints moved firmly into a new era. One measure of the change was Church response to the Spanish-American War in 1898: the First Presidency encouraged LDS young men to support the national effort, thereby demonstrating LDS patriotism and loyalty.

President Wilford Woodruff died on September 2, 1898, in San Francisco, California, at the age of ninety-one. In accordance with his instructions, a new First Presidency was immediately named, with Elder Lorenzo Snow becoming the Church's fifth President.

BIBLIOGRAPHY

Alexander, Thomas G. *Mormonism in Transition: A History of the Latter-day Saints, 1890–1930*. Urbana and Chicago, 1986.

Arrington, Leonard J. *Great Basin Kingdom: An Economic History of the Latter-day Saints 1830–1900*. Lincoln, Neb., 1966.

Larson, Gustive O. *The "Americanization" of Utah for Statehood*. San Marino, Calif., 1971.

Lyman, Edward Leo. *Political Deliverance: The Mormon Quest for Utah Statehood*. Urbana and Chicago, 1986.

Roberts, B. H. *A Comprehensive History of The Church of Jesus Christ of Latter-day Saints, Century I*, Vol. 6. Provo, Utah, 1965 (reprint).

WILLIAM G. HARTLEY
GENE A. SESSIONS

C. 1898–1945, TRANSITIONS: EARLY-TWENTIETH-CENTURY PERIOD

[*At the turn of the century the Church's finances suffered from the lingering effects of the federal crusade against* Polygamy, *and the public doubted that its recently declared cessation of* Plural Marriage *had indeed taken effect. After discussing developments in these two areas, this article looks at the Latter-day Saints' integration into the larger American society, including examining the Church's position on war and peace. It also reviews the efforts to systematize that accompanied the steady growth throughout this period.*

In addition to cross-references found in the text, see also Economic History. *Centennial observances accompanied the Church's one-hundredth anniversary in 1930. Lorenzo* Snow, *Joseph F.* Smith, *and Heber J.* Grant *were Presidents of the Church during this period.*]

The Church entered the twentieth century beleaguered and isolated. The LDS experience hitherto had involved founding, exodus to the isolated American West, building there a spiritual and temporal kingdom of God, and grappling with an unsympathetic and often hostile larger American community. The year 1898, however, was a watershed. Following the death of President Wilford WOODRUFF in September, Lorenzo SNOW (1898–1901) succeeded to office and began a series of changes aimed at renewal and redefinition. He, along with his successors President Joseph F. SMITH (1901–1918) and President Heber J. GRANT (1918–1945), reacted to the sweeping changes of the first half of the twentieth century and reached back to preserve old values in a rapidly changing world. The result by the middle of the century was a Church accepted by and integrated into American society, more vigorous and vital than anyone but its most stalwart defenders might have foreseen a half century earlier.

An immediate problem was finances. The antipolygamy crusade (*see* ANTIPOLYGAMY LEGISLATION) had severely impaired revenue and assets, first by incarcerating leaders who normally managed donations and second by seizing and mismanaging Church property. The Panic of 1893 and the resulting depression made the situation worse. In an effort to provide employment and stimulate the local economy, leaders had borrowed money to fund public works and business projects. President Snow quickly ended this practice. His administration slashed expenditures, sold nonessential property, and urged followers to increase their financial contributions.

He dramatically announced this new policy in a southern Utah preaching tour. In May 1899, speaking to assembled members in St. George, he promised that faithful compliance to the Church's longstanding tithing code would bless members and at the same time free the Church from its debts. A year after President Snow's tithing emphasis, Church income doubled. Leaders also encouraged cash donations instead of in-kind commodities and instituted systematic spending and auditing procedures. Because of these reforms, by 1907 President Smith was able to announce that the Church at last had retired its debt. Annual tithing receipts stood at $1.8 million, in contrast to the Church's 1898 debt of $1.25 million. Moreover, the Church had property worth more than $10 million. The Church never again resorted to deficit spending, not even during the Great Depression.

President Snow's reforms did not preclude the holding of investment property or controlling of businesses by Church officers and directors (*see* ECONOMIC HISTORY). While some enterprises were divested, such as the Deseret Telegraph, the Utah Light and Railway Company, and the Saltair Resort at the Great Salt Lake, the Church particularly invested in concerns that advanced its social or institutional purposes. It retained the *Deseret News,* and in the early 1920s leaders established one of the country's first radio stations, later known as KSL Radio. The SALT LAKE THEATRE, the pioneer playhouse, was returned to the Church to provide sanctioned recreation—only to close at the onset of the Depression because of reduced box office revenues and what Church leaders thought were declining theatrical values.

Drawing on the precedent of the NAUVOO HOUSE, Salt Lake City's Hotel Utah was built to draw tourists from hostile non-Mormon hoteliers and enhance the Church's image. The Beneficial Life Insurance Company provided low-cost insurance. The Utah Sugar Company, transformed into the Utah–Idaho Sugar Company, continued to provide local farmers a market for their most important cash crop, while Zion's Cooperative Mercantile Institution (ZCMI) and Zion's Savings Bank & Trust attended the public with competitive retailing and banking services. This altruistic investment policy was also pursued on a broader level. Church leaders sat on the board of other corporations important to the region.

These investments and the social concerns they expressed harked back to the pioneer ideals of community concern and uplift. They were not the only remnant of the past. PLURAL MARRIAGE continued to be a troublesome issue for Latter-day Saints and focused national attention on the Church, particularly during the Snow and Smith administrations. Although many members believed that the 1890 MANIFESTO ended plural marriage, others interpreted the pronouncement as simply shifting the responsibility for practicing it from the Church to the individual. As a result, from 1890 to 1904 some plural marriages continued, though on a greatly reduced level. Moreover, while some husbands stopped living with plural wives, most felt a moral and spiritual obligation to continue caring for their families.

This confusion and ambiguity spilled over visibly into politics. In 1898 Elder B. H. Roberts, a member of the First Council of Seventy and the husband of three wives, was elected to the U.S.

House of Representatives. The Salt Lake Ministerial Association and similar organizations elsewhere used Roberts's election to focus on continuing plural marriages, charging the Church with failure to abide by the agreements that had brought UTAH STATEHOOD. Anti-Roberts petitions containing seven million signatures flooded Congress, and the House eventually refused Roberts his seat.

Still more serious was the case of Reed Smoot. The 1903 election of Smoot, a monogamous member of the Quorum of Twelve Apostles, to the U.S. Senate once more stirred national uproar. The Senate Committee on Privileges and Elections commenced hearings on Smoot in 1904 (*see* SMOOT HEARINGS), but Congress focused more often on the Church itself. Were church and state truly separate in Utah? Did the Church control the conduct of its members? Did it encourage polygamy and polygamous cohabitation? During the two-year investigation, President Joseph F. Smith and other leaders testified before the committee. Others, such as Matthias F. Cowley and John W. Taylor, suspected of performing plural marriages since the Manifesto, refused. To close the controversy and demonstrate the Church's willingness to make the question a matter of discipline, President Smith announced a "Second Manifesto" that expressly forbade future plural marriages. He also required the resignations of both Cowley and Taylor from the Council of the Twelve. In 1907 the Senate narrowly voted to allow Smoot to retain his seat.

Plural marriage still failed to recede entirely, even in the face of the now resolute policy of President Smith and later President Grant. Elders Cowley and Taylor, for instance, each received further discipline for additional plural marriage activity, the former being "disfellowshipped," while Taylor, after taking an additional plural wife, was excommunicated. Their conduct was similar to that of a growing number of former Mormons in the twentieth century. Styled Fundamentalists, they accepted automatic excommunication rather than yield on plural marriage or discard other nineteenth-century practices. Unlike Latter-day Saints generally, who were strengthened by their belief in current prophetic revelation and therefore approached new times in new ways, the Fundamentalists faced the modern world by looking backward.

Nor did the plural marriage issue go away in the popular press. During the first decade of the twentieth century and even beyond, the

Church came under severe public scrutiny by muckrakers and political opponents in Utah. Newspapers, magazines, and cinema in both the United States and Europe focused on sensationalized (and often fictionalized) aspects of polygamy, depicted Church leaders as autocrats, and denounced the Church as un-American and un-Christian (*see* ANTI-MORMON PUBLICATIONS). Old charges of DANITE atrocities and blood atonement resurfaced. In Utah the assault was led by two former U.S. Senators, Frank J. Cannon and Thomas Kearns, who used the *Salt Lake Tribune* to launch bitter attacks on Smoot and the Church and to support the American Party. This short-lived, anti-Mormon political party controlled Salt Lake City government from 1905 to 1911.

The Church attempted to meet the barrage of abuse even though the tide flowed strongly against it. Early efforts included promoting Saltair Resort and Salt Lake City's TEMPLE SQUARE as visitors centers. With the TABERNACLE ORGAN and Mormon Tabernacle Choir as attractions, the latter site by 1905 annually drew 200,000 visitors. Attendance climbed steeply thereafter. When possible, leaders placed refutations in the muckraker publications. Moreover, a point-by-point rebuttal was read during the Church 1911 general conference. Perhaps the ablest and most enduring rejoinder came from B. H. Roberts. From 1909 to 1915, he issued a series of articles on Mormon history in the magazine *Americana*. These were later updated as Roberts's fair-minded, six-volume COMPREHENSIVE HISTORY OF THE CHURCH.

Increasingly men and women outside the Church also defended the Latter-day Saints. By 1900 C. C. Goodwin, a former editor of the anti-Mormon *Salt Lake Tribune* and longstanding critic, frankly labeled Mormons as successful, prosperous, and generally likable. Leading sociologist Richard T. Ely praised LDS group life. Morris R. Werner produced a Brigham YOUNG biography devoid of previous stereotypes and hostility. These path-breaking ventures were followed by others. By the late 1920s President Grant conceded that virtually anything the Church might request could be placed in the media. Indeed *Time Magazine* gave President Grant cover treatment, while Hollywood studios completed such favorable motion pictures as *Union Pacific* and *Brigham Young*.

In part the change in public attitude came from the integration of Church members into the larger American society. Nineteenth-century Latter-day Saints expanded their agricultural settlements throughout the mountain West and even into Canada and Mexico (*see* COLONIZATION), although their agrarian communities were often tightly knit, provincial enclaves. In contrast, as LDS outmigration continued in the twentieth century, Church members now rubbed shoulders with fellow Americans in urban settings. During the 1920s, for instance, the percentage of Latter-day Saints living in the Intermountain West declined while those living on the American West Coast rose. In 1923 the Los Angeles Stake, the first modern stake outside the traditional Mormon cultural area, was created. Between 1919 and 1927 the number of Latter-day Saints in California increased from fewer than 2,000 to more than 20,000. The twentieth-century Church dispersion had begun, first with the migration of large numbers to the West Coast, then also with increasing volume to the East and Midwest.

Direct contact with neighbors lessened cultural, religious, and even emotional barriers, bringing Mormons and non-Mormons an increased appreciation for each other. The growing number of successful Americans who were also Latter-day Saints or Utah-born accelerated the process. Maud Adams was lionized for her widely popular stage portrayal of Peter Pan. Philo T. Farnsworth's inventions brought about television. Cyrus Dallin and Mahonri Young achieved distinction in the arts.

Latter-day Saints were particularly drawn to public affairs. Edgar B. Brossard became a member and then chairman of the United States Tariff Commission. J. Reuben Clark, Jr., rose in the higher levels of the State Department bureaucracy, finishing his government career as ambassador to Mexico. During the New Deal, Marriner S. Eccles was chairman of the Federal Reserve System. James H. Moyle served as assistant secretary of the treasury from 1917 to 1921, while William Spry was commissioner of public lands from 1921 to 1929. Heber M. Wells was the treasurer of the U.S. Shipping Board. Richard W. Young became a U.S. commissioner of the Philippines and returned from the First World War as Utah's first regular army general. For members of a once persecuted religious minority, each such personal success betokened the Church's growing acceptance and prestige. "Outsiders" were becoming "insiders."

Two Church members had disproportionate influence in shaping the Church's new image. One was Reed Smoot. Aloof, but honest and utterly tireless in his devotion to government duty and Church interests, Smoot remained in the Senate for thirty years. As chairman of the powerful Senate Finance Committee, he wielded major influence over American economic policy. More than any other Latter-day Saint in public service, he personified the Church, assuaging questions about its patriotism and integrity by his personality and presence.

The other was President Heber J. Grant. A businessman by inclination and early profession, President Grant's homespun ways and business-mindedness charmed an age given to commercial enterprise. Non-Mormons delighted particularly in his speeches. Concluding an address before the San Francisco Commonwealth Club, he was greeted with cries of "Go on! Go on!" When he addressed the Second Dearborn Conference of Agriculture, Industry, and Science, the "Chemurgicians" twice gave him standing ovations. His public relations ministry included more than delivering speeches. He promoted tours of the Tabernacle Choir. He personally guided nationally prominent business and political leaders through Salt Lake City and cultivated their friendship. He visited U.S. Presidents Warren G. Harding, Calvin Coolidge, Herbert Hoover, and Franklin D. Roosevelt at the White House. While President Grant was respected by his own people, non-Mormons also liked and idealized him.

The Church's sturdy growth during the period reflected its more positive image. Membership more than tripled during the half century; from the years 1900 to 1945 totals grew from 268,331 to 979,454. Prior to 1898 the Church had organized 37 stakes (16 were discontinued); by 1945 another 116 had been added. The Church's missionary force changed and increased accordingly, growing younger, attracting more unmarried individuals, and after 1898, including an increasing number of young women. At the turn of the century, fewer than 900 missionaries were called annually; by 1940 there were 2,117.

Missionary work continued to be a major preoccupation. The most ambitious new mission was Japan, opened in 1901 by missionaries led by Elder Heber J. Grant, then an apostle. Three years later the Mexican mission was reopened. The 1920s saw more than 11,000

German-speaking converts, though most converts came from English-speaking areas: Great Britain, Canada, and the United States, with the Southern States Mission being the most successful. Unfortunately, there as elsewhere, missionaries were subject to acts of physical violence. At the beginning of the century, annual convert baptisms were 3,786; a half century later the total had reached 7,877.

The Church sought to make its proselytizing more effective. Instead of dispatching missionaries without "purse and scrip," most now were financially supported by their families or local congregations. Missionary training classes were organized at Church academies and colleges. In the mid-1920s a Salt Lake City "Mission Home" for departing sisters and elders was inaugurated, where missionaries typically received lessons on proper diet, hygiene, etiquette, and especially missionary techniques and Church doctrine for two weeks. The era also produced new proselytizing tracts. Charles W. Penrose wrote a series entitled *Rays of Living Light*, James E. Talmage completed *The Great Apostasy*, and Ben E. Rich authored *A Friendly Discussion*. To preserve a sense of its heritage and to help tell its story, the Church purchased sites of significance to its early history (*see* HISTORICAL SITES): the CARTHAGE JAIL in Illinois (1903), where Joseph Smith and his brother Hyrum had been killed; a part of the Independence, Missouri, temple site (1904); Joseph Smith's birthplace in Sharon, Vermont (1905–1907); and the Smith homestead in Manchester, New York (1907). At each of these locations, the Church eventually constructed visitors centers.

Perhaps more than by expansion, the era was characterized by internal consolidation. Lorenzo Snow's succession to office was symptomatic. For the first time the accession of the senior-tenured apostle to the office of Church president was completed within days instead of the past interregnums of about three years. Recognizing the Church's increasing complexity, President Snow urged General Authorities to devote their full time to their ministry. By 1941 the question no longer was simply leadership efficiency but expansion. "The rapid growth of the Church in recent times, the constantly increasing establishment of new Wards and Stakes . . . [and] the steadily pressing necessity for increasing our missions in numbers and efficiency," the First Presidency noted in 1941, "have built up an apostolic service of the greatest magnitude" (*CR* [Apr. 1941]:94–95). In response to these new requirements, five men were appointed Assistants to the Twelve. In contrast to the short-term laity that continued to occupy most Church positions, "general" Church officers—about thirty in number—now received compensation and served full-time, lifelong ministries.

Priesthood governance was also altered. The first half of the century saw a steady decentralizing of decision making as stake and local leaders received enlarged authority. The Church reduced the size of stakes to make them more functional and placed new emphasis on "ward teaching." With smaller districts and more boys and men assigned to teaching, the percentage of families receiving monthly visits grew from 20 percent in 1911 to 70 percent a decade later. Finally, in a major departure from pioneer practice, members were urged to take secular disputes to civil and criminal courts rather than to Church tribunals. Once a means of regulating social and economic issues, Church courts now concerned themselves exclusively with Church discipline.

Priesthood quorums were strengthened. Priesthood meetings were now held weekly, with meeting quality improved by centrally generated lesson materials. President Joseph F. Smith in 1906 outlined a program of progressive priesthood advancement for male youth. Contingent on worthiness, young men received ordination to the office of deacon at the age of twelve, teacher at fifteen, and priest three years later. In turn, worthy men typically received the offices of elder and high priest, altering the nineteenth-century dominance of the seventy among adult men. In 1910 quorums of high priest and seventy were realigned to coincide with stake boundaries, allowing closer direction by local authorities.

The tendency toward consolidation was also manifest in the Church's auxiliary organizations. Youth programs, once informal, diverse, and locally administered, increasingly yielded to centrally directed age group programs and unified curricula. The children's Primary Association no longer served older youth, while the Young Men's Mutual Improvement Association (YMMIA) and its young women counterpart (YWMIA) included adolescents as young as twelve. At first both the national Boy Scout and Campfire Girl programs were used for younger MIA members, but soon the latter was dropped in favor of an indigenous program. Activity programs received increasingly strong emphasis. With Sunday School and now priesthood quorums providing doctrinal instruction, the MIA increasingly turned to dance, drama, music, and sports. Church headquarters produced a magazine for each auxiliary: The Primary had the *Children's Friend* (1902) and the Sunday School the *Juvenile Instructor* (1900), later known as the *Instructor* (1929). YMMIA had the *Improvement Era* (1897), YWMIA the *Young Woman's Journal* (1889); in 1929 the two joined forces, and the *Improvement Era* became the publication for both. Articles, curricula, and programs were periodically reviewed and correlated. For instance, a general Church Correlation Committee and the Social Advisory Committee combined to issue a pivotal and far-reaching report in 1921.

The Relief Society experienced these same trends. Its first three twentieth-century presidents, Zina D. H. YOUNG (1888–1901), Bathsheba W. SMITH (1901–1910), and Emmeline B. WELLS (1910–1921), all remembered the Nauvoo organization. For them women's meetings were to be spontaneous, spiritually active, and locally determined. The new century, however, redefined their vision. In 1901 a few lesson outlines were provisionally provided. Twelve years later, with the recommendation of a Church correlation committee, Relief Society leaders adopted a uniform, prescribed curriculum. They also implemented uniform meeting days (Tuesday), record books, and a monthly message for the visiting teaching women who made monthly home visits. In 1915 an official *Relief Society Magazine* replaced the semi-independent *Woman's Exponent*, a voice for Relief Society since 1872. While the First Presidency at first endorsed the continuation of female prayer healing—often undertaken in meetings on an impromptu basis—the practice dwindled and by mid-century was abolished. As a further sign of centralization under priesthood leadership, the Relief Society was housed in the Bishop's Building and increasingly received its direction from the Presiding Bishopric rather than the First Presidency. Though Relief Society had once played a role in developing and supervising the Primary and YWMIA, their supervision of the children's and youth auxiliaries ended.

The Relief Society's later presidents, Clarissa S. WILLIAMS (1921–1928), Louise Y. ROBISON (1928–1939), and Amy Brown

LYMAN (1940–1945), cooperated in these changes. Speaking for modernism and efficiency, they and their advisory boards set aside such past tasks as HOME INDUSTRY, SILK CULTURE, and commission retailing in favor of community outreach; "scientific," or professionally trained, social work; campaigns against alcohol, tobacco, and delinquency; and, during the Great Depression, public relief. The latter effort was crucial. "To the extent that Relief Society Organizations in Wards are operating in cooperation with Priesthood Quorums and Bishoprics," declared Elder Harold B. Lee, who led the Church's relief efforts, "just to that extent is there a security [welfare] program in that ward" (*Relief Society Magazine* 24 [Mar. 1937]:143). These efforts reflected the early-twentieth-century Mormon feminine ideal. Women were to uplift, soften, and assist. While women leaders continued to play an active role in the National and International Council of Women, the rank and file were less active in political, social, and professional roles than in homemaking.

Several doctrinal issues were clarified, another indication of systematization at work. From the early years of the Snow administration, Church authorities discussed how strictly the 1833 health revelation, the Word of Wisdom, should be obeyed. In 1921 the question was answered by making abstinence from alcohol, tobacco, tea, and coffee one of the standards for admission to temples. During the century's first three decades, the health code led most Latter-day Saints to support local, state, and national prohibition.

In 1909 the First Presidency issued a statement designed to clarify the Church position on evolution. While the method of creation was not discussed, the declaration held that "Adam was the first man and that he was created in the image of God." The issue remained troublesome, however. Along with the question of higher biblical criticism, it led to the resignation of three Brigham Young University professors in 1911 and to extended private discussion among Church leaders two decades later.

In 1916 the First Presidency and Quorum of the Twelve issued a second important doctrinal exposition entitled "The Father and the Son." Apparently occasioned by anti-Mormon pamphleteering charging the Church leaders with conferring divinity on Adam, the statement delineated the respective roles of the first two members of the Godhead. Shortly before his death, Joseph F. Smith received a vision of missionary work and spiritual existence in the afterlife, which was eventually included as Section 138 in the Doctrine and Covenants. In addition to specific matters, general LDS doctrine and history received systematic treatment, often for the first time, by such works as President Smith's *Gospel Doctrine*, Elder James E. Talmage's *Articles of Faith* and *Jesus the Christ*, and Elder B. H. Roberts's three-volume *New Witnesses for God.*

With its membership still predominantly American, the Church was especially affected by the events occurring in the United States during this period. Almost from the outset, President Grant's administration was beset with hard times. Farming and mining, two of Utah's main industries, slumped badly in the 1920s and especially in the 1930s during the Great Depression. President Grant carefully conserved Church finances, trimming expenditures and construction projects. Using his contacts with national business and political leaders, he kept key Utah and Church-owned enterprises afloat. He was also concerned for the individual Saint. After careful preparation, he announced in 1936 the Church Welfare Program, which sought self-sufficiency and sustenance for the needy by simultaneously providing both work and needed commodities.

Despite difficult times, the Church maintained its primary functions. Just prior to the economic downturn, it completed an imposing five-story building in Salt Lake City. Temples were completed in Hawaii (1919); Cardston, Alberta, Canada (1923); and Mesa, Arizona (1927). Education also received attention. Between 1875 and 1911, the Church established thirty-four all-purpose academies. However, as the century progressed, financial distress and the rising acceptance of public education brought changes, and many of the academies were closed or transferred to state control. The Church, however, did not entirely surrender its educative role. A released-time seminary program for high school students began in 1912, and during the 1920s, institutes of religion for college students were established, the first at the University of Idaho.

Twentieth-century wars and warfare demonstrated the distance the Church had traveled from nineteenth-century alienation and isolation. Latter-day Saints supported the Spanish-American War effort and U.S. involvement in the two twentieth-century world wars. In the former the First Presidency issued a statement affirming the loyalty of the Latter-day Saints and telegraphed local leaders to encourage enlistment. Utah became one of the first states to fill its initial quota. Involvement in World War I was even more substantial. At first uncertain of its proper role, the Church eventually helped Utahans oversubscribe the government's financial quota for the state. By September 1918 Utah had more than 18,000 men under arms, almost half of them volunteers. Participation in the Second World War was more dutiful, perhaps because of the private misgivings of President Grant and his counselor J. Reuben Clark over New Deal policymaking. Nevertheless, by April 1942, 6 percent of the total Church population served in the American forces or in defense-related industries; others served for Canada, Britain, and Germany.

While each conflict saw some pacifist currents and even opposition, the general tendency was supportive of the need to yield loyalty to constituted government. "The Church is and must be against war," the First Presidency declared in April 1942. Yet when "constitutional law . . . calls the manhood of the Church into the armed service of any country to which they owe allegiance, their highest civic duty requires that they heed that call" (*CR*, pp. 88–97).

While documenting religiosity is difficult, statistics suggest the impact of the Church on the everyday life of its people. Meeting attendance showed sturdy growth throughout the era. In 1920 weekly average attendance at sacrament meeting was 16 percent; in 1930, 19 percent; in 1940, 23 percent; and 1950, 25 percent. Suggestive of Church family ideals, LDS birthrates exceeded the national average, as did marriage rates. No doubt the Church health code is reflected in the fact that in 1945 the LDS death rate was about half the national average.

A closer view of statistics reveals that in the decades of the early twentieth century the number of children born per LDS family declined, the age at time of marriage increased, and divorce ratios often mirrored national trends—lingering behind but moving in the same direction as national trends, as if assimilation were simply incomplete.

The half-century brought social, cultural, and political integration; growth and consolidation; and programs that redefined and reapplied earlier Church ideals. But the era also produced indications that Church members were not immune to such broad currents as secularism and even materialism. For observers, at mid-century basic questions remained: Could the Church preserve its traditional values and energy? Or would its journey into the modern world cost the movement its identity and mission?

BIBLIOGRAPHY

For general surveys of the period:

Alexander, Thomas G. *Mormonism in Transition: A History of the Latter-day Saints, 1890–1930*. Urbana, Ill., 1986.

Allen, James B., and Glen M. Leonard. *The Story of the Latter-day Saints*. Salt Lake City, 1976.

Arrington, Leonard J., and Davis Bitton. *The Mormon Experience*. New York, 1979.

Church Educational System. *Church History in the Fulness of Times*. Salt Lake City, 1989.

Cowan, Richard O. *The Church in the Twentieth Century*. Salt Lake City, 1985.

Roberts, B. H. *A Comprehensive History of The Church of Jesus Christ of Latter-day Saints*. Salt Lake City, 1930.

For LDS programs, policies, and teachings during the period:

Alexander, Thomas G. "Between Revivalism and the Social Gospel: The Latter-day Saints Social Advisory Committee, 1916–1922." *BYU Studies* 23 (Winter 1983):19–39.

———. "The Reconstruction of Mormon Doctrine: From Joseph Smith to Progressive Theology." *Sunstone* 5 (July–Aug. 1980):24–33.

———. "'To Maintain Harmony': Adjusting to External and Internal Stress, 1890–1930." *Dialogue* 15 (Winter 1982):44–58.

Hartley, William G. "The Priesthood Reform Movement, 1908–1922." *BYU Studies* 13 (Winter 1973):137–56.

Hefner, Loretta L. "This Decade Was Different: Relief Society's Social Services Department, 1919–1929." *Dialogue* 15 (Autumn 1982):64–73.

RONALD W. WALKER
RICHARD W. SADLER

C. 1945–1990, POST–WORLD WAR II INTERNATIONAL ERA PERIOD

[*Since World War II, the Church has enjoyed—and had to cope with—rapid international growth. After summarizing postwar revitalization and the attendant increases in membership, the article focuses on the adaptations that accompanied growth and internationalization. In surveying recent developments, it provides an introduction to the contemporary Church.*

For additional information about Church growth during this period, see articles about the Church in Africa; Asia, East; Asia, South and Southeast; Australia; British Isles; Canada; Europe; Hawaii;

Mexico and Central America; Middle East; New Zealand; Oceania; Scandinavia; South America; *and* West Indies. *Consult also the biographies of those who served as Church President in this period: George Albert* Smith *(1945–1951); David O.* McKay *(1951–1970); Joseph Fielding* Smith *(1970–1972); Harold B.* Lee *(1972–1973); Spencer W.* Kimball *(1973–1985); Ezra Taft* Benson *(1985–1994) and Howard W.* Hunter *(1994–).*]

Throughout his life and ministry, President George Albert SMITH's prevailing message was one of love. It was fitting, therefore, that it was during his administration that goods were sent from America to Europe to help relieve the suffering of the Saints following World War II, especially those in Germany who had been devastated by war. In 1946 Ezra Taft BENSON, of the Council of the Twelve Apostles, directed the reopening of the European Mission and the Church's relief efforts there. He found branches disorganized, meetinghouses destroyed, and many members without homes. Most had lost possessions and everywhere there was pressing need for food and clothing. The Church's Welfare Services became a significant factor in the recovery of many Saints as well as some nonmembers.

Since the war had postponed everything from missionary work to building construction, it was necessary to reestablish and revitalize Church programs everywhere. The missionary force was rapidly rebuilt and hundreds of meetinghouses were constructed. Half of all the chapels in use in the mid-1950s were erected in the years following World War II, a period when more than half of all Church expenditures went for building projects.

BECOMING AN INTERNATIONAL CHURCH. The close of World War II marked the dawn of a new era in Church history in which a dominant theme was international growth. In 1947 Church membership reached one million, and by 1990 the total was over seven million. Growth was especially strong along America's West Coast, in Latin America, and, after 1978, in Africa. In 1950 the Church had 180 organized stakes, nearly half of them in Utah; in 1990 there were 1,700 stakes, with less than one-fourth in Utah. In 1950 the Church was organized in fewer than 50 nations or territories, but by 1990 it had expanded to 128. Less than 8 percent of the Church lived outside the United States and Canada in 1950, but forty years later this was approximately 35 percent. During the same period the number of missionaries grew from 6,000 to 40,000 and the number of temples increased from eight, only one of which was outside the United States, to forty-four, with twenty-three outside the United States.

This remarkable growth resulted from renewed efforts to fulfill the revelation given to Joseph Smith "that the kingdom . . . may become a great mountain and fill the whole earth" (D&C 109:72). Early in his administration President David O. MCKAY, the first to travel so extensively as Church President, toured missions in Europe, Latin America, Africa, and the South Pacific, dedicating two temple sites in Europe and announcing that a temple would be built in New Zealand. In 1955 he declared that the Church must "put forth every effort within reason and practicability to place within reach of Church members in these distant missions every educational and spiritual privilege that the Church has to offer" (*CR* [Apr. 1955]:25). Building temples, increasing the number of missions, organizing stakes worldwide, persuading the Saints to build up Zion in their homelands rather than emigrate to America, and eventually putting Church leadership into the hands of each country's native people were all significant steps toward fulfilling that goal. In addition, increasing emphasis was placed on calling local missionaries who, in some areas, later essentially replaced American missionaries.

Growth did not come without its problems, however, not the least of which was sorting out which practices, teachings, and programs really constituted the essence of the gospel and which were reflections of the American culture in which the Church had grown. To open the eyes of members—particularly Americans—to the need for defining the gospel in terms of universal principles, Church leaders spoke out with increasing frequency. In 1971, for example, Elder Bruce R. McConkie reminded some American Saints that in New Testament times even the apostles were so indoctrinated with the idea that the plan of salvation was limited to a particular people that they found it difficult to take it to gentile nations, and he applied the lesson to the modern Church. He called upon American Saints to rise above their biases, though there would be "some struggles and some difficulties, some prejudices, and some uncertainties along the way." Other peoples, he noted, "have a different background than we have, which is of no moment to the Lord. . . . It is no different to have different social customs than it is to have different languages. . . . And the Lord knows all languages" (Palmer, pp. 143, 147). In 1987 Elder Boyd K. Packer reminded a group of Church leaders that "We can't move [into various countries] with a 1947 Utah Church! Could it be that we are not prepared to take the *gospel* because we are not prepared to take (and they are not prepared to receive) all of the things we have wrapped up with it as extra baggage?" (as quoted in *Dialogue* 21 [Fall 1988]:97). The goal was to ennoble people of diverse cultures and perspectives to more fully find true brotherhood and sisterhood within the common spiritual bounds of the Church.

In 1974 President Spencer W. KIMBALL challenged members to "lengthen our stride" in carrying the gospel to all the earth, and urged them to pray that barriers might be removed. He appointed David M. Kennedy, former U.S. secretary of the treasury and ambassador-at-large, as the Church's international representative to work with governments in resolving problems that had hindered the Church's activities. In 1977 the Church was legally recognized in Poland, and in 1985 a temple was dedicated in the German Democratic Republic. The dramatic political revolutions of 1989–1990 opened other eastern bloc countries and led to the beginnings of LDS missionary work in the Soviet Union.

One of the far-reaching changes in the twentieth century was the revelation received by President Spencer W. Kimball in June 1978 extending priesthood blessings to all worthy male members. The result of long and earnest prayer, the revelation meant that "the long-promised day has come when every faithful, worthy man in the Church may receive the holy priesthood . . . without regard for race or color." Without delay, worthy blacks were sealed in temples and many received assignments as missionaries and leaders. In Ghana and Nigeria, where blacks had been pleading for the establishment of the Church for years, the Church grew rapidly, but it also expanded in other areas with large black populations. The first black General Authority, Elder Helvécio Martins of Brazil, was sustained at the general conference of the Church in April 1990.

ADMINISTRATIVE CHANGES. Numerous administrative changes also reflected the demands of Church growth. In 1967 stakes were organized into regions. Beginning in 1975, several regions were organized into areas, and by 1984 area presidencies, each consisting of three General Authorities, were assigned responsibility for stakes throughout the world.

In 1975 President Kimball announced the organization of the First Quorum of the Seventy, members of which were General Authorities of the Church and included the former Assistants to the Twelve. In 1989 the Second Quorum of the Seventy was organized; these General Authorities serve for terms of three or five years. In 1978 the practice was begun of placing members of the Seventy on emeritus status for reasons of health or age, and the following year the Patriarch to the Church also became an emeritus.

General Authorities also took steps to more effectively coordinate Church programs and, beginning in 1961, placed greater emphasis on "priesthood correlation." Under the chairmanship of Elder Harold B. Lee, committees at Church headquarters planned, prepared, and reviewed curricula and activities for all organizations or age groups. They defined more carefully the unique roles of each organization and eliminated unnecessary duplication. Leaders focused on the home as the most effective place for teaching and applying gospel principles. Family home evening received renewed emphasis, and beginning in 1965 attractive manuals providing lesson helps were issued.

In the early 1970s there was also a consolidation of administrative responsibilities at Church headquarters. Agencies were grouped into several large departments, each under the jurisdiction of one or more General Authorities, with full-time professionals generally managing day-to-day operations. For example, the welfare, social services, and health programs were consolidated into a Welfare Services Department. A tangible symbol of this consolidation was the new twenty-eight-story Church office building in Salt Lake City, bringing most Church administrative units together. In 1970, functions of Aaronic Priesthood and the Young Men's Mutual Improvement Association were combined. In 1971 the publishing program was consolidated. Magazines in other languages than English were unified in 1967, with standardized content except for local matters.

Other changes came as rapid international growth increased the travel and administrative load of Church leaders. In the 1970s stake presidents were authorized to "set apart" full-time missionaries, ordain bishops and patriarchs, and dedicate chapels. General Authorities met in conference with individual stakes less frequently but, beginning in 1971, the Church began holding "area conferences," where a delegation of General Authorities met with the Saints gathered from geographic regions. In 1979 the number of stake conferences each year was reduced from four to two, and in the 1980s regional or multiregional conferences replaced area conferences.

CHURCH EDUCATION. Between 1950 and 1990 total enrollment in the Church's educational programs increased from 38,400 to 442,500. Full-time enrollment at Brigham Young University soared from 5,400 in 1950 to nearly 25,000 by 1975, leading to an enrollment ceiling. Rather than devoting ever larger amounts to higher education, funds increasingly went to meet more basic needs associated with worldwide growth. The major expansion in enrollment came in the area of religious education. Since the early twentieth century, students in predominantly LDS communities had attended "released time" seminary classes adjacent to their secondary schools. Beginning in California in the 1950s, "early morning" seminaries convened in church buildings near public secondary schools. After 1968, in areas where members were even more scattered, young people received "home study" seminary materials. The Church also increased the number of institutes of religion placed adjacent to college and university campuses. By 1990 seminary or institute programs were conducted in seventy-four nations or territories.

The Church also gave special attention to the religious life of college students. In 1956 the first student stake, with twelve wards, was organized on the Brigham Young University campus. This provided Church services that ministered directly to student needs and offered expanded opportunities for leadership. The plan spread to other areas where there were enough students to justify it. Subjective evidence suggested greater spiritual growth; and in such statistically measurable matters as temple marriage and attendance at meetings, student wards led the Church.

In some areas of the Pacific and Latin America, areas of particularly rapid Church growth where public education was not widely available, the Church returned to its earlier practice of establishing schools for religious instruction and to teach educational basics. It established forty elementary and secondary schools in Mexico, and established a junior college on the outskirts of Mexico City. As better public educational facilities developed, the Church closed many schools.

BUILDING PROGRAM. New congregations required new buildings. Even with two or three wards sharing most buildings, the Church found it necessary to complete more than one new meetinghouse every day. Potential costs were enormous, and in many areas the local Saints could not afford to raise their share.

One solution emerged when the Church encountered a labor shortage while erecting school buildings in the South Pacific. Beginning in 1950, it called young men as "building missionaries" to donate their labor for two years. As they completed buildings at a much lower cost, experienced builders taught them construction skills; labor missionaries also learned marketable skills from experienced builders. In the 1950s and 1960s building missionaries erected schools and chapels in the South Pacific, Latin America, Europe, and elsewhere. Later, in an effort to minimize construction and maintenance costs, the building department developed a series of standardized plans that could be adapted to different locations and expanded as needed.

Though general Church funds assisted with meetinghouses, local congregations were expected to contribute not only labor but also a significant portion of the money needed—in addition to paying regular tithes and offerings. With a view toward easing the financial burden on local congregations, the share borne by local Saints gradually diminished until, by 1989, local contribution was no longer required.

By the 1980s, new meetinghouses were generally smaller and sometimes more austere than earlier ones, but this approach allowed the Church to erect hundreds of chapels annually, and especially to provide badly needed meeting places in developing areas. It was also a move towards equality. Money that might have gone to build more expensive buildings in affluent areas instead provided comfortable places for worship throughout the Church.

TECHNOLOGY AND THE MODERN CHURCH. The Church actively seeks to harness the astonishing developments in modern technology to enhance its administrative capabilities and to aid in delivering its spiritual message. Since the Church installed its first computer in the

Financial Department in 1962, it has made use of this technology in myriad ways, including in architectural design, a computerized membership record system, automated accounting, processing missionary papers, record keeping at both the general and local level, and in providing resources for historical and genealogical research.

Perhaps no Church activity has felt the impact of modern technology more than genealogical work. As Church membership grew, so did the need for more effective means of gathering and processing names for temple work. The Genealogical Department (now the Family History Department) microfilmed vital records from around the world, making them available in its library in Salt Lake City and in hundreds of family history centers throughout the world. In the 1960s, the Genealogical Department also began using the computer to organize names obtained from these records. Since 1978, designated Church members have been devoting four or more hours of weekly service "extracting" information from microfilms for the sake of temple work. The Family History Department also produced Personal Ancestral File, a widely used computerized genealogical program, and began making key genealogical data available on laser disks.

Technology touched the temple in other ways. Motion picture and video technology allowed temple instructions to be presented more efficiently and more effectively. Because this could be done in one room instead of the former series of four rooms, temples could be built smaller and thus were less expensive to construct, making it possible for more members throughout the world to have a temple nearby. The new technology also made it possible to present the ordinances in several languages simultaneously, if necessary.

The effect of television on Church communications and the Church public image was also dramatic. General conferences of the Church were first broadcast on KSL Television in Salt Lake City in 1949, and by the mid-1960s one or more sessions of each conference were being televised coast-to-coast in the United States. In the 1980s the Church developed a satellite communication system connected to stake centers throughout the world so that Latter-day Saints could view both conference and other Church-initiated programs.

MISSIONARY WORK. By 1990 over two-thirds of the Church's annual growth came from convert baptisms. Approximately 30,000 of more than 40,000 full-time missionaries were young men ages nineteen to twenty-one; single women twenty-one years of age or older and couples who had reached retirement age made up most of the remainder.

Considerable attention was given to improving proselytizing techniques and abilities. After much experimentation, a systematic plan based on a series of regularized lesson discussions was officially adopted in the 1950s. After considerable refinement and modification, by 1990 the plan focused less on memorization on the part of the missionaries and more on their ability to rely on the Spirit in the presentation of outlined subject matter.

Missionaries were also given more effective training, especially in languages. In 1963 a Language Training Mission, later known as Missionary Training Center, was established near Brigham Young University, and five years later a similar program opened near the Church College of Hawaii. By 1990 missionaries were receiving intensive language and missionary training in fourteen missionary training centers around the world, though about 75 percent were attending the Provo center.

Innovations in the missionary program included encouraging more nonproselytizing activities and Christian service. In 1971, for instance, "health missionaries" began teaching the basics of nutrition, sanitation, and disease prevention, especially in developing countries. By 1990 all missionaries were urged to spend two to four hours a week in community service, in addition to proselytizing. Also, older missionary couples were often assigned to nonproselytizing Church service, including health and welfare work, leadership training, staffing visitors centers and doing other public relations activities, assisting patrons in the Church's various family history centers, temple service missions, and teaching missions.

PUBLIC ISSUES AND SOCIAL CONCERNS Though the Church attempted to distance itself from direct political involvement, Church leaders nevertheless from time to time declared official positions on moral issues. The First Presidency publicly lamented the growing flood of pornography, the widespread practice of birth control, and abortion, and the general decline in moral standards, including the rising number of divorces and the increased prominence of homosexuality. In 1968 the Church became directly involved in Utah's political process by openly opposing liquor-by-the-drink. It has also made public pronouncements in favor of Sunday closing laws and state right-to-work laws and against state lotteries.

Amid the intense civil rights conflict that characterized the United States in the 1960s the First Presidency openly called for "full civil equality for all of God's children," and specifically urged Latter-day Saints to work for civil rights for blacks. In the 1970s, as the controversy in America over women's rights escalated, the First Presidency took a public stance in favor of full equality before the law for women but, at the same time, publicly opposed the Equal Rights Amendment as anti-family. The First Presidency was also deeply concerned with the morality of the nuclear arms race and officially denounced it in 1980 and again in 1981.

In contrast to the early twentieth century when most Latter-day Saints lived in predominately rural settings, since mid-century, most have lived in urban centers. The hectic lifestyle in large cities created added emotional strains, and an array of attractions and temptations tended to pull family members in different directions. Responding to these and other needs, the Church instituted a series of social programs. Since 1919 the Relief Society had operated an adoption agency and provided foster homes for disadvantaged children. This was expanded. The Indian Student Placement Services, begun in the 1950s under the chairmanship of Elder Spencer W. Kimball, extended to thousands of Native American children the advantages of attending good schools while living in wholesome LDS family environments. A "youth guidance" program provided counseling to families in need. These three programs, required by law to employ licensed professional social workers, were combined in 1969 to form the Church's Social Services Department. This department also sponsored youth day camps, programs for members in prison, and counseling for alcohol or drug abusers.

Church leaders also began to show more concern for the special needs of unmarried men and women. Whether divorced, widowed, or simply never married, their social and spiritual needs were often not being met through traditional Church activity oriented toward couples and families. In the 1970s special programs for young single adults as well as older singles were created under the auspices of the priesthood and Relief Society. Through self-directed councils at the ward, stake, and regional level, they participated in dances and other cultural activities and found broader opportunities to become acquainted with other members their own age who shared common interests. In addition, wards for young singles were organized, first in the Emigration Stake in Salt Lake City, and then in other areas.

RETURN TO BASICS. One of President Ezra Taft Benson's clarion calls to the Saints in the 1980s was to return to traditional values. In particular, he urged regular study of the Book of Mormon as a means to strengthen faith in Christ and to receive guidance in meeting contemporary challenges. His call, however, was only one manifestation of the efforts of modern Church leaders to respond to the ever-deepening challenges of the world and to lead the Saints in a return to basics.

In 1972 the adult Gospel Doctrine class in Sunday School began a systematic study of the standard works. The scriptures were the only texts, and they were to be studied in an eight-year (later four-year) rotation. Soon all Church curricula were tied to the scriptures. To support the curriculum and encourage individual scripture study, Church leaders supervised the publication of new editions of the standard works, each cross-referenced to the others. The Church publication of the King James Version of the Bible, in 1979, contained an important 800-page appendix that included a Bible dictionary, a topical guide to all the scriptures, maps, and extracts from the Joseph Smith Translation of the Bible. In 1981 new editions of the other standard works appeared, including additional study helps.

The "return to basics" theme was echoed also in many other changes in Church policies and programs. In 1980 the Church meeting schedule was consolidated into a single three-hour block on Sundays, replacing the traditional schedule of priesthood meeting and Sunday School in the morning, sacrament meeting in the late afternoon or evening, and auxiliary meetings during the week. The move simplified transportation challenges for many members, but Church leaders emphasized that the central objective was to allow more time for families to study the scriptures or engage in other appropriate Sabbath activities together.

Beginning in 1990 in the United States and Canada and extended to other parts of the world in 1991, ward and stake budget donations were no longer required from members; all operating expenses of local units would be paid from tithes and offerings. The uniform system promoted greater equality, cutting many local operating budgets while increasing others. In explaining the new policy, Elder Boyd K. Packer of the Council of the Twelve called it an inspired "course correction," part of an overall effort to get back to basics (*Ensign* 10 [May 1990]:89–91). The metaphor could well be applied to much of what had happened since 1945.

Church members have generally accepted changes well, and have seen in them an opportunity for further spiritual growth. As a result, in 1990 the Church was moving more rapidly than ever before toward being able to accommodate diverse nationalities, language groups, and cultures. Church leaders continued to emphasize the traditional doctrines, but general conference addresses increasingly tended also to define Sainthood in terms of what Elder M. Russell Ballard characterized in April 1990, as the "small and simple things": love, service, home, family, and worship of the Savior (*Ensign* 10 [May 1990]:6–8). These are among the universals that constitute the essence of what it means to be a Latter-day Saint.

BIBLIOGRAPHY

Much has been written about this period in professional journals. A few broad treatments are mentioned in the introduction to this history section. See also Spencer J. Palmer, *The Expanding Church* (Salt Lake City, 1978). For additional information, consult the bibliographies accompanying the biographies of Church Presidents who served during this period: George Albert Smith, David O. McKay, Joseph Fielding Smith, Harold B. Lee, Spencer W. Kimball, and Ezra Taft Benson.

JAMES B. ALLEN
RICHARD O. COWAN

HISTORY OF THE CHURCH (HISTORY OF JOSEPH SMITH)

The seven-volume history of The Church of Jesus Christ of Latter-day Saints titled *History of the Church* covers less than two decades and might better be titled "The History of Joseph Smith." It is the official history of the Church's founding generation, still in print and still widely used. The motivation for compiling this early history was fourfold: (1) to obey a commandment of the Lord (D&C 21:1); (2) to preserve a record of the Church for later generations; (3) to combat and correct anti-Mormon publications; and (4) to provide a written record as a protection against false accusations and lawsuits (*see* SMITH, JOSEPH: LEGAL TRIALS OF JOSEPH SMITH).

Although the responsibility for keeping a history of the Church was delegated to the Church recorder and historian, Joseph Smith was the prime motivator. He selected able men, gave them regular encouragement and instruction, and provided space for them in his home or store. Because of his lack of formal education, Joseph Smith depended on others to do most of the actual writing of both the sources and the completed history. More than two dozen scribes and writers are known to have assisted him.

After several early attempts, Joseph Smith and his clerk, James Mulholland, began this history at Commerce, Illinois, on June 10, 1839 (*HC* 3:375–77). Originally titled "The History of Joseph Smith," it began with a first-person account of Joseph Smith's early visions (*see* VISIONS OF JOSEPH SMITH), which had been written in the spring of 1838 (*HC* 3:25–26). Although little of the subsequent history was dictated or written by the Prophet himself, writers used his diaries where available and retained the first-person narrative style throughout.

A series of scribes, clerks, and Church historians labored sporadically on the history for nearly twenty years, through difficult periods of persecution, pioneer travel, and western colonization. Written as annals rather than narrative history, the manuscript version fills six large journals called the "Manuscript History of the Church." Willard Richards, appointed as Joseph Smith's "private Sect. & Historian" on December 21, 1842, compiled most of the history—over half after the death of Joseph Smith on June 27, 1844. With the assistance of his adopted son and clerk, Thomas Bullock, Richards completed the narrative to March 1, 1843, before his own death in 1854. It was left to George A. Smith, his successor as Church Historian, to compile the history of the MARTYRDOM OF JOSEPH AND HYRUM SMITH, expand notes of the Prophet's sermons, and continue the narrative into August 1844, when Brigham YOUNG was sustained to lead the Church.

The Church published this history serially in its periodicals, first in the *Times and Seasons* at Nauvoo and then in Salt Lake City's *Deseret News* from 1852 to 1857. The seven-volume version published by the Church today is a product of the editing of B. H. Roberts of the Seventy, who worked intermittently on the project from 1902 to 1932. Because it quotes extensively from letters, minutes, and diaries of the day, the *History of the Church* has often been referred to as the *Documentary History of the Church*, or *DHC*.

Emphasizing the role of God in human affairs, this history falls within the Judeo-Christian tradition of "providential history." Because it was not written in a literary vacuum, it exhibits characteristics and flaws commonly found in the history and biography of its day: unacknowledged ghostwriting, edited sources, and a lack of balance. The most frequent distortion is the changing of an associate's third-person description of Joseph Smith's words and actions to a first-person account attributed to Joseph Smith, thereby conveying a false sense that he wrote it. Nonetheless, resting as it does on extensive documents from the period and compiled by persons who were eyewitnesses to the events, the factual content of the history has proven reliable.

BIBLIOGRAPHY

Jessee, Dean C. "The Writing of Joseph Smith's History." *BYU Studies* 11 (Summer 1971):439–73.

———. *The Personal Writings of Joseph Smith*. Salt Lake City, 1984.

———. *The Papers of Joseph Smith*, Vol. 1. Salt Lake City, 1989.

HOWARD C. SEARLE

HOME INDUSTRIES

From the earliest days of the Church, home industry, in one form or another, has been advocated among the Latter-day Saints. Included were the more common form of cottage industries and also both light and heavy manufacturing of most of the community's consumable goods. Home industry and manufacturing were to promote thrift and self-sufficiency among the members, to serve as a buffer against possible corrosive influences (greed, materialism, inequality), to provide employment for the poor, and to protect the Saints from persecution or to prepare them for further upheavals and expulsions such as had driven the Saints from state to state.

Home industries became Church policy in 1831, with the establishment of the law of CONSECRATION, which continued in various forms through the nineteenth century (*see* UNITED ORDERS). From 1831 to 1838, the Church sought to provide material necessities for all according to need. The Saints were to limit consumption voluntarily and, when production exceeded demand, to give the surpluses to the Church. Members pledged time, labor, energy, ability, and material possessions for the good of the group. In pioneer Utah it was not unusual for men to be called on missions to devote full time to establish specific industries (*see* PIONEER ECONOMY).

As European converts immigrated to the UTAH TERRITORY during the 1850s, they were encouraged to bring designs and tools for use in manufacturing. Home industries thrived through an abundance of skilled artisans among new immigrant converts. To support a self-sufficient regional economy (autarky), and to discourage a dependence on imports, the Saints developed an exchange economy. Leaders and members gave full patronage to home manufacturers, who were given preferential treatment and verbal support by leaders in Church conferences and in state legislative sessions.

Thus, in the Utah Territory, the Church, the government, and individuals were involved in a collective entrepreneurship that was supportive of immigration and public works programs. The mutual exchange of goods and labor among residents of the region developed the economic foundations of a commonwealth. Goods available in excess of personal needs were exported to bring money into the territory. This approach also involved dedication to building the kingdom of God, so encouragement of home manufacture included caution against exorbitant profits and speculation.

The contributions of women were fundamental to making these economic strategies a success. President Brigham YOUNG encouraged women to study mathematics, accounting, and medicine, among other things, so that they could provide clerking, bookkeeping, shop keeping, health care, and other professional services, thereby releasing the men to perform more strenuous physical labor (*JD* 13:61).

Both the poor and the not-so-poor were encouraged to live more frugally. Women learned not to waste anything of substance; and the desire, ideally, was for domestic and home manufacture to produce most necessary articles used for food, clothing, and shelter. Such industry was to sustain families religiously, politically, socially, and financially.

In 1867, the Church assigned to the Relief Society the responsibility of teaching the poor to provide for themselves. Female home manufacturing societies supported cottage industries that employed women and children and encouraged families to resist the purchasing of goods not made at home. The Relief Society became a major institutional sponsor of these self-sufficiency programs. For example, approximately 150 units of the Relief Society throughout the territory helped to raise silkworms and to reel and weave the filament produced for the fledgling silk industry (*see* SILK CULTURE). The need for production of materials not available locally engendered the establishment of substitute industries. Women experimented with the processing of such native plants as stinging nettle, milkweed, and red top grass for use as textiles.

Brigham Young and other leaders encouraged every branch of manufacture that could be adapted to the climate and the territory. A seemingly endless variety of products included downy beds, molasses, milk products, fruits, vegetables and grains, woolen and silk goods, woven rye and native grass products, all kinds of clothing articles, brooms, ink, leather, felt, alum, coppers, dyes, soap, matches, iron, school books, jewelry, perfume, paper, rope, harnesses, wagons, machinery, sacking, carpets, tools, sugar, flax, bonnets, and lumber.

In 1867–1869, home industries continued to be a major focus of both the Relief Society and the Young Women's Retrenchment Association. These organizations helped to make homemade articles fashionable and to discourage the purchase of imported goods. The coming of the railroad in 1869 and the resultant influx of outside businesses required a redoubling of these efforts to preserve the independence of the local economy.

Village cooperatives were established to provide the exchange and distribution of the products of home industry. Zion's Cooperative Mercantile Institution (ZCMI) was a major institution for carrying out such strategies, and the department store followed a policy of preference for the home industries of Mormon manufacturers. In addition, stake Boards of Trade were organized to help the cause of home manufacture. As late as 1878, ZCMI had a published policy of providing what was needed for home consumption but exporting the best for profit.

The success of Mormon home industry depended upon geography, economics, and ideology. The expansion of the United States through migration, facilitated by the transcontinental railroad, brought about an effective end to autarky and to LDS protectionist philosophy. Ultimately, however, the economic policies of Brigham Young and the Church had affected all of the mountain West and provided a pattern of economic survival copied and adapted by some other groups as they settled in the Great Basin. Later, the ideals of self-sufficiency, cooperation, and preparedness were reemphasized during the Great Depression of the 1930s and resulted in the implementation of a Church welfare services program.

Today, cottage industries still are a source of income, usually secondary and on a small scale, for some LDS households. A retail outlet known as Mormon Handicraft was established by the Church in 1937 to provide sale on consignment of high quality, hand-crafted products of household industries. In 1986 the Deseret Book Company purchased Mormon Handicraft and presently operates the store, which is renowned for hand-sewn quilts, needlework, and other craft items.

In harmony with the ideals that originally spawned the advocacy of home industry, Latter-day Saints today are counseled to grow vegetable gardens, make or preserve whatever commodities they can, and avoid debt and materialism. Work (industry) is expected to be the "ruling principle" in the lives of the Saints, and sharing of one's resources in service to the poor is considered a hallmark virtue of a true Saint.

[*See also* Economic History.]

BIBLIOGRAPHY

Arrington, Leonard J. *Great Basin Kingdom.* Cambridge, Mass., 1958.

Burgess-Olson, Vicky. *Family Structure and Dynamics in Early Utah Mormon Families 1847–1885.* Evanston, Ill., 1975.

Young, Brigham. *Discourses of Brigham Young*, ed. John A. Widtsoe. Salt Lake City, 1971.

MAXINE LEWIS ROWLEY

HORNE, MARY ISABELLA

From 1870 to 1904 Mary Isabella Hales Horne (1818–1905) was president of the Senior Cooperative Retrenchment Association, an organization that spearheaded a number of women's activities, including a Churchwide retrenchment from "worldly," or materialistic, pursuits in the 1870s, and a movement in support of plural marriage in the 1880s. During most of the three decades, she was also president of the Salt Lake Stake Relief Society and treasurer of the Central (later General) Board of Relief Society.

Mary Isabella Hales was born on November 20, 1818, in Rainham, Kent County, England. She was the oldest of seven children born to Stephen and Mary Ann Hales. Her father was a shoemaker and her mother a seamstress.

The Hales family immigrated to York (now Toronto), Canada, where Isabella met Joseph Horne at a Methodist camp meeting in 1834. They were married on May 9, 1836, and were baptized members of The Church of Jesus Christ of Latter-day Saints in July 1836 by Orson Hyde, an apostle. The newlyweds became friends of the Prophet Joseph SMITH, and both had a firm testimony of his prophetic calling. In 1838, they gathered with the Saints to Far West, Missouri, and subsequently suffered through the violent expulsion of the Saints from Missouri. They moved to Quincy and NAUVOO, Illinois, and then crossed the plains to the Salt Lake Valley in 1847. The Hornes had fifteen children, including three sets of twins.

In 1869 President Brigham YOUNG challenged Isabella Horne to encourage the women of the Church to spend less time preparing elegant meals and sewing fancy clothing, and more time nurturing their spiritual development. On February 10, 1870, the Senior Cooperative Retrenchment Association was formally organized, with Mary Isabella Horne as president. Under her direction, the association also supported local Relief Society, Primary, and young women's organizations; the *Woman's Exponent*; the 1876 centennial fair; and the UNITED ORDER. It also supported mass meetings in which resolutions were drafted in strong support of woman suffrage.

In December 1877, Isabella Horne was called to preside over the Salt Lake Stake Relief Society. She served twenty-six years, directing a total of sixty-five ward Relief Society presidencies. She presided over Relief Society sessions of the women's conferences of the stake, which were attended by many women from throughout the territory until the first general auxiliary conferences were inaugurated in 1889. She also instituted a nurse training program in the stake that was later adopted by Relief Society's general officers. In 1880 the Central Board of the Relief Society was organized and she was appointed treasurer, a position she held until 1901.

In addition to these assignments, Isabella Horne served as a member of the DESERET HOSPITAL committee (1882–1894); as a counselor to Zina D. H. YOUNG in the presidency of the Deseret Silk Association, established in 1876; and as president of the Women's Cooperative Mercantile and Manufacturing Institution from 1890 to 1905.

She died on August 25, 1905, at the age of eighty-six. At her death, Emmeline B. WELLS, another prominent leader among Utah women, said of her that she "was a born leader, a sort of General among women and indeed in this respect might surpass most men, of extraordinary ability. . . . A woman of great force of character, and wonderful ability, such a one as might stand at the head of a great institution and carry it on successfully. . . . Sister Horne can appropriately be called a stalwart, a champion for the rights of her own sex, and indeed for all mankind" [*Woman's Exponent* 36 (Apr. 1908):58].

BIBLIOGRAPHY

Horne, Mrs. Joseph. "Migration and Settlement of the Latter-day Saints." Typescript, 1884. Bancroft Library, University of California, Berkeley.

Kramer, Lyneve Wilson, and Eva Durrant Wilson. "Mary Isabella Hales Horne: Faithful Sister and Leader." *Ensign* 12 (Aug. 1982):63–66.

SUSAN ARRINGTON MADSEN

HUNTER, HOWARD W.

Howard William Hunter (1907–) is the fourteenth President of The Church of Jesus Christ of Latter-day Saints. Perhaps the best summary of his life is a statement he made in 1967. "Real Christians," he said, "must understand that the gospel of Jesus Christ is not just a gospel of belief; it is a plan of action. His gospel is a gospel of imperatives, and the very nature of its substance is a call to action" (*CR*, Apr. 1967, p. 115). His life bears witness to that imperative.

Howard Hunter was born in Boise, Idaho, on November 14, 1907, to John William Hunter and Nellie Marie Rasmussen. His mother was a lifelong member of the Church; her grandparents were baptized in Denmark and Norway before emigrating to Utah, where they met and married. Howard's father, known as Will, descended from Scottish emigrants who came to the American West from Scotland, and from early settlers in Colonial New England. His great-grandmother joined the Church in Nauvoo, Illinois, and crossed the plains in 1852. Will was not a Latter-day Saint, but he supported his wife's activity in the Church. Rather than allowing his children to be baptized at the customary age of eight, he insisted that they wait until they could better understand that commitment. So it wasn't until Howard was twelve and a half that he and his sister, Dorothy, two years younger than he, were baptized.

Howard's commitment to his faith was clear even before then. In the early 1920s, the ward members were asked in sacrament meeting to help fund a new meetinghouse; Howard was the first to stand. He pledged twenty-five dollars—a considerable sum for a boy in those days.

Howard attended Lowell Elementary School and later Boise High School, where he excelled as a student and served as a major in the ROTC—the highest rank awarded at the time. He was also a member of one of the first Boy Scout troops in Idaho and became the second Eagle Scout in Boise and perhaps in Idaho.

Howard was interested in music and learned to play several instruments, including the saxophone, clarinet, drums, and piano. As a junior in high school, he organized a dance orchestra, Hunter's Croonaders, that played in Boise and nearby communities. The orchestra also played for patrons of the SS *President Jackson* on a ten-week tour of the Orient. After the tour, in 1927, Howard returned to Boise to find that his father had joined the Church. Howard was elated.

The next year, Howard went to California to visit a friend. He liked what he saw and decided to stay. He moved in with an uncle and aunt in the Los Angeles area and soon found employment in banking. In April 1928, he started to work at the Bank of Italy (later

Bank of America), working his way up from a batch-proof clerk to a consolidation officer. When the First Exchange Bank later offered him a position with greater opportunities, he took it.

By then he had met a vivacious woman who was working as an assistant personnel director—Clara May (Claire) Jeffs. They became engaged early in 1931. The day before their marriage in the Salt Lake Temple on June 10, 1931, the couple received some valuable counsel: stay out of debt. Following that advice kept them from suffering the worst of the Great Depression.

Even so, the bank where Howard worked closed in January 1932. For a time, he worked at odd jobs. Then, in 1934, he was hired as a title examiner for the Los Angeles County Flood Control District. That economic success, however, was followed by personal tragedy: The Hunters' first child—Howard William, Jr.—died six months after birth.

Howard's work with the district included checking details at the courthouse, which whetted his interest in law. For the next five years he worked during the day and attended law school at night. He would get up early to study before catching a bus to work, and he studied most Saturdays as well. He even read his law books in hospital waiting rooms while Claire gave birth to their other sons, John and Richard. Howard graduated cum laude from Southwestern University Law School in June 1939, then took and passed the California bar exam a few months later.

With law school behind him, Howard flung himself into Church service. He had already served in the youth programs of both the Inglewood Ward and the Hollywood Stake, including service as stake representative to the Los Angeles Boy Scout Council. He had also taught a class in genealogy—one of his lifelong hobbies. But now much more was asked of him. The Hunters had moved to Alhambra in 1936, and in September 1940, the Alhambra Ward was divided, forming the new El Sereno Ward. Howard was called as bishop—one of the youngest in Southern California. He served during World War II, a time when many men and women were entering military service. Because of the manpower shortage, he also served for a time as Scoutmaster. Looking forward to a new meetinghouse after the war, he and his ward members spent many nights trimming onions at a pickle factory to raise funds.

As a lawyer, Howard had many opportunities to enter into business dealings. He formed a real-estate partnership with a friend, and they also organized a small oil company. His primary interest, though, was in church and family. In 1948, Howard and his family moved to Arcadia, where he was called to serve on the Pasadena Stake high council. Two years later, in February 1950, he was sustained as the president of the Pasadena Stake.

President Hunter became known as an indefatigable administrator. He oversaw a pilot program in Southern California of the Church's early-morning seminary program and served on the Los Angeles Temple building committee. He also became chairman of the regional council of stake presidents, responsible for members in an area stretching from San Luis Obispo to the Mexican border. President Hunter was much respected for his compassion, wisdom, and leadership style, which combined humility with a no-nonsense approach to getting the job done.

Then, unexpectedly, he was called to be a member of the Quorum of the Twelve Apostles. He was ordained October 15, 1959—the seventy-fourth to be so ordained in this dispensation.

His service as one of the Lord's special witnesses took him around the world and broadened his appreciation for different cultures. He served as president of the Polynesian Cultural Center in Hawaii, building it into a major tourist attraction that helps meet the educational costs for numerous Polynesian students at Brigham Young University—Hawaii. In the Holy Land, against great opposition from both Jewish and Arab groups, Elder Hunter worked tirelessly to gain approval for Brigham Young University to build the Jerusalem Center, which was dedicated in May 1989. As chairman of the advisory board for the New World Archaeological Foundation, he made many trips to archaeological sites in Guatemala and Mexico.

Elder Hunter served for ten years as president of the Utah Genealogical Society. In that capacity, he helped make far-reaching changes in the computerization and microfilming of records and in streamlining many administrative aspects of temple work. Elder Hunter also served as Church historian, and for many years he was on the board of trustees of Brigham Young University and the Church Educational System.

On June 2, 1988, after the death of President Marion G. Romney,

Elder Hunter was sustained and set apart as president of the Quorum of the Twelve Apostles. He continued to travel extensively and tirelessly in his service to Latter-day Saints around the world. He also served as chairman of the Church's Correlation Executive Committee, as a member of the Church Investment Advisory Committee, and on several other committees. In addition, he was chairman of the board and of the executive committee of Beneficial Life Insurance Company and served on the boards of many other corporations.

President Hunter's service on regional and national Boy Scout councils has kept him in close contact with the younger members of the Church. Scouting has always been close to his heart; some of his most treasured memories are of camping with his Scouts and of running Oregon's Rogue River in homemade kayaks with his sons. In 1978 he received the Distinguished Eagle Scout Award from the Great Salt Lake Council.

President Hunter's service has been distinguished by his compassion, his high personal and professional standards, and his patience, thoroughness, humor, and intelligence. His public addresses often exhibit his training in syllogistic argument as well as his gospel and historical scholarship, his empathy, and his love for the Savior. A common theme has been the divinity of Jesus Christ and the reality of his presence in our lives.

One of Elder Hunter's most insightful discourses was delivered in October 1984—a year after his wife Claire died. For twelve years, she had suffered a series of debilitating strokes and other medical problems. Elder Hunter had insisted on caring for her as long as he could. In that general conference address, he traced the history of Mary Ann Baker's hymn, "Master, the Tempest Is Raging," then said, "We will all have some adversity in our lives. . . . Some of it may even strain our faith in a loving God who has the power to administer relief in our behalf.

"To those anxieties I think the Father of us all would say, 'Why are ye so fearful? how is it that ye have no faith?' And of course that has to be faith for the whole journey, the entire experience, the fulness of our life, not simply around the bits and pieces and tempestuous moments. At the end of the journey, an end none of us can see now, we will say, 'Master, the terror is over. . . . Linger, Oh, blessed Redeemer! Leave me alone no more'" (*CR*, Oct. 1984, p. 43).

President Hunter has been no stranger to adversity and sorrow. He suffered, then recovered from, a heart attack; underwent quadruple bypass surgery; had cancer surgery; had major surgery on his spine; and had several other illnesses. But he has experienced a good measure of joy too. On April 12, 1990, he rejoiced to marry Inis Egan.

On June 5, 1994, Howard W. Hunter was called, sustained, and set apart as the President of The Church of Jesus Christ of Latter-day Saints.

In his first statement to the press as the President of the Church, President Hunter said: "I would invite all members of the Church to live with ever more attention to the life and example of the Lord Jesus Christ, especially the love and hope and compassion He displayed. I pray that we might treat each other with more kindness, more courtesy, more humility and patience and forgiveness. . . . I also invite the members of the Church to establish the temple of the Lord as the great symbol of their membership and the supernal setting for their most sacred covenants. It would be the deepest desire of my heart to have every member of the Church be temple worthy. . . . Let us be a temple-attending and a temple-loving people" (in Todd, pp. 4–5).

In his first conference address as President of the Church, President Hunter built upon and expanded those two themes, clearly identifying the two areas on which his administration would focus: living with increasing attention to the life and example of Jesus Christ and treating each other with more patience, courtesy, and forgiveness; and becoming a temple-attending and temple-worthy people. President Hunter added his testimony: "My greatest strength through these past months has been my abiding testimony that this is the work of God and not of men. Jesus Christ is the head of this church. He leads it in word and deed. I am honored beyond expression to be called for a season to be an instrument in his hands to preside over his church. But without the knowledge that Christ is the head of the Church, neither I nor any other man could bear the weight of the calling that has come. . . . I pledge my life, my strength, and the full measure of my soul to serving him" (Hunter, pp. 7–8).

BIBLIOGRAPHY

Faust, James E. "The Way of an Eagle." *Ensign* 24 (August 1994):2–13.

Green, Doyle L. "Howard William Hunter: Apostle from California." *Improvement Era* 63 (January 1960):18–21, 36–38.
Hunter, Howard W. "Exceeding Great and Precious Promises." *Ensign* 24 (November 1994):7–9.
Knowles, Eleanor. *Howard W. Hunter.* Salt Lake City, 1994.
Searle, Don L. "President Howard W. Hunter, Acting President of the Quorum of the Twelve Apostles." *Ensign* 16 (April 1986):21–25.
Todd, Jay M. "President Howard W. Hunter: Fourteenth President of the Church." *Ensign* 24 (July 1994):2–7.

R. VAL JOHNSON

HYDE, ORSON

As a member of the first Twelve Apostles (1835) of the modern dispensation and the first missionary to take the message of the restored gospel to continental Europe and the Near East, Orson Hyde was closely allied with the rise and the development of the LDS Church. Born on January 8, 1805, in Oxford, New Haven County, Connecticut, he was raised in the care of Nathan Wheeler of Derby, Connecticut. In 1819, Hyde walked some six hundred miles to the town of KIRTLAND, Ohio, where Wheeler had purchased land. There he found employment as a clerk in the N. K. Whitney & Co. store. Continuously searching for deeper religious truths, he came under the influence of Sidney RIGDON, a Reformed Baptist minister, and embraced restorationist ideals advanced by Alexander Campbell and Sidney Rigdon.

When Oliver COWDERY and other missionaries to the Lamanites came through the Kirtland region in October–November 1830, Orson spoke against the "Mormon Bible," a position he changed after carefully examining the Book of Mormon. After three months of studying and pondering the doctrines taught by the Latter-day Saints, he was baptized in the Chagrin River on October 30, 1831, by Sidney Rigdon, who also had been converted (Barron, pp. 15–25).

A succession of missions followed Hyde's conversion. He and Hyrum Smith preached in Elyria and Florence, Ohio, and in 1832 he joined Samuel Smith in journeying to the "eastern countries" of the United States. In 1833 he and John Gould were sent as Church emissaries to resolve difficulties in Jackson County, Missouri. He marched with ZION'S CAMP the following year. After returning to Ohio, he married Nancy Marinda Johnson in Kirtland, on September 4, 1834.

On February 15, 1835, Orson Hyde was ordained a member of the Quorum of the Twelve Apostles, and in 1837 he represented the Church in petitioning the Ohio state legislature for a bank charter for the Kirtland Safety Society. He went with Heber C. KIMBALL on the first mission to Great Britain (1837–1838). Their work led to the eventual conversion of thousands to the Mormon faith (*see* MISSIONS OF THE TWELVE TO THE BRITISH ISLES).

Hyde was in Far West, Missouri, by the summer of 1838, and in October he signed an affidavit against the Saints during the severe persecution of that period. John Taylor said that perhaps Hyde "had been sick with a violent fever" (*HC* 3:168). Whatever the reason, Hyde made things right with Joseph SMITH and in the spring of 1839 wrote to the Twelve in Illinois asking if he could return. Dropped from the Quorum of the Twelve on May 4, 1839, he was again sustained as an apostle on June 27, 1839.

Years before, it had been prophesied that Hyde "had a great work to perform among the Jews" (*HC* 4:106), and in 1840 he was directed to undertake a mission that took him to New York, London, Amsterdam, Constantinople (Istanbul), and Jerusalem, speaking to the Jewish communities wherever he could. On October 24, 1841, Elder Hyde climbed the Mount of Olives near Jerusalem and offered a prophetic prayer of dedication, asking the Lord to remove the "barrenness and sterility of this land" (Hyde, p. 21). He returned home via Cairo, Alexandria, Trieste, and Germany. In Germany he published the first LDS German tract, *Ein Ruf aus der Wüste (A Cry out of the Wilderness*; Frankfurt, 1842).

When the majority of the Saints left Nauvoo for Iowa Territory early in 1846, Orson Hyde was asked to remain behind to supervise the completion and dedication of the NAUVOO TEMPLE. Dedicatory services were conducted on April 30 and May 1, 1846. From 1846 to 1847 he presided over the British mission. When President Brigham YOUNG returned to the Salt Lake Valley in 1848, Hyde was placed in charge of the camps of Israel in the Midwest. He remained in Kanesville (Council Bluffs, Iowa) until 1852, publishing the *Frontier Guardian* (1849–1852).

In Utah, Elder Hyde was called to head the Carson Valley

Nevada Mission in 1855. He returned to Salt Lake in 1857 because of the UTAH EXPEDITION. Further implementing his plan to have the Twelve Apostles preside over designated settlement areas, President Young called Elder Hyde to supervise settlement in the Sanpete-Sevier district of Utah in 1858.

At a meeting of the Twelve Apostles held in 1875, Brigham Young made a decision affecting Hyde's standing as the senior member of the Quorum. It was ruled that since he and Orson PRATT had briefly separated themselves from the Quorum in 1838 and 1842, respectively, they should lose their seniority to Elders John TAYLOR, Wilford WOODRUFF, and George A. Smith, who had been ordained during their time away (Durham, *Succession in the Church* [Salt Lake City, 1970], pp. 73–76). Because of that decision, John Taylor rather than Orson Hyde succeeded Brigham Young as President of the Church.

Following a lingering illness, Orson Hyde died at his home in Spring City, Utah, on November 28, 1878. With his passing the Church lost a noted missionary, colonizer, eloquent speaker, and devoted servant.

BIBLIOGRAPHY

Barron, Howard H. *Orson Hyde, Missionary, Apostle, Colonizer*. Bountiful, Utah, 1977.

Hill, Marvin S. "An Historical Study of the Life of Orson Hyde, Early Mormon Missionary and Apostle from 1805–1852." Master's thesis, Brigham Young University, 1955.

Hyde, Orson. *A Sketch of the Travels and Ministry of Elder Orson Hyde*. Salt Lake City, 1869.

HOWARD H. BARRON

I

IDAHO, PIONEER SETTLEMENTS IN

Although the main thrust of Latter-day Saint COLONIZATION was to the south of Salt Lake City, Church members also established numerous settlements in the rich farm valleys of southern Idaho.

The first LDS excursion into Idaho followed President Brigham YOUNG's call of twenty-seven families to labor among the Indians in the Oregon Territory in 1855. The result was the founding of Fort Limhi on a tributary of the Salmon River near present-day Salmon, Idaho. As the U.S. Army approached Utah in 1857 (*see* UTAH EXPEDITION), conflict with local Indians erupted, two missionaries were killed, and, in 1858, the fort lost most of its stock. The settlers were called back to Salt Lake City and the colony was never reopened.

In 1860 the community of Franklin, near the present Utah-Idaho border, became the first permanent Anglo-American settlement in the future territory of Idaho. Indian problems plagued the settlement until the Battle Creek massacre, in which federal soldiers from Salt Lake City's Fort Douglas killed a large number of Indians in 1863. Additional settlers went east from Cache Valley (Franklin was its northernmost town) over the mountains into the Bear Lake region in southeastern Idaho, opening the settlements of Paris, Bloomington, St. Charles, Ovid, Montpelier, Fish Haven, Liberty, and Bennington. Charles C. Rich, an apostle, oversaw these communities, which by 1864 included nearly seven hundred settlers. Latter-day Saints started additional settlements in the Idaho part of northern Cache Valley, Malad Valley, and Marsh Valley beginning in the 1860s, and in Gentile Valley in the 1870s.

Church members helped construct the railroad between Ogden, Utah, and Franklin, Idaho, in 1871–1874, and beginning in 1878, they helped extend the line farther into Idaho through Blackfoot and Idaho Falls (then called Eagle Rock) to Monida Pass, on the present-day Idaho-Montana border. Many Latter-day Saints homesteaded near the railroad and established such communities as Chesterfield, Egin Bench, and Rexburg. For the next two decades, Mormon settlements increasingly dotted the landscape for two hundred miles between Pocatello and Victor in the Teton Basin. By 1890, the Bannock Stake, centered in Rexburg, reported 3,861 members. Because the Snake River Valley was arid, LDS settlers devoted considerable energies to canal building. By 1910, more than one hundred canals operated in the Upper Snake River Valley, and LDS settlements were established (Moreland, New Sweden, Thomas, Springfield, and Aberdeen) where there were canals.

Latter-day Saints also moved west from Pocatello. In 1879 William C. Martindale, from Tooele, Utah, explored the Goose Creek Valley and returned to Utah with a favorable report. Church families soon began homesteading areas that included Goose Creek and Raft River. Oakley, where the Oregon and California trails separated, became the central location of the colony.

LDS influence in Idaho in the nineteenth century was confined largely to the southeast, where the Saints were a majority in many settlements. In the twentieth century Latter-day Saints have become a significant minority in communities farther west, still primarily in the southern part of the state.

BIBLIOGRAPHY

Bitton, Davis. "Peopling the Upper Snake: The Second Wave of Mormon Settlement in Idaho." *Idaho Yesterdays* 23 (Summer 1979):47–52.

Campbell, Eugene E. *Establishing Zion: The Mormon Church in the American West*. Salt Lake City, 1988.

Rich, Russell R. *Land of the Sky-Blue Water: A History of the LDS Settlement of the Bear Lake Valley*. Provo, Utah, 1963.

Ricks, Joel E., ed. *The History of a Valley: Cache Valley, Utah-Idaho*. Logan, Utah, 1956.

ROBERT D. MARCUM

ILLINOIS, LDS COMMUNITIES IN

[*The Church was centered in western Illinois from 1839 to 1846. After their expulsion from Missouri in 1838–1839, Mormon refugees fled to Quincy, Springfield, and other locations in Illinois, where local residents gave them assistance. Church leaders purchased the village of Commerce and land in its vicinity, along with a large tract across the Mississippi River in* Iowa. *Commerce was renamed* Nauvoo *and became the principal LDS community of its time and one of the largest cities in Illinois.*

Numerous small settlements in the vicinity of Nauvoo fell within the city's sphere of influence (see Donald Q. Cannon, "Spokes on the Wheel: Early Latter-day Saints Settlements in Hancock County, Illinois," Ensign *16 [Feb. 1986]:62–68). The LDS town of Ramus (later Macedonia and now Webster), about twenty miles southeast of Nauvoo, became a Church stake, as did Lima, twenty-five miles south of Nauvoo. La Harpe, a few miles north of Ramus, also had a considerable LDS population. Warren, twenty miles southwest of Nauvoo, was a short-lived LDS community adjacent to Warsaw. Anti-Mormon violence focused on these outlying LDS communities and caused their evacuation in 1845.*

In addition to several entries under Nauvoo, see Carthage Jail; Historical Sites; *and* Martyrdom of Joseph and Hyrum Smith. *For information on the Illinois period see* Joseph Smith; History of the Church: c. 1831–1844; *and* History of the Church: c. 1844–1877.

For LDS immigration to Illinois and subsequent departure for the Rocky Mountains, see Immigration and Emigration *and* Westward Migration, Planning and Prophecy.]

IMMIGRATION AND EMIGRATION

The immigration of tens of thousands of converts, first into America's Midwest and then into the mountain West, was a major part of the growth of the Church in the United States during the nineteenth century. So closely interrelated were proselytizing and the gathering of the faithful in the vicinity of Church headquarters that President Brigham YOUNG declared in 1860 that emigration "upon the first feasible opportunity, directly follows obedience to the first principles of the gospel we have embraced" (Brigham Young to A. Lyman, et al., and Saints in the British Isles, Aug. 2, 1860, Brigham Young Letterbooks, LDS Church Archives). With millennial fervor, Latter-day Saint converts sought to flee the impending woes of a sinful world by gathering "home to Zion," where they could join their American counterparts in preparing for the second coming of Jesus Christ. This gathering made it possible for the Latter-day Saints to become a dominant economic, political, and religious force in the Great Basin. It reinforced a sense of group identity and shielded them from religious persecution while providing individuals and families with greater economic opportunity.

Most converts were poor; indeed, the majority lacked sufficient funds to emigrate. Individuals and families were encouraged to save systematically, and the few who had surplus funds after emigrating were asked to assist fellow converts. In 1849 the Church organized the PERPETUAL EMIGRATING FUND (PEF) to solicit donations and provide emigrants with loans, the repayment of which would aid others. Such loans were most often made available to individuals with needed skills, to those whose relatives or friends donated to the PEF, or to those who had been faithful Church members for ten years or longer. From 1852 until 1887 the PEF assisted some 26,000 immigrants—more than one-third of the total LDS emigrants from Europe during that period—with at least part of the journey to the mountain West. In the 1850s and 1860s there were three categories of immigrants: the independent, who paid their own way to Utah; "states" or "ordinary" immigrants, who paid only enough to reach a port of entry or other intermediate stopping place in the United States, hoping to earn enough there to finish the journey; and PEF immigrants, assisted by the Perpetual Emigrating Fund. In later years private assistance eclipsed the PEF in the amount of aid rendered. In the 1880s and 1890s, 20 to 50 percent of the immigrants each year received private assistance.

Enthusiasm for emigration was highest during periods of international unrest, with accompanying millennialist expectations of increasing troubles worldwide prior to Jesus' second coming. Thus, in 1855, during the Crimean War, more Latter-day Saints emigrated from Europe than during any other year. That year 4,225 emigrants—

about 2.4 percent of all Europeans who migrated in 1855 to the United States—were Latter-day Saints, even though the total number of Church members in Great Britain and on the Continent, from whom the emigrants were drawn, was fewer than 35,000. The American Civil War brought exceptionally high LDS emigration in the years 1861–1865, a time when the general emigration from Europe was relatively low.

Because Church funds, including those of the PEF, were never sufficient to help as many as wished to immigrate, Church leaders on both sides of the Atlantic utilized many approaches. After the 1855 season, when Church and PEF resources were exhausted, donations of Salt Lake City real estate were sold for cash to British arrivals with the proceeds applied to emigration; and the use of handcarts rather than large wagons cut costs for the overland journey from Iowa to Utah. The tragic loss of more than two hundred lives in the two last HANDCART COMPANIES of 1856, because they departed too late and were caught in early snowstorms, grimly underscored the necessity of careful planning and implementation.

While the PEF continued to assist with individual expenses for transatlantic voyages on a limited basis after 1856, most of its aid was applied to the overland portion of the trip. Beginning in 1861 this was made possible by the use of the "Church trains" system for conveying immigrants. Under Brigham Young's direction, oxen and wagons along with teamsters and other personnel from throughout Utah appeared in Salt Lake City as soon as spring grass began to grow along the immigrant trail. The men, for their labors, and the owners of teams and wagons received either credit for tithing or wages paid in goods from local tithing storehouses. This practice resulted in the Church's tithing system subsidizing the operation heavily: in 1868 teamsters and owners received about $200,000 in tithing credit, while immigrants were charged only $75,000, on credit. It often took immigrants years to pay their indebtedness for emigration, and many failed to complete payment. By 1887, about one-third of the emigrants had paid their debt to the PEF in full, one-third had paid part, and one-third had paid nothing.

After the completion of the transcontinental railroad in 1869, immigrants traveling by steam-powered ships and trains could make the trip from Liverpool, England, to Salt Lake City in just over three weeks. Earlier, the journey by ship and wagon often took nearly six months. Yet advantages in time, comfort, and health were countered by the fact that more cash—a scarce commodity in the PIONEER ECONOMY—was required for the trip. The PEF still provided full passage for more than one hundred emigrants yearly from Europe to Utah in the years 1871–1875 and 1878–1881.

Church personnel at both local and mission levels played important roles in organizing the emigration from Europe. Clerks in each branch (congregation) received deposits to individual emigration savings accounts, which were forwarded to headquarters for a larger area, called a "conference," and then sent on to the mission headquarters. Local leaders sought out potential emigrants who seemed deserving of assistance and forwarded information about them to mission headquarters. Expanding a system dating from 1840–1841, when the Quorum of the Twelve Apostles organized the first emigrant companies (*see* MISSIONS OF THE TWELVE TO THE BRITISH ISLES), mission publications gave notice of planned departures and costs and provided helpful information such as lists of items passengers should bring. Well in advance of the departure date, conference presidents collected deposits to reserve places on particular vessels. Mission personnel served as passenger agents, thus avoiding middlemen, and used the commission they received for the benefit of poor emigrants or missionaries. Where necessary, they made arrangements for provisions and for cookware and eating utensils. In hectic last-minute efforts they helped hundreds of passengers board ship and obtain their berths. Men traveling with the group, usually returning missionaries, were appointed as presidencies for the ship and were responsible for the conduct and morale of the passengers and for holding religious services. Generally the daily routine involved prayer, washing the decks, cooperative cooking arrangements, and special meetings to discuss problems that arose.

Because the Saints traveled as a Church family under priesthood leadership—and with the assistance of an experienced and well-organized system—LDS emigration impressed nonmember observers as orderly and civilized compared with the tumult generally surrounding emigrant ships. One writer noted:

> The ordinary emigrant is exposed to all the chances and misadventures of a heterogeneous, childish, mannerless crowd during the voyage, and

> to the merciless cupidity of land-sharks the moment he has touched the opposite shore. But the Mormon ship is a Family under strong and accepted discipline, with every provision for comfort, decorum, and internal peace. On his arrival in the New World the wanderer is received into a confraternity which speeds him onwards with as little hardship and anxiety as the circumstances permit and he is passed on from friend to friend, till he reaches the promised home [*Edinburgh Review*, Jan. 1862, p. 199].

When passengers arrived in America, they were usually met by a Church emigration agent who assisted them with arrangements for transportation to the frontier outfitting point. At the frontier the emigrants remained encamped until all arrangements could be completed for the arduous overland trek (*see* MORMON PIONEER TRAIL). Before the immigrants arrived, agents purchased teams and wagons or handcarts. During the era of "down and back" Church trains, flour was generally hauled from Salt Lake City—part of it stashed along the trail—and other provisions were purchased by agents near the outfitting point. After 1861, wagon trains sent periodic reports on their progress by telegraph, and, when necessary, relief parties met immigrants en route as they neared the end of the journey.

Immigrant companies were officially welcomed as they arrived at Salt Lake City, where they camped while awaiting assignments. Bishops or their representatives then escorted them to the various settlements to which quotas had been assigned.

LDS immigrants, particularly those from northern Europe, were usually assimilated into communities and congregations quickly. New arrivals who did not speak English availed themselves of Church-sponsored publications and activities in their mother tongue, while also attending worship services in English. There was a short-lived effort to produce materials in a phonetic alphabet to ease immigrant learning (*see* DESERET ALPHABET), but most of the immigrants and virtually all their children became fluent in English. With few exceptions, relatively little sense of ethnic community survived beyond the generation of immigrants themselves. Most descendants of the immigrants who served as missionaries to ancestral lands had to learn the native language during their service.

After the late 1880s, coinciding with a new wave of emigration from central and southern Europe and with negative publicity and

ANTIPOLYGAMY LEGISLATION, LDS immigration was frowned upon by many in the United States. The large number of LDS steamship passengers were still assisted with arrangements by Church personnel, but they were instructed to maintain a low profile and did not function visibly as Mormon emigrant companies. By the 1890s the number of Latter-day Saints in Europe had dwindled, and in view of economic conditions in the United States, Church leaders began to discourage emigration—though LDS immigration revived modestly during the following decade. More than 103,000 emigrated in the years 1840–1910, an average of some 2,000 annually. In the years 1911–1946, with two world wars and the Great Depression dampening interest in relocation, LDS emigration declined to an average of only 291 annually. Encouraging the Saints to remain in their native lands and strengthen the Church there—a temporary expedience in the 1890s—eventually became a firmer policy. Leaders obtained more substantial locations for Church meetings in major European cities and promoted a greater sense of permanence.

A resurgence of LDS emigration from Europe took place in the years immediately following World War II; an average of more than 1,000 Latter-day Saints emigrated annually in the years 1947–1953. Beginning in the late 1950s the Church moved to provide its members in Europe and other areas with greater access to opportunities found in the United States, including the temples, more substantial local meeting places, and local leadership. This reinforced the encouragement to build Zion wherever Saints were found, and emigration from Europe tapered off. The gathering of emigration statistics was discontinued after 1962. By that time approximately 127,000 Latter-day Saints had emigrated from Europe, and thousands more from Canada, the South Pacific, and Mexico, to bring the total to about 150,000 emigrants. The influx of Church members from such areas as Canada and the South Pacific to Utah, California, and Missouri remained at a significant level into the 1970s and 1980s. Additionally, conversions from among other recent immigrants, particularly refugees from Southeast Asia, continued to give the Church in the United States an international flavor. This was also true for other areas of the world, with converts from Africa and the West Indies becoming an important factor in the Church in the British Isles.

From the 1840s on, immigrants made vital contributions to Latter-day Saint life. Immigrant educators, artists, craftsmen, musicians, architects, clerks, and others all enriched life in their adopted land. Immigrants played a particularly significant role in local Church leadership in the nineteenth century. Of 605 bishops and presiding elders in Latter-day Saint congregations in the United States from 1848 to 1890, 40 percent were born outside the United States. Twenty-nine percent were born in the British Isles. Scandinavia, the next richest source of LDS immigrants, accounted for 8 percent. In addition, 29 percent of stake presidents in the period were born outside the United States, including 23 percent born in the British Isles. Other immigrants have served as General Authorities, including several who served in the First Presidency.

BIBLIOGRAPHY

Arrington, Leonard J. *Great Basin Kingdom: An Economic History of the Latter-day Saints 1830–1900*, pp. 96–240. Cambridge, 1958.

Larson, Gustive O. *Prelude to the Kingdom: Mormon Desert Conquest: A Chapter in American Cooperative Experience*. Francestown, N.H., 1947.

Mulder, William. *Homeward to Zion: The Mormon Migration from Scandinavia*. Minneapolis, 1957.

Sonne, Conway B. *Saints on the Seas: A Maritime History of Mormon Migration 1830–1890*. Salt Lake City, 1983.

Taylor, P. A. M. *Expectations Westward: The Mormons and the Emigration of Their British Converts in the Nineteenth Century*. London, 1965.

RICHARD L. JENSEN
WILLIAM G. HARTLEY

INDEPENDENCE, MISSOURI

The tenth Article of Faith of the Church states, "We believe in the literal gathering of Israel and in the restoration of the Ten Tribes; that Zion [the New Jerusalem] will be built upon the American continent." From the Book of Mormon (Ether 13:1–5), early Latter-day Saints realized they had a role in the fulfillment of prophecy and were looking forward to the establishment of the New Jerusalem in America.

Anxious to know exactly where the promised city would be and when it would be built, the Saints were excited when in 1831 a series of revelations identified Missouri as the general location of the city of Zion, that "Independence is the center place, and a spot for the temple is lying westward, upon a lot which is not far from the court-house" (D&C 57:1–3; 45:64–66; 48:4–6; 52:1–5, 42–43). Subsequently, Joseph Smith also indicated that the Jackson County area had been the location of the Garden of Eden.

Independence, Missouri, county seat of Jackson County, was the preparation and departure point in the 1830s and 1840s for trappers, explorers, and pioneers who were going to western America over the Santa Fe, Oregon, and California trails. The Latter-day Saints, however, anticipating permanent residence, purchased land, built homes, prepared their farms, and dedicated a temple site.

After one year of living peacefully in Independence and vicinity, the Saints began to be persecuted by their non-Mormon neighbors. Social, religious, and political differences finally developed into open hostilities, and the Latter-day Saints were driven into neighboring Clay County in 1833, where they petitioned for a peaceful settlement so that they could return to their homes. A settlement never came, but Latter-day Saints still look forward to a time when the city of Zion, the New Jerusalem, will be built in the area of Independence, Missouri.

BIBLIOGRAPHY

Anderson, Richard L. "Jackson County in Early Mormon Descriptions." *Missouri Historical Review* 65 (Apr. 1971):270–93.

Bushman, Richard L. "Mormon Persecutions in Missouri in 1833." *BYU Studies* 3 (Autumn 1960):11–20.

LAMAR C. BERRETT

INTELLECTUAL HISTORY

The Church encourages its members to be learned in gospel principles and in every edifying branch of knowledge that supports a life of Christian service. Latter-day Saints value intellectual activity because it can develop and enrich life and faith, beautify the earth and ameliorate mankind's temporal suffering, and further the growth of the kingdom of God on earth. LDS theology takes with utmost seriousness the divine injunction to learn to know, to love, and to serve

God with all one's heart, might, mind, and strength (Deut. 6:5; 1 Chr. 28:9; Matt. 22:37; D&C 4:2; cf. John 17:3). In this sense, intellectual activity can be an act of worship.

One of the divinely ordained purposes of life is to gain spiritual and intellectual experience in mind and spirit. The Prophet Joseph SMITH taught that "by proving contraries, truth is made manifest" (*HC* 6:248). To "study it out in your mind" is often a prerequisite to heavenly assistance (D&C 9:8), and communication from God may sometimes be recognized by its effect on the mind. Latter-day Saints were enjoined early to seek knowledge out of the best books (D&C 88:118) and to establish schools (*see* SCHOOLS OF THE PROPHETS) for instruction in both sacred and secular matters.

FLOW OF IDEAS. In LDS theology, revelation from God to his appointed prophets is the source of doctrine and of "knowledge of the things of God" (*TPJS*, p. 217). Thus, there is no formalized mechanism in the Church for achieving scholarly consensus on theological principles. But there is no doubt of the need for diligent inquiry after truth: Joseph Smith taught that "a man is saved no faster than he gets knowledge" (*TPJS*, p. 217) and that "if a person acquires more knowledge and intelligence in this life through his diligence and obedience than another, he will have so much the advantage in the world to come" (D&C 130:19).

The earliest written explorations of LDS beliefs by Church leaders were motivated primarily by missionary activities to teach the gospel. Orson PRATT wrote the two influential series *The Kingdom of God* (four parts, 1848–1849) and *Divine Authenticity of the Book of Mormon* (six parts, 1850–1851) as well as scientific investigations related to theological speculations. Parley P. PRATT, Orson Spencer, and Lorenzo SNOW also published significant missionary tracts. Parley Pratt's synthetic work *Key to the Science of Theology* captured the free-ranging spirit of LDS thought during the formative years of the Church.

The voluminous output of the missionary press was severely curtailed after 1857 for several reasons; scarce resources were required to bring Saints to Zion and to build temples. However, the *Journal of Discourses* recorded public addresses of Church leaders, particularly Brigham YOUNG, during this era on topics ranging from agriculture and politics to theology; and presentations of LDS history, doctrine, and philosophy continued in forums ranging from prayer circles to various Church magazines to pioneer lyceums.

With the urbanization of the Church in the twentieth century, Church periodicals, firesides broadcast from Temple Square, and books published by Church-owned and semi-official presses were widely supplemented by unofficial activities and publications. Pioneer lyceums gave way to various informal activities, including firesides, study groups, or gatherings held in homes. New periodicals, most unsanctioned by the Church and with varying editorial policies, investigated issues and ideas too controversial or too academic for the formal Church curriculum. Increasingly in recent years, scholarly publications from university presses, both in Utah and elsewhere, have been written on LDS topics by scholars inside and outside the Church.

INTELLECTUAL PROLOGUE TO THE RESTORATION. Latter-day Saints believe that God prepared the intellectual, political, and spiritual environment prior to the restoration of the gospel through such cultural and religious movements as the Renaissance and the Reformation, particularly as these were manifested in Puritanism and the English Enlightenment.

The Puritan critique of the Church of England stressed morality for its leaders, education for its members, and a vital relationship between individuals and God. The Puritan ideal of a covenant community imbued with a sense of divine mission sustained their first two generations in America; but by the early eighteenth century, the Puritan movement was shattered by its collision with Enlightenment ideas, in spite of periodic revivals of faith and devotion. Where Puritanism had stressed the magnificence of God and the depravity of fallen man in a sinful world, the Enlightenment emphasized the goodness of man and the beauty of the natural world and linked a natural theology to emerging scientific models.

The conflict between these paradigms polarized American society: Puritan ministers were replaced by patrician aristocrats and lay scientists as leaders of American society. Puritanism continued in a diluted form: Evangelical Methodist and Baptist ministers emerged with new followers after the Great Awakening of 1740. Stressing the "heart" over the "head," these religious movements swept through newly independent America after 1800, while the rationalism of the

Enlightenment continued through the Unitarian and Universalist societies.

Joseph Smith grew up in this setting, both directions being represented by his parents. His mother stressed the emotionalism of the revivals to which she regularly took her children. His father, who helped found a Universalist society in Vermont, stressed the rational dimensions of religion. This polarization, in his family and in the larger culture, helped to impel young Joseph to ask God directly for guidance in a "silent grove" in the spring of 1820 (*see* FIRST VISION). In subsequent visions and revelations, Joseph Smith received knowledge and authority from God to restore the Church of Jesus Christ, whose doctrines and practices are not limited by the former approaches but generate a dynamic interplay between both mind and spirit.

RESTORATION PERIOD (1830–1844). The key intellectual and spiritual figure in the early years of the Church was clearly Joseph Smith. The conceptual framework of the Restoration stems from his prophetic utterances on many key topics (*see* SMITH, JOSEPH: TEACHINGS OF JOSEPH SMITH). He translated the Book of Mormon; received and published additional revelations; gave doctrinal instructions; provided glimpses into former gospel dispensations; explicated and amended the biblical text in many places throughout the Old and New Testaments; and stimulated interest in previously neglected texts.

The central focus of Joseph Smith's teaching is the literal and infinite atonement of Jesus Christ and the restoration of the eternal gospel and its ordinances. In this expansive view (popularized under the label of "eternalism" by B. H. Roberts) men and women are eternal beings procreated by a Heavenly Father and Mother, a concept elaborated by Lorenzo Snow and his sister Eliza R. SNOW. Men and women are tested by choices between good and evil in mortal life as preparation for the eternities. The universe, filled with a myriad of worlds inhabited by sons and daughters of God, exists for the purpose of allowing individuals to progress toward becoming gods and goddesses. The divine potential in each individual is actualized by voluntarily obeying the first principles of the gospel and receiving all the ordinances of salvation, culminating in the ordinances of the temple, a place dedicated as a house of prayer, fasting, faith, and learning, "a house of glory, a house of order, a house of God" (D&C 88:119). Each temple is a meeting place of heaven and earth, where eternal relationships are formed by covenants; it is also a school, where eternal concepts are taught.

COMMUNITY, RENEWED CONSECRATION, AND RESPONSE (1844–1896). The exodus to the Salt Lake Valley and the drive to colonize the Great Basin saw the development of key ideas about economic, political, and social needs in the community and nation. Latter-day Saints rejected the temporal-spiritual separation in politics and economics and viewed the Mormon village as a covenant community based on the concept of gathering. Missionaries taught the gospel to those who would listen; converts gathered out of spiritual Babylon by changing their lives and removing to Utah to build Zion. This literal "gathering of scattered Israel" brought converts into communities that practiced principles of CONSECRATION and stewardship, in social settings hospitable to the making of Saints (*see* ECONOMIC HISTORY OF THE CHURCH).

The LDS economic order, based on the premise that the earth is the Lord's, holds that men are stewards over the property they hold and are responsible for consecrating their time, energy, and talents to the establishment of Zion. Dominion over the earth is not a license to plunder, but a sacred trust to conserve life and protect the environment. LDS cosmology teaches that all living things will be resurrected, that the earth itself has a celestial destiny, and that all people are accountable to God for their earthly stewardship.

Out of this sense of community, combined with living in a barren land, ideals of frugality, cooperation, and equality were nurtured. The earth exists that man "might have in abundance"; poverty exists because some "possess that which is above another" and waste flesh when they have "no need" (D&C 49:19–21). The divine standard mandates temporal and spiritual unity and equality based on individual needs, desires, and varying talents (D&C 78:6). Periodic reformations in the Brigham YOUNG era sought to reach these ideals; analogous concepts motivate the welfare programs in the wards of the contemporary Church, now extended well beyond its historic population centers in the western United States.

In the late pioneer period (1869–1896), the Church felt the need to teach its rising generation more systematically than before. In the

1880s, for instance, George Q. Cannon, a member of the First Presidency, published a "Faith-Promoting Series" of journals, biographies, and a periodical, *The Juvenile Instructor*, to instruct young men and women. President Cannon insisted that:

> Latter-day Saints are ardent friends of learning, true seekers after knowledge. They recognize in a good education the best of fortunes; it broadens the mind, creates liberal and noble sentiments, and fits the possessor for a more successful struggle with the obstacles of life. . . . The possession of knowledge is of itself the highest pleasure [*Juvenile Instructor* 27 (1892):210].

Cannon's works filled a significant need, but the fact that these writings addressed primarily the youth of the Church limited their topics and approaches. During this same time President Young established academies throughout LDS-dominated areas. Brigham Young University, now the largest private university in the United States, began as such an academy in 1875.

President Young had attempted to insulate the LDS community from the influx of non-Mormons after completion of the transcontinental railroad in 1869. This economic move by Brigham Young, focusing on establishing ZCMI and the cooperative movement, reinforced a trend to isolate Church members from outside ideas, especially as persecution intensified. A contemporary reaction to many of Brigham Young's economic policies led some LDS intellectuals to oppose the Church. This group, known as the Godbeites (*see* SCHISMATIC GROUPS), became the prime illustration in Church circles of intellect unchecked that rejected prophetic leadership and the larger needs of the LDS community.

Few LDS students journeyed "East" to attend non-Mormon schools before the 1880s, and few LDS authors before 1900 addressed the critical issues being debated in the larger society. An important exception was the issue of women's rights, which found an outlet in the *Woman's Exponent* edited by LDS women.

ENCOUNTER WITH SCHOLARLY SECULARISM (1896–1918). The transformation of Mormon village life began as the first generation of Latter-day Saints started to pursue advanced studies of geology, agricultural science, chemistry, and engineering. Such studies brought the Saints face to face with a secular and skeptical society. James E.

Talmage studied geology at Lehigh and Johns Hopkins universities and returned to Utah in 1885 to teach and write about many topics, including evolution and the age of the earth. As president of the University of Utah and later as an apostle, he exerted an enormous influence by systematizing LDS theology in two seminal works, *The Articles of Faith* and *Jesus the Christ*. John A. Widtsoe, later an apostle, studied biochemistry at Harvard and Göttingen; he returned to Utah in 1900 and became president of Utah State University in 1907, playing a pivotal role first in agricultural education and research and later as an educational administrator and writer on intellectual issues facing Church members.

The Mutual Improvement Association chose as its study manual for 1909 Widtsoe's book *Joseph Smith as Scientist*, and the *Improvement Era* frequently ran articles by LDS scientists discussing Latter-day Saint doctrines in light of current scientific theories. Utah universities also began to invite the scholarly luminaries of the day to campus as guest lecturers. However, concerns were raised by the Church's educational administrators when some faculty members advanced evolutionary treatments of the creation accounts in Genesis. By 1911 these concerns led to a policy that temporarily discouraged discussions in Brigham Young University classrooms of such theories.

ADAPTATION AND CONFRONTATION (1918–1945). With worldwide industrialization and the ravages of World War I and the Bolshevik Revolution, agrarian idealism in America and the old order in Europe gave way before new political, economic, and social theories. For both Church leaders and lay members, deeply ingrained concepts of stewardship, cooperation, and individual moral responsibility clashed sharply with the militance of organized labor, the totalitarian excesses of fascism and communism, and the greediness of unregulated capitalism.

The need for teachers in Church schools and institutes of religion swelled to a small stream what had been only a trickle of Latter-day Saints sent "East" for professional training. The "Divinity School" group of Saints at the University of Chicago (*see* R. Swenson, "Mormons at the University of Chicago Divinity School," *Dialogue* 7 [Summer, 1972]:37–47) drew on their experience of LDS group life to write scholarly articles suggesting answers to the pressing social and economic problems of their day. In this academic setting, these LDS graduate students were also confronted with "higher criticism" of the Bible, stimulating some to take a moderate, conciliatory approach to scriptural interpretation, analogous to the neo-orthodox movement among Protestant theologians.

During this era, the Church and its members were recognized as a major force in American religious life. The *Encyclopedia Americana* commissioned a lengthy article by Elder B. H. Roberts for the centennial of the Church. Latter-day Saints who were influential outside the Great Basin included Harvey Fletcher in physics, E. E. Erickson in philosophy, J. Reuben Clark, Jr. in international affairs, Franklin S. Harris in agricultural science, and Henry Eyring in chemistry.

URBANIZATION AND GLOBAL MISSION (1945–1990). After World War II, a technocracy based on the positivist view of physical and social sciences dominated the intellectual landscape. Molecular biologists, armed with the tools of physics, seemed to be on the verge of controlling life itself; social scientists, bolstered by mathematics and computers, explained human behavior without reference to man's divine nature.

While existentialist theologians alternately despaired of or embraced the "secular city," LDS leaders again sounded the call to heed revelation as the source of ultimate truth while using science and technology to spread the gospel and alleviate human suffering. LDS emphasis on individual and group guidance through revelation created significant intellectual stresses for the increasing numbers of Church members being trained in the professions. A number of scholars wrote cogently to this generation of Latter-day Saint students about the historical, philosophical, and theological foundations of Church doctrines and advocated integrating intellectual pursuits with the spiritual need to love, to serve, and to have faith in Jesus Christ.

The horrors of world war had challenged conventional Christian ideologies. President J. Reuben Clark, Jr., warned that the alliance forged in wartime between science and governments had created a military-industrial complex. Some Church members were troubled by the issues of war and peace in the Korean and Vietnam conflicts and by the quasi-permanent state of war that endangered the world peace on which the missionary work of the Church depended.

As mission fields expanded, Zion, "the pure in heart" (D&C 97:21), was gathered into stakes in locations around the world. President Harold B. LEE foresaw that the demography and cultural uniformity of the Church would be significantly altered by the immense influx of converts. Scholars and lay leaders in the Church were challenged to differentiate between Church practices derived from fundamental universal gospel principles and those that could be treated as merely cultural practices of members.

The historic LDS affirmation of man as created literally in the image of God—with a Heavenly Mother as well as a Heavenly Father—led to a reinterpretation by Latter-day Saints of many conflicts felt in the larger society about the roles of men and women as individuals and as members of families and the Church. It also produced both a dramatic collision with fundamentalist Protestants and, to some extent, a reconciliation with Catholic and Protestant theologians who have rediscovered such ideas in the theology of the ancient Church.

In the Church, as in society, key roles were played by bureaucratic entities deriving their expertise from the study of human behavior. Knowledge of the social sciences, for example, stimulated the founding of a Church Social Services organization, using social science expertise consistent with Church norms. As the Church expands outside the Intermountain West, adapting Church programs to local cultures without sacrificing the essential core of gospel teaching is a matter of increasing urgency. Here the growing worldwide reservoir of LDS professionals is an increasingly valuable asset. This is particularly true in view of the primacy of the family and home as the center of Christ-centered learning and service.

During this period, some turned to engaging metaphors from the Book of Mormon as expressions for LDS thought. In some cases, the symbol of their moral and intellectual response was the iron rod that guided those who obediently held on to revealed truths through the mists of darkness; in other cases the Liahona, a divinely fashioned compass that gave direction in proportion to one's faith, symbolized the faithful search for divine guidance (see 1 Ne. 8, 16; R. Poll, pp. 107–118). In Latter-day Saint life, such approaches are not mutually exclusive.

LDS theology has consistently seen the mind in the service of and as a companion to the spirit. The two remain creatively engaged: The intellect tends to notice problems and to ask questions, while the spirit is drawn toward finding answers and receiving assurance (see Alma 32:21–34); the intellect is often solitary and introspective, while the life of the spirit fosters charitable service and yearns for the collective building of the kingdom of God. Pride is a threat to all: It can cause the intellectual to substitute human judgment for revelation in matters of doctrine and revealed truth or can cause people to "hearken not unto the counsel of God, for they set it aside, supposing they know of themselves" (2 Ne. 9:28; cf. 1 Cor. 2:5–7); pride can also transform faith and trust into overconfidence and dogmatism. The scripture states: "To be learned is good if they hearken unto the counsels of God" (2 Ne. 9:29).

BIBLIOGRAPHY

The history of ideas arises from revealed teachings of the prophets and the ongoing dialogue in which members of the Church seek to understand those teachings, to incorporate them into their daily life, and to teach them to others. Its history is largely unwritten. A useful introduction is Leonard J. Arrington, "The Intellectual Tradition of the Latter-day Saints," *Dialogue* 4 (Spring 1969):13–26. Other important sources include Leonard J. Arrington and Davis Bitton, *The Mormon Experience*, New York, 1979, chaps. 13 and 16; Philip L. Barlow, ed., *A Thoughtful Faith: Essays on Belief by Mormon Scholars*, Centerville, Utah, 1986; Maureen Ursenbach [Beecher], "Three Women and the Life of the Mind," *Utah Historical Quarterly* 43 (Winter 1974):26–40; Lowell L. Bennion, "The Uses of the Mind in Religion," *BYU Studies* 14 (Autumn 1973):47–55; Davis Bitton, "Anti-Intellectualism in Mormon History," *Dialogue* 1 (Autumn 1966):111–34, and response by James B. Allen; Marvin S. Hill, "The Shaping of the Mormon Mind in New England and New York," *BYU Studies* 9 (Spring 1969):351–72; Paul R. Green, comp., *Science and Your Faith in God*, Salt Lake City, 1958 (essays by Henry Eyring, et al.); Duane E. Jeffrey, "Seers, Savants and Evolution: The Uncomfortable Interface," *Dialogue* 8 (Autumn/Winter 1973):41–75; Sterling M. McMurrin, *The Theological Foundations of Mormon Religion*, Salt Lake City, 1965; Hugh W. Nibley, *The World and the Prophets*, in *CWHN* 3; Erich Robert Paul, *Science, Religion, and Mormon Cosmology*, Urbana, Ill., 1991; Richard D. Poll, "What the Church Means to People Like Me," *Dialogue* 2 (Winter 1967):107–18; Charles S. Peterson, "The Limits of Learning in Pioneer Utah," *Journal of Mormon History* 10 (1983):65–78; John L. Sorenson, "Mormon World View and American Culture," *Dialogue* 8 (Spring 1973):17–29.

RICHARD F. HAGLUND, JR.
DAVID J. WHITTAKER

IOWA, LDS COMMUNITIES IN

[*LDS refugees first settled in southeastern Iowa along the Mississippi River in 1839 after their expulsion from Missouri (see* Missouri Conflict*). The towns of Montrose, Keokuk, and Augusta had numerous LDS settlers. Latter-day Saints established Ambrosia, about three miles west of Montrose; Nashville (now Galland), three miles south of Montrose; and Zarahemla, their principal settlement, immediately west of Montrose. Because of anti-Mormon feelings, questionable land titles, and the desire to live closer to Church headquarters, most members eventually moved across the Mississippi River to* Nauvoo, *Illinois. See generally* History of the Church: c. 1831–1844.

In 1846, Latter-day Saints moving west from Illinois established way-station settlements at Garden Grove and Mount Pisgah to raise crops for those who would follow. The Mormon Battalion *was recruited first at Mount Pisgah. Also in 1846, numerous temporary settlements were established in the vicinity of* Council Bluffs. *In 1848 most Latter-day Saints remaining at the Missouri River withdrew from* Winter Quarters, *today part of Omaha, Nebraska, and settled across the river in present-day Council Bluffs, which they called Kanesville. LDS population in Pottawattamie County, Iowa, including Kanesville, may have reached as high as 8,000 in about forty settlements before the massive effort to move them to the Salt Lake Valley in 1852.*

In 1856–1858, Iowa City was the outfitting point for church emigrants, including Handcart Companies. *See* Immigration and Emigration; Mormon Pioneer Trail*; and, more generally,* History of the Church: c. 1844–1877.]

KANE, THOMAS L.

A courageous friend of the Latter-day Saints, Thomas Leiper Kane was born in Philadelphia on January 27, 1822. His great-grandfather John Kane (O'Kane) came to America from Ireland before the American Revolution. John's grandson John Kintzing Kane married June Duval Leiper, and they became the parents of Thomas L. Kane.

After completing his college training in Philadelphia in 1840, Thomas studied in England. Returning to America, he studied law under his father's direction and was admitted to the Pennsylvania bar in 1846. Then came a period of service with the U.S. Army, following which he became known as Colonel Kane.

Kane's introduction to the Mormon cause came in his native Philadelphia at a conference in May 1846 held under the direction of Jesse C. Little, presiding elder in the East, who was soliciting support for the Latter-day Saints' WESTWARD MIGRATION. Colonel Kane gave Little helpful letters of recommendation and later joined him in Washington, D.C., where they called on the secretary of state, secretary of war, and President James K. Polk. As a result of their negotiations, the United States agreed to enlist a battalion of 500 LDS men to serve in the campaign against Mexico (*see* MORMON BATTALION).

Later, after carrying government dispatches to Fort Leavenworth, Kane rejoined Little in the Mormon camp on the Missouri, where he became seriously ill with pulmonary tuberculosis. The Saints nursed him back to health, and during his long convalescence he abandoned plans for a political career and decided to devote himself to helping the Latter-day Saints and other downtrodden people. The Saints later named their principal Iowa settlement Kanesville (present-day COUNCIL BLUFFS) in recognition of his service. Although he was not a member of the Church, Colonel Kane received a patriarchal blessing from the Church's patriarch, John Smith, an uncle of Joseph SMITH. This blessing furnished encouragement, and it also provided a bond with the Saints.

Kane rendered his most significant service by assisting the Saints during the Utah War. Responding to reports from federal officials in Utah, President James Buchanan ordered the UTAH EXPEDITION of 2,500 U.S. Army troops to Utah. Traveling under the alias of Dr. Osborne, supposedly a botanist from Philadelphia, Dr. Kane came to Utah in 1858 and served as a mediator. He succeeded in convincing the newly appointed territorial governor, Alfred Cumming, that the Saints were not in a state of rebellion, and helped arrange a solution to the conflict that avoided a violent confrontation and preserved the peace.

Colonel Kane continued for many years as a friend and political adviser to the Saints. He promoted UTAH STATEHOOD in the nation's capital throughout the 1850s and defended the Church, its leaders, and its interests at every opportunity. After outstanding service in the Civil War, Kane was promoted to major general. In 1872 he and his wife, Elizabeth, spent the winter in Utah. They traveled throughout the territory and stayed as guests of Brigham YOUNG at his winter home in St. George.

When Brigham Young died in 1877, Kane returned to Utah to express his sorrow and to assure the Church of his continued support. Upon Kane's death in 1883, Church leaders eulogized him for his staunch friendship and assistance. Today the Church helps maintain as a historic site the Thomas L. Kane Memorial Chapel, in Kane, Pennsylvania, where Kane is buried.

BIBLIOGRAPHY

Arrington, Leonard J. "In Honorable Remembrance: Thomas L. Kane's Services to the Mormons." *BYU Studies* 21 (Fall, 1981):389–402.

Cannon, Donald Q. "Thomas L. Kane Meets the Mormons." *BYU Studies* 18 (Fall 1977):126–28.

Kane, Elizabeth [Mrs. Thomas L.]. *Twelve Mormon Homes Visited in Succession on a Journey Through Utah to Arizona*, ed. Everett L. Cooley. Salt Lake City, 1975.

Zobell, Albert L., Jr. *Sentinel in the East: A Biography of Thomas L. Kane*. Salt Lake City, 1965.

DONALD Q. CANNON

KIMBALL, HEBER C.

Heber Chase Kimball was First Counselor in the First Presidency of the Church from December 5, 1847, until his death in 1868. One of the foremost men in the early years of the Church, along with the Prophet Joseph SMITH and Brigham YOUNG, Heber marched in ZION'S CAMP in 1834, was ordained one of the original members of the Quorum of the Twelve Apostles in 1835, and experienced the spiritual manifestations that attended the dedication of the KIRTLAND TEMPLE in 1836. He served two missions to Great Britain, in 1837–1838 and 1839–1841 (*see* MISSIONS OF THE TWELVE TO THE BRITISH ISLES). Blunt, honest, loyal, and believing, Heber served the struggling Church well when steadfastness was among the most needed qualities. This is reflected in Joseph Smith's saying, "Of the Twelve Apostles chosen in Kirtland, . . . there have been but two [who have not] lifted their heel against me—namely Brigham Young and Heber C. Kimball" (*HC* 5:412).

Heber C. Kimball was born June 14, 1801, near Sheldon, Vermont, to Solomon F. and Anna Spaulding Kimball. In 1811 the family moved to western New York, where, after scanty schooling, young Heber became a potter. He grew to be a physically impressive man, six feet tall and weighing more than two hundred pounds, barrel-chested and dark-eyed. He married Vilate Murray in 1822. He, his friend Brigham Young, and their wives joined the Church in 1832, after a two-year period of inquiry, and in 1833 they moved to Church headquarters in KIRTLAND, OHIO.

In 1837 Elder Kimball received an assignment from the Prophet Joseph Smith to lead a group of missionaries to England. As the ship arrived in Liverpool, Kimball leapt ashore, thus becoming the first Latter-day Saint in Europe. His simplicity and spirit suited the men and women who heard him preach, and within a week nine persons sought baptism. On the morning of the baptism, Elder Kimball and his companions reported they experienced an attack by evil spirits, whom they saw distinctly in their room. Calling on God, they received deliverance from the dark power. Through their efforts groups of hundreds of English converts, commencing in 1840, began sailing to the United States to be with the main body of the Church.

After a year Elder Kimball returned to the United States and to Missouri, where the Saints experienced persecution. While Joseph

Smith sat imprisoned in the LIBERTY JAIL (Missouri), Heber and Brigham Young organized the removal of approximately 12,000 LDS refugees to Illinois.

When the Prophet Joseph Smith rejoined the Saints in Illinois and established NAUVOO on the Mississippi River, Elder Kimball prepared to return to England. On the appointed day he and Brigham Young took their leave from sick wives, each with a new baby, and were themselves so ill they had to be lifted into the wagon. Elder Kimball was gone from home for almost two years, until 1841.

Kimball participated in the building of the Nauvoo Temple and received the temple ordinances. Joseph Smith taught him privately that God required him to enter into PLURAL MARRIAGE. After initial resistance, Elder Kimball married Sarah Noon. His anguish at keeping this secret from Vilate ended when she told him that the Lord had shown her that plural marriage was right, and that she accepted his participation in it. Kimball married a total of forty-three women (in many cases a caretaking rather than an intimate relationship), and by seventeen of them he had sixty-five children. He perceived his plural marriages as a religious obligation; Vilate accepted the other wives as sisters. Heber C. Kimball's grandson Spencer W. KIMBALL was President of the Church from 1973 to 1985.

After Joseph Smith's assassination in 1844, Church leadership was carried forth by the Quorum of the Twelve Apostles under its president, Brigham Young. Elder Kimball stood next in leadership. The Saints soon had to abandon their homes in Nauvoo and flee to the Great Basin.

The brutal trek across Iowa, temporary settlement in Winter Quarters, and the pioneer journey of 1847 to the Great Salt Lake Valley occurred under Brigham Young's supervision, with Kimball as his assistant. In December 1847, at Kanesville (Council Bluffs, Iowa), the First Presidency was organized, with Brigham Young as president and Heber C. Kimball and Willard Richards as his counselors. In summer 1848 President Kimball led one of three large companies of Saints to the Salt Lake Valley, where he established his families and supported them by farming, ranching, milling, freighting, and Church and civic administration.

The organization of Utah Territory in 1850 brought hostile federal appointees, but since the population was predominantly LDS, Church leaders had de facto control of the legislature. Heber served as leader of the legislature. Friction between the federally appointed judges and the Latter-day Saints led to U.S. President James Buchanan's sending federal troops to suppress a supposed "rebellion" of the Mormons. President Kimball helped direct the resistance.

A notably outspoken preacher, President Kimball often urged self-sufficiency, resistance to the corrupting influences of the larger society, and faithfulness to the kingdom of God. He frequently used metaphors from his experience as a potter. He prophesied accurately many times, including a prediction that Parley P. Pratt would go on a mission to Toronto, Canada, and find a people prepared for his message. He likewise prophesied that from there the gospel would spread to England. He correctly predicted that Pratt's invalid wife would bear him a son, even though the couple had been childless for ten years (Whitney, p. 135). He also prophesied to hungry pioneers in early 1849 that "in less than one year there will be plenty of clothes and everything that we shall want sold at less than St. Louis prices" (Kimball, 1981, p. 190). That summer, people traveling to the California gold fields dumped their excess supplies and equipment on the market in Salt Lake City and the prophecy was true.

President Kimball also shouldered special responsibility for the British mission and for all temple ordinances. His journals constitute important sources of Church history.

Heber C. Kimball died June 22, 1868, from the effects of a carriage accident, ending thirty-six years of unexcelled, dependable service to the Church.

BIBLIOGRAPHY

Kimball, Stanley B. *Heber C. Kimball: Mormon Patriarch and Pioneer.* Urbana, Ill., 1981.

———, ed. *On the Potter's Wheel: The Diaries of Heber C. Kimball.* Salt Lake City, 1987.

Whitney, Orson F. *Life of Heber C. Kimball.* Salt Lake City, 1888; 2nd ed., 1945.

EDWARD L. KIMBALL

KIMBALL, SARAH GRANGER

Sarah Melissa Granger Kimball (1818–1898) was founder of the Ladies' Society of Nauvoo, a suffragist, an advocate of women's rights, ward

Relief Society president for forty years, and a strong presence in the history of The Church of Jesus Christ of Latter-day Saints for much of the nineteenth century. Described by one of her associates as possessing "the courage to say what she thought," Sarah Kimball labored for the advancement of women, arguing that "education and agitation are our best weapons of warfare" (*Woman's Exponent* 20 [1 May 1892]:159 and 18 [15 Feb. 1890]:139, respectively). Such militancy was tempered, however, by her strong commitment to the Church and her loyalty to its leaders. Indeed, she saw little discrepancy between her devotion to the Church and her dedication to women's rights, since Joseph SMITH's "turning of the key" of power to women in 1842 had, in her view, led to the beginnings of the national women's rights movement.

Born December 29, 1818, in Phelps, New York, to Oliver and Lydia Dibble Granger, Sarah joined the Church and moved with her family to KIRTLAND, OHIO, in 1833 at age fifteen. While she did not detail her own conversion, a dramatic vision of the Book of Mormon prophet $Moroni_2$ experienced by her father made a lasting impression on her. She, however, was never content to live vicariously, either intellectually or spiritually. She was one of the twenty-three women known to have attended Joseph Smith's SCHOOL OF THE PROPHETS in Kirtland, and she later urged the inclusion of substantive courses of study in her ward Relief Society, delivered strong addresses expounding doctrine, and spoke in tongues.

Perhaps most significant in her early adulthood was her formation of the Ladies' Society of Nauvoo, the antecedent of the Relief Society. Married at age twenty-one to Hiram Kimball, a wealthy Nauvoo merchant who later converted to the Church, she sought to help build the kingdom of God, which the Saints then saw as embodied in Nauvoo, especially in the temple. She and her seamstress, a Miss (Margaret?) Cook, determined to sew shirts for the temple workmen and subsequently invited other women to join forces with them in a ladies' society. When they approached Joseph Smith for his approval of the society's constitution, written by Eliza R. SNOW, he stated that although the constitution was excellent, the Lord wanted the women organized "under the priesthood after the pattern of the priesthood." According to Sarah Kimball's recollection, Joseph continued, "The Church was never perfectly organized until the women were thus organized" (Kimball, p. 51).

In light of her important early involvement with the Relief Society, it is not surprising that Sarah spent much of her life actively engaged in its work. After her 1851 move to Salt Lake City, where she taught school to support her family while her husband recovered from some serious financial losses, she was called in 1857 as president of the Fifteenth Ward Relief Society. She continued in that position until her death in 1898, also serving during twelve of those years as general secretary of the Relief Society under President Eliza R. Snow and later as a vice-president of the organization after its incorporation in 1892.

Sarah Kimball's tenure as ward Relief Society president was noted for its innovation and attention to the complete development of women. Her compassion and charity were legendary, and she organized the women of her ward to provide for the poor and needy. She directed their efforts to fund the first Relief Society hall, which functioned both as a store in which the women sold their items of home manufacture and as a meetinghouse devoted to secular and sacred education.

During her years of greatest involvement in the Relief Society, Sarah Kimball also became a major force in the suffrage fight as president of the Utah Woman Suffrage Association. Compared by one of her contemporaries to Susan B. Anthony, Sarah Kimball displayed the same courage and forthrightness in contending for women's rights. She argued not only for suffrage but for equal esteem of women with men. Further, many of her sermons spoke of the ultimate and divine equality of "the Father and Mother God" (*Woman's Exponent* 8 [1 July 1879]:22).

Sarah Kimball died in Salt Lake City on December 1, 1898. A widow for thirty-five years following her husband's death in a steamship explosion while en route to a mission in the Sandwich Islands (Hawaii), she was survived by three sons and one adopted daughter.

BIBLIOGRAPHY

Mulvay, Jill C. "The Liberal Shall Be Blessed: Sarah M. Kimball." *Utah Historical Quarterly* 44 (Summer 1976):205–221.

Kimball, Sarah M. "Auto-Biography." *Woman's Exponent* 12 (Sept. 1, 1883):51.

MARY STOVALL RICHARDS

KIMBALL, SPENCER W.

Spencer Woolley Kimball (1895–1985), twelfth President of The Church of Jesus Christ of Latter-day Saints (1973–1985), came to the Presidency at the age of seventy-eight. Little new had been expected of his administration because of his age and long history of serious health problems, but his personal energy, broad vision, and openness to change produced a dynamic period consistent with the Church's growing awareness of itself as an increasingly international institution. Under his leadership, access to the temple and the priesthood was extended, regardless of race; the number of missionaries greatly increased; administrative innovations significantly changed Church governance; and a burst of temple building occurred. His tenure proved to be one of the most active periods in twentieth-century Church history.

Spencer Woolley Kimball was born March 28, 1895, in Salt Lake City, Utah. His father, Andrew Kimball, was a son of Heber C. KIMBALL, a counselor to President Brigham YOUNG, and his mother, Olive, was the daughter of Bishop Edwin D. Woolley, Brigham Young's business manager. At that time, Andrew was serving as president of the Indian Territory Mission in what is now Missouri and Oklahoma, overseeing missionary work by correspondence and periodic visits while supporting his family as a traveling dry goods salesman through Utah and southern Idaho.

When Spencer was three, his father received a call from the First Presidency to move to Thatcher, a Mormon settlement in the Gila Valley of southeastern Arizona, to become president of the St. Joseph Stake. Andrew earned his living by farming and business while he presided over several thousand Latter-day Saints in the valley and the vast surrounding area.

As a child, Spencer suffered from typhoid fever and facial paralysis and once nearly drowned. Four of his sisters died in childhood, and his mother died when he was eleven. After high school, he served as a missionary in the Central States Mission from 1914 to 1916. During his second year in the mission, he served in the St. Louis area as a supervisor of twenty-five missionaries, all older than himself.

In 1917 he attended the University of Arizona for one semester. He then received an induction notice for army service in World War I. Although expecting to leave any day, he married Camilla Eyring, a school teacher, on November 16, 1917. They eventually had four children: Spencer L., Olive Beth, Andrew E., and Edward L.

Delay in organizing the army contingent from his area resulted in his being deferred, and he obtained work in a bank. When the bank failed in 1923, wiping out the Kimballs' life savings, another bank hired him almost immediately as chief teller. In 1927 he left that bank and, with Joseph W. Greenhalgh, established an insurance and real estate agency in Safford, Arizona. Despite hard times caused by the Great Depression, Kimball said he would set up a peanut stand before he would become another person's employee again. Operating his own business gave him flexibility to attend to Church responsibilities and, with his wife, to engage in many community activities—PTA, library, elections, city council, Red Cross, Boy Scouts, the local college, and the organization of a radio station. He was selected as statewide leader of the Arizona Rotary Club in 1936.

In the Church, Spencer Kimball served as his father's stake clerk from 1917 until the latter's death in 1924. He then became counselor to the new stake president. In 1938, when the St. Joseph Stake was divided, he was called as president of the new Mount Graham Stake, extending 250 miles from Safford, Arizona, where he lived, to El Paso, Texas. As stake president, he supervised Church Welfare Services relief for victims of a major flood in Duncan, Arizona, in 1943.

On July 8, 1943, the First Presidency notified President Kimball of his call to fill a vacancy in the Quorum of the Twelve Apostles. Though he had a slight premonition of the call, he felt shocked, knowing so well his own limitations. With assurance from Camilla and after a long personal struggle, he received spiritual confirmation several days later that the call came from God. He sold his business, moved his family to Salt Lake City, and at the October General Conference in 1943 received the sustaining vote of the Church's membership and was that same day ordained an apostle by President Heber J. GRANT.

For thirty years Kimball served in the Quorum of the Twelve Apostles helping with Church administration, dealing with the personal problems of individuals, visiting stakes and missions, and teaching the gospel of Jesus Christ. In 1946, President George Albert SMITH gave him the responsibility of working with Indians. Soon afterwards, he awoke sensing a horrible enemy, unseen but very real, trying to destroy him. After a struggle, he rebuked the evil spirit and obtained relief. He concluded that perhaps the work he had just begun presented a special threat to the powers of darkness. He publicized the suffering of Navajos during the harsh winter of 1947 and organized relief for them, but concluded that improved roads and education were the keys to long-term improvement. He helped establish the Church's Indian Student Placement Services, under which LDS families with access to good schools took Indian children from the reservations into their homes for the school year on a voluntary basis. The program grew in two decades from one child to nearly 5,000 a year, before improved schools among the Indians reduced the need. He preached vigorously against racial prejudice.

Among other assignments, Elder Kimball also headed the missionary committee. As he traveled about the Church he gave hundreds of twelve-year-old boys a dollar each to begin a mission saving fund. He visited all the missions of Europe in 1955, circled the world in 1960, supervised the Church in South America for four years—where he began missionary work among the Indians of the Andes—and then supervised the missions in Great Britain.

His experience in counseling hundreds of individuals about personal problems, especially sexual immorality, moved him to write *The Miracle of Forgiveness*, a book on the process of repentance that has been well received among Church members.

Elder Kimball suffered a heart attack in 1948 and throat cancer a few years later. Removal of most of his vocal cords left him with a distinctive weak, raspy voice. In 1972 successful open-heart surgery replaced an obstructed artery and a failing valve. Since he was then age seventy-seven, he considered foregoing the surgery, but President Harold B. LEE said his work was not finished and he should have the operation.

On December 26, 1973, when President Lee died, Spencer W. Kimball succeeded him. Though already seventy-eight, President Kimball led energetically until 1979, when a cerebral hemorrhage required two brain surgeries. He recovered well, but in mid-1981 a third such operation left him seriously weakened. From that time until his death in 1985, he left active leadership to his counselors, especially President Gordon B. Hinckley. On November 5, 1985, at age ninety, President Kimball died, and was succeeded as Church President by Ezra Taft BENSON. Camilla, notable in her own right, survived to age ninety-two.

Spencer W. Kimball's remarkable resolution and purity of spirit grew from a solid religious background provided by parents and a strong community. In his early teens he met a challenge to read the entire Bible. At age fourteen he taught Sunday School. Given a believing heart, he was serious but not solemn. Short but strong and quick, he enjoyed sports, especially basketball. He played the piano, sang, and all his life was the center of fun and activity. Annually his classmates elected him president of his small high school class. His verbal humor turned to wordplay rather than anecdote, his quick wit usually directed against himself. He often joked about his being short.

He greatly missed his mother and always desired to be a credit to his parents. He hungered for approval. His capacity for hard work as a General Authority was legendary. He had the ability to nap for a few minutes and start afresh. Despite his serious illnesses, including typhoid fever, smallpox, two bouts of Bell's palsy, a heart attack and later heart failure, recurring throat cancer, three subdural hematomas, minor strokes, and scores of boils, he never slackened his efforts. He was relatively uncomplaining in suffering and ever grateful for medical help.

Because his formal education ended at marriage, President Kimball feared people might judge the Church negatively because of his inadequacies. He compensated by working doubly hard. In fact, he was well educated by his wide reading. His addresses were carefully prepared, with his own poetic eloquence. A humble man, he felt completely at home with common folk. He expressed appreciation and love easily and generously. There was no presumptuousness in him; he made no demands. He encouraged publication of a candid biography that portrayed him as an imperfect man striving to meet a divine challenge.

He and Camilla celebrated sixty-eight years of devoted marriage. She was well-spoken, forthright, highly intelligent, and a committed Christian. Ever supportive, she perfectly complemented President Kimball in his calling.

People sometimes perceived him as a strict moralist because of his seriousness in preaching, but he understood individuals' failings. He was the soul of kindness and unfailingly thoughtful. He carried on a massive correspondence, answering children's letters and writing to people he had counseled. He had great compassion for those struggling physically, socially, and spiritually. He expended huge energies trying to improve the conditions of the American Indians. As President and Prophet of the Church, he sought and obtained revelation that Church members of black ancestry could be full participants in all aspects of the Church. Few Church leaders called forth the affection that this unassuming man did.

Many changes resulted from the explosive Church growth during his twelve-year administration: from 630 stakes to about 1,500; from organization in 50 countries to 96; and from 3.3 million members to nearly 6 million. At the time of his death, nearly half the Church's membership had known no other president.

Many of the accomplishments of President Kimball's administration came from the effort to cope with this growth, and particularly the expansion into new areas of the globe. He organized the First Quorum of the Seventy to enlarge the number of General Authorities and called as members of that quorum men from Europe, Asia, and South America. The world was divided into areas with a presidency made up of General Authorities in each area. He held numerous regional conferences and solemn assemblies. All of this reflected an effort to give the members closer contact with the general Church leadership. To meet leadership needs, additional General Authorities were called for limited terms of approximately five years and others were given emeritus status.

An influential address in 1974 set out his vision of expanded missionary effort. The total number of full-time missionaries increased during President Kimball's administration by more than 50 percent, with many young women and older couples swelling the ranks. The fastest growth of the Church occurred in Latin America and Asia, but the Church also began organized activity in Communist-dominated countries and in sub-Saharan Africa. A center established in Jerusalem under the aegis of Brigham Young University stirred up protest by some orthodox Jews. The fifteen temples in operation when he became President grew to thirty-one around the world at his death, with eleven more under construction or announced. The use of computers to maintain records greatly increased the efficiency of temple work.

All of this activity exemplified his challenge to the Church to "lengthen your stride," and his personal motto was Do It!

Despite all this growth, in his preaching and policies President Kimball emphasized the return of the Church to the simple basics of good living and Church service. He articulated a threefold mission for the Church: to proclaim the gospel, to redeem the dead, and to perfect the Saints. He preached about improved family life, planting gardens, cleaning up yards, maintaining personal journals, and writing family history. Church meetings were compressed into three hours on Sunday to reduce the demands on members and to allow more time for family activity. Streamlined Church organization was approved for small groups. He urged Church members to give charitable service and backed up his preaching with Church relief for victims of a burst dam in Idaho, an earthquake in Mexico City, and famine in Ethiopia.

Ironically, this peace-loving and kindly man became involved in a number of contentious public issues. First Presidency statements addressed the issues of homosexuality, abortion, and pornography, evincing serious concern about the permissiveness of American society. The First Presidency opposed installation of an MX missile system in the United States and objected doubly because it was projected for the Utah-Nevada desert. Controversy arose over the role of Church historical writing and was accentuated by the purported discovery of significant historical documents by forger Mark Hofmann (*see* FORGERIES OF HISTORICAL DOCUMENTS). The First Presidency endorsed equal rights for women but opposed the Equal Rights Amendment as an improper means to a desirable end. Sensitivity to women's issues resulted in Churchwide meetings for women and for girls, a statuary park in Nauvoo as a monument to women, authorization for women to pray in all meetings, speaking by women leaders in general conference.

No event in the twentieth-century Church matched the excitement attending President Kimball's announcement of receiving a revelation on priesthood in 1978, ending more than a century of limitation on admission of Church members of black African ancestry to priesthood office and temple ordinances. The announcement made no doctrinal statement, but simply said that the Lord had indicated that the time for change had come. The change was implemented immediately, giving great impetus to missionary work in Africa. The announcement of this revelation was added to the Doctrine and Covenants as Official Declaration—2.

From a man of whom little more than a brief caretaker administration was expected, remarkable achievements came. President Spencer W. Kimball's energetic leadership and willingness to break new ground produced twelve years of unequaled growth and change in the modern Church.

BIBLIOGRAPHY

BYU Studies 25 (Fall 1985):1–166 (issue devoted to articles about Spencer W. Kimball).

Kimball, Edward L., and Andrew E. Kimball, Jr. *Spencer W. Kimball*. Salt Lake City, 1977.

———. *The Story of Spencer W. Kimball: A Short Man, A Long Stride*. Salt Lake City, 1985.

Kimball, Edward L. "The Administration of Spencer W. Kimball." *Sunstone* 11 (Mar. 1987):8–14.

Kimball, Spencer W. *Faith Precedes the Miracle*. Salt Lake City, 1972.

———. *One Silent Sleepless Night*. Salt Lake City, 1975.

———. *The Miracle of Forgiveness*. Salt Lake City, 1969.

———. *The Teachings of Spencer W. Kimball*, Edward L. Kimball, ed. Salt Lake City, 1982.

Miner, Caroline E., and Edward L. Kimball. *Camilla*. Salt Lake City, 1980.

EDWARD L. KIMBALL

KINDERHOOK PLATES

In April 1843 some alleged New World antiquities were presented to Joseph SMITH for his opinion. The six 2 7/8-by-2 1/4-inch bell-shaped brass plates with strange engravings were reported to have been excavated in Kinderhook, Illinois, about seventy miles south of NAUVOO (*HC* 5:372–79). They were shown to Smith because of his claim to have translated the Book of Mormon from ancient gold plates taken from a New York hill in 1827.

The Kinderhook plates created a stir in Nauvoo; articles appeared in the Church press, an illustrated handbill was published, and some Latter-day Saints even claimed Joseph Smith said he could and would translate them. No translation exists, however, nor does any further comment from him indicating that he considered the plates genuine. After his assassination in June 1844, the incident was largely forgotten. Decades later two of the alleged discoverers announced that the plates were a hoax, an attempt to discredit Smith. By then, however, the Church was headquartered in Utah and little attention was paid to these strange disclosures.

Interest was kindled again in 1920 when the Chicago Historical

Society acquired what appeared to be one of the original Kinderhook plates. Later the Chicago plate was subjected to a number of nondestructive tests, with inconclusive results. Then in 1980, the Chicago Historical Society gave permission for destructive tests, which were done at Northwestern University. Examination by a scanning electron microscope, a scanning auger microprobe, and X-ray fluorescence analysis proved conclusively that the plate was one of the Kinderhook six; that it had been etched, not engraved; and that it was of nineteenth-century manufacture. There thus appears no reason to accept the Kinderhook plates as anything but a frontier hoax.

BIBLIOGRAPHY

Kimball, Stanley B. "Kinderhook Plates Brought to Joseph Smith Appear to be a Nineteenth-Century Hoax." *Ensign* 11 (Aug. 1981):66–74.

Ricks, Welby W. "The Kinderhook Plates." *IE* 65 (Sept. 1962):636–37, 656, 658, 660.

STANLEY B. KIMBALL

KING FOLLETT DISCOURSE

The King Follett Discourse is the name given to an address the Prophet Joseph SMITH delivered in Nauvoo, Illinois, on April 7, 1844, at a general conference of the Church. It was a commemorative oration for a Church member named King Follett, who had died in an accident on March 9, 1844. The discourse may be one of the Prophet's greatest sermons because of its comprehensive doctrinal teachings. It was his last general conference address, delivered less than three months before he was martyred. Key doctrinal topics in the sermon include the character of God, man's potential to progress in God's likeness, the Creation, and the tie between the living and their progenitors.

Joseph Smith delivered the sermon to several thousand people in a grove west of the Nauvoo Temple in a natural amphitheater, where benches and a rostrum had been placed. He spoke for two hours and fifteen minutes. Four experienced scribes took synoptic notes: Willard Richards, Wilford WOODRUFF, William Clayton, and Thomas Bullock.

The spring of 1844 was a time of tension and turmoil in the Prophet's life. On the one hand, the Church was flourishing in

Nauvoo and abroad, construction of the Nauvoo Temple was proceeding apace, and generally men and women were serving in the Church with dedication and effectiveness. On the other hand, apostates, political factions in Illinois and Missouri, and other groups were conspiring against Joseph Smith.

Of the kinship between God and man, Joseph Smith taught, "If men do not comprehend the character of God, they do not comprehend themselves" (*TPJS*, p. 343). "It is the first principle of the Gospel to know for a certainty the Character of God, and to know that we may converse with him as one man converses with another" (*TPJS*, p. 345). Echoing his FIRST VISION, the Prophet taught what he called the "great secret": "If the veil were rent today, and . . . God . . . [were] to make himself visible, . . . if you were to see him today, you would see him like a man in form—like yourselves in all the person, image, and very form as a man" (*TPJS*, p. 345).

Creation, he taught, was not by mere fiat or ex nihilo. God's role was to bring harmony to primal, unorganized elements and to "institute laws" whereby weaker intelligences might have the privilege of advancing like himself (*TPJS*, p. 354).

Of man's potential, the Prophet said that even as God is eternal and self-existent, so the intelligence of man is also eternal. The Father has become what he is through eternities of progress. Christ, who did nothing but what he had seen the Father do (cf. John 5:19), followed identical paths and patterns. Since all mankind have a divine Father, they are potential "heirs of God and joint-heirs with Jesus Christ" (*TPJS*, pp. 346–47; cf. Romans 8:17). In this sense, all the children of God are embryonic gods or goddesses. Obedience to the fulness of the gospel is the perfecting process through which they may go "from one small degree to another, and from a small capacity to a great one; from grace to grace, from exaltation to exaltation . . . until [they] arrive at the station of a God" (*TPJS*, pp. 346–47).

On the link between the living and their progenitors, the Prophet asked, "Is there nothing to be done?—no preparation—no salvation for our fathers and friends who have died without having had the opportunity to obey the decrees of the Son of Man?" (*TPJS*, p. 355). He answered, "God hath made a provision that every spirit in the eternal world can be . . . saved unless he has committed [the] unpardonable sin" (*TPJS*, p. 357). He explained these provisions as they apply both in mortality and in the world beyond. To the mourners, the Prophet testified, "We have reason to have the greatest hope and consolations for our dead of any people on the earth; for we have seen them walk worthily in our midst, and seen them sink asleep in the arms of Jesus; and those who have died in the faith are now in the celestial kingdom of God" (*TPJS*, p. 359).

The Prophet indicated some of his concerns: threats on his life, his love of the Saints, the loneliness of leadership ("You never knew my heart"), the wonderment he felt in retrospect ("I don't blame anyone for not believing my history. If I had not experienced what I have, I could not have believed it myself" [*TPJS*, p. 361]). He finished with a plea for peace and invoked God's blessing on the assembly.

BIBLIOGRAPHY

Cannon, Donald Q. "The King Follett Discourse: Joseph Smith's Greatest Sermon in Historical Perspective." *BYU Studies* 18 (Winter 1978):179–92.

———, and Larry E. Dahl, eds. *The Prophet Joseph Smith's King Follett Discourse: A Six-Column Comparison of Original Notes and Amalgamation.* Provo, Utah, 1983.

Hale, Van. "The Doctrinal Impact of the King Follett Discourse." *BYU Studies* 18 (Winter 1978):209–225.

Larson, Stanley. "The King Follett Discourse: A Newly Amalgamated Text." *BYU Studies* 18 (Winter 1978):193–208.

DONALD Q. CANNON

KIRTLAND ECONOMY

[*This article reports the main facts and points of interest regarding the economic events in Kirtland in the 1830s and the significance of this historical development in the overall growth of the Church.*]

In early 1830, Kirtland, Ohio, was a small rural trading center of approximately 1,000 people, none of whom was LDS (*see* HISTORY OF THE CHURCH: C. 1831–1844). Six years later, it was a bustling community of 3,000, with commercial, mercantile, and small manufacturing firms, and a temple serving the 2,000 Latter-day Saints in the town. Despite its rapid growth and apparent prosperity, within another two years Joseph SMITH departed Kirtland, leaving behind disgruntled creditors, warrants for his arrest, a failed banking experiment, and a divided Mormon population preparing to leave the temple and their homes. By 1840, only 200 Latter-day Saints remained in Kirtland.

The study of the Kirtland economy between 1830 and 1840 continues to generate controversy among historians. One question has to do with the precipitous increases in the land prices between 1832 and 1837. Were they the result of "reckless land speculation" by Joseph Smith and other Church leaders? The average price per acre of land sold in Kirtland rose from approximately $7 in 1832 to $44 in 1837, only to fall back to $17.50 in 1839. These dramatic changes, however, were related to movements in the general price level, trends in the value of land in neighboring communities, and the impact of population growth. Probably between 25 and 40 percent of the change in the nominal price of land was associated with generalized inflation during this period. As much as 84 percent of the remaining change in the real price of land was correlated with the rise and fall in population. Joseph Smith was primarily responsible for the call to gather to Kirtland; naturally, the newcomers needed land. An examination of land transactions reveals nothing in the buying, selling, or subdividing of land that was unusual for a frontier community.

Another question has to do with Joseph Smith's debts. Was his use of credit "irresponsible"? Early studies of the economic difficulties in Kirtland emphasized debts and ignored assets. Actually, Joseph Smith's potential cumulative indebtedness during this period, including all purchases of land and merchandise, totaled a little over $100,000, considerably below earlier estimates by some historians. At least $60,000 of this debt was eventually settled, and probably much more, since the remainder produced no lawsuits and primarily represented debt for land, which would likely have been paid for or the land reclaimed. At the same time, because of the increase in prices, President Smith and his associates held almost $60,000 equity in land. In the environment of rapid population growth from 1830 to 1837, many New York, Buffalo, and Cleveland merchants willingly extended Joseph Smith credit. His position of leadership in an expanding community, the value of his current assets, and the expectation of continued growth made these transactions reasonable at the time.

The financial problems of Church leaders arose from two circumstances. First, their debts were largely in the form of 90-to-180-day notes, while their assets were primarily in nonliquid land. Second,

Joseph Smith found it very difficult to demand cash from the sale of land or goods to his followers, many of whom were impoverished by the costly migration to Kirtland. The resulting cash-flow problem, common in frontier communities, could have been alleviated by a bank with the capacity to transfer long-term assets into short-term liquidity.

In the fall of 1836, Joseph Smith and his associates drew up a charter for such a bank, the Kirtland Safety Society. The question of fraud has long hovered over the Society. Its timing was unfortunate. During 1836 and 1837, the Ohio legislature, dominated by the hard-money wing of the Democratic party, refused all applications for bank charters. Within a week of realizing the hopelessness of their request for a charter, Church leaders, probably with legal counsel judging from the language of the document, formed a joint stock company and began issuing notes sometimes stamped "anti-banking" notes.

Because an 1816 Ohio law forbade the issuance of unauthorized money, some have thought that the Kirtland Safety Society notes were illegal. But the definition of what constituted "unauthorized" money remained controversial as late as 1873. Several other commercial institutions in Ohio issued notes or scrip, including the Ohio Railroad Company, which issued almost $100,000 of scrip during the same year as the Kirtland Safety Society. Whigs, soft-money Democrats, and several newspapers encouraged such action in opposition to what they considered the unlawful and unconstitutional behavior of the hard-money majority in the legislature.

Heavy demand for redemption of the Kirtland Safety Society's notes led to the suspension of specie payments within its first month of operation. Thereafter, the notes were backed by land values, rather than specie, and almost immediately its notes circulated at a heavy discount. It was further buffeted by the nationwide banking panic of May 1837, when all Ohio banks suspended specie payment. The tenacious Kirtland bank, or anti-bank, continued its faltering operations until November, when it closed its doors for the last time.

The Kirtland Safety Society's first note issue during January 1837 was probably not for more than $15,000. Subsequent note issues may have totaled as much as $85,000 in face value, but the increasing discounts against these issues probably kept the real value of outstanding notes at about the January level or lower. At the time of the initial issue, paid-in subscriptions were also approximately $15,000. That amount, plus the unusual loyalty of the LDS community and a $3,000 loan from the Bank of Geauga, might have provided resources sufficient for a legally chartered bank in Kirtland to experience modest success.

Whatever might have been, the institution did not have a bank charter and did not survive, thereby adding substantially to Joseph Smith's financial woes. He bought more stock, paid more per share than 85 percent of the other investors, and continued to add his own money to the assets of the bank as late as April 1837, well after it had suspended specie payments. After the banking panic of May, Joseph Smith transferred his interests in the bank and other financial assets to Oliver Granger and Jared Carter, who continued to attempt to settle Joseph's financial obligations as late as 1843.

BIBLIOGRAPHY

Adams, Dale W. "Chartering the Kirtland Bank." *BYU Studies* 23 (Fall 1983):467–82.

Fielding, R. Kent. "The Mormon Economy in Kirtland, Ohio." *Utah Historical Quarterly* 27 (Oct. 1959):331–56.

Hill, Marvin S.; C. Keith Rooker; and Larry T. Wimmer. "The Kirtland Economy Revisited: A Market Critique of Sectarian Economics." *BYU Studies* 17 (Summer 1977):391–475.

Parkin, Max H. "Conflict at Kirtland: A Study of the Nature and Causes of External and Internal Conflict of the Mormons in Ohio Between 1830 and 1838." M.A. thesis, Brigham Young University, 1966.

Sampson, D. Paul, and Larry T. Wimmer. "The Kirtland Safety Society: The Stock Ledger Book and the Bank Failure." *BYU Studies* 12 (Summer 1972):427–36.

LARRY T. WIMMER

KIRTLAND, OHIO

[*This entry presents the history of LDS settlement in Kirtland and gives an idea of what it would have been like to have lived among the Saints in this community in the 1830s.*]

During most of the 1830s there were two gathering places for Latter-day Saints, one in western Missouri and the other in northeastern Ohio. Although more members gathered to the Missouri frontier, Kirtland, Ohio, was the principal administrative headquarters of the

Church and the major base for directing missionary work from 1831 until early 1838.

Latter-day Saint growth in northeastern Ohio began not long after the Church was organized in 1830. The Church was introduced into Ohio in late October 1830 and within a month gained 135 new members, of whom about 35 lived in Kirtland township (*see* LAMANITE MISSION OF 1830–1831). Joseph SMITH and his family moved there early in 1831, and in the spring and early summer of that year, other Latter-day Saints, primarily from Ohio and New York, followed. Although the Prophet made two trips to Missouri and lived for a time in nearby Hiram, Ohio, from the summer of 1832 until 1838 the Kirtland area was his primary residence.

The larger part of the first wave of Latter-day Saint settlers in Kirtland moved to Missouri before the end of 1831. The major growth of the LDS population in Kirtland began in 1833. The number rose from approximately 100 in that year to 2,000 in 1838. During the decade preceding the Mormon immigration, the population of the township doubled, increasing from 481 in 1820 to 1,018 in 1830. During the ensuing seven years, primarily as a result of immigration of Latter-day Saints, the population tripled.

Describing conditions in the Kirtland community in the mid-1830s, one contemporary wrote, "They came, men, women, and children, in every conceivable manner, some with horses, oxen, and vehicles rough and rude, while others had walked all or part of the distance. The future 'City of the Saints' appeared like one besieged. Every available house, shop, hut, or barn was filled to its utmost capacity. Even boxes were roughly extemporized and used for shelter until something more permanent could be secured" (*History of Geauga and Lake Counties, Ohio*, p. 248).

The sudden influx of Latter-day Saints to Kirtland had a major impact on the community. One of the visible changes was the increase of small temporary dwellings. Although log and small frame houses dotted the landscape during the first two decades of colonization, larger and more permanent frame and brick structures were erected before 1830. Squatters or renters, comprising half of the population in 1830, lived in small frame houses. As Mormon immigration increased, however, clusters of small unadorned cabins, a throwback to the dwellings of the earliest settlers, appeared primarily in the northwestern section of the township.

Most Latter-day Saints were poorer than the older settlers, partly because the Mormons were recent immigrants. Prior to joining the Church, most members were not transients, nor were they from the lowest economic classes in the East. Many, however, lost economic ground by migrating to Kirtland. Some sold farms in New York or New England for less than the market value, and many left equipment in the East because of the expense of transporting it. All spent a portion of the money derived from such sales on moving their families and supplies westward. The few Saints who moved from Jackson County, Missouri, to Kirtland were also in a difficult economic situation. In the course of their expulsion from that county in 1833, their homes were burned and their property was stolen. On arrival in Kirtland the new settlers faced inflated land values. Since the price of land increased in relation to the growth of population, most newcomers (both Mormon and non-Mormon) could not afford to buy sufficient land to support their families.

After arriving in Kirtland, Latter-day Saints fell further behind economically as a result of contributing labor and scarce resources to Church projects. The Church erected a variety of buildings in Kirtland between the east branch of the Chagrin River and the eastern portion of a plateau that overlooked the river. The principal structure was the KIRTLAND TEMPLE. For almost three years, between the summer of 1833 and the spring of 1836, nearly all members united in building the three-story "House of the Lord" to be used as a meetinghouse and school. While women and girls were carrying on their usual household duties, preparing food for their families, caring for young children, knitting and making clothes, and working in kitchen gardens, they also provided food and clothing for temple workers and drove supply wagons to the temple site. Meanwhile, men and boys worked on farms, cut wood for winter, tanned hides, hunted game, and fished, in addition to hauling stone to the temple site. They also cut, milled, and transported lumber for the construction.

While working on the temple, Latter-day Saints constructed a smaller building to the west that was used as a school, printing establishment, and office building. They also erected a sawmill to assist with their building program, established a tannery and ashery, and constructed shops and stores that provided settlers with merchandise and employment opportunities.

Along with all these sacrifices, many of the men postponed improvement of their standard of living to serve on missions without pay. During the 1830s, traveling elders preached the gospel throughout the United States and eastern Canada, and Heber C. KIMBALL led a group of missionaries (many of them from Kirtland) to England in 1837.

While constructing the temple and supporting missionary work, the Kirtland Saints found time for school. Although growing out of their New England culture and impulses in the Ohio environment, the Saints' educational efforts received their greatest impetus from revelations recorded in Kirtland by Joseph Smith. While living in an apartment above the Newel K. WHITNEY STORE, the Prophet received a revelation that declared, "Teach one another words of wisdom; yea, seek ye out of the best books words of wisdom; seek learning, even by study and also by faith" (D&C 88:118; cf. D&C 88:78–79; 93:36).

As a result of this and other divine commands, Joseph Smith in 1833 invited about twenty elders to attend a SCHOOL OF THE PROPHETS. Following the initial sessions of that school, Church leaders and members established a school of the elders, a grammar school, and various private schools, in which adults and youth studied theology, philosophy, government, literature, history, geography, English grammar, penmanship, arithmetic, Latin, Greek, and Hebrew. In 1836 more than one hundred Latter-day Saints commenced studying Hebrew. Women attended and taught school in Kirtland, and studied various subjects with their husbands.

To assist the Latter-day Saints in their educational pursuits and to promote missionary work, Church leaders sponsored a major publishing program in Kirtland beginning in 1834. Within four years, the Saints published a periodical, the *Latter-day Saints' Messenger and Advocate*; a secular and political paper, *Northern Times*; a hymnal (1835); a second edition of the Book of Mormon; and a collection of 102 sections of revelations recorded by Joseph Smith in the first edition of the Doctrine and Covenants (1835), which included the "Lectures on Faith." Historical and doctrinal information that is now included in the Joseph Smith Translation of the Bible (JST) and portions of the Pearl of Great Price (book of Moses) were also printed in Missouri and Kirtland during the early 1830s.

In addition to working long hours and studying, Latter-day Saints participated in regular worship services. The first day of the week (Sunday) was observed as the Lord's Day, during which members rested from their daily labors. Meetings were initially held in homes and schools. Following the construction of the Kirtland Temple, meetings were also held there. By the mid-1830s a pattern of Sunday worship had been established. Members attended morning and afternoon services during which they sang, prayed, and listened to sermons delivered by leaders and other members. They generally partook of the Lord's Supper not only during the afternoon meetings but also sometimes during the week in their homes. Confirmations of new members and marriages were also performed on Sunday in the temple and in homes on other days. On the first Thursday of each month, a fast and testimony meeting was held in the temple, and many of these meetings continued from 10:00 A.M. to 4:00 P.M., with members singing, praying, bearing testimonies, and teaching one another.

During this decade Church members also participated in an unusual pentecostal season. Shortly before and after the dedication of the Kirtland Temple, many Latter-day Saints wrote of seeing visions, speaking in tongues, and receiving the spirit of prophecy. During a series of meetings held between late January and early May 1836, several Latter-day Saints declared that they saw the Savior, and many claimed to have communed with other heavenly messengers. Many also testified that they sang accompanied by a choir of heavenly personages.

Along with their other activities, Latter-day Saints found time for recreation. Hunting, fishing, swimming, sleighing, skating, wrestling, horseback riding, and riding in carriages were among the most popular leisure pursuits. Although children had few toys, they played with balls, marbles, whistles, and homemade dolls (Backman, pp. 275–83).

Some of the non-Mormon residents considered the intrusion of Latter-day Saints into the community a threat to their traditional pattern of living. Some complained that the Mormon practice of living in harmony with revelations recorded by a prophet was hostile to the American spirit of democracy. Residents not only rejected LDS beliefs regarding visions, revelations, and the restoration but also claimed that the Latter-day Saints had increased the poverty of the community and were a political and economic threat. The political competition reached a peak in 1837 when Latter-day Saints were elected to all local township offices except for the office of constable. Prior to that year, only four Latter-day Saints had been elected to a major office, and there had been a tendency for the citizens to reelect the earliest settlers. In addition to gaining control of the local government, Latter-day Saints transformed the township's voting pattern from Whig to Democratic. Since Kirtland was located in a Whig section of Ohio and all townships in Geauga County in the mid-1830s, except Kirtland, supported that party, Whigs in northeastern Ohio united in opposition to the Mormons. Complaints and charges escalated into threats and mob action.

Early in 1838, amid intensifying pressures from outside the Church and apostasy within, accentuated by the demise of the Kirtland Safety Society and the Panic of 1837 (*see* KIRTLAND ECONOMY), the exodus of Latter-day Saints from Kirtland and vicinity began. Joseph Smith, Sidney RIGDON, and other leaders fled from mobs in January. Other members gradually followed.

In most instances small groups of less than fifty traveled westward. On July 5, 1838, however, more than 500 members left in a stream of fifty-nine wagons—with twenty-seven tents, ninety-seven horses, twenty-two oxen, sixty-nine cows, and one bull. As this long wagon train, known as Kirtland Camp, moved across the states of Ohio, Indiana, Illinois, and Missouri, spectators gathered to watch the sight. Some gave encouragement, while others jeered and threatened violence. Because of financial problems, many in this group were asked by the leaders to leave the camp, so that only a portion of them reached the Missouri frontier.

By mid-July 1838, more than 1,600 Latter-day Saints in the Kirtland area had reluctantly left the temple, vacated their homes, and headed westward. Only a few Latter-day Saints remained in a neighborhood of predominantly empty cabins, and most of these people moved westward before the mid-1840s.

BIBLIOGRAPHY

Anderson, Karl Ricks. *Joseph Smith's Kirtland: Eyewitness Accounts*. Salt Lake City, 1989.

Backman, Milton V., Jr. *The Heavens Resound: A History of the Latter-day Saints in Ohio 1830–1838*. Salt Lake City, 1983.

Hill, S. Marvin; Keith Rooker; and Larry T. Wimmer. "The Kirtland Economy

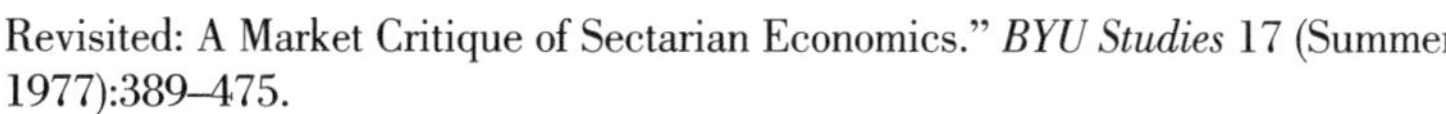

Revisited: A Market Critique of Sectarian Economics." *BYU Studies* 17 (Summer 1977):389–475.

History of Geauga and Lake Counties, Ohio. Philadelphia, 1878.

MILTON V. BACKMAN, JR.

KIRTLAND TEMPLE

The divine command that led to the building of the Kirtland Temple was given to the Prophet Joseph SMITH in January 1831 when the Church was beset by poverty and turmoil. At that time, the Saints were to gather to Ohio, where the Lord promised he would endow them "with power from on high" (D&C 38:32; cf. D&C 88:119; 95:3, 8, 11). Thus they began to build the first of the Latter-day Saint temples.

The Church then consisted of only a few hundred members, men, women, and children who labored together for the temple and contributed, as Eliza R. SNOW wrote, "brain, bone and sinew" and "all living as abstemiously as possible" so that "every cent might be appropriated to the grand object" (Tullidge, p. 82). According to Benjamin F. Johnson, "there was not a scraper and hardly a plow that could be obtained among the Saints," to prepare the ground for the foundation of the temple (Benjamin Johnson, *My Life's Review*, p. 16). Lumber was brought from nearby forests. Stone was hewn from a local quarry.

As the exact patterns of the Tabernacle of Moses and Solomon's temple had been revealed from on high (Ex. 25:9; 1 Chr. 28:11–12), so also were the design, measurements, and functions of the Kirtland Temple revealed. Its interior was to be fifty-five feet wide and sixty-five feet long and have a lower and a higher court. The lower part of the inner court was to be dedicated "for your sacrament offering, and for your preaching, and your fasting, and your praying, and the offering up of your most holy desires unto me, saith your Lord." The higher part of the inner court was to be "dedicated unto me for the school of mine apostles" (D&C 95:13–17).

The cornerstone was laid on July 23, 1833. Brigham YOUNG later explained that the first stone was laid at the southeast corner, the point of greatest light, and at high noon, the time of the greatest sunlight (*JD* 1:133). This was a symbolic reminder that the House of the Lord is a center of light and truth.

The external design of the Kirtland Temple is typical of other contemporary houses of worship at that time, but the arrangement of the interior is unique. On each of the two main floors are two series of four-tiered pulpits, one on the west side, the other on the east. These are symbolic of the offices of the Melchizedek and Aaronic Priesthoods and accommodated their presidencies.

The construction of the temple was abruptly slowed with the call of ZION'S CAMP to Missouri, though many of the women, older men, and the infirm remained in Kirtland. Sidney RIGDON, of the First Presidency, recorded walking the walls of the temple "by night and day and frequently wetting the walls" with his tears, praying for the completion of the temple. At other times the work was slowed because of harassment and threats by enemies of the Church. Elder George A. Smith recalled that sometimes guards attended the temple day and night and worked with a trowel in one hand and a gun in the other.

The women—who, Joseph once remarked, were "first in temple labors"—did spinning, knitting, and sewing so that temple laborers would have clothes to wear. To give the exterior glaze a sparkling appearance, the women contributed glassware to be broken in bits and applied to the plaster. In his dedicatory prayer, Joseph referred to the sacrifice of the Saints: "For thou knowest that we have done this work through great tribulation; and out of our poverty we have given of our substance to build a house to thy name, that the Son of Man might have a place to manifest himself to his people" (D&C 109:5).

An estimated 1,000 people attended the dedication on March 27, 1836. A repeat dedication ceremony was held on March 31. It was a time of great rejoicing. Dedicatory anthems were sung, including "The Spirit of God Like a Fire Is Burning," which was written for the occasion. The sacrament was administered. The inspired dedicatory prayer, filled with Hebraic overtones, became the pattern for all subsequent temple dedications. In it, the Prophet pleaded with the Lord for the visible manifestation of his divine presence (the *Shekhinah*), as in the Tabernacle of Moses, at Solomon's temple, and on the day of Pentecost, "And let thy house be filled as with a rushing mighty wind, with thy glory" (D&C 109:37; cf. Ex. 29:43; 33:9–10; 2 Chr. 7:1–3; Acts 2:1–4). Many recorded the fulfillment of that prayer. Eliza R. Snow wrote, "The ceremonies of that dedication may be rehearsed, but no mortal language can describe the heavenly manifestations of that memorable day. Angels appeared to some, while a sense of divine presence was realized by all present, and each heart was filled with 'joy inexpressible and full of glory'" (Tullidge, p. 95). After the prayer, the entire congregation rose and, with hands uplifted, shouted hosannas "to God and the Lamb."

The climax of the spiritual outpouring occurred on April 3, 1836, when the Savior appeared in the Kirtland Temple to Joseph Smith and Oliver COWDERY and said, "For behold I have accepted this house, and my name shall be here; and I will manifest myself to my people in mercy in this house" (D&C 110:7). Then three other personages of former dispensations, or eras, came and restored keys of the priesthood: Moses restored the keys of the gathering of Israel, Elias restored keys of the gospel of Abraham, and Elijah restored the keys of sealing. These keys represent three different aspects of the mission of the Church.

Without the keys restored in the Kirtland Temple, the Latter-day Saints would not have authority to perform the ordinances in their many temples. Washings and anointings had been given in January 1836. After attending to the washing of feet, Joseph assured the quorums that he "had given them all the instruction they needed" to go forth and build up the kingdom of God, having "passed through all the necessary ceremonies" (*TPJS*, p. 110). These ceremonies were preliminary to the fulness of the ordinances and the temple endowment later administered in the Nauvoo Temple.

Abandoned by the Saints after severe persecution, the Kirtland Temple was for a time in the hands of dissidents. Today it is owned by the REORGANIZED CHURCH OF JESUS CHRIST OF LATTER DAY SAINTS and is used as a visitors center. It has been recognized as a National Historic Site.

BIBLIOGRAPHY

Anderson, Karl Ricks. *Joseph Smith's Kirtland: Eyewitness Accounts.* Salt Lake City, 1989.

Backman, Milton V., Jr. *The Heavens Resound: A History of the Latter-day Saints in Ohio, 1830–1838*. Salt Lake City, 1983.

Madsen, Truman G. *Joseph Smith, the Prophet*, pp. 67–82. Salt Lake City, 1989.

Tullidge, Edward W. *The Women of Mormondom*. New York, 1877.

KEITH W. PERKINS

L

LAMANITE MISSION OF 1830–1831

The mission to western Missouri in 1830–1831 was important for three reasons: it demonstrated the Church's commitment to preach to the descendants of the Lamanites of the Book of Mormon; it helped establish a stronghold for the Church in KIRTLAND, OHIO, where the missionaries found numerous unexpected converts; and it ultimately brought Joseph SMITH to Jackson County, Missouri, to lay the foundation of Zion, or the New Jerusalem.

This mission, one of the Church's earliest missionary expeditions, commenced in October 1830 in New York State with the call of Oliver COWDERY, "second elder" in the Church; Peter Whitmer, Jr.; Parley P. PRATT; and Ziba Peterson (D&C 28:8; 32:1–3). It initiated the long continuing Church practice of taking the gospel to Native Americans. The Book of Mormon, in part a record of American Indian origins, prophesies that the Lamanites will assist in building the millennial New Jerusalem (3 Ne. 20–21), to be located in the Western Hemisphere (Ether 13:3–6; cf. D&C 28:9).

In the early 1800s the U.S. government began removing eastern Indians to the American frontier west of all existing states. In May 1830 the U.S. Congress passed the Indian Removal Law, further ensuring that the missionaries' ultimate destination was just west of Independence, Missouri, the last American outpost before "Indian country." To arrive there, the elders traveled on foot from New York, a distance of fifteen hundred miles, in midwinter.

These brethren soon found audiences of white settlers and some Indians. First, at nearby Buffalo, New York, they taught the Catteraugus Indians, who accepted two copies of the Book of Mormon. In northeastern Ohio they preached widely, and their message excited public curiosity. While visiting Mentor, Ohio, Cowdery and Pratt contacted Sidney RIGDON, a dynamic Reformed Baptist minister who was promoting New Testament restorationist beliefs in his congregation and was Pratt's friend and former pastor. They challenged Rigdon to read the Book of Mormon, which he promised to do. Rigdon also allowed the elders to speak in his Mentor church and to his congregation in Kirtland. Positive response to their message was almost immediate. Many members of the congregation, including Rigdon, were baptized. News of their success spread rapidly, sparking intense public feelings and leading to more conversions.

In four weeks in northeastern Ohio, the elders baptized approximately 130 converts, 50 of them from Kirtland. These new members made Kirtland their headquarters. Among the converts were men who would become leaders in the Church: Sidney Rigdon, Frederick G. Williams, Lyman Wight, Newel K. Whitney, Levi Hancock, and John Murdock. Two other prominent men, Edward Partridge and Orson HYDE, joined the Church soon after the missionaries departed. By the end of 1830, membership in Ohio had reached 300, nearly triple the number of members in New York. In December, after learning of the great Ohio harvest, Joseph Smith received a revelation directing the New York Saints to gather to the Kirtland area (D&C 37:1, 3), which most did in 1831.

Joined by Frederick G. Williams, a Kirtland physician, the four missionaries continued west in late November 1830, preaching as they traveled. They visited the Wyandot Indians at Sandusky, Ohio, where their hearers rejoiced over their message. However, during several days at Cincinnati, they were unable to interest other audiences. In late December, the elders took passage down the Ohio River toward St. Louis until encountering ice near Cairo, Illinois, which forced them to walk overland. Thereafter, their journey became increasingly arduous. Because of storms of rare severity, the winter of 1830–1831 is referred to in midwestern annals as "the winter of the deep snow." Food was scarce, and the missionaries were forced to survive on meager rations of frozen bread and pork.

In late January 1831, still in the midst of intense cold, the missionaries arrived at Jackson County (*see* MISSOURI: LDS COMMUNITIES IN JACKSON AND CLAY COUNTIES). Independence, the county seat, was a ragged and undisciplined frontier village twelve miles from the state's western border. Here the missionaries separated. Whitmer and Peterson set up a tailor shop to earn needed funds, while Cowdery, Pratt, and Williams crossed the state boundary, called by them "the border of the Lamanites," into Indian country. After first contacting the Shawnees, the elders crossed the frozen Kansas River and walked to the Delaware Indian village located about twelve miles west of the Missouri state line.

The Delaware Indians had arrived there only the previous November after a toilsome journey of their own. Because of their present poverty and mistreatment at the hands of whites, the aged Delaware chief, known to the white man as William Anderson Kithtilhund, viewed any Christian missionaries with suspicion. After his initial hesitation, however, Kithtilhund summoned his chiefs into council. For several days, through an interpreter, Cowdery shared with the receptive Delawares the Book of Mormon account of their ancestors.

Plans to establish a permanent school among the Delawares and to baptize converts were soon interrupted by an order to desist from the federal Indian agent, Richard W. Cummins. After issuing a second warning, he threatened to arrest the elders if they did not leave Indian lands. Pratt believed that the jealousy of the missionaries of other churches and Indian agents precipitated the order. In a letter to William Clark, superintendent of Indian affairs in St. Louis, Cummins indicated that the elders did not possess a certificate authorizing their presence on government Indian lands. Later in Independence, Cowdery wrote the superintendent requesting a license to return to Indian lands, but the request was never granted, and that effectively ended the Lamanite mission.

From Independence, Oliver Cowdery dispatched Parley P. Pratt to the East to report on the mission while the remaining four missionaries preached to white settlers in Jackson County. In the summer of 1831, Joseph Smith led a group from Kirtland to Jackson

County to meet the missionaries. Through revelation the Prophet identified a site a half mile from Independence as the temple lot for the New Jerusalem (D&C 57:1–3).

BIBLIOGRAPHY

Backman, Milton V., Jr. *The Heavens Resound*, pp. 1–12. Salt Lake City, 1983.

Pratt, Parley P. *Autobiography of Parley Parker Pratt*, pp. 47–58. Salt Lake City, 1938.

MAX H PARKIN

LEE, HAROLD B.

Harold Bingham Lee (1899–1973) became the eleventh President of The Church of Jesus Christ of Latter-day Saints on July 7, 1972, and served until his death on December 26, 1973. His 538-day tenure was the shortest service by a Church President in history, despite the fact that at age seventy-three President Lee was the youngest person to hold the office initially in nearly forty years. One of his greatest contributions to the Church, the organization of the correlation program, was made when he was still a member of the Quorum of the Twelve Apostles.

President Lee was born on March 28, 1899, in Clifton, Idaho, to Samuel Marion Lee and Louisa Emiline Bingham. He grew up in impoverished, rural conditions, and from childhood he advanced faster than his peers. He started school a year earlier than was the practice in his farming community because he could already write his name and knew the alphabet. As a young boy, he was large for his age, and when his friends were ordained to the priesthood, he became a deacon also, although he was technically not quite old enough for the honor.

In keeping with this pattern, he began his career in education at a young age. He earned a teaching certificate at Albion State Normal School in Idaho, and at seventeen was appointed to be principal of the one-room Silver Star School at Weston, Idaho, teaching twenty to twenty-five pupils, ranging from first to eighth grade. One year later, he was appointed principal of the larger grade school at Oxford, Idaho, where he served for three winters.

These responsibilities prepared him for his call in 1920 to the

Western States Mission, headquartered in Denver, Colorado. After nine months he became conference president, presiding over both missionaries and local Church members in Denver. During his two year missionary service, he baptized forty-five converts to the Church.

President Lee was one of the youngest stake presidents in the Church when at thirty-one, he was set apart as president of Pioneer Stake in Salt Lake City. Within a few years, he was faced with the suffering among stake members brought on by the Great Depression. With his counselors, he struggled to save his people from hunger and financial ruin. His ingenuity in helping them obtain basic necessities led to his appointment by the First Presidency in 1935 to organize a welfare program for the entire Church.

In 1932 President Lee was appointed to fill a vacancy in the Salt Lake City Commission and was assigned to direct the Department of Streets and Public Improvements. A year later, he was elected to the same position. For years Utah citizens urged him to run for the governorship or for the U.S. Senate.

Elder Lee was called as a member of the Quorum of the Twelve Apostles on April 6, 1941. As he looked around the council room in the Salt Lake Temple where the quorum held its meetings, Elder Lee, then forty-two, discovered that every man there was at least twenty years his senior. He thought of himself as a seedling among giant redwoods, causing his tutor and friend J. Reuben Clark, Jr., a counselor in the First Presidency, to refer affectionately to him as the "Kid."

Early in his apostleship, Elder Lee served on a committee to simplify Church organization and functions. For two decades, he studied the subject and prepared proposals. Finally when the time for implementing them came in the 1960s, the correlation program was introduced, with Lee serving as chairman of the Correlation Committee. Correlation emphasized the family and the home, the connection of auxiliary organizations with the priesthood, simplification of the curriculum, the teaching of the scriptures, and restructuring the Church magazines to serve children, youth, and adults better.

In January 1970, Elder Lee was called to serve as a counselor in the First Presidency while concurrently presiding over the Quorum of the Twelve Apostles. He was called to be President of the Church after President Joseph Fielding Smith died on July 2, 1972.

Following a long period when age and illness had prevented the previous Church Presidents from traveling, President Lee moved out among the people. He attended area conferences in England, Mexico, and Germany. President Lee also conscientiously and purposefully devoted much time to address youth conferences, to restore the prophetic image to the young members of the Church. He was the first to visit Israel and Palestine as President of the Church.

President Lee possessed a remarkable candidness about himself and the office of President. He talked openly of his feelings about his calling, allowing people to look into his heart. Sensitive spirituality was his greatest leadership quality. He sought answers to prayers for the Saints and boldly labeled the answers revelations. He was a forceful preacher of the gospel. His sermons were always based upon solid scriptural foundations, and yet the lessons were invariably illustrated with poignant and often tender stories of everyday life, appropriate to the day and its challenges. His counsel was practical; for him the most important commandment was the one a person was having difficulty living at the moment.

President Lee's spirituality resulted partly from his personal struggles. He learned to control a fiery temper and a quick, action-oriented disposition that had earlier in his life offended some. In his later years, President Lee was perceived as being more gentle in manner, compassionate, gracious, hospitable, and thoughtful of others. He was always a gentleman, impeccably dressed. At age seventy-four he served as though in the prime of life, with a rich, full voice and characteristic vigor. His sudden death on December 26, 1973, from cardiac and lung failure stunned the Church.

President Lee found great pleasure, and also experienced sorrows, in his family. In 1923 he married Fern Lucinda Tanner, whom he first met in the Western States Mission. To them were born two daughters, Maurine and Helen. They had ten grandchildren. Fern died September 24, 1962, and Maurine died shortly thereafter, making this a difficult period in President Lee's life. He married Freda Johanna (Joan) Jensen, an educator, on June 17, 1963.

In the conference meeting in which he was sustained as President of the Church, President Lee characterized his own life: "At times it seemed as though I, too, was like a rough stone rolling down from a high mountainside, being buffeted and polished, I suppose, by experiences, that I, too, might overcome and become a polished shaft in the quiver of the Almighty" (*CR*, Oct. 1972, p. 20).

BIBLIOGRAPHY

Arrington, Leonard J. "Harold B. Lee." In *The Presidents of the Church*, ed. Leonard J. Arrington, pp. 342–71. Salt Lake City, 1986.

Goates, L. Brent. *Harold B. Lee, Prophet and Seer*. Salt Lake City, 1985.

———. *He Changed My Life*. Salt Lake City, 1988.

L. BRENT GOATES

LEGAL AND JUDICIAL HISTORY OF THE CHURCH

The Church of Jesus Christ of Latter-day Saints has usually relied upon the law for protection and has honored its judgments in principle and practice. The one significant exception was its resistance to antipolygamy laws before PLURAL MARRIAGE was discontinued in 1890. Obedience to the law of the land is a tenet of LDS belief.

Despite this respect for law, nineteenth-century LDS history includes numerous encounters with the law. Peculiarities of doctrine and practice, accompanied by social cohesion that appeared threatening to outsiders, spawned both PERSECUTION and frequent litigation for the Church and its leaders. In western New York, where the Church had its genesis, and in OHIO, where the Prophet Joseph SMITH moved in 1831, evenhanded justice was generally available in the courts. Three times in New York, Joseph Smith was tried and acquitted for "vagrancy" and "disorderly conduct," the charges stemming largely from religious hostility (*see* SMITH, JOSEPH: LEGAL TRIALS). In Ohio the Prophet and other Church leaders used the courts affirmatively to obtain redress against religious persecution. Near the close of the Ohio period, the failure of the Kirtland Safety Society (*see* KIRTLAND ECONOMY), a lending institution, brought a host of lawsuits against individual Church leaders who had sponsored it. The society was engaged in banking activities without a legal charter and collapsed in the wake of bank failures that swept the nation in 1837. Numerous judgments were obtained against Joseph Smith and other principals, some of which they were unable to pay, but anti-Mormon bias appears not to have been a factor in the decisions.

In Missouri, where the Latter-day Saints began to gather in 1831 and where the Prophet went after fleeing Kirtland in January 1838, the courts were less sympathetic. In 1833–1834 the Saints were forcibly expelled from Jackson County and forced into Clay County, Missouri, by mob violence. After resettling in nearby Caldwell and other Missouri counties, they were again driven from their homes in 1838–1839 by armed mobs abetted by the state militia. In neither instance were they able to obtain judicial redress for loss of life and property. Instead, incident to the expulsion from Caldwell County, Joseph Smith and other Church leaders were arrested as instigators of the violence on charges of larceny, arson, and murder. Most of the prisoners, including the Prophet, were later allowed to escape, and they fled to Illinois. Two who reached trial were acquitted for lack of evidence.

In Illinois, for a time, the Saints had a more favorable experience with the law. Courted by Illinois politicians, they obtained a liberal state charter for their city of Nauvoo. Under the NAUVOO CHARTER the local court consisted of the mayor of Nauvoo and the city aldermen, who were also Church leaders. By ordinance, no legal process issued in any other jurisdiction could be served in Nauvoo except by the city marshal, and then only when countersigned by the mayor. The Nauvoo court made extensive use of the writ of habeas corpus to free persons held under arrest warrants issued by courts outside Nauvoo. Joseph Smith was discharged from arrest several times on writs issued by the Nauvoo court; he also obtained habeas relief from the federal district court in Springfield, Illinois. In June 1844 the Prophet accepted the need to stand trial at Carthage, the county seat, on charges arising from the Nauvoo city council's decision to declare the NAUVOO EXPOSITOR (a newly created opposition newspaper) a nuisance and destroy its printing press. While imprisoned in CARTHAGE JAIL awaiting trial, he and his brother Hyrum were killed by a mob. His accused assassins were tried and acquitted. The Illinois legislature repealed the Nauvoo Charter in January 1845, and in early 1846, threatened by mob violence, the Saints began a westward exodus that ultimately led to Utah.

In Utah, local government officials were usually Church leaders, and the territorial legislature and local judges were drawn almost exclusively from Church membership. When the UTAH TERRITORY was created in 1850, Brigham YOUNG, President of the Church, was appointed territorial governor. A system of ecclesiastical courts was established alongside the territorial courts, and most disputes between Church members were settled there rather than in the civil courts. Except in special circumstances, suing a brother or sister in a civil court constituted "un-Christianlike conduct," for which a penalty of Church disfellowshipment was often imposed. Nonmembers occasionally took their civil claims to Church courts as well. The county probate judge was usually a local Church leader, and probate courts were important in the judicial system because the territorial legislature had given them broad jurisdiction in both criminal and civil matters. Congress abolished the general jurisdiction of the probate courts in 1874 as part of the federal campaign against polygamy.

Tension between the Church and the federal government in Utah appeared almost from the beginning. Several federal appointees to the territorial government in 1851, including two of three federal judges, clashed with Church officials and the territorial legislature and quickly left the territory. Their negative reports to the President of the United States and to the public helped lay the foundation for future misunderstanding. The tension reached crisis proportions in 1857 when U.S. President James Buchanan, acting on false reports of a Mormon rebellion, sent an army of 2,500 men to ensure the authority of a new territorial governor, Alfred Cumming of Georgia (*see* UTAH EXPEDITION). The confrontation was resolved without bloodshed, but it signaled a conflict not to be mitigated until after 1890, when the Church officially discontinued the practice of plural marriage and adopted a less intrusive role in the political and economic life of Utah.

Courts and the law, rather than military force, became the means of enforcing Church capitulation to the mandates of the larger secular society. The U.S. Supreme Court, in *Reynolds v. United States* (98 U.S. 145 [1879]), ruled that the First Amendment right to free exercise of religion did not exempt Mormon polygamists from prosecution under the Morrill Anti-Bigamy Act (1862), and this paved the way for even harsher anti-Mormon legislation (*see* ANTIPOLYGAMY LEGISLATION). Unlawful cohabitation, easier to prove than a bigamous marriage, was made a crime in 1882. Other legislation found constitutional by the courts had the effect of excluding Latter-day Saints from territorial juries, denying them the right to vote or hold public office, denying polygamists' children the right of inheritance, and hindering the immigration of Church members from abroad. Church leaders were repeatedly harassed by vexatious lawsuits. Pressure on the Church climaxed when the U.S. Supreme Court, in *The Late Corporation of the Church of Jesus Christ of Latter-day Saints v. United States* (136 U.S. 1 [1890]), upheld provisions of the 1887 Edmunds-Tucker Act that disincorporated the Church and authorized confiscation of most of its property. On September 24, 1890, President Wilford WOODRUFF, by revelation, issued the MANIFESTO discontinuing the practice of plural marriage. Although a number of property issues remained, the Manifesto spelled the end of the nineteenth-century legal confrontation between the Church and the U.S. government.

In the twentieth century, the Church has avoided conduct that might bring it into conflict with the law of the land. Since the official discontinuance of plural marriage, no Church-sanctioned practices have posed a direct challenge to current legal norms. Disputes over property, business matters, and personal-injury claims have occasionally led to lawsuits, and legal claims sometimes have arisen out of specialized Church operations, such as LDS Social Services and Brigham Young University. Church activities outside the United States have also produced occasional lawsuits as the Church has expanded internationally. For the most part, this litigation has had little significance for the central mission of the Church or for issues of religious freedom. Compared with other large institutions in modern society, the Church has not been litigious.

A few court actions affecting the Church have had special significance, however. The decision of the U.S. Supreme Court in *Corporation of the Presiding Bishop of The Church of Jesus Christ of Latter-day Saints et al. v. Amos et al.* (483 U.S. 327 [1987]) was a notable affirmation of religious group rights under the U.S. Constitution. The suit was brought by former employees of the Church-owned Deseret Gymnasium, Beehive Clothing Mills, and Deseret Industries who were discharged for failing to meet religious qualifications for participation in LDS temple worship. The employees alleged religious discrimination in violation of the Civil Rights Act of 1964. In defense, the Church invoked section 702 of the act, which expressly exempts religious organizations from the statutory prohibition of religious discrimination in employment. The lower court found that the section 702 exemption violated the establishment clause of the First Amendment, a constitutional bar to laws having the purpose or primary effect of advancing religion. The Supreme Court unanimously disagreed, holding the statutory exemption to be a permissible governmental accommodation of religion, at least as to nonprofit activities. The *Amos* decision is an important statement of the right of religious organizations to preserve their institutional integrity by maintaining religious qualifications for employees.

In two other establishment clause cases, Church practices were implicated, although the Church was not a party. *Lanner v. Wimmer* (662 F.2d 1349 [10th Cir. 1981]) was a challenge to the Logan, Utah, school district policy of granting released time and high school credit for students attending weekday LDS seminary classes. The court decided that released time was permissible governmental accommodation of religion but that granting of credit was not. The second case, *Foremaster v. City of St. George* (882 F.2d 1485 [10th Cir. 1989]), involved a citizen's objection to the city's subsidization of exterior lighting of the LDS St. George Temple and to the use of a replica of the temple on the St. George city logo. Although St. George claimed it was using the temple to enhance the city's image, the federal appeals court ruled that the city was thereby endorsing the Church in violation of the constitutional rule against establishment of religion.

The Church and its members have helped to define the statutory rights of religious groups through litigation of tax exemption laws in a number of U.S. and foreign jurisdictions. In England the Church's claim to a statutory property tax exemption for its London Temple was ultimately decided by the House of Lords, the highest court of appeal (*Church of Jesus Christ of Latter-day Saints v. Henning*, 2 All E.R. 733 [1963]). The Lords denied the exemption because the temple, with its restrictive admission requirements, did not qualify under the statute as a place of "public worship." *Henning* has been frequently cited in British cases interpreting the property tax exemption statute. It was cited but not followed in the New Zealand Supreme Court decision of *Church of Jesus Christ of Latter-day*

Saints Trust Board v. Waipa County Council (2 N.Z.L.R. 710 [1980]), in which the court, interpreting a New Zealand statute, granted a property tax exemption to the LDS temple in New Zealand. Property tax exemptions for Church property have also been litigated in a number of U.S. states, most commonly in relation to Church welfare farms. Exemption for such property has been denied by courts in Arizona, Idaho, and Oregon, but upheld in South Carolina. In each case, the outcome has turned on the wording of the statute defining the tax exemption.

Of some practical importance for Church members in the United States was the 1990 decision of the U.S. Supreme Court in *Davis v. United States* (110 S.Ct. 2014 [U.S. 1990]). In an income-tax refund suit brought by parents of two former missionaries, the Court held that funds sent directly to missionaries for their support were not deductible as a charitable contribution. To qualify as a charitable deduction, the funds had to be given to the Church itself or else donated through a trust or other legally enforceable arrangement, for the benefit of the Church.

Occasionally other legal actions have been of interest to the Church, even though the Church was not a party and no Church activities were directly at issue. One highly publicized case was the prosecution of Mark Hofmann for two 1985 Utah murder-bombings and various document FORGERIES. The Church was interested because many of the Hofmann forgeries purported to shed new light on the early history of the Church and had been widely accepted as authentic. After a preliminary hearing, the prosecutors accepted a plea bargain mandating life imprisonment. Another widely noted case indirectly affecting the Church arose from an Idaho court challenge to the Equal Rights Amendment (ERA). The Church had taken a strong official stand against the ERA, and proponents of the amendment claimed that U.S. District Judge Marion J. Callister would be biased on the issue because he was a prominent local Church leader. Judge Callister refused to disqualify himself (*Idaho v. Freeman*, 478 F. Supp. 33 [1979], 507 F. Supp. 706 [1981]) and subsequently ruled against the ERA on the major issues. On appeal to the U.S. Supreme Court, the case was dismissed as moot because the time for ratification of the ERA had expired (*National Organization for Women, Inc., et al. v. Idaho et al.*, 459 U.S. 809 [1982]).

BIBLIOGRAPHY

Allen, James B., and Glen M. Leonard. *The Story of the Latter-day Saints*. Salt Lake City, 1976.

Burman, Jennifer Mary. "*Corporation of Presiding Bishop v. Amos*: The Supreme Court and Religious Discrimination by Religious Educational Institutions." *Notre Dame Journal of Law, Ethics and Public Policy* 3 (1988):629–62.

Driggs, Kenneth David. "The Mormon Church-State Confrontation in Nineteenth-Century America." *Journal of Church and State* 30 (1988):273–89.

Firmage, Edwin Brown, and Richard Collin Mangrum. *Zion in the Courts: A Legal History of the Church of Jesus Christ of Latter-day Saints, 1830–1900*. Urbana, Ill., 1988.

ROBERT E. RIGGS

LIBERTY JAIL

In 1833 a small jail was constructed in Liberty, the seat of Clay County, Missouri. In 1856 the building was abandoned. After a short tenure as an ice house, it fell into disrepair and was finally demolished near the turn of the century. Today, thousands of Latter-day Saints and other tourists visit the partially reconstructed jail and view it as what the LDS historian B. H. Roberts called a "prison temple" because of a notable prisoner it housed: the Prophet Joseph SMITH languished within its four-foot-thick walls from December 1, 1838 until April 6, 1839. Sharing this incarceration were his brother Hyrum (*see* HYRUM SMITH), who served as his second counselor in the presidency of the Church; Sidney RIGDON, his first counselor; and three other brethren—Lyman Wight, Alexander McRae, and Caleb Baldwin.

They were held on a variety of unsubstantiated charges stemming from the "Mormon War" (*see* MISSOURI CONFLICT), which had culminated in their betrayal and the fall of the LDS settlement of Far West, Missouri, a few weeks earlier. As they awaited trial, they suffered severe privation. Confined to the lower level, or dungeon portion of the building, they slept on the straw-strewn stone floor with little light and scant protection from the Missouri winter. Alexander McRae described the food they were served as "very coarse, and so filthy that we could not eat it until we were driven to it by hunger" (*CHC* 1:521). He also recorded that several attempts were made to poison them.

Notwithstanding these trying physical conditions, Joseph Smith's greater suffering seemed to come from his anguish for the thousands of Latter-day Saints, including his own family, who were being driven from the state under the executive order of Governor Lilburn W. Boggs calling for the extermination of the Mormons (*see* EXTERMINATION ORDER). In a very long, two-part letter to the Church, written between March 20 and March 25, Joseph cried out, "O God, where art thou? And where is the pavilion that covereth thy hiding place? How long shall thy hand be stayed, and thine eye, yea thy pure eye, behold from the eternal heavens the wrongs of thy people and of thy servants, and thine ear be penetrated with their cries? Yea, O Lord, how long shall they suffer these wrongs and unlawful oppressions?" (D&C 121:1–3).

In answer, he was told to be of good cheer: "My son, peace be unto thy soul; thine adversity and thine afflictions shall be but a small moment; And then, if thou endure it well, God shall exalt thee on high; thou shalt triumph over all thy foes" (D&C 121:7–8). Some of Joseph Smith's most sublime writings are found in this letter. The counsel of the Lord concerning the proper exercise of priesthood authority (D&C 121:33–46) is among the most quoted latter-day scripture. Excerpts from the letter make up sections 121, 122, and 123 of the Doctrine and Covenants.

In early April 1839, the prisoners were moved to Daviess County for trial; and then while being taken to Columbia, Boone County, on yet another change of venue, they learned from their captors that, for a variety of reasons, it would be agreeable to the officials if they would escape. With the aid of their guards, the prisoners hastened to join the exiled Latter-day Saints who were gathering in western Illinois.

Today, a commodious visitors center houses Liberty Jail that, in cutaway form, has been partially rebuilt from the original stones.

BIBLIOGRAPHY

Dyer, Alvin R. *The Refiner's Fire*. Salt Lake City, 1968.

Maxwell, Neal A. *But for a Small Moment*. Salt Lake City, 1986.

Roberts, B. H. *CHC*, chap. 38.

LAWRENCE R. FLAKE

LYMAN, AMY BROWN

Amy Brown Lyman (1872–1959) was the eighth general president of the Relief Society, an author, Utah state legislator, teacher, and social worker. She possessed an active mind, warm personality, good humor, indomitable spirit, and strong desire to serve.

Born in Pleasant Grove, Utah, on February 7, 1872, to pioneers John and Margaret Zimmerman Brown, Amy was a beautiful, popular, and intelligent child, with dark hair and eyes and a joyous zest for living. She attended public school in Pleasant Grove, then the Brigham Young Academy from 1888 to 1890. Her enthusiasm for learning blossomed under Dr. Karl Maeser, with whose family she boarded for several years. She taught at the academy for four years and then in Salt Lake City elementary schools two more years.

On September 9, 1896, she married Richard R. Lyman, a professor of civil engineering at the University of Utah; he later served as a member of the Quorum of the Twelve Apostles for twenty-five years. The Lymans had two children, Wendell Brown and Margaret; they also raised their granddaughter, Amy Kathryn Lyman, after the death of her parents.

Amy continued to develop her talents while raising her family and accompanying her husband on travels for his doctoral studies. She took classes at the University of Utah, the University of Chicago, and Cornell University. While in Chicago, she became interested in social work and spent several days at Hull House, where she met Jane Addams and gained experiences that changed her life. During summers, she studied family welfare work at the University of Colorado, earned a special certificate in social service, and received in-service training at the city and county welfare departments in Denver.

In 1909 she began her long service to the Relief Society, in which she displayed great organizational and leadership skills. She served two years as a general board member, two years as assistant secretary, and fifteen years as general secretary-treasurer. As secretary-treasurer, she brought to the Relief Society office up-to-date practices, introducing the use of secretaries, office machines, and new filing systems; prepared the first uniform record books for ward Relief Societies; and collected all the minutes and historical documents of the Relief Society since its inception in Nauvoo in 1842. For eleven years she served as first counselor in the general presidency, and she also presided over the women's organizations in the European Mission while her husband served as mission president.

Amy Brown Lyman was authorized by President Joseph F. SMITH to organize and promote family welfare work. She established and directed the Relief Society general board's Social Service Department, with its employment bureau and child-placement agency; taught thousands of volunteer Relief Society workers fundamental principles of family welfare; developed extensive health and nurse training programs; and served in public and private welfare agencies through both world wars and the Great Depression of the 1930s.

During this time, she also rendered important service in many civic organizations and in the Utah state legislature (1923–1924), where she sponsored legislation to provide for maternity and infant care. She held offices in the National Council of Women and in 1929 helped establish the Utah State Training School, where she served as a trustee for eleven years.

In January 1940, the centennial year for the Relief Society, Amy Brown Lyman became general president of the Relief Society. In this position she reemphasized the Relief Society's unique position among women's groups in providing opportunities for education and service outside the home. Under her presidency, the Relief Society actively supported the new Church welfare program, especially sponsoring sewing projects to supply Church welfare storehouses and to meet Red Cross needs in World War II.

Amy Brown Lyman experienced much personal tragedy in her life. Besides the early deaths of her son and daughter-in-law, she endured a great ordeal when her husband was released from the Quorum of the Twelve Apostles and subsequently excommunicated from the Church in November 1943. She continued to serve as general president of the Relief Society until she asked to be released in September 1944; the following spring her request was granted. She continued to stand by her husband, who was rebaptized in the Church in 1954.

Her testimony sustained and strengthened her throughout her life. She wrote, "My testimony has been my anchor and my stay, my satisfaction in times of joy and gladness, my comfort in times of discouragement" (Lyman, pp. 160–61). Her vision, wisdom, spirituality, and concern for others made Amy Brown Lyman a fitting president to usher in the Relief Society's second century.

BIBLIOGRAPHY

History of Relief Society 1842–1966. Salt Lake City, 1966.

Lyman, Amy B. *In Retrospect: Autobiography of Amy Brown Lyman.* Salt Lake City, 1945.

Peterson, Janet, and LaRene Gaunt. *Elect Ladies, Presidents of the Relief Society.* Salt Lake City, 1990.

ANN WILLARDSON ENGAR
AMY LYMAN ENGAR

M

MANIFESTO OF 1890

The Manifesto of 1890 was a proclamation by President Wilford WOODRUFF that the Church had discontinued PLURAL MARRIAGE. It ended a decade of persecution and hardship in which Latter-day Saints tenaciously resisted what they saw as unconstitutional federal attempts to curb polygamy. While the Manifesto is often referred to as a revelation, the declaration was actually a press release that followed President Woodruff's revelatory experiences. In this respect, the Manifesto is similar to Doctrine and Covenants Official Declaration—2.

Following the passage of the Edmunds-Tucker Act in 1887, the Church found it difficult to operate as a viable institution (*see* ANTIPOLYGAMY LEGISLATION). Among other things, this legislation disincorporated the Church, confiscated its properties, and even threatened seizure of its temples. After visiting with priesthood leaders in many settlements, President Woodruff left for San Francisco on September 3, 1890, to meet with prominent businessmen and politicians. He returned to Salt Lake City on September 21, determined to obtain divine confirmation to pursue a course that seemed to be agonizingly more and more clear. As he explained to Church members a year later, the choice was between, on the one hand, continuing to practice plural marriage and thereby losing the temples, "stopping all the ordinances therein," and, on the other, ceasing plural marriage in order to continue performing the essential ordinances for the living and the dead. President Woodruff hastened to add that he had acted only as the Lord directed: "I should have let all the temples go out of our hands; I should have gone to prison myself, and let every other man go there, had not the God of heaven commanded me to do what I do; and when the hour came that I was commanded to do that, it was all clear to me."

The final element in President Woodruff's revelatory experience came on the evening of September 23, 1890. The following morning, he reported to some of the General Authorities that he had struggled throughout the night with the Lord regarding the path that should be pursued. "Here is the result," he said, placing a 510-word handwritten manuscript on the table. The document was later edited by George Q. Cannon of the First Presidency and others to its present 356 words. On October 6, 1890, it was presented to the Latter-day Saints at the General Conference and approved.

While nearly all Church leaders in 1890 regarded the Manifesto as inspired, there were differences among them about its scope and permanence. Some leaders were understandably reluctant to terminate a long-standing practice that was regarded as divinely mandated. As a result, a limited number of plural marriages were performed over the next several years. Not surprisingly, rumors of such marriages soon surfaced, and beginning in January 1904, testimony given in the SMOOT HEARINGS made it clear that plural marriage had not been completely extinguished. The ambiguity was ended in the general conference of April 1904, when the First Presidency issued the "second manifesto," an emphatic declaration that prohibited plural marriage and proclaimed that offenders would be subject to Church discipline, including excommunication.

The Manifesto of 1890 should be regarded as a pivotal event in the history of The Church of Jesus Christ of Latter-day Saints and of the state of Utah. Not only did it mark the beginning of the end of the official practice of plural marriage, but it also heralded a new age as Latter-day Saints relinquished the isolationist practices of the past and commenced a period of greater accommodation and integration into the fabric of American society (*see* UTAH STATEHOOD).

BIBLIOGRAPHY
Alexander, Thomas G. *Mormonism in Transition*, pp. 3–15. Urbana, Ill., 1986.
Gibbons, Francis M. *Wilford Woodruff*, pp. 353–61. Salt Lake City, 1988.

PAUL H. PETERSON

MARTYRDOM OF JOSEPH AND HYRUM SMITH

The violent deaths of the Prophet Joseph SMITH at the age of thirty-eight and his brother Hyrum SMITH (age forty-four), Associate President and patriarch of the Church, dramatically ended the founding period of the LDS Church. On June 27, 1844, they were mobbed and shot while confined at CARTHAGE JAIL in Hancock County, in western Illinois. Climaxing more than two decades of persecution across several states, this event gave them an enduring place as martyrs in the hearts of Latter-day Saints.

NAUVOO in 1844, gathering place for the Saints on the Mississippi River, contained elements of both greatness and dissension. Almost overnight, it grew from a village of religious refugees and new converts to the point where it rivaled Chicago as the largest city in Illinois. With Democrats and Whigs both vying for the Mormon vote, Nauvoo was granted one of the most liberal city charters in the state, an independent military force, and a strong judicial system (*see* NAUVOO CHARTER). However, as in Missouri during the 1830s, natural rivalry with older citizens in neighboring towns like Carthage (the county seat) and Warsaw (the next largest port city) turned to jealousy and hatred as Nauvoo's economic and political power grew (*see* NAUVOO ECONOMY; NAUVOO POLITICS).

These tensions coalesced around Joseph Smith. In addition to being prophet and President of the Church, he also served as mayor, commander of the NAUVOO LEGION state militia, justice of the peace, and university chancellor. Non-Mormon fears of this concentration of powers were intensified by the Church's belief in the theocratic union of spiritual, economic, and political matters under the priesthood. This and other "unorthodox" doctrines, such as continuing revelation, temple ordinances for the living and the dead, new scripture, and plural marriage, further intensified political and economic rivalries.

Illinois anti-Mormons, perhaps assisted by old enemies from Missouri, joined with a handful of determined Mormon defectors within Nauvoo. Several had held high Church positions and, when excommunicated, fueled efforts to destroy Joseph Smith and the Church.

The Prophet's life and his plans to resettle many of the Saints in the West (*see* WESTWARD MIGRATION) were cut short by a series of explosive confrontations with these conspirators. The igniting spark was the destruction of the defectors' intemperate newspaper, the *Nauvoo Expositor*, as a public nuisance by the Nauvoo city marshal, under orders from Joseph Smith and the city council. Removal of this press came after the first and only issue had vilified Joseph Smith, pledged to cause repeal of the protective Nauvoo charters, and invited mob action against the Saints. Joseph Smith's enemies countered the destroying of the press with criminal charges against him and his brother for inciting a riot. The brothers soon gained release from arrest on a habeas corpus before an LDS tribunal. Then, following the advice of a state circuit court judge, they appeared before a non-Mormon justice in Nauvoo and were exonerated of the charges against them.

However, threats of mob violence increased. In Warsaw and Carthage, newspapers called for extermination of the Mormons. On June 18, Joseph Smith mobilized his troops to protect Nauvoo. When Illinois governor Thomas Ford apparently sided with the opposition and ordered the Church leaders to stand trial again on the same charges, this time in Carthage, Joseph and Hyrum first considered appealing to U.S. President John Tyler, but then decided instead to cross the Mississippi and escape to the West. Pressured by family and friends who felt abandoned and who believed Joseph to be nearly invincible, he agreed to return and surrender; but he prophesied that he would be going "like a lamb to the slaughter" and would be "murdered in cold blood" (*HC* 6:555, 559). Joseph urged Hyrum to save himself and succeed him as prophet, but Hyrum refused and accompanied his brother to Carthage.

Despite his promises of protection and a fair trial, Governor Ford allowed the Smiths to be imprisoned by their enemies without bail and without a hearing on a wholly new charge of treason for having declared martial law in Nauvoo. Stating that he had to "satisfy the people," the Governor ignored clear warnings of danger and disbanded most of the troops. He then left the hostile Carthage Greys to guard the jail and took the most dependable troops with him to Nauvoo.

During the governor's absence, a mob of between one hundred and two hundred armed men—many of them from the disbanded Warsaw militia—gathered in late afternoon, blackened their faces with mud and gunpowder, and then stormed the jail. In less than two minutes, they overcame feigned resistance from the Greys, rushed upstairs, and fired through the closed door. Hyrum, shot first, died instantly. John TAYLOR, an apostle, tried to escape out a window and was shot five times, but survived to later become the Church's third President. Only Willard Richards, another apostle, survived unharmed. Trying to go out the window to deflect attention from the two survivors inside, Joseph Smith was hit in the chest and collarbone with two shots from the open doorway and two more from outside the window. His final words as he fell to the ground outside the jail were, "O Lord, my God!" (*HC* 6:618). As rumors spread that the Mormons were coming, the mob dispersed.

Several times during his last days Joseph Smith told the Saints that while he had enjoyed God's safekeeping until his mission was fulfilled, he had now completed all that God required of him and could claim no special protection. Early in his career, the Prophet had recorded that the Lord told him, "Even if they do unto you . . . as they have done unto me, blessed are ye, for you shall dwell with me in glory" (D&C 6:30). Church leaders then and now have taught that the shedding of these martyrs' innocent blood was necessary to seal their testimony of the latter-day work that they "might be honored and the wicked might be condemned" (D&C 136:39).

BIBLIOGRAPHY

Esplin, Ronald K. "Joseph Smith's Mission and Timetable: 'God will Protect Me Until My Work Is Done.'" In *The Prophet Joseph Smith: Essays on the Life and Mission of Joseph Smith*, ed. L. Porter and S. Black, pp. 280–319. Salt Lake City, 1989.

HC 6:519–631, esp. 561–622.

Jessee, Dean C. "Return to Carthage: Writing the History of Joseph Smith's Martyrdom." *Journal of Mormon History* 8 (1981):3–19.

Madsen, Truman G. *Joseph Smith the Prophet*, pp. 109–126, 174–83. Salt Lake City, 1989.

Miller, David E., and Della S. Miller. *Nauvoo: The City of Joseph*, pp. 130–74. Salt Lake City, 1974.
Oaks, Dallin H., and Marvin S. Hill. *Carthage Conspiracy: The Trial of the Accused Assassins of Joseph Smith*. Urbana, Ill., 1979.

JOSEPH IVINS BENTLEY

MCKAY, DAVID O.

David O. McKay (1873–1970), sustained as the ninth President of The Church of Jesus Christ of Latter-day Saints on April 9, 1951, served as a General Authority for nearly sixty-four years, longer than any other person in Church history. During that time he served as a counselor in the First Presidency for seventeen years and was President for nearly nineteen years. He is remembered for his contributions to education, his exemplary family life, his emphasis on missionary work, his humanitarianism, his practical advice on achieving a happy life, and his participation in civic affairs, and for leading the Church toward increased internationalism.

The third child of David and Jennette Evans McKay, David Oman McKay was born in Huntsville, Utah, on September 8, 1873. While growing up on his father's farm, he faced tragedy and privation much earlier than many children. When he was six, his two older sisters died, and just a year later, his father was called on a two-year mission to his native Scotland. Young David matured quickly when he was left to help his mother care for the farm and the family, which included a younger brother and two younger sisters, one a two-year-old and the other a baby girl born ten days after his father left. The enterprising family, with the help of neighbors, had realized enough profit to surprise their father and husband with a much-needed addition to the house when he returned from his mission.

Young David continued to attend school, work on the farm, and, during the summer, deliver the *Ogden Standard Examiner* to a nearby mining town. He had an insatiable hunger for learning, and during his round trips on horseback, he spent much of the time reading and memorizing passages from the world's great literature that were later to permeate his sermons and writings. He also loved riding horses, swimming, and other sports; dramatics; debate; singing; and playing the piano with the Huntsville town orchestra.

After completing the eighth grade, David enrolled in the Church's Weber Stake Academy in Ogden, Utah. Two years later, he was back in Huntsville as principal of the community school, but after a year he decided that he needed more schooling for a career in teaching and enrolled at the University of Utah. He graduated in June 1897 as class president and valedictorian. The theme of his valedictory address, "An Unsatisfied Appetite for Knowledge Means Progress and Is the State of a Normal Mind," characterized his life.

After graduation Elder McKay accepted a mission call to Great Britain. He arrived in Liverpool on August 25, 1897, and, like his father before him, was soon appointed to preside over the Scottish conference (later known as district). During a special priesthood meeting, he received a powerful spiritual manifestation confirming the truthfulness of the gospel. He had been seeking that confirmation since childhood, and it remained with him throughout his life. In Liverpool in 1899, he discovered a saying that became a lifetime motto. Homesick and discouraged, he noticed over the doorway of an unfinished house an unusual stone arch bearing the inscription "What-E'er Thou Art, Act Well Thy Part." His attitude changed, and that perspective exemplified his life.

He returned home in the fall of 1899 and accepted a teaching position at Weber Stake Academy. On January 2, 1901, he married Emma Ray Riggs in the Salt Lake Temple; they had seven children.

As a teacher, McKay was popular, effective, and deeply concerned that his students absorb more than facts. He believed that teachers must lead students to stretch their minds into the world of ideas. "If you will give your class a thought, even one new thought during your recitation period," he later told other educators, "you will find that they will go away satisfied. But it is your obligation to be prepared to give that new thought" (1953, p. 439). He also believed that teachers must develop in students the moral and ethical values that lead to responsible citizenship. "Teaching is the noblest profession in the world," he proclaimed, for "upon the proper education of youth depend the permanency and purity of the home, the safety and perpetuity of the nation" (1953, p. 436). "True education," he said, "seeks . . . to make men and women not only good mathematicians, proficient linguists, profound scientists, or brilliant literary lights, but also honest men, combined with virtue, temperance, and brotherly love—men and women who prize truth, justice, wisdom, benevolence, and self-control as the choicest acquisitions of a successful life" (1953, p. 441). Teachers must be the exemplars, and he scolded the nation for not recognizing the need to pay for outstanding teachers in the classroom.

In 1902 McKay became the principal of Weber Stake Academy, and he soon instituted a number of progressive and innovative program changes. His Church assignments during these years also centered on education, as he served on the Weber Stake Sunday School board and then as a member of the superintendency. He was fully satisfied with what he believed would be a lifelong career in education when in 1906 everything changed: three members of the Quorum of the Twelve Apostles died, and David O. McKay, at age thirty-two, was called to that quorum.

In addition to his new responsibilities, Elder McKay remained active in educational administration. He stayed on as head of Weber Academy until 1908 and then served on its board of trustees until 1922. He was a member of the Board of Regents of the University of Utah in 1921–1922, and in 1940–1941 he was a member of the Board of Trustees of Utah State Agricultural College (later Utah State University). As a General Authority of the Church he became a member of the superintendency of the Church's Sunday School, and from 1918 to 1934 was the superintendent. In 1919 he became the Church's first Commissioner of Education, and in this assignment he had some difficult decisions to make. In 1920 he advised the closing of most Church-owned academies and the establishment of seminaries adjacent to all high schools with sufficient LDS population. Religious instruction would still be given to high school students, but without the expense of full high school programs. A seminary adjacent to Granite High in Salt Lake City had already proved successful, and the new recommendation was quickly put into effect. He also recommended that Brigham Young University adopt a full college curriculum and that the other five Church colleges (four in Utah and one in Idaho) develop just two-year programs, primarily for training teachers. Within the next ten years, all the Utah colleges except Brigham Young University were transferred to the state.

Elder McKay became the most widely traveled Church leader of his day, an emissary to the growing worldwide Church. In 1920–1921 he toured the missions of the world, stopping at many places never before visited by a General Authority. From 1922 to 1924, he was back in Europe, this time as president of the European Mission (*see* EUROPE, THE CHURCH IN). His success there became legendary, as he did much to improve the public image of the Church. He also revitalized missionary work by urging every Latter-day Saint to make a commitment to bring one new member into the Church each year. In later years he became famous for his motto "Every member a missionary," an emphasis that began in Europe in 1923. In addition, he urged the Saints to remain in Europe rather than to emigrate to America, promising them that one day the full program of the Church, including sacred temples, would be made available in their homelands.

In 1934 President Heber J. GRANT chose David O. McKay to be his Second Counselor in the First Presidency of the Church. In 1951, the same year that he and Emma Ray celebrated their golden wedding anniversary, he became President of the Church. Tall, still robust despite his seventy-seven years, possessing a full head of wavy white hair, and with eyes that one man characterized as "fiercely tender," David O. McKay looked every bit the prophet his followers revered him to be.

President McKay's administration covered an important period of transition. As he guided the Church into the last half of the twentieth century, he faced critical new challenges connected with numerical growth, international expansion, and a variety of political and social problems related to the rapidly changing world. Church membership nearly tripled, from 1.1 million to 2.8 million; the number of stakes grew from 184 to 500; the number of missions more than doubled; the missionary force expanded six times; temples were erected in Switzerland, New Zealand, and Great Britain, as well as California; and the Church was established in several new countries. As an experienced leader with both a firm hand and a humanitarian nature, President McKay was admirably suited for the task of moving the Church toward the new internationalism that would characterize the later twentieth century.

In the summer of 1952 he visited nine European countries on

what may have been the most significant tour of his career. His announcement that a site had been selected for the erection of a temple just outside Bern, Switzerland, ushered in a new era, symbolizing the establishment of the full program of the Church in nations outside North America. Having temples within traveling distance strengthened the Saints spiritually and encouraged them to remain in their homelands to build up the Church. President McKay dedicated the Swiss Temple in 1955, and soon temples began to dot the world. Smaller and less expensive than previous temples, the new temples introduced design changes and technological innovations (including special films) that made the temple ceremonies available in many languages.

Another step in the maturation of the Church outside North America was the organization of stakes. Having local stakes indicated that the local leaders were experienced enough to assume leadership in place of American mission presidents and that local members, rather than missionaries, could direct Church activities. The first stakes outside North America were organized in Hawaii (1935 and 1955) before President McKay's administration, and the second, in New Zealand (1958). These were followed, during his time as President, by stakes in Australia, England, the Netherlands, Germany, Switzerland, Mexico, Samoa, Scotland, Brazil, Argentina, Guatemala, Uruguay, Tonga, Peru, and Japan.

President McKay's humanitarian impulse, even in controversial areas of Church policy, was demonstrated during a mission tour of South Africa in 1954. There he was reminded of the difficulties involved with the Church's policy of not allowing blacks or people with black ancestry to hold the priesthood. At that time, to be ordained, members in South Africa had to trace their ancestral lines beyond the continent of Africa because of the high possibility of black ancestry. President McKay listened with great empathy to those whose inability to trace their genealogy kept them from bearing the priesthood, and he felt inspired to modify the policy so that the genealogical test would not apply. It remained for one of his successors, President Spencer W. KIMBALL, to be given the revelation on priesthood in 1978.

Other controversial questions confronted President McKay, one concerning education. In 1954 the continued state support of Utah's junior colleges became a heated political issue. At the urging of Governor J. Bracken Lee and as a money-saving device for the state, the legislature authorized the transfer of Snow, Weber, and Dixie colleges back to the Church. Citizens placed the issue on the ballot as a referendum measure, and President McKay, concerned that the colleges would deteriorate if the state continued to operate them without adequate financing, announced that the Church was willing to take the schools back and operate them on a sound financial basis. In the referendum, however, the people of the state voted against the move.

President McKay made a myriad of far-reaching administrative decisions. As an avid missionary, he approved a new proselytizing plan, A Systematic Program for Teaching the Gospel, and in 1961 he presided over the first world seminar for mission presidents, where the plan was introduced. He promoted the continuing expansion of seminaries, institutes of religion, and Church schools in areas where public educational opportunities were limited. Other administrative decisions demonstrated his willingness to innovate as needs arose. In 1961 he authorized ordaining members of the First Council of the Seventy to the office of high priest, which gave them the right to preside at stake conferences and thus eased the growing administrative burdens of the Quorum of the Twelve, and in 1967 he inaugurated the position of Regional Representative of the Twelve. In 1965 he also took the unusual step of expanding the number of counselors in the First Presidency, as his own ability to function effectively became impaired with age.

President David O. McKay believed that Church leadership also implied civic responsibility. Throughout his career he remained active in public affairs and was frequently asked to head important civic committees. During most of his presidential administration, he held weekly breakfast meetings with the head of the Salt Lake area Chamber of Commerce and the publisher of the *Salt Lake Tribune*, which gave him an opportunity to share concerns with these civic leaders and reach agreements on many areas of mutual interest. Politically, he made every effort to keep the Church nonpartisan and constantly encouraged Church members in the United States to be active in both major political parties. At times, however, he took clear stands on controversial political issues when it was apparent to him that they were also moral issues. His denunciation of communism, for example, was uncompromising, on the grounds of its atheistic nature and its threat to the democratic institutions he valued. In 1969, amid the tense civil rights struggles that were dividing Americans as they had seldom been divided since the Civil War, he authorized the issuing of a strong official statement calling upon Church members everywhere to do their part to see that civil rights for all races were held inviolate.

President McKay kept up a steady pace of travel and administrative work until, in his nineties, his age required him to slow down. On January 18, 1970, at age ninety-six, he died in Salt Lake City.

David O. McKay's values were enunciated in his sermons and writings. His emphasis on education included equal emphasis on good reading. "Good reading is to the intellect what good food is to the body," he observed. "Thoughts, like food, should be properly digested" (1967, p. 53). He was vitally concerned with the family and constantly called upon parents to spend time with their children and to train them in all the virtues of good citizenship. His main religious message concerned the reality of Christ, his atonement and resurrection, and the restoration of the gospel of Christ through the Prophet Joseph Smith. He taught that Christ's gospel was meant to transform the individual and thus change society. The sanctity of the home, kindness, mercy, tolerance, spirituality, love of freedom, the power of prayer, charity, personal integrity—these were the subjects of his sermons and writings.

BIBLIOGRAPHY

Allen, James B. "David O. McKay." In *The Presidents of the Church*, ed. L. Arrington, pp. 274–313. Salt Lake City, 1986.

McKay, David Lawrence. *My Father, David O. McKay*. Salt Lake City, 1989.

McKay, David O. *Gospel Ideals: Selections from the Discourses of David O. McKay*. Salt Lake City, 1953.

———. *Secrets of a Happy Life*, comp. Llewelyn R. McKay. Salt Lake City, 1967.

McKay, Llewelyn R. *Home Memories of President David O. McKay*. Salt Lake City, 1956.

Middlemiss, Clare, comp. *Man May Know for Himself: Teachings of President David O. McKay*. Salt Lake City, 1966.

Morrell, Jeanette McKay. *Highlights in the Life of President David O. McKay*. Salt Lake City, 1967.

Symposium. "President David O. McKay, 1873–1970." *Dialogue* 4 (Winter 1969):47–62.

JAMES B. ALLEN

MEXICO, PIONEER SETTLEMENTS IN

LDS COLONIZATION in Mexico was planned as a place of refuge from PERSECUTION in the United States and as a springboard for teaching the gospel in Latin America.

In 1875, President Brigham YOUNG sent Daniel W. Jones and others to Mexico to look for possible places to settle. They found the Mexican government anxious for colonization in the sparsely settled areas of northern Chihuahua and Sonora. LDS colonization in Mexico did not begin, however, until after the first severe persecution precipitated by the passage of the 1882 Edmunds Act (*see* ANTIPOLYGAMY LEGISLATION). In 1885, hundreds of families, many of which practiced POLYGAMY, crossed the border into Mexico. In the next several years, seven colonies were founded on the Casas Grandes River and its tributaries in northwestern Chihuahua: Colonia Díaz, Colonia Dublan, Colonia Juárez, and the mountain colonies Cave Valley, Pacheco, García, and Chuichupa. In addition, Latter-day Saints established Colonia Oaxaca and Colonia Morelos on the Bavispe River in northern Sonora.

Hardship marked the early years as land-title problems, hunger, drought, hostile Apache Indians, and such diseases as smallpox and diphtheria challenged the Saints' determination to make the desert valleys their home. With capable leadership they persevered. In addition to local leaders, at one time or another six of the Twelve Apostles of the Church resided in the Mexican colonies.

Most of the settlers had already helped establish colonies in the western United States. With this experience, they imported to Mexico the best varieties of fruit trees for their orchards and selected breeds of cattle and horses. Within ten years, the colony lands were covered with canals, dams, man-made lakes, and irrigated crops. Thriving villages had wide streets lined with maple trees and lilacs and red-brick homes reminiscent of villages where many of the settlers had had their roots. There were stores, mills, and factories. Each community built schools to ensure the acquisition of cultural, literary, and technical skills. Through hard work, the colonists achieved a high degree of self-sufficiency.

On December 8, 1895, the first stake in Mexico was formed, with Colonia Juárez as its center and Anthony W. Ivins as stake president.

In 1912, during the Mexican Revolution, local Church leaders led a general exodus and abandoned the colonies as the members sought refuge in the United States. Before the revolution, more than 4,000 Latter-day Saints lived in the colonies. Nearly one-fourth later returned and became part of Mexico's revolutionary history, enduring the raids of Pascual Orozco's "Red Flaggers" and American General John J. ("Black Jack") Pershing's search for Pancho Villa.

In 1990, there were again approximately 4,000 Latter-day Saints in the area, about 500 of them descendants of the original pioneers, and the area was still a major supplier of fresh fruits to other parts of Mexico. The Church schools in Mexico are bilingual, with the Juárez Academy a regional center of culture and learning. A striking number of Church leaders have roots in the Mexican colonies. The area also produces a high number of Spanish-speaking missionaries and mission presidents, whose work has extended beyond Latin America to Spain and the Spanish-speaking population worldwide.

While visiting Colonia Juárez on November 11, 1989, Carlos Salinas de Gortari, the president of Mexico, commended the LDS colonists in Mexico in these words:

> We appreciate your dedication, honesty, sobriety, and respect for law. You have contributed to the elevation of the regions where you live together, work and labor intensely, and with this you also elevate the level of our nation. You have incorporated new technology, more efficient productive processes, and have shared your knowledge and experience with the rest of your fellow citizens, adding generosity to the characteristics that distinguish you. We know that you are a good people who do good [transcribed and translated by Guillermo Toscano Arrambí, on file at Juárez Academy].

BIBLIOGRAPHY

Hatch, Nelle Spilsbury. *Colonia Juárez: An Intimate Account of a Mormon Village*. Salt Lake City, 1954.

Johnson, Annie R. *Heartbeats of Colonia Díaz*. Salt Lake City, 1972.

Romney, Thomas Cottam. *The Mormon Colonies in Mexico*. Salt Lake City, 1938.

Tullis, F. LaMond. *Mormons in Mexico: The Dynamics of Faith and Culture*. Logan, Utah, 1987.

SHIRLEY TAYLOR ROBINSON

MEXICO AND CENTRAL AMERICA, THE CHURCH IN

MEXICO

The Church of Jesus Christ of Latter-day Saints first sent missionaries into Mexico in 1875. It had long been a hope of Church leaders to teach the gospel to these descendants of the Book of Mormon peoples, and to show them the sacred record of their ancestors. President Brigham YOUNG also looked at Mexico as a possible place of refuge for the Saints in the event of further persecution from the United States government. The Church established colonies in northern Mexico in 1885. Though Church growth in Mexico, and later in Central America, was sporadic and beset with political difficulties, the deep roots of nearly a century began to produce abundantly in the 1970s, so that by the end of 1990 the Church had twenty-seven missions and hundreds of stakes and wards serving approximately a million members in these areas. There are also temples in both Mexico City and Guatemala City.

FIRST MISSIONARIES. The first LDS missionaries sent to Mexico in 1875 included Daniel W. Jones, his son Wiley, Anthony W. Ivins, James Z. Stewart, and Helaman Pratt. This group was also to scout out good colonizing areas in the southwestern United States and northern Mexico. Though they recorded no baptisms, the missionaries found many possible sites for the Saints to settle, the most promising being in Chihuahua, Mexico.

From Chihuahua the group also mailed a booklet, *Trozos Selectos del Libro de Mormon* (selections of the Book of Mormon), to well-known citizens and government officials. The selections had been translated by Melitón González Trejo and Daniel W. Jones. Meanwhile, a second group of missionaries, called in September 1876, left for Mexico directly following the October general conference. This group was composed of two of the original missionaries, Stewart and Pratt, and four new ones—Stewart's brother Isaac, George Terry, Louis Garff, and Melitón G. Trejo. They separated in Tucson, Arizona, with Pratt and Trejo going south to Hermosillo, Sonora, Mexico, where the first five baptisms in Mexico occurred in 1877. The other four missionaries were not so fortunate as they were driven from the country by the warring Yaqui Indians.

Two of the booklets mailed by the first expedition fell into the hands of two influential citizens who wrote for more information: Ignacio Manuel Altamirano and Dr. Plotino Rhodakanaty (also spelled Rhodacanaty). Dr. Rhodakanaty studied the materials with several of his friends, and when Elder Moses Thatcher, of the Quorum of the Twelve Apostles, and other missionaries arrived in Mexico City in November 1879, they soon baptized him and his study group. Within a week Thatcher organized the Mexico City branch and appointed Rhodakanaty as branch president, with Silviano Arteaga and Jose Ybarola serving as his counselors.

Thatcher dedicated Mexico for missionary work on January 25, 1880, but because many of the original members left the Church, he rededicated the land and mission on April 6, 1881, from the rim of the volcano Popocatepetl—which has great historical significance to Mexico's Indian people. He formed a second branch that August in Ozumba, a small town nestled at the base of Popocatepetl.

COLONISTS. By 1885, the U.S. persecution of the Church for polygamy resulted in many Church leaders in the United States going into foreign countries to find homes for their multiple families, and some of them founded Colonia Juárez in the state of Chihuahua, Mexico. Later colonies were founded at Díaz, Dublán, and also in Pacheco, Oaxaca, Morelos, and San José, Sonora (*see* MEXICO, PIONEER SETTLEMENTS IN).

The American colonists suffered greatly from the political instability in Mexico. Sonora permanently exiled all foreign settlers, and the Chihuahua Saints were evacuated for a time, with the loss of food, possessions, and sometimes lives. However, many of the Saints returned and rebuilt their colonies and had no further trouble.

MISSION CLOSURES (1889–1946). The Mexican Mission was closed in 1889 and the missionaries recalled because of the worsening persecution in the polygamy crisis, but it was reopened in 1901 by Elder John Henry Smith, an apostle, and Presidents Anthony W. Ivins and Henry Eyring from the Juárez Stake. Missionary work continued with lengthy interruptions due to the Mexican Revolution and counterrevolutions (1910–1928).

Elder Rey L. Pratt, of the Seventy, presided over the Mexican

Mission from 1907 until his death in 1931, but did not live in Mexico much of that time because the missionaries were often banned. When all foreign missionaries were exiled from 1913 until 1921, President Pratt placed Presidents Isaias Juárez, Abel Paez, and Bernabe Parra, the district presidency, in charge of the Church in Mexico, and the work of the mission continued under local leadership. Local priesthood brethren also led the Church from 1926 to 1946, when the Mexican government prohibited foreigners from doing religious work in Mexico. Church membership continued to grow.

1946 TO PRESENT. With its rapid growth in Mexico, and noting the need for education among its members there, the Church established thirty-seven schools in Mexico between 1960 and 1974, most of them elementary schools. The largest, most widely known LDS school in Mexico is its preparatory school, Centro Escolar Benemerito de las Américas, established in 1964.

The Mexican Mission was divided into four missions between 1952 and 1960. In December 1961, Mexico City established its first stake with Harold Brown, an Anglo who was reared in the Mormon colonies, as president. The second stake was organized in 1967 with Agrícol Lozano, a native Mexican, as president. On November 9, 1975, Elder Howard W. Hunter, of the Quorum of the Twelve Apostles, organized eleven new stakes in the Mexico City area, among them the Mexico City Zarahemla Stake for the students of Benemerito. From 1976 to 1978 nearly 150 full-time missionaries were called from the membership of this stake. By 1983 Mexico had eight missions, seventy-six stakes, and several hundred thousand members (second only to the United States in membership), and the majority of the missionaries in the country were local Mexicans. Hundreds of the members had been blessed to attend Church schools.

MEXICO CITY TEMPLE. On March 21, 1977, President Spencer W. KIMBALL announced that the Church would build a temple in Mexico City. The Mexico Temple was dedicated on December 2, 1983, by President Gordon B. Hinckley, a counselor in the First Presidency. Its design was a modern adaptation of ancient Mayan architecture, showing respect for the culture and history of Mexico. Harold and Leanore Jespersen Brown were its first president and matron.

CENTRAL AMERICA

The expansion of the Church into Central America is more recent than that of Mexico. The first missionary effort beyond Mexico came in 1941, when John (Juan) O'Donnal, who had grown up in the LDS Mexican colonies, was assigned to Guatemala City by the U.S. Department of Agriculture. He taught the gospel informally in Guatemala for several years and petitioned the Church to send missionaries to what he considered a humble people ready to hear the gospel. In 1947 four missionaries were sent to Guatemala and Costa Rica, as part of the Mexican Mission. On September 7, 1947, the first sacrament meeting was held in Guatemala. Central America was dedicated for preaching the gospel and the Central America Mission was organized on November 16, 1952, by Elder Spencer W. Kimball, then of the Quorum of the Twelve. On August 1, 1965, the Guatemala-El Salvador Mission was divided from the Central American Mission. By 1990 missions had been organized in five Central American countries: Guatemala, Honduras, Panama, El Salvador, and Costa Rica. Guatemala had three missions, and El Salvador opened its second mission in July 1990. In December 1990 the Church had forty-three stakes in Central America.

THE GUATEMALA TEMPLE. While the Mexico City Temple was being built, plans were already being made to build a temple in Guatemala City. Construction of this temple was completed in three years, and it was dedicated in December 1984, one year after the dedication of the Mexico City Temple. The construction of the temples enables thousands of Mexican and Central American Latter-day Saints to participate regularly in temple ordinances in their own language and without undertaking the long trip to the Arizona Temple in Mesa as they had done before.

In the April 1989 general conference of the Church, the first General Authorities from Mexico and Central America were called to the quorums of Seventy: Horacio Tenorio from Mexico and Carlos H. Amado from Guatemala. On April 6, 1991, Jorge A. Rojas of Mexico was also called to the Seventy.

BIBLIOGRAPHY

"Central America: Saints in Six Nations Grow in the Gospel." *Ensign* 7 (Feb. 1977):25–26.

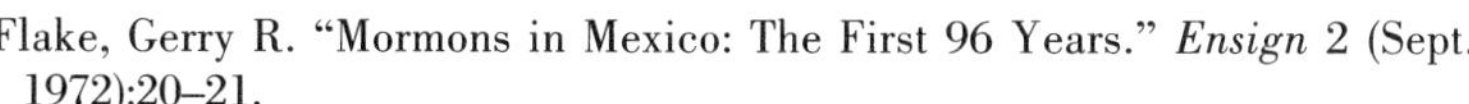

Flake, Gerry R. "Mormons in Mexico: The First 96 Years." *Ensign* 2 (Sept. 1972):20–21.
Gardner, Marvin K. "Taking the Gospel to Their Own People." *Ensign* 18 (Oct. 1988):12–16.
Hansen, Terrence L. "The Church in Central America." *Ensign* 2 (Sept. 1972):40–42.
Lozano, Agrícol. *Historia de la Iglesia en México.* México, D.F., 1980.
Tullis, F. LaMond. *Mormons in Mexico.* Logan, Utah, 1987.

BOANERGES RUBALCAVA

MIDDLE EAST, THE CHURCH IN THE

Political turmoil in the Ottoman empire, two world wars, and restrictions imposed by local governments have challenged the efforts of The Church of Jesus Christ of Latter-day Saints to establish an official presence in the Middle East. Despite these difficulties, the Church has small congregations in several Middle Eastern countries, mostly because of the influx of expatriate (mainly American) Church members working there. Before 1950, Church activities were limited to the Levant (Turkey, Palestine, Lebanon, and Syria), but since then some have also occurred, temporarily at least, in Iran, Egypt, Jordan, Israel, the West Bank, Lebanon, and the Arab countries of the Gulf.

The history of LDS Church activity in the Middle East dates from 1841, when Orson Hyde, an apostle, prayed on the Mount of Olives near Jerusalem for the ingathering of Abraham's children (especially the Jews) to Palestine, for the building up of Jerusalem, and for the rearing of a temple. LDS missionary work in the Middle East began in 1884, when Jacob Spori opened the Turkish Mission in Constantinople. Branches of the Church, consisting mostly of Armenian and European converts, were eventually established in Aintab, Aleppo, and Haifa, but the mission closed in 1896. It reopened in 1897, but closed again in 1909 because of the increasing political turmoil in the Ottoman empire.

After World War I, the mission was reopened in Aleppo and renamed the Armenian Mission. In 1928 it was headquartered in Haifa, but was closed that December with the sudden death of Joseph Booth, the mission president. It reopened in 1933 as the Palestine-Syrian Mission, but was closed again in 1939 because of World War

II. In 1947 the mission was reopened with Badwagan Piranian as president; it was renamed the Near East Mission in 1950 but closed again later that year. From 1950 to 1969, Church activity in the Middle East consisted mostly of small groups scattered in various countries and of a few missionaries from the Swiss Mission assigned to work in Lebanon. In September 1969 a Church group was organized in Jerusalem to accommodate Brigham Young University (BYU) faculty and students involved in a Near Eastern Studies program. Other events there included the organization of the Israel District (1977), the dedication of the Orson Hyde Memorial Garden on the Mount of Olives (1979), and the dedication of the BYU Jerusalem Center for Near Eastern Studies on Mount Scopus (1989).

The Church has established a few congregations in other Middle Eastern countries since 1950 as economic expansion, related mostly to the oil industry, has brought an influx of Western workers to the area. A branch of the Church has been operating in Cairo, Egypt, since 1974. The Iran Tehran Mission was organized in July 1975, the first formal mission in the Middle East since 1950, but it was closed in December 1978 with the worsening political situation between Iran and the United States. In 1989, Jordan became the first Arab country to grant formal recognition to the Church, allowing it to establish the Center for Cultural and Educational Affairs in Amman. The governments in these countries have allowed the Church, along with other non-Muslim groups, to hold services and other activities as long as they are unobtrusive and their members respect Islamic laws and traditions, including the restriction against proselytizing among the Muslim populace.

ISSUES AND CHALLENGES. The manner in which the Church has handled a number of sensitive issues in the Middle East illustrates its capacity to adapt to local needs and customs. Between 1841 and 1950, the most vexing problem for the missionaries was how to deal with the poverty and poor health of the members. The Church attempted to alleviate the suffering of members by teaching them new skills, organizing cooperatives to market goods in Salt Lake City, soliciting clothing and food donations from members in Utah, and arranging for relocation to Europe, Mexico, and the United States. Since 1950 the Church has adjusted to issues of a cultural and political nature. One example is the First Presidency's decision to allow members to hold

Sabbath services, customarily reserved for Sunday, on the day of worship designated by local religious tradition: Friday in Muslim countries and Saturday in Israel. The Church has refrained from taking an official stand on the Arab-Israeli question; rather, the position of Church leaders is best revealed by the manner in which they have quietly sought to cultivate good relations and a reputation for impartiality with both Israelis and Palestinians. The following statement by Elder Howard W. Hunter, an apostle, is characteristic of this attitude: "Both the Jews and the Arabs are children of our Father. They are both children of promise, and as a church we do not take sides. We have love for and an interest in each" (pp. 35–36).

The greatest obstacle to Church growth today is the prohibition against proselytizing that prevails in every country in the Middle East. Despite its reputation for vigorous missionary activity in other areas of the world, the Church has observed religious restrictions in the Middle East by making nonproselytizing commitments to government leaders and by issuing strict instructions for members to honor these commitments.

BIBLIOGRAPHY

Baldridge, Steven W. *Grafting In: A History of the Latter-day Saints in the Holy Land.* Murray, Utah, 1989.

Hunter, Howard W. "All Are Alike Unto God." *BYU Speeches of the Year, 1979*, pp. 35–36. Provo, Utah.

Lindsay, Rao H. "A History of the Missionary Activities of The Church of Jesus Christ of Latter-day Saints in the Near East, 1884–1929." Master's thesis, Brigham Young University, 1958.

JAMES A. TORONTO

MISSIONS OF THE TWELVE TO THE BRITISH ISLES

Between 1837 and 1841 there were two apostolic missions to the British Isles. In 1837–1838 Heber C. KIMBALL and Orson HYDE established the first mission, concentrating in the area of Preston and the Ribble Valley. Their efforts saw about 1,500 people baptized into the Church. From 1839 to 1841, nine members of the Quorum of the Twelve Apostles labored in Britain and added another 4,000 converts to the Church. These missions were extremely important. In a relatively short time, the Twelve Apostles established the foundation for the most successful missionary program of the Church in the nineteenth century, organized an extensive emigration program, and established a major publication program. In these activities, they also shared experiences that welded them together as a quorum. The spiritual and administrative dimensions of these missionary experiences prepared the Quorum of the Twelve Apostles to assume their key role in the leadership of the Church following their return to Nauvoo, and especially after the death of the Prophet Joseph SMITH in 1844. These missions were a manifestation of the early LDS recognition of the divine command to take the gospel "into all the world" (D&C 84:61–63; cf. Matt. 28:19) and to "gather" to Zion those who would accept the gospel message. Even as Jesus had commanded his apostles anciently, so had he done with his apostles in the nineteenth century.

THE 1837–1838 MISSION. The Church was barely seven years old when Elders Kimball and Hyde departed for England in July 1837. The Prophet Joseph Smith had directed men to go on missions from the beginning, and the early missionaries had first concentrated in the smaller hamlets and villages of New England and nearby Canada. By 1836, LDS missionaries were venturing into larger cities. On April 3, 1836, the keys of the holy priesthood were bestowed by heavenly messengers upon the Prophet Joseph and Oliver Cowdery in the Kirtland (Ohio) Temple (D&C 110:11–16). These keys included the authority to gather Israel from the four parts of the earth, which is a missionary activity.

In April 1836, Parley P. PRATT, an apostle, was sent to Toronto with a prophetic promise that the fruits of missionary work there would lead to the introduction of the gospel into England (pp. 130–31). Elder Pratt helped to convert, among others, John TAYLOR, Isaac Russell, and Joseph Fielding, all of whom had family contacts in Britain and several of whom accompanied Elders Kimball and Hyde when the Prophet assigned them to go to the British Isles on the first mission.

Elders Kimball and Hyde were in England from July 1837 to April 1838. Landing at Liverpool, they traveled north to Preston, where relatives of the Canadian converts provided various assistance, including a place to preach. Finding ready acceptance of their message, they baptized more than 140 people by October 1837. They moved up the Ribble Valley, finding other audiences, particularly among the textile workers throughout Lancanshire. By the time they returned home in April 1838, Church membership had grown to about 1,500 people in Britain, in spite of growing opposition, particularly from local clergy.

THE 1839–1841 MISSION. Dissension and apostasy had arisen among the leading brethren, reflecting the larger troubles of the Church in Ohio and Missouri. Seeking Joseph Smith's counsel in 1837, the Twelve were instructed by revelation to be united (D&C 112), but by 1838, some of the original Quorum of the Twelve did not wholeheartedly support Joseph Smith, and quorum president Thomas B. Marsh weakened the quorum further by his personal apostasy. With the death of David W. PATTEN in 1838, Brigham Young became the senior member of a quorum greatly hampered by defection. The second apostolic mission was also initiated by divine revelation. On July 8, 1838, from the new headquarters at Far West, Missouri, the Prophet Joseph Smith inquired, "Show us thy will, O Lord, concerning the Twelve," and received a revelation that the Twelve Apostles were to leave Far West on April 26, 1839, on a mission "over the great waters" (D&C 118:4). The revelation promised success in their mission and care for their families.

This overseas mission was an opportunity for the Twelve to prove themselves and to take their rightful place next to the First Presidency in leading the Church. The July 8, 1838, revelation gave specific direction, including the naming of four new apostles—John Taylor, John E. Page, Wilford WOODRUFF, and Willard Richards—to fill existing vacancies (D&C 118:6).

Departing in conditions of poverty and illness and trusting in the promises of God that all would be well with them and their families, most of the members of the Twelve made their way in various groups to Liverpool. By April 1840, they were together for the first time as a quorum in a foreign land. On April 14, 1840, in Preston, they ordained Willard Richards an apostle and sustained Brigham Young as "standing president" of their quorum. They held a general conference the next day in which they conducted Church business and further organized the mission. On the 16th they met again as a quorum and further planned their work. On the next day, they separated to various assigned geographical areas: Brigham Young and Willard

Richards were to assist Wilford Woodruff with the work he had already begun among the United Brethren in Herefordshire; Heber C. Kimball was to return to the areas of his 1837–1838 missionary successes; Parley P. Pratt was to establish a mission home and publishing concern in Manchester; Orson PRATT was assigned to Scotland, where the work had already begun; John Taylor was to go to Liverpool, Ireland, and the Isle of Man; and George A. Smith was assigned to the area of the Staffordshire potteries. In time, Wilford Woodruff and George A. Smith would extend their work to London.

Under Brigham Young's direction, these apostles diligently supported each other and showed their love for the British people. In their journals and letters to each other they shared the burdens and joy of the hard work they were assigned to do. Truly on their own for the first time, they were forced to depend on the Lord and upon each other for assistance in the challenges they faced. Although they sought the Prophet Joseph's counsel on a variety of items, the distance from him often forced them to make decisions before a response could be received. In all major decisions the Prophet Joseph seems to have approved of their course of action.

In addition to providing leadership to the expanding British Mission, which saw an additional 4,000 converts join the Church by 1841, their efforts had at least three other related consequences: (1) the establishment of a successful emigration program that saw the first converts gathered to Nauvoo, with at least 50,000 members emigrating from the British Isles to America (*see* PERPETUAL EMIGRATING FUND); (2) the use of Britain as a base for further LDS missionary activity into continental Europe and other countries, such as South Africa, India, and Australia; and (3) the laying of the foundation for extensive LDS publishing in the nineteenth century. The *Millennial Star*, begun in 1840, became one of the most important LDS periodicals. Later editions of the Book of Mormon and the Doctrine and Covenants followed the text and format of those published by the Quorum of the Twelve Apostles in England. The same is true of the Manchester Hymnal. Also, various pamphlets defending and explaining Church doctrine were issued in regular editions in England. In fact, Liverpool became the LDS book supply depot for most of the nineteenth century.

A major consequence of the 1839–1841 mission was the impact

it had on the quorum itself. Beginning in 1841, following the return of the Twelve to Nauvoo, Joseph Smith gave them more direct responsibility in administering the affairs of the Church. They were assigned management of the Church press in Nauvoo, were directed to supervise emigration, were placed on the Nauvoo City Council, and were given direct responsibility over Church finances. They were then brought into closer association with Joseph Smith and entrusted with greater responsibilities in many areas as they took their position as the quorum next to the First Presidency (D&C 107:23–24; 124:127–28).

Perhaps the greatest indication of their true calling as apostles was their vital role of leadership in the Church just before and following Joseph Smith's death in 1844. This mantle of authority, both spiritual and administrative, had been clearly established during the period of their British Mission experience.

BIBLIOGRAPHY

Allen, James B.; Ronald K. Esplin; and David J. Whittaker. *Men with a Mission: The Quorum of the Twelve in Great Britain—1837–1841*. Salt Lake City, 1991.

Bloxham, V. Ben; James R. Moss; and Larry C. Porter, eds. *Truth Will Prevail: The Rise of The Church of Jesus Christ of Latter-day Saints in the British Isles, 1837–1987*. Solihull, England, 1987.

Crawley, Peter, and David J. Whittaker. *Mormon Imprints in Great Britain and the Empire, 1836–1857*. Provo, Utah, 1987.

Esplin, Ronald K. "Joseph, Brigham and the Twelve: A Succession of Continuity." *BYU Studies* 21 (Summer 1981):301–341.

———. "A Preparation for Ascendancy: Brigham Young and the Quorum Experience in England, 1840–41." In "The Emergence of Brigham Young and the Twelve to Mormon Leadership, 1830–1841," pp. 427–98. Ph.D. diss., Brigham Young University, 1981.

———. "A Great Work Done in That Land." *Ensign* 17 (July 1987):20–27.

Evans, Richard L. *A Century of "Mormonism" in Great Britain*. Salt Lake City, 1937.

Jensen, Richard L., and Malcolm R. Thorp, eds. *Mormons in Early Victorian Britain*. Salt Lake City, 1989.

Pratt, Parley P. *The Autobiography of Parley Parker Pratt*. New York, 1874.

Taylor, P. A. M. *Expectations Westward: The Mormons and the Emigration of their British Converts in the Nineteenth Century*. Edinburgh and London, 1965; Ithaca, N.Y., 1966.

Whittaker, David J. "Mormonism in Victorian Britain: A Bibliographic Essay." In *Mormons in Early Victorian Britain*, ed. R. Jensen and M. Thorp, pp. 258–71. Salt Lake City, 1989.

DAVID J. WHITTAKER
JAMES R. MOSS

MISSOURI

[*This entry consists of two articles:*

LDS Communities in Jackson and Clay Counties
LDS Communities in Caldwell and Daviess Counties

The first article identifies the importance of Jackson County, Missouri, in the teachings of the Church and traces LDS history there and in Clay County. The second article discusses how the Missouri State Legislature created Caldwell and Daviess counties especially for the Latter-day Saints to settle in. The Church was driven from Missouri in the winter of 1838–1839, when its leaders were arrested and held for trial and the state militia enforced Governor Boggs's Extermination Order.]

LDS COMMUNITIES IN JACKSON AND CLAY COUNTIES

LDS interest and settlement in Jackson County, Missouri, came as a direct result of a revelation designating it as the location for Zion and the New Jerusalem. Both the Book of Mormon (Ether 13:2–3; 3 Ne. 20:22) and revelations to Joseph Smith (D&C 28:9; 29:7–9; 35:24; 42:9, 35–36, 62; 45:65–71) filled the Latter-day Saints with a zeal to know the time and place for the establishment. Elders from the LAMANITE MISSION had traveled to western Missouri in early 1831, knowing they were near the location of Zion (D&C 28:9). The day after a significant June 1831 conference in Ohio, a revelation directed Joseph SMITH and other Church leaders to go to Missouri, where the land of their inheritance would be revealed (D&C 52:3–5, 42–43).

Three new groups of Saints proceeded to western Missouri in the summer of 1831: Joseph Smith's party of leaders; an entire branch of the Church from COLESVILLE, NEW YORK, who were commanded to relocate in Missouri (D&C 54:8); and thirteen pairs of missionaries who were instructed to preach along the way (D&C 52:7–10, 22–33; 56:5–7). The Prophet's group, traveling by foot, investigated other counties near the western Missouri border before determining that Jackson County was to be their ultimate destination. Their observation of Missouri's frontier communities was in harmony with a general feeling even in the West that the society of western Missouri, composed as it was of recent arrivals who had sought out the frontier to escape society's constraints, was not a model of civilization. "Our reflections were many, coming as we had from a highly cultivated state of society in the east," reads Joseph Smith's official history, "to observe the degradation . . . of a people that were nearly a century behind the times" (*HC* 1:189).

In response to the question "When will Zion be built up in her glory, and where will Thy temple stand?" (*HC* 1:189), the Lord declared, "Wherefore, this is the land of promise, and the place for the city of Zion. . . . The place which is now called Independence is the center place; and the spot for the temple is lying westward, upon a lot which is not far from the court-house" (D&C 57:2–3).

In the summer of 1831, Church leaders explored the county, wrote a description of it for future Saints, established the first settlement in Kaw Township (now in Kansas City), dedicated the land for a gathering place, dedicated the temple lot, and conducted a conference for all Saints thus far gathered. The following men were assigned to prominent Church positions in Missouri: Edward Partridge, bishop; A. Sidney Gilbert, financial agent; W. W. Phelps, printer and editor; and Oliver COWDERY, assistant printer and editor. After Joseph Smith returned to Ohio, Bishop Partridge began buying land for the Saints' new inheritances.

LDS settlers who spent the winter of 1831–1832 in Jackson County struggled to cut timber; build ferries, bridges, mills, dams, homes, outbuildings, and fences; and prepare land for cultivation. Even though up to ten families lived in each log cabin, "there was a spirit of peace and union, and love and good will manifested in this little Church in the wilderness" (Pratt, p. 56). Plainly, it was not what Zion was but what it could become that buoyed up the Saints and lifted sagging spirits.

Early in 1832, Gilbert established a Church storehouse and Phelps the printing office. Proceeds from the store were used to buy and develop more land. Phelps began publishing a religious monthly, the *Evening and the Morning Star*, and a secular weekly, the *Upper Missouri Advertiser*; work also proceeded on the Book of Commandments, a compilation of revelations that had been received by Joseph Smith, and on a compilation of hymns. Establishing schools also became a high priority. By fall, schools were started in Kaw Township (called the Colesville School) and in Independence near the temple lot. Proper observance of the Lord's Day also received special emphasis (see D&C 59).

The subject that received the most attention was "gathering to Zion." Through the *Star*, Phelps reminded migrating Saints not to gather without adequate preparation, including carrying a recommend from the bishop in Ohio or from three elders. Bishop Partridge assigned land "inheritances" to new arrivals. Some three to four hundred arrived in the spring and summer of 1832, and by November there were 810 Latter-day Saints in Missouri. Up to this time, five settlements had easily absorbed the immigrants: a community in Independence near the temple lot; a branch on the Blue River three miles to the west; the Whitmer Branch three miles farther west; the Colesville Branch in Kaw Township two miles south of the Whitmer Branch; and the Prairie Branch on the Missouri state border. Editorials in the *Star* reflected the Saints' optimism.

The year 1833 brought numerous new challenges to the Church in Jackson County. Some members circumvented appointed leaders and ignored their authority to preside. Others tried to obtain property through means other than the revealed laws. Joseph Smith and Sidney RIGDON had visited the area in the spring of 1832, but now there arose a general concern among Missouri Latter-day Saints that their Prophet should move permanently from Ohio to the new Zion. Additionally, there were petty jealousies, covetousness, and general neglect in keeping the commandments. None of this helped the newcomers to cope with the worst problem—increasing hostility with the "old settlers" of Jackson County. As the LDS population in the county reached twelve hundred by the summer of 1833, concerns of the local citizens reached fever pitch. It did not help that some members unwisely boasted that nonmembers would be driven from the county.

However, not everything was gloomy in the Jackson County settlements. Solemn assemblies in each branch had brought about a new spirit of humility, diligence, and order to the Church. A school for elders was established on the model of the SCHOOL OF THE PROPHETS in Kirtland, Ohio. Joseph Smith sent a plan for the building-up of the city of Zion and its accompanying temple (*see* CITY PLANNING). The Book of Commandments was nearing completion. But all of this seemed only to increase hostility.

Mob violence broke out against the Saints in late July 1833. The printing press was destroyed, the page sheets of the Book of Commandments were scattered, and Bishop Partridge was tarred and feathered. Under duress, Church leaders signed an agreement to vacate Jackson County (*see* MISSOURI CONFLICT). Church members sought redress from the government, but were granted only sympathy, not help. When the old settlers saw that the Saints intended not to depart immediately but to hold their ground and defend themselves, they resumed acts of violence. After small battles erupted and led to several fatalities, the local militia succeeded in disarming the Mormons and driving them from Jackson County in early November.

Although some Saints fled to Van Buren and LaFayette counties, most found refuge north across the Missouri River in Clay County. The citizens of Liberty, the seat of Clay County, charitably offered shelter, work, and provisions. The refugees moved into abandoned slave cabins, built crude huts, pitched tents, and lived on meager subsistence until spring. Most Clay County citizens were friendly but considered the settlement of the Saints in their midst as only temporary.

To help the Missouri Saints, Joseph Smith arrived in June 1834 at the head of ZION'S CAMP, a paramilitary body of Latter-day Saints from the East. All efforts to achieve either reentry into Jackson County or redress of grievances came to naught. Outright war between Missourians and Mormons seemed imminent. By revelation (D&C 105) Joseph Smith was told to disband the camp because Zion could not yet be redeemed; bloodshed was thereby averted.

Before returning to Ohio, the Prophet established a presidency and high council for the Missouri Saints with David WHITMER as president and W. W. Phelps and John Whitmer as his counselors. Church members began establishing more permanent residences in Liberty and the surrounding Clay County countryside. They won a reputation for retrenchment and thrift and were generally able to live at peace with their neighbors.

Gradually, however, citizens of Clay became concerned about the permanence of LDS settlements. This concern became acute after the arrival of additional Church members in 1835 and 1836. In June 1836 a public meeting was held at the courthouse in Liberty to discuss objections to the Mormons remaining in the county. The citizens reminded the Saints of their original pledge to leave the county when they were no longer welcome, but promised to control any violence until they left.

Bishop Partridge and W. W. Phelps explored new gathering spots for the Saints in relatively uninhabited territory in northern Missouri, and by early 1837, Church members began moving out of Clay County into the newly created "Mormon county" of Caldwell (*see* MISSOURI: LDS COMMUNITIES IN CALDWELL AND DAVIESS COUNTIES).

BIBLIOGRAPHY

Jennings, Warren A. "Zion Is Fled: The Expulsion of the Mormons from Jackson County, Missouri." Ph.D. diss., University of Florida, 1962.

Parkin, Max H. "A History of the Latter-day Saints in Clay County, Missouri, from 1833 to 1837." Ph.D. diss., Brigham Young University, 1976.

Pratt, Parley P. *Autobiography of Parley Parker Pratt.* Salt Lake City, 1938.

CLARK V. JOHNSON

LDS COMMUNITIES IN CALDWELL AND DAVIESS COUNTIES

The Missouri legislature created Caldwell and Daviess counties in December 1836 in an attempt to resolve "the Mormon problem." After the Latter-day Saints were driven from Jackson County in 1833, they were given temporary refuge in Clay County (*see* MISSOURI: LDS COMMUNITIES IN JACKSON AND CLAY COUNTIES), but three years later, they still lacked a homeland. The small, newly created county of Caldwell in unsettled northern Missouri was to be *their* county; later, they also moved north into Daviess County.

When the Saints sought shelter in Clay County, both they and the local citizens expected their stay to be temporary. Consequently, in the spring of 1836, Bishop Edward Partridge and W. W. Phelps explored potential sites for LDS settlements in northern Ray County, an expansive region commonly known as the Far West, which stretched north to the Iowa border. Most of the territory was prairie covered by tall grass, with timber only along the streams and rivers. They identified suitable sites and the Saints began purchasing land along Shoal Creek in northern Ray County, about thirty miles northwest of Liberty. In the summer of 1836, when Clay County officially requested the Latter-day Saints to leave, Church leaders announced their intent to move to northern Ray.

Ray County residents opposed the plan, however, an opposition made firmer when approximately one hundred families of migrating

Saints from Ohio camped on the Crooked River in lower Ray County. Although many of the Saints in the camp were ill and most without funds to purchase either provisions or lands, the local citizens threatened them with violence if they did not leave. Another hundred impoverished LDS families were already traveling toward Missouri. Only after Church leaders assured Ray County officials of their intent to settle uninhabited and generally unwanted prairies to the north and to apply for a new county did opposition wane. Both parties agreed to establish a six-mile buffer zone or a no-man's land where neither Mormons nor non-Mormons would settle.

Early in August 1836, W. W. Phelps and John Whitmer, members of the Missouri stake presidency, located a site for a city on Shoal Creek and called it Far West. It was twelve miles west of Haun's Mill, a small LDS settlement created by Jacob Haun a year earlier. The Saints began gathering near Far West in late summer and fall and soon built numerous smaller settlements.

Alexander W. Doniphan, state legislator and friend to the Saints, introduced a bill in December 1836 to create two new small counties from sparsely settled northern Ray County. Doniphan named the new counties Daviess and Caldwell after two famous Kentucky Indian fighters. Caldwell County, the location of the Far West and Shoal Creek settlements, would be exclusively for Mormons; they would have their own militia and their own representation in the state legislature. Since many considered this segregation of the Latter-day Saints an excellent solution to the Mormon problem, the bill passed and was signed into law December 29, 1836. By early 1837, Missouri Saints were pouring into Caldwell County and began constructing log houses and preparing the soil for spring planting. The standard government rate was $1.25 per acre for unimproved land, and within a year most of the land was claimed and much of it was under cultivation. Civil officers were selected, and as in other counties, a county militia was organized as an arm of the state militia.

Some of the land around Far West was purchased by W. W. Phelps and John Whitmer using nearly $1,500 that had been raised to aid the poverty-stricken incoming Saints. Without consulting other local leaders, they developed the land, sold it, and retained some of the profit for themselves, thus creating discord. Conflict festered in Far West throughout 1837 until Joseph SMITH, visiting from Ohio in

November, temporarily resolved differences among the leaders. During his visit he also established committees to identify additional settlement sites.

New tension arose among the Saints during the winter, however, when Oliver COWDERY and Frederick G. Williams arrived in Far West from KIRTLAND, OHIO. With Phelps and Whitmer, Cowdery sold Church land in Jackson County, violating a policy that the Saints should retain their claims in Zion (D&C 101:99). The local high council tried the three for disobedience and excommunicated them, along with Williams, who apparently sided with them. As prominent "dissenters," they stirred up trouble among the Saints through the first half of 1838.

In March 1838 Joseph Smith moved the headquarters of the Church to Far West. Other Ohio Saints planned to follow later in the year. That summer, the population in Caldwell County reached five thousand, a large percentage living in Far West, where the Saints had built hundreds of homes, four dry-goods stores, three family grocery stores, several blacksmith shops, two hotels, a printing shop, and a large schoolhouse that doubled as a church and courthouse.

The rapidly increasing LDS population required more new settlements. In mid-May, Joseph Smith led an exploring expedition northward into Daviess County, where a few members had previously settled under a gentleman's agreement with the old settlers. The explorers found a beautiful townsite on the Grand River. While there, the Prophet received a revelation that this was also the site of ADAM-ONDI-AHMAN, mentioned in a revelation three years earlier as the valley where Adam had gathered his righteous posterity "and there bestowed upon them his last blessing" (D&C 107:53; cf. 78:15–16). This news helped confirm the decision to create a stake there and designate the area as a gathering place for Ohio members traveling to Missouri. At a June 28, 1838, conference in the newly laid-out community, affectionately nicknamed Di-Ahman, Joseph Smith's uncle, John Smith, was called as stake president. Throughout the summer of 1838, Latter-day Saints poured into Daviess County, where a plentiful harvest helped provide for the impoverished members of the Kirtland Camp when they arrived in early October. That same spring, the Saints also began to settle in DeWitt, in nearby Carroll County near the confluence of the Grand and Missouri rivers, where they established a steamboat landing from which immigrants could move to the other LDS settlements.

The Saints in northern Missouri industriously planted crops and built log houses throughout the summer, and prospects for peace appeared good. They still hoped for eventual reconciliation with the citizens of Jackson County so that they could return to their center place, but in the meantime they intended to prosper where they were. By revelation, Far West was to become a temple city (D&C 115:7), and the following spring, the Quorum of the Twelve would dedicate the temple site before departing on a mission to Great Britain (D&C 118:4). Revelation in Far West also prescribed the formal name of the Church, "even The Church of Jesus Christ of Latter-day Saints" (D&C 115:4), and established the tithing system, which continues to provide financial stability to the Church and to bless its members (D&C 119, 120).

But new difficulties arose. First, Sidney RIGDON publicly threatened dissenters in his June "Salt Sermon," intimating that they should leave Far West or harm would befall them. News of this threat reinforced anti-Mormon hostility throughout Missouri. Second, LDS militia officer Sampson Avard formed an underground group of vigilantes labeled DANITES. Avard convinced this oathbound group that they operated with the approval of Church leaders and that they were authorized to avenge themselves against the Church's enemies, even by robbery, lying, and violence if necessary. Third, in an inflammatory Independence Day speech, Sidney Rigdon thundered out a declaration of independence from further mob violence. He warned of a war of extermination between Mormons and their enemies if they were further threatened or harassed.

Finally, and perhaps most important, the new LDS settlements in Adam-ondi-Ahman and DeWitt angered other Missourians who thought that the Mormons had agreed to stay in Caldwell County. Church leaders countered that as American citizens they had the right to buy land and live wherever they chose. Soon, depredations occurred, and with mobilization of militias on both sides, the stage was set for war. After violence erupted in October 1838, Governor Lilburn W. Boggs issued his infamous EXTERMINATION ORDER, declaring that all Mormons should be driven from Missouri or be exterminated.

At first, Church members attempted to defend themselves in their respective settlements, but the outlying towns were not defensible. Before all the Saints could gather to safety in fortified Far West, lives were lost in several confrontations, including the HAUN'S MILL MASSACRE, where seventeen LDS men and boys died. The siege of Far West took place during the last three days of October. Joseph Smith and other Church leaders were arrested and incarcerated, several in LIBERTY JAIL, and the Saints were forced to abandon their improved lands to their enemies and leave Missouri (*see* MISSOURI CONFLICT). Brigham YOUNG and Heber C. KIMBALL, members of the Twelve Apostles who were not imprisoned, and John TAYLOR, who was ordained an apostle in December, led the heroic efforts to relocate the approximately 12,000 Missouri Saints across the Mississippi River into Illinois.

BIBLIOGRAPHY

Gentry, Leland H. "A History of the Latter-day Saints in Northern Missouri from 1836 to 1839." Ph.D. diss., Brigham Young University, 1965.

LeSueur, Stephen C. *The 1838 Mormon War in Missouri*. Columbia, Mo., 1987.

LELAND H. GENTRY

MISSOURI CONFLICT

Incidents of discord between Latter-day Saints and their neighbors in Missouri from 1831 to 1839 are sometimes known as the Missouri War. In 1838 the tensions that had intermittently produced violence escalated into large-scale conflict that ended with the forced expulsion of the Latter-day Saints from the state.

The first Latter-day Saints entered Missouri in January 1831 as part of the LAMANITE MISSION. These zealous missionaries soon drew the ire of both U.S. Indian agents and local clergy in Independence, the rough-hewn and sometimes disorderly seat of Jackson County and the head of the Santa Fe Trail. Joseph SMITH arrived in July 1831. In August he selected a site for a temple and designated Jackson County as the location of the millennial Zion, or New Jerusalem, and as the gathering place for the Saints.

That summer more than one hundred Church members arrived in Jackson County from KIRTLAND, OHIO, and from other northern and eastern states; hundreds more soon followed. By the summer of 1833, more than a thousand were grouped into four settlements west of Independence, while others lived in the village itself.

Tension between the Latter-day Saints and their neighbors in frontier Jackson County mounted for several reasons. First, marked cultural differences set them apart. With New England roots, most Saints valued congregational Sabbath worship, education of their children, and refined personal decorum. In contrast, many Jackson County residents had come to the Missouri frontier from other states precisely to avoid such interference in their lives. Many held no schools for their children, and Sunday cockfights attracted more people than church services did. Often hard drinking intensified violent frontier ways. In the opinion of non-LDS county resident John C. McCoy in the *Kansas City Journal* (Apr. 24, 1881, p. 9), such extreme differences in customs made the two groups "completely unfitted to live together in peace and friendship."

Second, Missourians considered the Latter-day Saints strange and religiously unorthodox. Many LDS Church members aggressively articulated belief in revelation, prophets, the Book of Mormon, spiritual gifts, the Millennium, and the importance of gathering. Some went further and claimed Jackson County land as a sacred inheritance by divine appointment. Even David WHITMER, presiding elder of one branch, thought these boasts excited bitter jealousy. Articles on prophecy and doctrine published in the Church newspaper at Independence, the *Evening and the Morning Star,* added to hard feelings. In addition, local Protestant clergy felt threatened by LDS missionary activity.

Third, because the Saints lived on Church lands and traded entirely with the Church store or blacksmith shops, some original settlers viewed them as economically exclusive, even un-American. Others accused LDS immigrants of pauperism when, because of diminished Church resources, they failed to obtain land.

A fourth volatile issue was the original settlers' fear that Latter-day Saints might provoke battles with either slaves or Indians. They accused the Saints of slave tampering. As transplanted Southerners who valued their right to hold slaves, the settlers erroneously feared that the Saints intended to convert blacks or incite them to revolt.

They also correctly asserted that the Latter-day Saints desired to convert Indians and, perhaps, ally themselves with the Indians.

Finally, Missourians feared that continued LDS ingathering would lead to loss of political control. "It requires no gift of prophecy," stated a citizens' committee, "to tell that the day is not far distant when the civil government of the county will be in their hands; when the sheriff, the justices, and the county judges will be Mormons" (*HC* 1:397). These monumental differences between the Latter-day Saints and the Missourians eventually led to violence.

Vandalism against LDS settlers first occurred in the spring of 1832. Coordinated aggression commenced in July 1833, after the article "Free People of Color" appeared in the *Evening and the Morning Star*. Even though the article was written to curtail trouble, it so outraged local citizens that more than 400 met at the courthouse to demand that the Mormons leave. When the Latter-day Saints refused to negotiate away or abandon lands they legally owned, some citizens formed a mob and destroyed the press and printing house, ransacked the Mormon store, and violently accosted LDS leaders. Bishop Edward Partridge was beaten and tarred and feathered. Meeting three days later, the mob issued an ultimatum: One-half of the Mormons must leave by year's end and the rest by April (1834).

Local Church leaders sought counsel from Joseph Smith at Kirtland and assistance from Missouri Governor Daniel Dunklin. The Prophet urged them to hold their ground, and the governor advised them to seek redress through the courts. They did both. They employed lawyers from Clay County, including Alexander W. Doniphan and David R. Atchison.

Determined to settle the matter decisively, the old settlers mobilized to drive the Mormons out. Renewed violence began on October 31, 1833, with an attack on the Whitmer Branch a few miles west of the Big Blue River, near Independence. The mob demolished houses, whipped the men, and terrorized the women and children. For a week, attacks, beatings, and depredations against the Saints continued. On November 4 a mob again attacked the Whitmer settlement, making its streets a battleground. Two Missourians and one defender died.

The following day men led by Lyman Wight arrived from the Prairie Branch, twelve miles west, to protect members threatened at

Independence. Colonel Thomas L. Pitcher then called out the county militia to quell the mob and negotiate a truce with Wight. According to John Corrill, a Church officer at Independence, after the Saints surrendered their arms to the militia, the troops joined the mob in a general assault against them. Some county residents recoiled at this barbarism. John McCoy, whose father rode with the mob, later wrote in the *Kansas City Journal* (Jan. 18, 1885, p. 5) that the Mormons "were unjustly and outrageously maltreated." But neither Colonel Pitcher nor Lieutenant Governor Lilburn W. Boggs, a resident of the county, interfered.

The terrified Saints fled Jackson County in disarray. Most went north, across the Missouri River, and sought refuge in Clay County, whose citizens were generally sympathetic and hospitable. Even there, however, these refugees endured a miserable winter without sufficient shelter, clothing, or food—either in extemporized camps along the river or above the bluffs in abandoned summer slave quarters. By spring, though, industry, better weather, and the aid of Clay County citizens improved their desperate condition.

After the Missouri governor promised militia assistance, about 200 Saints marched from Ohio to Missouri to escort the exiles back to their homes. This paramilitary relief party was known as ZION'S CAMP. But reports of the camp's coming mobilized anti-Mormons throughout Missouri's western counties, and when it arrived in Missouri, it encountered hundreds of armed adversaries. The promised military assistance from the governor was not forthcoming, and the camp disbanded in June 1834 without crossing into Jackson County. The revelation disbanding Zion's Camp declared that, because the Saints had not been blameless and must yet learn much, their anticipated Zion would not be redeemed for "many days" (D&C 105:2–10, 37).

All parties considered the Saints' exile in Clay County to be temporary. Joseph Smith still hoped for the strength to return to Jackson County in the near future. But the Clay County old settlers, fearful of the flood of new LDS arrivals, grew impatient. On the night of June 28, 1836, a Clay County mob, determined to drive the Mormons from the county, commenced to harass and beat them. The following day a convention of leading citizens entreated the Saints to leave the county before the mob struck further. Grateful for the refuge provided by Clay County citizens at a time of deep crisis, Church leaders agreed to move.

An uninhabited area north of Richmond became the new gathering place. Friends of the Saints, including state legislator Alexander W. Doniphan, guided the formation of a new "Mormon county" called Caldwell. By late 1836, with the county seat of Far West surrounded by other settlements, Latter-day Saints streamed into Caldwell County. In early 1838, after experiencing difficulties in Ohio, Joseph Smith arrived at Far West, and the settlement became Church headquarters. Many of the Ohio Saints soon followed. As LDS settlement extended into nearby Daviess and Carroll counties, competition with the old settlers resumed, eventually erupting into conflict.

Internal dissent, the aftermath of problems in Kirtland, also plagued the Church at Far West. Oliver COWDERY, the Missouri stake presidency (David WHITMER, William W. Phelps, and John Whitmer), and three apostles (Luke S. Johnson, Lyman E. Johnson, and William E. McLellin) were all excommunicated. Trying to prevent them from damaging the Church, Sidney RIGDON, a counselor to Joseph Smith, demanded in his June 19 "salt sermon" that the dissenters leave or be punished. Soon after, in a vigorous July 4 address, Rigdon declared the Church's independence from "mobocracy." These two sermons further incensed the public against expanding LDS influence.

Hostilities that began on August 8, 1838, election day, ended a few months later with the expulsion of the Latter-day Saints from the state. At Gallatin, county seat of Daviess County, a fight ensued when Mormons were prevented from voting. Joseph Smith quickly took measures to protect his people in Daviess County, but matters worsened. As false rumors of his efforts and of the election day battle reached surrounding counties, hundreds of self-appointed regulators congregated in Daviess, Caldwell, and Carroll counties. State militia commanded by Major General David R. Atchison worked to keep an uneasy peace.

Fearing that Latter-day Saints, reinforced regularly by new arrivals, would soon control their counties, non-Mormons determined to attack. On October 2, 1838, a mob laid siege to the LDS settlement of DeWitt in Carroll County. The Saints petitioned recently elected Governor Lilburn W. Boggs for protection, only to be told that they must take care of themselves. Atchison's militia, weakened by mutiny and insubordination and lacking the firm support of the governor, failed to quell the mob. After ten days, the DeWitt Saints fled to Far West for safety; some in weakened condition died.

Faced with a heedless governor and an ineffective militia, Latter-day Saints reconsidered their long-standing position of passive defense. Concluding that without civil protection they had to protect themselves, in mid-October LDS leaders mobilized their own state-authorized militias in Caldwell and Daviess counties. These units actively confronted threatening mobs; there may also have been activity by units not strictly part of the militia (*see* DANITES).

Raiders from Gallatin and Millport in Daviess County harassed the LDS community of ADAM-ONDI-AHMAN. Throughout October both sides engaged in burning, stealing, and intimidation. While clearly acting first in self-defense, some Latter-day Saints nevertheless felt that military measures were excessive. In late October, Thomas B. Marsh and Orson Hyde, both apostles, signed affidavits critical of Mormon actions.

Hostilities escalated into outright warfare. Far West Militia Captain David W. PATTEN, an apostle, pursued a renegade band of Missouri militia overnight to the Crooked River in northern Ray County where, at dawn on October 25, they clashed. Two died on the battlefield, one on each side, and two mortally wounded Saints died soon after, including Patten.

From the Battle of Crooked River, rumors of LDS aggression spread like wildfire. On the strength of these rumors, Governor Boggs issued his infamous EXTERMINATION ORDER on October 27, authorizing the state militia to drive all Mormons from Missouri or exterminate them. Three days later Colonel William O. Jennings launched an unprovoked attacked on an LDS settlement at Haun's Mill, east of Far West, leaving seventeen men and boys dead (*see* HAUN'S MILL MASSACRE). Survivors joined other refugees fleeing to Far West. On October 31, the militia under the command of Major General Samuel D. Lucas laid siege upon Far West.

To avoid bloodshed, Joseph Smith and others agreed to meet with militia leaders, who instead arrested them. A court-martial that evening summarily sentenced Joseph Smith and his associates to be shot, and Lucas ordered Brig. General Alexander Doniphan to execute them at dawn. Doniphan thought the order illegal and heroically refused to carry it out, declaring that he would bring to account anyone who tried to do it. After Far West defenders were disarmed, Missouri attackers committed numerous outrages against women and property; a number of men were shot and at least one was killed.

While Joseph Smith and some of the others were jailed at Independence, in RICHMOND JAIL, and finally in LIBERTY JAIL, the rest of the Latter-day Saints were forced from the state. That winter, under the leadership of Brigham YOUNG, approximately 12,000 suffering Saints fled Missouri, most crossing the Mississippi River into Illinois at Quincy.

Joseph Smith and several others spent five months in jail awaiting trial for alleged murder, treason, arson, and other charges growing out of the fall violence and attempts at defense. For the Prophet, this imprisonment evoked a legacy of strength and revelations from heaven. A trial was never held. On April 15, 1839, while being transported on a change of venue to Boone County, Joseph and his brother Hyrum were allowed to escape to join Saints and their families in Illinois.

BIBLIOGRAPHY

Gentry, Leland H. "A History of the Latter-day Saints in Northern Missouri from 1836 to 1839." Ph.D. diss., Brigham Young University, 1965.

Jennings, Warren A. "Zion Is Fled: The Expulsion of the Mormons from Jackson County, Missouri." Ph.D. diss., University of Florida, 1962.

Johnson, Clark V. *The Missouri Petitions: Documents from the Missouri Conflict, 1833–1838*. Provo, Utah, 1991.

LeSueur, Stephen C. *The 1838 Mormon War in Missouri*. Columbia, Missouri, 1987.

Roberts, B. H. *The Missouri Persecutions*. Salt Lake City, 1900.

MAX H PARKIN

MORMON BATTALION

Though it never fought a battle, the Mormon Battalion, a volunteer unit in the 1846 U.S. campaign against Mexico, earned a place in the history of the West. Its men cleared a wagon road from Santa Fe to San Diego and helped secure California as United States territory. Members of the Battalion helped preserve a tenuous peace in southern California before the Treaty of Guadalupe Hidalgo ended hostilities. A wagon road they established between the Gila and the Rio Grande influenced the U.S. government to make the Gadsden Purchase. They also opened wagon roads via Carson and Cajon passes that linked California with Salt Lake City. Some former members of the Battalion eventually participated in the gold discovery and helped stimulate economic development in the Great Basin (*see* CALIFORNIA, PIONEER SETTLEMENTS IN). These former LDS soldiers ultimately received favorable recognition both from their military commanders and from other non-Mormons for their industriousness and loyalty.

After Brigham YOUNG had determined a timetable for moving west from Winter Quarters early in 1846 (*see* HISTORY OF THE CHURCH: C. 1844–1877; WESTWARD MIGRATION), he instructed Jesse C. Little, president of the Eastern States Mission, to seek government assistance. With the help of Thomas L. KANE, Little explored the matter with Amos Kendall, an influential political adviser, and later directly with U.S. President James K. Polk. After making a decision to send an overland army to California under the command of Stephen W. Kearny, Polk confided in his diary on June 2, 1846: "Col. Kearny was also authorized to receive into service as volunteers a few hundred of the Mormons who are now on their way to California, with a view to conciliate them, attach them to our country, & prevent them from taking part against us" (Polk, p. 109).

President Polk authorized this enlistment despite several concerns. One was the danger of internal conflict because Kearny's fighting regiments were mainly Missouri recruits, and Mormons and Missourians had little respect for each other since the Saints had been forced from the state in 1838–1839 (*see* MISSOURI CONFLICT). Polk also wanted to avoid the possibility that Mormon troops could be the first and possibly only American troops to reach California overland in 1846. The President's confidential orders therefore gave Colonel Kearny almost unlimited authority to deal with such matters.

Kearny dispatched Captain James Allen to raise five hundred volunteers from the LDS camps on the Missouri River. The initial reaction to Allen's call was overwhelmingly negative. Some feared that this call was part of a government conspiracy designed to ascertain their strength and to obstruct or prevent their movement west.

The five hundred enlistees would be drawn from the able-bodied men most needed for the trek west, and few saw any potential benefit.

However, by early June Brigham Young realized after struggling through the rain-soaked quagmires of southern Iowa, that the Saints could not safely reach the Rocky Mountains that year as planned. The proposed enlistment, he recognized, could bring military pay that would be helpful for purchasing supplies; moreover, it would provide for transporting several hundred families to the West, allay fears about LDS loyalty to the United States, and secure the privilege of establishing temporary quarters on Indian land near the Missouri (*see* WINTER QUARTERS).

As a result, Church leaders began vigorously recruiting volunteers from COUNCIL BLUFFS to Mt. Pisgah. Heber C. KIMBALL called the enlistment a great blessing from heaven, and Brigham Young explained that the soldiers would be mustered out in California, much closer to their new home in the West. Official rolls record an enlistment of 497 volunteers. In addition, as many as 80 women and children marched with the battalion, some of the women serving as paid laundresses.

Brigham Young selected LDS officers for the five companies, and the recruits voted to sustain his selection. The death of Colonel Allen en route to Santa Fe led to conflict: Should leadership fall to Captain Jefferson Hunt, senior Latter-day Saint officer, or to Lieutenant Andrew Jackson Smith of the regular army? Smith led the Battalion to Santa Fe, and the problem was solved when Kearny's new appointee, Philip St. George Cooke, took command.

When it became apparent that some soldiers and most of the families lacked the stamina for the desert march to San Diego, three "sick" detachments, including nearly all the women and children, went to Fort Pueblo, Colorado. Pueblo was an ideal location, partly because it was the temporary home of more than forty Latter-day Saints from Mississippi who had proceeded farther west than the general exodus. Altogether about 275 Latter-day Saints spent an unusually mild winter at Fort Pueblo under the command of Mormon Battalion captain James Brown. The next spring they proceeded to the Salt Lake Valley, arriving July 29, 1847, just five days after Brigham Young's party.

Commander Cooke, meantime, prepared the Battalion for the

trek to San Diego. After sending the sick detachments to Pueblo, he reorganized the command staff and acquired provisions, including thirty-seven wagons. He left Santa Fe with 397 soldiers. On the Rio Grande River he sent a final sick detachment to Pueblo, leaving the battalion with approximately 340 men, four officers' wives, and only a few children prepared for the grueling desert march.

After a strenuous desert march, the battalion reached the Pima villages scattered along the Gila River. From there it followed the previously established Gila Trail to the Colorado River, forded the Colorado, then struggled from water hole to water hole along the southern edge of the Imperial Sand Dunes and across the Imperial Valley. Finally, it followed the dry Vallecito Wash to the infamous Box Canyon. As the sidewalls of the wash became too narrow for wagons, the men hewed a route through the rock outcroppings and brought the five remaining wagons into southern California.

The Mormon Battalion's only engagement of the war, the Battle of the Bulls, occurred December 11, 1846, when several of the battalion's hunters opened fire on wild cattle that had stampeded into the rear companies. The toll was ten to fifteen bulls killed, two mules gored to death, three men wounded. When the battalion later neared Tucson, Mexican soldiers and residents chose to flee rather than fight.

After reaching San Diego in January 1847, LDS soldiers were given a variety of garrison responsibilities, with fifteen serving as Kearny's escort back to Fort Leavenworth. After more than 300 were discharged in Los Angeles on July 16, 1847, Captain Hunt led about fifty northward to Monterey. Some of the 300 worked near San Francisco before reuniting for the trip to Salt Lake City. The largest group, about 164 men, met Captain James Brown of the Pueblo detachments on the Truckee River in the Sierra Nevada Mountains on September 7, 1847. Brown was en route to collect his men's pay in San Francisco. He brought news of the safe arrival of the pioneers in the Salt Lake Valley, along with word that the men were free to work in California or to proceed to Salt Lake City, depending upon their financial circumstances and desire.

While a few went eastward, the majority of the destitute men scattered for odd jobs, including about forty who worked at Sutter's Fort and a few who were at Sutter's Mill when James Marshall discovered gold. Eighty-one men reenlisted as the California Volunteers and performed garrison duty at San Diego. After their discharge in the spring of 1848, these men opened a wagon road via Cajon Pass to Salt Lake City.

Though leaving their families behind was difficult and their desert march arduous, by their sacrifice the men of the Mormon Battalion facilitated the Saints' move to the Salt Lake Valley and helped develop the West.

BIBLIOGRAPHY

Polk, James K. *Polk, the Diary of a President 1845–1849*, ed. Allan Nevins, pp. 108–109. London, 1929.

Tyler, Daniel. *A Concise History of the Mormon Battalion in the Mexican War 1846–1847*. n. p., 1881; Chicago, 1964.

Yurtinus, John F. "A Ram in the Thicket: A History of the Mormon Battalion in the Mexican War." Ph.D. diss., Brigham Young University, 1975.

———. "The Mormon Volunteers: The Recruitment and Service of a Unique Military Company." *Journal of San Diego History* 25 (Summer 1979):242–61.

JOHN F. YURTINUS

MORMON PIONEER TRAIL

The approximately 1,300-mile-long trail from NAUVOO, ILLINOIS, to Salt Lake City, Utah, was certified by the National Trails Act of 1986 as a National Historic Trail—officially The Mormon Pioneer National Historic Trail. Contrary to popular belief, however, the famous trail was not a Mormon creation. The Latter-day Saints did very little trailblazing. They followed territorial roads and Indian trails across Iowa; various segments of the Oregon Trail from the Missouri River to Fort Bridger in present western Wyoming; and the year-old trail of the ill-fated California-bound Reed–Donner party from Fort Bridger into the valley of the Great Salt Lake.

Although the trail was not blazed by the Latter-day Saints, and parts of it have at times been known as the Council Bluffs Road, the Omaha Road, the Great Platte River Road, or even the North Branch of the Oregon Trail, the entire route is today almost universally known as "The Mormon Trail" because the Latter-day Saints used it for twenty-three years in such large numbers (at least seventy thousand; no one knows just how many), because of the high drama of their "Exodus," and because they developed separate strands or *trails* and wove them into their great *road* (*see* IMMIGRATION AND EMIGRATION).

The trail divides into two unequal sections:

1. The approximately 265-mile-long section from Nauvoo on the Mississippi across Iowa to present-day Council Bluffs on the Missouri. This part of the trail was used relatively little: mainly by Latter-day Saints fleeing Illinois in 1846, by some immigrants "jumping off" from Keokuk, Iowa, in 1853, and in 1856–1857 by seven HANDCART COMPANIES from Iowa City who entered the Mormon Trail at present-day Lewis, Cass County, Iowa. Thousands of other Latter-day Saints crossed Iowa on variants of the 1846 route or on other trails, but all these intersected the trail of 1846 somewhere in western Iowa.
2. The approximately 1,032-mile-long trans-Missouri River segment from present North Omaha (one-time WINTER QUARTERS) and Florence, Nebraska, across Nebraska and Wyoming, into Utah. This part of the trail was used extensively from 1847 until completion of the transcontinental railroad in 1869. As in Iowa, variants evolved, but all LDS immigrants used all or parts of this trans-Missouri trail.

While the 1846–1847 trek from Nauvoo to Salt Lake City is by far the best-known part of the twenty-three-year-long Mormon overland migration, it is only part of the story. Between 1848 and 1868, LDS immigrants traveling west from the Missouri River developed or utilized at least a dozen other points of departure and followed many other trails, such as the Oxbow Trail (1849–1864), the Mormon Grove Trail (1855–1856), and the Nebraska City Cutoff (1864–1866). In one way or another, however, all these trails eventually intersected *the* Mormon Trail. Furthermore, with the Union Pacific Railroad moving west from Omaha beginning in 1865, during 1867–1868 Latter-day Saints took trains from Omaha to four different railheads (North Platte, Nebraska; Julesburg, Colorado; and Laramie and Benton, Wyoming), from which they eventually picked up the Mormon Trail.

Across the monotonous, undifferentiated, rolling central lowlands of Iowa, the Mormon Trail of 1846 generally followed primitive territorial roads as far as Bloomfield, Davis County, and then vague

Pottawattamie Indian and trading trails along ridges from one water source to another, always within fifty miles of the present Missouri state line. Today this part of the Mormon Trail is difficult to follow, not because of the terrain but because modern roads seldom parallel it and because the plow has destroyed most vestiges of it.

West of the Missouri River the Saints passed along river valleys, across grasslands, plains, steppes, deserts, and mountains, and through western forests. Topographically, the trail led across the central lowlands and high plains of eastern and central Nebraska, then the upland trough of western Nebraska and eastern Wyoming, through the Wyoming basin and the middle Rocky Mountains, and into the desert valleys of the Great Basin.

From the Missouri River, Mormon companies followed the broad, flat valleys of the Loupe and Platte rivers for some six hundred miles to present-day Casper, Wyoming, then the Sweetwater River for about ninety-three miles to South Pass, thence along branches of the Sandy River and Blacks Fork to Fort Bridger, finally zigzagging through a series of canyons into the valley of the Great Salt Lake.

In Nebraska, as in Iowa, there is little left today of the Mormon Trail, but modern roads do parallel the old trail closely. In Wyoming, however, with proper maps much of this old trail can still be found because the harsh terrain has held the ruts better and agriculture has obliterated little. In Utah, although modern roads follow the trail closely, very few of the original ruts remain.

BIBLIOGRAPHY

Kimball, Stanley B. *Historic Sites and Markers Along the Mormon and Other Great Western Trails*. Urbana, Ill., 1988.

Kimball, Stanley B., and Hal Knight. *111 Days to Zion*. Salt Lake City, 1978.

Stegner, Wallace. *The Gathering of Zion: The Story of the Mormon Trail*. New York, 1971.

STANLEY B. KIMBALL

MORONI, VISITATIONS OF

From 1823 to 1829, the angel Moroni$_2$ appeared at least twenty times to Joseph SMITH and others. Those appearances opened the way for the translation and publication of the Book of Mormon and laid the foundation of many of the Church's most characteristic teachings. As a resurrected messenger of God, Moroni told Joseph Smith about the Nephite record on gold plates and taught him concerning the gathering of Israel, the forthcoming visit of Elijah, the imminence of the second coming of Jesus Christ, and the judgments to be poured out on the world prior to that event.

Of Moroni's first appearance on the night of September 21, 1823, Joseph Smith recorded:

> After I had retired to my bed for the night, I betook myself to prayer and supplication to Almighty God for forgiveness of all my sins and follies, and also for a manifestation to me, that I might know of my state and standing before him. . . . While I was thus in the act of calling upon God, I discovered a light appearing in my room, which continued to increase until the room was lighter than at noonday, when immediately a personage appeared at my bedside, standing in the air. . . . He had on a loose robe of most exquisite whiteness. It was a whiteness beyond anything earthly I had ever seen. . . . His hands were naked, and his arms also, a little above the wrist; so, also, were his feet naked, as were his legs, a little above the ankles. His head and neck were also bare. . . . His whole person was glorious beyond description, and his countenance truly like lightning [JS—H 1:29–32].

The angel introduced himself as Moroni, and as he told about the Nephite record, its contents, and the interpreters buried with it, Joseph saw in vision their location in the hill Cumorah. Moroni warned Joseph not to show the plates or the interpreters to anyone except those whom the Lord designated. Moroni also quoted certain prophecies from the Bible, including Malachi 3–4, Isaiah 11, and Acts 3:22–23.

After the angel left, Joseph lay contemplating this experience, and Moroni returned a second time and repeated verbatim everything he had said in his first visit, adding more detail about the coming judgments, and then returned a third time to repeat his instructions and to warn Joseph that he must put all thoughts of worldly wealth aside and concentrate solely on the translation of the record and the establishment of the kingdom of God.

As Moroni left the third time, Joseph said he heard the cock crow, the visitations having occupied the entire night. He arose and went into the fields with his father and his older brother Alvin, but felt tired and feeble. His father, noticing his son's condition, told him to return to the house. As Joseph was climbing over a fence, he fell to the ground unconscious.

The next thing he remembered seeing was Moroni standing over him, repeating his instructions of the night before, adding that Joseph should now tell his father about the visitations. Joseph did so, and his father, assured that the vision came from God, told Joseph to follow the angel's instructions (JS—H 1:46–50).

Joseph Smith then went to the hill and found the place shown him the night before in vision. He uncovered the plates and was about to remove them when Moroni appeared again, counseling Joseph that the time was not yet right. Instead, he instructed Joseph to return to this spot at the same time the following year and that he should continue to do so until the time had come for obtaining the plates (JS—H 1:51–54).

It is reported that during those years Joseph Smith also received visits from Mormon, Nephi, and other "angels of God unfolding the majesty and glory of the events that should transpire in the last days" (*HC* 4:537; cf. *JD* 17:374; Petersen, p. 131). Joseph shared with his family some of his experiences. His mother, Lucy Mack SMITH, recalled, "From this time forth, Joseph continued to receive instructions from the Lord, and we continued to get the children together every evening for the purpose of listening while he gave us a relation of the same. . . . He would describe the ancient inhabitants of this continent, their dress, mode of traveling, and the animals upon which they rode; their cities, their buildings, with every particular; their mode of warfare; and also their religious worship. This he would do with as much ease, seemingly, as if he had spent his whole life among them" (pp. 82–83).

Moroni temporarily reclaimed the plates and the interpreters after Martin HARRIS had lost the first 116 manuscript pages of the translation. Later, when Joseph Smith moved from Harmony, Pennsylvania, to Fayette, New York, in June 1829, Moroni returned them to him (Smith, pp. 149–50). Still later, Moroni showed the plates to the Three Witnesses (*HC* 1:54–55), took them after the translation had been completed (JS—H 1:60), and once more returned them briefly to Joseph to show to the Eight Witnesses.

In addition to Joseph and the Three Witnesses, Mary Whitmer also saw the angel and talked with him. Mary Whitmer said she was shown the gold plates when she conversed with Moroni (Peterson, pp. 114, 116). Other sources indicate that Moroni appeared also to W. W. Phelps, Heber C. KIMBALL, John TAYLOR, and Oliver Granger (Peterson, pp. 151–52).

BIBLIOGRAPHY

Backman, Milton V., Jr. *Eyewitness Accounts of the Restoration*, rev. ed. Salt Lake City, 1986.

Cheesman, Paul R. *The Keystone of Mormonism*, rev. ed. Provo, Utah, 1988.

Peterson, H. Donl. *Moroni: Ancient Prophet, Modern Messenger*. Bountiful, Utah, 1983.

Smith, Lucy Mack. *History of Joseph Smith*. Preston Nibley, ed. Salt Lake City, 1958.

ELDIN RICKS

MOUNTAIN MEADOWS MASSACRE

In September 1990, some two thousand persons gathered in Cedar City, Utah, to effect a reconciliation among those whose ancestors died or participated in what may be considered the most unfortunate incident in the history of the LDS Church, the Mountain Meadows Massacre. The massacre occurred between September 7 and 11, 1857, when a group of Mormon settlers in southern Utah joined with nearby Indians in killing all but some of the youngest members of a group of non-Mormon emigrants en route to California.

After years of painstaking research, Juanita Brooks, author of an oft-cited book on the tragedy, concluded, "The complete—the absolute—truth of the affair can probably never be evaluated by any human being; attempts to understand the forces which culminated in it and those which were set into motion by it are all very inadequate at best" (Brooks, p. 223). Yet, as Brooks makes clear, a few elements that helped contribute to the tragedy are evident.

Among these is the fact that a large contingent of United States troops was marching westward toward Utah Territory in the summer of 1857 (*see* UTAH EXPEDITION). Despite having been the federally appointed territorial governor, Brigham Young was not informed by

Washington of the army's purpose and interpreted the move as a renewal of the persecution the Latter-day Saints had experienced before their westward hegira. "We are invaded by a hostile force who are evidently assailing us to accomplish our overthrow and destruction," he proclaimed on August 5, 1857. Anticipating an attack, he declared the territory to be under martial law and ordered "[t]hat all the forces in said Territory hold themselves in readiness to march, at a moment's notice, to repel any and all such threatened invasion" (Arrington, p. 254).

Part of Brigham Young's strategy in repelling the approaching army was to enlist local Indian tribes as allies. In an August 4 letter to southern Utah, for example, he urged one Latter-day Saint to "[c]ontinue the conciliatory policy towards the Indians, which I have ever recommended, and seek by works of righteousness to obtain their love and confidence, for they must learn that they have either got to help us or the United States will kill us both" (Brooks, p. 34).

Meanwhile, owing to the lateness of the season, a party of emigrants bound for California elected to take the southern route that passed through Cedar City and thirty-five miles beyond to the Mountain Meadows, which was then an area of springs, bogs, and plentiful grass where travelers frequently stopped to rejuvenate themselves and their stock before braving the harsh desert landscape to the west. Led by John T. Baker and Alexander Fancher, the diverse party consisted of perhaps 120 persons, most of whom left from Arkansas but others of whom joined the company along their journey.

As the Baker-Fancher party traveled from Salt Lake City to the Mountain Meadows, tensions developed between some of the emigrants, on the one hand, and Mormon settlers and their Native American allies, on the other. Spurred by rumors, their own observations, and memories of atrocities some of them had endured in Missouri and Illinois, Mormon residents in and around Cedar City felt compelled to take some action against the emigrant train but ultimately decided to dispatch a rider to Brigham Young seeking his counsel. Leaving September 7, 1857, the messenger made the nearly 300-mile journey in just a little more than three days.

Approximately one hour after his arrival, the messenger was on his way back with a letter from Brigham Young, who said he did not expect the federal soldiers to arrive that fall because of their poor stock. "They cannot get here this season without we help them," he explained. "So you see that the Lord has answered our prayers and again averted the blow designed for our heads." Responding to the plea for counsel, he added, "In regard to the emigration trains passing through our settlements, we must not interfere with them until they are first notified to keep away. You must not meddle with them. The Indians we expect will do as they please but you should try and preserve good feelings with them" (Brooks, p. 63). The messenger arrived back in Cedar City on September 13.

By that time, however, it was too late, and nearly all the men, women, and children of the Baker-Fancher party lay dead. Besides a few persons who left the party before the attack, only about eighteen small children were spared. Two years later, seventeen of the children were returned to family members in northwestern Arkansas. Two decades after the tragedy, one of the Mormon settlers who were present at the massacre, John D. Lee, was executed by a firing squad at the Mountain Meadows, symbolically carrying to the grave the responsibility for those who "were led to do what none singly would have done under normal conditions, and for which none singly can be held responsible" (Brooks, p. 218).

Yet for more than another century after Lee's death, the community guilt of those who participated in the massacre continued to fester alongside the collective pain of both the children who survived it and the relatives of those who did not. Then in the late 1980s, the descendants of those affected by the tragedy began meeting to bind the wounds and achieve a reconciliation. On September 15, 1990, many of them gathered to dedicate a memorial marker to those who died at the Mountain Meadows.

One speaker at the marker dedication was Judge Roger V. Logan, Jr., of Harrison, Arkansas, a man related to twenty-one of the massacre victims listed on the marker, as well as to five of the children who survived. "I am happy to say that thanks to the work, cooperation and gifts of many of you," he said, "there is now an appropriate monument standing in the place of the emigrants' demise; a monument containing the names of eighty-two persons who died and seventeen who survived and [that] also contains reference to many others who may have been a part of the caravan." As he read the victims' names, he asked all related to them to stand in their honor.

Brigham Young University President Rex E. Lee, a descendant of John D. Lee, also spoke at the memorial service, saying he found little solace in recognizing that similar tragedies had occurred across time and space. "Any attempt to recreate the human dynamics that were at work in southern Utah in the fall of 1857 can only leave us bewildered as to how rational human beings at any time, in any place, under any circumstances could have permitted such a tragedy to occur."

"Fortunately," he added, "full comprehension of the reasons is as unnecessary as it would be impossible. Our task for today is not to look backward, nor to rationalize, nor to engage in any kind of retroactive analysis nor apology. Our focus is not on 1857. It is on 1990. It is on our generation, and on those that are yet to come. And whatever drove the actions of those who came before, ours must be driven by something higher and more noble."

Gordon B. Hinckley, First Counselor in the LDS Church First Presidency, offered the prayer dedicating the new monument. In a talk delivered before the prayer, President Hinckley said he came "not as a descendant of any of the parties involved at Mountain Meadows" but "as a representative of an entire people who have suffered much over what occurred there."

"In our time," he said, "we can read such history as is available, but we really cannot understand nor comprehend that which occurred those tragic and terrible September days in 1857. Rather, we are grateful for the ameliorating influence that has brought us together in a spirit of reconciliation as new generations gather with respect and appreciation one for another. A bridge has been built across a chasm of cankering bitterness. We walk across that bridge and greet one another with a spirit of love, forgiveness, and with hope that there will never be a repetition of anything of the kind." (Excerpts from the talks are all taken from unpublished manuscripts found in the Mountain Meadows Memorial collection, LDS Church Historical Department, Salt Lake City, Utah.)

BIBLIOGRAPHY

Arrington, Leonard J. *Brigham Young, American Moses.* New York, 1985.

Brooks, Juanita. *The Mountain Meadows Massacre.* Rev. ed., Norman, Okla., 1991.

CHC 4:139–80.

RONALD K. ESPLIN
RICHARD E. TURLEY, JR.

N

NAUVOO

Nauvoo, Illinois, headquarters of the Church and home for many of its members from 1839 to 1846, began and ended as a community in exile. In 1838–1839 Latter-day Saints fled from Missouri seeking religious refuge from mob persecution. They found shelter in eastern Iowa and western Illinois, where they established new communities. Joseph Smith named the principal city Nauvoo, meaning, he said, "a beautiful location, a place of rest." When the Saints left Nauvoo for the Rocky Mountains seven years later, they were again religious exiles in search of a home.

The community at Nauvoo grew rapidly on land purchased from settlers and speculators willing to sell on contract. Joseph Smith, acting as agent for the Church, bought the Illinois farms of Hugh and William White and investment tracts from Isaac Galland and Horace Hotchkiss—in all, 660 acres. He resold one-acre Nauvoo lots surveyed on the flats along the river, in competition with other LDS developers who platted land on nearby bluffs. A survey established streets three rods wide within city boundaries overlaying existing "paper" towns of Commerce and Commerce City. In December 1840, Nauvoo became a legal entity under the NAUVOO CHARTER, issued by the Illinois legislature and providing the Saints better legal protection than they had ever known. Nauvoo was now home.

As exiled Latter-day Saints from Missouri and Ohio gathered to their new stake of Zion, missionaries in the United States and Great Britain baptized many new converts (*see* MISSIONS OF THE TWELVE TO THE BRITISH ISLES). Encouraged by Joseph Smith, American and Canadian converts moved westward to Nauvoo. Some used canal boats and lake steamers, others covered wagons and horseback, and a few simply walked. Beginning in 1840, thousands sailed the Atlantic from Liverpool, England, and took steamboats up the Mississippi from New Orleans. This was a religious migration, an individual and family response to religious beliefs, aided by Church emigration agents in Liverpool, who organized companies and appointed shepherds for those fleeing to Zion (*see* IMMIGRATION AND EMIGRATION).

Newcomers were welcomed in Nauvoo by friends, relatives, missionaries, and the Prophet Joseph Smith himself. Renting a room or finding other temporary quarters became increasingly difficult during the boom years 1841–1843. As quickly as possible, new settlers hired scarce contractors and craftsmen to build houses. Lumber, harvested from nearby virgin forests or shipped in, and, later, bricks made in Nauvoo, went into hundreds of comfortable but small, new homes. Nauvoo became a boom town.

Gardens on the city lots furnished vegetables, herbs, fruits, and berries. Meat and potatoes, when available, and corn—ground into meal for boiling, baking, and frying—were staples in everyone's diet. On nearby prairies, farmers plowed, cooperatively enclosed, and then planted hundreds of acres in corn, wheat, and potatoes. LDS tradesmen found ready work in Nauvoo, as did merchants eager to import manufactured goods from St. Louis, Cincinnati, and the East Coast.

Nauvoo boosters and their political opponents in neighboring towns exaggerated their estimates of Nauvoo's population for differing purposes. Illinois census takers in 1845 counted 11,057 residents. Adding growth through late 1845 and including the city's environs boosted the estimate to 15,000 at Nauvoo's peak, almost equal to a faster-growing Chicago.

To meet public needs, civic groups built a music hall and cultural hall, and priesthood quorums planned their own meeting halls. Church-sponsored construction of the NAUVOO HOUSE, a grand hotel, and the NAUVOO TEMPLE gave Nauvoo's growth religious meaning.

Though all members contributed as means and faith allowed

toward erection of the temple, they did not all live in Nauvoo. Some remained in their hometowns because of economic or family pressures. Others joined the march to Nauvoo but found homesites and land away from headquarters. On a 13,000-acre, Church-purchased site in Lee County, Iowa, just across the river from Nauvoo, the Saints founded a town called Zarahemla and nine other smaller settlements. Joseph Smith organized an Iowa stake and approved settlement there and in several new towns in western Illinois. Besides Nauvoo, Church members in Hancock County lived at Ramus (now Webster); in Adams County at Lima, Quincy, Mount Hope (now Columbus), and Freedom (near Payson); in Morgan County at Geneva; in Sangamon County at Springfield; and in Pike County at Pleasant Vale (now Canton). Additionally, presiding elders organized Church branches wherever clusters of members lived in North America and the British Isles.

Wherever they lived, Latter-day Saints looked to the Prophet Joseph Smith for religious leadership. His revelations and sermons published in Nauvoo achieved Churchwide distribution. For residents, the Prophet offered firsthand preaching, teaching, and counseling. Besides these, his influence in Nauvoo was enlarged through his roles as land agent, mayor, militia leader, magistrate, and merchant. No wonder that after his death and the repeal of its charter, the city was renamed the City of Joseph.

During his last years at Nauvoo, the Prophet unfolded additional aspects of the restored gospel. He responded to questions about basic LDS beliefs with thirteen Articles of Faith, which described fundamental doctrines. He published another revealed scriptural record, the book of Abraham. He taught new insights into the common origins of all mankind and their eternal destiny, particularly in a eulogy for a member, King Follett (*see* KING FOLLETT DISCOURSE). Many of the new teachings pointed toward the temple, and looked toward a collective effort to perform ordinances for the salvation of deceased ancestors and the exaltation of faithful Saints. The first baptisms for the dead were done in the Mississippi River, but by late November 1841, proxy baptisms commenced in the temple font. Meanwhile, with the temple not yet complete, several men, including two of the Twelve, received the first temple endowments on May 4, 1842, in an upstairs room at the President's office-store. The following year their wives and other men and women received the same ordinances, providing a corps of initiates to administer temple ordinances to thousands of others in the Nauvoo Temple beginning in December 1845.

The temple was a central focus of Nauvoo religious life. The Saints supported its construction with tithes of time and means, and they longed to receive anticipated temple blessings. For those privileged to live in Nauvoo, the temple and its associated theology gave new and eternal meaning to birth, marriage, life, and death.

Though Joseph Smith's personal leadership dominated Nauvoo's religious life, an institutional structure supported his efforts and carried on after his death in 1844 (*see* MARTYRDOM OF JOSEPH AND HYRUM SMITH). During the Nauvoo years, the Quorum of the Twelve accepted an increased role. First organized in 1835, members gained experience first as mission leaders in England and then as administrators in Nauvoo. With the First Presidency and other authorities, they shared opportunities to preach scriptural commentaries on Sunday from the stand in the grove near the temple, and to address the Saints at general conferences. Among the most significant meetings in Nauvoo, these April and October conferences brought together thousands of the Saints for business and instruction. Similar gatherings convened elsewhere for scattered branches. Minutes published in the British *Millennial Star* and Nauvoo *Times and Seasons* helped keep members elsewhere informed of Church business, membership growth, and preachings. Church periodicals issued the first installments of Joseph Smith's HISTORY OF THE CHURCH, a project he pursued diligently with his clerks from 1838 until his death in 1844.

The women's Relief Society, organized in 1842, administered to the needs of the poor and taught principles of sexual purity. In this, they assisted the bishops of Nauvoo's fledgling wards—new administrative units for tending to temporal needs and monitoring religious worthiness. After Brigham YOUNG and the Twelve succeeded the Prophet as leaders, the Seventy and other Melchizedek Priesthood quorums grew rapidly in numbers and importance. The Seventy built a hall, sponsored a library, and prepared themselves for missions and for temple blessings.

While Latter-day Saints in Nauvoo gave primary allegiance to their religious affiliation, their lives reflected experiences typical of others in Jacksonian America. Non-Mormons living in and around

Nauvoo joined with them in the celebration of Independence Day. Military processions, band music, patriotic speeches, and other festivities attracted citizens who arrived on horseback and in carriages and riverboats. Christmas observances were highlights for family and friends, with progressive dinners, singing, and dancing. Membership in Mormon Freemasonry lodges, organized in 1841–1842, affirmed group loyalty within the Church and encouraged fraternal ties with others. Contrary to expectations, however, the rapid growth of the lodges created controversy that strained relationships with other masons.

Mormon-American society in Nauvoo, leavened increasingly by a British and Scandinavian immigrant influence, included typical nineteenth-century entertainment and recreational opportunities. Brass bands played at dances and patriotic gatherings, accompanied Church choirs, and performed for temple capstone ceremonies. Adult and youth choirs, instrumentalists, and vocalists entertained and edified at social and religious gatherings. The music performed came out of the host society, though some hymns were newly written for LDS services. Mormon poets regularly memorialized events and people and set significant religious messages to rhyme for biweekly periodicals. Thespians in Nauvoo presented popular theatricals or sponsored traveling performing troupes in the Nauvoo cultural hall. Other occasional attractions included art exhibits, the circus, and riverboat excursions.

Children had few toys, mostly homemade wagons, tops, and dolls. They enjoyed games such as fox and geese or leapfrog. Youths engaged in pastimes such as playing with marbles, wrestling, foot racing, hunting, fishing, stick-pulling, bowling, and baseball. Adults joined in many of these recreational activities and sometimes passed the time with card games, carriage rides, or parlor socials. When not providing necessities, Nauvooans also pursued education and learning. To get basic training in reading, writing, and arithmetic for their families, parents hired tutors or enrolled children in one of dozens of classes offered by Nauvoo's part-time teachers. Tuition was paid through providing teachers board and room and scarce cash. The University of Nauvoo existed only in a few scattered classes. Male adults and younger men organized lyceums and debating societies to develop rhetorical skills. They argued religious as well as political topics to prepare participants for missionary and civic service. Books were scarce in private homes, but a membership lending library offered two hundred donated volumes on science, world religion, history, and literature. Nauvoo's religious and secular newspapers, the *Times and Seasons* and *Nauvoo Neighbor* (originally *The Wasp*), edited by prominent LDS citizens, circulated to Latter-day Saints on two continents. In an "Age of the Common Man," Nauvoo's social and educational life was one of broad enjoyment and participation.

As elsewhere in American society, the family was the focus of everyday life. Women met domestic needs through a combination of their own labor and income from their husbands' work. The family produced and prepared food, though Nauvoo merchants imported or traded many foodstuffs. Women often made everyday clothing, bed coverings, rugs, and such things as towels and curtains from purchased cloth. Furniture, kitchen utensils, and tools for trades were imported or brought along by immigrants. Home remedies, supplemented by priesthood blessings, were administered in faith for healing. Infant mortality was high, and death for all a constant possibility from malarialike diseases, untreatable illnesses, and accidents.

For Latter-day Saints in Nauvoo, the family took on new religious meaning. Conversion unfortunately often divided families, though letters from Nauvoo nurtured bonds and encouraged reunion. Proxy temple ordinances offered opportunity for uniting families across generations and beyond the grave. Select associates accepted the Prophet's private challenge to make covenants of marriage with plural wives (*see* PLURAL MARRIAGE), though the doctrine was not preached publicly until 1852 in Utah. In preparation for the temple, teaching of the doctrine of eternal families added a unique touch to LDS family life. Sealing ordinances for husbands and wives gave marriage and the family in Nauvoo an eternal perspective.

Just when life appeared to be back to normal after the martyrdom, the loss of Nauvoo's charter and mob harassment in 1845 threatened the peace of Joseph Smith's City Beautiful. Political and schismatic opponents predicted "the end of 'Mormonism.'" Disaffected Latter-day Saints threatened religious unity and offered guardianship and new prophetic leadership in opposition to the Twelve. The Church survived, but Nauvoo's position as the Church center ended. The governing Quorum of the Twelve announced plans at the October 1845 conference to evacuate by the following spring.

Throughout the winter, residents organized for the exodus even as they rushed to complete their temple and receive its ordinances (*see* WESTERN MIGRATION, PLANNING AND PROPHECY). They purchased oxen, made wagons, sold properties, and outfitted themselves for the long trek into the western wilderness as they also prepared temple clothing and did finishing work inside the temple on the hill. Brigham Young and the Twelve appointed agents to dispose of unsold property and organized emigration companies as they oversaw construction details on the temple. By December, just before departure began, thousands of the Nauvoo faithful began to receive their long-awaited temple endowments. Before winter's end more than 6,000 received temple ordinances and thus were willing to leave. After seven eventful years, the Latter-day Saints moved on again, transplanting their covenant society to a new promised land.

BIBLIOGRAPHY

Flanders, Robert B. "To Transform History: Early Mormon Culture and the Concept of Time and Space." *Church History* 40 (1971):108–17.

Godfrey, Kenneth W. "Some Thoughts Regarding an Unwritten History of Nauvoo." *BYU Studies* 15 (1975):417–24.

———. "The Nauvoo Neighborhood: A Little Philadelphia or a Unique City Set Upon a Hill?" *Journal of Mormon History* 11 (1984):78–97.

Hill, Marvin S. "Mormon Religion in Nauvoo: Some Reflections." *Utah Historical Quarterly* 44 (1976):170–80.

Kimball, Stanley B. "Nauvoo West: The Mormons of the Iowa Shore." *BYU Studies* 18 (1978):132–42.

Miller, David E., and Della S. Miller. *Nauvoo: The City of Joseph*. Salt Lake City, 1974.

GLEN M. LEONARD

NAUVOO CHARTER

By legislation signed into law on December 16, 1840, the Illinois General Assembly granted corporate city status to Nauvoo. Among literally hundreds of Illinois settlements, only Alton, Chicago, Galena, Quincy, and Springfield shared such distinctive legal status. Expectations of what would result ran high for both Latter-day Saints and their neighbors.

Many Illinoisans, shocked at the harsh treatment given the Latter-day Saints by the Missourians (*see* MISSOURI CONFLICT), sought to succor the beleaguered followers of Joseph SMITH by helping them politically and providing legal safeguards. Moreover, the economic fabric of the state suffered from the deepening effects of the panics of 1837 and 1839, and many legislators saw an economic boon in the future immigration of several thousand new settlers. Encouraged by state political leaders, the Saints believed that a city charter would guarantee them a kind of security they had never yet enjoyed. Even State Supreme Court Justice Stephen A. Douglas, despite prior judicial decisions to the contrary, opined that a corporate charter was irrevocable and perpetual.

The Nauvoo document, neither the longest nor the shortest city charter, was much like the charters of other Illinois cities. More than half the sections were modeled on the Springfield charter. City status allowed governance by a council chosen by an electorate; unlike other city councils in Illinois, the Nauvoo Council contained aldermen, councillors, and a mayor. The Nauvoo instrument also differed from others in being not one but three charters, granting corporate status to the city, a university, and a city militia. Previous practice was to establish schools and also militia units by separate acts. The University of the City of Nauvoo, governed by the city council, was the only city-operated university in the state.

One important provision stated that the Nauvoo Council could pass any ordinances not repugnant to the constitutions of the United States or that of Illinois. This, in effect, empowered the Nauvoo body to stand in a federated position with the Illinois General Assembly. Ordinances passed by the Nauvoo Council could be in direct violation or disregard of state law and still be valid in Nauvoo, provided they did not conflict with specific powers granted by the federal and state constitutions. Leaders of the city militia, known as the NAUVOO LEGION, and the university trustees could also pass laws, limited only by state and federal constitutions.

Almost at once this power became a focal point of misunderstanding and controversy, though the same delegation of authority was also in three of the other five city charters. Since this provision was not unique, adverse reaction to it clearly had a good deal to do with how others viewed Latter-day Saints and the implementation of the provision by Nauvoo and its leaders. The Nauvoo Municipal Court, the third such court provided for by the Illinois General Assembly, also became a point of contention. While the city courts of Chicago and Alton convened under one judge, the principal Nauvoo judge was the mayor of the city, sitting as chief justice, with the aldermen as associate justices. Adversaries argued that the way Joseph Smith, as mayor of Nauvoo, used the legislative and judicial powers granted by law resulted in "anti-republican" abuses.

In granting the charter, some legislators may have hoped to protect Latter-day Saints from PERSECUTION, but it proved to be a two-edged sword. When the Illinois majority turned against Nauvoo but lacked legal tools to curb the city's power and influence, it turned to extralegal means. Later, after violence, it also succeeded in getting Nauvoo's charter repealed. Although based solidly on precedents not termed "anti-republican" until Latter-day Saints obtained and used them, the Nauvoo Charter nevertheless ultimately fell short of providing the Saints the peace and protection they desired.

BIBLIOGRAPHY

Kimball, James L., Jr. "The Nauvoo Charter: A Reinterpretation." *Journal of the Illinois State Historical Society* 54 (Spring 1971):66–78.

JAMES L. KIMBALL, JR.

NAUVOO ECONOMY

Nauvoo, for seven years the headquarters of the Church, was a river city with an agricultural hinterland set amid a preestablished, second-generation frontier society of non-Mormons. Founded in 1839 by LDS refugees from the MISSOURI CONFLICT, it existed as an LDS community only until 1846. Additions to its fast-growing population came mostly through new converts, many from England, who almost always brought skills and sometimes wealth. Though commerce in goods and services was brisk, Nauvoo's primary import was converts (*see* IMMIGRATION AND EMIGRATION), and its primary export, missionaries.

Nauvoo was neither communal nor communitarian. Still, the influences of the corporation of the Church pervaded society and economy. In Nauvoo, Joseph SMITH voiced a prophetic, hurrying urgency to build the city and its temple, an urgency that loomed over all. Nauvoo was the first full-scale model of the kingdom of God on earth as envisioned by Joseph Smith. The Nauvoo Saints thus directed great energy toward "building up the Kingdom," which, in economic terms, meant building the city and establishing its economic infrastructure.

Like other communities of its day, Nauvoo had blacksmiths, coopers, potters, gunsmiths, and tinsmiths, but most in demand were the sawyers, brick makers, and carpenters. Construction was the principal industry. The hamlet of Commerce, Illinois, whose site Nauvoo overran, had few buildings, so the demand for housing was great. The Saints did not envision group housing in the fashion of Moravians, Shakers, and other communitarian societies, but they wanted detached single-family dwellings of Anglo-American rural tradition. The same was true for commercial and industrial buildings. With numerous small buildings reared upon large lots in more or less orderly rows, organized in a grid of wide streets with open land between for outbuildings, gardens, orchards, and grazing plots, Nauvoo became the prototypical Mormon city (*see* CITY PLANNING).

Public works made up a major part of Nauvoo construction. Work never started on an ambitious plan to dam the Mississippi to facilitate industrial development, but work did begin on a canal across the town peninsula. The plan was to bypass the Des Moines Rapids of the Mississippi, an obstacle that made the site a river portage much of the year; but the project was abandoned when the workers encountered limestone bedrock. The stone was subsequently quarried for the NAUVOO TEMPLE.

The Nauvoo Temple, a focal point of Nauvoo religious and economic life, was essential for Nauvoo to be a literal manifestation of the kingdom. Temple building tested the religious zeal and the economic resources of all the Saints, both in Nauvoo and elsewhere. Residents were expected to "tithe for the temple" in time, goods, or money. Saints not yet gathered to Nauvoo were urged to do so quickly so that they could be part of the enterprise. Those who could not do so were to support temple construction with cash. The Twelve Apostles wrote the English Saints in 1841, "The first great object before us, and the Saints generally, is to [complete] the Temple . . .

to secure the salvation of the Church" (*HC* 4:449). For Joseph Smith, completion of the temple was the first priority. The 1841 revelation authorizing the temple also threatened rejection of the Church unless the building was completed in "a sufficient time" (D&C 124:30–32). Even so, when Joseph Smith was killed in 1844, the walls were only half built.

Though building the temple was a labor of love, its economic cost put a severe drain on the city's resources. Capital was diverted from enterprises needed to provide goods and employment. Even Joseph Smith, though enthusiastic about the temple, recognized the problem. "I prophesy," he said in 1843, that "as soon as we get the Temple built, so that we shall not be obliged to exhaust our means thereon, we will have means to gather the Saints by thousands and tens of thousands" (*HC* 5:255).

Nauvoo's economy developed during the national depression of 1839–1843. The refugee founders were virtually destitute, but few Americans of any station had sound money during that period. The banks had failed, and specie had fled. The Saints fashioned an ingenious but shaky exchange system based on barter, letters of credit, informal IOUs, and "bonds-for-deed"—bonds given in land sales in lieu of deeds, a necessity because the whole Nauvoo tract was purchased on a long-term contract without deed until full payment. The system worked because the economy was generally expanding and the Saints trusted each other and were bound by common purpose.

The land purchase, the temple, the NAUVOO HOUSE (a large hotel), and the whole kingdom-building project upon which the Saints believed their salvation depended were headed by Joseph Smith and his ecclesiastical organization. Because Nauvoo represented an intermingling of the sacred and the secular under a prophet-leader, when he was killed in 1844, the survival of the project depended upon how and by whom he was succeeded. Those who accepted the leadership of Brigham YOUNG and the Quorum of the Twelve transplanted the system of political economy fashioned in Nauvoo to the West (*see* PIONEER ECONOMY; WESTWARD MIGRATION, PLANNING AND PROPHECY). Some who did not and who chose to move away from the model of Nauvoo later joined the REORGANIZED CHURCH OF JESUS CHRIST OF LATTER DAY SAINTS.

BIBLIOGRAPHY

Flanders, Robert. *Nauvoo: Kingdom on the Mississippi.* Urbana, Ill., 1965.

Miller, David, and Della Miller. *Nauvoo: The City of Joseph.* Santa Barbara and Salt Lake City, 1974.

Rowley, Dennis. "Nauvoo: A River Town." *BYU Studies* 18 (Winter 1978):255–72.

ROBERT B. FLANDERS

NAUVOO EXPOSITOR

The *Nauvoo Expositor* was the newspaper voice of apostates determined to destroy the Prophet Joseph SMITH and The Church of Jesus Christ of Latter-day Saints in the spring of 1844. During the last few months of Joseph Smith's life, an opposition party of disgruntled members, apostates, and excommunicants coalesced into a dissenting church. The principals claimed to believe in the Book of Mormon and the restoration of the gospel, but rejected what they termed Nauvoo innovations, notably PLURAL MARRIAGE. Claiming that Joseph was a fallen prophet, the dissenters set out, through the *Expositor*, to expose the Prophet's supposed false teachings and abominations. They held secret meetings, made plans, and took oaths to topple the Church and kill Joseph Smith. The publication of the newspaper was crucial to their stratagem.

When the press for the *Expositor* arrived in Nauvoo on May 7, 1844, it stirred great excitement among Mormons and non-Mormons alike, but there was no immediate interference. Within three days the owners, all leaders of the opposition movement, issued a broadside prospectus for their newspaper. One month later, on June 7, the first and only issue of the *Nauvoo Expositor* appeared and caused an immediate furor in the community. Nauvoo residents were incensed at what they saw as its sensational, yellow-journalistic claims about Nauvoo religion, politics, and morality. They were also struck with sharp foreboding. Francis Higbee, one of the proprietors of the newspaper, set an ominous tone when he described Joseph Smith as "the biggest villain that goes unhung."

The literary quality of the paper was inferior. A contemporary non-Mormon critic described it as "dull or laughable," with "lame grammar and turgid rhetoric" (Oaks, p. 868). But the *Expositor*'s polemics against the Church and Joseph Smith were threatening and polarizing. The anti-Mormons were exultant about the *Expositor*, but Church members demanded that something be done.

As mayor of Nauvoo, Joseph Smith summoned the city council. Following fourteen hours of deliberation in three different sessions, the council resolved on Monday, June 10, about 6:30 P.M., that the newspaper and its printing office were "a public nuisance" and instructed the mayor "to remove it . . . without delay." Joseph Smith promptly ordered the city marshal to destroy the press and burn all copies of the paper. At 8:00 P.M. the marshal carried out the mayor's orders (*HC* 6:432–49). That action, justified or not, played into the hands of the opposition. It riled anti-Mormon sentiment throughout Hancock County and provided substance for the charges used by the opposition to hold Joseph Smith in CARTHAGE JAIL, where he was murdered on June 27, 1844 (*see* MARTYRDOM OF JOSEPH AND HYRUM SMITH).

BIBLIOGRAPHY

Godfrey, Kenneth W. "Causes of Mormon/Non-Mormon Conflict in Hancock County, Illinois, 1839–1846." Ph.D. diss., Brigham Young University, 1967.

Oaks, Dallin H. "The Suppression of the Nauvoo Expositor." *Utah Law Review* 9 (Winter 1965):862–903.

Oaks, Dallin H., and Marvin S. Hill. *Carthage Conspiracy: The Trial of the Accused Assassins of Joseph Smith*. Urbana, Ill., 1979.

REED C. DURHAM, JR.

NAUVOO HOUSE

A revelation to Joseph Smith in January 1841 commanded the Saints to build both the NAUVOO TEMPLE and the Nauvoo House, a hotel that would be "a delightful habitation for man, and a resting place for the weary traveler" (D&C 124:60). The Saints were not to isolate themselves from the world, but to provide attractive accommodations for strangers and tourists while they "contemplate the word of the Lord; and the corner-stone I have appointed for Zion" (D&C 124:23).

Joseph Smith donated the land for the Nauvoo House, and many Latter-day Saints purchased stock. The design of architects Lucien Woodworth and William Weeks called for an L-shaped brick building forty feet deep and three stories high. Construction began in the spring of 1841 and progressed (with interruptions) into 1845. Eventually, the work was discontinued in an effort to complete the Nauvoo Temple.

When the Saints left Nauvoo in 1846, the Nauvoo House walls were up above the windows of the second story. The large unfinished building on the south end of Main Street facing the Mississippi River became the property of Joseph Smith's widow, Emma SMITH. Subsequently, Emma's second husband, Lewis C. Bidamon, tore down the extremities of the L-shaped structure and used their bricks to complete the central portion as a smaller hotel, variously known as the Bidamon House and the Riverside Mansion. He and Emma lived there from 1871 until they died. After Bidamon's death, the REORGANIZED CHURCH OF JESUS CHRIST OF LATTER DAY SAINTS purchased the Nauvoo House and still owns it.

BIBLIOGRAPHY

Flanders, Robert Bruce. *Nauvoo: Kingdom on the Mississippi*, pp. 179–90. Urbana, Ill., 1965.

Holzapfel, Richard N., and T. Jeffery Cottle. *Old Mormon Nauvoo, 1839–1846*. Provo, Utah, 1990.

HELENE HOLT

NAUVOO LEGION

The Illinois legislative act of December 1840 that incorporated the city of Nauvoo also authorized creation of a military body or militia that came to be known as the Nauvoo Legion. Perhaps influenced by genuine disgust with the way the Latter-day Saints had been treated in Missouri, the Illinois legislature acted liberally. Under the NAUVOO CHARTER, Latter-day Saints could manage their own affairs, provided they did not violate the state or federal constitutions.

The organization of a militia unit was customary in settlements with sufficient population, a practice as old as the Republic. Nauvoo residents were particularly anxious to have their own military protection after having been victims of mob violence and having suffered expulsion from Missouri (*see* HAUN'S MILL MASSACRE; MISSOURI CONFLICT). By 1840, they realized that they could not always rely on federal or state authorities for protection from such violence.

The Nauvoo Court Martial, consisting of the legion's commissioned officers, was given extensive authority. Among other things, it could "make, ordain, establish, and execute all such laws and ordinances as may be considered necessary for the benefit, government, and regulation of said Legion; provided [that] said Court Martial shall pass no law or act, repugnant to, or inconsistent with, the Constitution of the United States, or of this State [Illinois]" (*HC* 4:244).

As part of the state militia, the Nauvoo Legion was at the disposal of the governor of Illinois "for the public defense, and the execution of the laws of the State or of the United States." Significantly, it was also at the disposal of the mayor of Nauvoo for "executing the laws and ordinances of the city corporation" (*HC* 4:244).

The city council ordinance that created the Nauvoo Legion authorized the rank of lieutenant general for its commanding officer, an extraordinary authorization, since no other militia officer in the United States held rank above that of major general. The court martial elected Joseph SMITH commander of the legion.

The parades and other activities of the legion—which included mock battles—attracted visitors from near and far. Indeed, the legion became so popular that many non-Mormons joined the ranks. At its peak, it is said to have numbered 5,000 men, the largest such body in Illinois. But there were problems. According to historian B. H. Roberts:

> [The Nauvoo Legion] excited the jealousy and envy of the rest of the militia in surrounding counties, and all the laudable efforts of the legion to become an efficient body with a view of assisting in the execution of the state and national laws, if occasion should require, were construed by their enemies to mean a preparation for rebellion. . . . Hence that which was to be a bulwark to the city, and a protection to the saints, was transformed by their enemies into an occasion of offense, and an excuse for distrusting them [*CHC* 2:59–60].

Joseph Smith mobilized the Nauvoo Legion to defend the city and declared martial law in June 1844 as tensions mounted between the Latter-day Saints, dissenters, and hostile neighbors. Joseph Smith and his brother Hyrum were among those arrested by another Illinois militia and placed in CARTHAGE JAIL, where they were killed by members of yet another militia (*see* MARTYRDOM OF JOSEPH AND HYRUM

SMITH). Six months later, the Illinois legislature revoked the Nauvoo Charter. At that point, the Nauvoo Legion ceased to exist as a state militia, although as an unofficial body it continued to provide some protection to the beleaguered Latter-day Saints.

During the exodus westward later, some former members of the Nauvoo Legion served in the MORMON BATTALION. This 500-man body, authorized by the U.S. government in 1846 as part of the campaign against Mexico, marched from Council Bluffs to San Diego.

The name Nauvoo Legion was revived in Utah and applied to the organized militia of the state of DESERET and later of UTAH TERRITORY. This legion was called upon in 1849 to subdue marauding Indians, and its members served in the so-called Walker War of 1853–1854, named after Wakara, a Ute chieftain. With the approach of the UTAH EXPEDITION in 1857–1858, the Utah militia harassed and burned U.S. Army supply trains and prepared, if necessary, to prevent the entry of U.S. troops into Salt Lake City. In 1862, during the American Civil War, two units of the Nauvoo Legion protected overland mail and telegraph lines. Later, with a force of some 2,500 men, it fought against Indians in Utah's Black Hawk War (1865–1868).

Always more responsive to Mormon leadership than to the federal appointees who succeeded Brigham Young as governor of Utah, the legion was rendered inactive by an 1870 proclamation of Acting Governor J. Wilson Shaffer, who forbade gatherings of the militia except on his express orders. The Nauvoo Legion was finally disbanded as a result of the Edmunds-Tucker Act of 1887. In 1894 the National Guard of Utah was organized as Utah's militia.

BIBLIOGRAPHY

Gardner, Hamilton. "The Nauvoo Legion, 1840–1845—A Unique Military Organization." *Journal of the Illinois State Historical Society* 54 (Summer 1961):181–97.

PHILIP M. FLAMMER

NAUVOO POLITICS

Political power played an important role both in the development of the LDS community in Illinois and in its demise. The political situation was complex, inviting rivalry and controversy.

On the eve of the arrival of the Latter-day Saints, Commerce (NAUVOO), in Hancock County, Illinois, was situated in a pro-Whig enclave in a state where Democrats dominated all political offices except the supreme court. In Hancock County, however, the two parties were so evenly matched that a few hundred votes could be decisive. But in the state legislature, even voting as a unit, a community the size of that of the Latter-day Saints could have only moderate influence. County offices were more vulnerable; the number of votes needed for election to such offices as sheriff, county commissioner, and probate judge was under one thousand. A liberal provision in the Illinois constitution enfranchised all adult immigrants after only six months' residence—a contentious issue in a state where party lines were sharply drawn, especially with the regular arrival of new British immigrants in Nauvoo (*see* IMMIGRATION AND EMIGRATION).

Joseph Smith's decision to use LDS voting strength sprang from a desire for security from PERSECUTION and for self-government. Conscious of the divine imperative to gather the Saints and build the physical kingdom of God on earth, he came to see politics as one means of enlarging and protecting his community. At first, the Saints were politically neutral. But in 1840–1841 they voted solidly Whig in Illinois, though they had voted Democrat in Missouri. This alienated some Democrats, but most politicians courted the LDS bloc vote in Illinois, just as others courted the Roman Catholic vote in New York.

The first example of possible "vote trading" by Latter-day Saints was the legislative vote in favor of the NAUVOO CHARTER in December 1840, promoted by Democrats but also voted for by the Whig Abraham Lincoln. The resulting Nauvoo Municipal Court, NAUVOO LEGION, and Agricultural and Manufacturing Association formed the backbone of a self-governing theocracy, which was anathema to frontier Illinoisans.

The prevalence of lawyer-politicians and the frequency of Missouri arrest warrants enmeshed Joseph Smith in vote trading. One clear example was LDS support for the Whig John T. Stuart in the congressional election of 1841, a direct result of assistance rendered to Joseph Smith by the Whigs Orville H. Browning and Cyrus Walker when Smith was arrested following a Missouri extradition order. Joseph Smith was technically a fugitive, having fled Missouri after six months in LIBERTY JAIL awaiting trial (*see* SMITH, JOSEPH: LEGAL TRIALS OF JOSEPH SMITH). However, not all lawyers were Whigs. The judge in the 1841 case was Stephen A. Douglas, an ambitious Democrat determined to win the LDS vote. His efforts were successful in December 1841 when Joseph Smith declared for the Democrats; Hancock County subsequently lost its Whig identity.

Seeing Nauvoo as a political threat, non-Mormons in Hancock County organized politically on an anti-Mormon platform. Successful in the county elections in 1841 (they were unopposed in many contests), they were singularly unsuccessful in 1842 with nominations for the state legislature. Existing partisan affiliations were too strong for the emergence of a third party, and the Whigs had usurped the anti-Mormon cause in the 1842 gubernatorial elections. The Democratic candidate for governor, Thomas Ford, an opponent of the Nauvoo Charter, won the election.

Governor Ford advised Joseph Smith to stay out of politics. Smith seemed inclined to do that until Ford, in June 1843, issued another writ for the Prophet's arrest on a Missouri requisition. After the Whig Cyrus Walker, a prominent criminal lawyer, using the controversial habeas corpus provisions of the Nauvoo Charter, effected Joseph Smith's release from custody, the Prophet pledged his vote to Walker. But his brother Hyrum SMITH, a Democrat, announced that he believed the Saints should vote for Walker's opponent, Joseph P. Hoge. The Latter-day Saints in Nauvoo, part of the Sixth Congressional District, voted for Hoge, but those in the Fifth Congressional District voted for the Whig O. H. Browning, running against Douglas.

This marked the beginning of disillusionment with the LDS vote by both parties. In particular the Whigs, who had retreated from anti-Mormonism in 1842–1843 in the hope of finding favor, now openly opposed LDS political and judicial power. In 1843, even within Nauvoo, Joseph Smith found politics problematic. There was internal dissent over city elections in February, and in August, Mayor Smith complained of being roughly treated by pro-Democrats in city elections. Also, the prominent Church leader William Law publicly challenged Hyrum's "Hoge testimony."

In January 1844, after canvassing U.S. presidential hopefuls for support in obtaining redress for Missouri depredations and finding none, Joseph Smith announced his own candidacy. Some saw this as a bid for political power, consistent with the goal of furthering the political kingdom of God; others felt that because Joseph Smith was not likely to win national election, he simply wanted a platform for presenting his message. The leading anti-Mormon newspaper in Illinois, the *Warsaw Signal*, greeted the move with customary derision but nonetheless viewed it as an audacious and threatening development.

All Joseph Smith's attempts to gain political influence were objectionable to the apostate group that launched the NAUVOO EXPOSITOR newspaper, the destruction of which set in motion the events leading to Smith's death in June 1844 (*see* MARTYRDOM OF JOSEPH AND HYRUM SMITH). In this volatile atmosphere, anti-Mormons gained strength by accusing Governor Ford of pursuing pro-Mormon policies in order to secure Democratic votes. The Latter-day Saints gradually lost support until, in January 1845, their charter was repealed, disincorporating Nauvoo. Unauthorized municipal elections continued in Nauvoo, however, and Latter-day Saints voted in county and state elections, still favoring the Democrats. From then until the Saints left in 1846 (*see* WESTWARD MIGRATION, PLANNING AND PROPHECY), this persistent involvement of Mormons in politics continued to inflame non-Mormons and rally them to press for Mormon expulsion.

Politics and political power were indispensable to the rise and strength of Nauvoo and to the protection of the Prophet Joseph Smith. But mismanagement of political power may also have contributed to the city's downfall.

BIBLIOGRAPHY

Flanders, Robert B. *Nauvoo: Kingdom on the Mississippi*. Urbana, Ill., 1965.

Gayler, George R. "The Mormons and Politics in Illinois: 1839–1844." *Journal of the Illinois State Historical Society* 49 (1956):48–66.

Hampshire, Annette P. *Mormonism in Conflict: The Nauvoo Years*. New York, 1985.

ANNETTE P. HAMPSHIRE

NAUVOO TEMPLE

The Nauvoo Temple, its tower and spire visible from a distance of twenty miles, was the principal structure in the city of NAUVOO.

Facing west, it stood on the summit of a gently sloping bluff overlooking the lower part of the city and the Mississippi River.

Built from a high-quality grayish-white to tan limestone, its imposing walls were erected and finished with great skill. The walls were three feet thick at ground level, with some individual stones weighing as much as 4,000 pounds. The building measured 128 feet long and 88 feet wide. The top of the tower stood 158 feet above ground level and was graced by a golden statue of an angel flying in a horizontal position (doubtless inspired by the prophecy in Rev. 14:6–7).

Prominent features of the stone walls were thirty tall, heavily ornamented pilasters, nine on each side and six on each end. Each pilaster was embellished by a large moonstone at the base and a sunstone at the top. The moon-and sunstones were bas-relief features, hand-chiseled in solid stone. A stone star also graced each pilaster. These cosmic symbols typified the three degrees of glory in the life to come (1 Cor. 15:41; D&C 76).

Construction of the building began in the fall of 1840. Cornerstones were set with impressive ceremonies during a general conference on April 6, 1841. Financial setbacks and persecution continually interfered with the construction, even up to the days of its completion and dedication.

William Weeks became the official architect and supervised most of the construction. The building was a complexity of architectural styles, yet much of it was also original, inspired by what the Prophet Joseph SMITH had seen in vision. He closely guided Weeks in the design of the temple as he had seen it, requiring, for example, that it have round windows on the second level (*HC* 6:196–97).

The call to build so large a structure taxed the resources of a destitute people. The final cost exceeded $1,000,000. Funds came largely from tithes and offerings of Church members, some donating their life savings. Many gave months of physical labor with little or no remuneration, working from early morning until sundown, even during harsh weather.

Stone for the building was quarried near the city. Wood was brought in from Wisconsin in the form of huge rafts of sawed lumber, which were floated down the Mississippi to Nauvoo. Some British converts contributed a large bell weighing over 1,500 pounds. As the Saints left Nauvoo, the bell was removed and taken west as part of the migration, where it was later mounted on a tower on Temple Square, Salt Lake City.

The main feature at the basement level was a large white limestone laver resting on the backs and shoulders of twelve life-sized stone oxen. This was the baptismal font to be used particularly for the ordinance of baptism for the dead. The basement floor was paved with brick. The first story contained a large room in the center, which served as an auditorium. At each end of this large hall were elaborate pulpits, each graded into four tiers of seats to accommodate the Aaronic Priesthood and Melchizedek Priesthood leaders. The main floor was fitted with seats, the backs of which could be reversed, allowing congregations to face either direction. The second story was an exact duplicate of the first. The attic story contained two main sections. A half-story on the west end was divided by cloth partitions and used for the endowment ordinances. The main attic section, under the pitched roof, was used for sealing ordinances and celestial or eternal marriages. The entire attic was plastered and painted, and the floors were covered with carpets.

Occasional ceremonial use took place during construction, especially baptisms for the dead. Even though not fully completed, the temple was filled to capacity by members coming for ordinances during the months just prior to the exodus—ordinances on behalf both of the living and the dead. In addition to its sacral uses, the temple served as a multipurpose meeting place. Regular Sunday services and even some general conferences were held in the building. The structure also provided some facilities as a Church office building. The planning and organization of the western migration took place in the temple.

As most of the Saints left Nauvoo under threat of mob violence in early February 1846, a special crew stayed behind and completed the temple. Three months later the building was considered complete and was publicly dedicated on May 1, 1846. Dedication services were repeated over a three-day period and witnessed by thousands. Visitors paid a one-dollar admission fee, and the funds were used to help workmen move their families and join the main body of the Church on the plains to the west.

When most of the remaining Church members were driven from the city in September of 1846, the temple was temporarily abandoned. Mob forces desecrated and defiled the sacred structure. Some physical damage, though not extensive, was sustained. Attempts were later made to sell the temple, but these proved unsuccessful. The building was consumed by fire in October 1848, by the deliberate act of arson. Only the bare walls were left standing. A French Icarian community purchased the site and was preparing to reclaim the structure when it was struck by a tornado, which knocked down some of the walls and damaged others so severely that they had to be razed. Much of the structural stone was later reused in other Nauvoo buildings.

Today the temple site has been repurchased by the Church. A Nauvoo Temple exhibit is a key part of the Nauvoo Visitors Center. A small model built to scale is on the exact location of the original temple. The well that supplied water for the baptismal font is preserved. Some sunstones and moonstones that once adorned the building remain here and in museums as a reminder of the beauty of this once majestic temple.

BIBLIOGRAPHY

Colvin, Don F. "A Historical Study of the Mormon Temple at Nauvoo, Illinois." Master's thesis, Brigham Young University, 1962.

Harrington, Virginia S. *Rediscovery of the Nauvoo Temple*. Salt Lake City, 1971.

DON F. COLVIN

NEVADA, PIONEER SETTLEMENTS IN

Latter-day Saints constructed Nevada's first log cabins and founded what became the state's first permanent white settlement when, in 1849, would-be gold miners established a trading post at present-day Genoa (Carson Valley, near Reno) to supply those en route to the goldfields in northern California.

The present state of Nevada lay within the original boundaries of Utah Territory as established by Congress in 1850, and in 1855 territorial governor Brigham YOUNG appointed Orson HYDE, an apostle, as probate judge and sent him to Carson Valley to organize a county government. Hyde called for more LDS settlers to establish political control of the area and to proselytize and "civilize" the Indians of that region. The following year about 250 Latter-day Saints arrived. Problems promptly developed between them and non-Mormons who resented LDS political control. Reports that they were to be recalled to Utah kept the LDS settlers off balance, and some of the leading members soon departed. As the U.S. Army approached Utah from the east in 1857 (*see* UTAH EXPEDITION), the remaining colonists were recalled to Salt Lake City.

The Las Vegas Mission was founded in 1855 to proselytize local Indians and teach them agriculture and peaceful ways. Latter-day Saints there labored among the Paiutes, converting many of them and establishing a farm for them. In 1856 the colony, reinforced by men sent from Salt Lake City, established a lead-mining mission. Lead mining was largely unsuccessful, partly due to silver in the ore and the difficulty of separating them. In 1857, after the lead miners returned to Utah, the remainder of the missionaries received permission to return as well. Most departed later that year, after word reached them of the army's approach to Utah.

In 1865 Brigham Young sent colonists to settle on the Muddy River, in present-day Moapa Valley, to grow cotton and other semitropical crops and to assist with possible LDS overland immigration from a projected port on the Colorado River. In 1867 the boundaries of Nevada Territory, which was created from the western part of Utah Territory in 1861, were extended southward, annexing part of Arizona Territory, including the Muddy settlements. Most Latter-day Saints abandoned these towns in 1871 when they were ordered to pay back taxes to Nevada; farming marginal lands, the settlers lacked the cash to meet additional assessments. The LDS resettlement of the Moapa Valley area was resumed in 1877 with the founding of Bunkerville, a UNITED ORDER community.

LDS families founded several small communities north of the Muddy River beginning in 1864. Some of these settlers remained despite the problems with taxation, particularly in Panaca, which has remained largely LDS.

In 1898 the LDS settlements of Lund, Preston, and Georgetown were established in White Pine County on land ceded to the Church in lieu of property confiscated under the provisions of the Edmunds-Tucker Act of 1887 (*see* ANTIPOLYGAMY LEGISLATION).

BIBLIOGRAPHY

Arrington, Leonard J. *The Mormons in Nevada*. Las Vegas, 1979.

Hunter, Milton R. *Brigham Young the Colonizer*. Santa Barbara, Calif., 1973.

TED J. WARNER

NEW MEXICO, PIONEER SETTLEMENTS IN

Although the MORMON BATTALION traversed New Mexico from its northeast to its southwest corner in 1846, the next significant LDS contact in that territory did not occur until nearly three decades later. In 1876 two members of a group of LDS missionaries otherwise assigned to Mexico found notable success in proselytizing among the Zuni in western New Mexico. Subsequent labors among the Zuni were less successful, but a number of Navajos were converted. In 1876, missionaries founded the settlement of Savoia, about twenty miles east of the Zuni village, and were joined by LDS converts from the southern states. The southerners soon moved to LDS settlements on the Little Colorado River in Arizona, and in 1882 the remaining settlers, reinforced by expatriates from the Little Colorado, relocated a few miles south. Eventually named Ramah, the village continues as a predominantly LDS community. Ramah was a major focus in a landmark interdisciplinary study of five cultures by Harvard University scholars in the mid-twentieth century.

Meanwhile, Latter-day Saints settled along the San Juan River at Fruitland, in northwestern New Mexico, in 1878. Kirtland and Waterflow, additional LDS villages along the San Juan, were initiated in the early 1880s, and Bluewater, a short distance to the north, was founded in 1894. In 1912, Fruitland became headquarters for the Young Stake, which also included wards and branches in nearby southwestern Colorado.

Farther south but also near New Mexico's western border, a group of Latter-day Saints settled in the Luna Valley, beginning in 1883. The Luna Ward was closely associated with LDS congregations across the border in Arizona.

Additional LDS congregations were established in western New Mexico at Pleasanton, Socorro County (1882–1889); and at Virden, Hidalgo County (from 1915). The latter was settled by refugees from the Mormon colonies in Mexico dislodged by the Mexican Revolution.

Most LDS wards and branches established in the twentieth century served minorities in communities east of these predominantly Mormon villages. In the first third of the century, congregations were organized at Albuquerque, Gallup, Taos, Silver City, Clovis, Tres

Piedras, Pagosa Springs, and Thoreau. By 1990, as a result of widespread proselytizing and of in-migration, there were 49,000 Latter-day Saints in New Mexico.

BIBLIOGRAPHY

Divett, Robert T. "New Mexico and the Mormons." *Greater Llano Estacado Southwest Heritage* 6 (Spring 1976):14–19.

Telling, Irving. "Ramah, New Mexico, 1876–1900: An Historical Episode with Some Value Analysis." *Utah Historical Quarterly* 21 (Apr. 1953):117–36.

Vogt, Evon Z., and Ethel M. Albert, eds. *People of Rimrock: A Study of Values in Five Cultures.* Cambridge, Mass., 1966.

RICHARD L. JENSEN

NEW YORK, EARLY LDS SITES IN

[*Many events in early Latter-day Saint history occurred in the Finger Lakes region of western New York and nearby northern Pennsylvania from 1820 to 1831. Western New York became known as the Burnt-over District because of the intense religious revivals that swept the area from the 1790s to the 1840s, affecting the families of many early LDS converts. See, generally,* Historical Sites *and* History of the Church: c. 1820–1831.

The Palmyra-Manchester neighborhood was the home of the Joseph Smith family and the location of Joseph's First Vision; *see* Sacred Grove. *In this area he obtained the gold plates; see* Moroni, Visitations of. *In 1830 the Book of Mormon was published in Palmyra with the financial assistance of a local resident, Martin* Harris.

Joseph Smith was employed near Harmony, Pennsylvania, *in 1825. There he met his future wife, Emma Hale* Smith; *they were married at nearby* South Bainbridge (Afton), New York, *in 1827. Joseph and Emma lived until 1830 in Harmony, where Joseph translated most of the Book of Mormon. The restoration of the Aaronic Priesthood occurred in this vicinity in May 1829, and the Melchizedek Priesthood was restored between Harmony and* Colesville. *Some of the earliest converts to the Church belonged to its Colesville branch.*

In Fayette, New York, *Joseph Smith completed the Book of Mormon translation in June 1829, at the home of Peter Whitmer, Sr., where the organization of the Church also took place, April 6, 1830.*]

NEW ZEALAND, THE CHURCH IN

The Church of Jesus Christ of Latter-day Saints first reached New Zealand on October 27, 1854, when President Augustus Farnham, of the Australian mission, Elder William Cooke, and Thomas Holder, a priest in the Aaronic Priesthood, arrived from AUSTRALIA. The missionaries worked first among European immigrants and then among the native Maoris, and the Church grew slowly at first, then steadily, so that by 1990 New Zealand had about 70,000 Latter-day Saints, two missions, and sixteen stakes.

The first two people baptized into the LDS Church in New Zealand were Martha Holder and her daughter Louisa. The first Church branch was established in April 1855 among the European immigrants in Karori, a suburb of Wellington. The April 15, 1881, assignment of Elder William J. McDonnel to go to the Maori people coincided with prophecies of at least five separate Maori *tohungas* (tribal priests) that the true church of God would soon come to New Zealand. The best-known of these prophecies was the one given by Paora Potangaroa in 1881. Collectively they helped the Maoris to readily identify with the Church when its missionaries came among them (Britsch, pp. 274–76). In 1883–1884, Elders Alma Greenwood and Ira Hinckley, Jr., were especially successful among the Maoris, baptizing several hundred converts and organizing thirteen branches.

SCRIPTURES IN THE MAORI LANGUAGE. Before the LDS missionaries arrived, the Bible had already been published in Maori by earlier Christian missionaries, but expanding Maori membership created an urgent need to have the Book of Mormon translated. Ezra F. Richards and Sondra Sanders, assisted by Henare Potae, Te Pirihi Tutokohi, and James Jury, local Maori members, published the first translation in 1889. During World War I, President Joseph F. SMITH approved a second translation of the Book of Mormon, and Elder Matthew Cowley, a young missionary with unusual skill in the Maori language, was assigned to the work. He made changes in approximately 2,500 verses in the original translation, and the second edition appeared in 1917. Elder Cowley was then assigned to translate the Doctrine and Covenants and the Pearl of Great Price, assisted by Wiremu Duncan and Stuart Meha. These translations appeared in 1919.

RELIEF SOCIETY, PRIMARY, AND THE MUTUAL IMPROVEMENT ASSOCIATION. The first branch Relief Society in New Zealand was organized in 1878, with Ann Jones as president. The first Maori Relief Society was organized in 1901, with Sister Mangu Reweti as president. In 1904, Sister Emma E. Wright, the wife of a missionary, was called as the first president of the Mission Relief Society, which coordinated the local units. Thereafter until 1931, the wife of the mission president presided over the mission Relief Society, Primary, and Young Women Mutual Improvement Association (YWMIA, now Young Women). Then in 1931, Hepera Takare Duncan became the first local sister to preside over the Mission Relief Society.

The first MIA was organized in the Auckland branch in 1907, and the first units among the Maoris came in 1918. Sister Una Thompson is remembered for her leadership of the MIA in those early years. The first Primaries were organized in 1913, with Sisters Ere Hapati Mete and Bessie Greening as presidents. Between 1928 and 1931, Sister Arta Romney Ballif, wife of the principal of the Maori Agricultural College, was instrumental in building the Primary association throughout the mission.

CHURCH SCHOOLS. Because many Maori converts lived in outlying areas with no schools for their children, the Church established schools in local branch meetinghouses as early as 1886. In 1907 the First Presidency of the Church authorized creation of a secondary school to train boys in farming, technology, and leadership skills, and to teach them religion. Accordingly, Maori Agricultural College was dedicated on April 6, 1913, in Korongata, Hastings, Hawkes Bay. A February 1931 earthquake rendered the buildings unsafe, and the Church closed the college.

Because many of the alumni of the college had become prominent Church leaders by the 1940s, Mission President Matthew Cowley recommended that a coeducational secondary school be established in New Zealand, with capacity increased from eighty to more than five hundred students. The First Presidency approved building the present Church College of New Zealand (CCNZ) at Temple View, near Hamilton. Since its inception in 1955, CCNZ has played a significant role in the educational and spiritual development of thousands of LDS high school students.

New Zealand Temple. Prior to 1958, Latter-day Saints in New Zealand had to travel to the Hawaii Temple to receive the significant ordinances available only in temples. The decision to build a temple in New Zealand was announced by President David O. MCKAY in February 1955 and brought great joy among the local Saints. The temple and college buildings were to be built simultaneously under the newly conceived Church Building Missionary Program, which provided for supervisory craftsmen to be called from the United States to construct the buildings with a local voluntary missionary labor force of hundreds of members, mainly Maoris, who would learn construction skills on the job. In less than two and a half years, both the temple and the college were completed at minimal expense, and hundreds of previously unskilled and unemployed Maori members had learned building skills and were qualified for gainful employment. E. Albert and Vernice Gold Rosenvall were called as the first president and matron. President McKay dedicated the temple on April 20, 1958, and the college on April 26. The Building Missionary Program was so successful that it was used for several years to construct Church buildings in other parts of the world. For years the New Zealand Temple served Church members living throughout the South Pacific, but since September 1984, temples have been in service in Australia, Samoa, Tonga, and Tahiti.

Matthew Cowley. With the coming of World War II, all American missionaries were called home, but President Matthew and Sister Elva Taylor Cowley chose to remain in New Zealand with their family to supervise the work during the war. It was September 1945 before the Cowleys were released after seven and a half years of service. At the October 1945 general conference, Matthew Cowley was called to be a member of the Quorum of the Twelve Apostles and was affectionately called their "Polynesian Apostle" by the Saints of the South Pacific. Six other men with New Zealand connections have been called as General Authorities, all in the quorums of the Seventy: Douglas J. Martin, a native New Zealander, and former New Zealand mission presidents Rufus K. Hardy, John J. Lasater, Glenn L. Rudd, Robert L. Simpson, Philip T. Sonntag, and Rulon G. Craven.

The year 1958 was pivotal for the Church in New Zealand. In that year the temple and the college were completed, the first stake was organized in Auckland, and the mission was divided into two missions. Since then, the Church has shown increasing growth in New Zealand.

BIBLIOGRAPHY

Britsch, R. Lanier. "New Zealand." In *Unto the Islands of the Sea: A History of the Latter-day Saints in the Pacific*, pp. 215–345. Salt Lake City, 1986.

Clement, Russell T., comp. *Mormons in the Pacific: A Bibliography.* Laie, Hawaii, 1981.

ROBERT L. SIMPSON

OCEANIA, THE CHURCH IN

The Church of Jesus Christ of Latter-day Saints has been established in Oceania (the islands of the central and southern Pacific) since 1844, when its missionaries first arrived in French Polynesia and organized a branch there. The Church moved into Hawaii in 1850, New Zealand in 1854, Samoa in 1888, Tonga in 1891, and other islands after World War II. By 1990 the Church in Oceania had grown to over 100,000 members living in several missions and hundreds of stakes, wards, and branches, and it had temples in Samoa, Tahiti, and Tonga (*see also* HAWAII and NEW ZEALAND).

FRENCH POLYNESIA. The Prophet Joseph SMITH sent four missionaries, Addison Pratt, Benjamin Franklin Grouard, Noah Rogers, and Knowlton F. Hanks (who died at sea), to the islands of the Pacific in May 1843. Arriving at Tubuai Island, 350 miles south of Tahiti, on April 30, 1844, they established the first branch of the Church in Oceania in July 1844, with eleven members. When friction with the French territorial government ended the first period of missionary work in 1852, the Church had nearly 2,000 converts scattered on at least twenty islands.

The mission was refounded in 1892, when William A. Seegmiller and Joseph W. Damron, Jr., were sent to Tahiti from the Samoan mission. Growth was negligible until 1950, when the Church placed leadership in the hands of local members and moved the proselytizing missionaries from the Tuamotu Islands to Tahiti. This move accelerated Church growth. Three other factors also contributed to more rapid growth after 1953: increased use of the French language, use of organized proselytizing plans, and the building of modern meetinghouses.

The first stake organized in French Polynesia was the Papeete Tahiti Stake, on May 14, 1972, with Raituia Tehina Tapu as stake president. Church President Spencer W. KIMBALL broke ground for the Papeete Tahiti Temple on February 13, 1981, and Gordon B. Hinckley, first counselor in the First Presidency, dedicated the completed structure on October 27–29, 1983. LDS scriptures are available in Tahitian and French.

SAMOA. LDS missionary work in Samoa officially began on June 18, 1888, when Joseph Harry Dean and Florence Ridges Dean arrived on Tutuila. There had been an unofficial start in January 1863, when Walter Murray Gibson sent two Hawaiian elders, Kimo Pelio and Samuela Manoa, to Samoa to teach the restored gospel; they baptized about fifty people. Pelio died in 1876, and Manoa married and settled on the little island of Aunuu, from which he wrote letters to Hawaii and Church headquarters asking for assistance. One of those letters prompted the Deans to go to Samoa from Hawaii.

Growth of the Church in Samoa was steady from 1888 on. During their first four months the Deans baptized forty people and formed a branch. By 1899 the Church had 1,139 Samoan Latter-day Saints scattered across the major islands. Local leaders led most branches, and Samoan priesthood holders and their wives served missions. Church schools were operated in a number of villages, and three "central" residential schools were created on the islands of Tutuila, Upolu, and Savai'i. The Church has continued to operate many schools, the most important being the Church College of Western Samoa, a high school in Apia, Western Samoa. Gathering places for Church families to establish homes were founded at Mapusaga on Tutuila, American Samoa, in 1903 and at Sauniatu, Upolu, in Western Samoa, in 1904.

In 1902, Church headquarters were established at Pesega, near Apia, on land donated by Ah Mu, a Chinese member. The Apia Samoa Temple, the Church College of Western Samoa, a stake center, the mission headquarters, and the missionary training center are all built on that land. The Book of Mormon was translated and published in Samoan in 1903, and the Doctrine and Covenants and the Pearl of Great Price, in 1963.

On March 18, 1962, the Apia Stake was organized with Percy John Rivers, a descendant of Ah Mu, as stake president. On February 19, 1981, President Spencer W. Kimball broke ground for the Samoa Temple at Pesega, and the completed structure was dedicated on August 5–7, 1983.

TONGA. LDS missionaries first visited the "Friendly Islands" on July 15, 1891, when Brigham Smoot and Alva J. Butler arrived at Nuku'alofa, Tongatapu Island, from Samoa. However, this first phase of the Tongan mission was short-lived because of political and religious circumstances. In June 1907, William O. Facer and Heber J. McKay reopened missionary work in Tonga, this time at Vava'u, the northern island group. Until 1916, when Willard L. Smith arrived as the first mission president, Tonga was part of the Samoan mission. Until the early 1950s, Church growth in Tonga was slow, being retarded by misunderstandings with the government. When those difficulties were resolved, the Church showed significant growth in Tonga, reflecting the maturity in leadership, understanding of Church organization, and depth of spirituality of the Tongan Saints. The Nuku'alofa Stake was organized on September 5, 1968, with Orson Hyde White as stake president. As growth continued, Church President Spencer W. Kimball broke ground for a temple near Nuku'alofa on February 18, 1981. It was dedicated August 9, 1983, by his counselor, President Gordon B. Hinckley.

Education has played an important role in the Church in Tonga. Of the many schools established, the most important are Liahona High School (1952) on Tongatapu and Saineha High School (1978) on Vava'u. The Book of Mormon was published in Tongan in 1946 and the Doctrine and Covenants and the Pearl of Great Price, in 1959.

FIJI. Although Tongan and other Latter-day Saints had lived and held Church meetings in Fiji for many years, not until May 1954 were missionaries sent to Suva from the Samoan mission to officially commence LDS proselytizing. Boyd L. Harris and Sheldon L. Abbott organized the Suva Branch on September 5, 1954. An initial boost in Church growth occurred when Church President David O. McKay visited Suva in January 1955 and decided that a large chapel should be built, which he dedicated three years later on May 4, 1958. That building was part of President McKay's vision for Fiji and manifested to the government and people alike that the LDS Church was in Fiji to stay.

Fiji was assigned to the Samoan and Tongan missions until July 1971, when it was made an independent mission. Since then, the Fiji Suva Mission has had many South Pacific areas assigned to it for a time, such as New Caledonia, Niue, the Cook Islands, Kiribati, Vanuatu, and Rotuma. Church growth and development in Fiji have been steady. In 1969 the Suva chapel also housed a Church-sponsored elementary school. Seminary classes began in 1973, and two years later, the LDS Fiji Technical College (equivalent to a U.S. vocational high school) opened on a new campus in Suva. By 1984, 372 students, mostly LDS, were enrolled.

Overall Church membership also continued to grow in Fiji, and in February 1976, one thousand Fijian Latter-day Saints attended an area conference held by President Spencer W. Kimball. On June 5, 1983, Howard W. Hunter organized the Suva Fiji Stake, with Inosi Naga as stake president. The Book of Mormon was published in Fijian in 1980.

NEW CALEDONIA. Some LDS Tahitian laborers migrated to New Caledonia during the 1950s and established small units of the Church there. Under the direction of the French Polynesia (Tahiti) mission president, the Noumea Branch was organized in October 1961. Years of negotiations between mission leaders and the New Caledonian government led to permission for LDS missionaries to proselytize. On May 2, 1968, Elder Thomas S. Monson, of the Quorum of the Twelve Apostles, dedicated New Caledonia for the preaching of the gospel. Two months later, the first missionary couple arrived. In 1990 the full program of the Church had been established, and New Caledonia was under the Fiji Suva Mission.

GUAM AND MICRONESIA. Latter-day Saints have lived on many of the Micronesian islands since World War II. But only Guam has had LDS servicemen's groups and branches consistently. President Joseph Fielding SMITH dedicated Guam to the preaching of the gospel on

August 25, 1955, and the first full-time missionaries were sent there in January 1957. However, until the mid-1970s, missionary work was confined primarily to U.S. military personnel and their families. Since that time, expansion into the many islands of Micronesia has been rapid. In the spring of 1980, the Church created the Micronesia Guam Mission, with Ferron C. Losee as president. Book of Mormon selections were published in Marshallese and Pohnpeian in 1984 and 1987, respectively.

KIRIBATI. LDS missionary efforts in the Republic of Kiribati (formerly the Gilbert Islands) have proven quite fruitful. On October 19, 1975, six Gilbertese students who had studied at Liahona High School in Tonga returned to the island of Tarawa and commenced missionary work. They had been ordained elders and were serving in the Fiji Suva Mission. At about the same time, the Church took over a small middle school in 1977 and renamed it Moroni Community School. It has served as the physical focus of the Church in Kiribati. Relative to the small population, Church growth has been rapid. In 1990 the Church was also established in Belau, the Cook Islands, Marshall, Niue, Nauru, Northern Marietta, Tuvalu, and Vanuata.

BIBLIOGRAPHY

Britsch, R. Lanier. *Unto the Islands of the Sea: A History of the Latter-day Saints in the Pacific*. Salt Lake City, 1986.

Clement, Russell T., comp. *Mormons in the Pacific: A Bibliography*. Laie, Hawaii, 1981.

R. LANIER BRITSCH

OHIO, LDS COMMUNITIES IN

[*The Church became established in Ohio after Sidney* Rigdon *and his Reformed Baptist congregations at Mentor and* Kirtland *converted in October–November 1830. Others around the vicinity of Kirtland joined the Church. A December 1830 revelation initiated a gathering of Church members to Ohio (D&C 37:1–2), where they were to be "endowed with power from on high" (D&C 38:32). See* History of the Church: c. 1831–1844.

Joseph Smith *and Sidney Rigdon lived at* Hiram, Ohio, *from*

September 1831 to September 1832, where both were tarred and feathered. There Joseph Smith received sixteen revelations later published in the Doctrine and Covenants.

Between 1831 and 1838, Kirtland served as Church headquarters. See such entries as Kirtland, Ohio; Schools of the Prophets; *and* Whitney Store. *Here many more revelations were received, and in the* Kirtland Temple, *in 1836, Latter-day Saints experienced an increased outpouring of spiritual manifestations and visitations.*

By 1838, the Church had organized more than two dozen branches in communities mostly in northeastern Ohio.

Some early Ohio converts had formed a communal society prior to their conversion. This communitarian impulse was redirected by a revelation, Doctrine and Covenants section 42; see Consecration: Consecration in Ohio and Missouri. *Management of temporal affairs was seen as an integral part of building the kingdom of God on the earth. Joseph Smith's role in the development of the* Kirtland Economy *became a focal point of dissent in the wake of the failure of an unchartered Kirtland bank during the Panic of 1837.*

In early 1838, threatened by malcontents, Joseph Smith and other Church leaders fled Kirtland, moving Church headquarters to Missouri. Most Latter-day Saints soon left Ohio, although a Church organization was maintained at Kirtland for several years.]

P

PALMYRA/MANCHESTER, NEW YORK

The Palmyra/Manchester area of New York is significant to the LDS Church because the Joseph SMITH, Sr., family settled there in 1816, and the hill Cumorah, from which came the gold plates of the Book of Mormon, is nearby. Many events in early Church history occurred in the vicinity, including Joseph Smith's FIRST VISION, and also the visits of the angel Moroni leading to the translation and publication of the Book of Mormon in Palmyra. A number of persons, including Martin HARRIS, Oliver COWDERY, and E. B. Grandin, prominent in the early scenes of the Church, also lived in the vicinity. Four revelations now published in the Doctrine and Covenants were received in the area (see D&C 2, 19, 22, 23).

The Joseph Smith, Sr., family arrived in the village of Palmyra, New York, in 1816 from their home in Norwich, Vermont. By the fall of 1817 they made a down payment on a 100-acre farm two miles south of the village in the adjoining township of Farmington (which became Manchester in 1822). During the winter of 1817–1818, they began the construction of a log house, which was completed by the fall of 1818 (Enders, p. 16). A 1982 archaeological dig revealed the exact location of the log cabin on the southern edge of Palmyra township (Berge, pp. 24–26).

In the early spring of 1820, Joseph Smith, Jr., sought the Lord in prayer and experienced the First Vision, in a grove of trees near the home, and three years later, on the evening of September 21–22, 1823, the angel Moroni visited him in the log cabin and gave him instructions about the coming forth of the Book of Mormon. The hill Cumorah where Joseph first viewed the gold plates and received annual visits from Moroni is about three miles to the southeast, on the Canandaigua Road.

From 1822 to 1826 the Smiths built a frame house in Manchester; and in January 1827 Joseph and his new bride, Emma Hale Smith, came to that home to work on the farm. Attempts to steal the gold plates required their being concealed both under the hearthstone of the house and in the cooper's shop.

The Book of Mormon was printed by Egbert B. Grandin in his Palmyra Bookstore, with Martin Harris's mortgaged farm guaranteeing that the printing costs would be met. With the organization of the Church on April 6, 1830, at Fayette, the Manchester/Palmyra area was identified as one of three branches.

The Church still has interest in the area, maintaining visitors centers in the Grandin printing shop and bookstore; at the Smith farm and SACRED GROVE; and also at the hill Cumorah, where an appropriate monument and building have been erected, and where an annual pageant is held. A portion of the Martin Harris farm is also owned by the Church. Members of the Smith family and others prominent in the early History of the Church are buried in the cemeteries of the area.

[*See also* History of the Church, c. 1820–1831; New York: Early LDS Sites in.]

BIBLIOGRAPHY

Berge, Dale L. "Archaeological Work at the Smith Log House." *Ensign* 15 (Aug. 1985):24–26.

Enders, Donald L. "A Snug Log House": A Historical Look at the Joseph Smith, Sr., Family Home in Palmyra, New York." *Ensign* 15 (Aug. 1985):14–23.

Porter, Larry C. "A Study of the Origins of The Church of Jesus Christ of Latter-day Saints in the States of New York and Pennsylvania, 1816–1831." Ph.D. diss., Brigham Young University, 1971.

LARRY C. PORTER

PARMLEY, LAVERN WATTS

Martha LaVern Watts Parmley (1900–1980) served as general president of the Primary of The Church of Jesus Christ of Latter-day Saints from 1951 to 1974, a period when the Church was adapting its programs to serve the needs of a rapidly growing, worldwide membership. She was born January 1, 1900, in Murray, Utah, to LDS parents. LaVern served as a Primary teacher at age fourteen. She married Thomas Jennison Parmley on June 28, 1923. After her husband completed a doctorate at Cornell University in New York, the Parmleys returned to Utah. They were the parents of three children.

When she returned from New York, LaVern Parmley became a member of a stake Primary board. After serving on that board for three years, she was called as a member of the Primary General Board in 1942. Six months later, she was appointed second counselor to Primary President May Green Hinckley. She became first counselor to a new president, Adele Cannon Howells, a year later, a position she held until her call as Primary general president in 1951.

As president, LaVern Parmley was instrumental in adapting the Primary programs to meet a new set of challenges. When the Boy Scouts of America lowered its admission age to eleven, Church and Primary leaders discussed whether the Primary or the Young Men's organization should direct the activities of the eleven-year-old boys. Although the National Scout Committee initially opposed having women leaders direct a scouting program, the Primary obtained permission for women to administer scouting activities for boys until they turned twelve. The Primary also adopted Cub Scouting, thereby assuming responsibility for four years of scouting. LDS women helped open the Boy Scouts program to women leaders nationwide. They served not only in local troops but eventually on local and national boards. In 1967 Parmley became the first woman member of a national scouting committee and later served on several scouting boards. She received the highest honors awarded by the Boy Scouts of America, including the Silver Buffalo award.

President Parmley also supervised the adaptation of the Primary organization to serve the needs of a growing, widely distributed world membership. When Primary membership doubled during her first decade as president, she doubled the members on the Primary

General Board. She set up committees to establish new activities, including an annual sacrament meeting presentation by the children, special Primaries for handicapped children, and a reverence program. As editor of the *Children's Friend,* she restructured its format to make it a magazine for children. Under her direction, teacher training, which began with Primary, developed into a well-ordered general Church program.

As the Church grew, stake Primary conventions and general Primary conferences were discontinued. The Church began to centralize the publication of educational materials, and Primary publications were reduced. President Parmley responded to these challenges by standardizing lesson materials and by preparing audiovisual and printed materials for presentation to Primary leaders in regional meetings.

A major challenge during her administration was the need to accommodate the Primary program to the correlation process implemented in 1961 to place all Church programs under the authority and direction of the priesthood. As part of the process, responsibility for Primary lessons was transferred to the Church Correlation Committee. In a spirit of cooperation, President Parmley helped merge the goals and programs of the Primary into a larger Church-sponsored program for children.

President Parmley helped promote the construction of a new Primary Children's Hospital (later Primary Children's Medical Center), completed in 1952, and encouraged donations from Primary children. As Primary president, she served as chairman of the board for the hospital until 1970. When the Health Service Corporation was organized later that year to oversee all LDS hospitals, she was appointed a board member. In 1975, after she was released as Primary president, the Primary Children's Hospital was transferred to Intermountain Health Care, a private nonprofit corporation.

LaVern Parmley presided over the Primary Association at a time when its programs became more complex and wide-ranging than at any earlier time in its history. As its president during a period of rapid Church growth and expansion, she traveled more than any Primary president before her, providing firsthand supervision and unity in an organization otherwise subject to much local variation.

Her contributions are reflected in the organization and direction of Primary today.

BIBLIOGRAPHY

Madsen, Carol Cornwall, and Susan Staker Oman. *Sisters and Little Saints*. Salt Lake City, 1979.

Parmley, Martha LaVern Watts. Oral history interview with Jill Mulvay Derr, 1974–1976. Church Archives, Historical Dept., Salt Lake City.

JESSIE L. EMBRY

PATTEN, DAVID W.

David Wyman Patten (1799–1838), son of Benenio (Benoni) Patten and Abigale (Edith) Cole, was born in Theresa, Jefferson County, New York, on November 14, 1799. He left his home at an early age and settled near Dundee, Monroe County, Michigan. In 1828 he married Phoebe Ann Babcock. They had no children.

Patten first became acquainted with the Book of Mormon around 1830. In May 1832 he received a letter from his brother John, who was living in Green County, Indiana, noting that he had joined The Church of Jesus Christ of Latter-day Saints. Patten journeyed to Indiana and was baptized by his brother on June 15, 1832. Two days later he was ordained an elder by Elisha H. Groves. On September 2, 1832, he was ordained a high priest by Hyrum Smith.

Until his death in 1838, Patten served almost continuously as a missionary for the Church. He established numerous branches of the Church on each of his proselytizing journeys and was renowned for his spiritual gift of healing.

On February 14, 1835, Patten was chosen as one of the Twelve Apostles and was ordained the following day by Oliver COWDERY. On May 2, 1835, the Prophet Joseph SMITH directed that the seniority of the Twelve be determined according to the members' ages. Patten was uncertain of his exact birth date, and Thomas B. Marsh (born 1800) was mistakenly adjudged to be the older of the two, and thus was made the President of the Quorum.

During the latter part of 1836, Elder Patten settled in Far West, Missouri. Following Church action taken against the presidency of the stake in Missouri (David Whitmer, William W. Phelps, and John

Whitmer) in early February 1838, Thomas B. Marsh and Patten were appointed as Presidents pro tem of the Church in Missouri. On April 6, 1838, Patten and Brigham Young were sustained as assistant presidents of the Church in Missouri, with Thomas B. Marsh as President pro tem.

In April 1838, Joseph Smith received a revelation instructing Patten to prepare for a mission with the Twelve the following spring (D&C 114); however, Patten did not live to fulfill the assignment. He died on October 25, 1838, from a wound suffered in a battle at Crooked River when a contingent of Caldwell County militia (all Mormons), under his leadership, attempted to rescue three Latter-day Saints who had been taken prisoners by a company of Missourians from Ray County. He was buried in Far West, Missouri, two days later. In January 1841 a revelation was given to Joseph Smith in which the Lord indicated that David W. Patten "is with me at this time" (D&C 124:19, 130).

BIBLIOGRAPHY

Jenson, Andrew. *Latter-day Saint Biographical Encyclopedia*, Vol. 1, pp. 76–80. Salt Lake City, 1901.

Wilson, Lycurgus A. *Life of David W. Patten, the First Apostolic Martyr*. Salt Lake City, 1900.

ALEXANDER L. BAUGH

PERPETUAL EMIGRATING FUND (PEF)

To assist Latter-day Saints in the eastern United States and Europe to gather to Church headquarters in the West, the Church inaugurated the Perpetual Emigrating Fund Company in 1849. It is probable that before its demise in 1887, the Emigrating Company assisted more than 30,000 individuals to travel to Utah.

The PEF used Church assets and private contributions to assist individuals commensurate with their inability to pay. With limited funds, fewer individuals could be assisted than wished to participate. Those receiving priority included individuals with skills urgently needed in the West, those whose relatives or friends had contributed to the PEF, and those with longest membership in the Church. Cost-cutting measures, including group contracting, doubling up families in wagons, and organizing HANDCART COMPANIES, were also adopted to make the available funds stretch as far as possible.

PEF assistance was always extended as a loan rather than as a gift. Sponsored emigrants signed a note obligating themselves to repay the PEF as they were able. Though it sometimes required years, and some never fully retired their debt, many repaid their loan in cash, commodities, or labor. In 1880, on the fiftieth anniversary of the organization of the Church, President John TAYLOR, in the tradition of the Israelite jubilee year, forgave half of the outstanding debt owed by the poor to the fund, while those who were able to pay were still expected to do so. In late 1887, under provisions of the Edmunds-Tucker Act (*see* ANTIPOLYGAMY LEGISLATION), the U.S. government dissolved both the Corporation of The Church of Jesus Christ of Latter-day Saints and the Perpetual Emigrating Fund Company.

[*See also* Immigration and Emigration.]

BIBLIOGRAPHY

Arrington, Leonard J. *Great Basin Kingdom*. Cambridge, Mass., 1958.

Jensen, Richard J. "The British Gathering to Zion." In *Truth Will Prevail: The Rise of The Church of Jesus Christ of Latter-day Saints in the British Isles, 1837–1987*, pp. 165–98. Cambridge, England, 1987.

DAVID F. BOONE

PERSECUTION

Jesus told his followers that they would be persecuted, but promised them a great reward in heaven (Matt. 5:11–12). Latter-day Saints believe that righteously enduring persecution can bring blessings in both this life and the next. Although suffering is as unwelcome to Latter-day Saints as to any other people, they strive to respond with patience and faith and to avoid bitterness or revenge (Matt. 5:43–47; D&C 101:35; cf. 98:23–27).

Although Latter-day Saints claim no greater suffering than many others who have also been persecuted for their religious beliefs through the ages, many Latter-day Saints have been persecuted, beginning with Joseph SMITH (see JS—H 1:33). As the Church grew, persecutions increased; the Latter-day Saints faced threats, murder, rape, mayhem, property damage, and revilement in Kirtland, Ohio (1831–1838), in Missouri (1831–1839), and in the area of Nauvoo, Illinois (1839–1846), culminating in the assassinations of Joseph and Hyrum Smith at Carthage, Illinois, in 1844 (Hull, pp. 643–52).

The isolation and safety of the Great Basin in the American West, to which the main body of the Church fled beginning in 1846–1847, lasted only a few years before persecutions were renewed. The Great Basin area became part of the United States in 1848 after the Mexican-American War, and soon federal laws against the practice of plural marriage forced many Latter-day Saints into hiding or to settlements in Mexico and Canada. More than one thousand Latter-day Saints, mostly polygamous husbands, were fined and imprisoned. Ultimately, ANTIPOLYGAMY LEGISLATION disenfranchised the Saints and disincorporated the Church, allowing confiscation of Church property. After the 1890 MANIFESTO enjoining plural marriage, anti-Mormon persecution declined substantially, but other hostilities persisted.

Anti-Mormon literature has often incited and precipitated persecution, from early attempts to discredit Joseph Smith and the Book of Mormon, to recent films misrepresenting LDS doctrine. LDS missionaries have sometimes especially been persecuted. Some missionaries sent to England and Scandinavia in the 1830s and 1850s were confronted by mobs, threats, imprisonment, and physical harm. Several missionaries and potential converts were murdered in the United States at the height of antipolygamy agitation during the 1870s. As recently as 1990, two LDS missionaries were killed in Huancayo, Peru, by anti-American terrorists, and Church property was vandalized or destroyed in several South American countries.

Scriptural examples provide comfort and perspective to Latter-day Saints by showing that in God's eternal plan persecutions are sometimes allowed, with blessings then coming to the persecuted (Ivins, pp. 408–413). The biblical stories of Joseph (Gen. 37–46) and Esther (Esth. 2–9) demonstrate that faith can overcome persecution and bring honor to the persecuted. In the Book of Mormon, the Ammonites provide a poignant example of a people who became dedicated to righteousness, willing to suffer persecution and death rather than break their covenants (Alma 24). Many have also been comforted by the Lord's words to Joseph Smith when he was falsely accused and wrongfully imprisoned. Despite his many trials, the Lord reminded Joseph that the Savior had endured even more, and promised him, "All these things shall give thee experience, and shall be for thy good" (D&C 122:7). He expanded the Prophet's perspective to eternity with the statement "Fear not what man can do, for God shall be with you forever and ever" (D&C 122:9).

The LDS response to persecution is to temper sorrow and anger in accordance with scriptural counsel. The Savior's admonition to turn the other cheek (Matt. 5:39–42) is expanded in the Doctrine and Covenants: Great rewards are promised to those who do not seek retribution and retaliate, but the persecuted may seek for justice after they have suffered repeated offenses and given their adversaries adequate prior warnings (D&C 98:23–31). Patience and tolerance are admonished in the Book of Mormon (Alma 1:21) and in Articles of Faith 11 and 13. A true Latter-day Saint hopes to be reconciled to, and perhaps even to convert, an enemy.

BIBLIOGRAPHY

Allen, James B. "Why Did People Act That Way? Some Observations on Religious Intolerance and Persecution in the American Past." *Ensign* 8 (Dec. 1978):21–24.

Arrington, Leonard J., and Davis Bitton. *The Mormon Experience*, chaps. 3–5, 9. New York, 1979.

The Church of Jesus Christ of Latter-day Saints, ed. *My Kingdom Shall Roll Forth*, chap. 8. Salt Lake City, 1979.

Hull, T. "Persecution: The Heritage of the Saints." *IE* 4 (July 1901):643–52.

Ivins, A. "Is Persecution a Result of Transgression or Righteousness?" *IE* 27 (Mar. 1924):408–413.

LISA BOLIN HAWKINS

PIONEER DAY

July 24, Pioneer Day, is celebrated yearly in "Mormon Country" and increasingly on an international scale among Latter-day Saints. On this date in 1847, the first Mormon pioneers (143 men, 3 women, 2 children) led by Brigham YOUNG, entered the uninhabited Salt Lake Valley. They began the pioneer settlement of more than 400 communities in the intermountain West, Canada, and Mexico. Before the completion of the transcontinental railroad in 1869, 80,000 Mormon refugees and converts went west in perpetual immigration. Six thousand lost their lives and were buried along the way.

"In the annals of the American Frontier," wrote historian Purnell H. Benson, there is "no more thrilling story" (p. 423). On July 24 this story is commemorated annually by a huge parade in Salt Lake City and is also celebrated frequently in drama (e.g., the *Promised Valley* musical), poetry, and song. The holiday is typically marked by sunrise services and, throughout LDS communities, by Old West reenactments. In Church programs, commemorative addresses are given and family journals and reminiscences are revived. The close conjunction of the festivities of July 4 and 24 tends to focus on the Mormon exodus as a quest for religious freedom. But like the Puritan movement and the Jewish *aliyah*, it was at root a quest for the sacred. It grew out of the vision of a consecrated community, the kingdom of God on earth. The festivities of July 24 attempt to regain and extend that vision.

BIBLIOGRAPHY

Benson, Purnell H. *Religion in Contemporary Culture*, pp. 420–27. New York, 1960.

Shipps, Jan. *Mormonism: The Story of a New Religious Tradition*, pp. 64, 129. Urbana, Ill., 1985.

D. JAMES CANNON

PIONEER ECONOMY

The Church of Jesus Christ of Latter-day Saints was the major force contributing to the economic development of the Great Basin region in the nineteenth century. This was true until the completion of the transcontinental railroad in 1869, and to a large extent even through the remainder of the century. Though the railroad ended the isolation of the Great Basin and brought both economic benefits and new challenges to HOME INDUSTRIES, the Church's economic role did not decline significantly until the end of the pioneer period (*see* ECONOMIC HISTORY OF THE CHURCH).

Church involvement in the economy was rooted in theology. According to LDS belief, building up the kingdom of God on earth—developing it and beautifying it for the return of the Savior—is a prime task of God's people. LDS pioneers believed that the Church was the agent of God and his people in building the kingdom. The responsibility to promote its progress and perfection rested upon Church officials. It thus became a religious duty to produce, to build, and to prepare for the Millennium. Digging canals, tending herds, cultivating crops, and constructing telegraph lines, railroads, and factories were all viewed as acts of religious devotion similar to prayer, worship, and other strictly religious activities.

Partly because economic activity had religious significance, it was clearly understood that all such was to be conducted in harmony with gospel principles. Precious-metal mining and other economic activities that did not contribute to basic production and stable communities were not endorsed. Individualism, profiteering, and speculation were eschewed. Instead, the individual member was enjoined to be "one with his brethren." Not only were they to work together in harmony, but Latter-day Saints were also expected to maintain relative equality in the possession and enjoyment of this world's goods.

President Brigham Young recognized early on the economic importance of women in making a harsh land productive. Not only were women partners with men in agriculture and home production—the more so with many men called away on missions—but they were also specifically encouraged by President Young to be involved as telegraph operators and shopkeepers, and he enlisted them throughout the territory to work in SILK CULTURE.

Building the pioneer kingdom required the erection of a "two-decker" economy—a foundation of agricultural and handicraft production to satisfy the most pressing wants of the settlers and the steady increment of immigrants, along with a superstructure of investment to provide for future growth. In general, programs were concerned with three types of activities. First, leaders sought to increase the agents of production by a widespread missionary program and by promotion and organization of emigration (*see* IMMIGRATION AND EMIGRATION; PERPETUAL EMIGRATING FUND). Between 1847 and 1880 more than 70,000 converts immigrated to the Great Basin to work on farms, in factories, and to participate in COLONIZATION projects.

Second, Church leaders sought to aid capital formation. This they did by sending out exploration parties to discover new resources, by developing these resources under Church sponsorship, by mobilizing the savings of its members in the Great Basin and in Europe, and by diverting resources from the production of consumables to the production of reproducible wealth. Sizable groups were sent to southern Utah to mine and manufacture iron, to southern Nevada to mine silver and lead, to northern and central Utah to mine coal, to southern California to establish an entrepôt, to southern Utah to raise cotton and other semitropical products, to various places in northern Utah and southern Idaho to utilize grazing lands, and to hundreds of irrigable areas throughout the Great Basin to establish colonies, construct irrigation systems, and engage in farming (*see also* CITY PLANNING).

In mobilizing savings to support these developmental projects, the basic organizational device was the office of the trustee-in-trust. Usually the president of the church, as trustee-in-trust, held, bought, and sold property; collected donations and expended them; and in general used the common fund of the community in constructing the infrastructure of communications, transportation, merchandising, and education. This was sometimes done by chartered companies such as the Deseret Iron Company, the Deseret Sugar Manufacturing Company, and the Deseret Telegraph Company. The President of the Church could also direct regionwide economic initiatives such as the 1850s CONSECRATION movement, the 1860s cooperative movement, and the 1870s UNITED ORDERS.

A second organizational device was the network of tithing houses, that received contributions in kind of butter, eggs, calves, chickens, hay, wheat, and other produce that were then used to support workers on school buildings, tanneries, woolen factories, gristmills, roads, and other projects. In the largely cashless pioneer economy, the tithing house system also made it possible to spend credit earned for labor or goods in one community in another. Tithing Office script and credits, ultimately controlled and reconciled through the books of the trustee-in-trust, thus helped to grease the wheels of commerce in the Great Basin.

Third, pioneer Church leaders also sought to overcome an adverse balance of trade for the region. They solicited investments by members wherever they were located and promoted sales outside the region of livestock, grain, salt, cotton, dried fruits, wool products, and other exportables. In this connection, the Church was able to turn to advantage the discovery of gold in California in 1848. The Church acquired about $150,000 in gold dust during the 1850s from returning miners, from contributions of its members in California, and from men assigned to California expressly for the purpose of obtaining specie to help boost the Utah economy.

The balance of payments problem was one reason the Church discouraged the importation of unnecessary consumables. Leaders urged Latter-day Saints to refrain from using imported tea, coffee, tobacco, liquor, or "fashionable" clothing from the East (homemade was considered more saintly). In order to prevent "outside" merchants from becoming wealthy in this trade, Church leaders bought out most of them, imposed a boycott on trading with others, and channeled the bulk of the territory's imports through the Church-controlled Zion's Cooperative Mercantile Institution (ZCMI).

The Church assumed much of the burden of promoting economic activity that, under different circumstances, might have been assumed by eastern capitalists or the federal government. By influencing the movement of population and new investment, and by controlling community pricing through the tithing houses, the Church regulated the allocation of resources to maximize the gross product. By continuously funneling new families into the various settlements and valleys, the Church also prevented the creation of a class system and contributed to a greater equality of income. In so doing, LDS leaders expressed greater confidence in the efficacy of their own administered economy than in the ability of an impersonal price system to optimally allocate resources and induce rapid and diversified economic development.

BIBLIOGRAPHY

Arrington, Leonard J. *Great Basin Kingdom: An Economic History of the Latter-day Saints, 1830–1900*. Cambridge, Mass., 1958.

———. "Religion and Planning in the Great Basin, 1847–1900." *Proceedings of the Thirty-second Annual Conference of the Western Economic Association*, pp. 37–41. Salt Lake City, 1957.

LEONARD J. ARRINGTON

PIONEER LIFE AND WORSHIP

The first members of The Church of Jesus Christ of Latter-day Saints worshiped like the converts of many new religions: their devotions were democratic, fervent, local, and spontaneous. "High Church" priestly gowns, sacerdotal objects, or complicated liturgy were not used—then or later. Equally remote were the formal creeds and confessions of the frontier sects. Only as Church growth brought the need for orderly administration, toward the last third of the nineteenth century, did the Latter-day Saints gain a measure of formal devotion.

The early Saints were not left without direction. As early as June 1829, ten months prior to the formal organization of the Church, Joseph SMITH and Oliver COWDERY sought guidance about Church performances. "The church shall meet together oft for prayer & supplication," read an early copy of the manuscript that resulted. "Each member shall speak & tell the church of their progress in the way of Eternal life" (Oliver Cowdery, "Articles of the Church of Christ," 1829, LDS Library Archives). The document, which drew on previous revelations and Book of Mormon injunctions, later became the Church's "Articles and Covenants." The first revelation to be canonized, it became, arguably, the Church's single most important statement on religious worship and procedure (see Doctrine and Covenants sections 20–21).

It defined a simple structure. There were three sacramental ordinances: baptism by immersion, confirmation of the Spirit, and the bread and the cup of the Lord's Supper. Routines were equally modest, prescribing prayer, frequent meetings, home visits by teachers, local priesthood governance, and quarterly conferences to regulate Churchwide business. Traveling elders took this blueprint to the early, scattered congregations.

KIRTLAND, OHIO, one of the Church's early centers, typified the resulting system. There were many meetings. Leaders might hold frequent "councils" and "schools" at the Newel K. Whitney store. They joined members in private homes on Sundays and on weekdays for prayer and worship meetings, often with millennial singing and testifying accompanied by the display of pentecostal gifts. Fast and testimony meetings might be held on Thursdays, with attention given to the needs of the poor. Abstinence from food brought piety to worshipers, and what was saved assisted the needy. Kirtland members also attempted wider, congregational assemblies. With no other gathering place at first available, they met in the open air or in Kirtland's sixteen-by-twenty-four-foot schoolhouse. After the completion of the KIRTLAND TEMPLE in 1836, meetings were held there with as many as several hundred people in attendance.

These routines set the pattern for Latter-day Saint worship as the Church moved from Ohio to Missouri, Illinois, and Nebraska. While leaders might organize and direct meetings, individual Saints could also do so. Prayer meetings, often the redoubt of women, proceeded at times without ecclesiastical direction. General Church meetings were often as democratic. Members simply summoned others by ringing the community bell. Content was also unstructured. "We shall devote this day to preaching—exhortation—singing—praying and blessing children," promised a Church leader prior to the start of the Church's April general conference in 1845 (*T&S*, 6:953–57). With congregational sessions still held in open air, some might chat on the perimeters while the more centrally situated struggled to hear.

NAUVOO brought the innovation of ward worship. At first a political division as in other American cities, wards in Nauvoo became religious units. Church-appointed bishops presided over the jurisdictions, levying quotas for Church building projects, conducting neighborhood (block) or ward teaching, and overseeing the needs of the poor and, increasingly, the holding of meetings. Here began, for the first time, Church-directed neighborhood worship. The system was regularized at WINTER QUARTERS, Nebraska, during the exodus west. Brigham YOUNG instructed bishops to "organize and watch over their wards, have weekly meetings therein; also see that those under their charge have work and that none suffer through want, also [they should] instruct their wards to establish schools" (Manuscript History of Brigham Young, 1846, p. 474, Church Archives).

The Saints' propensity for "going to meeting," as they called congregational worship, increased after they settled in the Great Basin. Community meetings were first held in the Salt Lake City fort, with a haystack affording shade and a small cannon serving as a podium. Later a "bowery" was built within the fort by erecting posts, interlacing them with beams, and covering the affair with boughs and leaves. Boweries became a staple of Salt Lake and outlying community worship—in some communities they were not replaced by tabernacles for several decades. After the abandonment of the fort bowery, Salt Lake City settlers erected another on TEMPLE SQUARE, eventually giving it adobe walls and a ceiling of debris and soil. Still bigger boweries followed, largely to attend to the needs of the Church's general conferences when no community building could seat the flood of the people who attended.

During the pioneer period the most prominent building on Temple Square was the TABERNACLE (later called the "Old Tabernacle" to differentiate it from the present-day tabernacle built in the 1860s). Unlike the stopgap adobe and soil bowery, it boasted stone walls and had no interior posts. "The Tabernacle on the inside is built quite in the form of a Theatre," wrote a traveler, "benches rising one behind another until the outer row is a great way from the pulpit. The building is executed on the inside so that it is one story under ground and in entering its steps descend" (Reminiscence of Addison Moses Crane, Huntington Library, San Marino, California). While lacking architectural distinction, it answered practical purposes. Finished in 1852, its 60-by-120-foot expanse provided 2,500 unobstructed seats and fairly good acoustical quality.

At first Temple Square community worship services were most important. The entire settlement was expected to gather each Sunday, usually at ten in the morning and two in the afternoon. A brass band might begin the preliminaries, followed by the "crying out" of the recently arrived post, notices of lost and found articles, or the announcement of upcoming political, social, and religious events. These newsy routines generally ended with the establishment of the *Deseret News* in 1850.

During opening exercises, leaders might enter the hall to assume positions on the "stand," while followers drifted to their unassigned benches (increasingly members were asked not to occupy the rostrum without invitation). The lack of prepared sermons sometimes brought problems. Without a seasoned speaker present, authorities might summon a Church officer from other activity. The afternoon meeting was occupied by the administration of the Lord's Supper and a continuation of impromptu sermonizing, often by members of the congregation. Each meeting usually lasted for two hours or more.

There was variety and sometimes even theater. Leaders might

invite LDS preachers, Indian chiefs, or, more frequently, returning missionaries to speak. Church leaders often preached gospel "discourses" that mixed spiritual and temporal themes—and sometimes the serious and the humorous. Elder Joseph Young, President of the First Quorum of Seventy, "got up lively & spirited & caused much merriment," recorded the minutes on one occasion. "Pres[iden]t [Brigham] Young followed—on Charity—amusingly" (September 9, 1855, Minutes of Meetings, Church Archives). Speakers might preach, dialogue with the congregation, issue reproof and correction, and on occasion disfellowship or excommunicate wayward members.

With Temple Square meetings disadvantaged by a growing lack of intimacy due to increased membership and uncomfortable conditions during inclement weather, emphasis slowly shifted to local and ward activity. There, "blessing meetings" were held to confirm the baptized or rebaptized, and to bless. One ward boasted a "singing school." Thursday fast and testimony meetings continued in most neighborhoods, and bishops also held youth meetings. While the male priesthood quorums generally met on a multiward basis, special men's meetings were held in wards to aid immigration, levy taxes, or oversee road, canal, school, and chapel construction. Women continued their prayer meetings, Relief Society meetings in the 1850s for Indian relief, and restructured Relief Society gatherings in the 1870s for instruction, testimony, and relief for the unfortunate.

The most important ward gathering was the Sunday evening worship service, held usually an hour or two after the Temple Square afternoon service. "Meeting at E. M. Saunder's house," read the minutes of one. "Filled to overflowing. Pres John Young opened the meeting by singing and prayer. [He] made some remarks, ex[h]orted the brothern to use their privelages in occupying the time. Was followed by the Brotheren in quick succession. Brotheron and sisters delivered their testimony concerning the work of the Lord. [Many] spake in toungs, and prophesied" (Jan. 18, 1852, Nineteenth Ward Book A, Church Archives). The meeting began at 6 P.M. and ended three and one-half hours later.

Music played an important part in any LDS service. "My soul delighteth in the song of the heart," read an early revelation; "yea, the song of the righteous is a prayer unto me" (D&C 25:12). Emma

SMITH, Joseph's wife, collected and published in 1835 the first hymnal, which was actually a diminutive volume of poetry (music was borrowed from popular or favorite melodies). The settlers continued their musical tradition in the intermountain West. Only two weeks after their arrival, the nucleus of what would become the TABERNACLE CHOIR formed around a group of English and Welsh singers. As pioneering progressed, President Young insisted that each colonizing party have a music leader, called "musical missionaries," to sing, lead choirs, and play instruments in outlying settlements. He personally subsidized the Nauvoo Brass Band, which became a prototype. By the 1860s there were at least forty bands in the territory; by 1875 there were twice that number. Travelers Jules Remy and Julius Benchley were impressed. "Mormons have a feeling for sacred music," they concluded. "Their women [particularly] sing with soul" (A Journey to Great-Salt-Lake City, 1861, 2:56, 374–75).

Latter-day Saints also expressed their devotions in sacramental ordinances. Communion, or "the sacrament," as Latter-day Saints call it, was a primary means. Occasionally suspended due to the unworthiness or insouciance of partakers, the sacrament generally was a weekly ritual on Temple Square and at least a monthly one in local wards. Forms varied. Sometimes speakers stopped in mid-discourse to bless the emblems, which priesthood teachers then passed to the congregation's men, women, children, and even non-Mormon visitors as the preaching resumed. On other occasions bishops or young men consecrated the bread and water, which increasingly was substituted for wine. For Latter-day Saints the ordinance was a symbolic remembrance of Christ's flesh and blood and a renewal of the covenant of discipleship. Simple and unadorned, avoiding complex formulations such as transubstantiation, it was the central LDS public act of worship.

There were others. During a pioneer's lifetime, baptism might be administered several times as a token of special covenant. In addition to the original baptismal vow, accepting Christ and establishing Church membership, Saints were baptized on such special occasions as the dedication of the Nauvoo Temple, the exodus west, arrival in the SALT LAKE VALLEY, and during the Churchwide reformations of 1856–1857 (*see* REFORMATION [LDS] OF 1856–1857) and 1875–1876, when "reconfirmations" were also administered. Moreover, members used rebaptism in the process of personal repentance and faith healing, and they also performed proxy baptisms in behalf of deceased ancestry. At a time when the acceptance of the restored gospel often severed a convert's ties to family, neighborhood, and vocation, the outward sign of baptism provided powerful emotional and psychological reconfirmation. With weekly meeting attendance figures starkly low, it was the means by which many Latter-day Saints expressed their continuing religious commitment.

The temple endowment was another way of uniting pioneer life with the sacred. With no temple completed during the pioneer period, members received their endowments on hills or mountaintops or in an upper room, but more frequently, after its dedication in 1855, in the Salt Lake Endowment House. Here they were instructed on mankind's spiritual journey through the eternities and performed ordinances pertaining to eternal life. Without the opportunity for doing frequent proxy endowments, a ritual that became common in the twentieth century, these ceremonies entered everyday pioneer life in two ways. Members wore temple garments or marked shirts as a sign of their temple commitments, and many joined a prayer circle. Salt Lake City had more than seven of these groups, at least one scheduled for each night of the week, and outlying settlements had at least one. At these gatherings, members bore testimony, discussed doctrine, consecrated oil for anointing the sick, reviewed personal and group needs, and united in temple ritual and prayer.

There were broader, community devotions as well. In the early years, quorums of seventy held jubilees, which united dance, exhortation, music, socializing, and general celebration. Starting in 1849 annual, communitywide Pioneer Day fetes used similar activities to mark the coming of the first pioneers. Reminiscent of the community worship and socializing of the biblical feast days, general conferences twice each year gathered thousands to Salt Lake City for worship and mingling. Finally, the Saints often united for "reform." While most often a local phenomenon, at times the "spirit of reformation" spread through the territory or was officially initiated and sanctioned. During these periods, Latter-day Saints subjected themselves to preaching, religious catechizing, confession, and the cleansing of sin, followed by a renewal of the sacramental ordinances.

There was a final expression of LDS worship. Beyond their traditional expressions and devotions, nineteenth-century Saints acted on their religious feeling by seeking to establish the temporal kingdom of God. They "gathered to Zion," settled, had children, built homes and communities, and refined themselves. Leaders might complain of their wayward meeting attendance or inattention to detail. Yet their community building, at least in a broad sense, was a sacral experience that revealed their formidable religious energy and devotion.

BIBLIOGRAPHY

Though no comprehensive survey of nineteenth-century Latter-day Saint worship exists, several narrower studies are especially helpful. Consult Leonard J. Arrington and Davis Bitton, "The Nineteenth Century Ward," in *The Mormon Experience*, pp. 206–219, New York, 1979; Joseph Heinerman, "The Mormon Meetinghouse: Reflections of Pioneer Religious and Social Life in Salt Lake City," *Utah Historical Quarterly* 50 (Fall 1982):340–53; and Ronald W. Walker, "'Going to Meeting' in Salt Lake City's Thirteenth Ward, 1849–1881: A Microanalysis," in *New Views of Mormon History*, ed. Davis Bitton and Maureen Ursenbach Beecher, pp. 138–61, Salt Lake City, 1987. For an example of Temple Square preaching rhetoric, see Ronald W. Walker, "Raining Pitchforks: Brigham Young as Preacher," *Sunstone* 8 (May–June 1983):4–9.

RONALD W. WALKER

PLURAL MARRIAGE

Plural marriage was the nineteenth-century LDS practice of a man marrying more than one wife. Popularly known as polygamy, it was actually polygyny. Although polygamy had been practiced for much of history in many parts of the world, to do so in "enlightened" America in the nineteenth century was viewed by most as incomprehensible and unacceptable, making it the Church's most controversial and least understood practice. Though the principle was lived for a relatively brief period, it had profound impact on LDS self-definition, helping to establish the Latter-day Saints as a "people apart." The practice also caused many nonmembers to distance themselves from the Church and see Latter-day Saints more negatively than would otherwise have been the case.

Rumors of plural marriage among the members of the Church in the 1830s and 1840s led to persecution, and the public announcement of the practice after August 29, 1852, in Utah gave enemies a potent weapon to fan public hostility against the Church. Although Latter-day Saints believed that their religiously-based practice of plural marriage was protected by the U.S. Constitution, opponents used it to delay Utah statehood until 1896. Ever harsher ANTI-POLYGAMY LEGISLATION stripped Latter-day Saints of their rights as citizens, disincorporated the Church, and permitted the seizure of Church property before the MANIFESTO OF 1890 announced the discontinuance of the practice.

Plural marriage challenged those within the Church, too. Spiritual descendants of the Puritans and sexually conservative, early participants in plural marriage first wrestled with the prospect and then embraced the principle only after receiving personal spiritual confirmation that they should do so.

In 1843, one year before his death, the Prophet Joseph Smith dictated a lengthy revelation on the doctrine of marriage for eternity (D&C 132). This revelation also taught that under certain conditions a man might be authorized to have more than one wife. Though the revelation was first committed to writing on July 12, 1843, considerable evidence suggests that the principle of plural marriage was revealed to Joseph Smith more than a decade before in connection with his study of the Bible, probably in early 1831. Passages indicating that revered patriarchs and prophets of old were polygamists raised questions that prompted the Prophet to inquire of the Lord about marriage in general and about plurality of wives in particular. He then learned that when the Lord commanded it, as he had with the patriarchs anciently, a man could have more than one living wife at a time and not be condemned for adultery. He also understood that the Church would one day be required to live the law (D&C 132:1–4, 28–40).

Evidence for the practice of plural marriage during the 1830s is scant. Only a few knew about the still unwritten revelation, and perhaps the only known plural marriage was that between Joseph Smith and Fanny Alger. Nonetheless there were rumors, harbingers of challenges to come.

In April 1839, Joseph Smith emerged from six months' imprisonment in LIBERTY JAIL with a sense of urgency about completing his mission (*see* HISTORY OF THE CHURCH: C. 1831–1844). Since receiving the sealing key from Elijah in the KIRTLAND TEMPLE (D&C 110:13–16) in April 1836, the Prophet had labored to prepare the Saints for additional teachings and ordinances, including plural marriage.

Joseph Smith realized that the introduction of plural marriage would inevitably invite severe criticism. After the Kirtland experience, he knew the tension it would create in his own family; even though Emma, with faith in his prophetic calling, accepted the revelation as being from God and not of his own doing, she could not reconcile herself to the practice. Beyond that, it had the potential to divide the Church and increase hostilities from outside. Still, he felt obligated to move ahead. "The object with me is to obey & teach others to obey God in just what he tells us to do," he taught several months before his death. "It mattereth not whether the principle is popular or unpopular. I will always maintain a true principle even if I Stand alone in it" (*TPJS*, p. 332).

Although certain that God would require it of him and of the Church, Joseph Smith would not have introduced it when he did except for the conviction that God required it *then.* Several close confidants later said that he proceeded with plural marriage in Nauvoo only after both internal struggle and divine warning. Lorenzo Snow later remembered vividly a conversation in 1843 in which the Prophet described the battle he waged "in overcoming the repugnance of his feelings" regarding plural marriage.

> He knew the voice of God—he knew the commandment of the Almighty to him was to go forward—to set the example, and establish Celestial plural marriage. He knew that he had not only his own prejudices and pre-possessions to combat and to overcome, but those of the whole Christian world . . . ; but God . . . had given the commandment [*The Biography and Family Record of Lorenzo Snow*, pp. 69–70 (Salt Lake City, 1884)].

Even so, Snow and other confidants agreed that Joseph Smith proceeded in Nauvoo only after an angel declared that he must or his calling would be given to another (Bachman, pp. 74–75). After this, Joseph Smith told Brigham Young that he was determined to press ahead though it would cost him his life, for "it is the work of God, and He has revealed this principle, and it is not my business to control or dictate it" (Brigham Young Discourse, Oct. 8, 1866, Church Archives).

Nor did others enter into plural marriage blindly or simply because Joseph Smith had spoken, despite biblical precedents. Personal accounts document that most who entered plural marriage in Nauvoo faced a crisis of faith that was resolved only by personal spiritual witness. Those who participated generally did so only after they had obtained reassurance and saw it as religious duty.

Even those closest to Joseph Smith were challenged by the revelation. After first learning of plural marriage, Brigham Young said he felt to envy the corpse in a funeral cortege and "could hardly get over it for a long time" (*JD* 3:266). The Prophet's brother Hyrum Smith stubbornly resisted the very possibility until circumstances forced him to go to the Lord for understanding. Both later taught the principle to others. Emma Smith vacillated, one day railing in opposition against it and the next giving her consent for Joseph to be sealed to another wife (see comments by Orson Pratt, *JD* 13:194).

Teaching new marriage and family arrangements where the principles could not be openly discussed compounded the problems. Those authorized to teach the doctrine stressed the strict covenants, obligations and responsibilities associated with it—the antithesis of license. But those who heard only rumors, or who chose to distort and abuse the teaching, often envisioned and sometimes practiced something quite different. One such was John C. Bennett, mayor of Nauvoo and adviser to Joseph Smith, who twisted the teaching to his own advantage. Capitalizing on rumors and lack of understanding among general Church membership, he taught a doctrine of "spiritual wifery." He and associates sought to have illicit sexual relationships with women by telling them that they were married "spiritually," even if they had never been married formally, and that the Prophet approved the arrangement. The Bennett scandal resulted in his excommunication and the disaffection of several others. Bennett then toured the country speaking against the Latter-day Saints and published a bitter anti-Mormon exposé charging the Saints with licentiousness.

The Bennett scandal elicited several public statements aimed at arming the Saints against the abuses. Two years later enemies and dissenters, some of whom had been associated with Bennett, published the NAUVOO EXPOSITOR, to expose, among other things, plural marriage, thus setting in motion events leading to Joseph Smith's death (*see* MARTYRDOM OF JOSEPH AND HYRUM SMITH).

Far from involving license, however, plural marriage was a carefully regulated and ordered system. Order, mutual agreements, regulation, and covenants were central to the practice. As Elder Parley P. Pratt wrote in 1845,

> These holy and sacred ordinances have nothing to do with whoredoms, unlawful connections, confusion or crime; but the very reverse. They have laws, limits, and bounds of the strictest kind, and none but the pure in heart, the strictly virtuous, or those who repent and become such, are worthy to partake of them. And . . . [a] dreadful weight of condemnation await those who pervert, or abuse them [*The Prophet*, May 24, 1845; cf. D&C 132:7].

The Book of Mormon makes clear that, though the Lord will command men through his prophets to live the law of plural marriage at special times for his purposes, monogamy is the general standard (Jacob 2:28–30); unauthorized polygamy was and is viewed as adultery. Another safeguard was that authorized plural marriages could be performed only through the sealing power controlled by the presiding authority of the Church (D&C 132:19).

Once the Saints left Nauvoo, plural marriage was openly practiced. In WINTER QUARTERS, for example, discussion of the principle was an "open secret" and plural families were acknowledged. As early as 1847, visitors to Utah commented on the practice. Still, few new plural marriages were authorized in Utah before the completion of the Endowment House in Salt Lake City in 1855.

With the Saints firmly established in the Great Basin, Brigham Young announced the practice publicly and published the revelation on eternal marriage. Under his direction, on Sunday, August 29, 1852, Elder Orson Pratt publicly discussed and defended the practice of plural marriage in the Church. After examining the biblical precedents (Abraham, Jacob, David, and others), Elder Pratt argued that the Church, as heir of the keys required anciently for plural marriages to be sanctioned by God, was required to perform such marriages as part of the Restoration. He offered reasons for the practice and discussed several possible benefits (see *JD* 1:53–66), a precedent followed later by others. But such discussions were after the fact and not the justification. Latter-day Saints practiced plural marriage because they believed God commanded them to do so.

Generally plural marriage involved only two wives and seldom more than three; larger families like those of Brigham Young or Heber C. KIMBALL were exceptions. Sometimes the wives simply shared homes, each with her own bedroom, or lived in a "duplex" arrangement, each with a mirror-image half of the house. In other cases, husbands established separate homes for their wives, sometimes in separate towns. Although circumstances and the mechanics of family life varied, in general the living style was simply an adaptation of the nineteenth century American family. Polygamous marriages were similar to national norms in fertility and divorce rates as well. Wives of one husband often developed strong bonds of sisterly love; however, strong antipathies could also arise between wives.

Faced with a national antipolygamy campaign, LDS women startled their eastern sisters, who equated polygamy with oppression of women, by publicly demonstrating in favor of their right to live plural marriage as a religious principle. Judging from the preaching, women were at least as willing to enter plural marriage as men. Instead of public admonitions urging women to enter plural marriage, one finds many urging worthy men to "do their duty" and undertake to care for a plural wife and additional children. Though some were reluctant to accept such responsibility, many responded and sought another wife. It was not unheard of for a wife to take the lead and insist that her husband take another wife; yet, in other cases, a first marriage dissolved over the husband's insistence on marrying again.

As with families generally, some plural families worked better than others. Anecdotal evidence and the healthy children that emerged from many plural households witness that some worked very well. But some plural wives disliked the arrangement. The most common complaint of second and third wives resulted from a husband displaying too little sensitivity to the needs of plural families or not treating them equally. Not infrequently, wives complained that husbands spent too little time with them. But where husbands provided conscientiously even time and wives developed deep love and respect for each other, children grew up as members of large, well-adjusted extended families.

Plural marriage helped mold the Church's attitude toward divorce in pioneer Utah. Though Brigham Young disliked divorce and discouraged it, when women sought divorce he generally granted it. He felt that a woman trapped in an unworkable relationship with no alternatives deserved a chance to improve her life. But when a husband sought relief from his familial responsibilities, President Young consistently counseled him to do his duty and not seek divorce from any wife willing to put up with him.

Contrary to the caricatures of a hostile world press, plural marriage did not result in offspring of diminished capacity. Normal men and women came from plural households, and their descendants are prominent throughout the Intermountain West. Some observers feel that the added responsibility that fell early upon some children in such households contributed to their exceptional record of achievement. Plural marriage also aided many wives. The flexibility of plural households contributed to the large number of accomplished LDS women who were pioneers in medicine, politics and other public careers. In fact, plural marriage made it possible for wives to have professional careers that would not otherwise have been available to them.

The exact percentage of Latter-day Saints who participated in the practice is not known, but studies suggest a maximum of from 20% to 25% of LDS adults were members of polygamous households. At its height, plural marriage probably involved only a third of the women reaching marriageable age—though among Church leadership plural marriage was the norm for a time. Public opposition to polygamy led to the first law against the practice in 1862, and, by the 1880s, laws were increasingly punitive. The Church contested the constitutionality of those laws, but the Supreme Court sustained the legislation (*see* REYNOLDS V. UNITED STATES), leading to a harsh and effective federal antipolygamy campaign known by the Latter-day Saints as "the Raid." Wives and husbands went on the "underground" and hundreds were arrested and sentenced to jail terms in Utah and several federal prisons. This campaign severely affected the families involved, and the related attack on Church organization and properties greatly inhibited its ability to function (*see* HISTORY OF THE CHURCH: C. 1877–1898). Following a vision showing him that continuing plural marriage endangered the temples and the mission of the

Church, not just statehood, President Wilford WOODRUFF issued the Manifesto in October 1890, announcing an official end to new plural marriages and facilitating an eventual peaceful resolution of the conflict.

Earlier polygamous families continued to exist well into the twentieth century, causing further political problems for the Church, and new plural marriages did not entirely cease in 1890. After having lived the principle at some sacrifice for half a century, many devout Latter-day Saints found ending plural marriage a challenge almost as complex as was its beginning in the 1840s. Some new plural marriages were contracted in the 1890s in LDS settlements in Canada and northern Mexico, and a few elsewhere. With national attention again focused on the practice in the early 1900s during the House hearings on Representative-elect B. H. Roberts and Senate hearings on Senator-elect Reed Smoot (*see* SMOOT HEARINGS), President Joseph F. Smith issued his "Second Manifesto" in 1904. Since that time, it has been uniform Church policy to excommunicate any member either practicing or openly advocating the practice of polygamy. Those who do so today, principally members of Fundamentalist groups, do so outside the Church.

BIBLIOGRAPHY

Bachman, Danel W. "A Study of the Mormon Practice of Plural Marriage before the Death of Joseph Smith." M.A. thesis, Purdue University, 1975.

Bashore, Melvin L. "Life Behind Bars: Mormon Cohabs of the 1880s." *Utah Historical Quarterly* 47 (Winter 1979): 22–41.

Bennion, Lowell ("Ben"). "The Incidence of Mormon Polygamy in 1880: 'Dixie' versus Davis Stake." *Journal of Mormon History* 11 (1984): 27–42.

Bitton, Davis. "Mormon Polygamy: A Review Article." *Journal of Mormon History* 4 (1977): 101–118.

Embry, Jessie L. *Mormon Polygamous Families: Life in the Principle*. Salt Lake City, 1987.

Foster, Lawrence. *Religion and Sexuality: The Shakers, The Mormons, and the Oneida Community*. Oxford, 1981.

James, Kimberly Jensen. "'Between Two Fires': Women on the 'Underground' of Mormon Polygamy." *Journal of Mormon History* 8 (1981): 49–61.

Van Wagoner, Richard S. *Mormon Polygamy: A History*. Salt Lake City, 1986.

Whittaker, David J. "Early Mormon Polygamy Defenses." *Journal of Mormon History* 11 (1984): 43–63.

DANEL W. BACHMAN
RONALD K. ESPLIN

POLYGAMY

[*The main article on this subject is* Plural Marriage. *Under the direction of the Prophet Joseph Smith, some members of The Church of Jesus Christ of Latter-day Saints began to practice plural marriage, also referred to as "celestial marriage." This was viewed as a divine commandment to "raise up seed unto" God (Jacob 2:30). The revelation of God concerning eternal marriage is D&C 132. See* Doctrine and Covenants: Sections 131–32. *The latter also contains strong warnings against marital infidelity.*

On the federal and public opposition to Mormon polygamy, see Antipolygamy Legislation; Legal and Judicial History of the Church; *and* Reynolds v. United States.

The Church of Jesus Christ of Latter-day Saints officially discontinued the practice of plural marriage in 1890. See Manifesto of 1890.

Some schismatic groups have not accepted the revelation of God to Wilford Woodruff, fourth President of the Church, ending Church-sanctioned plural marriage and therefore continue the practice today.

See generally History of the Church: c. 1844–1877 *and* c. 1878–1898; Smith, Emma; Smith, Joseph: Teachings of; Snow, Eliza R.; Woodruff, Wilford; *and* Young, Brigham.]

PRATT, ORSON

As a member of the first Quorum of the Twelve Apostles of the modern dispensation, Orson Pratt participated in almost every phase of the Church's history from 1830 until his death in 1881. As a missionary, editor, pioneer, and pamphleteer, he was one of the most influential leaders of the Church in the nineteenth century.

Pratt was born September 19, 1811, at Hartford, Washington County, New York. At the age of eighteen he began seeking a religious experience, and within a year he had been taught the gospel by his brother Parley P. Pratt, who had himself recently joined the Church. On his nineteenth birthday, Orson was baptized into the Church by his brother.

Orson Pratt spent his first years in the Church on a variety of short-term missions in the eastern United States and Canada. He also attended the SCHOOL OF THE PROPHETS in Kirtland, Ohio, marched to Missouri with ZION'S CAMP in 1834, was ordained one of the Standing High Council in Missouri (July 1834), and in February 1835 was chosen as a member of the newly organized Quorum of the Twelve Apostles.

From 1839 to 1841 he participated in the very successful MISSION OF THE TWELVE TO THE BRITISH ISLES, spending much of his time in Scotland. At Edinburgh in September 1840, he published his first missionary tract, *A[n] Interesting Account of Several Remarkable Visions*. An important pamphlet, it contained the first *public* recording of Joseph SMITH's FIRST VISION and also summarized basic LDS beliefs, a list that bears some resemblance to the 1842 Articles of Faith in the WENTWORTH LETTER of Joseph Smith.

Orson Pratt's return to America in 1841 thrust him into a maelstrom of rumors and gossip in Nauvoo: that the Prophet Joseph Smith was teaching PLURAL MARRIAGE. His reactions to the situation led to his excommunication in August 1842. However, after several months of seeking the truth regarding both Joseph Smith's revelations and the newly introduced practice of plural marriage, Pratt accepted both with such assurance that he spent the rest of his life in their defense. He was reinstated in the Quorum of the Twelve Apostles in January 1843.

Following Joseph Smith's death in 1844, Pratt supported the right and responsibility of the Quorum of the Twelve Apostles to preside over the Church. In 1847 he was a member of the Pioneer Company traveling to the Great Basin. On July 21 of that year he and Erastus Snow were the first of that company to enter the Salt Lake Valley. Several days later he preached the first sermon there. His journals are an important source for pioneer history.

From 1848 to 1851 Pratt presided over the Church in Europe. In addition to his many responsibilities regarding proselytizing, immigration, and editing the LDS *Millennial Star*, he wrote and published sixteen pamphlets in defense of LDS doctrines. These include his treatises *Divine Authority, or the Question, Was Joseph Smith Sent of God?* (1848); *The Kingdom of God* (1848–1849); and *Divine Authenticity of the Book of Mormon* (1850–1851).

When he returned to Salt Lake City, Elder Pratt was assigned by President Brigham Young to publicly preach a sermon announcing the doctrine of plural marriage at a special missionary conference in August 1852. Following the meetings he was assigned by Brigham Young to publish in Washington, D.C., a periodical in defense of plural marriage. The twelve-month run of *The Seer* in 1853 provides the most detailed defense of the doctrine in LDS literature.

In 1856, again presiding over the European Mission, Elder Pratt produced additional pamphlets on specific gospel principles. Eight tracts were issued separately, then bound together in 1857 under the title *Tracts by Orson Pratt. . . .* After Brigham Young's death in 1877, Pratt was assigned by John Taylor to help prepare new editions of the modern LDS scriptures. He had provided much of the critical work for the 1876 edition of the Doctrine and Covenants, and he did the same for the 1879 edition of the Book of Mormon (dividing it into chapters and verses and adding references), and for the 1879 American edition of the Pearl of Great Price.

Throughout his life Orson Pratt pursued his strong interest in mathematics and astronomy. In 1866 he published his major mathematical work, *New and Easy Method of Solution of the Cubic and Biquadratic Equations*, and in 1879 issued *Key to the Universe*. In these works and in various lectures to many early LDS audiences, he was a positive force in the scientific education of the American pioneers. By the time his last scientific work was published, he was suffering from diabetes. He preached his last public discourse on September 18, 1881, and died on October 3 in Salt Lake City. He had married seven wives and fathered forty-five children.

Elder Pratt's greatest impact upon the Church came through his precisely written theological studies. Within each work he moved carefully from one axiom to the next, developing his position with the same exactness he used in presenting a mathematical proof. His concern for definitiveness and his ability to simplify, to reduce things to their lowest common denominator, made his written works valuable to missionaries defending the faith in mission fields throughout the world.

Orson Pratt's religious pamphlets grew out of a missionary context. Their importance lies partly in the extended arguments and "proofs" for the central tenets of LDS theology. In most of his writing, however, he was an elaborator, a systematizer, and a popularizer of LDS thought, rather than an innovator or an originator. In almost every area he learned the substance either directly from the Prophet Joseph Smith or indirectly from his dynamic and visionary older brother Parley, also an LDS apostle and author. Orson Pratt was at his best in developing the ideas of others and expanding them into fully elaborated statements.

BIBLIOGRAPHY

England, Breck. *The Life and Thought of Orson Pratt.* Salt Lake City, 1985.

Hogan, Edward R. "Orson Pratt as a Mathematician." *Utah Historical Quarterly* 41 (Winter 1973):59–68.

Lyon, T. Edgar. "Orson Pratt—Early Mormon Leader." Master's thesis, University of Chicago, 1932.

———. "Orson Pratt, Pioneer and Proselyter." *Utah Historical Quarterly* 24 (July 1956):261–73.

Skabelund, Donald. "Cosmology on the American Frontier: Orson Pratt's Key to the Universe." *Centaurus: International Magazine of the History of Mathematics, Science, and Technology* 11 (1965):190–204.

Whittaker, David J. "Orson Pratt: Prolific Pamphleteer." *Dialogue* 15 (Autumn 1982):27–41.

———. "The Bone in the Throat: Orson Pratt and the Public Announcement of Plural Marriage." *Western Historical Quarterly* 18 (July 1987):293–314.

DAVID J. WHITTAKER

PRATT, PARLEY PARKER

One of the most significant LDS missionaries, writers, poets, and thinkers to emerge during the early years of the LDS Restoration was Parley Parker Pratt (1807–1857). He was a central figure in expounding the doctrines of the gospel, and his publications set a standard for future pamphleteers. He was a member of the original Quorum of the Twelve Apostles in this dispensation and a leader in the migration to the Great Basin.

Pratt was born April 12, 1807, in Burlington, Otsego County, New York, the third son of Jared and Charity Pratt. He married Thankful Halsey on September 9, 1827, at Canaan, New York, and they made their home in Amherst township, Lorain County, Ohio. In Ohio, Parley became a member of the Reformed Baptist Society (Campbellite) through the preaching of Sidney RIGDON. While traveling on the Erie Canal in western New York, Parley came in contact with a Baptist deacon named Hamblin, who introduced him to a copy of the Book of Mormon. He then investigated the LDS Church and was baptized in Seneca Lake by Oliver COWDERY on September 1, 1830. In turn, he converted his younger brother, Orson PRATT, and baptized him on September 19, 1830.

From 1830 to 1857, Parley P. Pratt was constantly engaged in a variety of missionary assignments. Of special note was a 1,500-mile journey from Fayette, New York, to the western boundaries of Missouri with Oliver Cowdery, Peter Whitmer, Jr., and Ziba Peterson (D&C 32:1–2) on a mission to the Lamanites, beginning in October 1830 (*see* LAMANITE MISSION). En route, these missionaries converted some 130 persons in the Kirtland-Mentor area, including Sidney Rigdon and Frederick G. Williams, future members of the First Presidency. Upon reaching Missouri, Pratt was among the first members of the Church to stand upon the land later designated for the City of Zion, Independence, Jackson County (cf. D&C 57:2–3).

Parley Pratt was ordained an apostle on February 21, 1835, and sustained as a member of the Quorum of the Twelve. The first LDS hymnal (1835) included three hymns he had written. During a mission to the eastern states with the Twelve in the summer of 1835, Parley published eleven more hymns in conjunction with a long narrative poem in six chapters entitled *The Millennium, A Poem*. This volume became the first book of LDS poetry.

Pratt proselytized extensively in Upper Canada, leading to the conversion of John TAYLOR and his wife Leonora, Joseph Fielding, and Joseph's sisters, Mary and Mercy Fielding (*see* SMITH, MARY FIELDING). In 1838, he suffered persecution with the Saints in Missouri and spent nine months imprisoned in Richmond and Columbia before escaping to Illinois in July 1839.

Parley and Orson Pratt left Nauvoo, Illinois, on August 19, 1839, on an apostolic mission to the British Isles (*see* MISSIONS OF THE TWELVE TO THE BRITISH ISLES). At a conference in Preston, England, Parley was named editor of the newly created *Latter-day Saints' Millennial Star*, which became the Church's longest continuous periodical—1840 to 1970.

Upon his return to Nauvoo, Parley was called to preside over the branches of the Church in New England and the Mid-Atlantic states with headquarters in New York City. Here he published a periodical entitled *The Prophet*.

February 1846 found Parley and his family crossing the territory of Iowa on a forced move from Illinois. During the summer and autumn of 1847, he traveled with his household to the Salt Lake Valley.

In 1851 the First Presidency called Elder Pratt to preside over a "General Mission to the Pacific" with headquarters in San Francisco. Sensing a duty to the peoples of Latin America, he, with his wife Phebe Soper, and Elder Rufus Allen, sailed to Valparaiso, Chile, in September 1851. Frustrated by language difficulties, poverty, the death of an infant son, and the ecclesiastical and political conditions in Chile, the missionaries returned to San Francisco in March 1852.

His publication *A Voice of Warning* (1837) became a model for other writers. The format, which employed descriptions of basic LDS doctrines and biblical references, arguments, and examples, was used by most Church writers for the next century. It was the first use of a book, other than the standard works, to spread the gospel message (Crawley, 1982, p. 15). His contributions to the dissemination of doctrine were extensive, and among his most significant works are *Late Persecutions of the Church of Jesus Christ of Latter-day Saints . . . With a Sketch of Their Rise, Progress and Doctrine* (1840); *Key to the Science of Theology* (1855); *The Millennium and Other Poems: To Which Is Annexed, a Treatise on the Regeneration of Matter* (1840); and the *Autobiography of Parley Parker Pratt* (1874). (For additional publications, see Crawley, 1990; Robison, 1952.)

In 1856 Elder Pratt was called to another mission to the Eastern states. While returning to the West on May 13, 1857, he was killed by a man who had been seeking to murder him. This occurred about twelve miles northeast of Van Buren, Arkansas (S. Pratt, 1975). A monument now marks the site of his burial. Through the enduring legacy of his doctrinal writings, hymns, and poems, Parley Parker Pratt continues to instruct and inspire each new generation.

BIBLIOGRAPHY

Crawley, Peter L. "Parley P. Pratt: Father of Mormon Pamphleteering." *Dialogue* 15 (Autumn 1982):13–26.

———. *The Essential Parley P. Pratt*. Salt Lake City, 1990.

Pratt, Parley P. *Autobiography of Parley P. Pratt*, ed. Parley P. Pratt, Jr. Salt Lake City, 1874 and 1938.

Pratt, Steven. "Eleanor McLean and the Murder of Parley P. Pratt." *BYU Studies* 15 (Winter 1975):225–56.
Robison, Parley Parker. *The Writings of Parley Parker Pratt*. Salt Lake City, 1952.

LARRY C. PORTER

PROPHET JOSEPH SMITH

[*Joseph Smith, Jr., Prophet and first President of The Church of Jesus Christ of Latter-day Saints, is the primary subject of several entries and is mentioned prominently in many more. For a brief biography and articles on his teachings and writings, see* Smith, Joseph: the Prophet. *See also* History of the Church: c. 1820–1831 *and* c. 1831–1844 *and numerous articles relating to Joseph Smith cross-referenced there. For a history of Joseph Smith's prophetic ministry prepared under his direction, see* History of the Church (History of Joseph Smith).

Regarding Joseph Smith's early prophetic experiences, see First Vision; Moroni, Visitations of; *and* Sacred Grove. *During one of Moroni's visits in 1827, Joseph Smith received the* Gold Plates *from which he translated by the "gift and power of God" the Book of Mormon. For other visions and visitations, see* Visions of Joseph Smith.

In company with Oliver Cowdery, *Joseph Smith received divine authority. Thus authorized, they proceeded with the organization of the Church in 1830. Numerous revelations given through Joseph Smith guided the infant organization.*

Joseph Smith's mission focused on the restoration of the gospel of Jesus Christ, including the first principles of the gospel and its ordinances; he encouraged the gathering of the Saints and laid the foundation for the establishment of Zion and the New Jerusalem in preparation for the second coming of Christ.]

R

REFORMATION (LDS) OF 1856–1857

A reform movement initiated by Church leaders in 1856–1857 to rekindle faith and testimony throughout the Church has long been known as the Mormon Reformation. Motivations for reform had as much to do with the lofty expectations of Church leaders as with the spiritual complacency or deficiency of the Saints. The Reformation occurred in a period of optimism and anticipation, as Church leaders hoped to create the unified society viewed as a necessary precursor to the Millennium. With the Saints now secluded in their Rocky Mountain retreat, a reemphasis of basic principles seemed especially appropriate.

The Mormon Reformation commenced in early September 1856, when President Brigham YOUNG sent his counselor Jedediah M. Grant to preach reform in settlements north of Salt Lake City. While speaking to assembled Saints, Grant was prompted to commit them to reform and to instruct them to signify that commitment through rebaptism. Grant's success had a contagious effect, and within days Saints in other settlements were also being rebaptized.

Early reform efforts, influenced by President Grant's unbridled enthusiasm, were somewhat spontaneous. The revivalistic spirit, the anxious confession, and the mass rebaptisms, however, gradually gave way to more judicious and ordered reform. The reform became especially systematic at Church headquarters, where a policy was established to have two home missionaries assigned to each ward. Equipped with a twenty-seven-question catechism to help measure the worthiness of the Saints, the home missionaries assisted families with everything from hygiene and church attendance to obeying the Ten Commandments. Only after some months of missionary-member visits were Saints in the Salt Lake City wards rebaptized in early spring of 1857. In Salt Lake City, rebaptism generally marked the formal end of the Reformation, though reform fervor continued until mid-1858.

Under instructions from President Young, the Reformation was carried to settlements and missions throughout the world. While procedures differed somewhat in areas away from Utah, rebaptism was a requirement for all faithful Saints. It symbolized both forgiveness of sin and a recommitment to obey commandments. Those who refused to be rebaptized might lose their membership in the Church. In Britain, zealous application of Reformation principles resulted in trimming from Church rolls a large number of the less-committed.

The era of the Reformation is often regarded as a controversial period. Some critics have claimed that blood atonement was practiced at this time. While President Young did preach that forgiveness for certain sins could come only through the sinner's shedding his blood, such comments reflect his style more than his intent. Many of Brigham Young's utterances were rhetorical and designed to encourage (or even frighten) Saints into gospel conformity. While publicly he threatened, privately he instructed Church leaders to forgive those who expressed sorrow for sin and repented.

For many Latter-day Saints, the Reformation was a period of spiritual rejuvenation. Attending meetings, paying tithing and other free-will offerings, and showing other outward indicators of renewal increased dramatically. The Reformation also had the effect of separating "wheat from chaff." Some members were disconcerted by the processes and the effects of reform and chose to leave LDS settlements. Perhaps the most damaging legacy from the point of view of Latter-day Saints was the grist the Reformation provided anti-Mormon writers who for decades would inaccurately characterize the period as a "reign of terror."

It may be that both critics and apologists have claimed too much for the Reformation. Certainly the reform impulse was on the whole more structured and restrained than has often been believed. Conversely, it appears that the major impact was of short duration and only moderate consequence—perhaps because the UTAH EXPEDITION and impending armed conflict abruptly ended the main thrust of the movement less than a year after it began.

BIBLIOGRAPHY

Larson, Gustive O. "The Mormon Reformation." *Utah Historical Quarterly* 26 (Jan. 1958):45–63.

Peterson, Paul H. "The Mormon Reformation of 1856–1857: The Rhetoric and the Reality." *Journal of Mormon History* 15 (1989):59–87.

PAUL H. PETERSON

REORGANIZED CHURCH OF JESUS CHRIST OF LATTER DAY SAINTS (RLDS CHURCH)

The RLDS church emerged during the 1850s from the conflict and schism that arose in Mormonism after the June 27, 1844, murder of Joseph SMITH, Jr., its founding PROPHET. From 1834 to 1844, Smith had indicated as many as eight possible modes of prophetic succession. One of these was a designation of his son Joseph III (1832–1914) to succeed him as prophet-president. He had not, however, chosen anyone to lead pro tempore until his son should be old enough to preside. During the decade following Smith's assassination, Mormonism split into more than a dozen factions. The main body of believers accepted the Quorum of the Twelve Apostles as their leaders. They remained headquartered at Nauvoo, Illinois, until 1846, when they fled to the Great Salt Basin of present-day Utah. Brigham YOUNG, the senior apostle, who had been President of the Quorum of the Twelve since April 14, 1840, organized the westward trek and was sustained as President in the First Presidency of The Church of Jesus Christ of Latter-day Saints in 1847.

Jason W. Briggs (1821–1899), leader of the Beloit, Wisconsin, branch, rejected Brigham Young's leadership in 1848 to affiliate with the faction led by James J. Strang (1813–1856). After Strang opted for polygamy in 1850, Briggs left to join a colony led by the slain prophet's younger brother, William B. Smith (1811–1893). Briggs left

Smith in the fall of 1851 on learning that Smith was also a polygamist.

On November 18, 1851, Briggs sought and received what he felt to be divine revelation regarding the future of the church. His followers distributed copies of the record of Briggs's revelation to nearby branches. The four major thrusts of the document were to denounce other claimants to prophetic authority; to enjoin the elders to preach against false doctrines that had overtaken the church; to instruct the elders to teach the original gospel law as found in the Bible, the Book of Mormon, and the Doctrine and Covenants; and to promise that from the lineage of Joseph Smith, Jr., would come the proper leader of the church. Zenas H. Gurley, Sr. (1801–1871), pastor of a church branch at Yellow Stone, Wisconsin, read the Briggs message to his people. Gurley had also rejected the leadership of Brigham Young, James Strang, and William Smith at about the same time as Briggs, his new ally. During the winter and spring of 1852 a nucleus of Saints in Wisconsin and northern Illinois began to effect what they felt to be a bona fide continuation of the original church.

The first formal conference of church elders of this emerging movement met on June 12–13, 1852, near Beloit, Wisconsin. The conference passed measures endorsing and enlarging on the sentiments expounded in the record of Briggs's revelation. The conference also ordered publication of a pamphlet supporting those measures and called for the convening of a second conference in October.

The October conference heard the pamphlet read, and authorized Jason Briggs to publish 2,000 copies of it as a means to inform the public of the basis of the emerging RLDS movement. In the publication process, three more pages were added condemning polygamy. A pivotal conference convened in April 1853, at which seven new apostles were chosen by a committee and ordained. This interim group presided over the church until the lineal successor to the founding prophet became available. The autumn conference of 1856 sent two representatives to the home of Joseph Smith III near Nauvoo, Illinois, to officially invite him to head the church. Smith firmly declined, but on the strength of later revelatory experiences, he accepted in early 1860. On April 6, 1860, Joseph Smith III became prophet-president of the RLDS church at its conference, at

Amboy, Illinois. For early "reorganizers," the long-held conviction of lineal succession in presidency was now enacted.

Smith was both strongly opposed to polygamy and deeply convinced that his father could have had nothing to do with its inception in the church. He and other RLDS leaders, writers, missionaries, and members fought for decades to project the image of original Latter Day Saintism as nonpolygamous. The public outcry against Utah Latter-day Saints for their polygamous doctrine and practice, however, together with the similarity of the two churches' names, greatly complicated the RLDS effort to mark itself as separate from Utah Mormonism.

Polygamy was the most clear-cut issue that RLDS people used to disassociate themselves from the LDS Church, and to arouse public antipathy against Utah Mormonism. Other issues, however, also placed Utah Mormonism and the RLDS church on opposite sides of an ideological boundary. Some of these stemmed from teachings Joseph Smith, Jr., had put in place in the Nauvoo setting (1839–1844). By the end of the century, the RLDS church was either repudiating them or taking a wait-and-see posture. Rejected were such doctrines as the political kingdom of God, militarism (i.e., military organizations such as the Nauvoo Legion), the Adam-God theory (*see* YOUNG, BRIGHAM: TEACHINGS), plural gods, exclusion of blacks from priesthood offices, and absolute theocracy. In the wait-and-see category were the temple and its system of saving rituals for both dead and living, the book of Abraham, and strictly enforced restrictions on the use of coffee, alcohol, and tobacco.

In finding much of its nineteenth-century identity along this "Mormon boundary," the RLDS church marked out a difficult course of development. Missionaries working among Utah Mormons tried to convince their audiences that the RLDS church adhered to the "true Mormonism." When trying to persuade Protestant prospects, on the other hand, RLDS ministers were inclined to deemphasize aspects linking them with Mormonism and to focus on the common ground they shared with mainstream Christianity.

The resulting ambiguity within the RLDS church created recurring seasons of internal theological conflict. The church elders and leaders, until well into the twentieth century, tried to resolve much of that friction in the setting of their general conferences. Joseph Smith III and other leaders felt inclined to resolve only the most critical conflicts through revelatory fiat of the prophet. This means that for the most part the RLDS church has pursued a delicate, operational balance between the democratic and theocratic modes of church governance.

Joseph Smith III's early policy of restraining the scattered RLDS membership from gathering to one central location had a lasting effect on church development. Smith remembered the persecution the early Saints had suffered wherever they colonized en masse. He urged his followers to embody their Christian religion as fully as possible wherever they lived, widely dispersed as they were. From his headquarters office in Plano, Illinois, Smith repeatedly editorialized in the church periodical, the *True Latter Day Saints' Herald*, cautioning the widely scattered church branches to put down their roots where they were. He urged them to build solid foundations of Christian witness and community responsibility as a prerequisite to any ultimate recolonization to Independence, Missouri.

The "gathering" impulse within the membership, however, remained strong. In 1870 a group of men of means incorporated the "First United Order of Enoch." Under its charter, stockholders bought several thousand acres of land in Decatur County, Iowa, and began farming and related agri-business enterprises. There they built up the town of Lamoni (a Book of Mormon name), which in 1881 became the church headquarters and home of the church press and of its editor in chief, President Joseph Smith III.

A number of Mormons either on the trail west through Iowa or newly arrived in the Great Salt Lake Basin left the West or the trail to unite with RLDS branches in southwest Iowa. By 1890 the center of RLDS church population (about 25,000) had shifted from Illinois to Iowa. Even Missouri, with rapidly expanding membership in and around St. Louis and Independence, had pulled ahead of Illinois. The church in 1895 founded Graceland College at Lamoni (its 1990 enrollment was more than 1,300).

Smith's death in December 1914 brought his son Frederick M. Smith (1874–1946), a counselor in the First Presidency since 1902, to the prophetic office. The primary emphases of Frederick M. Smith's thirty-one-year presidency were centralization of administrative control into a more theocratic mode; practical and theological training for the church's ministry; physical, cultural, and educational development of the "Center Place" in and around Independence, Missouri, as the new headquarters of the church (moved from Lamoni in 1920) and the primary place of Zionic witness; mobilization of the membership into stewardship communal enterprises, especially in and near the Center Place; and a heightened effort to streamline and expand the church's missionary effort.

Smith's plans for church expansion and development suffered from resistance to change within the church, both at the General Officer and local levels. Even more vexing were economic dislocations in the larger world. Two worldwide armed conflicts, the severe economic panic of 1920–1921, and the Great Depression of the 1930s deferred many of his hoped-for church goals. Several years of deficit spending brought the church to a financial crisis in 1931. An austere fiscal management policy designed by Presiding Bishop L. F. P. Curry (1887–1977) and his counselor, G. L. DeLapp (1895–1981), inspired the confidence of the members. Their sacrificial giving enabled liquidation of the nearly $2 million debt by January 1942. The membership ranks grew throughout F. M. Smith's presidency, from 74,000 in 1915 to nearly 133,000 at his death on March 20, 1946. One of his building enterprises, the vast Auditorium in Independence—headquarters and General Conference center—begun in 1926, was in use by 1928, but remained unfinished until 1962.

Israel A. Smith (1876–1958), brother of Frederick, became RLDS president in April 1946. During his twelve-year tenure, the church built financial reserves and greatly expanded its missionary forces. In Independence it founded Resthaven, a home for the elderly; the School of the Restoration, for education of church leaders and members; and the Social Service Center, a facility for various helps to the needy. The church's hospital, with financial aid from the community at large, expanded greatly. This period was also a time of local church-building activity, with hundreds of branches either building new churches or expanding old ones. The church also added to its educational facilities at Graceland College.

William Wallace Smith (1900–1989), the third son of Joseph Smith III to serve as church president, was ordained to that office in October 1958. Utilizing the skills of many, he planted the RLDS church in more than twenty nations. This expansion has continued steadily in the years since his retirement in April 1978.

This recent crossing of cultural boundaries has stimulated much ideological and theological ferment within the church. Leaders soon realized that the task was more than merely extending an American church into other cultures. International diversity required the church to seek ways to magnify the Christian witness in other cultures in terms compatible with the life experiences and expectations of divergent peoples and worldviews. This quest prompted RLDS leaders to attempt to identify the "universal" aspects of the gospel that might find a place in other cultures while being adapted to indigenous values and needs. The church's General Officers then realized the necessity for pluralism, since what were earlier thought to be universals were now seen as particulars.

An urgently felt task issuing from this realization was the development of a theological base appropriate to a worldwide, multicultural church. This task required rigorous theological study, consultation, and synthesis. RLDS leaders participated in seminars on history, theology, evangelism, planning, Zionic concepts and procedures, higher education, and professional development. In the early stages of these programs, the First Presidency and the Council of Twelve Apostles in 1966 announced five new objectives to guide future church development. The first of these called the church to clarify its theology and unify the members in their faith. A special committee on basic beliefs, appointed years earlier, gained several new members who had pursued formal theological training. The newly constituted committee compiled essays explicating the various aspects of the faith. Its report, *Exploring the Faith*, issued in 1971, called the whole church to serious theological exploration and reflection.

As they entered into this complex process, many RLDS leaders and members experienced considerable anxiety. The neo-orthodox Christian theological stances taken in *Exploring the Faith* and in many other works from the church's press in the 1960s and 1970s did not fit some of the more traditional views. For example, the fifth objective of 1966 called for an interpretation of Zion "in worldwide terms." As church leaders pursued this process, they began to speak and write of Zion, not only as a remnant colony of Saints in Missouri but also as a leavening process—a source of redemptive social change all over the world. This called the church to be a covenant people, transforming culture from within, wherever they lived.

A vocal minority of RLDS members viewed this concept and its implications as a total rejection of the early "remnant" image. They began to resist the church's pastoral, theological, educational, and programmatic efforts to nurture a wider, pluralistic application of the Zionic dimension. The resistance inhered in the fact that the expanding interpretation of Zion appeared to some to be a loss of loyalty by current leaders to the perpetual authority of the scriptures and to other statements of Joseph Smith, Jr., about the Zionic endeavor.

W. Wallace Smith's revelatory instruction of 1968 called the church to begin preparations for building a temple in Independence. This stirred much discussion, among both leaders and members, about the extent to which such an edifice would fit earlier temple purposes, either at Kirtland, Ohio (1834–1836) or Nauvoo (1840–1846). Very little along these lines was determined during W. Wallace Smith's tenure in office. The consensus was that the proposed temple was to have more in common with Kirtland's House of the Lord than with the Nauvoo Temple, in terms of educational and worship functions. The Temple School came into being in 1974, with a focus on leadership education related to the future temple. Graceland College president Dr. William T. Higdon (1929–), was called into the Council of Twelve Apostles at that time and assigned as president of Temple School. Clearly RLDS leadership was committed to a strong educational component as part of temple planning. Also during the late 1970s, the church took on a heavy financial and personnel commitment when it began to sponsor and operate Park College in Kansas City, Missouri.

Wallace B. Smith (1929–), son of W. Wallace Smith, became prophet of the RLDS church on April 5, 1978, having been chosen as "prophet and president designate" two years earlier. Leaving his practice of ophthalmology, Smith spent two years in rigorous theological studies to prepare for his presidency. The two most far-reaching leadership moves since his ordination are reflected in his revelatory instruction to the 1984 World Conference: section 156 of the RLDS Doctrine and Covenants.

Section 156:9–10 meant that the church would now move ahead with women's ordinations, a breakthrough foreshadowed by events dating back to 1970. Local pastors had been initiating priesthood calls for women since 1974, but no clear precedent permitted actual ordination. Now, the conference's approval of section 156 created the context for the ordination of women, the first ones being ordained November 17, 1985. This cluster of events led to intense conflict in scattered areas of the RLDS Church. An effort to rescind section 156 at the 1986 world conference failed decisively. Proponents of rescission continued to work to strengthen networks of resistance. Some formed what they call "independent branches," which defy the authority of the RLDS church on all matters. It is impossible to measure the extent of the disaffection, but it probably numbers about 3 percent of the 240,000 total membership.

Section 156:3–6 pointed the church in a new direction by setting forth the general purposes of the temple. The document declared that the primary purpose of the temple would be the "pursuit of peace, reconciliation, healing of the spirit." It would be built also to nurture "an attitude of wholeness of body, mind, and spirit." Furthermore, the temple would express the "essential meaning of the church as healing and redeeming agent, inspired by the life and witness of the redeemer of the world." Finally, the temple would require and enable new programs of leadership education in expansion of the ministries of all the priesthood and members of the church.

Section 156 also enjoined the church to redouble its efforts to finance and build the temple. Ground was broken for the temple at the 1990 World Conference, where it was also announced that more than $61 million had been pledged toward the $75 million needed for its completion and its supporting endowment fund.

As of 1990, the RLDS church stood at a new turning point in its history. More than 3,000 women ordained to all offices of priesthood except the General Officer category were adding new styles and depths of caring ministries not before experienced in the church. The developing Temple School courses and the programs of the Temple Ministries Division have begun to create new life and energy in RLDS branches and members in many of the forty nations where the church is established. Since World War II, the RLDS church has also become much more ecumenical than at any previous time. A resolution passed at the 1990 World Conference requested the First Presidency to go beyond the bounds of the church for help. The specific intent was that the RLDS church would seek those whose experience and expertise would equip them to give valuable help to the forthcoming temple programs in the area of peace and justice.

The RLDS church seems intent on shedding many of the vestiges of its sectarian background of early Mormonism. To what extent it can discard these while retaining its identity as a recognizable part of Latter Day Saintism remains to be seen.

BIBLIOGRAPHY

Blair, Alma R. "The Tradition of Dissent—Jason W. Briggs." In *Restoration Studies I*, pp. 146–61. Independence, Mo., 1980.

Booth, Howard J. "Recent Shifts in Restoration Thought." In *Restoration Studies I*, pp. 162–75. Independence, Mo., 1980.

Davis, Inez Smith. *The Story of the Church*. Independence, Mo., 1969.

Edwards, F. Henry. *The History of The Reorganized Church of Jesus Christ of Latter Day Saints*, Vols. 5–8. Independence, Mo., 1970–1976.

Higdon, Barbara. "The Reorganization in the Twentieth Century." *Dialogue* 7 (Spring 1972):94–100.

Judd, Peter, and Bruce Lindgren. *An Introduction to the Saints' Church*. Independence, Mo., 1976.

Launius, Roger D. *Joseph Smith III: Pragmatic Prophet*. Chicago, 1988.

McMurray, W. Grant. "True Son of a True Father: Joseph Smith III and the Succession Question." In *Restoration Studies I*, pp. 131–45. Independence, Mo., 1980.

Newell, Linda King, and Valeen Tippetts Avery. *Mormon Enigma: Emma Hale Smith: Prophet's Wife, "Elect Lady," Polygamy's Foe, 1804–1879*. New York, 1984.

Smith, Joseph, III, and Heman C. Smith. *The History of The Reorganized Church of Jesus Christ of Latter Day Saints*, Vols. 1–4. Lamoni, Iowa, 1896–1903.

Vlahos, Clare D. "Images of Orthodoxy: Self-Identity in Early Reorganization Apologetics." In *Restoration Studies I*, pp. 176–88. Independence, Mo., 1980.

RICHARD P. HOWARD

REYNOLDS V. UNITED STATES

Reynolds v. United States (98 U.S. 145 [1879]) was the first U.S. Supreme Court decision to interpret the "free exercise" language of the First Amendment to the U.S. Constitution. In giving an extremely narrow interpretation to that guarantee of religious freedom, the *Reynolds* decision opened the way for legal suppression of the Mormon practice of PLURAL MARRIAGE.

The Morrill Act (Act of July 1, 1862, 12 Stat. 501), which defined the crime of bigamy in U.S. territories, had been adopted for the express purpose of outlawing Mormon polygamous marriages. The First Amendment, however, expressly states that Congress shall "make no law . . . prohibiting the free exercise" of religion. The issue posed by the *Reynolds* case was whether a federal bigamy statute could constitutionally be applied to a person who practiced polygamy as a matter of religious duty. The Court held that it could.

George Reynolds, an English immigrant to Utah, private secretary to Brigham Young, and husband of two wives, was found guilty in March 1875 of violating the antibigamy provision of the Morrill Act. The conviction was overturned by the Utah Supreme Court on procedural grounds (*United States v. Reynolds*, 1 Utah 226 [1875]), but on retrial he was again convicted and was sentenced to two years in prison with a $500 fine. This conviction was upheld by the U.S. Supreme Court.

In applying the First Amendment's free exercise clause, Chief Justice Morrison R. Waite concluded that "Congress was deprived of all legislative power over mere opinion, but was left free to reach actions which were in violation of social duties or subversive of good order" (98 U.S. 164). This distinction between protected religious *belief* and unprotected religious *actions* was followed for several decades, and this specific holding regarding plural marriage is still the law. Since 1940, however, the Court has said that religious conduct also may fall within the free exercise guarantee (*Cantwell v. Connecticut*, 310 U.S. 296).

The Morrill Act was not an effective weapon against polygamy because of the difficulty of obtaining testimony to prove the plural marriages. Nevertheless, the *Reynolds* decision paved the way for other, more enforceable federal laws that penalized "unlawful cohabitation," disincorporated the Church, and forfeited its property. Ultimately at the direction of its Prophet, President Wilford Woodruff, the Church submitted to those laws and discontinued the practice of plural marriage.

[*See also* Antipolygamy Legislation; Manifesto of 1890.]

BIBLIOGRAPHY

Davis, Ray J. "Plural Marriage and Religious Freedom: The Impact of *Reynolds v. United States*." *Arizona Law Review* 15 (1974):287–306.

Firmage, Edwin Brown. *Zion in the Courts*, pp. 151–59. Urbana, Ill., 1988.

ROBERT E. RIGGS

RICHMOND JAIL

When the Latter-day Saints at Far West, Caldwell County, Missouri, surrendered to the state militia in late October 1838, seven Church leaders—Joseph SMITH, Hyrum SMITH, Sidney RIGDON, Parley P. PRATT, Lyman Wight, Amasa Lyman, and George W. Robinson—were arrested (*see* MISSOURI CONFLICT). They were first taken under guard to Independence, Jackson County, Missouri, and then to Richmond, the county seat of Ray County. They were confined on November 9, not in the county jail but in a small vacant house on the town square. Here they were imprisoned for three weeks to await a court inquiry into charges of treason, murder, arson, robbery, and perjury. Other Saints were also arrested and brought to Richmond for trial.

At the inquiry on November 28, the prisoners were bound over for trial, and Joseph Smith and five others were removed to a jail in Liberty, Clay County, Missouri, to await further hearings (*see* LIBERTY JAIL). Pratt and four others remained in the Richmond County Jail, some until late April 1839 and others until June 1839.

During the time Joseph Smith was incarcerated in Richmond, the prisoners were chained together under miserable conditions and constant harassment. One incident during the imprisonment has become a legend. Pratt recalled that Joseph Smith, chagrined at the verbal abuse, boasting, and obscenity by the guards, stood up in chains and commanded, "SILENCE, ye fiends of the infernal pit. In the name of Jesus Christ I rebuke you, and command you to be still; I will not live another minute and hear such language. Cease such talk, or you or I die this instant!" (p. 221). The tormenters reportedly fell silent.

The Richmond Jail no longer stands, and no marker designates its location.

BIBLIOGRAPHY

Gentry, Leland H. "A History of the Latter-day Saints in Northern Missouri from 1836 to 1839." Ph.D. diss., Brigham Young University, 1965.

LeSueur, Stephen C. "'High Treason and Murder': The Examination of Mormon Prisoners at Richmond, Missouri." *BYU Studies* 26 (Spring 1986):3–30.

Pratt, Parley P. *Autobiography of Parley Parker Pratt*. Salt Lake City, 1980.

HOWARD A. CHRISTY

RIGDON, SIDNEY

Sidney Rigdon (1793–1876) was one of Joseph SMITH's closest friends and advisers. He was also a renowned early convert to the Church, its most persuasive orator in the first decade, and First Counselor in the First Presidency from 1832 to 1844. Following the Prophet Joseph Smith's martyrdom, Rigdon became one of the Church's best-known apostates.

Rigdon was born February 19, 1793, on a farm in St. Clair Township, near Pittsburgh, Pennsylvania, the fourth child and youngest son of William and Nancy Briant Rigdon. In 1817, while supporting his widowed mother on the family farm, Rigdon experienced Christian conversion and a year later qualified himself to become a licensed preacher with the Regular Baptists. He moved to eastern Ohio to preach under the tutelage of Adamson Bentley, a popular Baptist minister, and in June 1820 he married Phebe Brooks, Bentley's sister-in-law. After ordination as a Baptist minister, Rigdon became pastor of the First Baptist Church in Pittsburgh in 1821. Famed for his dynamic preaching, Rigdon attracted listeners until his congregation became one of the largest in the city. One of his critics, William Hayden, described him as being of "medium height, rotund in form; of countenance, while speaking, open and winning, with a little cast of melancholy. His action was graceful, his language copious, fluent in utterance, with articulation clear and musical" (quoted in Chase, p. 24).

Throughout his early ministry, Rigdon kept looking for the pure New Testament church that practiced laying on of hands for the gift of the Holy Ghost and healing the sick. Drawn to Alexander Campbell and Walter Scott, fellow ministers with similar views, Rigdon associated with leading members of the Mahoning Baptist Association, the forerunner of the restorationist Disciples of Christ movement. In 1826 he became the pastor of a Grand River Association congregation in Mentor, Ohio. In 1830, however, Rigdon broke with Campbell and Scott, who went on to form the Disciples of Christ, while Rigdon established a communal "family" near Kirtland.

In late October 1830 four Mormon missionaries visited Rigdon in Ohio. One was Parley P. Pratt, whom Rigdon had converted to the reformed Baptists a year earlier. Pratt told Rigdon about the Book of

Mormon and the restoration of the gospel through Joseph Smith. After two weeks of earnest investigation, Rigdon announced that he believed the new church to be the true apostolic church restored to the earth. In mid-November 1830 he was baptized and ordained an elder. More than a hundred members of his Kirtland congregation and common stock community followed him into the Church.

Rigdon, along with Edward Partridge, a young hatter who was interested in Mormonism, left almost immediately for Fayette, New York, to meet Joseph Smith. After their arrival, a revelation to Joseph commended Rigdon for his previous service, but called him to "a greater work," including that of scribe to the Prophet on his "new translation" of the Bible then under way (D&C 35). In December 1830, Smith, with Rigdon's help, worked on the manuscript that eventually became the seventh and eighth chapters of the Book of Moses in the Pearl of Great Price.

Rigdon's report of the harvest of souls in the Mentor-Kirtland area in Ohio may have encouraged Joseph to ask for guidance on moving the headquarters of the Church; in December 1830 a revelation commanded them to leave New York for Ohio (D&C 37; cf. 38). On February 1, 1831, Joseph and Sidney arrived in Kirtland, where they renewed their work on the inspired translation of the Bible.

In the summer of 1831, Joseph, Sidney, and other leaders journeyed to Independence, Missouri, which a revelation identified as the location of the latter-day Zion and the New Jerusalem. Sidney was instructed to dedicate the land of Zion for the gathering of the Saints and to write a description of the country for publication (D&C 58:50). Upon their return to Ohio, Joseph and Sidney resumed the translation of the scriptures, and on February 16, 1832, they jointly received the vision of the degrees of glory that is now Doctrine and Covenants section 76. In March 1832 they were brutally attacked by a mob and tarred and feathered. Sidney received head injuries that occasionally affected his emotional stability for the rest of his life. His friend Newel K. Whitney said that thereafter he was "either in the bottom of the cellar or up in the garrett window" (Chase, p. 115).

In March 1833 Sidney Rigdon and Frederick G. Williams were formally set apart as counselors to Joseph Smith in the First Presidency. Sidney had already been called as a counselor to Joseph a year earlier, before there was a First Presidency. In 1833 Rigdon was also called to be a "spokesman" for the Church and for Joseph Smith. Rigdon was promised that he would be "mighty in expounding all scriptures" (D&C 100:11). At this same time, Joseph said of him, "Brother Sidney is a man whom I love, but he is not capable of that pure and steadfast love for those who are his benefactors that should characterize a President of the Church of Christ. This, with some other little things, such as selfishness and independence of mind . . . are his faults. But notwithstanding these things, he is a very great and good man; a man of great power of words, and can gain the friendship of his hearers very quickly. He is a man whom God will uphold, if he will continue faithful to his calling" (*HC* 1:443).

In 1834 Rigdon assisted in recruiting volunteers for ZION'S CAMP and, while Joseph was away on that undertaking, had charge of affairs in Kirtland, including the construction of the temple (*see* KIRTLAND TEMPLE). He was a leading teacher at the Kirtland school and helped arrange the revelations for publication in the 1835 edition of the Doctrine and Covenants (*see* SCHOOLS OF THE PROPHETS). Under the Prophet's direction, Sidney helped compose and deliver many of the doctrinally rich Lectures on Faith. He often preached long, extravagant biblically based sermons, notably one at the dedication of the Kirtland Temple. In the persecution that followed the failure of the Kirtland Safety Society, Rigdon, along with Joseph Smith and other Saints, fled for their lives to Far West, Missouri, in 1838. There Rigdon delivered two famous volatile speeches, the Salt Sermon and the Independence Day oration, both of which stirred up fears and controversy in Missouri and contributed to the EXTERMINATION ORDER and the Battle of Far West (*see* MISSOURI CONFLICT). With Joseph and Hyrum Smith, Rigdon was taken prisoner and locked up in LIBERTY JAIL, but was released early because of severe apoplectic seizures.

Rigdon took an active part in the founding of Nauvoo and in 1839 accompanied Joseph Smith to Washington, D.C., to present the grievances of the Saints to the federal government. He was elected to the Nauvoo City Council and served also as city attorney, postmaster, and professor of Church history in the embryonic university projected for the city. Despite his many appointments, however, he was nearly silent during this time and often sick. He was accused of being associated with John C. Bennett and other enemies of the Church in their seditious plans to displace Joseph Smith, but this he always denied. He did not endorse the principle of plural marriage, although he never came out in open opposition to it. Joseph Smith eventually lost confidence in Rigdon and in 1843 wished to reject him as a counselor, but because of the intercession of Hyrum SMITH, retained him in office.

Early in 1844, when Joseph Smith became a candidate for president of the United States, Rigdon was nominated as his running mate and he established residence in Pittsburgh to carry on the campaign. He was there when news arrived of Joseph Smith's murder. He hastened to Nauvoo to offer himself as a "guardian of the Church," promising to act as such until Joseph Smith was resurrected from the dead. His claims were duly considered, but at a memorable meeting in Nauvoo on August 8, 1844, Church members rejected him as guardian. The Twelve Apostles were sustained as the head of the Church. When he undertook to establish a rival leadership, Rigdon was excommunicated in September 1844 and left with a few disciples for Pennsylvania, where they organized a Church of Christ. Acting erratically, he lost most of his followers in less than two years. In 1863, he made another effort, founding the Church of Jesus Christ of the Children of Zion, which continued into the 1880s. From 1847 to his death in 1876, Rigdon resided in Friendship, New York, usually in a state of emotional imbalance and unhappiness.

In 1834, in *Mormonism Unvailed*, Eber D. Howe attacked the authenticity of the Book of Mormon by adopting Philastus Hurlbut's argument that Sidney Rigdon purloined the "Manuscript Story" of Solomon Spaulding, plagiarized it to compose the Book of Mormon, and gave it to Joseph Smith to publish under his name. During his lifetime Rigdon and members of his family consistently denied any connection with Spaulding, and after the discovery in 1885 of one of Spaulding's manuscripts, the story was discredited.

BIBLIOGRAPHY

Backman, Milton V., Jr. *The Heavens Resound: A History of the Latter-day Saints in Ohio, 1830–1838*. Salt Lake City, 1983.

Chase, Daryl. "Sidney Rigdon—Early Mormon." Master's thesis, University of Chicago, 1931.

McKiernan, F. Mark. *The Voice of One Crying in the Wilderness: Sidney Rigdon, Religious Reformer 1793–1876*. Lawrence, Kan., 1971.

BRUCE A. VAN ORDEN

ROBISON, LOUISE YATES

Louise Yates Robison (1866–1946) succeeded Clarissa Williams to become the seventh general president of the Relief Society of The Church of Jesus Christ of Latter-day Saints in October 1928 and led that society through the difficult years of the Great Depression (1928–1939). She had previously served as second counselor to President Williams in the general presidency. These two women had become friends while they prepared surgical dressings for the Red Cross during World War I. Louise Robison's name rarely appears on lists of outstanding LDS women, an obscurity that would have pleased this unassuming, down-to-earth woman of plain appearance and quiet ways; nevertheless, she deserves recognition for several unique contributions to the Church and for the important principle of service she exemplified.

Born May 27, 1866, in the small rural town of Scipio, in south-central Utah, Louise grew up in a log house where she learned pioneer values from her parents, Thomas and Elizabeth Yates. Her early marriage to Joseph L. Robison and subsequent rearing of six children shortened her studies at Brigham Young Academy, but her love of books and learning was lifelong. A six-month course in dressmaking at age fifteen helped prepare her for future service on the Relief Society General Board, where she directed the Temple and Burial Clothing Department.

As General President of the Relief Society, one of her practical responses to women's needs during the Depression of the 1930s was to establish Mormon Handicraft in 1937. This shop enabled Relief Society women to sell homemade gift items on consignment. The shop reflected President Robison's appreciation both for the handiwork of women and for their role as mothers in the home. It flourished under the Relief Society until 1986, when management of the store was transferred to the Deseret Book Company.

Louise Robison believed that burdens could be lightened with song. A daughter later remembered that she sang, or sometimes whistled, while doing her work at home. "A singing mother makes a happy home," she said when she named the popular Relief Society choral groups Singing Mothers in 1934.

Several modest historic achievements can be credited to

President Robison. She was the first Relief Society general president to address a regular session of a general conference (October 1929). She was the first to visit the Relief Societies in Great Britain, and on that trip she also served as a delegate to the Tenth World Congress of the International Council of Women, held in Paris. In 1933 she instigated the erection of a monument to the Relief Society on the site of its founding in NAUVOO, Illinois. Later relocated in the Monument to Women gardens, it is thought to be the first Church effort to mark its historic sites in Nauvoo.

Welfare Services was the greatest concern of President Robison's administration. Her longtime friend and coworker Belle SPAFFORD said that Louise Robison "stressed the volunteer compassionate services. 'Go where you're needed, do what you can'; that was her theme" (Spafford). She practiced what she preached, and the principle of personal service she exemplified was a needed counterpoint to the more structured Church welfare system.

After being released from service as Relief Society general president in 1939, Louise Robison lived in San Francisco with her daughter Gladys Winter. She died March 30, 1946.

BIBLIOGRAPHY

Gladys Robison Winter Collection. LDS Church Archives, Salt Lake City.

Mulvay Derr, Jill, and Susan Oman. "These Three Women." *Ensign* 8 (Feb. 1978):66–70.

Spafford, Belle S. *Oral History Interview with Jill Mulvay Derr*, November 1975–March 1976. LDS Church Archives, Salt Lake City.

JANATH RUSSELL CANNON

ROGERS, AURELIA SPENCER

Aurelia Spencer Rogers (1834–1922), the first Primary president of the Church, was born October 4, 1834, in Deep River, Connecticut, to Catherine Curtis and Orson Spencer, a Protestant minister. When Aurelia was six years old, her parents joined the Church and traveled to Nauvoo, Illinois. Years later, Aurelia's suggestions helped establish the Primary Association, the Church organization for children.

"Aurelia came by her concern for children through a long

apprenticeship in mothering" (Madsen, p. 1). At the age of twelve, she and her older sister, Ellen, cared for four younger siblings when their mother died and their father was called by Church leaders to head the missionary work in Great Britain. The children lived on their own in WINTER QUARTERS, Nebraska, with limited provisions and then made the arduous trek to the Great Salt Lake basin. Wilford Woodruff, a member of the Quorum of the Twelve Apostles, wrote their father that "although in childhood, their faith, patience, . . . longsuffering and wisdom . . . [were] such as would have done honor to a Saint of thirty years" (Rogers, pp. 103–104).

At age seventeen Aurelia married Thomas Rogers. Through the next twenty-two years, she gave birth to twelve children, of whom only seven survived infancy. When three infants died in succession, she despaired and nearly lost her faith and belief in God; but a letter from her father came to mind and helped her gradually overcome her malaise. Her travail through the loss of children heightened her sensitivity to the preciousness of life and to the importance of nurturing the young.

Thomas and Aurelia Rogers lived all their married life in Farmington, Utah, a community sixteen miles north of Salt Lake City. Observing the rowdiness of children on the street, Aurelia Rogers wondered if an organization could be formed to teach them better deportment and moral and spiritual values. She brought the matter to the attention of Eliza R. SNOW, president of the Relief Society, who shared her concern and subsequently gained the support of Church leaders.

On August 11, 1878, Aurelia Spencer Rogers was set apart as president of the Farmington Ward Primary, the first Primary in the Church. Her counselors, Louisa Haight and Helen M. Miller, helped her organize the children into age groups; and on August 25, 1878, they held the first Primary meeting, with 224 children present, beginning what is today a fully developed curriculum for children.

Although Eliza R. Snow and her immediate associates organized most of the Primaries throughout Church settlements, important impetus came from the work of Rogers in the development of Primary in and near Farmington, for which she received many honors. In 1897, in recognition of her role in founding the Primary, the children of the Church raised the funds to publish her book, *Life Sketches* (1898).

In the winter of 1894–1895, Aurelia Rogers also served as one of three Utah suffragist delegates to the Woman's Suffrage Convention in Atlanta and attended the Second Triennial Congress of the National Council of Women in Washington, D.C.

Although she suffered ill health for much of her life, Aurelia Rogers often said, "Cheerfulness and pleasant thoughts help to produce longevity" (p. 298). She must have practiced this principle, as she lived to be eighty-seven. She died August 19, 1922.

BIBLIOGRAPHY

Madsen, Carol Cornwall, and Susan Staker Oman. *Sisters and Little Saints: One Hundred Years of Primary*. Salt Lake City, 1979.

Rogers, Aurelia Spencer. *Life Sketches of Orson Spencer and Others, and History of Primary Work*. Salt Lake City, 1898.

SHIRLEY A. CAZIER

S

SACRED GROVE

A grove of trees on the Joseph SMITH, Sr., farm near Palmyra, New York, is revered by Latter-day Saints as the vicinity where Joseph SMITH experienced his FIRST VISION, the divine manifestation of God the Father and his Son Jesus Christ that began the restoration of the gospel in this dispensation. For that reason, Latter-day Saints honor the place as sacred. The grove is part of the forest that once covered the Smiths' 100-acre farm in Manchester Township as well as much of western New York.

The forest was some 400 years old when the family of Joseph Smith, Sr., moved to the site in 1818 or 1819. The large trees of the forest—maple, beech, elm, oak, and hickory—reached heights of up to 125 feet and diameters of 6 feet or more. Beneath this natural canopy grew hop hornbeam, wild cherry, and ash. The woodland floor was carpeted with leaves, ferns, grasses, wildflowers, and clumps of chokecherry and dogwood.

The Smiths cleared the trees from sixty acres of their property. The Sacred Grove was part of a fifteen-acre wooded tract at the farm's west end, reserved as a sugarbush, where trees were tapped for making maple syrup and sugar.

Subsequent owners of the farm maintained the grove, associating it with Joseph Smith's vision, although the exact location of the vision is unknown. In 1907 the Church purchased the farm and grove from William A. Chapman, and these sites formed the nucleus of the Church HISTORICAL SITES program, which at present includes properties from Vermont to Utah.

Through an ongoing professional maintenance program, the Church has retained much of the primeval beauty of the Sacred Grove. Trees that were mature at the time of Joseph Smith's boyhood still grace this forest. People from many lands visit the Sacred Grove each year. In 1989 the number of visitors exceeded 36,000.

BIBLIOGRAPHY

Backman, Milton V., Jr. *Joseph Smith's First Vision*, 2nd ed. Salt Lake City, 1980.

Enders, Donald L. "A Snug Log House." *Ensign* 15 (Aug. 1985):14–23.

Jessee, Dean C. "The Early Accounts of Joseph Smith's First Vision." *BYU Studies* 9 (Spring 1969):275–96.

DONALD L. ENDERS

SALT LAKE CITY, UTAH

Between July 21 and 23, 1847, an advance party of LDS men under Orson Pratt, an apostle, entered the Salt Lake Valley, placed a dam across City Creek, and began plowing and planting. President Brigham YOUNG arrived on July 24, and four days later designated the spot on the valley floor between City Creek's two forks as a site for the Salt Lake Temple, establishing what was then thought of as the center of Salt Lake City.

The valley had been inhabited by Indians—particularly Ute, Shoshone, and Gosiute—and had been visited by explorers before the Latter-day Saints entered the valley. Reports by explorers such as John C. Frémont and the blazing of the 1846 Donner-Reed trail helped further the LDS migration.

The city grew rapidly. Dividing it into what became twenty ecclesiastical wards in the nineteenth century, the Mormon pioneers laid out ten-acre blocks. The business district developed southward from the temple block on Main Street. At first most people engaged in agricultural, industrial, and merchandising enterprises, but eventually Salt Lake City became principally a commercial, manufacturing, and governmental center. By 1870, only 16.1 percent of the heads of households were farmers, compared with 33.6 percent in 1850.

Dominated by the LDS population in the nineteenth century, the city's non-Mormon population began to grow after the construction of the Utah Central Railroad in 1870 and the subsequent boom in mining, milling, and smelting. The city owed much of its growth in the nineteenth century to European immigration. In 1870, more than 65 percent of the 12,800 people in the city had come from abroad—principally from the British Isles. After 1900, immigrants from southern and eastern Europe came in larger numbers.

City government changed over time. It operated at first with a mayor-council-alderman system. Until the February 1890 election, the Mormon People's party governed the city. With the division of the citizens of the two religion-based parties (Mormon People's party and non-Mormon Liberal party) into both the national Republican and the Democratic parties, politics became much more like that of other American cities except for a brief period between 1905 and 1912, when the American party, organized by non-Mormons, controlled city government. The city commission system was adopted in 1911.

The city faced a number of problems in the nineteenth and early twentieth centuries, not the least of which was providing urban services. In general, private companies, such as those that operated street railways and provided electricity and telephone services, offered those services under franchise and expected to earn a profit. The city provided services not anticipated to pay their way, such as streets, water, and sewers.

During the 1920s, the city faced special problems of air pollution, zoning regulations, and budgetary concerns. Before these could be fully solved, the decade of the Great Depression arrived and was as difficult for citizens of Salt Lake City as for those elsewhere. In spite of economic problems, the city continued to play a dominant role as a key regional city in the Rocky Mountains. This was due in part to the planning of nineteenth-century LDS pioneers who had emphasized commercial, financial, educational, transportation, and religious activities, and in part to the admixture of non-Mormons. In April 1936, the Church announced its welfare plan, which, along with federal work programs, softened the blow of the Great Depression on city residents.

Strategic placement of military industries benefited Salt Lake City during World War II and brought some prosperity to the city.

Fort Douglas, Kearns Army Air Base, Hill Air Force Base, Tooele Ordnance Depot, and other military facilities contributed to the economic vitality that was centered in the city.

Space industries based on rocket fuels and high technology gradually replaced defense-based employment after World War II. During the 1960s the Salt Lake City metropolitan area became one of the fastest-growing in the United States. The LDS Church, under the guidance of N. Eldon Tanner, a counselor in the First Presidency, became a major contributor to downtown development. Investment by Church-owned businesses helped in the building of the Salt Palace Convention Center, the Beneficial Towers, the ZCMI Mall, and the Crossroads Mall, some of the first downtown malls in the nation.

In 1979, a dispute in city government over administrative practices resulted in a vote by the public to change the commission form of government to a mayor-council form. This led the way for other Utah cities, and by 1986 all commission governments in the state had changed to the mayor-council form.

In 1983, Salt Lake City residents became nationally known for their volunteer efforts in controlling floodwaters through the city. A strong volunteer network and ethic grew in the city, which was later recognized when Salt Lake City was designated the United States bid city for the Winter Olympic Games by the United States Olympic Committee in 1989.

In 1990, Salt Lake City enjoyed renewed economic vitality after a period of recession in the mid-1980s. Though the city proper continues to lose population as younger people move to the suburbs, it remains the heart of the LDS community. The activities established by the pioneer founders continue to make Salt Lake City a vital and important Rocky Mountain center.

[*See also* Temple Square; "This Is the Place" Monument.]

BIBLIOGRAPHY

Alexander, Thomas G., and James B. Allen. *Mormons and Gentiles: A History of Salt Lake City*. Boulder, Colo., 1984.

McCormick, John S. *Salt Lake City: The Gathering Place*. Woodland Hills, Calif., 1980.

Tullidge, Edward W. *History of Salt Lake City*. Salt Lake City, 1886.

THOMAS G. ALEXANDER
TED L. WILSON

SALT LAKE TEMPLE

The Salt Lake Temple is an impressive structure standing on the ten-acre TEMPLE SQUARE in the heart of Salt Lake City. For many years after its construction, the temple physically dominated the Salt Lake Valley. While other buildings now tower over it, the gray granite structure is still recognized as the religious symbol of The Church of Jesus Christ of Latter-day Saints worldwide. Millions of visitors annually have seen the building. Photographs of the temple have gone to scores of countries where people who have never personally seen the structure identify its striking presence with the Church and the city.

SITE SELECTION. Several days after the LDS pioneers entered the Salt Lake Valley in July 1847, Brigham Young planted his walking stick at a certain point while traversing the ground with some associates and exclaimed, "Here we will build the temple of our God" (Gates, p. 104).

CONSTRUCTION. Construction on the temple began on February 14, 1853, with Brigham Young turning the first shovelful of dirt in ground-breaking ceremonies. That April 6, the cornerstones were laid, following the pattern established for temples by Joseph Smith (cf. *TPJS*, p. 183). By this date, Truman O. Angell and William Ward, architect and assistant, had completed plans for the foundation and part of the basement, and Brigham Young had approved them. Sandstone from nearby Red Butte Canyon provided the basic material for the foundation and footings. The great walls of the building were to be granite from a vast mountain deposit in Little Cottonwood canyon about twenty miles away.

The foundation was completed in 1855, and some granite blocks were assembled on the site. Then, in 1858, under threat of an approaching U.S. army unit (*see* UTAH EXPEDITION), the Saints evacuated Salt Lake City and temporarily moved southward. They buried the foundation of the temple, leaving the appearance of a plowed field.

Work on the temple was not resumed for several years. Some deterioration of the foundation was discovered when it was re-excavated, and replacements were made with stone of the best quality. The exterior walls from the ground up, eight feet thick at ground level and six feet thick at the top, were painstakingly prepared and fitted from solid granite.

Transporting the granite from the mountain quarry proved to be a severe challenge. The builders tried using a wooden railroad spur, a canal, special roads, and even a uniquely constructed wagon. Although it was less than forty miles, a round trip required four days. The arrival of the transcontinental railroad in 1869 and the later laying of a spur into the canyon for mining purposes resolved the transportation problem.

As many as 150 men worked on the temple at any given time. During the forty years from the beginning to the end of the project, they also completed the construction of the great domed Tabernacle, the Assembly Hall, the Temple Annex, and a 15-foot-high wall that, a century and a half later, still sequesters Temple Square from the city that surrounds it.

COMPLETION AND DEDICATION. The capstone was laid April 6, 1892, one year before the dedication, amidst a tremendous spiritual outpouring of appreciation and anticipation. After the large spherical capstone was put in place, the people unanimously adopted a resolution to complete and dedicate the building one year from that date. That afternoon, the 12-foot-high gold-leafed copper statue representing the angel Moroni was placed on the central eastern spire, anchored through the capstone with huge weights suspended into the tower below.

The temple was completed within the year, and the dedication was held on the appointed date—April 6, 1893—forty years after Brigham Young laid the cornerstone. More than 2,250 people crowded the large Assembly Room on the fourth floor of the temple for the first of twenty-three dedicatory sessions that continued over almost three weeks. Many reported having spiritual experiences at the dedications. President Wilford WOODRUFF offered the dedicatory prayer, and the hosanna shout and original inspirational music were rendered. The sacred celebration was concluded with the singing of a special hymn saluting the sentiments of the people: the Hosanna Anthem.

INTERIOR DIVISIONS (DESIGN). Entrance to the temple for patrons is through an annex outside the main building. For the instructions and ordinances within, a processional plan is followed through several rooms, each signifying a stage in man's path of eternal progression. Each room is decorated with murals depicting that stage of the journey.

First is the Creation Room, where the creative periods of the earth are considered. Next, the events of Eden are the subject in the Garden Room. The World (or Telestial) Room depicts conditions following the expulsion of Adam and Eve from the Garden of Eden, providing a background for the atonement of Christ, the great apostasy, and the restoration of the gospel.

In the Terrestrial Room, the requirements of the pure life and of complete commitment to the work of the Lord are taught. The path then leads through the veil of the temple to the Celestial Room, representing the "heaven of heavens," the glorious kingdom of God. On this level also are small rooms with altars for marriage and sealing ordinances.

The building also includes in the lower area a baptistry, and on other levels, a large assembly room, rooms where the leaders of the Church meet, lecture rooms, administrative offices, and dressing rooms.

SYMBOLISM. Notable among all LDS temples, the Salt Lake Temple includes significant symbolism in its architecture. The six major towers and finial spires signify the restoration of priesthood authority. Earth stones, sun stones, moon stones, star stones, cloud stones penetrated with rays of light, the all-seeing eye, the clasped hands, Ursa Major pointing to the North Star, and the inscriptions "The House of the Lord" and "I Am Alpha and Omega" all appear on its exterior.

UNIQUE FUNCTIONS. Notwithstanding the increasing availability of temples nearer to them offering the same religious experience, many members of the Church still travel long distances to receive their individual endowment in the Salt Lake Temple or to be married or sealed as families in the same building in which parents or perhaps grandparents or other family members were married long ago.

This temple is also unique among LDS temples in that the highest quorums of the priesthood meet there. The First Presidency, the Quorum of the Twelve Apostles, and the Presidents of the Seventy gather separately as quorums weekly, and the First Presidency and

Quorum of the Twelve also meet conjointly. All General Authorities meet there monthly.

It is also, as already noted, architecturally and artistically unique and is the most widely known and recognized building in the Church.

BIBLIOGRAPHY

Anderson, James H. "The Salt Lake Temple." *Contributor* 14 (Apr. 1893):243–303.
Gates, Susa Young. *The Life Story of Brigham Young*. New York, 1931.
McAllister, D. M. *The Great Temple* (pamphlet). Salt Lake City, 1935.

MARION D. HANKS

SALT LAKE THEATRE

The Salt Lake Theatre was built in downtown Salt Lake City in 1861–1862 at a cost of over $100,000. President Brigham YOUNG donated more than half of the funds because he believed the Saints needed a theater to bring recreation, relaxation, and additional unity to the pioneer community. Visitors from other areas were shocked and even a little scandalized by his support because the theatrical stage did not have a good reputation in the 1860s. However, a glance at his talk given at the dedication shows that President Young made very clear his expectations for good, moral theater (*JD* 9:242–45).

The Salt Lake Theatre, with a seating capacity of 1,500, was one of the finest buildings in pioneer Salt Lake City, comparing well to theaters worldwide. It was praised by many of the professional actors who performed in it, including such theatrical greats as Sarah Alexander, Julie Dean Hayne, E. L. Davenport, and John McCullough. "There was scarcely a 'star' of the American stage who did not make a Salt Lake Theatre appearance" (Walker and Starr, p. 73).

After more than half a century of significant productions, however, the financially troubled and aging playhouse was sold in 1928 to be razed for a commercial office building. But the elements of theater—music, dance, and drama—established by the Salt Lake Theatre by the Mormon pioneers through six decades of continuous operation could not be torn down or destroyed. In 1962 the Pioneer Memorial Theatre, commemorating the old Salt Lake Theatre, was dedicated on the University of Utah campus and has since played a full season each year.

BIBLIOGRAPHY

Asahina, Roberta Reese. "Brigham Young and the Salt Lake Theater, 1862–1877." Ph.D. diss., Tufts University, 1980.

Maughan, Ila Fisher. *Pioneer Theatre in the Desert*. Salt Lake City, 1961.

Walker, Ronald W., and Alexander M. Starr. "Shattering the Vase: The Razing of the Old Salt Lake Theatre." *Utah Historical Quarterly* 57 (Winter 1989):64–88.

CHARLES L. METTEN

SALT LAKE VALLEY

In 1847 Brigham YOUNG, like a modern Moses, led the first pioneer Saints across a 1,300-mile stretch of "wilderness" into a large valley, surrounded by high mountain peaks and bordered on the northwest by a large lake of salty water, which gave the valley its name. Religious persecution of the 1830s and 1840s in the more populated eastern states necessitated the movement of the Latter-day Saints to the West, where they could be more isolated. The Prophet Joseph SMITH had designated Jackson County, Missouri, on the fringes of civilization, as the Zion of the latter days. However, continued persecution in Ohio, in Missouri, and later in Illinois caused the Latter-day Saints to seek a refuge in the Rocky Mountains, farther to the west, where they could worship God and practice their religious beliefs in the absence of religious bigotry, in land claimed by Mexico. To approximately 80,000 LDS pioneers who gathered from many nations and traveled across the great American desert by wagons before the advent in 1869 of the railroad, and to the thousands who followed afterward, the LDS presence in the Salt Lake Valley was compared to a fulfillment of Isaiah's prophecy of the latter days, the City of God, established in the top of the mountains where people from all nations could gather to the House of the Lord to learn his ways (Isa. 2:1–3). To the Latter-day pioneers, President Brigham Young's words expressed their feelings: "This is the place."

The seventeen-mile-wide by twenty-five-mile-long Salt Lake Valley is some 4,500 feet above sea level and is surrounded by towering mountain peaks of the Wasatch Range that rise to over 11,000 feet. The valley is part of the Great Basin, where river waters are kept from flowing into the Pacific Ocean by high mountains. Lake Bonneville once lay within the Great Basin, and geologists say that it measured 1,000 feet deep where Salt Lake City is now located. The current Great Salt Lake is the evaporation remnant of that inland sea.

Though the valley floor was very dry and covered with sagebrush when the LDS pioneers arrived in July 1847, it did not take long for them to divert the clear, snow-fed mountain streams onto the parched soil and make a productive farming community. Fur trappers and traders, explorers, and Roman Catholic priests had "passed through," but the Latter-day Saints were in the valley to stay.

Salt Lake City, in the north end of the valley, became the "big city," the headquarters of the Church. But as immigrants gathered from far-flung countries to their Zion, numerous smaller towns were established in the valley along the mountain streams.

With the coming of the transcontinental railroad in 1869, Gentiles (non-Mormons) began to move into the valley, diluting the LDS population; but Latter-day Saints continued to be a majority. The railroad helped foster more manufacturing, mining, and commerce, and the valley took on a decided change. By 1870 modern houses were replacing the log and adobe brick cabins, and green trees lined the streets and roads. Farms were fenced and well groomed.

The 1880s saw the introduction of the telephone and electricity to Salt Lake City, and in 1893 the Salt Lake Temple was finished. In the early 1900s money from Utah's mining industry was being invested in the valley's first skyscrapers, and a modern capital city emerged with hospitals, colleges, business buildings, libraries, and thousands of homes. Salt Lake City had changed from the all-Mormon village of 1847 to a cosmopolitan city.

By 1990 the population within the formal city boundaries was 165,000, but the greater Salt Lake Valley population totaled over 715,000. With shopping malls, freeways, and employment opportunities scattered throughout the valley, the population shift away from the city became valleywide on both sides of the Jordan River, which flows north from Utah Lake to the Great Salt Lake. Mountains surrounding the valley have been extremely valuable. Mining in the west side Oquirrh Mountains has brought many jobs to the people of the valley and the world's largest open-pit copper mine is a major employer. The mountains to the east provide precious drinking water and are used chiefly for recreational purposes, especially for skiing in the winter.

As travelers drive down out of the mountains today, they view a beautiful tree-filled Salt Lake Valley below. The scene stirs feelings of gratitude for the labor of the pioneers, who, in many cases, were their forefathers. The faithful Saints may feel that Isaiah's words have literally been fulfilled, that "The wilderness and the solitary place shall be glad for them; and the desert shall rejoice, and blossom as the rose. . . . They shall see the glory of the Lord, and the excellency of our God" (Isa. 35:1–2).

BIBLIOGRAPHY

Alexander, Thomas G., and James B. Allen. *Mormons and Gentiles: A History of Salt Lake City*. Boulder, Colo., 1984.

McCormick, John S. "The Valley of the Great Salt Lake." Reprint of the *Utah Historical Quarterly* 27 (July 1959); rev. ed., 1963.

———. *Salt Lake City, the Gathering Place*. Woodland Hills, Calif., 1980.

LAMAR C. BERRETT

SCANDINAVIA, THE CHURCH IN

At the general conference of the Church in Salt Lake City on October 6, 1849, Elder Erastus Snow, an apostle, and Peter Olsen Hansen were called to serve missions to Scandinavia. John Erik Forsgren asked that he might also be called to his native Sweden. They were joined by George Parker Dykes, who was already a missionary in England, and these four men formally introduced the Church into Scandinavia. Successful in finding converts from the beginning, the Church has had two very dynamic periods of growth there, from 1850 to 1870, and from 1947 to 1967. Emigration of Church members to the United States was particularly high between 1861 and 1891 and after World War II. By the end of 1990, the Church had over 20,000 members living in seven stakes and 119 wards and branches throughout Scandinavia, served by a temple in Västerhaninge, Sweden. Records show that 57 percent of the LDS converts in Scandinavia have been women and 43 percent men.

EARLY CONVERTS. Hansen arrived first in Copenhagen on May 12, 1850, and immediately visited a Baptist congregation. The first

Danish Mormon converts later came from that group. Elder Snow, Forsgren, and Dykes arrived on June 14, 1850.

Forsgren visited his family in Gävle, Sweden, and baptized his brother Peter Adolf Forsgren on July 26, 1850. This was the first LDS baptism in Scandinavia. On August 12, eight men and seven women were baptized at Øresund, near Copenhagen. The first Danish branch of about fifty members was organized in Copenhagen a month later.

Dykes was sent to Ålborg in Jutland in northern Denmark, where he also contacted a Baptist congregation. The first converts in Ålborg included Hans Peter Jensen, a prominent Baptist, who owned an iron foundry employing over one hundred men, and his conversion to the LDS Church became widely known. Within four months the branch in Ålborg included sixty members.

A Norwegian ship's captain named Svend Larsen first encountered the Church in Ålborg. He was taught by Elder Snow in Brother Jensen's home, and noted in his diary that an inner voice whispered to him that this was a man of God. Baptized in Ålborg on September 23, 1851, he became the first resident Norwegian to join the Church. Larsen gave important support to spreading the Church in Norway. On September 11, 1851, he brought Hans F. Peterson, the first LDS missionary to Norway, who baptized master blacksmith John Olsen and his assistant Peter Adamsen on November 26 at Risør. With the help of missionaries from Denmark, the work was extended to Brevik and Fredrikstad. The first convert there was Svend Peter Larsen, a stepson of one of the leading Methodists in Fredrikstad. His wife, Berthine Randine, was baptized four days later. In spite of mob disturbances and occasional brief imprisonment of the missionaries, the Church grew. The first branch in Norway was organized in Risør on July 16, 1852. During the next six years branches were organized in Fredrikstad, Brevik, Christiania (Oslo), Drammen, Stavanger, Halden, Trondheim, and Bergen.

John Erik Forsgren's missionary work in Sweden ended quickly as he and Mikel Johnson were deported to Copenhagen. The first highly successful missionary in Sweden was Anders W. Winberg, who began his work in Skåne in April 1852, and organized the first branch in Skönabäck with thirty-six members on April 24, 1852. Soon thereafter branches were established in Malmö, Lomma, and Lund. On June 25, 1853, the Skåne Conference was organized.

The Church was introduced into Iceland by two young Icelanders, Thorarinn Halflidasson and Gumundur Gudmundsson, who were baptized in Denmark in 1851 and returned to their homeland to proselyte as instructed by Elder Snow. Benedikt Hanson and his wife were baptized, but when Halflidasson accidentally drowned on a fishing trip, no one was left with priesthood authority to baptize in Iceland. On April 10, 1853, Johan P. Lorenzen of the Copenhagen Branch arrived to continue the missionary work. He organized a branch in Iceland on June 19, 1853. The Church has had only moderate success in Iceland.

Thus by 1853 the Church had gained a foothold in all the Scandinavian countries except Finland. In 1876, Carl August and John E. Sundström of the Stockholm Conference were called to Finland. They organized a small branch in Larsmo, under difficult conditions because of the lack of religious freedom. After having been ruled by Sweden for 600 years, Finland was a Russian Grand Duchy from 1809 until 1917, and the authorities confiscated LDS books and tracts. Post offices in Finland opened packages containing *Nordstjärnan*, the LDS Swedish publication, and sent the empty wrappers to subscribers with the explanation that no Mormon literature would be allowed into the country. In 1903 Elder Francis M. Lyman, an apostle, dedicated Finland for the preaching of the gospel, but it was not until after World War II that missionary work showed any significant success. C. Fritz Johansson and Karl Lagerberg were sent to Finland in May 1946, and Elder Ezra Taft BENSON, an apostle, rededicated the country on July 16, 1946, at Larsmo, where the small branch had been established earlier. Henry A. Matis became the first mission president of the Finnish mission in August 1947. At the end of 1990 Finland had two stakes and one mission of the Church.

EMIGRATION. Since 1852, many Scandinavian members have emigrated to the United States. Particularly in the nineteenth century, poverty, starvation, persecution, and hopelessness motivated people to seek a better life and, for Latter-day Saints, the spirit of gathering to the "promised land" in Utah was strong. There they could enjoy religious freedom and practice their religion without ridicule or harassment.

The Church in Western America has been significantly augmented by these immigrants. From 1850 to 1950, 27,000 members of record emigrated from Scandinavia. If unbaptized children under eight years of age were counted, the total would be much higher. A little more than half of these emigrants were Danish, a third Swedish, and the balance Norwegians. Emigrating Icelanders amounted to less than one percent. A 1950 survey concluded that about 45 percent of the Church membership was at least partly of Scandinavian descent.

CLASH OF CULTURES. To understand the environment in which early missionaries to Scandinavia found themselves, it is necessary to know that a strong liberal movement prevailed there in the mid-1800s. On June 5, 1849, only months before the first LDS missionaries came to Denmark, King Frederik VII signed the new Danish Constitution, which guaranteed the people freedom of speech, press, and religion. In Norway a Dissenter Law guaranteeing religious freedom to all Christian denominations was passed as early as 1845. As soon as Mormon missionaries began to proselytize in Norway, some of the clergy and public officials questioned whether Latter-day Saints could be considered Christians. On November 4, 1853, the Supreme Court of Norway ruled that Mormons could not enjoy protection under the Dissenter Law, and missionaries were arrested and fined for preaching, baptizing, or administering the sacrament. Unable to pay, they had to go to jail, where they studied the scriptures, sang hymns, and taught the gospel to the jailers, who often were sympathetic and provided them with the best cells. In Sweden limited religious freedom was granted by law in 1858, but it was not until 1952 that the Church was given full legal religious freedom. For Scandinavians, plural marriage was a real problem. It took a long time after the 1890 Manifesto to convince the public that Mormons who lived their religion were law-abiding and hard-working citizens with strict moral principles. The right to exercise full religious freedom has come slowly to the Latter-day Saints in Scandinavia. But the resentment long prevalent among Scandinavian public officials and clergy has gradually turned into respect and, in some instances, into admiration for the Church, which can now legally pursue full worship and perform all its ordinances in all the Scandinavian countries.

LANDMARK TRANSLATIONS. Using the standard translations of the Bible, the missionaries in Copenhagen realized the pressing need to have the Book of Mormon translated into Danish. Peter Olsen Hansen and Elder Snow's translation was printed by F. E. Bordings Bogtrykkeri in May 1851. This was the first foreign language edition of the Book of Mormon.

Because the Norwegians could read the Danish translation, the Book of Mormon was not translated into Norwegian until 1950. The first Swedish translation was published in 1878, the Finnish in 1954. Selected passages were published in Icelandic in 1981. The Doctrine and Covenants and the Pearl of Great Price have also been printed in all Scandinavian languages.

LOCAL PUBLICATIONS. Peter Olsen Hansen also wrote the first Mormon tract published in Scandinavia, *En Advarsel til Folket* (*A Warning to the People*). When Elder Snow arrived in June 1850, he wrote *A Voice of Truth*, which Hansen translated as *En Sandheds Røst*, which has seen many reprintings. *Skandinaviens Stjerne* (*The Scandinavian Star*), published in 1851, was the first official periodical of the Church in Scandinavia. It later became *Den Danske Stjerne* (*The Danish Star*), presently *Stjernen*. Comparable Norwegian and Finnish magazines, *Lys Over Norge* (*Light over Norway*) and *Valkeus*, were published monthly in 1990. The Swedish journal is called *Nordstjärnan* (*The North Star*). March 1851 saw publication of the first Danish LDS book of hymns.

GENERAL AUTHORITIES BORN IN SCANDINAVIA. Three native-born Scandinavians have become General Authorities of the Church. Anthon H. Lund, born in Ålborg, Denmark, became an apostle (1889) and counselor in the First Presidency (1903–1921). John A. Widtsoe, born at Dalöe, Island of Fröya, Norway, was an apostle (1921–1952). And Christian D. Fjeldsted from Sundbyvester, Copenhagen, Denmark, was a member of the Seventy (1884–1905).

ORGANIZATION OF MISSIONS AND STAKES. Copenhagen became the center for the Church in Scandinavia as communication from Salt Lake City went through the Scandinavian Mission office located there. As membership increased, branches were organized into conferences. In 1900 the Scandinavian Mission consisted of sixty organized branches in nine conferences: three in Denmark (Copenhagen, Århus, and Ålborg), three in Sweden (Stockholm, Göteborg, and Skåne), and three in Norway (Christiania, Bergen, and

Trondheim). Even after thousands of Saints had emigrated, Church membership in Scandinavia totaled 4,535, with 165 American missionaries. The Swedish Mission was divided from the original Scandinavian Mission on July 1, 1905, and the Norwegian Mission was organized on April 1, 1920.

In the fall of 1939, the American missionaries were withdrawn from Europe, and local leaders were made acting presidents over the missions: Orson B. West in Denmark, Olaf Sønsteby in Norway, and C. Fritz Johansson in Sweden. Even though Denmark and Norway were occupied by Germany from 1940 until 1945, the local members were able to continue Church activity. When the new American mission presidents arrived in 1945–1946, they found the missions to be in good condition in spite of the ravages of war.

On February 15, 1946, Elder Ezra Taft Benson began administering a relief program of food and clothing to Latter-day Saints in Scandinavia. Many members emigrated to the United States after World War II, and most were educated people who left good jobs to go to Zion. Yet, recent growth of the Church in all of the Scandinavian countries has led to organized stakes. The first stakes organized in each country are: the Copenhagen Denmark Stake on June 16, 1974; the Stockholm Sweden Stake on April 20, 1975; the Oslo Norway Stake on May 22, 1977; and the Helsinki Finland Stake on October 16, 1977.

THE STOCKHOLM SWEDEN TEMPLE. In 1985, the Church dedicated a temple in Västerhaninge, Sweden, eighteen miles south of Stockholm, with John and Edna Fluge Langeland, Norwegian-Americans, as temple president and matron. Scandinavian members who have temple recommends perform sacred temple ordinances in their own languages there. It was the first place in Europe where Latter-day Saints could receive temple sealings for time and eternity without first being married by civil authority. With stakes and wards in their countries and the temple in Västerhaninge, Scandinavian Latter-day Saints can enjoy the full program of the Church.

BIBLIOGRAPHY

Haslam, Gerald M. *Clash of Cultures: The Norwegian Experience with Mormonism, 1842–1920.* New York, 1984.

Jenson, Andrew. *History of the Scandinavian Mission.* Salt Lake City, 1927.

Mulder, William. "Mormons from Scandinavia 1850–1905." Ph.D. diss., Harvard University, 1955.

———. *Homeward to Zion: The Mormon Migration from Scandinavia.* Minneapolis, 1957.

Zobell, Albert L., Jr. *Under the Midnight Sun: Centennial History of Scandinavian Missions.* Salt Lake City, 1950.

JOHN LANGELAND

SCHISMATIC GROUPS

Like any large religious body, The Church of Jesus Christ of Latter-day Saints has had a number of variously disaffected members break away. Some have taken a group of members with them and started rival organizations, based on their interpretations of the teachings of Joseph SMITH. There have been about 130 such groups; only a few have existed for more than ten years.

The first was known as the Pure Church of Christ, founded in 1831 by Wycam Clark, Northrop Sweet, and others. Asserting that Joseph Smith was a false prophet, Clark claimed that he was the true leader of the Church. The group held only two or three meetings and died out.

The most prominent schismatic group organized during Joseph Smith's lifetime was the Church of Christ, established by Warren Parrish in Kirtland, Ohio, in 1837. A few months earlier Parrish was accused of embezzling funds from the Church's bank, the Kirtland Safety Society, and was excommunicated. Alleging that Joseph had fallen from his divine calling as leader of the Church, Parrish claimed the authority to lead it. He gained the support of three members of the Quorum of the Twelve Apostles, some of the presidents of the Seventies, and several other influential leaders who had become alienated from Smith during the 1837–1838 economic crisis in Kirtland. That group broke up in less than a year (*CHC* 1:403–407).

The death of Joseph Smith in 1844 produced another flurry of new groups seeking to take advantage of the loss of the Church's leader. There were people in these organizations who agreed that Joseph Smith had been a true prophet, although many of them rejected or ignored some of the doctrines or practices he had established; the question in their minds was who was to take his place.

Joseph's counselor in the First Presidency, Sidney RIGDON, was one of the first to press his claim, telling the Saints that there could be no successor to Joseph Smith and that he should be named guardian of the Church, to watch over it in Joseph's name and build it up to the memory of the slain prophet. His claim was rejected by most members, who sustained Brigham YOUNG and the Quorum of the Twelve Apostles. Rigdon was excommunicated, and he returned to Pittsburgh, Pennsylvania, where he established the Church of Christ, which lasted less than two years. In 1863 he organized the Church of Jesus Christ of the Children of Zion. This group lasted into the 1880s.

In August 1844, James J. Strang, converted only a few months before Joseph Smith's death, produced a letter supposedly from Joseph Smith appointing Strang to lead the flock (*see* FORGERIES OF HISTORICAL DOCUMENTS), and claimed that an angel had appeared to him shortly after the martyrdom and ordained him to that calling. Strang was immediately excommunicated. A few weeks later, he moved with a group of converts to Voree, Wisconsin, the area he claimed as the new gathering place for the church. His followers included two apostles, John E. Page and William Smith (younger brother of Joseph Smith), and William Marks, former president of the Nauvoo Stake. For a short time, Martin HARRIS accompanied a Strangite leader on a mission to England.

Strang moved his group to Beaver Island, a small island in northern Lake Michigan, where in 1850 Strang was crowned king in an elaborate ceremony. There he established a theocracy that thrived for most of the decade with an estimated 3,000 members; he also continued the practice of PLURAL MARRIAGE. On June 16, 1856, two assassins, part of a larger conspiracy, shot Strang; he did not appoint a successor before he died eleven days later. His group was broken up by the combined action of federal and local forces, and the majority was forcibly exiled from the island. A small remnant of Strang's order, however, still exists in Wisconsin, Michigan, Colorado, and New Mexico (Van Noord, pp. 48–177, 233–66; Lewis, pp. 274–91).

A move toward creating a larger reorganization began early in the 1850s. Some former Strangites, including William Marks, Jason Briggs, and Zenas H. Gurley, met in 1850 to decide on a new leader. Briggs and Gurley had been members of William Smith's group, called the Church of Jesus Christ of Latter Day Saints, which had been organized in 1846 after the excommunication of William Smith from the Strangites. Marks, Briggs, and Gurley were convinced that succession in the presidency of the Church must be lineal, descending from father to son. In an intense proselytizing effort, they drew to them a number of other Mormons and former Mormons in the Midwest of the same idea. A group met in Beloit, Wisconsin, on June 12–13, 1852, to organize. In 1853 they held another conference and apostles were chosen. In 1859 Joseph Smith III formally accepted the call to become the new president and prophet, and in April 1860 the group formally incorporated under the name of the Reorganized Church of Jesus Christ of Latter Day Saints. Most of Joseph Smith, Jr.'s immediate family joined this church in the early 1860s, and many descendants remain active members today (Launius, pp. 77–139).

Other groups broke away during Brigham Young's administration in Utah. One of the most significant was the Godbeites, organized in 1868 under the leadership of William S. Godbe. Several years earlier, Godbe had joined with E. L. T. Harrison, Edward W. Tullidge, Eli B. Kelsey, William H. Shearman, and other disaffected Mormon businessmen and intellectuals to protest the economic self-sufficiency policy of Brigham Young. Godbe and his group favored a less structured society, free trade inside Utah Territory, and open trade with the outside world. Their social protest soon developed into a thorough rejection of doctrine and practice. They discarded all of the Church's theological structure, claiming loyalty to no single prophet or set of scriptures. Instead, they proclaimed the universal brotherhood of man and the universal love of God. This led to involvement with the Spiritualist movement, popular in the nineteenth century. They participated in a number of séances, in the belief that they were speaking with deceased LDS Church leaders, Jesus Christ, and the ancient apostles. The Salt Lake Stake High Council excommunicated Godbe and Harrison on October 25, 1869. Others in the group eventually brought on their own excommunication. In 1870 they formally organized the Church of Zion, an openly anti-Mormon organization, both religiously and economically, which founded the *Salt Lake Tribune*. The movement failed to attract many new followers and died out by 1880 (Walker, 1974, 1982).

Other splinter groups have followed from time to time, especially following the termination of plural marriage in 1890.

BIBLIOGRAPHY

Anderson, C. LeRoy. *For Christ Will Come Tomorrow: The Saga of the Morrisites.* Logan, Utah, 1981.

Carter, Kate B. *Denominations That Base Their Beliefs on the Teachings of Joseph Smith.* Salt Lake City, 1969.

Launius, Roger D. *Joseph Smith III: Pragmatic Prophet.* Urbana, Ill., 1988.

Lewis, David Rich. "'For Life, the Resurrection, and the Life Everlasting': James J. Strang and Strangite Mormon Polygamy, 1849–1856." *Wisconsin Magazine of History* 66 (Summer 1983):274–91.

Morgan, Dale L. *Bibliographies of the Lesser Mormon Churches.* Salt Lake City, n.d.

Rich, Russell R. *Those Who Would Be Leaders: Offshoots of Mormonism.* Provo, Utah, 1959.

Shields, Steven L. *Divergent Paths of the Restoration: A History of the Latter Day Saint Movement*, 3rd ed. Bountiful, Utah, 1982.

Van Noord, Roger. *King of Beaver Island: The Life and Assassination of James Jesse Strang.* Urbana, Ill., 1988.

Walker, Ronald W. "The Commencement of the Godbeite Protest: Another View." *Utah Historical Quarterly* 42 (Summer 1974):216–44.

———. "When the Spirits Did Abound: Nineteenth-Century Utah's Encounter with Free-Thought Radicalism." *Utah Historical Quarterly* 50 (Fall 1982):304–324.

MARTIN S. TANNER

SCHOOLS OF THE PROPHETS

Between 1833 and 1884, Church leaders from time to time organized schools for instructing members in Church doctrine and secular subjects and for discussing political and social issues relevant to the Church's mission. Although they varied greatly in form and purpose, these schools were called Schools of the Prophets, or sometimes Schools of the Elders.

The first such school met on January 23, 1833, in Kirtland, Ohio, in response to a revelation (D&C 88:119–33) instructing the Church to prepare priesthood members to carry the gospel to the world. Following prayer and an outpouring of spiritual gifts, the Prophet Joseph SMITH invited each man present to receive the ordinance of washing of feet and a blessing. They ended their daylong fast by partaking of the Lord's Supper, after which they sang a hymn and were dismissed.

The School of the Prophets met in Kirtland through the winter and early spring of 1833, usually in a room above Newel K. WHITNEY'S STORE. Joseph Smith presided, and Orson Hyde was the instructor. Enrollment was limited to selected priesthood holders and probably never exceeded twenty-five. In accordance with the revelation about the school, members were initiated through the washing of feet, then reaffirmed their commitment and mutual goodwill by exchanging a formal salutation at the commencement of each class. School usually convened at sunrise and dismissed in late afternoon. Instruction focused on scripture and doctrine, though some time was devoted to secular topics such as grammar. During the February 27, 1833, meeting, Joseph Smith received the revelation known as the Word of Wisdom (D&C 89), which thereafter was binding upon members of the school.

The school ended in April 1833, when spring weather permitted active missionary work to begin, and never reconvened. Instead, a series of educational efforts expanded on the original idea and took on added responsibilities. Two of these later schools, known as the School of the Elders or School of the Prophets, convened in Jackson County, Missouri, during the summer of 1833 and in Kirtland, Ohio, from late fall to early spring in 1834–1835 and 1835–1836. These had larger enrollments than the first School of the Prophets and, in addition to the spiritual preparation of priesthood members, taught students an expanded secular curriculum, including penmanship, English, Hebrew, grammar, arithmetic, philosophy, literature, government, geography, and history. These later schools did not observe the earlier initiation rite and formalized salutation. Parley P. Pratt led the Missouri school, and Joseph Smith, Sidney Rigdon, Frederick G. Williams, and William E. McLellan taught in Kirtland. During the 1834–1835 school year, students in Kirtland heard the lectures later published in the Doctrine and Covenants as the Lectures on Faith.

Following the closure of the School of the Elders in 1836, the School of the Prophets did not meet again until the Church moved west. In December 1867, President Brigham Young reorganized the School of the Prophets in connection with the University of Deseret. The Church's First Presidency presided over a theological class of ecclesiastical officers and selected priesthood holders that served as a forum for the discussion of questions related to the spiritual and temporal concerns of the Church. The class later separated from the University, and branch classes were established in major LDS communities throughout the Intermountain West. Total enrollment eventually exceeded 1,000 members. Locally elected priesthood leaders presided over meetings of active priesthood members in discussions of religious, civic, and economic issues as well as of the spiritual and temporal concerns of the Church. Meetings were confidential, and admission was by tickets given to an invited membership.

President Brigham Young dissolved these branches of the Schools of the Prophets late in the summer of 1872 and then reorganized in November 1872 a Salt Lake City School of the Prophets for General Authorities and other invited priesthood leaders. Participants numbering more than 200 discussed theology and also temporal concerns. This school helped introduce cooperative enterprises into LDS communities. When united order organizations were incorporated in the spring and summer of 1874 to facilitate economic cooperation, the Salt Lake City School of the Prophets dissolved and some of its functions were absorbed by local united orders.

President John Taylor, who succeeded Brigham Young as Church President, reconvened the School of the Prophets in the fall of 1883. Inviting Church General Authorities and a select group of other Church leaders to participate, President Taylor followed the ceremonies of the original school. A branch of the school was established in St. George, Utah, in December 1883. These schools probably ceased to operate in early 1884, with no subsequent attempt by the Church to organize further Schools of the Prophets.

BIBLIOGRAPHY

Backman, Milton V., Jr. *The Heaven's Resound: A History of the Latter-day Saints in Ohio 1830–1838*. Salt Lake City, 1983.

Cook, Lyndon W. *The Revelations of the Prophet Joseph Smith: A Historical and Biographical Commentary of the Doctrine and Covenants*. Provo, Utah, 1981.

Patrick, John R. "The School of the Prophets: Its Development and Influence in Utah Territory." Master's thesis, Brigham Young University, 1970.

STEVEN R. SORENSEN

SEAGULLS, MIRACLE OF

The first LDS pioneers entered the SALT LAKE VALLEY in July 1847 (*see* PIONEER DAY). Nearly 2,000 made the journey that year, with another 2,400 emigrants arriving in 1848. From the beginning, having so many dependent on first harvests from an untried land with an unknown growing season produced concern. That first summer, pioneers observed Indians harvesting "millions" of crickets for winter food. The crickets were driven into fires and roasted, and then stored in baskets and bags. Survival—individual and group survival—was clearly on the minds of these first Mormon settlers as they watched the Indians prepare to endure the winter.

During the first year in the Great Basin, most Latter-day Saint settlers resided in the Salt Lake Valley, although small settlements were also begun to the north at Kaysville, along the Weber River, and at Bountiful. Through the summer and fall of 1847, they planted 2,000 acres of winter wheat near the main settlement. A mild winter and thaw permitted plowing in early 1848, making it possible to plant more wheat and another 3,000 to 4,000 acres in corn and garden vegetables by spring.

As spring arrived, pioneer farmers reported with pride that their crops appeared to be doing very well. But April and May frosts leveled some of the crops, and late May brought another devastation—hordes of insects began to destroy the crops. These insects, later dubbed "Mormon crickets," were as large as a man's thumb. Not a true cricket but a member of the katydid family, the Mormon cricket has only small wings and cannot fly. Pioneer diarists reported the invaders in the fields as early as May 22. Some described them as numbering in the millions; John Steele wrote that they appeared by the "thousands of tons." For more than a month, the crickets devastated the fields, devouring the new corn, beans, wheat, pumpkins, squash, cucumbers, melons, and other crops. Farmers battled the crickets with a variety of defensive measures but had little success.

By early June, relief arrived in the form of the seagull. The appearance of gulls was described in a letter of June 9 to Brigham YOUNG in the following manner: "The sea gulls have come in large flocks from the lake and sweep the crickets as they go; it seems the hand of the Lord is in our favor" (Hartley, p. 230). For the next three weeks, gulls appeared daily. They fed on the crickets, drank water, and then regurgitated before eating more crickets. There would be a harvest that year, after all.

Some 1848 pioneer journals mention the problems of frost, crickets, and drought without mentioning the gulls. However, several autumn accounts credited the counterinvasion by the gulls for the scanty crops that survived and acknowledged the hand of God in the event.

Ornithologists have noted that gulls, whose spring and summer habitat centers on the shores of the Great Salt Lake, regularly return to the valleys of the Great Basin to devour crickets, grasshoppers, and other insects, and that the 1848 appearance of the gulls was therefore not unusual. Some skeptics thus saw the 1848 activities of both crickets and gulls as simply natural phenomena. On the other hand, many Latter-day Saints, with faith in a God whose hand is in history and who often acts through "natural" events, believed that their crops had been saved in part by God's intervention. Over time, the 1848 "cricket war," now called "the miracle of the gulls," became a prominent part of the Saints' collective memory. In honor of this occasion, the indigenous California gull became the Utah state bird, and in 1913 the Seagull Monument on TEMPLE SQUARE was dedicated to commemorate the birds' role in the 1848 crisis.

In the Salt Lake Valley, crickets, frost, and lack of water played havoc on the harvest of 1848, and crop losses were severe. But the losses would have been much worse without the appearance of the gulls, which was thus a significant factor in the survival of Utah's pioneer settlers.

BIBLIOGRAPHY

Hartley, William G. "Mormons, Crickets, and Gulls: A New Look at an Old Story." *Utah Historical Quarterly* 38 (Summer 1970):224–39.

RICHARD W. SADLER

SILK CULTURE

President Brigham YOUNG conceived sericulture in the Great Basin as an important component in economic stability. He regarded locally produced silk as a practical textile and as a light industry that could be maintained at home by women and children, requiring less intensive labor and capital outlay than cotton, flax, or wool. He planted the first mulberry trees in Deseret, which were imported from France in 1855.

In 1856, Elizabeth Whitaker produced cocoons from worms that her husband brought from England as eggs; in 1858, Nancy Barrows planted mulberry seeds, feeding her worms on lettuce leaves until the mulberry trees matured. She reeled thread, wove it into fabric, and made the first silk dress in the territory of Deseret in 1859. In 1863, Octave Ursenbach and his wife exhibited 3,000 cocoons they had produced in Salt Lake City. Paul and Susanna Cardon produced silk in Cache Valley during the early 1860s, and Paul A. Schettler and his family set up a loom for weaving silk in 1867 and began raising cocoons in Salt Lake City.

In 1867, President Young offered free eggs and mulberry leaves to any persons willing to "undertake the work" of hatching, tending, and feeding the worms. He called George D. Watt to promote silk culture throughout the territory and Zina D. H. Young, of the newly reorganized Relief Society, to head the silk project. She traveled widely over the territory, delivering speeches, and organizing and teaching classes.

Carolyn Jackson raised the first silk in St. George in 1869. In Ogden Mariana Comb Bens was independently producing silk before the Relief Society took it on. By 1870, most ward Relief Societies produced silk, and by 1880 every Relief Society in the territory had a silk project. Important promoters of silk culture were A. K. Thurber in Spanish Fork, Daniel Graves in Provo, and Anson Call and Mary Carter in Layton. Susan B. Anthony and Mrs. Rutherford B. Hayes both enjoyed gifts of silk articles.

The silk industry continued moderately healthy through most of the 1880s, but a lull marked the late 1880s and the early 1890s. The last surge of Utah's silk works began when officials decided to feature silk at the state exhibit at the 1893 World's Fair. The exhibit was a stunning success, and the attention it received resulted in renewed activity.

Headed by Zina D. H. Young, the Utah Silk Commission was established by the state legislature in 1896 to replace the older

Deseret Silk Association, simultaneously authorizing payment of a bounty of twenty-five cents per pound for cocoons produced in the state. During 1897–1904, bounties were paid on 4,769, 7,493, 6,479, and 8,647 pounds of cocoons. Although production nearly doubled during these years, the crop was never profitable. In 1905, the legislature could not justify renewing the cocoon bounty, and except for individuals scattered throughout the state who maintained silk culture as a hobby, sericulture ended in Utah in 1905.

BIBLIOGRAPHY

Arrington, Chris Rigby. "The Finest of Fabrics: Mormon Women and the Silk Industry in Early Utah." *Utah Historical Quarterly* 46:376–96.

Arrington, Leonard J. "The Economic Role of Pioneer Mormon Women." *The Western Humanities Review* 9(2):145–64.

Potter, Margaret Schow. "The History of Sericulture in Utah." Master's thesis, Oregon State College, 1949.

ELIZABETH HUNTINGTON HALL

SMITH, BATHSHEBA BIGLER

Bathsheba Wilson Bigler Smith (1822–1910) was the fourth general president of the Relief Society, matron of the SALT LAKE TEMPLE, woman suffrage leader, and member of the Deseret Hospital Board of Directors.

Bathsheba was the eighth of nine children born to Mark and Susannah Ogden Bigler at Shinnston, Harrison County, Virginia, on May 3, 1822. She was reared in a genteel, upper South culture. The Biglers provided a substantial living for the family on their 300-acre plantation. Bathsheba was trained in management, hospitality, handiwork, and art, and was a cheerful, dignified, and prayerful woman.

At the age of fifteen, Bathsheba and her family joined The Church of Jesus Christ of Latter-day Saints. One of the missionaries serving in the area, George A. Smith, later to be the youngest member called to the Quorum of the Twelve Apostles, became acquainted with this tall, sophisticated southern belle; before he left Virginia, they pledged that "with the blessings of the Almighty in preserving us, in three years from this time, we will be married."

The Bigler family gathered with the Saints in Nauvoo in 1839.

Following his return from a mission in England, George and Bathsheba were married on July 25, 1841. While in Nauvoo, they became parents of two children, George A., Jr., and Bathsheba. Their son was killed in 1860 by Indians while serving a mission.

From the time of her marriage, her life was closely intertwined with the Church's movements and programs. She was one of the twenty founding members of the Female Relief Society. She received the ordinance of anointing from Emma SMITH and, with her husband, received the endowment under the direction of the Prophet Joseph SMITH. Her relationship with the Smiths provided Bathsheba with a solid conviction of the prophetic calling of Joseph Smith.

Bathsheba was a diversely talented woman. She studied portraiture with William W. Major, a British convert, and carried her paintings of her husband, her parents, and Joseph and Hyrum SMITH in a covered wagon to Utah. She was a full participant in the heritage of leadership prescribed to LDS women; she gave blessings to the sick, washed and anointed women in confinement prior to childbirth, and served in leadership positions in the Church and community. A loyal and committed friend, she exchanged names with a childhood girlfriend surnamed Wilson, adding that name to her established signature.

During the early 1870s, Bathsheba made frequent trips with her husband, then first counselor to President Brigham YOUNG, through settlements north and south of Salt Lake City on preaching and pioneering tours. After the death of her husband in 1875, Bathsheba pursued with customary vigor her commitments to civic and ecclesiastical affairs. Representative of such verve, at a women's meeting in 1870 she made the motion "that we demand of the Governor the right of franchise." This proposal was subsequently signed into law, making the Territory of Utah one of the first places in the nation to give women the right to vote.

In addition to her service as a ward and stake Relief Society leader, and as second counselor and later general president of the Relief Society, Bathsheba also officiated in each of the temples constructed during her lifetime: Nauvoo, Logan, Manti, St. George, and Salt Lake. For seventeen years, she also participated with Eliza R. SNOW in conducting sacred ceremonies in the Endowment House.

As general president of the Relief Society (1901–1910),

President Smith maintained the forward pace of women. She sent representatives to national and international women's meetings, sponsored nurses' training and free services for the poor, and organized lessons for Relief Society classes. She promoted funding for construction of the Women's Building, from which the programs for the women of the Church were directed. It was this building that Church leaders later elected to rename the Bishops' Building, to accommodate the offices of both the Presiding Bishopric and the women's organizations.

Bathsheba Smith died on September 20, 1910, in Salt Lake City. Her funeral was held in the Salt Lake Tabernacle.

BIBLIOGRAPHY

Horne, Alice M., ed. *Autobiography of Bathsheba Smith.* Salt Lake City, 1901.

Mulvay-Derr, Jill, and Susan Oman. "The Nauvoo Generation: Our First Five Relief Society Presidents." *Ensign* 7 (Dec. 1977):40–42.

Whitney, Orson F. *History of Utah*, Vol. 4, pp. 578–80. Salt Lake City, 1901–1904.

HARRIET HORNE ARRINGTON

SMITH, EMMA HALE

Emma Hale Smith (1804–1879), wife of the Prophet Joseph SMITH, was born July 10, 1804, in the Susquehanna Valley in HARMONY township (now Oakland), Pennsylvania, to Isaac and Elizabeth Lewis Hale, the first permanent settlers in the valley. As the seventh of nine children, Emma spent a happy childhood learning to ride horses and to canoe on the Susquehanna with her brothers, while honing her quick wit among her other siblings. She attended school whenever opportunity permitted, including a year beyond the common grammar school education of her brothers and sisters. Tall and gangly as a youth, she grew to be a stately, handsome, dark-haired woman.

Emma met Joseph Smith when he and his father arrived in Harmony to work for an acquaintance of the Hales, Josiah Stowell (sometimes spelled Stoal). During the two years he worked in the area, Joseph twice asked Isaac Hale for permission to marry Emma, but was twice refused, because he was "a stranger." At age twenty-two, Emma Hale married Joseph Smith on January 18, 1827, in South Bainbridge, New York, without her father's permission, and moved to Manchester, New York, to make her home with Joseph's parents. That experience marked the beginning of a warm, supportive, and enduring relationship between Emma and her mother-in-law, Lucy Mack SMITH. Returning briefly to Harmony to collect her belongings, Emma and Joseph were told the Hales's door would always be open to them, despite her father's continuing reservations about the man she had chosen to marry.

In the fall of 1827, Joseph, accompanied by Emma, finally obtained the gold plates from which he was to translate the Book of Mormon. Though never permitted to see the plates, Emma handled them frequently within their protective cover and helped hide them against the violent intrusion of townspeople in New York who sought the plates for the fortune they represented. Harmony offered refuge to Joseph and Emma, and so the young couple fled there, where Joseph hoped to translate the plates without disturbance. He bought a small farm from his father-in-law and engaged in sporadic farming. Emma became the first of several scribes who assisted in the translation. On June 15, 1828, she gave birth to their first child, a boy, who lived only a few hours. When the threats of Harmony residents began to hinder the work there, Emma and Joseph moved to Fayette, New York, where in June 1829 the translation was completed. In March 1830 the work was published in Palmyra, New York, as the Book of Mormon.

On April 6, 1830, Joseph Smith formally organized the Church of Christ, as The Church of Jesus Christ of Latter-day Saints was first known. Emma was baptized at Colesville, New York, on June 28, 1830, but before she could be confirmed a member of the Church the following day, Joseph was arrested "for being a disorderly person and setting the country in an uproar by preaching the Book of Mormon." He was vilified by his captors and subjected to two spurious trials, but was finally released. For the remainder of his life, Joseph would seldom be free of such encounters, and Emma would never again, during her husband's lifetime, know more than temporary respite from the anxiety she felt on that occasion.

Returning to Harmony in July 1830, Emma was the subject of a revelation received by Joseph but addressed specifically to Emma (D&C 25). In it she was designated the "Elect Lady," which Joseph would later explain means one elected "to preside." She was told that her calling was to be a support and comfort to her husband, to continue to act as his scribe, and "to expound scriptures and to exhort the church." She was also commissioned to prepare a hymnal for the Church, which was published five years later. Emma received her long-awaited confirmation in August 1830, almost two months after her baptism.

In August, Joseph and Emma moved back to Fayette, living there until January 1831, when they moved to Kirtland, Ohio. Like many other early converts, Emma was never to see her parents again, nor was she able to effect a lasting reconciliation between her father and husband.

On April 30, 1831, three months after moving to Kirtland, Emma gave birth to twins, both of whom died within hours. Nearby, a friend, Julia Clapp Murdock, wife of John Murdock, died after also giving birth to twins. Unable to care for them alone, her husband asked the bereft Joseph and Emma to raise his twins as their own. This they gladly did, naming the infants Joseph and Julia.

Emma faced continued difficulties during her eight-year residence in Kirtland. To the alarm of original settlers, Latter-day Saint converts swelled the community, inflating land values and creating hardship and dissension both within and outside the Church (*see* KIRTLAND ECONOMY). Scarcity of goods plagued the new residents. Emma witnessed again both the abuse and the fierce loyalty her husband and his work engendered. On March 24, 1832, she saw him dragged from the John Johnson house in the night and tarred and feathered by an angry mob. Five days later, she mourned the death of her adopted son, Joseph, from exposure to the cold as a result of mob action. Enduring her husband's frequent absences on Church business, Emma was obliged to support herself and her children by taking boarders into her already crowded quarters, an expedient that she would frequently employ throughout her life.

When the Saints in Missouri, like those in Kirtland, began experiencing the hostility of earlier settlers, Emma helped gather supplies for the men of Zion's Camp, who accompanied Joseph to Missouri to assist the beleaguered members there. She also provided room and board for builders of the temple in Kirtland and shared her means with new converts flooding into the area. With the assistance of William W. Phelps, she completed the first edition of the hymnal before the dedication of the Kirtland Temple in 1836, fulfilling the charge given her by revelation in 1830. She also gave birth to two more sons, Joseph (later known as Joseph III), born November 6, 1832, and Frederick Granger Williams, born June 20, 1836, both of whom lived to manhood.

In 1838, as relations with their Kirtland neighbors deteriorated and the Church experienced increasing internal difficulties, Emma followed her husband and other members to Missouri to consolidate the Church in one central location. Emma, Joseph, and their three children joined the settlement in Far West, the new center of the Church, and Emma gave birth to another son, Alexander Hale, on June 2, 1838. Missourians, however, continued to resist the LDS incursion, resentful of their growing political power. When feelings erupted into widespread violence and an order from the governor expelled the Mormons, they turned eastward to Illinois, leaving their Prophet imprisoned in Liberty Jail (*see* MISSOURI CONFLICT). While her husband languished there through the winter of 1838–1839, Emma, with two babies in her arms and two at her skirts, walked across Missouri, finally crossing the frozen Mississippi to refuge in Quincy, Illinois, carrying the manuscript of her husband's translation of the Bible hidden in pockets in her clothing. From there she wrote to her husband of the trials she had endured, but vowed that she was "yet willing to suffer more if it is the will of kind heaven" (Joseph Smith Letterbook, Mar. 7, 1839, HDC).

While Emma suffered physical deprivation, harassment, and mob violence in New York, Pennsylvania, Ohio, and Missouri, the emotional and spiritual challenges she experienced in Nauvoo, Illinois, where the Church finally established itself, had more than personal ramifications. She and Joseph moved into a small house near the southern edge of the new town, later building a home they called the Mansion House, which also served as an inn or hotel for travelers. During the next five years, Emma gave birth to three more sons, losing one at birth and a second at eighteen months to a fever. Her last child, David Hyrum, was born November 17, 1844, five months after her husband's murder.

At the inception of the Female Relief Society of Nauvoo in 1842, Emma was elected president of the organization. As the Elect Lady, she was to preside "during good behavior" and "as long as [she] shall continue to fill the office with dignity" (Record of the Female Relief Society of Nauvoo). From March until October, Emma presided regularly and Joseph frequently attended, counseling the women on the charitable mission of the society and how they would "come in possession of the privileges, blessings, and gifts" associated with the priesthood (*HC* 4:602). Emma pressed for vigilance in watching over the morals of the community and diligence in succoring the poor. She saw the organization grow from a charter membership of twenty women to more than 1,100 at the end of the first year.

The following year, Emma became the first woman to receive the endowment, an ordinance that would later be administered to all worthy members in the temple then under construction in Nauvoo. Joseph Smith had earlier introduced these ordinances to some of his closest associates, and before his death as many as sixty-five men and women would receive them, with Emma officiating for the women. Joseph did not live to see the completion of the temple, and Emma chose not to participate during the brief period when temple ordinances were administered there before the Saints' exodus from Nauvoo in 1846.

The suspension of the Relief Society in 1844, only two years after its organization, was later attributed by John Taylor to Emma's opposition to plural marriage or polygyny (more commonly, polygamy) and concern over her use of the society to preach against it ("Minutes of the General Meeting," [of the Retrenchment Association], July 17, 1880, reported in the *Woman's Exponent* 9 [Sept. 1, 1880]:53–54). The practice had been privately disclosed as a Church principle in 1840, and Emma's ambivalence enabled her husband to act on her brief acceptance of the doctrine long enough to take additional wives. But her rejection of the principle soon became paramount. Loyal to her husband for seventeen years through all the vicissitudes that his mission had entailed, Emma Smith was unable, at the end, to make the sacrifice that the doctrine of plural marriage required. She struggled between her faith in her husband's prophetic role and her aversion to a principle that he, as Prophet, had been instructed to institute.

After Joseph's martyrdom in June 1844, Emma unfortunately became a symbol of the dissension within the Church. Unable to condone continuation of the practice of plural marriage or the leadership of Brigham YOUNG, who supported it, and ambivalent about the proper line of succession to her husband, Emma made her first priority after her husband's death the preservation of an inheritance for her five living children. Distinguishing Joseph's personal property from that of the Church defied easy solution, however, and involved Brigham Young and Emma Smith in a series of complex and often bitter legal entanglements. Brigham Young, as president of the Quorum of the Twelve Apostles and steward of the Church, claimed all that he felt rightfully belonged to its members. Emma Smith, as guardian of Joseph's children, just as vigorously claimed their share, to which she had contributed throughout her marriage to Joseph. Unable to reach an amicable solution and unwilling to accept plural marriage even in principle, Emma elected to remain in Nauvoo with her family while Brigham Young led the majority of Church members to the Rocky Mountains in 1846. On December 23, 1847, Emma Smith married Lewis Bidamon, a non-Mormon, further estranging her from the Church, to which she had once been known as the Elect Lady. Bidamon assisted Emma in raising her five children and remained her companion until her death in 1879 in Nauvoo.

In 1860, Emma's eldest son, Joseph Smith III, after four years of refusal, accepted the invitation to serve as prophet and first president of the Reorganized Church of Jesus Christ of Latter Day Saints. It was offered by a group of men who formerly had been members of the Church, many of whom had left to follow James J. Strang for a time. As a group they chose not to go west with the body of the Church. Emma, who had heretofore rejected connection with any of the splinter Mormon groups, was admitted into membership in 1860. In his acceptance speech, Joseph III firmly rejected polygamy as a practice of the new church, and Emma denied that her husband had participated in the practice.

Still devoted to her mother-in-law, Emma cared for her until Lucy died in 1856. The Prophet's mother had always admired Emma. "I have never seen a woman in my life, who would endure every species of fatigue and hardship, from month to month, and from year to year," she wrote, "with that unflinching courage, zeal, and patience, which she has ever done" (Smith, pp. 190–91).

Emma Smith Bidamon's final years in Nauvoo were family-focused and private. She shared the Nauvoo House, her final home, with relatives and friends and basked in the love and care of her children and grandchildren. She continued to live her life with genteel qualities, meeting adversity and difficulty with grace and equanimity. She was polite to the "Utah Mormons" who occasionally visited, but was firm in her decision to remain apart from them.

Though Emma was publicly criticized by Church leaders for her failure to remain faithful to her husband's mission, she was sympathetically remembered by some of her former Nauvoo friends. Many of them, unlike Emma, had found the courage to accept the doctrine of plural marriage. "I know it was hard for Emma, and any woman to enter plural marriage in those days," wrote Emily Partridge Young, a plural wife, "and I do not know as anybody would have done any better than Emma did under the circumstances" (*Woman's Exponent* 12 [Apr. 1, 1884]:165).

In 1892 at the jubilee celebration in Salt Lake City of the founding of the Nauvoo Relief Society, a motion to hang a life-size portrait of Emma Smith in the Tabernacle brought mixed responses from the Relief Society board members. To settle the question, Relief Society president Zina D. H. Young took the matter to Church President Wilford Woodruff, who replied that "anyone who opposed it [hanging the portrait in the Tabernacle] must be very narrow minded indeed" (Emmeline B. Wells Diary, March 11, 1892, HDC). Fifty years had softened bitter memories, and Emma Smith could once again be honored as a leader of women and remembered for the essential part she had played in the restoration of the gospel and the support she gave her Prophet-husband through the difficult years of his ministry.

BIBLIOGRAPHY

Newell, Linda King, and Valeen Tippetts Avery. *Mormon Enigma: Emma Hale Smith.* Garden City, N.Y., 1984.

Smith, Lucy Mack. *History of Joseph Smith.* Salt Lake City, 1958.

Youngreen, Buddy. *Reflections of Emma, Joseph Smith's Wife.* Orem, Utah, 1982.

CAROL CORNWALL MADSEN

SMITH, GEORGE ALBERT

George Albert Smith (1870–1951), the eighth President of the Church, was born April 4, 1870, in Salt Lake City, the son of John

Henry Smith and Sarah Farr. His grandfather, George A. Smith, was an apostle and counselor to President Brigham YOUNG, and his father, John Henry Smith, was an apostle and counselor to President Joseph F. SMITH. His mother was a daughter of Lorin Farr, the pioneer founder and early mayor of Ogden, Utah. On May 25, 1892, George Albert Smith married Lucy Emily Woodruff, the daughter of Wilford Woodruff, Jr., and Emily Jane Smith. They had three children: Emily (Mrs. Robert M. Stewart), Edith (Mrs. George O. Elliott), and George Albert, Jr. George Albert Smith was ordained an apostle at thirty-three years of age on October 8, 1903, by President Joseph F. Smith.

In his youth he worked in the ZCMI factory and as a salesman, traveling by wagon throughout Utah. He attended Brigham Young Academy and the University of Deseret (later the University of Utah). When he was on a railroad surveying job in eastern Utah, the glare of the sun permanently impaired his eyesight. In 1896 he declared for the Republican party and campaigned for William McKinley, which won him appointment in 1897 as receiver for the Land Office in Utah, a position to which he was reappointed in 1902 by Theodore Roosevelt.

At the time of his call to the apostleship in 1903, George Albert Smith was president of the Young Men's Mutual Improvement Association (YMMIA) in the Salt Lake Stake, with some forty wards to supervise. In 1891 he had undertaken a short mission for the Church among the young people in Juab, Millard, Beaver, and Parowan stakes, and in June 1892, a week after his marriage, he was called to the Southern States Mission under President J. Golden Kimball. Elder Smith was soon appointed mission secretary. His wife joined him, and they served in the mission office until June 1894.

His call to the apostleship entailed continual weekly visiting to the established stakes of the Church, organizing new wards and stakes, and supervising the missions of the Church. His travels averaged 30,000 miles yearly, and his attendance at meetings averaged more than ten per week.

Under this pressure, his already frail health broke, and his life became a constant struggle against physical weakness. Through his remaining years he guarded his energies and rationed them to fulfill his responsibilities. His illness was diagnosed only at end of life as lupus erythematosus, a disease that produces chronic weakness.

President Smith was a master of the art of making friends. Wherever he went he especially cultivated the acquaintance and companionship of the leaders of the people. Whether it was the President of the United States or the Lord Mayor of London, he established a friendship. His friends were legion, throughout the Church and around the globe.

Some of his finest work was done with youth. Over a lifetime he served in every capacity in the YMMIA, and shortly after becoming an apostle, he was called to the YMMIA General Board, serving from 1904 to 1921. As general superintendent of that organization from 1921 to 1935, he was influential in setting policies, establishing programs, and directing youth activities throughout the Church.

President Smith gained international prominence as a scout. When scouting came to the United States in 1910, he recommended its incorporation into the YMMIA program, where it came under his leadership. Beginning in 1931, he served on the advisory board of the National Council of Boy Scouts of America. At this time Utah and the Church came to lead the world in the percentage of boys registered as scouts and explorers. In 1932 he was awarded the Silver Beaver, and in 1934, the Silver Buffalo, two of scouting's highest awards.

As president of the European Mission from June 1919 to July 1921, he won the love and admiration of the missionaries and the Saints and made many friends for the Church. As World War I had just ended, a major task was to reestablish missionary work and help the Saints adjust. President Smith inaugurated friendly relations with governments and visited missionaries and Saints in Ireland, Scotland, France, Switzerland, Norway, Denmark, Sweden, and Germany. Between January and July 1938, he and Rufus K. Hardy of the First Council of the Seventy visited the missions of the Pacific Ocean area: Hawaii, the Fiji Islands, New Zealand, Australia, Tonga, and the Samoa Islands.

Throughout his life George Albert Smith maintained intense personal interests rooted in his pioneer family and Church heritage. He carried on his father's interest in irrigation, dry farming, and reclamation. Between 1913 and 1918 he attended the meetings of the International Irrigation Congress, the International Dry-farm Congress, and their successor, the International Farm Congress. At each of these congresses he was elected either a vice-president or president, increasing his friendships throughout the United States and Canada.

He had a keen interest in identifying and marking HISTORIC SITES. He was at Sharon, Vermont, for the 1905 dedication of the monument noting the centennial anniversary of the birth of the Prophet Joseph SMITH. In June 1907 he and others negotiated for the purchase of the Joseph Smith, Sr., farm in Manchester, New York. In 1937 he took the initiative in organizing the Utah Pioneer Trails and Landmarks Association, whose first purpose was to erect a monument at the mouth of Emigration Canyon to honor the arrival of the pioneers of 1847, a project realized in July 1947 with the "THIS IS THE PLACE" MONUMENT. More than a hundred historic monuments and markers were erected by the association, from Nauvoo to Utah and throughout the West.

Proud of his American patriot ancestry, President Smith affiliated with the Sons of the American Revolution. He was active in the Utah chapter and was elected a trustee of the national society.

His appreciation for his Smith family heritage included cordial relations with his cousins, the descendants of Joseph Smith III, and with other leaders of the REORGANIZED CHURCH OF JESUS CHRIST OF LATTER DAY SAINTS.

President George Albert Smith both taught and lived the two great commandments to "love the Lord thy God" and to "love thy neighbour as thyself" (Matt. 22:37–39). To him, all people were the children of God, and he could in no way hurt a child of God. "All the people of the earth are our Father's children, . . . regardless of race, creed, or color, all men are our brothers." He taught that "men cannot approach the likeness of God except by the practice of love to their fellow men. Only by love can peace and joy be made to cover the earth." Other recurring themes and aphorisms in his teachings include: "This is our Father's work." "Keep on the Lord's side of the line." "Seek ye first the Kingdom of God and his righteousness." "There is only one aristocracy that God recognizes, and that is the aristocracy of righteousness" (Papers, Box 96). He preached of honest work, thrift, self-reliance, good homes, education, and progress. He gave comfort and cheer, praise and encouragement, without offense and without guile. He was the apostle of kindness and love.

There was no room in his heart for hatred, anger, envy, resentment, or fear. "To him have been given many of the qualities which can only be described as being Christlike" (John D. Giles, *IE* 48 [July 1945]:388).

President Smith exemplified these qualities in all aspects of his personal life. He measured his life by the yardstick of service and was happiest when assisting the poor, the widows, and the fatherless, or visiting the sick among his neighbors or in hospitals. He was always polite, gentlemanly, tactful, forgiving, and kind, a man of peace who cultivated goodwill among all people. He lifted the burdens from the shoulders of both friends and strangers, planted hope in the human heart, and restored confidence. He practiced the divine law of love.

Upon the death of Elder Rudger Clawson on June 21, 1943, George Albert Smith was selected president of the Quorum of the Twelve Apostles, which office he held for two years. When President Heber J. Grant died, George Albert Smith was sustained President of the Church, May 21, 1945, at the age of seventy-five.

World War II ended that summer, and President Smith led a group to Washington, D.C., to facilitate the sending of Church welfare goods to Church members in war-devastated Europe. During the weeks that followed, the Church shipped 133 railroad carloads of food, clothing, and bedding, along with thousands of individual eleven-pound packages.

During President Smith's administration, he asked Spencer W. KIMBALL, an apostle, to assist in supervising the Navajo-Zuni Indian Mission, and he himself headed a delegation to the nation's capital to initiate plans to help Native Americans.

Missionary work was revitalized throughout the world after cutbacks during World War II. New stakes and missions were organized. The number of missionaries rose to more than 5,000, and the number of wards and branches increased from 1,273 to 1,492, and stakes from 149 to 179. Some 200 new meetinghouses were built. New hospitals were constructed and old ones enlarged. Microfilming of vital records was accelerated so that by February 1950 a total of 24,579 microfilm records had been catalogued. On September 23, 1945, President Smith dedicated the Idaho Falls Temple.

President George Albert Smith died on April 4, 1951, on his

eighty-first birthday, leaving as his chief legacy an example of Christlike living.

BIBLIOGRAPHY

Pusey, Merlo J. *Builders of the Kingdom: George A. Smith, John Henry Smith, George Albert Smith*, pp. 203–364. Provo, Utah, 1981.

Smith, George Albert. Papers, Folders 1–4, Box 96. Special Collections, University of Utah Library, Salt Lake City.

Stubbs, Glen R. "A Biography of George Albert Smith, 1870–1951." Ph.D. diss., Brigham Young University, 1974.

S. GEORGE ELLSWORTH

SMITH, HYRUM

Among early Mormon leaders, Hyrum Smith (1800–1844) stands next to his brother the Prophet Joseph SMITH in the esteem of many Latter-day Saints. Although nearly six years older than his prophet brother, Hyrum became Joseph's closest adviser and confidant. When he died a martyr with Joseph on June 27, 1844, Hyrum was Associate President of the Church, second in authority.

Hyrum was born to Joseph SMITH, Sr., and Lucy Mack SMITH on February 9, 1800, in Tunbridge, Vermont. During his childhood, the family moved to eight different locations near the Connecticut River while the father struggled as a farmer, storekeeper, and tenant farmer. At age eleven, Hyrum was sent to Moor's Charity School, associated with Dartmouth College. About two years later, a severe epidemic of typhoid fever broke out and Hyrum returned home ill to find several siblings ill as well. Joseph, Jr., was stricken with the dreaded disease, which developed into osteomyelitis in his left leg. Hyrum, who was already recognized for his tender and compassionate nature, became young Joseph's nurse, developing an enduring bond between the brothers.

After the family moved to New York, Hyrum and the other Smith brothers helped the family finances by hiring out as farm laborers, coopers, and masons, in addition to clearing their own land for farming. On November 2, 1826, Hyrum married Jerusha Barden (1805–1837).

After Joseph received the plates and started translating the Book of Mormon, Hyrum journeyed to Harmony, Pennsylvania, in 1828, and again in May 1829, to learn how the work was progressing. Joseph sought a revelation at Hyrum's earnest request in which Hyrum learned that after he had prepared himself by studying the Bible and the teachings soon to come forth in the Book of Mormon, he was called to "assist to bring forth my work" and to preach "nothing but repentance" (D&C 11:9, 22). Early in June 1829, Hyrum was baptized in Seneca Lake, New York. Toward the end of June, he became one of the Eight Witnesses, examining and "hefting" the plates of gold. He served as Oliver Cowdery's bodyguard as he delivered a few pages of the Book of Mormon manuscript each day to the printer in Palmyra.

When the Church was organized under New York state law on April 6, 1830, Hyrum was the oldest at age thirty of the six men who signed their names as charter members. He was told, "Thy duty is unto the church forever" (D&C 23:3), a duty he faithfully fulfilled. Hyrum became one of the first preachers of the Church in surrounding communities in New York, baptizing some of the earliest converts. When a substantial branch of the Church was formed in Colesville, Hyrum was called as its presiding officer.

In 1831 Hyrum Smith moved, along with most Church members, to Kirtland, Ohio. Between 1831 and 1833 he served three proselytizing missions to Missouri and Ohio. In 1834 he helped recruit members for Zion's Camp and served as Joseph Smith's chief aide in that military March. Upon his return, Hyrum became foreman of the stone quarry for the rising Kirtland Temple. Having proved his ability and faithfulness, Hyrum was ordained an Assistant President of the Church in December 1834. His responsibilities were further increased in November 1837 when he became Second Counselor in the First Presidency with Joseph Smith and Sidney Rigdon, and with Oliver Cowdery as Associate President.

In Missouri in October 1838, when the Latter-day Saints clashed with their neighbors, Joseph, Hyrum, Sidney Rigdon, and several other Mormons were arrested on false charges of treason, murder, arson, and stealing. They were taken to Richmond, Missouri, for trial, while the rest of the Saints were driven from the state (*see* MISSOURI CONFLICT). After a preliminary hearing in November, Joseph and Hyrum were bound over for trial. For nearly five more months, they and three others shared a jail cell in the village of Liberty, Missouri, while state officials deliberated on their fate. On April 16, 1839, during a second change of venue, they were allowed to escape.

In the Saints' new home along the Mississippi in Illinois, Hyrum Smith was ordained to two prominent positions in the Church: Presiding patriarch, in place of his deceased father (D&C 124:91), and Associate President of the Church, in place of Oliver Cowdery (D&C 124:95). When Joseph Smith traveled to Washington, D.C., to seek redress from federal officials for the Saints' Missouri grievances, Hyrum served as Acting President of the Church in Nauvoo. Hyrum pronounced hundreds of patriarchal blessings upon the members of the Church, including numerous converts arriving from Britain. He was a founding leader of the Nauvoo Masonic lodge. In 1842 he clarified that "hot drinks" in the Word of Wisdom (D&C 89:9) referred to tea and coffee (*T&S* 3:800), a point that had been controversial. He was also the chairman of the Nauvoo Temple Building Committee and stood close to the Prophet Joseph, acting "in concert" with him in all leadership capacities (D&C 124:95).

Latter-day Saints revered their "Prophet Joseph" and "Patriarch Hyrum"; enemies of the Church despised both them and the power they represented. As events led toward Joseph's assassination in Carthage, Hyrum refused to leave him, even though Joseph requested that Hyrum flee with his family to Cincinnati. He went with Joseph to Carthage in June 1844 and was charged with riot and treason, along with his brother. When a mob stormed the jail where they were confined awaiting trial, Hyrum, standing to hold the door shut, was the first to die from gunfire through the door. Joseph and Hyrum became dual martyrs. Like many of "the Lord's anointed in ancient times," they sealed their works with their own blood; "in life they were not divided, and in death they were not separated" (D&C 135:3; *see also* CARTHAGE JAIL; MARTYRDOM OF JOSEPH AND HYRUM SMITH).

Hyrum Smith is credited in Church history with being an astute organizer who gave ecclesiastical leadership to the emerging Church. As a person, he was considered a man without guile. One scripture concerning him reads, "I, the Lord, love him because of the integrity of his heart" (D&C 124:15). With a love for Hyrum that was stronger than death, Joseph once described him as possessing "the mildness of a lamb, and the integrity of a Job, and in short, the meekness and humility of Christ" (*HC* 2:338). When John Taylor looked upon Hyrum's slain body, he reflected, "He was a great and good man, and my soul was cemented to his. If ever there was an exemplary, honest, and virtuous man, an embodiment of all that is noble in the human form, Hyrum Smith was its representative" (*HC* 7:107).

Hyrum and his first wife, Jerusha, had four daughters and two sons. After Jerusha's death, he married Mary Fielding in 1837, and she bore him a son and a daughter. When Joseph Smith introduced PLURAL MARRIAGE to him, Hyrum at first opposed the idea, but when converted to the principle, he became one of its staunchest advocates.

Many of Hyrum's descendants have played significant roles in Church history. A son, Joseph F. SMITH, became the sixth President of the Church, and a grandson, Joseph Fielding SMITH, became the tenth President. Four of the six patriarchs to the Church since 1845 have been descendants of Hyrum Smith.

BIBLIOGRAPHY

Corbett, Pearson H. *Hyrum Smith, Patriarch.* Salt Lake City, 1963.

Smith, Joseph Fielding. "The Martyrs." *IE* 47 (June 1944):364–65, 414–15.

BRUCE A. VAN ORDEN

SMITH, JOSEPH

[*This entry is divided into four parts:*

The Prophet
Teachings of Joseph Smith
Writings of Joseph Smith
Legal Trials of Joseph Smith

The Prophet *is a biography of Joseph Smith;* Teachings of Joseph Smith *sketches his thought and teachings;* Writings of Joseph Smith *examines his personal writings and the body of scripture, revelations, and history resulting from his ministry; and* Trials of Joseph Smith *recounts his legal and judicial history. See also* Visions of Joseph Smith.

Historical overviews of LDS history during the Joseph Smith period are History of the Church: c. 1820–1831; c. 1831–1844. *For entries dealing with his prophetic calling consult* Prophet Joseph Smith. *For Joseph Smith's family background, see* Smith Family *and* Smith Family Ancestors; *see also entries for his mother,* Lucy Mack Smith; *his father,* Joseph Smith, Sr.; *his brother* Hyrum Smith, *and his wife,* Emma Hale Smith.]

THE PROPHET

Joseph Smith, Jr. (1805–1844), often referred to as the Prophet Joseph Smith, was the founding prophet of The Church of Jesus Christ of Latter-day Saints. Latter-day Saints call him "the Prophet" because, in the tradition of Old and New Testament prophets, he depended on revelation from God for his teachings, not on his own learning. They accept his revelations, many of them published as the Doctrine and Covenants and as the Pearl of Great Price, as scripture to accompany the Bible. As a young man, Joseph Smith also translated a sacred record from ancient America known as the Book of Mormon. These revelations and records restored to the earth the pure gospel of Christ. Joseph Smith's role in history was to found the Church of Jesus Christ based on this restored gospel in preparation for the second coming of Christ.

Little in his background pointed toward this momentous life. Joseph Smith's ancestors were ordinary New England farm people. His Smith ancestors emigrated from England to America in the seventeenth century and settled in Topsfield, Massachusetts, where they attained local distinction. His grandfather Asael Smith, unable at the time to pay the debts on the family farm, sold the farm, liquidated the debts, and migrated in 1791 to Tunbridge, Vermont, where he purchased enough land to provide for his sons. Joseph Smith's Mack ancestors, from Scotland, settled in Lyme, Connecticut, prospered for a while, and then fell on hard times. Joseph's grandfather Solomon Mack attempted various enterprises in New England and New York, with little financial success. One of the Mack sons moved to Tunbridge, and through him Lucy Mack met Joseph Smith, Sr., one of Asael's sons. The pair married in 1796. They had eleven children, nine of whom lived to adulthood. Joseph Smith, Jr., born December 23, 1805, in Sharon, Vermont, was the third son to live and the fourth child.

Young Joseph had little formal schooling. His parents lost their

Tunbridge farm in 1803 through a failed business venture and for the next fourteen years moved from one tenant farm to another. In 1816 they migrated to Palmyra, New York, just north of the Finger Lakes, where in 1817 they purchased a farm in Farmington (later Manchester), the township immediately south of Palmyra. Clearing land and wresting a living from the soil left little time for school. "As it required the exertions of all that were able to render any assistance for the support of the Family," Joseph wrote in 1832, "we were deprived of the bennifit of an education suffice it to say I was mearly instructid in reading writing and the ground rules of Arithmatic which constuted my whole literary acquirements" (Jessee, 1989–, 1:5). His mother described him as "much less inclined to the perusal of books than any of the rest of the children, but far more given to meditation and deep study" (Smith, p. 84). His knowledge of the Bible and his biblical style of writing suggest that much of his early education came from that source.

One subject he pondered was religion. His parents had been reared under the influence of New England Congregationalism but, dissatisfied with the preachers around them, they were not regular churchgoers. Both parents had deep religious experiences and an intense longing for salvation, without having a satisfactory way to worship. A few years after settling in Palmyra, Lucy Smith and three of the children joined the Presbyterians; Joseph, Sr., and the others stayed home, Joseph, Jr., among them. Young Joseph was deeply perplexed about which church to join, and the preaching of the revival ministers in the area intensified his uncertainty.

In the spring of 1820, when he was just fourteen, Joseph turned directly to God for guidance. The answer was astonishing. As he prayed in the woods near his house, the Father and the Son appeared to him. Assuring him that his sins were forgiven, the Lord told him that none of the churches were right and that he should join none. Latter-day Saints call this Joseph Smith's FIRST VISION, the initial event in the restoration of the gospel. At the time, it made little impression on the people around Joseph Smith. He told a minister about the vision and was rebuffed. Believing the Bible sufficient, ministers were skeptical of direct revelation. The scorn upset Joseph, who had only tried to report his actual experience, and alienated him still further from the churches.

After three years with no further revelations, Joseph wondered if he still was in favor with God and prayed again for direction and forgiveness. The vision he received on September 21, 1823, set the course of his life for the next seven years. An angel appeared and instructed him about a sacred record of an ancient people. This angel, $Moroni_2$, told Joseph that he was to obtain the record, written on gold plates, and translate it. He also told him that God's covenant with ancient Israel was about to be fulfilled, that preparation for the second coming of Christ was about to commence, and that the gospel was to be preached to all nations to prepare a people for Christ's millennial reign. In a vision Joseph saw the hill near his home where the plates were buried. When he went the next day to get the plates, the angel stopped him. He was told that he must wait four years to obtain the plates and that, until then, he was to return each year for instructions. On September 22, 1827, he obtained the plates from which he translated the Book of Mormon (*see* MORONI, VISITATIONS OF).

The discovery of gold plates in a hillside resonated strangely with other experiences of the Smith family. Like many other New Englanders, they were familiar with searches for lost treasure by supernatural means. Joseph Smith's father was reputed to be one of these treasure-seekers, and Joseph Smith himself had found a stone, called a seer stone, which reportedly enabled him to find lost objects. Treasure-seekers wanted to employ him to help with their searches. One, a man named Josiah Stowell (sometimes spelled Stoal), hired Joseph and his father in 1825 to dig for a supposed Spanish treasure near HARMONY, PENNSYLVANIA. The effort came to nothing, and the Smiths returned home, but the neighbors continued to think of the Smiths as part of the treasure-seeking company. Joseph Smith had to learn, in his four years of waiting, to appreciate the plates solely for their religious worth and not for their monetary value. The angel forbade Joseph to remove the plates on his first viewing because thoughts of their commercial worth had crossed his mind. Joseph had to learn to focus on the religious purpose of the plates and put aside considerations of their value as gold.

While working in Harmony in 1825, Joseph Smith met Emma Hale at the Hale home where he and his father boarded. He continued seeing her through the next year while working at other jobs in the area, and on January 18, 1827, they married. She was tall, straight, slender, and dark-haired; he stood over six feet tall with broad chest and shoulders, light brown hair, and blue eyes. After the wedding they went to live with the Smith family in Manchester, close to the hill Cumorah where the plates still lay buried.

On September 22, 1827, Joseph Smith went to the hill for the fifth time. This time the angel permitted him to take the plates, with strict instructions to show them to no one. Designing people tried strenuously to get the plates, however, and he was not left in peace to begin translation. Eventually he and Emma were compelled to move, for their safety, to Harmony, near Emma's family.

For the next three years, Joseph's work depended on the support of a few loyal friends who came to his aid and helped buffer him from troublesome inquirers. His open manner inspired confidence, and his candor in simply narrating what had happened to him disarmed skepticism. His brother later wrote that Joseph's youth, his lack of education, and his "whole character and disposition" convinced the family that he was incapable of "giving utterance to anything but the truth" (*William Smith on Mormonism*, Lamoni, Iowa, 1883, pp. 9–10). By the time the translation was completed and the Book of Mormon published, three or four dozen people believed in his mission and divine gifts.

Martin HARRIS, a prosperous Palmyra farmer, was one of these friends. He helped Joseph move to Harmony and then moved there himself to help with the translation. To enable him to translate, Joseph received with the plates a special instrument called interpreters or Urim and Thummim. As he dictated, Martin Harris wrote. In the spring of 1828, after three months of work, Martin Harris took the 116 pages of the translation home to show his wife, and they were lost or stolen. This interrupted the translation and left Joseph desolate. Soon after, he received a scathing rebuke in a revelation (D&C 3). About this time, Joseph and Emma's firstborn son died on the day of his birth, June 15, 1828, wrenching Joseph's feelings even further.

Translation resumed in the fall of 1828, continuing intermittently until the spring of 1829. Then Oliver COWDERY, a schoolteacher who learned of the plates from Joseph's parents, believed in Joseph and agreed to take dictation. From April to June 1829 they labored together. When the two friends prayed on May 15 for an understanding of baptism, a messenger who announced himself as John the

Baptist appeared, conferred priesthood authority upon them, and instructed them to baptize each other. Oliver later wrote: "These were days never to be forgotten—to sit under the sound of a voice dictated by the inspiration of heaven, awakened the utmost gratitude of this bosom" (JS—H 1:71n).

Oliver was not the only additional witness to the revelations. When opposition began to build in Harmony, Oliver and Joseph moved in June 1829 to Fayette, New York, to the family home of Oliver's friend David WHITMER. Here again Joseph received needed support from people who believed in him. Once the translation was completed, Joseph was told that others would be allowed to see the plates, which until that time only he had viewed. The angel Moroni appeared to Martin Harris, Oliver Cowdery, and David Whitmer and showed them the gold plates while a voice from heaven declared that the translation was done by the power of God and was true. Joseph's mother reported that Joseph came into the house after this revelation and threw himself down beside her, exclaiming that at last someone else had seen the plates. "Now they know for themselves, that I do not go about to deceive" (Smith, p. 139). His words suggest the pressure he felt in being the only witness of his remarkable experiences.

In March 1830 the Book of Mormon was published, ending one phase of Joseph's life but not his divine mission. Revelations in 1829 instructed him to organize a church. On April 6, 1830, at the Whitmers' house in Fayette, New York, the Church of Christ was organized with Joseph Smith and Oliver Cowdery as first and second elders.

Leadership of the Church set Joseph Smith's life on a new course. Up to this time he had been a young man with a divine gift and a mission to translate the Book of Mormon; now, without any previous organizational experience, he was responsible for organizing a church and leading a people. He had to rely on revelation. Over the next six years, he received many revelations, 90 of which fill 190 pages in the Doctrine and Covenants. They range from instructions on mundane details of administration to exalted depictions of life hereafter. Typically, when problems had to be solved, whether administrative or doctrinal, the Prophet sought divine guidance and by virtue of this help led the Church.

The course the revelations laid out for the new Church was extraordinarily challenging. The Prophet received instructions for ventures reaching halfway across the continent and involving a reorganization of society. At the core of the instruction was the establishment of Zion. Book of Mormon teachings of Christ made reference to a New Jerusalem, a city of Zion that would be established in America (3 Ne. 20:22). Later revelations outlined the nature of the new order. The central concept was the gathering of the pure and honest from among the nations into communities where they could learn to live in unity and love under divine direction, and where temples could be built to administer the sacred ordinances of salvation.

In September–October 1830, missionaries were called to teach Native Americans who resided near the western boundary of Missouri (*see* LAMANITE MISSION). These missionaries were told that the city of Zion would be located somewhere in that region. Later revelations called for a gathering to Missouri to organize Zion, and a new economic order designed to enable the Saints to live together in unity (*see* CONSECRATION). Joseph and other leading figures in the Church journeyed to Jackson County, Missouri, in the summer of 1831, and there learned by revelation that the city was to be constructed and a temple built near Independence, Missouri (*see* MISSOURI: LDS COMMUNITIES IN JACKSON AND CLAY COUNTIES). The gathering was to commence immediately.

When it is remembered that Joseph Smith was not yet twenty-six, and five years earlier was an uneducated farmer notable only for his spiritual gifts, the daring of these plans is hard to comprehend. The magnitude of his conceptions never troubled him. "I intend to lay a foundation that will revolutionize the whole world," he later remarked (*HC* 6:365). He acted in the certainty that the directions were from God and that the Church would triumph against all odds.

In the spring of 1831 virtually all Latter-day Saints left New York for Ohio. Joseph and Emma settled in KIRTLAND, OHIO, near a body of new converts, and for the next six years this was Church headquarters. The other focal point of Church life until 1838 was Missouri, first Independence, the site of the future city of Zion, then northern Missouri. As Latter-day Saints migrated to Missouri, tensions with old settlers increased. In Jackson County, in 1831–1833, and again in Caldwell County, in 1836–1838, efforts to establish Zion aroused violent opposition to what non-Mormons perceived as a threat to their way of life (*see* MISSOURI CONFLICT).

Joseph Smith also made efforts to realize his vision of Zion during the seven years that the Latter-day Saints were in Ohio. He organized the first stakes and set up the presiding priesthood structure of the Church. The Prophet established a bank, a newspaper, and a printing office; he supervised the building of the Church's first temple, and initiated extensive missionary work in the United States, Canada, and England. His revelations, including a law of health, tutored the Saints in the conduct of daily life. He made a translation of the Bible. He introduced a school system to prepare the Saints for leadership and missionary roles and was himself a student of Hebrew in the school. The high point of the Kirtland years was the dedication of the temple. Although Joseph Smith had received priesthood authority several years earlier, in 1836, in the KIRTLAND TEMPLE, he received important additional keys of authority from Moses, Elias, and Elijah pertaining to the gathering of Israel and the eternal sealing of families.

Opposition had beset the Prophet from the time he first told people about his visions. In 1832 he was tarred, feathered, and beaten by a mob who broke into the house where he was staying at Hiram, Ohio, an intrusion that led to the death of a child. At Kirtland, dissent arose within the Church over the nature of the new society and the Prophet's involvement in economics and politics; some accused him of attempting to control their private lives and labeled him a fallen prophet. By early 1838, opposition, especially among Ohio leadership, grew to the point that the Prophet and loyal members moved to Missouri.

Joseph Smith arrived with his family at Far West, Caldwell County, Missouri, in March 1838, where he sought once again to establish a gathering place for the Saints and to build a temple (*see* MISSOURI: LDS COMMUNITIES IN CALDWELL AND DAVIESS COUNTIES). But, as before, the influx of outsiders with differing social, religious, and economic practices was unacceptable to the old settlers. Opposition flared into violence at Gallatin, Daviess County, on August 6, 1838, when enemies of the Church tried to prevent Latter-day Saints from voting. The ensuing fight produced injuries on both sides. A subsequent misunderstanding with a local justice of the peace led to charges against the Prophet. As rumors spread, citizens of several counties, then militias, mobilized to expel the Latter-day Saints (*see* MISSOURI CONFLICT; EXTERMINATION ORDER).

The crisis came to a head on October 31, 1838, when Joseph Smith and several others, expecting to discuss ways to defuse the volatile situation, were arrested—it was the beginning of five months of confinement. A November court of inquiry at Richmond, Ray County, accused the Prophet and others with acts of treason connected with the conflict and committed them to LIBERTY JAIL to await trial. Meanwhile, the Saints were driven from the state.

Harsh imprisonment made worse by forced separation from his family and the Church left Joseph time to reflect on the meaning of human suffering. His writings from prison contain some of the most sublime passages of his ministry. Excerpts from his letters were added to the collection of his revelations. Acknowledging all that he had experienced, one of the revelations reminded him that however great his sufferings, they did not exceed the Savior's: "The Son of Man hath descended below them all. Art thou greater than he?" (D&C 122:8).

The following April, while being taken under guard to Boone County, Missouri, for a change in venue, the Prophet and his fellow prisoners were allowed to escape. Within a month of rejoining family and friends at Quincy, Illinois, Joseph Smith had authorized the purchase of land on the Mississippi River near Commerce, Hancock County, Illinois, and had moved his family into a two-room log cabin. During the summer of 1839, the Saints began settling their new gathering place, which they named NAUVOO.

Like many areas along the river bottoms, Nauvoo was at first poorly drained and disease-infested. During a malaria epidemic, the Prophet gave up his home to the sick and lived in a tent. Witnesses reported miraculous healing under his administration. "There was many sick among the saints on both sides of the river and Joseph went through the midst of them taking them by the hand and in a loud voice commanding them in the name of Jesus Christ to arise from their beds and be made whole" (Wilford Woodruff Diary, July 22, 1839, Ms., LDS Church Archives). Deaths were so frequent that a mass funeral was held.

Late in 1839 the Prophet traveled to Washington, D.C., to seek redress from the federal government for losses sustained by his people in Missouri. While there he obtained interviews with President Martin Van Buren and prominent congressmen, but came away frustrated and without relief.

Nauvoo was soon incorporated under the state-authorized NAUVOO CHARTER. Within the next few years the city grew to rival Chicago as the largest in Illinois. Joseph served on the city council and eventually became mayor. As mayor he also served as presiding judge of the municipal court and as registrar of deeds. With the rank of lieutenant general, he led the NAUVOO LEGION, or municipal militia. He was also proprietor of a merchandise store and became editor and publisher of the newspaper *Times and Seasons*.

The relative security of Nauvoo provided Joseph Smith with an opportunity to move forward the work of the kingdom with renewed vigor. He sent the Quorum of the Twelve Apostles to Great Britain, where they expanded missionary work and launched an emigration program that provided a stream of immigrants into the new place of gathering (*see* MISSIONS OF THE TWELVE TO THE BRITISH ISLES). At Nauvoo the Prophet organized the first wards, the basic geographical units of the Church. He expanded the ecclesiastical authority of the Twelve to include jurisdiction within stakes, placing them for the first time in a position of universal authority over the Church under the First Presidency. He supervised the building of the NAUVOO TEMPLE and established the Female Relief Society of Nauvoo.

The Prophet faced a dilemma as he began to restore long-lost divine principles. Prompted by forebodings that his remaining time was short, he wished to hasten his efforts, but because many did not understand his mission and opposed him, he had to move slowly. "I could explain a hundred fold more than I ever have of the glories of the kingdoms manifested to me . . . were the people prepared to receive them," he wrote in 1843 (*HC* 5:402). To resolve this dilemma, the Prophet presented some principles privately to a small number of faithful members, intending to plant the seeds before he died. As early as 1841, he introduced PLURAL MARRIAGE, a necessary part of the restoration of the ancient order of things, to members of the Twelve and a few others. Although he had understood the principle since 1831 and apparently had married one plural wife several years earlier, he married his first recorded plural wife, Louisa Beaman, in

1841. During his remaining years, he married at least twenty-seven others.

In May 1842 the Prophet introduced the full endowment, religious ordinances subsequently observed in all LDS temples, to a small group in the upper room of his Nauvoo store. A year later he performed the first sealings of married couples for time and eternity. In addition, he taught the Saints important doctrines pertaining to the nature of God and man (*see* KING FOLLETT DISCOURSE). In March 1844 he organized the COUNCIL OF FIFTY, the political arm of the kingdom of God. By the time of his death three months later, he had completed all that he felt was essential for the continuation of the kingdom. By then he had transferred to the Twelve the keys of authority, confident that the program he had initiated would now continue regardless of what befell him.

Teaching these principles privately to a small circle enabled Joseph Smith to fulfill his mission but complicated the situation at Nauvoo and unleashed forces that eventually led to his death. Some Saints had difficulty in accepting these unusual teachings. Upon being taught plural marriage, Brigham YOUNG said it was the first time in his life that he had desired the grave. Joseph's wife Emma at one point became "very bitter and full of resentment" ["Statement of William Clayton," *Woman's Exponent* 15 (June 1, 1886): 2]. As knowledge of the private teachings leaked into the community, speculation and distorted rumors proliferated.

While the Prophet pursued his objectives, forces outside the Church organized against him. Missouri authorities tried three times to extradite him from Illinois, resulting in lengthy periods of legal harassment. Because of the loss of property in earlier persecutions, he was unable to pay his debts and had to fend off creditors. When Illinois political leaders turned against the Latter-day Saints and no national leaders would champion their cause, the Prophet declared his candidacy for president of the United States, gaining a platform from which to discuss the rights of his people (*see* NAUVOO POLITICS).

Despite the adversity that dogged him from youth until death, Joseph Smith was not the somber, forbidding person his contemporaries generally envisioned in the personality of a prophet. An English convert wrote that Joseph was "no saintish long-faced fellow, but quite the reverse" [John Needham to Thomas Ward, July 7, 1843,

Latter-Day Saints' Millennial Star 4 (Oct. 1843):89]. It was not uncommon to see him involved in sports activities with the young and vigorous men of a community. He is known to have wrestled, pulled sticks, engaged in snowball fights, played ball, slid on the ice with his children, played marbles, shot at a mark, and fished. Tall and well built, Joseph Smith did not hesitate to use his strength. Once in his youth he thrashed a man for wife-beating. In 1839, as he was en route to Washington, D.C., by stagecoach, the horses bolted while the driver was away. Opening the door of the speeding coach, the Prophet climbed up its side into the driver's seat, where he secured the reins and stopped the horses.

Joseph was also deeply spiritual. His mother said of him that in his youth he "seemed to reflect more deeply than common persons of his age upon everything of a religious nature" (Lucy Smith, Biographical Sketches of Joseph Smith, preliminary manuscript, p. 46, LDS Church Archives). When he was just twelve, as he later wrote, his mind became "seriously imprest with regard to the all importent concerns for the wellfare of my immortal Soul" (*PJS* 1:5). Years after he began receiving revelations, he continued to seek spiritual comfort. In 1832 while on a journey, he wrote of visiting a grove "which is Just back of the town almost every day where I can be Secluded from the eyes of any mortal and there give vent to all the feelings of my heart in meaditation and prayr" (*PWJS*, p. 238). Clearly he spoke from the heart in declaring that "the things of God are of deep import: and time, and experience, and careful and ponderous and solemn thoughts can only find them out" (*HC* 3:295).

Joseph Smith deeply loved his family, and his personal writings are filled with prayerful outpourings of tenderness and concern. "O Lord bless my little children with health and long life to do good in this generation for Christs sake Amen" (*PWJS*, p. 28). His family consisted of eleven children, including adopted twins. Of these, four sons and a daughter died in infancy or early childhood; five were living when their father was killed, and a sixth, a son, was born four months after his death. Occasional glimpses into his family life show him sliding on the ice with his son Frederick, taking his children on a pleasure ride in a carriage or sleigh, and attending the circus.

He was also a loyal friend and cared deeply about others. He repeatedly extended a forgiving hand to prodigals, some of whom had caused him pain and misery. "I feel myself bound to be a friend to all . . . wether they are just or unjust; they have a degree of my compassion & sympathy" (*PWJS*, p. 548). One observer noted that the Prophet would never go to bed if he knew there was a sick person who needed assistance. He taught that "love is one of the leading characteristics of Deity, and ought to be manifested by those who aspire to be the sons of God. A man filled with the love of God, is not content with blessing his family alone but ranges through the world, anxious to bless the whole of the human family" (*PWJS*, p. 481). One Church member who stayed at the Smith home and witnessed the Prophet's "earnest and humble devotions . . . nourishing, soothing, and comforting his family, neighbours, and friends," found observation of his private life a greater witness of Joseph Smith's divine calling than observing his public actions (*JD* 7:176–77).

Joseph Smith spent his life bringing forth a new dispensation of religious knowledge at great personal cost. He noted that "the envy and wrath of man" had been his common lot and that "deep water" was what he was "wont to swim in" (D&C 127:2). A little more than a year before his death he told an audience in Nauvoo, "If I had not actually got into this work and been called of God, I would back out. But I cannot back out: I have no doubt of the truth" (*HC* 5:336). He lived in the hope of bringing that truth to life in a society of Saints, and died the victim of enemies who did not understand his vision.

BIBLIOGRAPHY

Anderson, Richard L. *Joseph Smith's New England Heritage*. Salt Lake City, 1971.

Brodie, Fawn M. *No Man Knows My History*. New York, 1946.

Bushman, Richard L. *Joseph Smith and the Beginnings of Mormonism*. Urbana, Ill., 1984.

Ehat, Andrew F., and Lyndon W. Cook. *The Words of Joseph Smith: The Contemporary Accounts of the Nauvoo Discourses of the Prophet Joseph*. Provo, Utah, 1980.

Gibbons, Francis M. *Joseph Smith: Martyr, Prophet of God*. Salt Lake City, 1982.

Hill, Donna. *Joseph Smith, The First Mormon*. Garden City, New York, 1977.

Jessee, Dean C., ed. *The Personal Writings of Joseph Smith*. Salt Lake City, 1984.

———. *The Papers of Joseph Smith*. Salt Lake City, 1989– .

Millet, Robert L., ed., *Joseph Smith: Selected Sermons and Writings*. New York, 1989.

Porter, Larry C., and Susan Easton Black, eds. *The Prophet Joseph: Essays on the Life and Mission of Joseph Smith*. Salt Lake City, 1988.

Smith, Lucy. *Biographical Sketches of Joseph Smith the Prophet*. Liverpool, 1853.

RICHARD L. BUSHMAN
DEAN C. JESSEE

TEACHINGS OF JOSEPH SMITH

The written and spoken words of the revelations to Joseph Smith are clear, direct, and unequivocal, yet his teachings are difficult to characterize or summarize, since they do not fit easily into traditional theological categories, and they always presuppose that more can, and probably will, be revealed by God. Audiences eagerly listened to the Prophet's bold proclamations and reasoning on hundreds of topics, although his was not a work of systematic analysis or synthesis. His teachings, sayings, counsels, instructions, blessings, responses, and commentaries from 1820 to 1844 are scattered over thousands of pages of revelations, scriptures, histories, journals, letters, and minute books (*see* JOSEPH SMITH: WRITINGS OF JOSEPH SMITH).

The teachings of Joseph Smith may be approached in many ways. Some collections arrange them topically; other commentaries focus on the historical settings of his revelations and discourses; still others compare published versions with recorded recollections of his sayings. In any case, one finds continuity and consistency rather than conspicuous breaks or reversals.

The record shows that Joseph Smith's access to sources and his own understanding entailed growth processes. He said in 1842, two years before his death, that he had "the whole plan of the kingdom" before him (*HC* 5:139). But it is not clear how early in his life the "whole plan" reached maturity in his mind.

Some of his teachings now have scriptural status; others are authoritative but not sustained as scripture. As he himself explained, a prophet is not always a prophet, but "only when he was acting as such" (*TPJS*, p. 278). Careful scholarship will distinguish original utterances of the Prophet from later accretions; also, some statements that he did not make or endorse have been published under his name. The following sketch treats his revelations, his scriptural translations, and his most characteristic sayings as comprising his teachings.

Joseph Smith never claimed to establish a new religion but to initiate a new beginning, a restoration of the everlasting gospel of Jesus Christ. "The fundamental principles of our religion are the testimony of the Apostles and Prophets, concerning Jesus Christ, that He died, was buried, and rose again the third day, and ascended into heaven; and all other things which pertain to our religion are only appendages to it" (*TPJS*, p. 121). He anticipated "a whole and complete and perfect union, and welding together of dispensations, and keys, and powers, and glories . . . from the days of Adam even to the present time" (D&C 128:18). This restoration would encompass "all the truth the Christian world possessed" (*TPJS*, p. 376)—including much that had been lost or discarded—and, in addition, revelations "hid from before the foundation of the world" (*TPJS*, p. 309). His teachings were often in contrast to postbiblical additions, subtractions, and changes. He said that he intended "to lay a foundation that will revolutionize the whole world" (*TPJS*, p. 366).

The following are selected from among the dozens of topics and insights that typify the teachings of the Prophet Joseph Smith:

GOD AND DIVINITY. Joseph Smith taught that God is properly called Father. He is a glorified, exalted person, with personal attributes. Jesus Christ is the mediator between man and God. He is not identical with God, but has become like the Father. This strips away the mystery of many classical creeds. This doctrine is refined anthropomorphism, and it permeates ancient and modern scriptures.

Because God is the preeminent person, he may be approached, encountered, and known. He is subject to, and involved in, man's struggles. He can be trusted to move, act, respond, love, serve, and give. From the presence of God and his Son proceeds forth a Spirit that gives light to everyone who comes into mortality. This light is in all things, gives life to all things, and is the law by which all things are governed, even the power of God (D&C 88:13).

TRUTH. Experience points to a plural universe. The highest knowledge is of things, existences, in all their varieties (D&C 93:24–25). The revelations to Joseph Smith speak of independent spheres of existence and an array of glorious degrees (D&C 76; cf. 88:37). Thus, any mystical thrust toward metaphysical union in which individuality is lost is abandoned.

SCRIPTURE. The Prophet taught that the scriptures are the written records of revelatory experiences. He rejected equally the dogmas of verbal inerrancy, of "merely human" origin, and of allegorical excess in interpreting the scriptures. The limits of the canon are fluid, as they were originally in early Judaism and Christianity. Scripture, spoken or written, is light to those who are quickened by divine life and light. The need for living prophets to supplement, clarify, and apply the written sources to contemporary needs is continual. "I told the brethren that the Book of Mormon was the most correct of any book on earth, and the keystone of our religion, and a man would get nearer to God by abiding by its precepts, than by any other book" (*TPJS*, p. 194).

CREATION AND COSMOS. Joseph Smith's teachings have been characterized by the word "eternalism": "Every principle that proceeds from God is eternal" (*TPJS*, p. 181). The "pure principles of element" and of intelligence coexist eternally with God: "They may be organized and re-organized, but not destroyed" (*TPJS*, p. 351). God created the universe out of chaos, "which is Element and in which dwells all the glory" (*WJS*, p. 351). "The elements are the tabernacle of God" (D&C 93:35). God is related to space and time, and did not create them from nothing. Change occurs through intelligence. The universe is governed by law. There were two creations: All things were made "spiritually" before they were made "naturally" (Moses 3:5). Through his Son, God is the Creator of multiple worlds. God is the Father of the human spirits that inhabit his creations. His creations have no end.

NATURE OF MAN. As eternal intelligence, "man was in the beginning with God" (D&C 93:29–30). But his unfolding from grace to grace is dependent on the nurture of God. Because of the gospel and the Atonement, the children of God are heirs of all the Father has and is, and can become gods themselves (D&C 76:58–61; 84:35–39; 88:107).

Spirit is refined matter. Individual spirits "existed before the body, can exist in the body; will exist separate from the body, when the body will be mouldering in the dust; and will in the resurrection be again united with it" (*TPJS*, p. 207). Thus, extreme dualism between spirit and matter is rejected.

Man is free to resist or to embrace either the powers of God or those of evil. God, man, Satan, and his hosts are independent. One cannot force another.

PLAN OF SALVATION. Finding himself in the midst of spirits and glory, God saw fit to institute laws whereby his children might advance like himself and have glory upon glory. "At the first organization in heaven we were all present, and saw the Savior chosen and appointed and the plan of salvation made, and we sanctioned it" (*TPJS*, p. 181). Like embraces like (D&C 88:40); harmonies are restored: knowledge replaces ignorance, sanctity replaces sin, and life replaces death.

FALL. The Prophet rejected the traditional theory of original sin and returned to the doctrine of man's innocence before the Fall. Adam and Eve transgressed, as planned, to open the way for the contrasting experiences of mortality. The Fall was not inevitable, but free. All men and women are, in their infant state, innocent before God. It follows that infant baptism is unnecessary, that accountability comes later (at the age of eight), and that accountability for sin is personal, not inherited (D&C 68:25–27; 93:38). One becomes what one chooses to become.

God himself has a body "as tangible as man's" (D&C 130:22), and the human body is a temple. "The great principle of happiness consists in having a body" (*TPJS*, p. 181, 297). Redemption is of the whole soul, meaning spirit and body.

ATONEMENT. The power of redemption is the atonement of Jesus Christ, the Son of God. In the unfolding drama, the Son inherited the fulness of the Father; he was not "eternally begotten," nor were two absolutely unlike natures inherent in the person of Christ.

The atonement of Jesus Christ was necessary to reconcile the demands of justice and mercy. Christ responded to this need in a voluntary act, a descent in order to ascend (D&C 88:6).

Christ could not have known, except by experience, the depths of compassion. He suffered pains and afflictions and temptations "that his bowels might be filled with compassion according to the flesh," for only thus could he "succor his people according to their infirmities" (Alma 7:12). Gethsemane was the place and time of his most intense suffering for mankind; the cross was its final hour (D&C 19:16–20; JST Matt. 27:54).

Christ saves men from their sins, not in them. He does not impute righteousness where there is none. One who seeks to become a law unto himself and abides in sin cannot be sanctified unless he repents (D&C 88:35).

The infinite Atonement is intended to bring life and redemption to all the children of the Eternal Father, including those of other worlds who "are saved by the very same Savior of ours" (*T&S* 4:82–85).

KNOWLEDGE. Intelligence, as light and truth, is the glory of God (D&C 93:36). Mind is eternal, with access to the vast reaches of the eternities, and knowledge is essential to salvation: "One is saved no faster than he gets knowledge" (*TPJS*, p. 217); and he gains knowledge of the truths of the gospel no faster than he is saved—that is, no faster than he receives Christ into his life. "Knowledge through our Lord and Savior Jesus Christ is the grand key that unlocks the glory and mysteries of the kingdom of heaven" (*TPJS*, p. 298). "God hath not revealed anything to Joseph, but what He will make known unto the Twelve, and even the least Saint may know all things as fast as he is able to bear them" (*TPJS*, p. 149).

Knowledge of God and divine things comes through the Spirit. Revelation includes the visible presence, visions, dreams, the visitations of angels and spirits, impressions, voices, prophetic flashes of inspiration and light, and the flow of pure intelligence into mind and heart. Such direct communications are essential to the religious life of every person. At least one gift of the spirit is given to each person of faith. "It is impossible to receive the Holy Ghost and not receive revelation" (*TPJS*, p. 256). "No man can know that Jesus is the Lord but by the Holy Ghost" (*WJS*, p. 115). "No generation was ever saved or destroyed upon dead testimony neither can be; but by living" (*WJS*, p. 159). Within limits, these experiences can be verbalized and communicated.

PURPOSE OF LIFE: JOY. "Happiness is the object and design of our existence" (*TPJS*, p. 255). "We came to this earth that we might have a body and present it pure before God in the Celestial Kingdom" (*TPJS*, p. 181). Glorified bodies have powers and privileges over those who have not, and to be denied or separated from the body is bondage. The combination of spirit body and physical body can maximize joy (D&C 93:33–34).

God's glory is to work for the benefit of other beings. Likewise, man cannot find himself until he loses himself in the Christlike desire to elevate, benefit, and bless others (*PWJS*, p. 483). Even in mortality, members of the family of God may begin to experience the joy that will be in full hereafter (*TPJS*, p. 296).

TRIALS AND AFFLICTION. Evil and pain are real, losses are real, temptation is real, overcoming is real. Both risk and reward attend the mortal experience. These are the conditions of soul growth. God's purpose is to lift his children, but he cannot do so without their co-operation; nor can he intervene in a way that removes the need for experience, even bitter experience.

Life is a trial, a probation: "All these things shall give thee experience" (D&C 122:7). Abraham's willingness to sacrifice Isaac was a similitude of the Father's sacrifice of his Only Begotten Son. One cannot attain the heirship of the Son without being willing to sacrifice all earthly things. The overcoming of such trials is the foundation of perfected love, and until one has perfect love, one is liable to fall (*TPJS*, p. 9). The view that all suffering in the world is punishment for sin is "an unhallowed principle" (*TPJS*, p. 162). The Saints must expect to wade through much tribulation, but afflictions may be consecrated to their gain.

PRIESTHOOD. Priesthood is authority and power centered in Christ. It is conferred only by tangible ordination, by the laying on of hands of one having authority. Joseph Smith taught the importance of priesthood keys: Jesus Christ "holds the keys over all this world" (TPJS, p. 323). John the Baptist, Peter, James, John, Moses, Elijah, and Elias held various keys of priesthood functions and restored them to the earth by conferring them upon Joseph Smith and Oliver COWDERY.

Priesthood is not indelible; it can be lost. It is not infallible; only under the influence of the Spirit can one speak for and with the approval of God.

The opportunity for the fulness of priesthood blessings is conferred on both men and women when they make and keep unconditional covenants with Jesus Christ and then with each other as husband and wife.

In The Church of Jesus Christ of Latter-day Saints, Joseph Smith explained and established the roles of apostles, prophets, bishops, evangelists, pastors, teachers, and so on, in analogue to their New Testament functions. He dissolved the distinction between laity and a priestly class: All priests, teachers, and administrators are lay people, and all worthy laymen are priesthood holders.

ORDINANCES. Joseph Smith restored and taught a progressive series of ordinances that confer spiritual enlightenment and power. These ordinances were "instituted in the heavens before the foundation of the world" (*TPJS*, p. 308). "Being born again comes by the Spirit of God through ordinances" (*TPJS*, p. 162). All essential ordinances, from baptism to temple marriage, involve prayer, covenant making, and divine ratification.

TEMPLES. Some ordinances pertain to the holy temple, where "the power of godliness is manifest" (D&C 84:20). Temples embody and manifest sacred truths, "the mysteries and peaceable things" (D&C 42:61). They will enable the children of God to overcome the corruptible elements of their lives and enter the realms of light and fire, the presence of the Father and the Son. All of the temple functions and powers are reestablished today, with the authority of the high priesthood: baptism for the dead, the holy endowment, and the sealing of families are their essence. "We need the Temple more than anything else," Joseph Smith taught (*Journal History*, May 4, 1844).

All temple ordinances point to Christ. The temple is presently, as it was anciently, his sanctuary, endowed with his glory, blessed with his name and ultimately with his presence. Christ is a living temple, and through him one may become a living temple (D&C 93:35; cf. Rev. 21:22).

MARRIAGE, FAMILY, AND HOME. Reversing the Augustinian tradition that celibacy is preferable to marriage in this life and universal in the next, the Prophet taught that the Christlike life reaches its zenith in marriage and parenting. The greatest prophets and prophetesses are also patriarchs and matriarchs. The highest ordinance is marriage, when king and queen begin their eternal family kingdom: The symbols are ordination, coronation, and sealing.

SOCIAL, ECONOMIC, AND POLITICAL THOUGHT. In the earthly government of God, a theodemocracy is contemplated: a covenant kingdom led by Jesus Christ, the benevolent King of Kings. The kingdom of God on earth is to become like Enoch's city of Zion, with utopian thought and culture realized in a community of the pure-hearted.

Joseph taught a law of stewardship and CONSECRATION. All the earth is the Lord's; property in Zion is, in effect, held in trust for the establishment of Zion. In the infancy of the Church, the Saints tried to live this economic system and failed, foundering on what it was designed to overcome: greed, covetousness, jealousy. Consequently, the Prophet was instructed to substitute the law of tithing to prepare the Saints to live this higher law.

"The Constitution of the United States is a glorious standard; it is founded in the wisdom of God" (*TPJS*, p. 147). The protections of constitutional government should extend to all. Wilford WOODRUFF recalled Joseph Smith's saying "that if he were the Emperor of the world and had control over the whole human family he would sustain every man, woman and child in the enjoyment of their religion" (*Journal History*, Mar. 12, 1897). This would allow, without compulsory means, the growth of a kingdom of God eventually to be administered in two world capitals, Jerusalem in the East and the New Jerusalem in the West.

The Church is the body of members who have entered the covenant and formed a community for the perfecting of its individual members. The living prophets, seers, and revelators are the authority nucleus of the kingdom of God, but the Church performs its work in intimate communities: families, wards, and stakes.

RESURRECTION. Eternal family life is perfected only in the highest degree of God's celestial kingdom. In the resurrection and judgment, each body with few exceptions will receive a degree of glory. One's identity in both spirit and body is secure and eternal. God's celestial being, perfected and glorified, is the ideal. The earth itself, having been baptized by water and then by fire, will die, be resurrected, glorified (D&C 88:25–26), and rolled back into the presence of God. The beauty, glory, perfection, and powers of a glorified resurrected body are unspeakable: "No man can describe it to you—no man can write it" (*TPJS*, p. 368). "All your losses will be made up to you in the resurrection provided you continue faithful. By the vision of the Almighty I have seen it" (*TPJS*, p. 296).

ESCHATOLOGY. Joseph Smith uttered many prophetic statements about the future. His eschatology is extensive and inclusive. The gospel will be taught to all mankind, either on this earth or in the world of the spirits, so that all may receive it. The family of Abraham, which has permeated all races of men, will be united. The families of Judah and Joseph will join hands in redemptive fulfillment. Many of these expectations and realizations are beyond the power of man to achieve or to impede. The work is "destined to bringing about the destruction of the powers of darkness, the renovation of the earth, the glory of God, and the salvation of the human family" (*TPJS*, p. 232).

BIBLIOGRAPHY

Burton, Alma P., comp. *Discourses of the Prophet Joseph Smith*, 3rd ed. Salt Lake City, 1968 (arranged topically).

Ehat, Andrew F., and Lyndon W. Cook, eds. *The Words of Joseph Smith: The Contemporary Accounts of the Nauvoo Discourses of the Prophet Joseph*. Provo, Utah, 1980 (excerpts from 173 addresses).

Roberts, B. H. *Joseph Smith: The Prophet Teacher*. Salt Lake City, 1908; rep., Princeton, N.J., 1967.

Smith, Joseph Fielding, comp. *Teachings of the Prophet Joseph Smith*. Salt Lake City, 1938 (arranged chronologically).

Widtsoe, John A. *Joseph Smith: Seeker After Truth, Prophet of God*. Salt Lake City, 1957.

TRUMAN G. MADSEN

WRITINGS OF JOSEPH SMITH

The Prophet Joseph Smith's writing career began at age twenty-two when he commenced translation of the Book of Mormon. At his death seventeen years later, in 1844, he had left a substantial archive for the study of his life and the church he was instrumental in founding. In addition to the Book of Mormon, his papers include diaries covering intermittently the period 1832–1844; correspondence; reports of discourses; more than 130 revelations, published as the Doctrine and Covenants; a record of Abraham; a Bible revision, including some restored writings of Enoch and Moses; and the beginnings of a multivolume documentary HISTORY OF THE CHURCH based upon his papers.

Several factors influenced and initially limited the extent of Joseph Smith's writings and the literary style of his prose. Because of the indigent circumstances of his family, his formal schooling was very little, the basics of reading, writing, and arithmetic constituting, so he said, his entire scholastic preparation. Some who heard him noted that he seemed to have little native talent or training as a speaker. He felt inadequate as a writer, referring on one occasion to "the little narrow prison almost as it were total darkness of paper, pen, and ink."

But whatever the Prophet lacked in formal rhetorical training was compensated for by his message. Beginning in his early life, religious experiences inspired him with a strong sense of mission that propelled him onto the stage of public controversy. He saw his mission as laying a foundation that would revolutionize the whole world, not by sword or gun but by "the power of truth." The articulation of that truth was the impetus of his writings. Many who heard him were awed by his ability to make plain the way of life and salvation. Many outsiders found his views striking and magnetic. His writings carry the same sense of purpose and conviction.

A study of early Mormon sources indicates that only a fraction of Joseph Smith's writings and teachings were preserved. This was the result of haphazard record-keeping procedures during his early lifetime; the incompetence or untimely death of some of his clerks; long imprisonments; vexatious and repeated lawsuits; poverty; and disruptive conditions that forced the migration of the Latter-day Saints across two-thirds of the American continent.

Joseph Smith's dependence upon others to write for him also complicates the record. His philosophy was that "a prophet cannot be his own scribe." Hence, most of his writings were dictated, and some ghostwritten, but approved and accepted by him. While the presence of clerical handwriting in his papers helps date the source material, it does obscure his own image and necessitates a careful look at the sources for those who would distinguish the Prophet's mind and personality from those who assisted him.

Joseph's writings are characterized by long, unbroken sentences connected by conjunctions, descriptive images, and an astute narrative sense. As a keen student of the scriptures, his prose is interspersed with biblical word forms and examples, and breathes a positive tone, reflecting a sense of vitality and love. His writing style and personality show up most clearly in his holograph writings. These show a conversational style, in contrast to the more formal manner of associates like Sidney RIGDON. Typical of his handwritten prose is this extract from an 1838 letter to his wife Emma written while in jail at Richmond, Missouri:

> . . . Brother Robison is chained next to me he ~~he~~ has a true heart and a firm mind, Brother Whight, is next, Br. Rigdon, next, Hyram, next, Parely, next Amasa, next, and thus we are bound together in chains as well as the cords of everlasting love, we are in good spirits and rejoice that we are counted worthy to be per = secuted for christ sake, tell little Joseph, he must be a good boy, Father loves him <With> a per = fect ~~l~~love, he is the Eldest must not hurt those that <Are> smaller then him, but cumfor <t> them tell little Frederick, Father, loves him, with all his heart, he is a lovely boy. Julia is a lovely little girl, I love hir also She is a promising child, tell her Father wants her to remember him and be a good girl, tell all the rest that I think of them and pray for them all, . . . little ~~baby~~ Elexander is on my mind continuly Oh my affectionate Emma, I want you to remember that I am <a> true and faithful friend, to you and the children, forever, my heart is intwined around you[r]s forever and ever, oh may God bless you all amen ~~you~~ I am your husband and am in bands and tribulation &c— [Jessee, 1984, p. 368].

JOSEPH SMITH'S WRITINGS

Writings	*Dates*	*Scribes**
Book of Mormon MSS	1827–1829	Oliver Cowdery and others
Original MS		
Printer's MS		
Diaries	1832–1844	William Clayton, Oliver Cowdery, Warren A. Cowdery, James Mulholland, Warren Parrish, Parley P. Pratt, Willard Richards, Sidney Rigdon, George W. Robinson, Joseph Smith, Sylvester Smith, and others
Revelations	1828–1844	William Clayton, Oliver Cowdery, Warren A. Cowdery, Orson Hyde, James Mulholland, Edward Partridge, William W. Phelps, Sidney Rigdon, Joseph Smith Sr., John Whitmer, Newel K. Whitney, Frederick G. Williams, and others
Kirtland revelation book		
Unbound revelations		
Bible revision		
Book of Abraham		
Correspondence	1829–1844	Thomas Bullock, William Clayton, Howard Coray, Oliver Cowdery, Warren A. Cowdery, James
Letter Bk. 1		
Letter Bk. 2		

Writings	*Dates*	*Scribes**
Bound correspondence		Mulholland, Willard Richards, Sidney Rigdon, James Sloan, Joseph Smith, Robert B. Thompson, John Whitmer, Frederick G. Williams, and others
Egyptian MSS	1835?–1841	Oliver Cowdery, Warren Parrish, William W. Phelps, Joseph Smith, Willard Richards
Autobiographical/ historical writings	1832–1844	Oliver Cowdery, Warren A. Cowdery, James Mulholland, Warren Parrish, William W. Phelps, Willard Richards, Joseph Smith, Robert B. Thompson, Frederick G. Williams, and others

*Known scribes for Joseph Smith with life dates (in parenthesis) and approximate years of their clerical involvement: Thomas Bullock (1816–1885), 1843–1844; William Clayton (1814–1879), 1842–1844; Howard Coray (1817–1908), 1840–1841; Oliver Cowdery (1806–1850), 1829–1838; Warren A. Cowdery (1788–1851), 1836–1838; Orson Hyde (1805–1878), 1833–1836; James Mulholland (1804–1839), 1838–1839; Warren Parrish (1803–1887), 1835–1837; William W. Phelps (1792–1872), 1831–1844; Willard Richards (1804–1854), 1841–1844; Sidney Rigdon (1793–1876), 1830–1838; George W. Robinson (1814–1878), 1836–1840; James Sloan (1792–?), 1840–1843; Sylvester Smith (c.1805–?), 1834–1836; Robert B. Thompson (1811–1841), 1839–1841; John Whitmer (1802–1878), 1829–1838; Newel K. Whitney (1795–1850), 1831–1838; Frederick G. Williams (1787–1842), 1832–1839.

BIBLIOGRAPHY

Works by Joseph Smith

Ehat, Andrew F., and Lyndon W. Cook., comps. and eds. *The Words of Joseph Smith: The Contemporary Accounts of the Nauvoo Discourses of the Prophet Joseph.* Provo, Utah, 1980. A compilation of original reports of Joseph Smith's discourses during the Nauvoo years (1839–1844) of his life.

Faulring, Scott H., comp. and ed. *An American Prophet's Record: The Diaries and Journals of Joseph Smith.* Salt Lake City, 1987. A compilation of Joseph Smith's diaries, but missing his 1842 journal, one of his largest.

Jessee, Dean C., comp. and ed. *The Personal Writings of Joseph Smith.* Salt Lake

City, 1984. A compilation of all of Joseph Smith's known holograph writings and core dictated material.

———. *The Papers of Joseph Smith*, Vol. 1, *Autobiographical and Historical Writing*. Salt Lake City, 1989. The first volume of a comprehensive edition of Joseph Smith's papers.

Smith, Joseph, ed. *History of the Church of Jesus Christ of Latter-day Saints*. Period 1. History of Joseph Smith, the Prophet, by Himself. Introduction and notes by B. H. Roberts. 2nd ed., 6 vols., Salt Lake City, 1964. Written in the form of a first-person daily journal, using the text of Joseph Smith's diaries interspersed with his correspondence and other documents, this work is the most extensive publication of the Prophet's papers to date. Its main limitation is the outdated editorial treatment of the sources.

Smith, Joseph Fielding, comp. and ed. *Teachings of the Prophet Joseph Smith*. Salt Lake City, 1938. A compilation of excerpts from sermons, letters, and other writings of Joseph Smith taken almost exclusively from *History of the Church* and arranged in chronological order.

Secondary Literature

Jessee, Dean C. "The Writing of Joseph Smith's History." *BYU Studies* 11 (Summer 1971):439–73.

King, Arthur Henry. *The Abundance of the Heart*. Salt Lake City, 1986.

Partridge, Elinore H. "Characteristics of Joseph Smith's Style." Task Papers in LDS History, No. 4, 1976. Typescript, LDS Church Archives.

Searle, Howard C. "Early Mormon Historiography: Writing the History of the Mormons 1830–1858." Ph.D. diss., UCLA, 1979.

DEAN C. JESSEE

LEGAL TRIALS OF JOSEPH SMITH

Joseph Smith believed that his enemies perverted legal processes, using them as tools of religious persecution against him, as they had been used against many of Christ's apostles and other past martyrs. Although he often gained quick acquittals, numerous "vexatious and wicked" lawsuits consumed his time and assets, leading to several incarcerations and ultimately to his martyrdom. Beginning soon after his ministry began and continuing throughout his life, Joseph Smith was subjected to approximately thirty criminal actions and at least that many civil suits related to debt collection or failed financial ventures.

The first charge of being a "disorderly person" involved treasure hunting for hire, brought against him at South Bainbridge, New York, in 1826 by a disgruntled Methodist preacher related to Josiah Stowell, Joseph's employer. When Stowell refused to testify against him at the trial, Joseph was discharged. In July 1830 in the same venue, Joseph was tried and acquitted by another magistrate on charges of "being a disorderly person, of setting the county in an uproar by preaching the Book of Mormon, etc." (*HC* 1:88). The trial ended at midnight. The next day, he was seized and tried in neighboring Broome County on the same charges, as well as charges of casting out a devil and using pretended angelic visitations to obtain property from others. Following a twenty-three-hour trial involving some forty witnesses, Joseph was again acquitted (*HC* 1:91–96).

After the Church moved to KIRTLAND, OHIO, in 1831, several religious-based charges were prosecuted against Smith and other LDS leaders, but were dismissed on the grounds listed following each charge: assault and battery (self-defense), performing marriages without a valid license (one was procured), attempted murder or conspiracy (lack of evidence), and involuntary servitude without compensation during the ZION'S CAMP military crusade to Missouri (won on appeal). In turn, Church leaders successfully instituted charges and recovered damages for assaults occurring while they were acting in a religious capacity. However, the financial Panic of 1837 swamped the Prophet and others with civil debt-collection litigation. Worse still were suits for violating Ohio banking laws when the Kirtland Safety Society Anti-Banking Company (*see* KIRTLAND ECONOMY) failed soon after it was organized in 1836 without a state charter. Charges of fraud and self-enrichment were raised but not proven; a jury conviction was appealed, but Joseph Smith left Ohio for Missouri before it was heard.

In Missouri, most actions against the Latter-day Saints were extralegal, brought by non-Mormon vigilantes prejudiced against the Saints' opposition to slavery, their collective influx, and Smith's religious teachings concerning modern revelation and the territorial establishment of Zion in Jackson County. Civil magistrates routinely refused to issue peace warrants for Mormons or to redress their personal injuries or property damage. For example, despite being beaten and tarred and feathered and having the printing office destroyed, the LDS printer was awarded less than his legal fees and the Presiding Bishop received "one penny and a peppercorn." All three branches of state government seemed paralyzed or supportive of mob action, as the Saints were repeatedly dispossessed and expelled from county to county.

Finally, election-day violence between Mormons and non-Mormons erupted at Gallatin in Daviess County, Missouri, on August 6, 1838. Joseph Smith and others called on Justice of the Peace

Adam Black to obtain an "agreement of peace" from Black to support the law and not attach himself to any mob. This resulted in Joseph Smith's and Lyman Wight's being arrested, based on an affidavit alleging riot and assault by them, while obtaining the writs from Black (*HC* 3:61). Smith and Wight appeared before Judge Austin King and were ordered to appear at the next hearing of the grand jury in Daviess County (*HC* 3:73).

On October 25, 1838, Moses Rowland, a Missouri state militiaman, was killed at the Battle of Crooked River in a clash with a company of Saints who were attempting to rescue three kidnapped brethren. Upon hearing of this engagement, coupled with other reports, Governor Lilburn W. Boggs issued his infamous EXTERMINATION ORDER. Joseph and other leading Saints were arrested, and received a preliminary court hearing before Judge Austin King in Richmond, Missouri, on November 12–29, 1838. Joseph Smith and some other defendants were confined for four and a half months in LIBERTY JAIL pending a grand jury indictment on such charges as murder, arson, theft, rebellion, and treason. While en route to stand trial in a more impartial venue, Joseph and others were allowed to escape, thereby preventing widespread official embarrassment on the part of the state.

In 1838–1839 the Saints settled in NAUVOO, Illinois, after their wrongful expulsion from Missouri. To avoid the "legal" persecutions suffered in earlier states, they obtained a liberal city charter for Nauvoo, which granted broad habeas corpus powers to local courts. These helped to free Joseph Smith and other Latter-day Saints when they were sought on writs by arresting officers from outside of Nauvoo. In 1841 state judge Stephen A. Douglas set aside a Missouri writ to extradite Joseph for charges still pending there, and in 1843 a federal judge did the same for a similar requisition after the alleged shooting of then ex-governor Boggs. However, the increasing use of the writ of habeas corpus by Nauvoo magistrates, preempting even state and federal authority, escalated distrust among non-Mormons who felt that Joseph Smith considered himself above the law.

The Prophet's final use of habeas corpus came after his arrest in June 1844 by a county constable for inciting a "riot" by ordering suppression of the NAUVOO EXPOSITOR. This action climaxed a series of lawsuits between the Prophet and several apostates, who had charged him with perjury and adultery; he had countercharged with perjury, assault, defamation, and resisting arrest. After a subsequent trial on the merits and his acquittal in Nauvoo, the governor persuaded the Prophet to let himself be arrested and tried again for the "riot," this time in Carthage, where he was incarcerated without bail on a new charge of "treason" for declaring martial law and ordering out the Nauvoo militia to keep peace. Joseph Smith's enemies charged that he was going on the offensive against citizens of Illinois. Two days later, he and his brother Hyrum were killed by a mob in disguise.

Even after death, legal trials involving the Prophet continued. Of sixty potential assassins named before a grand jury, nine were indicted and five stood trial at Carthage for the murder of Joseph (a separate trial was to follow for the murder of Hyrum). After a six-day trial, all defendants were acquitted in June 1845 for insufficient evidence. The final legal indignity to Joseph Smith and the Church in Illinois was a series of federal court decrees in 1851 and 1852 that liquidated all remaining personal and Church assets held by Joseph Smith during his lifetime, in order to discharge an 1842 default judgment. He had guaranteed a promissory note to the federal government in an early Nauvoo business transaction; when the note was unpaid, a succession of lawsuits followed, forestalling his efforts in bankruptcy and prompting charges of fraud and misconduct. Although plagued by bad advice and misfortune in business matters, the Prophet was never found guilty of any misconduct.

BIBLIOGRAPHY

Firmage, Edwin B., and Richard C. Mangrum. *Zion in the Courts: A Legal History of the Church of Jesus Christ of Latter-day Saints, 1830–1900*. Urbana, Ill., 1988.

Gentry, Leland H. "A History of the Latter-day Saints in Northern Missouri from 1836 to 1839," pp. 167–85, 352–401. Ph.D. diss., Brigham Young University, 1965.

History of the Church, Vol. 1, pp. 88–96, 377, 390–493; Vol. 2, pp. 85–450; Vol. 3, pp. 55–465; Vol. 4, pp. 40–430; Vol. 5.

Madsen, Gordon A. "Joseph Smith's 1826 Trial: The Legal Setting." *BYU Studies* 30 (Spring 1990):91.

Oaks, Dallin H. "The Suppression of the Nauvoo Expositor." *Utah Law Review* 9 (Winter 1965):862–903.

Oaks, Dallin H., and Joseph I. Bentley. "Joseph Smith and Legal Process: In the Wake of the Steamboat *Nauvoo*." *BYU Law Review* 3 (1976):735–82; repr. *BYU Studies* 19 (Winter 1979):167.

Oaks, Dallin H., and Marvin Hill. *Carthage Conspiracy*. Urbana, Ill., 1975.

Walters, Wesley P. "Joseph Smith's Bainbridge, N.Y., Court Trials." *Westminster Theological Journal* 36 (Winter 1974):123–55.

JOSEPH IVINS BENTLEY

SMITH, JOSEPH, SR.

Joseph Smith, Sr. (1771–1840), father of the Prophet Joseph SMITH, believed in the religious experiences of his son and supported him from the time of his FIRST VISION. He later received significant callings in the newly formed Church. Joseph, Sr., died following the expulsion of the Latter-day Saints from Missouri and was considered a martyr for the cause.

Joseph Smith, Sr., was born in Topsfield, Massachusetts, July 12, 1771, the third of eleven children born to Asael and Mary Duty Smith (*see* SMITH FAMILY ANCESTORS). As a young man, he moved with his parents to Tunbridge, Vermont, where he met Lucy Mack (*see* SMITH, LUCY MACK). They were married January 24, 1796, in Tunbridge (*see* SMITH FAMILY).

The couple began married life as part owners in the Asael Smith farm and received a $1,000 wedding present from Lucy's brother Stephen and his business partner, John Mudget. Joseph and Lucy's finances declined, however, after they opened a mercantile store in Randolph and invested in ginseng, a root that grew wild in Vermont and was prized in China as a medicine. A failed exporting venture required them to sell their farm and sacrifice their wedding gift to pay their debts. Now tenants instead of landowners, they moved from one rented farm to another in Vermont and New Hampshire. After three successive crop failures in Norwich, Vermont, they moved to Palmyra, New York, in 1816.

Like his father, Joseph, Sr., was a religious man, but remained aloof from conventional religion. From 1811 to 1819 he had seven dreams that reflected his yearnings for redemption and may have prepared him to believe in his son Joseph's VISIONS, despite the fierce opposition that they aroused among others who heard of them.

The Smiths purchased a 100-acre farm in Manchester, New York, soon after their arrival from Vermont in 1816, but lost it in 1825 when they were unable to make the final yearly payment of $100. In an effort to raise the money, Joseph, Sr., and his son Joseph joined Josiah Stowell in a venture to dig for purported treasure in Harmony, Pennsylvania. Critics of the Smith family have used this incident as evidence of their interest in money digging. While the practice of seeking buried treasure was common at that time in the Northeast and Joseph, Sr., may have participated in searching for it, his digging for Stowell was a desperate attempt to earn money to meet a mortgage payment. After they lost their farm, the Smiths again became tenant farmers.

In 1829 a revelation to Joseph SMITH, Jr., called his father to participate in the "marvelous work" about to be accomplished (D&C 4), and soon thereafter, Joseph, Sr., became one of the Eight Witnesses to the Book of Mormon and saw and held the gold plates. He was present when the Church was organized on April 6, 1830, and was baptized on the same day. He was ordained the first Patriarch to the Church in 1833 and in that office gave blessings of comfort and inspiration throughout the remainder of his life. In Kirtland, Ohio, in 1834 he was called also as a member of the high council.

Joseph, Sr., and Lucy moved with the Church from New York to Ohio, Missouri, and finally Nauvoo, Illinois. They operated a farm in Kirtland, Ohio, and a boardinghouse in Far West, Missouri. In 1839, they assisted hundreds of Saints fleeing from Missouri to Quincy, Illinois (*see* MISSOURI CONFLICT).

Father Smith, as Church members came to call him, suffered more than his share of life's vicissitudes. In 1830 he was arrested in New York and spent a month in jail because of a $14 debt. In Ohio in 1837 he was charged with riot in connection with a confrontation with apostates in the KIRTLAND TEMPLE. He also suffered a serious illness in Ohio and was healed through a blessing given him by Joseph, Jr.

During the Missouri persecutions in the fall of 1838, Joseph, Sr., again became ill. He made the forced exodus from Missouri to Illinois in 1839 in cold and rain, and illness continued to plague him in Nauvoo, where he died on September 14, 1840. Before his death, he called his children to his bedside to give them final blessings. He assured his son Joseph that he would live to finish his work. In his final moments, Smith said he saw Alvin, a son who had died nearly seventeen years earlier.

BIBLIOGRAPHY

Anderson, Richard L. *Joseph Smith's New England Heritage.* Salt Lake City, 1971.

Bushman, Richard L. *Joseph Smith and the Beginnings of Mormonism.* Urbana, Ill., 1984.

Skinner, Earnest M. "Joseph Smith, Sr., First patriarch to the Church." Master's thesis, Brigham Young University, 1958.

Smith, Lucy Mack. *History of Joseph Smith.* Salt Lake City, 1958.

A. GARY ANDERSON

SMITH, JOSEPH F.

Joseph F. Smith (1838–1918), sixth President of The Church of Jesus Christ of Latter-day Saints (1901–1918), led the Church in the first two decades of the twentieth century and helped it win increasing respect in American society. He was a son of Hyrum SMITH and Mary Fielding SMITH and a nephew of the Prophet Joseph SMITH.

Joseph Fielding Smith (his full name) was born in Far West, Missouri, on November 13, 1838, during one of the most strife-torn years in the Church's history. He was named after his uncle, the Prophet, and a maternal uncle, Joseph Fielding. Less than two weeks earlier, Joseph and Hyrum Smith had been arrested by the Missouri militia during the Battle of Far West (*see* MISSOURI CONFLICT). Mary Fielding, a Canadian convert to the Church who married Hyrum after the death of Jerusha Barden Smith, was severely ill when she gave birth to Joseph, her firstborn. Fortunately, Mary's sister Mercy Fielding Thompson, already nursing a five-month-old daughter, was able to nurse Joseph. One day soon after his birth, hostile men entered the house and ransacked the family's valuables. In the commotion, they threw bedding on the baby Joseph, and he nearly suffocated.

In January 1839, Mary and her two-month-old son visited Hyrum in LIBERTY JAIL and in February fled Missouri with other Latter-day Saints to refuge in Quincy, Illinois. In May, after Hyrum escaped from Missouri authorities, the Smith family moved to the new gathering spot of the Church in Nauvoo, Illinois. Joseph, although only five and a half years old when his father and Joseph Smith were murdered in 1844, retained many impressions of the two men in Nauvoo.

In 1846 Mary Fielding Smith left Nauvoo for the West with Joseph and three other children. Another son, John, met her in Iowa. Mary had only two children herself, Joseph and Martha Ann, but she was also mothering the five children of Hyrum and his deceased first wife, Jerusha. Although only seven, young Joseph drove a team of oxen across Iowa. From the fall of 1846 to the spring of 1848, the fatherless family endured the privations of WINTER QUARTERS, Nebraska, where many of the Saints suffered from sickness and some 359 died. Several of the family's horses and cattle, which Joseph tended, also died. At age nine he drove his mother's wagon across the plains to the valley of the Great Salt Lake.

In the early years in the Salt Lake Valley, Joseph tended cattle and sheep, cut wood, and hired out at harvest time. In 1852, when he was thirteen, his mother died from overwork and malnutrition. Throughout his long life, Joseph never forgot her example of faith and integrity and frequently told stories about her. Her death made him a substitute father to his sister, Martha Ann. While the two children were attending school in the winter of 1853–1854, a harsh schoolmaster took out a leather strap to punish the little girl. "Don't whip her with that," Joseph cried. Later he explained, "At that he came at me and was going to whip me; but instead of whipping me, I licked him, good and plenty" (Gibbons, pp. 26–27). During his youth, he struggled with a fiery temper before he eventually conquered it.

This incident both ended Joseph's short formal education and launched his long ecclesiastical career. In the next general conference he was called at age fifteen to serve in the Church's mission in the Sandwich Islands (Hawaii). Parley P. Pratt, an apostle, set Joseph apart and promised that he would master the Hawaiian language by study and the gift of the Spirit. Joseph served a remarkably successful mission, which lasted nearly four years. While in Hawaii, he served as conference president on the islands of Maui and Hawaii. He also overcame his own attacks of "island sickness" and became well known for his gifts of healing and of casting out evil spirits.

Immediately upon his return to Salt Lake City in 1858, Joseph joined the Nauvoo Legion, Utah Territory's militia, and started with an expedition of a thousand men to intercept Johnston's army. From his return until the end of the war in June he was almost constantly in the saddle, patrolling the region between Echo Canyon, in Utah, and Fort Bridger, in Wyoming. Upon the peaceful settlement of the Utah War, Joseph assisted his relatives in returning to Salt Lake City from the southern settlements where they had gone in anticipation of the invading army (*see* UTAH EXPEDITION).

In April 1859 twenty-one-year-old Joseph married his sixteen-year-old cousin Levira, daughter of Samuel Harrison Smith. With Levira's permission Joseph then married Julina Lambson in PLURAL MARRIAGE. Later, he also married Sarah Ellen Richards, Edna Lambson, Alice Ann Kimball, and Mary Taylor Schwartz. He eventually was the father of forty-three children, thirteen of whom preceded him in death. Joseph was known as a kind and loving husband and father among members of his family.

Joseph served a mission in Great Britain from 1860 to 1863 and returned briefly to Hawaii in 1864 to help straighten out irregularities in Church affairs. While in Hawaii, he selected the site for a Church plantation on Oahu at Laie, presently the location of the Hawaii Temple, Brigham Young University—Hawaii Campus, and the Polynesian Cultural Center. Returning to Salt Lake City, he began work in 1865 as a clerk in the Church Historian's office. He was elected to the Territorial House of Representatives in 1865 and to the Salt Lake City Council in 1866. Later he served several consecutive terms in the Utah legislature. He was also a member of the Salt Lake Stake high council.

In 1866 Brigham YOUNG ordained the twenty-seven-year-old Joseph an apostle. In 1867 he accompanied Abraham O. Smoot, former mayor of Salt Lake City, and fellow apostles John TAYLOR and Wilford WOODRUFF to Provo, Utah, where they acted as civic officials in an effort to suppress and redirect some "rowdy elements" that had arisen in the town's citizenry. He returned to Salt Lake City in 1869, resumed his duties in the Historian's office, and began officiating in ordinances in the Endowment House.

In 1874, now known as President Smith, he presided over both the European and British missions. Upon his return in late 1875, he was called as stake president over the Saints in Davis County, Utah, and was also president of the Davis County Cooperative Company, one of a chain of Church cooperatives established during the United Order era, initiated by Brigham Young in 1874. In April 1877, Elder Smith was again sent to Great Britain to preside over the European Mission. The death of Brigham Young in August 1877 interrupted this call. Elder Smith returned to Salt Lake City to help with the settlement of President Young's estate, putting in long hours and painstakingly going over financial records and correspondence in this complicated matter.

Joseph F. Smith's labors in the Church took a significant turn in October 1880 when, at age forty-one, he was set apart as second counselor to John Taylor in the First Presidency. The first counselor was George Q. Cannon, a close friend for many years. The two men also served as counselors to Presidents Wilford Woodruff and Lorenzo SNOW. Both were experienced missionaries and Church administrators, well versed in Church history and doctrine.

In the 1870s and 1880s, mass rallies throughout the United States protesting the Church's practice of plural marriage were adding impetus to the federal government's increasingly stern antipolygamy crusade. Rather than submit to what they considered unjust laws, President Taylor and his counselors chose civil disobedience. Joseph spent much of 1883 and 1884 in seclusion, and in 1885, when a warrant was issued for the arrest of the members of the First Presidency, he went into hiding in Hawaii under the assumed name of J. F. Speight. Over the next two and a half years, he grieved that he could do little to provide for his wives and children. In June 1887 he was called back to Utah to the deathbed of President Taylor, who died on July 25.

Continuing to serve in his position as a member of the Twelve Apostles during the period from President Taylor's death to the sustaining of Wilford Woodruff as President of the Church, Joseph fulfilled an assignment as the chief lobbyist for the Church in Washington, D.C., during the terms of Congress in 1888 and 1889. The First Presidency was reorganized in April 1889, with Joseph called as second counselor to President Woodruff.

The new presidency continued further political negotiations concerning the principle of plural marriage in an effort to lift the burdens imposed by the federal government. These negotiations were inconclusive, but a revelation to President Woodruff, known as the MANIFESTO of 1890, advised the Saints to refrain from contracting plural marriages where such were forbidden by law. The Manifesto gradually achieved the desired effect: prosecution of polygamists ceased, Church property was returned, and Utah obtained statehood. Joseph sought and obtained amnesty from U.S. President Benjamin Harrison and was able, for the first time in nearly a decade, to mingle openly in society and resume a normal life. After the Manifesto, Joseph continued to care for each of his wives and to have children by them.

He also took an active role in politics. The Church had been criticized for dominating politics in Utah through the People's party. In 1891 the People's party disbanded, and its members were encouraged to join the two national parties. To make sure of genuine diversity, the First Presidency asked Joseph F. Smith to join the Republican party, then the less popular of the two parties because of its leading part in the antipolygamy campaign. To strengthen the Republicans, in 1892 he published a pamphlet, *Another Plain Talk: Reasons Why the People of Utah Should Be Republicans.*

Following the death of Wilford Woodruff, Joseph continued as Second Counselor in the First Presidency from 1898 to 1901 while Lorenzo Snow was President. President Snow died on October 10, 1901, and at the next regular meeting of the Twelve in the temple on October 17, the First Presidency was reorganized, with sixty-two-year-old Joseph F. Smith as President and John R. Winder and Anthon H. Lund as counselors.

President Smith vigorously assumed the reins of leadership, determined to improve public opinion of the Church and its members. For half of his seventeen years as Church President, he was frustrated in this goal. He was forced to endure grueling interrogation before the U.S. Senate during the Smoot hearings, local editorial attacks from the *Salt Lake Tribune*, and diatribes from some of the nation's leading magazine editors. Gradually, however, partly through his genuine charity and his grandfatherly image, tension between the Church and the federal government and society diminished. President Smith labored indefatigably to strengthen the Church and improve its image by careful spending and getting out of debt; by purchasing and developing significant HISTORICAL SITES, such as Joseph Smith's birthplace in Vermont, the Smith farm in New York, important sites in Missouri, and CARTHAGE JAIL in Illinois; by completing the Church Administration Building, the LDS Hospital, a Church visitors bureau, and the Hotel Utah in Salt Lake City; and by promoting the expansion of the Church's missionary and educational systems.

One of Joseph F. Smith's legacies was through his exposition of various Church doctrines and of principles of priesthood government. He felt strongly that Church members should be taught "sound doctrine." Following his death in 1918, some of his voluminous teachings, recorded during five decades of instructing the Saints as a General Authority, were published under the title *Gospel Doctrine*. Possibly President Smith's most significant doctrinal contribution was his "Vision of the Redemption of the Dead," which he received on October 3, 1918, just six weeks prior to his death on November 19. In it he saw the world of departed spirits and many individuals who reside there, including ancient and modern prophets, and he viewed the visit of Jesus Christ to the spirit world, where Jesus declared liberty to the righteous and organized a mission to preach the gospel to the wicked spirits. In 1981 his account of this vision was added to the Doctrine and Covenants as section 138.

BIBLIOGRAPHY

Gibbons, Francis M. *Joseph F. Smith: Patriarch and Preacher, Prophet of God*. Salt Lake City, 1984.

Smith, Joseph F. *GD*.

Smith, Joseph Fielding. *Life of Joseph F. Smith*. Salt Lake City, 1969.

BRUCE A. VAN ORDEN

SMITH, JOSEPH FIELDING

Joseph Fielding Smith (1876–1972), the tenth President of the Church, was born July 19, 1876, in Salt Lake City, the firstborn son of Joseph F. SMITH, an apostle who would become the sixth President of the Church, and Julina Lambson, the first of his six plural wives. His grandfather was the Patriarch Hyrum SMITH. Under the tutelage of his parents, Joseph Fielding, as he became known in the Church, grew up with a deep affection for the Prophet Joseph SMITH and his teachings. Upon learning to read, he constantly studied Church magazines, pamphlets, and other publications, reading the Book of Mormon twice by age ten. A few years later, he read the lengthy History of the Church, published in the *Millennial Star*. In his late teens he studied the New Testament in transit to and from his merchandizing job at ZCMI (Zion's Cooperative Mercantile Institution), the Church department store. He built the lasting scholarship on this foundation of constant learning that later distinguished his prolific writings.

He married Louie Emily (Emyla) Shurtliff in the Salt Lake Temple on April 26, 1898. One year later, he accepted a two-year mission call in the Nottingham conference of the British Mission (1899–1901). Upon his return, he secured employment in the Church

Historian's office. In April 1906 he was appointed an assistant Church historian.

As antipolygamy sentiment raged in the early 1900s, Joseph Fielding felt the injustice of the attacks upon the Church and the men whom he knew and loved, such as his father. Some of his first publications were defenses of historical Church doctrine and practice, including *Blood Atonement and the Origin of Plural Marriage* (1905) and *Origin of the "Reorganized" Church: The Question of Succession* (1907).

In March 1908 his wife, Louie, died leaving him with two daughters. That November he married Ethel Georgina Reynolds, who bore him five sons and four daughters. Ethel died in August 1937, and he married Jessie Ella Evans in April 1938. She died on August 3, 1971, one year before President Smith.

Family influence powerfully shaped Joseph Fielding Smith's feeling about religion and his understanding of the gospel. In his later years he often commented that he had been tutored by his father, who was called to preside over the Church when Joseph Fielding was only twenty-five. "I have a great love for my father," he said. "It was marvelous how the words of living light and fire flowed from him" (remarks at Smith family reunion, Nov. 13, 1970; copies in family possession). "In all my life," he continued, "whenever I have been tempted, one thought has always come to me. 'What would my father think of that?'" A year later, dramatizing the impact of his father on his own gospel scholarship, he said, "I feel a closeness to my father, and my grandfather, and my granduncle the Prophet [Joseph Smith] himself, and to the other early brethren of this dispensation. I believe what they believed and am sure that in large measure I think as they thought" (fireside speech to Latter-day Saint Student Association, Nov. 21, 1971, LDS Institute of Religion, University of Utah).

Family influences in turn became the molding forces in the lives of Joseph Fielding's children, who tell of his constant efforts to teach them. At meals, in family gatherings, while walking children to school or church, and later in letters to those in the military and on missions, he was always instructing his children in gospel principles. His letters, like his sermons, were filled with scriptural quotations, often interpreting world events or family activities in terms of what the scriptures said. Through these constant teachings he earned what he considered to be one of life's greatest blessings: all of his children remained faithful Latter-day Saints. Each married in the temple, and each of his sons served a mission for the Church. Following Joseph Fielding's death, Harold B. LEE, his successor as President of the Church, said, "Truly, the greatest monument to him is the great posterity which he has given to the world" (Letter to the Joseph Fielding Smith family, July 14, 1972, Salt Lake City, Historical Department of the Church [HDC]).

When Joseph Fielding Smith was ordained an apostle on April 7, 1910, the *Salt Lake Tribune* published criticisms against him, his father, and the Smith family for nepotism. This vilification ignored his qualifications for the apostleship. In this difficult time, he took refuge in his family, which had special reason to have confidence in the call because of a revelation to his mother that her son would become an apostle (Bruce R. McConkie, pp. 24–31). In a patriarchal blessing he received at nineteen, Joseph Fielding Smith had also been told, "It shall be thy duty to sit in council with thy brethren, and to preside among the people" (John Smith, Patriarchal Blessing to Joseph Fielding Smith, Jan. 19, 1896; copy in LDS Church Historian's Library).

During his apostolic tenure, amid many responsibilities and duties, Joseph Fielding Smith was best known, and is best remembered, as a theologian and gospel scholar. President Heber J. GRANT called him "the best posted man on the scriptures of the General Authorities of the Church that we have" (Letter to Joseph Fielding Smith, Dec. 31, 1938, *HDC*). He published more books and articles than any other man who became President of the Church, though it was never his main intent to become an author. Many of his writings were discourses, answers to questions posed to him, instructions for Church leaders, and efforts to clarify common uncertainties.

One book, *The Signs of the Times* (1942), was published after requests mounted for copies of lectures he had given on the last days. *The Restoration of All Things* (1945) was a compilation of radio talks; the two-volume *Church History and Modern Revelation* (1953) was a manual of instruction for the Melchizedek Priesthood quorums; and the five-volume *Answers to Gospel Questions* (1957–1966) was a compilation of answers to gospel questions printed in Church magazines over a period of years.

At a time when many were concerned with the issues of organic evolution, Elder Smith published *Man: His Origin and Destiny* (1954), in which he provided a scriptural and theological defense of the Church position that mankind is the offspring of and placed on earth by God, not a product of random evolutionary processes. His calm throughout this intellectual storm showed both his serenity and wisdom.

He always built his sermons on scriptural themes. "I never did learn to deliver a discourse," he said, "without referring to the scriptures" (Joseph F. McConkie, pp. 44–45). In his sixty-two-year ministry as an apostle and prophet, Joseph Fielding Smith preached on almost every facet of the gospel. Few Latter-day Saints have spoken so emphatically on the fact that God is a personal being, that he is the creator of all things, that he is literally the Father of Jesus Christ, and that the atonement of Christ grows out of the fact of his divine Sonship. His defense of the Prophet Joseph Smith, the Book of Mormon, and the doctrine of a latter-day restoration fulfilled a promise in a second patriarchal blessing that his teachings and writings would stand as a "wall of defense against those who are seeking and will seek to destroy the evidence of the divinity of the mission of the Prophet Joseph Smith" (Joseph D. Smith. Patriarchal Blessing to Joseph Fielding Smith, May 11, 1913; copies in family possession).

He explained the doctrine of the "divine law of witnesses" (*CR*, Apr. 1930) with a force and clarity not found elsewhere in the literature of the Latter-day Saints. *The Way to Perfection* (1931) and *Elijah the Prophet and His Mission* (1957) stand as classic expositions of the doctrines of salvation for the dead. His compilation *Teachings of the Prophet Joseph Smith* (1938) is one of the most widely used reference texts in LDS literature. *Essentials in Church History* (1922) and *The Life of Joseph F. Smith* (1938) are examples of interpreting history through scriptural and prophetic eyes.

Yet, while he is remembered as a gospel scholar, Joseph Fielding Smith's love of life and those he worked with was broader than his scholarship. When President Smith was ninety-three, Elder Gordon B. Hinckley said, "I have never heard him say a mean or evil or unkind thing. . . . He speaks generously of those he discusses." He repeatedly said, "I love my brethren," and with regard to the wayward, he urged giving "them the benefit of the doubt; there are two sides to the story." His counsel to bishops was similar: "If you make any mistakes in judgment, make them on the side of mercy." He frequently financed missions, paid the hospital bills of the sick, and sent groceries to the needy. He always disciplined his children with love, avoiding physical punishment, preferring to look them in the eyes and say, "I wish my children would be good." "No spanking or whipping," said one daughter, "could accomplish what this kindly father did with love" (Joseph F. McConkie, pp. 71–90).

Joseph Fielding Smith became President of the Church on January 23, 1970, following the death of President David O. McKay. His two-and-one-half-year tenure was marked by steady missionary growth; the dedication of the Ogden and Provo temples; some significant organizational restructuring, including reorganizations in the Church Sunday School system and the Church Department of Social Services; and a revamping of portions of the Church internal communication systems, which led to the consolidation of all general Church magazines into three.

After a long life of scholarship and influence, one of his most significant acts was his reaffirmation, as President of the Church, of the doctrines that he had taught throughout his apostolic ministry. "What I have taught and written in the past," he said in the October general conference of 1970, "I would teach and write again under the same circumstances" (*CR*, Oct. 1970, p. 5). He died July 2, 1972, in Salt Lake City.

BIBLIOGRAPHY

McConkie, Bruce R. "Joseph Fielding Smith, Apostle, Prophet, Father in Israel." *Ensign* 2 (Aug. 1972):23–31.

McConkie, Joseph F. *True and Faithful: The Life Story of Joseph Fielding Smith.* Salt Lake City, 1971.

Smith, Joseph Fielding, Jr., and John J. Stewart. *The Life of Joseph Fielding Smith.* Salt Lake City, 1972.

AMELIA S. MCCONKIE
MARK L. MCCONKIE

SMITH, LUCY MACK

Lucy Mack Smith (1775–1856) was the mother of the Prophet Joseph SMITH and his main biographer for the crucial formative years of the restored Church. A marked tenderness existed between the Smith parents and children, and Lucy lived near or in the Prophet's household through hardships in New York, Ohio, Missouri, and Illinois. Mother and son maintained the strongest mutual respect throughout these years of change, sacrifice, and persecution.

Faith in God was central to Lucy Smith's personality. When a young mother, she became critically ill and spent a night very near death, but a voice promised her life after she pleaded for the power to "bring up my children, and comfort the heart of my husband," with a vow to serve God completely. More than forty years later, she publicly reviewed the result of her parental leadership with her husband, Joseph SMITH, Sr. Of eleven children, nine reached maturity, and with typical intensity, Lucy said, "We raised them in the fear of God. . . . I presume there never were a family that were so obedient as mine" (MS conference minutes, Oct. 8, 1845, HDC).

Her father, Solomon Mack, was a dynamic venturer who showed courage and self-reliance in close combat in the French and Indian Wars and afterward as merchant, land developer, contractor, miller, seafarer, and farmer. Unsatisfied with the seeming meaninglessness of his way of life, he finally found God after severe sickness. He then published his concise biography—the saga of how God protected him in his wanderings and at the end showered his soul with love and insight. Lucy Mack Smith identified deeply with her mother, Lydia Gates, who came from the home of a prosperous Congregational deacon. Lydia used her schoolteaching skills in the home, creating what Solomon called an atmosphere of "piety, gentleness, and reflection" (Anderson, 1971, p. 27). All of the Mack children possessed mixtures of the daring enterprise of their father and the assertive piety of their mother. Lucy was true to this heritage of seeking light and then sharing it.

Lucy was born in Gilsum, New Hampshire, where town records enter her birthday as July 8, 1775, the year the American Revolution began. Her education included attending school there and at Montague, Massachusetts, supplemented by private instruction by her mother. Lucy Smith's speeches and writing reveal an intelligent believer who used English capably. In her late teens Lucy was also greatly influenced by the courageous deaths of her older sisters; each died in her early thirties, after testifying to personal revelations of the hereafter and of Christ's love.

Lucy's entrepreneur brother, Stephen Mack, took her to Tunbridge, Vermont, where she met her future husband, Joseph Smith, Sr. She evaluated his family as "worthy, respectable, amiable, and intelligent." To their marriage on January 24, 1796, Lucy brought a dowry of a thousand dollars, a gift of her brother and his business partner; her husband owned a farm of almost equal value. A huge exporting investment failed because of the dishonesty of their agent, and the couple used their total assets to pay the debt rather than default on merchandise obtained for their Vermont store. Their first twenty years of marriage were spent in neighboring Vermont and New Hampshire towns. They climbed back to prosperity through the schoolteaching of Joseph Smith, Sr., assisted with farming and home industry. Yet setbacks came with agonizing sickness in the family in 1812–1813 and frozen crops in 1814–1816, which precipitated their move to Palmyra, New York.

Lucy and Joseph Smith, Sr., were active seekers. As a young, sensitive woman, Lucy sought the conversion that she heard preached in churches. As she "perused the Bible and prayed incessantly," Lucy concluded that the biblical church "was not like" any existing church. Thus, after a miraculous healing in early marriage, she asked a minister to baptize her without commitment to attend his denomination. Finding New England Presbyterianism wanting, she investigated Methodism, only to be opposed by her unaffiliated husband. In these years, he received periodic dreams promising future answers. And Lucy in turn dreamed of Joseph Smith, Sr., as a pliant tree; she concluded that he would yet receive the full truth from God.

Lucy Smith was a vigorous forty years of age when regional crop failure forced the family to the opening wheat land of western New York. Their move was evidently in 1816, and her husband preceded her, sending Lucy the means to bring a few goods and their eight children, ranging from eighteen-year-old Alvin to the new baby, Don Carlos. Mother Smith showed independence in publicly dismissing her unprincipled teamster (who had been hired to help the family, but proved to be selfish and undependable). She also showed tender emotions in the reunion of "throwing myself and my children upon the care and affection of a tender husband and father" (Coray MS).

In the Palmyra area the family rebuilt financial security, only to have it slip away again amid the hostility of their neighbors to their son's revelations. Lucy first began to "replenish" her home furnishings by continuing "painting oil cloth coverings for tables, stands, etc." Like many new settlers, the Smiths signed a short-term contract to purchase about a hundred acres of uncleared land. Over several years the family cleared forty acres, built fences and outbuildings, kept up a coopering business, and ran farm operations for a large sugar maple harvest, orchard production, and the main wheat crop. These activities objectively contradict one of two charges in neighborhood affidavits that Lucy and her family were lazy and superstitious. The realities behind such accusations were poverty and a belief in the miraculous. Obvious attempts were made to discredit the new religion by denigrating its founders and their families.

Mother Smith's history admits that the family was accused of occult treasure searching, but it passes over the issue by stating the intense goal of their New York years: "Whilst we worked with our hands we endeavored to remember the service of [God] and the welfare of our souls" (Coray MS). In this context, she relates how the prayers of her son Joseph were answered. The Prophet does not suggest that he confided his FIRST VISION to his family, and his mother reports only that she had early knowledge that an angel later revealed the Book of Mormon. Lucy carefully describes that she handled the Urim and Thummim and the ancient breastplate. Her conviction of the divinity of the Book of Mormon was total, as suggested by a letter to her brother in 1831: "I want you to think seriously of these things, for they are the truths of the living God" (Kirkham, p. 67).

For a time, Lucy affiliated with a Presbyterian church in Palmyra, though she was excommunicated for nonattendance the month before the LDS Church was organized. Her powerful faith in the young Church was expressed in her taking a large New York group to Ohio by canal boat to Buffalo and by steamer across a partially frozen Lake Erie in 1831. She braved cold weather and discouragement, leading in prayer, missionary work, and practical arrangements until again united with her husband and sons in upper Ohio. She then went to teach her Mack relatives in Detroit, converting Stephen Mack's widow, Temperance. Mother Smith endured two later migrations, one in the spring rains on the way to Missouri in 1838 and a move to Illinois in the wet snows of early 1839.

Joseph Smith, Sr., died in late 1840, a casualty of a decade of trauma and exposure. Shortly before he died, he blessed his children and expressed love for his "most singular" wife, promising her that her last days would be her best days. But other searing partings preceded the fulfillment of this promise of peace. Lucy early had lost two infant sons, and later came the sudden death of her oldest son, Alvin, during her New York days. She buried her husband in Illinois and, within the next four years, endured the deaths of four more sons—Samuel and Don Carlos in sickness and Joseph and Hyrum murdered by a mob.

"O God, why were my noble sons permitted to be martyred?" was her cry upon seeing their corpses (Anderson, 1977, p. 135). An inner voice assured her that divine purpose was accomplished in the tragedy. Lucy never lost her faith in God, in the revelations to her son, and in the destiny of her family. She was cared for by Joseph and Emma Smith until 1844, by her daughter Lucy Millikin some years thereafter, and by Emma once more in her final years in Nauvoo. Feeble and unable to write, she impressed visitors with her spiritual and social vitality. She passed from life May 14, 1856, at nearly eighty-one.

For a time after 1844, Lucy Smith depended emotionally on her only surviving son. Yet William seems to have overused her name in his cause. In 1845 he sought to expand his patriarch's office, and John TAYLOR'S journal records visions briefly circulated from Lucy about William's supposed authority to lead the Church. Perhaps William helped her write them, since the apostles who met with Lucy found her questioning whether they had "a correct copy." Taylor described her "good feelings" toward the Twelve (pp. 63–68). She and most of her sons' widows were in the first companies receiving higher ordinances in the NAUVOO TEMPLE. She received washings and anointings on December 11, 1845, and the endowment the following day (*HC* 7:542–44).

Lucy Smith gave a spirited talk before the October 1845 conference, expressing her need to stay with her children in Nauvoo but giving her blessing to the Twelve and their plans for the exodus: "I feel that the Lord will let Brother Brigham take the people away." She also said that her memoirs were complete: "I have got all in a history, and I want this people to be so good as to get it printed" (MS conference minutes, Oct. 8, 1845, HDC). This was dictated to Martha Jane Knowlton Coray, whose first narrative survives. Lucy's history was not printed until Orson PRATT obtained a copy and published it in England in 1853.

The first edition of Lucy's memoirs was recalled by Brigham YOUNG. However, his goal was accuracy, not suppression, since he initiated a second edition. According to Wilford WOODRUFF's journal, the President charged the careful Woodruff and two Smith family members to "correct the errors in the History of Joseph Smith as published by Mother Smith, and then let it be published to the world" (Apr. 22, 1866).

Lucy Smith's history gives more than two hundred names in its various drafts and hundreds of details. Nearly all of these individuals and episodes are confirmed by independent contemporary records. Astute John Taylor evaluated her capacity after talking with her about her history: "Though now quite an aged woman, the power of her memory is surprising; she is able to relate circumstances connected with the family, with great distinctness and accuracy" (p. 52). Beyond facts, her history burns with the dedication that made the events of the Restoration possible. She achieved religious greatness—as a mother and as a dynamic contributor to the infant Church. Furthermore, her history is irreplaceable, judged by her expressed goal to give "the particulars of Joseph's getting the plates, seeing the angels at first, and many other things which Joseph never wrote or published" (Lucy Smith to William Smith, Jan. 23, 1845, HDC).

BIBLIOGRAPHY

Anderson, Richard Lloyd. "The Reliability of the Early History of Lucy and Joseph Smith." *Dialogue* 4 (Summer 1969):13–28.

———. *Joseph Smith's New England Heritage.* Salt Lake City, 1971.

———. "Joseph Smith's Home Environment." *Ensign* 1 (July 1971):57–59.

———. "His Mother's Manuscript: An Intimate View of Joseph Smith." BYU Forum address, Jan. 27, 1976.

———. "The Emotional Dimensions of Lucy Smith and Her History." In *Dedication Colloquiums, Harold B. Lee Library*, pp. 129–37. Provo, Utah, 1977.

Kirkham, Francis W. *A New Witness for Christ in America*, 4th ed., Vol. 1. Salt Lake City, 1967.

Smith, Lucy. All unidentified quotations from Lucy Smith in this article are from Martha Jane Knowlton Coray's preliminary manuscript in the Historical Department of the Church. Most are also found in edited form in Lucy Mack Smith, *Biographical Sketches of Joseph Smith, the Prophet, and His Progenitors for Many Generations* (Liverpool, 1853). Among reprints, the most widely distributed is the

early Utah edition, lightly modified by editor Preston Nibley, *History of Joseph Smith, by His Mother, Lucy Mack Smith* (Salt Lake City: n.d.).
Taylor, John. "The John Taylor Nauvoo Journal," ed. Dean C. Jessee. *BYU Studies* 23 (Summer 1983):63–68.
Youngreen, Buddy. "The Death Date of Lucy Mack Smith." *BYU Studies* 12 (Spring 1972):318.

RICHARD LLOYD ANDERSON

SMITH, MARY FIELDING

Mary Fielding Smith (1801–1852) has the unique distinction of being the mother of one President of The Church of Jesus Christ of Latter-day Saints (Joseph F. SMITH) and the grandmother of another (Joseph Fielding SMITH).

Born on July 21, 1801, at Honidon, Bedfordshire, England, Mary Fielding was the sixth child of John Fielding and Rachel Ibbotson, staunch Methodists. In 1834, Mary migrated to Toronto, Canada, where her brother and sister, Joseph and Mercy, had moved two years earlier. Nearby at Charleton, the three Fieldings were baptized into the Church in May 1836. The following year, Mary moved to KIRTLAND, OHIO.

Attractive and well educated, Mary became a live-in governess and teacher for various families in Kirtland. On December 24, 1837, Mary Fielding married the widower Hyrum SMITH, whose first wife had died while giving birth to their fifth child. Though reluctant to become a stepmother, Mary accepted this responsibility as the will of the Lord.

Mary and Hyrum were forced to flee Kirtland for FAR WEST, MISSOURI, in early 1838. That November 13th, while Hyrum was incarcerated in LIBERTY JAIL in Clay County, MISSOURI, and the Missouri Saints were under siege, Mary gave birth to a son, whom she named Joseph Fielding Smith, and who would become the sixth President of the Church in 1901.

Ill for several months after the birth of her son, Mary was transported on a bed in a wagon to Quincy, Illinois, in February 1839. Freed from imprisonment in April, Hyrum joined her there. Soon they settled in nearby Commerce, which became NAUVOO. On May 14, 1841, Mary gave birth to a daughter, Martha Ann. Mary assisted Hyrum as he served as vice-mayor of Nauvoo, Patriarch to the Church, and Associate President of the Church. She and her sister Mercy helped organize the women of the Church to raise funds for the NAUVOO TEMPLE. Tragedy befell the entire Church on June 27, 1844, with the MARTYRDOM OF JOSEPH AND HYRUM SMITH in Carthage Jail.

Mary and her children left Nauvoo in the fall of 1846. After living in WINTER QUARTERS eighteen months, they crossed the plains to the SALT LAKE VALLEY in 1848. Her son Joseph F., only nine years of age, drove one of the wagons. When Peter Lott, captain of their company, complained that Mary was underequipped and would be a burden on the entire company, she replied that she would beat him to the valley—and without his help. A deeply spiritual person, Mary often relied on prayer. On one occasion while crossing the plains, two of her finest oxen disappeared. Several men looked for them at length but without success. Back in camp, Mary knelt in prayer and then walked straight to a ravine, where she found her oxen caught in a clump of willows. Her family arrived in Salt Lake City on September 22, 1848—ahead of Captain Lott.

Mary secured a lot in Salt Lake City and a farm in Mill Creek. Her two-room adobe farmhouse is preserved in the pioneer village near the "THIS IS THE PLACE" MONUMENT in Salt Lake City. Although a widow with few means, she directed her children to pick the best of their farm produce for the tithing office. When a clerk at the office suggested that the Widow Smith should not tithe when she had so little, she scolded him. It was a privilege to pay tithing, she insisted, and to recommend that she not pay her tithing was to deny her the blessings that she needed.

Mary Fielding Smith died September 21, 1852, probably from pneumonia, at the age of fifty-one. She was widely respected and admired during her lifetime. Later generations saw her through the eyes of her son, President Joseph F. Smith, who often spoke of her as a model of courage and faithfulness.

BIBLIOGRAPHY

Arrington, Leonard J., and Susan Arrington Madsen. *Mothers of the Prophets*, pp. 89–107. Salt Lake City, 1987.

Corbett, Don C. *Mary Fielding Smith: Daughter of Britain.* Salt Lake City, 1966.

Smith, Joseph Fielding. *Life of Joseph F. Smith.* Salt Lake City, 1938.

SUSAN ARRINGTON MADSEN

SMITH FAMILY

Joseph and Lucy Mack SMITH, parents of the Prophet Joseph SMITH, were married in Tunbridge, Vermont, in 1796. Joseph, Sr., worked as a cooper, shopkeeper, schoolteacher, farmer, and laborer to provide for a growing family. Accounts of these years describe hard work, severe economic reversals, and strong family loyalty. Both parents were dissatisfied with the religions of their time, but family members believed in God, prayed, read the Bible, and were concerned about the salvation of their souls.

After the failure of a number of business and farming ventures, they moved to the village of Palmyra, New York, in 1816, near which Joseph Smith, Jr., experienced his early visions (*see* VISIONS OF JOSEPH SMITH). From the beginning, the Smith family supported young Joseph's claim to angelic visitations and prophetic power. Nine children grew to adulthood (a first son was stillborn; another, Ephraim, died shortly after birth in 1810), and all were loyal to their belief in their brother Joseph's divine mission.

Alvin (1798–1823), the oldest son, was a great strength to his family as he cleared land and worked to build a house for the family in Manchester. He died in November 1823 of an overdose of calomel prescribed for a stomach ailment. On his deathbed Alvin encouraged the seventeen-year-old Joseph to "be a good boy, and do everything that lies in your power to obtain the Record," referring to the Book of Mormon plates (Smith, p. 87). In an 1836 vision, Joseph saw Alvin in the celestial kingdom (D&C 137).

The Smiths participated in the early events of the Restoration and followed young Joseph first to Ohio and then to Missouri and Illinois, suffering hardship and persecution, but continuing faithful. Don Carlos Smith (1816–1841), the youngest brother, was president of the high priests at Kirtland and Nauvoo and an editor of the *Times and Seasons*. He died in August 1841 at the age of twenty-five.

The close relationship of Hyrum SMITH (1800–1844) and his younger brother Joseph is a prominent theme in the history of the Church. John TAYLOR declared of them, "In life they were not divided, and in death they were not separated!" (D&C 135:3). Hyrum became Second Counselor in the First Presidency and was named patriarch and assistant Church President in 1841. He married Jerusha Barden in 1826, and after her death in 1837 he married Mary Fielding (*see* SMITH, MARY FIELDING). He was the father of eight children and was assassinated with Joseph at CARTHAGE JAIL on June 27, 1844.

Samuel Harrison Smith (1808–1844) was the first missionary in the Church. Along with Hyrum and his father, Joseph, Sr., he was one of the eight witnesses of the Book of Mormon. He married Mary Bailey and, after her death, Levira Clark. Upon hearing of the danger to his brothers at Carthage, Samuel attempted to ride to their aid, but was fired upon and chased away by the mob. He eluded his pursuers with hard riding, but arrived too late to intervene. He died within the month, apparently of an injury sustained in that ride. Samuel's family went west with the Saints, as did the family of Hyrum Smith.

William Smith (1811–1893) was the only brother in the family to survive the Nauvoo period. He became a member of the Quorum of the Twelve Apostles in 1835 and Church Patriarch after the death of his brother Hyrum in 1844. Unwilling to accept the leadership of the Twelve over the Church after the death of Joseph, he was excommunicated in 1845. He may have been a pivotal influence in the decision of the Smith sisters and their mother to remain in Illinois after the main body of the Church moved west. He vigorously encouraged Mary Fielding Smith and Hyrum's children to remain in the area, but they chose to follow Brigham YOUNG and the Twelve. William joined the REORGANIZED CHURCH OF JESUS CHRIST OF LATTER DAY SAINTS in 1878.

The three sisters in the Smith family were Sophronia, Catherine, and Lucy. Sophronia (1803–1876) married Calvin Stoddard in 1828 and bore him two daughters. After Calvin's death in 1836, she married William McCleary. Their temple endowments are recorded after Joseph and Hyrum's martyrdom, which indicates that they were in harmony with Church leadership at that time, but they did not go west with the Saints.

Catherine (1813–1900) fulfilled her father's blessing that she would live to a good old age. She married Wilkins Jenkins Salisbury in 1831, and they were the parents of eight children. After his death in 1856, she remained in Hancock County, Illinois, a prominent member of the community.

Lucy (1821–1882), the youngest, was especially beloved by all the family. She married Arthur Millikin when almost nineteen and became a welcome support to her mother, who lived with the couple for seven years after the death of Joseph, Sr. Lucy stayed in Illinois and with her sisters joined the RLDS church in 1873. The sisters maintained cordial relationships with their Utah relatives throughout their lives.

BIBLIOGRAPHY

Anderson, Richard Lloyd. "What Were Joseph Smith's Sisters Like?" *Ensign* 9 (Mar. 1979):42–44.

———. "Joseph Smith's Brothers: Nauvoo and After." *Ensign* 9 (Sept. 1979):30–33.

Bushman, Richard L. *Joseph Smith and the Beginnings of Mormonism.* Chicago, 1984.

Smith, Lucy Mack. *History of Joseph Smith by His Mother, Lucy Mack Smith.* Salt Lake City, 1956.

SYDNEY SMITH REYNOLDS

SMITH FAMILY ANCESTORS

Five generations of the Prophet Joseph SMITH'S ancestors lived in Topsfield, Massachusetts. The first was his great-grandfather's grandfather, Robert Smith, who came from England to Boston in 1638. He married Mary French in 1659 at Topsfield. They were the parents of ten children. When Robert died at Boxfield, Massachusetts, in 1693, he left an estate valued at the comparatively large amount of 189 pounds. Robert and Mary's son Samuel was born in 1666. He was listed on the town and county records as a "gentleman" and apparently held public office. He married Rebecca Curtis, and the third of their nine children, also named Samuel, was born in 1714.

Samuel Smith, Jr., was a distinguished community leader and supporter of the American War of Independence. He served six terms in the Massachusetts state legislature and twelve as a town selectman. He was chairman of the Tea Committee at Topsfield in 1773, which sustained the action of the Boston Tea Party, and he was elected to the First Provincial Congress in Massachusetts in 1774. Samuel married Priscilla Gould, a descendant of Zaccheus Gould, the founder of Topsfield.

Asael Smith, the Prophet Joseph Smith's grandfather, was born to this couple in 1744. His mother died just six months after he was born. Asael married Mary Duty at Topsfield in 1767. Their son Joseph SMITH, Sr., was born in Topsfield in 1771. They later moved to New Hampshire. Asael served in the Revolutionary War, following which he was town clerk of Derryfield, New Hampshire, from 1779 until 1786. When his father died, Asael returned to Topsfield at great personal sacrifice and worked for five years to liquidate his father's debts. In 1791 Asael left Topsfield to make a new life, first in Ipswich, Massachusetts, and then that same year in Vermont. He continued his trade as a cooper, settling in Tunbridge, Vermont, where he served as selectman, grand juror, and surveyor of highways. Over the years, he held nearly every public office in Tunbridge.

Although Asael believed in a personal God and Savior, he came to oppose the established churches. He served as moderator of a meeting that established one of the early Universalist societies in Vermont in 1797. He always subscribed to the Universalist doctrine that the atonement of Christ was sufficient to redeem all men. Despite this departure from traditional New England orthodoxy, his writings show him to have been a man of warm Christian faith. Asael said that he felt that God intended to raise a branch of his family to be of great benefit to mankind (R. L. Anderson, p. 112).

The maternal ancestors of the Prophet Joseph Smith were named Mack(e). John Macke was born in 1653 at Inverness, Scotland, a descendant of a line of clergymen. He emigrated to Salisbury, Massachusetts, in 1669, and then on to Lyme, Connecticut. His son Ebenezer inherited his father's large estate in Lyme and married Hannah Huntley. For a while Ebenezer was able to keep his family in good style, but their prosperity was short-lived. Their son Solomon, born in 1732, was apprenticed to a neighboring farmer in Lyme at the age of four. Solomon later reported that he was treated as a slave and never given instruction in religion or taught to read and write, which was a great hardship to him in later life.

In 1759 Solomon Mack married Lydia Gates, a young schoolteacher and a member of the Congregational church. She was well educated and from a well-to-do religious family. Although Solomon and Lydia came from contrasting backgrounds, theirs was an enduring marriage. Lydia took charge of both the secular and religious

Genealogy of Joseph Smith, Jr.

Joseph SMITH Jr.
B. 23 Dec 1805 Sharon, Windsor, VT
M. 18 Jan 1827 S. Bainbridge, Chenango, NY
D. 27 June 1844 Carthage, Hancock, IL

Joseph SMITH Sr.
B. 12 July 1771 Topsfield, Essex, MA
M. 24 Jan 1796 Tunbridge, Orange, VT
D. 12 Sept 1840 Nauvoo, Hancock, IL

Asael SMITH
B. 7 Mar 1743/4 Topsfield, Essex, MA
M. 12 Feb 1767 Topsfield, Essex, MA
D. 31 Oct 1830 Stockholm, St. Lawrence, NY

Samuel SMITH
B. 26 Jan 1714/5 Topsfield, MA
M. 27 May 1734 Topsfield, MA
D. 14 Nov 1785

Samuel SMITH
B. 26 Jan 1666/7
D. 12 July 1748

Rebecca CURTIS
B. 20 Jan 1667/8
D. 2 Mar 1753

Priscilla GOULD
B. 4 Aug 1707 Topsfield, MA
D. 25 Sept 1744

Zaccheus GOULD
B. 26 Mar 1672
D. 29 Apr 1739

Elizabeth CURTICE
B. 15 Dec 1679
D. 21 June 1740

Mary DUTY
B. 11 Oct 1743 Rowley, Essex, MA
D. 27 May 1836 Kirtland, Geauga (Lake), OH

Moses DUTY
B. 2 Sept 1700 Rowley, MA
M. 1 May 1741 Rowley, MA
D. 1778

William DUTY
B. 5 Aug 1658
D. 11 Apr 1738

Elizabeth HIDDEN
B. 19 Feb 1665/6
D. 7 Feb 1742/3

Mary PALMER
B. 1 June 1717 Rowley, MA
D. 2 Nov 1763

John PALMER
B. 21 June 1689
D. 2 Jan 1763/4

Mary STICKNEY
B. 1 Mar 1686/7
D. 2 Nov 1763

Lucy MACK
B. 8 July 1775 Gilsum, Cheshire, NH
D. 14 May 1856 Nauvoo, Hancock, IL

Solomon MACK
B. 15 Sept 1732 Lyme, New London, CT
M. 4 Jan 1759
D. 23 Aug 1820 Gilsum, Cheshire, NH

Ebenezer MACKE
B. 8 Dec 1697 Lyme, CT
M. 30 Apr 1728
D. 1777

John MACKE
B. 6 Mar 1653/4
D. 24 Feb 1721/2

Sarah BAGLEY
B. 2 Mar 1663/4

Hannah HUNTLEY
B. 22 July 1708 Lyme, CT
D. 1796

Aaron HUNTLEY
B. 1 Dec 1680
D. 26 Sept 1748

Deborah DEWOLF
B. 25 July 1690

Lydia GATES
B. 3 Sept 1732 East Haddam, Middlesex, CT
D. 1818 Royalton, Windsor, VT

Daniel GATES
B. 5 Feb 1706/7 East Haddam, CT
D. 7 Jan 1777/8

Daniel GATES
B. 6 May 1680
D. 24 Nov 1761

Rebecca DUTTON
B. 13 Aug 1686

Lydia FULLER
B. 1 Sept 1709 East Haddam, CT
D. 14 Aug 1778

Shubael FULLER
Ch. 21 Oct 1688
D. 29 May 1748

Hannah CROCKER
B. 26 Mar 1688

Note: Double dates before 1752 are due to the change from the Julian calender to the Gregorian calender.

BYU Geography Department

education of their eight children. They pioneered the upper Connecticut River Valley and settled Marlow, New Hampshire. They later moved to Gilsum, New Hampshire, where the Prophet Joseph's mother, Lucy Mack, was born in 1775 (*see* SMITH, LUCY MACK).

During the American Revolution, Solomon helped with the manufacture of gunpowder, served in an artillery company, and shipped aboard a privateer. Although he worked hard as a merchant, land developer, shipmaster, mill operator, and farmer, fortune did not favor him, and accidents, hardships, and financial reverses beset him most of his life.

Solomon Mack was not outwardly religious, though he was a God-fearing and good-hearted man. He showed little inclination toward scripture reading or churchgoing until 1810, when rheumatism forced him to reassess his values. "After this I determined to follow phantoms no longer, but devote the rest of my life to the service of God and my family" (quoted in Smith, pp. 7–8). That winter, he read the Bible and prayed earnestly, eventually finding peace of soul and mind. From then on until his death in 1820, Solomon spent much of his time telling others of his conversion and admonishing them to serve the Lord. He wrote an autobiography in the hope that others would not become enamored with the desire for material gain as he had. He enthusiastically shared his religious conviction with his grandchildren, among whom was young Joseph Smith, Jr. Solomon Mack died in 1820, three weeks before his eighty-eighth birthday and shortly after his grandson's remarkable FIRST VISION of the Father and the Son.

BIBLIOGRAPHY

Anderson, Mary Audentia Smith. *Ancestry and Posterity of Joseph Smith and Emma Hale*. Independence, Mo., 1929.

Anderson, Richard L. *Joseph Smith's New England Heritage*. Salt Lake City, 1971.

Bushman, Richard L. *Joseph Smith and the Beginnings of Mormonism*. Urbana, Ill., 1984.

Hill, Donna. *Joseph Smith, the First Mormon*. Garden City, N.Y., 1977.

Smith, Lucy Mack. *History of Joseph Smith*. Salt Lake City, 1958.

A. GARY ANDERSON

SMOOT HEARINGS

Before seating senator-elect Reed Smoot, a member of the Quorum of the Twelve Apostles, the U.S. Senate conducted lengthy hearings into his alleged involvement in PLURAL MARRIAGE and into the policy and government of the Church. Few events have had greater impact on the Church and its public image than the highly publicized Smoot Hearings of 1903–1907.

The 1890s had seen the Church pass through some of its most challenging times, including the tumultuous political fight for Utah statehood following the MANIFESTO OF 1890 (officially curtailing new plural marriages) and presidential amnesty for Church officers who had practiced POLYGAMY, initiating the process of accommodation and acculturation to mainstream America. Euphoria, however, was short-lived.

The election to the U.S. Senate of Reed Smoot, a highly visible Church leader, unleashed intense anti-Mormon sentiment, which had subsided after statehood. Within a year of his election, more than 3,100 petitions arrived in Washington, D.C., protesting his seating and creating a furor that forced the Senate to examine the case. The prosecution focused on two issues: Smoot's alleged polygamy and his expected allegiance to the Church and its ruling hierarchy, which, it was claimed, would make it impossible for him to execute his oath as a United States senator. Although the proceedings focused on senator-elect Smoot, it soon became apparent that it was the Church that was on trial.

The case opened with Church leaders subpoenaed to testify as to the power the Church exerted over its members in general and over General Authorities in particular. Investigators probed into past and present polygamous relationships of leaders and lay members alike. They raised questions on points of doctrine that affected how Church members and their leaders interacted with American society at large.

Some of the testimony revealed situations and circumstances that put the Church in an unfavorable light. President Joseph F. SMITH received especially harsh treatment in cross-examination. Some members of the Quorum of the Twelve refused to testify, which increased the hostility of senators already concerned about the Church's motives and conduct. Faced with intense pressure, Church leaders accepted the resignations of apostles Matthias Cowley and

John W. Taylor, who were rumored to have performed plural marriages after the Manifesto. To further evidence good faith, in the annual April conference of 1904 President Smith issued a "Second Manifesto" that added ecclesiastical teeth to the Manifesto of 1890. Excommunication would now follow for those who refused to relinquish the practice of plural marriage.

Despite some damaging testimony, Senator Smoot gradually won support for three reasons. First, his character was found to be above reproach, and charges against him and the Church proved groundless. Second, U.S. President Theodore Roosevelt was sympathetic to Smoot's position; his motivation was partly personal but also political, as Senator Smoot and a Republican Utah were important to him. Third, the defense convinced a majority of senators that Smoot's apostleship would not impair his ability to put the oath of the senator first in executing his responsibilities.

The victory for Elder-Senator Smoot was a victory for the Church, providing the political legitimacy it had been seeking since 1850. It also launched a thirty-year career in the Senate that saw Senator Smoot reach the pinnacle of political success as one of the two or three most powerful senators in America during the 1920s. Perhaps more than any other individual, Reed Smoot molded and shaped the positive national image the Church was to enjoy throughout the twentieth century.

BIBLIOGRAPHY

Alexander, Thomas G. *Mormonism in Transition: A History of the Latter-Day Saints, 1890–1930.* Chicago, 1986.

Heath, Harvard. "Reed Smoot: The First Modern Mormon." Ph.D. diss., Brigham Young University, 1990.

Merrill, Milton R. *Reed Smoot: Apostle in Politics.* Logan, Utah, 1990.

United States Senate, Committee on Privileges and Elections. *In the Matter of the Protests Against the Right of Hon. Reed Smoot, A Senator from the State of Utah to Hold His Seat,* 4 vols. Washington, D.C., 1904–1906.

HARVARD S. HEATH

SNOW, ELIZA R.

Dubbed "Zion's poetess" by Joseph SMITH, Eliza Roxcy Snow (1804–1887) is still noted widely for her hymn-texts, ten of which are included in the 1985 LDS Hymnal. Of those, "O My Father," written in Nauvoo in 1845 and sung to various tunes since its first publication, is one of Mormondom's favorites. Her poems "How Great the Wisdom and the Love" and "Though Deepening Trials" are also sung frequently. Her most significant legacy, however, was not her poetry but her 1867 assignment to organize Relief Societies throughout the Church, and her involvement in the organization of the Young Ladies Mutual Improvement Association (later Young Women), the Primary Association, and other economic and ecclesiastical movements. She was unchallenged in her position as "captain of Utah's woman-host."

She is described by her contemporaries as being of average height, and delicate in appearance. In her sixties she seemed to observers to be as young as forty, despite the fact that her dark brown hair was silvered with gray. She had dark eyes and a high forehead, and she habitually wore a cap over her center-parted hair and dangling earrings. Her manner was quiet and dignified. She was simple in her attire, calm, ladylike, and rather cold, observed several of her contemporaries. At age seventy, her now wrinkled face appeared to many to be stern. Most remarkable are the descriptions of her in her eighties, however, revealing a woman with mental faculty in full vigor, industrious beyond her physical strength, and tireless as a woman half her age. Throughout her life she was perceived as neat and orderly, with "old school" manners. Where her detractors saw her as outrageously bigoted, her friends admired her precision and enthusiasm in defense of her faith.

Born in Becket, Berkshire County, Massachusetts, on January 21, 1804, Eliza Roxcy (most often Eliza R. or misspelled Roxey) Snow was raised from her second year in Mantua, Portage County, Ohio. Her father, Oliver Snow, of Becket, and mother, Rosetta Pettibone, of Simsbury, Connecticut, along with daughters Leonora and Eliza, and family members on both sides, were 1806 pioneers to Connecticut's "Western Reserve" in northeastern Ohio. They cleared a good farm and in 1814 built one of Mantua's first permanent homes. Oliver was a town and county official, and Eliza, as she matured, served often as his secretary.

A precocious child, Eliza was gifted in language, reading, and writing beyond her years. Her earliest publications, odes in the neoclassical style of the century past, indicate wide knowledge of the literary masters, Shakespeare, Milton, and the ancients. "Trained to the kitchen," as she later wrote in her autobiography, she was skilled in domestic arts as well. She completed an education in the local grammar school; unlike her younger brother Lorenzo SNOW, however, she did not attend secondary schools.

Eliza claimed to have had suitors as a young woman, yet did not marry in Ohio. A member of the Reformed Baptist congregation of Sidney RIGDON, she was, with her family, introduced to Joseph Smith within a year of his arrival in Ohio. Not until 1835 did she follow her mother and older sister into the new faith, she having had first to "prove all things." Shortly after her baptism she moved to KIRTLAND, where she lived in the household of Joseph and Emma Smith. There she taught a school for their children and others. She witnessed and recorded the dedication of the KIRTLAND TEMPLE, purchased land, and brought her family to Kirtland, but was, with them, compelled to move with the Saints to Missouri.

Settling in ADAM-ONDI-AHMAN, north of Far West, the Snows stayed only nine months before they were forced to leave with the migration to Illinois. There the family was split three ways: Lorenzo had gone on a mission through the southern states; the parents and younger boys moved to LaHarpe; and Eliza with Leonora and her two daughters stayed in Quincy. The local newspaper, the *Quincy Whig*, published several of Eliza's verses in defense of the Saints.

On invitation from Sidney Rigdon, Eliza moved to what would become NAUVOO, again to teach a school. Though Father Snow eventually came to Nauvoo, he soon became disaffected from the Church and took his remaining family to settle in Walnut Grove, Illinois, where he and Rosetta died.

Left alone in Nauvoo, Eliza continued to publish verses in the several Latter-day Saint newspapers. When in March 1842 the women's Relief Society was organized, she was invited first to draft its bylaws and then to be its secretary. At the discontinuance of that organization in 1844, she was custodian of the minute book. That record would prove invaluable as a guide to the reorganization of the Relief Society in Utah in the 1860s, containing as it did reports of the Prophet Joseph Smith's instructions to the women.

Less than ten weeks after the founding of the Nauvoo Relief Society, on June 29, 1842, Eliza Snow was sealed as a plural wife to

Joseph Smith, and lived for six months in the Smith home (*see* PLURAL MARRIAGE). Again she taught a school, which included the Smith children. Following the death of Joseph, by which time she was living in the attic room of the Stephen Markham home, she was married "for time" to President Brigham YOUNG. She never took President Young's name, however, and at his death claimed the name—and was buried as—Eliza Roxcy Snow Smith.

With the Markhams, and later with the Robert Peirce family, she made her way across the plains in the pioneer migration to the Great Basin. The winter that divided the two seasons of travel she spent at WINTER QUARTERS, Nebraska, much of it in ill health. Recovering, she found a place in the network of "leading sisters," those wives and daughters of the leaders of the Church who would, in years to come, direct the activities of LDS women in the Utah settlements. Traveling with the "big company," she arrived in the Salt Lake Valley on October 9, 1847.

Little is known of her activities in her first decade in Utah. Susa Young GATES, who knew her later, wrote that she was ill with tuberculosis, from which she recovered in the late 1850s; other indications suggest something less severe. During the first two decades in Utah she wrote and compiled poetry until she had enough for two volumes. The first, *Poems: Religious, Historical, and Political*, was published in Liverpool in 1856. Eliza Snow's reputation as poet and thinker made her the center of a female intelligentsia in Utah society. In 1854, she and her brother Lorenzo founded a Polysophical Society, where a select group of friends met regularly to perform for and address one another. Some of her most thoughtful writings were composed for those occasions. The assembly displeased some Church authorities, and so was discontinued in 1856.

The same year as the founding of the Polysophical Society, Relief Societies sprang up in various Salt Lake City wards, later to be encouraged by Brigham Young. Eliza Snow was herself only peripherally involved in the movement, and only in her own Eighteenth Ward. The reborn societies were interrupted by the Utah War (*see* UTAH EXPEDITION), however, and few survived.

In December 1866, following the Civil War, President Young once more saw need for the women to be organized, and called Eliza R. Snow to "head up" the movement, this time on an all-Church basis. Thus began the Relief Society as it has continued to the present: a central board setting directions to be followed by stake and ward officers wherever the Church has members. Loosely organized at first, the movement took advantage of existing networks of women until lines of responsibility were firmly established. Always at the center was "Sister Snow," or "Aunt Eliza," visiting or sending envoys to the various settlements to instruct, aid, and encourage. The Cooperative Junior and Senior Retrenchment Association, established in 1869 to promote frugality and HOME INDUSTRY, served as an early central meeting place for the sisters, meeting semimonthly in the Fourteenth Ward meetinghouse. It was replaced gradually by more directed organizations.

Included under her direction as "presidentess" of the women's organizations were, by 1884, the Relief Society, Young Ladies' Mutual Improvement Association, and Primary Association, all of which she helped found. She also held responsibility for the women's work of the Endowment House, and sat on an advisory board of the *Woman's Exponent,* the semimonthly newspaper edited for Mormon women by Lula Greene [Richards] and Emmeline B. Wells.

Various ad hoc projects came under Eliza Snow's direction: the encouragement of women to attend medical schools and then to offer classes in practical nursing and midwifery; the celebration of the United States Centennial by the preparation of handicrafts, later sold in the Ladies' Commission Store; the preparation, with Edward Tullidge, of a manuscript later published in New York as *Women of Mormondom*; and the establishment of the DESERET HOSPITAL, the first to be founded by the Latter-day Saints.

In addition to all of her public efforts, Eliza Snow carried on her private projects. She wrote, or edited, and published nine books, including her two poetry volumes, a biography of her brother Lorenzo, a collection of letters from her 1872–1873 tour of Europe and the Holy Land, and five instructional books for children.

Revered in her own time, she was honored during her many visits to the settlements of the Saints by feasts, celebrations of her birthday, odes in her praise, and invitations to address meetings of both men and women. Accounts of her healings, blessings, and prophesies are extant; her instructions to the women were accepted as binding. There was no intended exaggeration in the Kanab Relief Society's 1881 acknowledgment of her position as president "of all the feminine portion of the human race" and as "leading Priestess of this dispensation" (*Woman's Exponent* 9 [Apr. 1, 1881]:165), and Primary children two decades after her death in 1887 were encouraged in reverence for "the prophet, the priesthood, and Eliza R. Snow."

BIBLIOGRAPHY

Autobiographical writings:

Three holograph diaries and a brief autobiography are extant, two diaries at the Huntington Libraries, San Marino, Calif., one at the LDS Church Archives, and the autobiography at the Bancroft Library, Berkeley, Calif.; they have been published, in greater or lesser completeness, in the following places: Trail journals, 1846–1849, serially in the *Improvement Era*, in 1943–1944; "Sketch of My Life" in *Relief Society Magazine*, March to October 1944; also in part in Edward Tullidge, *Women of Mormondom* (New York, 1877). Parts of the trail journals are found, with other writings, in *Eliza R. Snow: An Immortal* (Salt Lake City, 1957). The Nauvoo diary and notebook, 1842–1844, are published as "Eliza R. Snow's Nauvoo Journal" in *BYU Studies* 15 (Summer 1975):391–416.

Publications by Eliza R. Snow:

Poems, Religious, Historical, and Political, 2 vols. Liverpool, 1856, and Salt Lake City, 1877.

Correspondence of Palestine Tourists . . ., edited. Salt Lake City, 1875.

Biography and Family Record of Lorenzo Snow. . . . Salt Lake City, 1884.

Publications about Eliza R. Snow:

Beecher, Maureen Ursenbach. "The Eliza Enigma." *Dialogue: A Journal of Mormon Thought* 11 (Spring 1978):30–43.

———. "'The Leading Sisters': A Female Hierarchy in Nineteenth Century Mormon Society." *Journal of Mormon History* 9 (1982):26–39.

———. "Leonora, Eliza, and Lorenzo: An Affectionate Portrait of the Snow Family." *Ensign* 10 (June 1980):64–69.

———; Linda King Newell; and Valeen Tippetts Avery. "Emma and Eliza and the Stairs." *BYU Studies* 22 (Winter 1982):87–96.

Madsen, Carol Cornwall, and Susan Staker Oman. *Sisters and Little Saints: One Hundred Years of Primary*. Salt Lake City, 1979.

Mulvay Derr, Jill, and Susan Staker Oman. "The Nauvoo Generation: Our First Five Relief Society Presidents." *Ensign* 7 (Dec. 1977):36–43.

Terry, Keith, and Ann Terry. *Eliza*. Santa Barbara, Calif., 1981.

MAUREEN URSENBACH BEECHER

SNOW, LORENZO

Lorenzo Snow (1814–1901) was the fifth President of The Church of Jesus Christ of Latter-day Saints, from 1898 to 1901. A well-educated and refined man, he served many missions for the Church, traveling to England, Italy, and the Pacific, as well as in the southern and northwestern United States. Coming to the presidency when the Church suffered under a crushing weight of debt, President Snow reinvigorated tithe-paying among the Saints and put the Church on the road to financial solvency.

Born on April 3, 1814, the oldest son of Oliver and Rosetta Pettibone Snow, Lorenzo was the fifth of seven children. He grew to manhood in Mantua, Portage County, Ohio, where his parents had established themselves as leaders in the community. His father's public duties often took him from home, so the responsibility of the farm fell to Lorenzo and his younger brothers. Bookish by nature, Lorenzo pursued his education beyond the common schools in Mantua to the high school in nearby Ravenna, and completed one term at newly founded Oberlin College.

The family were Baptists with broad religious interests. While Lorenzo was in his teens, the Prophet Joseph SMITH took up residence in Hiram, four miles from the Snow farm. Although Lorenzo's sister Eliza, in her biography of him, claims to have whetted his interest in Mormonism while he was at Oberlin, his own account tells of hearing the Book of Mormon being read in his home in Mantua and of later meeting with the Prophet at Hiram in 1831. Contrary to the common accusations that Joseph Smith was a "false prophet," Lorenzo judged him to be "honest and sincere." He later said that at that time "a light arose in my understanding which has never been extinguished" (*IE* 40 [Feb. 1937]:82–83; Lorenzo Snow journal, Church Archives).

Lorenzo's mother, his two oldest sisters, and probably his father were soon baptized into the Church, but Lorenzo left for Oberlin uncommitted. A chance meeting with David W. PATTEN, an apostle, provided further information on the new Church, and as the young scholar began his work at Oberlin, he lost favor among the students and faculty by arguing in defense of Mormonism. Seeing an opportunity to continue his studies in Kirtland, he joined his two sisters there and on June 19, 1836, was baptized. He soon after received a manifestation that confirmed for him "a perfect knowledge that God lives, that Jesus Christ is the Son of God, and of the restoration of the holy Priesthood, and the fulness of the Gospel" (Smith, pp. 7–8). That conviction directed his actions for the remainder of his life.

Giving up his plans for further formal education, Lorenzo set out on a series of missions for the Church in early spring 1837, first to the Mantua area, where he baptized some of his friends and relatives, and then to other Ohio counties before returning to Kirtland. In 1838 the Snows joined the Saints in Missouri, and Lorenzo left for another mission, this time to Illinois and Kentucky. While the Saints settled Nauvoo and his parents moved farther on, to Walnut Grove, Illinois, Lorenzo went as a missionary to England.

Elder Snow taught in and around Birmingham for three months, during which time he baptized people in Greet's Green and organized a branch in Wolverhampton. In February 1841 the twenty-six-year-old missionary was called to preside over the ten established branches in London. He returned to Nauvoo in 1843 as leader of a shipload of 250 converts. En route, Elder Snow's quiet confidence, his healing of a dying steward, and the faith of his company of Saints led to the baptism of the ship's first mate and several of the crew. The party arrived in Nauvoo on April 12, 1843.

In accordance with the revelation on plural marriage, Snow married Charlotte Squires, Mary Adaline Goddard, Sarah Ann Prichard, and Harriet Amelia Squires before leaving Nauvoo in the 1846 exodus. On the way west, the family had to stop at Mt. Pisgah, Iowa, because of his illness. Two of his three children born there survived. Called to preside over the temporary settlement, Snow actively raised money to assist the Saints in the move west. The family moved on to Salt Lake City in 1848.

On February 12, 1849, Lorenzo Snow was ordained a member of the Quorum of the Twelve Apostles. Assigned that summer to direct the first celebration of the Saints' entry into the Salt Lake Valley, Elder Snow established a reputation for pageantry as a way of building morale and group identity. For decades afterward, settlements throughout the Church followed his lead in celebrating significant events.

At the October 1849 conference, Elder Snow was assigned to fill a mission in Italy. Traveling with the first company of missionaries from Utah, he went first to England and there determined by study and by "a flood of light" that the work should begin among the Waldenses in the Piedmont area of northern Italy. He and his companions were successful in bringing several Waldensian converts to Utah, but the mission itself did not remain active. Snow extended the work to Switzerland, left missionaries there, and sent two more to India. Returning to Britain, he superintended the publication of an Italian translation of the Book of Mormon. Crossing France once more, he visited Switzerland and the Piedmont and concluded his mission in Malta.

After an absence of nearly three years, Elder Snow returned to Utah, arriving July 30, 1852, to discover that his wife Charlotte had died in his absence. He was immediately caught up in community activities. He organized the Polysophical Association to promote cultural refinement for the community. That fall, he was elected to the Utah legislature, where he served with distinction for twenty-nine years, ten of them as president of the Legislative Council.

In 1853, Elder Snow was called to lead a colonization group of fifty families and preside over the Saints in Box Elder County, Utah, headquartered in a struggling settlement of modest adobe huts later known as Brigham City. He established a dramatics society, a public school system, and the Brigham City Mercantile and Manufacturing Association, with forty departments. The association, a branch of the United Order, became the most successful cooperative in the territory; its production for 1875 was valued at $260,000.

In 1864, Elder Snow accompanied four other missionaries on a short-term mission to the Sandwich (Hawaiian) Islands. He drowned when their small boat capsized in Lahaina Harbor but was restored to life when his friends were impressed to perform mouth-to-mouth resuscitation, a procedure unknown at that time. On Lanai the elders excommunicated the self-appointed Hawaiian mission president, Walter Murray Gibson, for organizing a new church, selling priesthood offices to men and women, and usurping Church property.

After all these missions abroad, still more were to come. Eight years later, Elder Snow accompanied George A. Smith, a member of the First Presidency, and others to Palestine, where, on the Mount of Olives, they blessed the land to be fruitful and dedicated the country for the return of the Jews. In 1885 he served a short-term mission among the Native Americans in the Pacific Northwest.

Shortly after his return to Utah, Snow was tried and imprisoned for violation of the 1882 Edmunds Act, which prohibited the practice of polygamy. The territorial governor, Caleb W. West, promised amnesty if he would renounce plural marriage, but Elder Snow replied, "I thank you, Governor, but having adopted sacred and holy principles for which we have already sacrificed property, home and life on several occasions, . . . we do not propose, at this late hour, to abandon them because of threatened danger" (Romney, p. 381). He remained in prison for eleven months before being released under mandate of the U.S. Supreme Court.

Elder Snow radiated a purity and holiness that were extraordinary. He dedicated the Manti Temple in south-central Utah in 1888. Rhoda W. Smith, who was present, wrote, "When Apostle Lorenzo Snow arose, a beautiful heavenly light enveloped his head and shoulders; he looked angelic" (Spiritual Manifestations in the Manti Temple, *Millennial Star*, 50, Aug. 13, 1888, p. 522).

About the time of his conversion as a young man, Elder Snow had been promised an ancient apostolic power by Joseph Smith, Sr.: "If expedient the dead shall rise and come forth at thy bidding" (Romney, p. 406). In 1891, he restored life to a young woman, Ella Jensen, after she had been dead for two hours.

During the April 1889 general conference, Lorenzo Snow was sustained as President of the Quorum of the Twelve Apostles. He became the first president of the Salt Lake Temple in 1893, and on September 13, 1898, at age eighty-four, he was sustained as the fifth President of the Church. Worried about his advanced age, he pleaded for a manifestation of divine will. He testified that the Lord appeared to him in the Salt Lake Temple and affirmed that he should serve and that he should immediately reorganize the First Presidency (pp. 677–79). The reorganization took place without the lengthy interval that had followed the deaths of the first four Presidents of the Church and established a custom of immediate succession.

Another question firmly resolved by his succession was that seniority among the Twelve was determined not by chronological age but by date of ordination to the quorum.

Humble and self-effacing, President Snow told the Council of the

Twelve, "I do not want this administration to be known as Lorenzo Snow's administration, but as God's in and through Lorenzo Snow" (*L.D.S. Biographical Encyclopedia*, Vol. 1, p. 30, Salt Lake City, 1901).

By 1898 the Church owed $2.3 million, an overwhelming burden of debt considering its resources. The major cause of debt was the U.S. government's escheat of Church properties under the provisions of the Edmunds-Tucker Act of 1887. Most of the Church's assets, including tithing funds, had been seized by federal agents. Many Saints reacted by curtailing financial donations; tithing receipts declined from more than $500,000 a year in the 1880s to about $350,000 in the 1890s.

The First Presidency consolidated debts, offered two $500,000 bond issues, and sold its controlling interest in many businesses. These measures, though helpful, were not sufficient. In 1899, President Snow, addressing the debt problem in a talk in the St. George (Utah) Tabernacle, received a spiritual manifestation: "This is the answer to our financial problems. Even though as a Church we are heavily in debt, I say unto you that, if this people will pay a full and honest tithing, the shackles of indebtedness will be removed from us" (*MFP* 3:322; see also Journal History entry for May 8, 1899). Carrying this message to the Saints throughout the territory, he stimulated a renewed commitment to tithing, and the Church's debt problems were resolved before he died.

As the new century dawned in 1901, President Snow stressed the worldwide mission of the General Authorities of the Church: "Here are the Apostles and the Seventies, their business is to warn the nations of the earth and prepare the world for the coming of the Savior" (*CHC* 6:377). He also encouraged the Saints in foreign lands to remain there and build up the Church rather than migrate to Salt Lake City.

President Snow spoke of introducing missionary work in Russia, Austria, and Latin America. He reopened the Mexican Mission and assigned Heber J. Grant of the Quorum of the Twelve Apostles to establish a proselytizing mission in Japan. Locally, young men were called to serve as stake missionaries of the Young Men's Mutual Improvement Association (YMMIA) to recommit youth to participation in the YMMIA.

Suffering from declining health, President Snow died of

pneumonia in the Beehive House, the residence of the President, on October 10, 1901. At the time of his death, there were 50 stakes and 292,931 members in the Church, an increase of 10 stakes and 25,680 members during his three-year presidency.

Lorenzo Snow was small and slender in appearance. He stood five feet, six inches tall, weighed 140 pounds, and had tranquil gray eyes and a full beard. He was a scholar, schoolmaster, missionary, legislator, cooperative leader, financier, temple worker, and prophet. He had a profound effect upon Latter-day Saints and non-Mormons alike, with his heavenly countenance and sweet, gentle dignity. Meeting him for the first time, a Protestant minister said, "I was startled to see the holiest face I had ever been privileged to look upon. . . . The strangest feeling stole over me, that I stood on holy ground." Another minister said, "The tenor of his spirit is as gentle as a child. You are introduced to him. You are pleased with him. You converse with him, you like him. You visit with him long . . . , you love him" (Romney, pp. 14–16).

BIBLIOGRAPHY

Gibbons, Francis M. *Lorenzo Snow, Spiritual Giant, Prophet of God.* Salt Lake City, 1982.

Romney, Thomas C. *The Life of Lorenzo Snow, Fifth President of the Church of Jesus Christ of Latter-day Saints*. Salt Lake City, 1955.

Smith, Eliza R. Snow. *Biography and Family Record of Lorenzo Snow*. Salt Lake City, 1884.

Snow, Leroi C. "An Experience of My Father." *IE* 36 (Sept. 1933):677–79.

Swinton, Heidi S. "Lorenzo Snow." In *Presidents of the Church*, ed. Leonard J. Arrington. Salt Lake City, 1987.

Williams, Clyde J. *The Teachings of Lorenzo Snow, Fifth President of the Church of Jesus Christ of Latter-day Saints.* Salt Lake City, 1984.

MAUREEN URSENBACH BEECHER
PAUL THOMAS SMITH

SOUTH AMERICA, THE CHURCH IN

[*This entry consists of three articles:*

Brazil
South America, North
South America, South

The first article discusses the establishment, growth, and development of the Church in Brazil. The second article covers the same points in Bolivia, Colombia, Ecuador, Peru, and Venezuela; and the third article covers Argentina, Chile, Paraguay, and Uruguay.

After Parley P. Pratt, an apostle, his wife Phoebe Soper Pratt, and Elder Rufus C. Allen were unsuccessful in establishing a foothold in Valparaiso, Chile, in 1851–1852, it was not until 1925 that The Church of Jesus Christ of Latter-day Saints sent Melvin J. Ballard, another apostle; and Elders Rulon S. Wells, who spoke German, and Rey L. Pratt, who spoke Spanish, both of the Seventy, to open the South America Mission. Under assignment from President Heber J. Grant, these men dedicated the vast area of South America for the preaching of the gospel in Buenos Aires on December 25, 1925. The establishment of the Church in South America began in Argentina when some German LDS families emigrated there in the 1920s, and requested that missionaries and Church supplies be sent to Buenos Aires to help them build the Church among their families and friends. The Church moved into Brazil in 1928, also in answer to requests of LDS German emigrants living there. The first Latter-day Saints in Chile apparently were North American miners who worked in the mining district in northern Chile. The first missionaries were sent there from Argentina in 1956, and the Chilean Mission was established in 1961. The Church moved into Uruguay from Argentina in 1944, and into Paraguay from Uruguay in 1948. The first missionaries were sent to Peru from Uruguay in 1956.

Speaking at a sacrament meeting in Buenos Aires in 1926, Elder Ballard likened the Church's potential in South America to a strong, mighty oak growing from a tiny acorn. He said there would be thousands of members and many missions growing from the tiny beginnings of the Church there, and South America would become one of the strongest areas of the Church. True to that prophecy, although the work went slowly for a number of years, with the location of a General Authority, Elder A. Theodore and Sister Marné Whittaker Tuttle, in South America in the 1960s to supervise missionary work, a dramatic surge of conversions began. The Church moved into the northern countries with the creation of the Andes Mission in Peru and Chile in 1959. The first units were established in Bolivia in 1964; in Ecuador in 1965; and in Colombia and Venezuela in 1966. Many of the LDS missionaries in South America are local members who have been strengthened and prepared for service and leadership by attending seminary and institute programs of the Church Educational System. Where the Church originally had only one mission in all of South America, in January 1991 it had 43 missions, 381 stakes and districts, and 3,791 wards and branches serving over 1.35 million members.]

BRAZIL

The LDS Church first came to Brazil in 1928, when several German converts emigrated to the German colonies in the southern states of Brazil and asked the Church for materials to teach their children. The Church grew slowly in Brazil until the 1960s and 1970s, when great numbers of Brazilians began joining. The first mission was divided to make new missions, stakes were organized and then divided, and in 1985 Brazil became an area with a resident area presidency of General Authorities. In January 1991 Brazil had an LDS temple, an area presidency, 12 missions, more than 2,100 LDS missionaries (over half local Brazilians), 87 stakes and districts, and over 800 wards and branches serving 366,000 members of the Church.

When President Reinhold Stoof visited the German members in Brazil in 1928 as president of the South American Mission, he was impressed with the potential he saw for missionary work there. The first LDS missionaries assigned to Brazil spoke German rather than Portuguese and began their missionary labors in the German colonies at Joinville, Santa Catarina State, on September 12, 1928. The first converts were baptized on April 14, 1929. Although the work progressed slowly at first, by October 1931 Joinville had the first LDS meetinghouse chapel in South America. The first Relief Society was organized there in 1933 with twenty-four members.

In 1935 the Brazil Mission was divided from the South American Mission with only 143 members of the Church in the entire mission. President Rulon S. Howells began preparing Church materials in Portuguese and then assigned some of the missionaries to learn Portuguese so that they could work with the Brazilians and not just with the German immigrants. In 1938 the Brazilian government prohibited the use of the German language in public meetings and schools, which made Church activities very difficult for the German-speaking members. With the advent of World War II and the North

American missionaries being called home, many of the local branches of the Church were closed. However, some units, such as the Campinas Branch, had developed sufficient local leadership to be able to keep the branch functioning throughout the war and to bring in new members.

With the return of the North American missionaries in 1945 and the calling of local Brazilians to serve missions, the Church began to grow more rapidly in Brazil. That growth was aided by the visit of Stephen L Richards, an apostle, who toured the mission in 1948, and of President David O. MCKAY in 1955. Lifting the members spiritually, and recognizing their strength, President McKay authorized the building of meetinghouses (chapels) in which the Saints could worship. With this manifestation of confidence by the President of the Church, the local members reached out to share the gospel with their friends and neighbors. They especially shared the Church youth auxiliary program, which attracted many converts and became the center of proselytizing for the mission. They also developed pageants and theatrical presentations that showed the Brazilians what blessings being a member of the Church brings.

Another important event in the history of the Church in Brazil was the organization of its first stake, the São Paulo Brazil Stake, on May 1, 1966, with Walter Spät as president. By mid-1990 that first stake had grown to fifty-six stakes and almost six hundred wards and branches, all presided over by local Brazilian priesthood bearers.

The most significant event in the history of the Church in Brazil was the construction of the São Paulo Temple in 1978. That brought all the blessings of the Church to the Brazilian and other South American Saints. Former Mission President Finn B. Paulsen was called as temple president, and his wife, Sara Broadbent Paulsen, as the temple matron. With a temple in Brazil, the Church organized the first missionary training center in South America at São Paulo in 1979.

One of the most effective missionary tools the members used to present the message of the Church was a theatrical presentation, "The Gate," written by Ana Gláucia Ceciliato and presented to more than 20,000 people at the open house for the São Paulo Temple before it was dedicated. To make the presentation required some sixty talented Church children, youth, and adults to travel many miles from several cities to São Paulo for rehearsals. The introduction of the Church seminary and institute programs also greatly strengthened the youth of the Church in Brazil.

The first translation of the Book of Mormon into Portuguese was printed in 1940. Some of the missionary tracts were translated and published a year earlier. The Portuguese translation of the Doctrine and Covenants was published in 1950, and the Pearl of Great Price in 1952, making all the latter-day scriptures available in the language of the people. The Church magazine for Portuguese-speaking members, *A Gaivota* (now *A Liahona*), began publication in 1948. Other Church materials are translated into Portuguese in Brazil for all Portuguese-speaking countries. The work of Elder William Grant and Sister Geri Hamblin Bangerter and of Elder James E. and Sister Ruth Wright Faust greatly expanded the Church in Brazil.

Two native Brazilians have been called as General Authorities of the Church. Hélio da Rocha Camargo, born in Rezende, Rio de Janeiro, on February 1, 1926, became a Seventy on April 7, 1985. A former Protestant minister, he was baptized a member of the Church on June 1, 1957. He was released from the Seventy in October 1990 and called as the president of the São Paulo Temple. Helvécio Martins, born in Rio de Janeiro on June 27, 1930, and baptized on July 2, 1972, was called to the Seventy on March 31, 1990. He is the first General Authority of African lineage.

BIBLIOGRAPHY

Grover, Mark L. "Mormonism in Brazil: Religion and Dependency in Latin America." Ph.D. diss., Indiana University, 1985.

Labarca, Ana Rosa. "Dias inesquecíveis de 1978 Uma nova era para a Igreja no Brasil." *A Liahona* 41 (Oct. 1988):4–5.

Williams, Frederick S., and Frederick G. Williams. *From Acorn to Oak Tree: A Personal History of the Establishment and First Quarter Century Development of the South American Missions*. Fullerton, Calif., 1987.

FLAVIA GARCIA ERBOLATO

SOUTH AMERICA, NORTH

BOLIVIA. The Church became legally established in Bolivia in 1963 through the work of North American LDS families living in La Paz and in Cochabamba. The first Bolivian was baptized and the first branch organized in 1964. The Bolivian Mission was organized in

1968, with headquarters in La Paz. Some of the first families who joined the Church are still active in leadership roles.

The first Bolivian stake was organized in January 1979 in Santa Cruz de la Sierra, with Noriharu Ishigaki Haraguichi as president. In March of the same year, the La Paz Stake was established, with Jorge Leano as president. In January 1991, he was serving as president of the Colombia Cali Mission.

Church materials going to Bolivia are printed in the three principal languages of the country: Spanish, Quechua, and Aymara. The LDS Bolivian youth, strengthened by the seminary and institute programs, have responded enthusiastically to the call to share the restored gospel; they currently make up 70 percent of the missionaries serving in the country. As a result of the dedicated missionary effort, approximately 64,000 members of the Church lived in Bolivia in January 1991. The Church enjoys the respect and admiration of the citizens and of government authorities because of the members' stability, spiritual contribution, and exemplary lifestyle. The construction of one hundred meetinghouses between 1987 and 1990, has given the members places in which to worship, as well as work opportunities to many Bolivians. The meetinghouses are also used as classrooms wherein the Bolivians are given the advantage of religious education and literacy training.

COLOMBIA. On March 20, 1966, the first branch of the Church was organized in Bogotá, Colombia, with Harold M. Rex as president. When the government officials signed the record of the proceedings, The Church of Jesus Christ of Latter-day Saints was established in Colombia. Elder Spencer W. Kimball rededicated the country to the preaching of the gospel in Bogotá on May 11, 1966. Colombia was part of the Andes Mission until 1968, when it became part of the Colombia-Venezuela Mission. The Colombia Bogotá Mission began operations on July 1, 1971. That mission was divided in 1975, creating the Colombia Cali Mission. On July 1, 1988, a third mission, the Colombia Barranquilla Mission, was established.

The first chapel built in Colombia was built at Cali in 1975, in a section of the city where the Versalles Ward is located. The First Presidency has announced plans for the construction of a temple in Bogotá.

The first stake in Colombia was organized at Bogotá on January

23, 1977, by Elder Bruce R. McConkie, of the Quorum of the Twelve Apostles, with Julio E. Dávila as president. On April 6, 1991, President Dávila became the first native Colombian called to be a General Authority. In January 1991 there were nine stakes in the country: Bogotá, Kennedy, Ciudad Jardín, El Dorado, Cali, Américas, Medellín, Bucaramanga, and Barranquilla. The progress of the Church in Colombia is noteworthy. More than 83,000 members are enjoying the benefits of the spiritual and temporal programs offered by the quorums of the priesthood, the auxiliary organizations, and the religious educational courses, as well as literacy classes in seminaries and institutes.

The feeling of unity has grown strong among Church members in Colombia, as was shown during the 1983 earthquake in the city of Popayán, in the southern part of the country. The Colombian Saints united to help provide the necessities of life as well as housing for the thousands injured and made homeless by the quake.

The March 1977 area conference with President Spencer W. Kimball was of great significance to the people of Colombia, as were the regional conferences of 1987 and 1989 with Elder M. Russell Ballard, of the Quorum of the Twelve Apostles, presiding.

ECUADOR. On April 27, 1964, Sterling Nicolaysen, president of the Andes Mission, was instructed by Elder A. Theodore Tuttle to register the "Corporation of the Church" in Ecuador. On Saturday, October 9, 1965, Elder Spencer W. Kimball, then of the Council of the Twelve Apostles, dedicated the land of Ecuador to the preaching of the restored gospel, offering the dedicatory prayer from the top of Panecillo Hill in Quito. In June 1969, the Ecuador Quito Mission was organized, with Louis Latimer as president. In January 1991 there were two missions in Ecuador, headquartered in Quito and Guayaquil.

The first nine members in Quito were baptized on October 31, 1965. Missionary work began in Guayaquil on January 20, 1966. Napoleón Trujillo, the first local missionary called from Ecuador, served in Uruguay. His father, José G. Trujillo, was serving as the patriarch of the Quito Stake in 1991.

Church materials for Ecuador are prepared in Spanish and Quechua, its two official languages. In 1978 Amado Ruíz, a member from Otavalo, translated some the materials needed by the Otavalo

Indians, who received their own stake on December 6, 1981, with Luis Alfonzo Morales C. as president. Having Church materials in their native language has been a great help to the indigenous peoples who inhabit the diverse regions of the country.

Elder Mark E. Petersen, of the Quorum of the Twelve Apostles, organized the first stake in Guayaquil on June 11, 1978, and called Lorenzo Garaycoa as president. The first stake in Quito was organized on August 22, 1979, by Elder Gordon B. Hinckley, then of the Quorum of the Twelve, with Ernesto Franco as president.

The Church Educational System has performed an important role in the religious education of the Ecuadorian youth in seminaries and institutes and has made great strides in the area of literacy, especially among the indigenous Indian peoples. The many youths of Ecuador who serve as missionaries among their countrymen have brought the missionary work of the Church to all corners of their country. As of January 1991, the Church had 81,000 members served by two missions, 18 stakes and districts, and 121 wards and branches in Ecuador.

The First Presidency of the Church has announced plans to construct a temple in Guayaquil, Ecuador.

PERU. The first LDS contact with the people of Peru was in 1926, when Elder Melvin J. Ballard, returning to the United States after dedicating South America to the preaching of the gospel, visited Peru and was impressed that it would be a good place to send missionaries. Although several members lived in Peru in the 1940s and possibly even earlier, it was not until July 8, 1956, that Elder Henry D. Moyle, of the Quorum of the Twelve, and Frank K. Parry, president of the Uruguayan Mission, organized the first branch in Lima. Frederick S. Williams, former president of the South American and Uruguay missions, was called to be president of the branch, which began in his home. On November 1, 1959, Elder Harold B. Lee, then of the Quorum of the Twelve Apostles, organized the Andes Mission, which included Peru and Chile, and later Bolivia, Ecuador, Colombia, and Venezuela. Headquarters were in Lima. Two years later Peru had twelve branches of the Church and more than a thousand members.

Selected passages of the Book of Mormon and other Church materials have been translated into the Quechua and Aymara languages to help the new indigenous members gain a better understanding of the gospel.

The Lima Peru Stake was organized on February 22, 1970, with Roberto Vidal as president. It had six wards, three branches, and approximately 5,000 members. In January 1991 there were 5 missions, 57 stakes and districts, and over 500 wards and branches serving the 178,000 members of the Church in Peru. At the April 1989 multiregional conference held in Lima, more than 10,000 Latter-day Saints from nine of Lima's eighteen stakes attended. The Lima Peru Temple was dedicated by President Gordon B. Hinckley, First Counselor in the First Presidency, on January 10, 1986, with Samuel and Clara Lorenzi Boren as the first president and matron. In 1990 the Lima Temple operated with an average of nine endowment sessions a day.

The Church is received with respect and enthusiasm throughout the country, where an ever-increasing number of local missionaries carry the message of the restored gospel to their people. Much credit for this success among the youth has been given to the significant role played by the Church members' religious education. More than 12,500 young Peruvians between the ages of fourteen and thirty have benefited from the courses available in the Church Educational System's seminaries and institutes. Sixty percent of the members of the Church in Peru are under thirty years of age.

VENEZUELA. On November 2, 1966, on special assignment from President David O. McKay, Elder Marion G. Romney, of the Quorum of the Twelve, dedicated the land of Venezuela for the preaching of the restored gospel. Present at that dedication was Elder F. Burton Howard, who was responsible for the legal registration of the Church in Venezuela, and Ted E. Brewerton, president of the Central American Mission (to which Venezuela belonged). Both men were later called to the Seventy.

From 1966 to 1968 there were only a few LDS missionaries in Venezuela, and progress was slow. From July 1968 to 1971, Venezuela formed a part of the Colombia-Venezuela Mission, but in 1971 the Venezuela Caracas Mission was organized, and the Church began a new era of growth. In 1978 the Venezuela Maracaibo Mission was divided from the Venezuela Caracas Mission, and President Alejandro Portal Campos, who had been the president of the Caracas Mission and the first Venezuelan to preside over a mission, was assigned the new mission.

The Caracas Stake, the first in Venezuela, was organized on May

15, 1977, under the direction of Elder Bruce R. McConkie; Adolfo Mayer was the president. In January 1991 there were seven stakes in Venezuela: two in Caracas, two in Maracaibo, and one each in Valencia, Oriente, and Guayana. There were also nine districts in the two missions. More than fifty thousand members of the Church in Venezuela have benefited from Church influence and have contributed significantly to the quality of life in their country. Because of the leadership training and skills that Church members receive and develop, many businesses and industries prefer to hire members of the Church. The Church seminary and institute programs have made significant contributions to the Venezuelan LDS youth. The influence that daily scripture study has had in their lives has made them want to participate in missionary work.

BIBLIOGRAPHY

Cowan, Richard O. "The Church in Latin America." In *The International Church*, ed. James R. Moss et al., pp. 157–91. Provo, Utah, 1982.

Williams, Frederick S., and Frederick G. Williams. *From Acorn to Oak Tree: A Personal History of the Establishment and First Quarter Century Development of the South American Missions*. Fullerton, Calif., 1987.

JULIO E. DÁVILA

(Translated from Spanish by Lyman Sidney Shreeve and Afton Kartchner Shreeve.)

SOUTH AMERICA, SOUTH

ARGENTINA. The Church was brought into Argentina by a few German immigrant families who had joined it in their homeland before they emigrated. They felt they needed to await the visit of Elder Melvin J. Ballard before they could baptize even their family members who wished to join. The first non-German convert was baptized in 1926. For several years the missionaries spoke only English and German, but emphasis was later placed on teaching also in Spanish, and that brought limited success to the Church's missionary work. The Church grew slowly in Argentina until the 1960s, when the emphasis was placed on training local member leadership. Mission President C. Laird Snelgrove organized a mission council in which he trained most of the men who would become the leaders during the next twenty-five years. A member of that council, Juan Carlos Avila, became the first native Argentine to be called as a mission president (1974–1977). The first Argentine stake was organized on November 20, 1966, presided over by a local priesthood bearer, Angel Abrea, who in 1976 would become the first Latin American General Authority. The mission was first divided in 1962, and by January 1991 the Church had nine missions, 64 stakes and districts, and over 500 wards and branches serving Argentina's 171,000 Latter-day Saints. The Buenos Aires Temple was dedicated on January 17, 1986, by Thomas S. Monson, Second Counselor in the First Presidency. Angel and Maria Victoria Chiapparino Abrea were the president and the matron. Argentina received a missionary training center in Buenos Aires, established in 1986 under President Lyman Sidney and Sister Afton Kartchner Shreeve, who had served missions in Argentina and presided over the Uruguay Mission.

CHILE. After Parley P. Pratt's unsuccessful attempt to establish a Church foothold in Chile in 1851–1852, the Church did not officially come to Chile until Brother William Fotheringham moved to Santiago, Chile, in 1952, and requested that the Church send missionaries there. The first regular missionaries arrived in Santiago just two weeks before Elder Henry D. Moyle, then of the Quorum of the Twelve Apostles, called Brother Fotheringham as the president of the first Chilean branch on July 5, 1956. It was made up primarily of expatriate members, the first local Chilean convert being baptized that same year.

The first mission in Chile was organized on October 8, 1961, with A. Delbert Palmer presiding. That single mission has grown to become six missions, with more than 50 percent of the missionaries called from the local members, many of whom have been prepared in large measure by their seminary and institute training. They are generally called to attend the Missionary Training Center in Santiago, the second such center in South America. The Church has grown rapidly in Chile, with almost 298,000 members on March 31, 1990. On January 1991, Carlos Cifuentes, one of those local converts, became the first native Chilean branch president and stake president. On September 15, 1983, the Santiago Chile Temple was dedicated. Eugene F. and Rae Stephens Jones Olsen were the president and matron. On March 31, 1990, Elder Eduardo Ayala, a former mission president in Uruguay, became the first native Chilean called to be a Seventy.

PARAGUAY. Even though in 1939 President Frederick S. Williams of the Argentine Mission traveled to the upper Pilcomayo River and visited Indian tribes there, as well as the people in Asunción, it was not until 1948 that the Church baptized its first Paraguayan convert. The Church was officially established when missionaries were sent to Paraguay from the Uruguay Mission in October 1949. Since the first baptism, Church growth has been steady. The Paraguay Mission was created in 1977, and the first stake was organized in Asunción on February 25, 1979, with Carlos R. Espinola as president. In 1980, the Church established an active branch made up of Indian converts from the Churupi-Nivacle tribe, in Mistolar village, about 800 kilometers northwest of Asunción.

URUGUAY. The first member of the Church to gain attention in Uruguay was Elder Rolf L. Larson, a missionary in the Argentina Mission who was named the most valuable basketball player in South America during the championship games held at Montevideo in January 1940. The first branch in Uruguay was organized with twelve members on June 25, 1944; the mission was organized on August 30, 1947, with the first converts being baptized on November 1, 1948. In the 1960s President and Sister A. Theodore Tuttle moved the headquarters of the South American Mission to Montevideo, which then became the center for the development of the Church throughout South America. The headquarters were later moved to Buenos Aries. The Montevideo Uruguay Stake was organized on November 12, 1967, with Vicente C. Rubio as president. Although the first plans for a temple in South America called for it to be built in Uruguay, it was eventually built in São Paulo, Brazil, in 1978. On January 1991, the Church had one mission, 18 stakes and districts, and 111 wards and branches serving over 50,000 Uruguayan Latter-day Saints.

BIBLIOGRAPHY

Cowan, Richard O. "The Church in Latin America." In *The International Church*, ed. James R. Moss et al., pp. 157–91. Provo, Utah, 1982.

Tullis, F. LaMond, ed. *Mormonism: A Faith for All Cultures*. Provo, Utah, 1978.

Williams, Frederick S., and Frederick G. Williams. *From Acorn to Oak Tree: A Personal History of the Establishment and First Quarter Century Development of the South American Missions*. Fullerton, Calif., 1987.

TOMÁS FREDERICO LINDHEIMER

SOUTH BAINBRIDGE (AFTON), NEW YORK

In October 1825, Josiah Stowell (sometimes spelled Stoal) of Bainbridge Township (now Afton), Chenango County, New York, hired Joseph SMITH and his father to assist in digging for Spanish treasure near the Susquehanna River in Harmony Township (now Oakland), Pennsylvania. The men lodged with Isaac Hale, where Joseph Smith met his future wife, Emma Hale, and began their courtship. The treasure hunters gave up excavating in mid-November 1825, but Joseph continued his employment at the Stowell farm.

Josiah Stowell's home was situated on the west side of the Susquehanna River about two miles southwest of the village of South Bainbridge (Afton since 1857), on the road to Nineveh, twenty-six miles northeast of the Hale home in Harmony. Joseph Smith worked as a farmhand, a laborer in the Stowell sawmill, and as a "wool carder." Josiah Stowell, Jr., remembered that Joseph "went to school with him one winter" and that "he was a fine likely young man" (letter of Josiah Stowell, Jr., to John S. Fullmer, Feb. 17, 1843, HDC).

Joseph Smith encountered difficulty when Peter G. Bridgman (Bridgeman), who was Stowell's nephew, swore out a complaint against him for being a "disorderly person." He appeared before Justice of the Peace Albert Neeley in South Bainbridge during March 1826 and was acquitted (Madsen, pp. 106–107; *see* SMITH, JOSEPH: LEGAL TRIALS OF JOSEPH SMITH). That same year Joseph Smith found employment with Joseph Knight, Sr., in Colesville Township, Broome County, a few miles south of the Stowells. He continued to call on Emma Hale in Harmony, and requested her hand in marriage. Isaac Hale strenuously objected and Joseph Smith found himself "under the necessity of taking her elsewhere" (*HC* 1:17). The couple were married in South Bainbridge on January 18, 1827, by Justice of the Peace Zachariah Tarbell. Joseph Smith was twenty-one and Emma Hale was twenty-two.

On June 28, 1830, while proselytizing at the home of Joseph Knight, Sr., in Colesville, Joseph Smith was arrested on a warrant from Chenango County, taken to South Bainbridge for trial before Justice of the Peace Joseph Chamberlain, and was again acquitted (Firmage, pp. 50–51). Despite strong sectarian opposition, Joseph and other LDS missionaries were successful in converting a number of individuals in the South Bainbridge area, including Josiah Stowell.

BIBLIOGRAPHY

Firmage, Edwin B., and Richard C. Mangrum. *Zion in the Courts*. Urbana, Ill., 1988.

Hill, Marvin S. "Joseph Smith and the 1826 Trial: New Evidence and New Difficulties." *BYU Studies* 12 (Winter 1972):223–33.

Madsen, Gordon A. "Joseph Smith's 1826 Trial: The Legal Setting." *BYU Studies* 30 (Spring 1990):91–108.

Porter, Larry C. "A Study of the Origins of The Church of Jesus Christ of Latter-day Saints in the States of New York and Pennsylvania, 1816–1831." Ph.D. diss., Brigham Young University, 1971.

GORDON A. MADSEN

SPAFFORD, BELLE SMITH

Marion Isabelle (Belle) Sims Smith Spafford (1895–1982) was a gifted administrator and an able assistant and adviser to six Presidents of the Church during her twenty-nine years as general president of the Relief Society (1945–1974).

President Spafford served through the late 1940s, when the Church rallied to rebuild war-weary Saints both physically and emotionally; the 1950s, when the Church endeavored to bridge its tremendous national and international growth; and the 1960s, when the Church correlated its programs and reemphasized the family and selfless service. Commanding in stature, she displayed invaluable energy, stamina, wisdom, and forthrightness during those turbulent decades.

Belle Smith was born October 8, 1895, in Salt Lake City, to Hester Sims and John Gibson Smith. Following her graduation from LDS High School, she completed a two-year degree at the University of Utah. After her marriage to widower Earl Spafford on March 23, 1921, she studied at the BYU Training School, and later, while her children, Mary and Earl, were growing up, she took courses at the University of Utah. A lifelong student, she designated daily study hours during which she was not to be called or disturbed; as a grandmother, she established "scholar night" on which she would study with each of her grandchildren, on a one-to-one basis.

Called early to leadership, Belle Spafford served as president of her ward YWMIA at age seventeen, and she also taught religion classes. She later served as a counselor in her ward Relief Society presidency and on the Relief Society stake board of Salt Lake Belvedere Stake. In 1935 she was called to the Relief Society General Board, and in 1942 she became a counselor to General Relief Society President Amy Brown LYMAN. She edited the history of Relief Society, *A Centenary of Relief Society* (1942), and also the *Relief Society Magazine* from 1937 until her call as general president in 1945.

Named as general president of the Relief Society near the end of World War II, Spafford felt an urgent need to aid the members of the Church in Europe who had suffered from the conflict. Within weeks, Relief Society members had gathered and shipped thousands of items of food, clothing, and bedding to the members abroad. In addition to providing for physical needs, President Spafford placed special emphasis in the *Relief Society Magazine*, as well as in the lesson manuals, on social and spiritual issues of love and tolerance, in an attempt to lessen some of the anger and bitterness that existed as a result of the war. The leadership of the Relief Society organization was restructured to meet local needs worldwide. With increased emphasis on training, members of the Relief Society General Board visited every stake to develop leadership skills in local officers and to establish or reestablish local units.

Amid all the aid and effort aimed at repairing war damage, the Relief Society gained permission and raised money to construct a new Relief Society Building in Salt Lake City. Having their own headquarters building, dedicated on October 3, 1956, gave the Relief Society new cohesion and support. The early 1960s brought new emphasis on music and choirs at the local level and almost every stake in the Church formed a women's chorus called "The Singing Mothers." These groups appeared both nationally and internationally over the next twenty years.

In an effort to solidify the family, the First Presidency and the Quorum of the Twelve Apostles assigned the Relief Society the responsibility of reemphasizing the Family Home Hour. These efforts grew into the regular Monday night family home evening program in 1964.

In the 1960s, the Relief Society also placed special emphasis on strengthening the community by encouraging women to do volunteer service at the Red Cross, Traveler's Aid, March of Dimes, child-care clinics, and hospitals. A health missionary program was instituted in 1971, using specially trained nurses and others to teach health principles and welfare concepts to the disadvantaged. Under President Spafford's direction the Social Service and Child Welfare departments provided specialized services, including programs for abused children, unwed mothers, and youth guidance, and established licensed agencies for adoption, foster care, and Indian student placements in Utah, Nevada, Arizona, and Idaho. For her pioneering efforts in social work, the Utah State Conference of Social Work awarded her an honorary life membership, and the University of Utah established the Belle S. Spafford Endowed Chair in Social Work.

President Spafford traveled the world widely and was affiliated with a number of national and international organizations. She served two terms as president of the National Council of Women (1968–1970). Recognized as one of the leading women in the world, she was presented with the National Council of Women's highest honor (1978). She died on February 2, 1982.

BIBLIOGRAPHY

History of the Relief Society, 1842–1966. Salt Lake City, 1966.

Peterson, Janet, and LaRene Gaunt. *Elect Ladies*. Salt Lake City, 1990.

Spafford, Belle S. *A Woman's Reach*. Salt Lake City, 1974.

MAREN M. MOURITSEN

T

TABERNACLE, SALT LAKE CITY

This dome-shaped building on TEMPLE SQUARE in SALT LAKE CITY is one of the most impressive achievements of Latter-day Saint architectural design and engineering skill. Since 1867, this unique pioneer structure has been the site of nearly all of the Church's general conferences; addresses by prominent visitors, including several U.S. Presidents; and many significant cultural events. The site of weekly Tabernacle Choir broadcasts since 1929, it is renowned for its organ. The Salt Lake Tabernacle culminated Latter-day Saint pioneer efforts to construct a very large auditorium for important meetings. On July 28, 1847, Brigham YOUNG designated Temple Square as the center of the new Latter-day Saint capital. By July 31, the first of a series of open-sided boweries had been erected on the square. With wood posts supporting a roof made of leafy boughs and dirt, this rough shelter provided some protection for religious worship and other public gatherings. In 1851–1852, the Old Tabernacle, the first major building on the block, was built in the southwest corner of Temple Square, later the site of the Assembly Hall. Truman O. Angell, architect of public works, designed the building with low adobe walls, a gabled roof, and a floor below ground level. Although it could accommodate 2,500 people, it was soon inadequate for conference crowds, and in 1854 the general conferences were again held outdoors.

At the April 1863 conference, Daniel H. Wells, counselor to President Brigham Young, announced plans to build a new tabernacle "that will comfortably seat some ten thousand people" (*JD* 10:139). The construction of so large an auditorium in an isolated territory without railroad access to manufactured building materials was an extraordinary undertaking. Church architect William H. Folsom prepared the first plans under President Young's direction. The design called for a structure 150 feet wide and 250 feet long with semicircular ends and a peaked roof similar to that of the Old Tabernacle. The cornerstone was laid July 26, 1864, and forty-four sandstone piers to support the roof were begun that year.

The next year, President Young appointed an experienced bridge builder, Henry Grow, to superintend the construction. In consultation with the President, Grow modified a type of lattice truss used in bridge construction into huge elliptical arches that spanned the entire width of the structure without intermediate supports, an innovation without parallel for a building of these dimensions. The trusses were constructed of timbers pegged together with wooden dowels that were split and wedged at each end. Cracked timbers were wrapped with green rawhide, which contracted when dry and made a tight binding. When the building was completed, the roof structure was nine feet thick, and the plaster ceiling was 68 feet above the floor.

Truman O. Angell, who replaced Folsom as Church architect early in 1867, designed the exterior cornice and the interior woodwork, including the gallery added in 1869–1870. This 3,000-seat balcony increased the building's seating capacity to approximately 10,000 and improved its acoustics by reducing echoes. Although the Tabernacle was used for the October 1867 conference, it was not formally dedicated until October 1875. A baptismal font was installed in 1890; the rostrum area was extensively remodeled in 1882, 1933, and 1977; the shingle roof was replaced with aluminum in 1947; and a basement was added in 1968. The building was designated as a National Historic Landmark in 1970 and as a National Civil Engineering Landmark in 1971.

BIBLIOGRAPHY

Anderson, Paul L. "William Harrison Folsom: Pioneer Architect." *Utah Historical Quarterly* 43 (Summer 1975):240–59.

Angell, Truman O. Journals. LDS Church Archives.

Grow, Stewart L. *A Tabernacle in the Desert*. Salt Lake City, 1958.

"The New Tabernacle." *Salt Lake Telegraph*, Oct. 6, 1867.

PAUL L. ANDERSON

TABERNACLE ORGAN

While not the world's largest, the organ in the SALT LAKE TABERNACLE is one of the most famous musical instruments ever produced. Thanks to the widely disseminated "Music and the Spoken Word" weekly radio (and later TV) broadcast, this organ has probably been heard by more people than any other. Year-round daily recitals (inaugurated in 1915 and attended by millions of visitors to TEMPLE SQUARE each year) and numerous performances at Church conferences and other public recitals and concerts add to the number of people whose lives have been enriched by this remarkable instrument.

The present organ was built in 1948 by the Aeolian-Skinner Company of Boston, under the supervision of its president and tonal director, G. Donald Harrison. However, the person most responsible for the project was Tabernacle organist Alexander Schreiner, who, with colleagues Frank Asper and Roy Darley, shared the goal of creating an organ for Temple Square to equal the greatest ever known. Given the enthusiastic acceptance of this instrument by organ experts and the general public, they did indeed succeed.

This organ is the most recent of a line of fine Tabernacle instruments. Pioneer organ builder Joseph Ridges (1827–1914) installed the first one in 1867. Some pipes and parts from that organ and its successors have been incorporated into the present instrument not only to provide a link with the past but also to preserve the superb quality of those artifacts. The most notable feature from pioneer days is the central portion of the large organ case. The famous golden pipes, made of wood staves fashioned from Utah timber, still play today. Over the years, the case has been enlarged, but always following the style of the original, which was influenced by the Boston Music Hall organ (Walcker, 1863), the most sensational instrument of its day.

Neils Johnson enlarged the organ in 1885. Then an instrument incorporating some of the pioneer pipes and parts was built by the Kimball Company at the turn of the century. Much of that organ was replaced by the Austin Company in 1915. Essentially this is the instrument that was heard on the first radio broadcasts from the Tabernacle in 1930.

Most organ historians consider the present organ to be the most complete and perfect example of the American Classic style. The prime mover in developing the American Classic organ was G. Donald Harrison, who brought this concept to maturity after World War II. Alexander Schreiner was impressed with this forward-looking approach and felt that an all-American instrument drawing on European and English traditions would be appropriate for the Tabernacle.

The organ presently contains 11,623 individual pipes organized into 147 voices (tone colors) and 206 ranks (rows of pipes). Grouped into 8 divisions, they are controlled from a console with five 61-note manuals (keyboards) and a 32-note pedalboard. All divisions of the organ are located behind the massive casework on the west end of the Tabernacle except the antiphonal division, which is in the lower attic at the east end and speaks through openings behind the center balcony seats. The longest pipe is 32 feet in speaking length; the shortest is three-quarters of an inch. Pipes are made of wood, zinc, and various alloys of tin and lead.

Between 1985 and 1989, Schoenstein and Co. of San Francisco directed a major renovation of the organ, regulating all pipework, rebuilding the console, and installing seventeen ranks of new pipes.

BIBLIOGRAPHY

Bethards, Jack M. "The Tabernacle Letters." *The Diapason* (June 1990):14–17; (July 1990):8–9; (Aug. 1990):10–11.

Callahan, Charles. *The American Classic Organ: A History in Letters*. The Organ Historical Society, Richmond, Virginia, 1989.

Owen, Barbara. *The Mormon Tabernacle Organ: An American Classic*. Salt Lake City, 1990.

JACK M. BETHARDS

TAYLOR, ELMINA SHEPARD

Elmina (Mina) Shepard Taylor (1830–1904), the first general president of the Young Ladies' Mutual Improvement Association, was born September 12, 1830, in Middlefield, New York. She was the eldest of three daughters of Methodist parents, David S. and Rozella (Rosella, Rozita) Bailey Shepard. Following her graduation from public school and Hardwick Academy, she left home in 1854 to teach school in Haverstraw, New York, where she met John Druce, a member of The Church of Jesus Christ of Latter-day Saints. She was converted and baptized into the LDS Church on July 5, 1856. In a later account of her conversion, she wrote, "I fought against my convictions, for I well knew how it would grieve my dear parents . . . and I also thought I should lose my situation. . . . However, I could not silence my convictions, and . . . I went forth and was baptized" (Crocheron, p. 49).

On August 31, 1856, she married George Hamilton Taylor. They left New York for Utah on April 15, 1859, and arrived in Salt Lake City on September 16. They located in the Salt Lake Fourteenth Ward, where Elmina lived until her death. She was the mother of seven children, three of whom died in infancy.

Elmina Taylor was appointed secretary of the Fourteenth Ward Relief Society on December 12, 1867, and served in that capacity for twenty-six years. On September 23, 1874, she was called as president of the Young Ladies' Association of the ward. On December 22, 1879, she was chosen as a counselor to Salt Lake Stake Relief Society president Mary Isabella Horne, a position she held for sixteen years.

At a conference of women's organizations held June 19, 1880, in the Assembly Hall on Temple Square, Elmina Taylor, although shy and reserved, was appointed the first general president of the Young Ladies' Mutual Improvement Association. Originally organized to help teenage girls focus more on spiritual and less on worldly pursuits, the association encouraged their study of gospel principles, development of individual talents, and service to those in need. Under her direction, the organization flourished. General, ward, and stake boards were appointed, lesson manuals produced, the *Young Woman's Journal* inaugurated (1889), and joint activities established with the Young Men's Association. President Taylor traveled thousands of miles yearly, giving instruction to ward and stake leaders. She became a member of the National Council of Women and, in 1891, three years after its organization, became an ex officio vice-president.

Elmina Taylor retained her office as president of the Young Ladies' Association through her last illness, reading reports in bed until the day of her death, December 6, 1904. Her funeral was held in the white-draped Assembly Hall. The choir and ushers were members of the Young Ladies' Association. President Joseph F. SMITH, one of the speakers, summarized her life's work: "She was one of the few in the world who had the light within her, and . . . power among her associates. . . . She was legitimately the head of the organization over which she was called to preside. . . . She was a strong character, . . . tempered and softened by the . . . spirit of kindness, of love, of mercy, and of charity" ("Death of Elmina S. Taylor," p. 221).

BIBLIOGRAPHY

Crocheron, Augusta Joyce. *Representative Women of Deseret*. Salt Lake City, 1884.

"Death of Elmina S. Taylor." *IE* 8 (Jan. 1905):218–22.

Jenson, Andrew. "Elmina Shepherd [*sic*] Taylor." *Latter-day Saint Biographical Encyclopedia*, Vol. 4, p. 267. Salt Lake City, 1971.

Romney, Thomas C. "Representative Women of the Church—Elmina Shepard Taylor." *Instructor* 85 (Aug. 1950):230–31.

FLORENCE SMITH JACOBSEN

TAYLOR, JOHN

John Taylor (1808–1887), the third President of The Church of Jesus Christ of Latter-day Saints, was born in Milnthorpe, Westmorland (now Cumbria), England, a son of James and Agnes Taylor. After John's formal schooling ended at the age of fourteen, he became a skilled woodturner and cabinetmaker. Much of his youth was spent in a picturesque region that inspired many of England's finest artists, poets, and writers. John himself would later be recognized for his cultural refinement and literary ability.

Although John was christened in the Church of England, he thought little of its creeds and at the age of sixteen joined the Methodist church. He was appointed a lay preacher a year later. He later remembered having a "strong impression on my mind" that he must "go to America to preach the gospel!" (Roberts, p. 28). He followed his parents to Canada in 1832, where he met and married Leonora Cannon, a refined and intelligent young woman from the Isle of Man. In Toronto he preached for the Methodists, but told his wife that "this is not the work; it is something of more importance"

(Roberts, p. 30). The Taylors belonged to a religious-studies group that prayed for the restoration of New Testament Christianity. They embraced Mormonism as the answer to their prayers and were baptized in 1836. Afterward, serving the Church became Taylor's life work. In 1837 the Taylors moved to Far West, Missouri, where Taylor was ordained an apostle on December 19, 1838. He played a prominent role in assisting the Saints as they fled from mob persecutions to a new gathering place at Commerce, Illinois. In 1839 he accompanied a number of his fellow apostles to the British Isles, where he opened Ireland and the Isle of Man for preaching the gospel and gained a reputation as a powerful debater (*see* MISSIONS OF THE TWELVE TO THE BRITISH ISLES). A bold advocate of the Church and the Prophet Joseph SMITH, John Taylor was called a "defender of the faith."

In Nauvoo he began a lifetime of community service. He served as a Nauvoo city councilman, a chaplain, a colonel, and a judge advocate for the NAUVOO LEGION, the city's militia. As a newspaper editor, he published the *Times and Seasons* (1842–1846) and the *Nauvoo Neighbor* (1843–1846).

John Taylor was with Joseph and Hyrum SMITH in the CARTHAGE JAIL when the Smiths were martyred as they awaited a hearing regarding the destruction of an anti-Mormon newspaper. Severely wounded himself, Taylor became known as a living martyr. His tribute to the fallen brothers was later canonized as Section 135 of the Doctrine and Covenants.

Two years after the death of Joseph Smith, the Church moved westward from Nauvoo under the direction of Brigham YOUNG. While in Winter Quarters, Nebraska, Taylor was sent on a short-term mission to England to resolve problems in Church leadership there. Upon his return, he and Parley P. PRATT led 1,500 Saints to the Salt Lake Valley, arriving in the fall of 1847.

Taylor applied for U.S. citizenship in 1849, and in that year was appointed an associate judge under the provisional state of DESERET (1849). Serving in the territorial legislature from 1853 to 1876, he was elected Speaker of the House for five consecutive sessions, beginning in 1857. For two years (1868–1870), he served as probate judge of Utah County, and in 1876 he was elected territorial superintendent of schools. In all of his offices, he felt dependent on the inspiration of God. "No man or set of men," he once declared, "of their own wisdom and by their own talents, are capable of governing the human family aright" (*JD* 9:10).

In 1849, Taylor returned to Europe, where he presided over missionary work in France and Germany and directed the translation and publication of a French-German edition of the Book of Mormon. He also wrote a short book, *The Government of God* (1852), in which he compared and contrasted the systems of God and man: "In God's government there is perfect order, harmony, beauty, magnificence, and grandeur; in the government of man, confusion, disorder, instability, misery, discord, and death" (p. 2). He described numerous examples of earthly societies that failed to resolve the problems of mankind, concluding that the only solution is "for his servants, to draw nigh to their Father, . . . throw themselves upon his guardianship, seek his wisdom and government, and claim a father's benediction" (p. 31).

While in Europe he founded the Deseret Manufacturing Company at the request of Brigham Young and purchased expensive sugar-processing equipment in Liverpool, that was shipped to Salt Lake City. It was his most notable failure. Lacking retorts, a key component, the assembled machinery produced only a good-quality molasses.

Following the death of Brigham Young in 1877, the Council of the Twelve governed the Church, with John Taylor as the senior apostle, presiding until he was set apart as the Church's third President in 1880. His motto as president was The Kingdom of God or Nothing. Although his most notable achievement was to hold the Church together under the intensifying pressure of the antipolygamy campaign, much else was achieved during his administration, especially in the early years. Under his direction, four new missions were organized; Mormon settlements were established in Colorado, Wyoming, and Arizona; construction continued on the Salt Lake and Manti temples; and the Logan Temple was dedicated. To encourage the Saints' economic independence, President Taylor established Zion's Central Board of Trade, a coordinating agency that encouraged cooperative economic activity in the Church's stakes.

On April 6, 1880, the fiftieth anniversary of the Church, President Taylor proclaimed a jubilee year, as observed in the Old

Testament. "It occurred to me," he said, "that we ought to do something, as they did in former times, to relieve those that are oppressed with debt, to assist those that are needy, . . . and to make it a time of general rejoicing" (Roberts, p. 333). One-half of the debts owed by the Saints to the PERPETUAL EMIGRATING FUND, borrowed on migrating to Utah, was forgiven ($802,000), and one thousand cows and five thousand sheep were distributed to the poor, replacing many animals that had been lost in severe winter storms.

In October 1880, during President Taylor's administration, the Pearl of Great Price, a collection of ancient and modern scriptures, was canonized. A new edition of the Doctrine and Covenants, incorporating extensive cross-references and explanatory notes, was also published. The Primary Association, a children's auxiliary, and the Young Ladies' Mutual Improvement Association, an organization for girls twelve through seventeen, were adopted Churchwide.

During the first years of his administration, while still President of the Quorum of Twelve Apostles, President Taylor continued work begun under Brigham Young in changing significant priesthood functions and defining important relationships. Members of the Seventy, one of the offices of the Melchizedek Priesthood, were organized into stake quorums. The relationship of the ward bishop to the priesthood and that of the Aaronic Priesthood to the Melchizedek Priesthood were clarified. Weekly bishopric meetings and monthly general stake priesthood meetings were inaugurated. Stake presidents were instructed to hold quarterly conferences under the direction of the First Presidency. President Taylor wrote a short work entitled *Items on Priesthood* (1881) to help the priesthood serve more effectively. He also wrote *The Mediation and Atonement of Our Lord and Savior Jesus Christ* (1882) as his witness of the preeminent role of the Son of God in the salvation of humankind; in it, he assembled scriptural passages pertaining to Christ's atonement and offered a commentary on their meaning.

Although he knew that obedience to authority brought strength and unity to the Church, President Taylor also stressed the importance of common consent: "The government of God is not . . . where one man dictates and everybody obeys without having a voice in it. We have our voice and agency, and act with the most perfect freedom" (1987, p. 321). A frequent theme expressed throughout his life was his love of liberty and hatred of slavery. "I'm God's free man," he said. "I cannot, will not be a slave!" (Roberts, p. 424). For such forthright determination he was called the "Champion of Liberty."

President Taylor was about six feet tall and weighed 180 pounds. He had large hands, an oval face, a high forehead, and deep-set gray eyes. As a young man, he had curly brown hair, which turned silver white in middle age. Erect in posture and fastidious in dress, he was polite, dignified, gracious, affable, and friendly. His speech was calm and deliberate, delivered in a voice that was clear, strong, and resonant. He enjoyed telling stories and had a keen sense of humor and a hearty laugh that shook his entire body. He generally did not prepare sermons ahead of time but depended upon inspiration as he spoke. He used gestures sparingly but with effect. An accomplished poet, his lyrics were used for several hymns published in the Church's hymnal.

In his private life, President Taylor was a kind and loving husband and father. He entered into PLURAL MARRIAGE, as counseled by Joseph Smith, and fathered thirty-five children by his seven wives. He went to great lengths to be fair and impartial with each of his families. The names and number of his wives are in dispute, but the women who were certainly married to him were Leonora Cannon, Elizabeth Haigham, Jane Ballantyne, Mary Ann Oakley, Sophia Whitaker, Harriet Whitaker, and Margaret Young.

During President Taylor's ministry, persecution of the Church grew in intensity. Three missionaries were killed in the southern states; and the U.S. secretary of state attempted to prevent Mormon immigrants from entering the United States, citing them as potential lawbreakers because of the Church's practice of polygamy. Congress passed the Edmunds Act in 1882, declaring polygamy to be a felony. Under its provisions, polygamists could not vote, hold public office, or serve on juries. The General Authorities discussed the Church's course of action as well as their hopes for achieving statehood. Wilford WOODRUFF later wrote that "President Taylor with the rest of us came to the conclusion that we could not swap of[f] the Kingdom of God or any of its Laws or Principles for a state government" (Wilford Woodruff Journal, Nov. 27, 1882). Mounting antipolygamy prosecution, known as "the Crusade," led to the arrest and imprisonment of hundreds of men and women. President Taylor instructed polygamous Saints to establish places of refuge in Mexico and Canada, and he and his counselors withdrew from public view to live in the "Underground." During his last public sermon he remarked, "I would like to obey and place myself in subjection to every law of man. What then? Am I to disobey the law of God? Has any man a right to control my conscience, or your conscience? . . . No man has a right to do it" (*JD* 26:152).

Persecution intensified in 1887 with the passage of the Edmunds-Tucker Act, which abolished women's suffrage, forced wives to testify against their husbands, disincorporated the Church, and escheated much of its property to the United States. For two and a half years, President Taylor presided over the Church in exile. The strain took a great toll on his health. He died on July 25, 1887, from congestive heart failure while living in seclusion at the farm home of Thomas F. Roueche in Kaysville, Utah. He was eulogized as a "double martyr" for his near-fatal wounds in Carthage Jail and for his sacrifice for religious principles.

BIBLIOGRAPHY

Gibbons, Francis M. *John Taylor: Mormon Philosopher, Prophet of God*. Salt Lake City, 1985.

Roberts, B. H. *The Life of John Taylor*. Salt Lake City, 1963.

Smith, Paul Thomas. "John Taylor." In *Presidents of the Church*, ed. L. Arrington, pp. 74–114. Salt Lake City, 1987.

Taylor, John. *The Gospel Kingdom: Selections for the Writings and Discourses of John Taylor*, ed. G. Homer Durham. Salt Lake City, 1987.

Taylor, Samuel W., and Raymond W. Taylor. *The John Taylor Papers, Records of the Last Utah Pioneer*: Vol. 1, *1836–1877, The Apostle*, and Vol. 2, *1877–1887, The President*. Redwood City, Calif., 1984–1985.

PAUL THOMAS SMITH

TEMPLE SQUARE

Temple Square is the architectural center of Salt Lake City, sacred ground for The Church of Jesus Christ of Latter-day Saints, and a primary point of interest for millions of visitors annually. Within the square are the SALT LAKE TEMPLE, the TABERNACLE (home of the Mormon Tabernacle Choir), the Assembly Hall, two visitors centers, several historical statues, and well-kept grounds. Its appearance today differs sharply from that of the treeless desert that greeted the first Mormon pioneers in 1847.

Only days after arriving in the SALT LAKE VALLEY, President Brigham Young identified the site for the temple. It was originally planned as a 40-acre block but was reduced to ten acres "for convenience." The ground-breaking ceremony for the temple was held on February 14, 1853, even though the ground was frozen and covered with snow. Construction continued for forty years, and the temple was dedicated on April 6, 1893.

Construction of the Tabernacle began in 1863. It was in use four years later and dedicated in 1875. A decade later the Assembly Hall was built to accommodate smaller gatherings. This building holds approximately 3,000 people and is often used for overflow of the Church's general conferences.

Almost from the beginning, keen interest in Temple Square and the Church made it an attraction for those visiting the "Crossroads of the West." In 1875 Charles J. Thomas was appointed the first official guide to Temple Square. In 1876 he greeted 4,000 visitors. The first visitors center, called the "Bureau of Information," was built in 1902, followed by larger buildings in 1904 and 1910. However, when the number of visitors increased, the depiction of the story and beliefs of the Church required additional exhibit areas. In 1963 the large visitors center at the northwest corner of the square was opened to the public. It houses theaters, artwork, displays, and dioramas. Its focal point is a copy of the 11-foot Christus statue originally carved by the Danish sculptor Bertell Thorvaldsen. It depicts the Savior with arms outstretched inviting all to come to him. The Christus represents the central focus of the Church's beliefs and worship: Jesus Christ.

An additional visitors center was built in the southeast corner of the square and dedicated on June 1, 1978. Its displays include an exact replica of the baptismal font of the Salt Lake Temple, like the biblical "molten sea" on the backs of twelve life-size oxen (see 2 Chr. 4:2–5).

Many monuments and statues adorn the square. They represent people and entertain the story of the beginnings of the Church and of the pioneers. The first statues to become a permanent part of the square were those of the Prophet Joseph SMITH and his brother Hyrum in 1911. In 1913, the Seagull Monument was placed on the square memorializing the gulls' providential intervention in 1848 that saved the Mormon pioneers' early crops from being devoured by crickets.

Other monuments include a statue honoring the Three Witnesses to the Book of Mormon: Oliver COWDERY, David WHITMER, and Martin HARRIS; the Handcart Monument representing approximately 3,000 pioneers who walked either from Iowa City, Iowa, or from the Missouri River near Florence, Nebraska, to the Salt Lake Valley; a small bronze and granite sundial provided by the young women of the Church in 1940; the Aaronic Priesthood Memorial Monument, which depicts John the Baptist bestowing the Aaronic Priesthood on Joseph Smith and Oliver Cowdery; and the Relief Society Memorial Campanile, a 35-foot tower in which the NAUVOO bell is preserved and displayed and upon which a tone is struck on the hour each hour of the day. The bell had originally hung in the NAUVOO TEMPLE and was brought to Utah by oxteam in 1847.

Visitors may choose to walk through the grounds and visitors centers at their leisure or may request a guide to accompany them. Guides are familiar with the state's pioneer history as well as the teachings and culture of the Church. Foreign visitors are provided, when possible, with guides who speak their language.

At every season, the temple grounds are colorful. Long before spring, workmen are trimming, planting, and cultivating flowers, shrubs, and trees. Since 1969, the limbs of almost every tree have been wrapped in lights for the Christmas season. On the day after Thanksgiving, a special program inaugurates the celebration and the lights are turned on. They remain on until New Year's Day.

BIBLIOGRAPHY

Grant, Carter E. "Zion's Ten Acres." *IE* (June 1970):16–19.

Johnson, Melvin Kay. "A History of the Temple Square Mission of The Church of Jesus Christ of Latter-day Saints to 1970." Master's thesis, Brigham Young University, 1971.

CAROLYN J. RASMUS

TESTATOR

A testator is one who at death leaves a valid will or testament. In certain usages, the word is synonymous with witness. The term appears twice in scripture, retaining the strictly legal sense in Hebrews 9:16–17, where the death of Jesus Christ makes valid the new testament, or covenant. In Doctrine and Covenants 135:5–6, testator includes the additional connotation of "martyr" when referring to the deaths of the Prophet Joseph SMITH and his brother Hyrum. The outline of Joseph Smith's accomplishments in verse 3 underscores why Latter-day Saints regard him as a valid testator.

ROBERT L. MARROTT

"THIS IS THE PLACE" MONUMENT

This monument depicts a dramatic moment in western and Church history. Brigham YOUNG entered the Great Salt Lake Valley on July 24, 1847, and said, according to Church tradition, "This is the right place."

In 1915 a committee including George Albert Smith, an apostle, and Church historians B. H. Roberts and Andrew Jenson identified the approximate spot at the mouth of Emigration Canyon where Brigham Young might have first seen the Salt Lake Valley and made his famous pronouncement. They placed a small board as a marker there that July.

One year later, a larger wooden marker was erected with the inscription "This is the place." In 1921 the Young Men's Mutual Improvement Association dedicated a cast stone marker at the same location and denominated the area Pioneer View.

In 1937 a more imposing monument was conceived and created by a state commission composed of persons of various faiths, in anticipation of the 1947 centennial celebration. Mahonri M. Young, a grandson of Brigham Young, was selected as sculptor. The monument is built of Utah granite, the rectangular base is 206 feet long and supports a centered 60-foot-high pylon surmounted by the bronze figures of Brigham Young, Heber C. Kimball, and Wilford Woodruff, each 12.5 feet high. On the pylon and base are seventeen bronze friezes depicting an Indian chief, Spanish and U.S. government explorers, trappers, groups of pioneers, and a wagon train. Two statuary groups, one at either end, symbolize the Dominguez-Escalante exploring party of 1776 and a group of mountainmen and trappers.

The monument, which cost $450,000, was dedicated on July 24, 1947, by Church President George Albert Smith. Today it is part of Pioneer Memorial State Park, a 221-acre area at the mouth of Emigration Canyon.

BIBLIOGRAPHY

Lyon, T. Edgar. *This Is the Place Monument, Story and History* (pamphlet). Salt Lake City, 1955.

Roberts, B. H. "Monument at Pioneer View." *IE* 24 (Sept. 1921):958–78.

"'This Is the Place' Monument Dedication." *IE* 50 (Sept. 1947):570–71, 627.

JAMES L. KIMBALL, JR.

U

UNITED ORDERS

"United orders" refers to the cooperative enterprises established in LDS communities of the Great Basin, Mexico, and Canada during the last quarter of the nineteenth century in an effort to better establish ideal Christian community and group economic self-sufficiency. The roots go back to Joseph Smith's 1831 revelations outlining the law of CONSECRATION and stewardship as the foundation for the ideal community. Economic goals of consecration included relative income equality, group self-sufficiency, and the elimination of poverty (*see* ECONOMIC HISTORY OF THE CHURCH). Under this plan, the head of each family would consecrate or deed all real and personal property to the Presiding Bishop of the Church and would receive, in turn, a stewardship, or "inheritance," from consecrated property. Thereafter, Church members would consecrate annually all surplus production from their stewardships to the bishop's storehouse. This system functioned briefly in a few LDS communities in the Midwest during the 1830s; in the Great Basin, Church members prepared deeds of consecration in 1855–1858, but they were never acted upon.

During the 1860s President Brigham YOUNG reemphasized economic cooperation and self-sufficiency, and a network of more than 150 cooperative mercantile and manufacturing enterprises was established in the region (*see* PIONEER ECONOMY). Designed to promote unity and to reduce dependence on non-Mormon merchants and traders, the cooperatives did not require consecration of property but issued and sold shares of stock and paid wages and dividends. Among the most successful cooperatives was the Brigham City Mercantile and Manufacturing Association, which operated forty departments and encompassed the economic activity of the entire community. President Young saw this cooperative movement as an important step toward the ideal society but recognized that a more comprehensive system was necessary to reach his political and economic goals.

Three events undoubtedly influenced Brigham Young to introduce the united order system in 1874. First, completion of the transcontinental railroad in 1869 led to an influx of Gentiles into the territory. The accompanying individualistic and competitive attitudes and institutions of nineteenth-century American capitalism seriously threatened to erode the bonds of selflessness and cooperation that held the LDS social fabric together. Second, congressional bills designed to reduce LDS political and economic power and individual rights led to persecution, including the arrest of Brigham Young in 1871. Third, the Panic of 1873 brought depression to Utah's mining industry and loss of jobs and markets to Mormon laborers, farmers, and merchants. Faced with general disruption of social, political, and economic life, Brigham Young introduced The United Order of Enoch.

He organized the first united order at St. George, Utah, on February 9, 1874. The last known Church-authorized united order was organized at Cave Valley, Chihuahua, Mexico, on January 9, 1893. In the interim more than 200 united orders were organized in LDS communities in several mountain states, including Utah, Idaho, Wyoming, Arizona, and Nevada, mostly in 1874 and 1875. This ambitious attempt to establish a utopian society was both a direct response to the forces that threatened LDS economic and political independence and a final effort by Brigham Young to build the ideal community envisioned by Joseph Smith (*see* CITY PLANNING).

Brigham Young saw the united order as an intermediate step between the cooperatives of the 1860s and Joseph Smith's ideal community based on consecration and stewardship. Though they differed from one another in form, nearly all united orders were organized as voluntary producer cooperatives where, rather than working for fixed wages, members shared the net income of the enterprise. United orders used two main types of producer cooperatives. In the St. George type, members contributed their economic property to the order and received dividends and labor income according to the relative amounts of capital and labor contributed. A governing board directed the enterprise.

The second category of united orders was communal. Members contributed all their property to the order, shared more or less equally in the common product, and functioned, ate, and worked as a well-regulated family. This system is called the Orderville type, after the most famous of the united orders. Established in southern Utah in 1875, the Orderville united order attained almost complete self-sufficiency. It produced its own food, fuel, fiber, and nearly all needed manufactured items, some of which it exported to other parts of the territory. The most successful of the communal-type orders, it disbanded in 1885. In addition to Orderville, communal united orders were established in several LDS communities in southern Utah, Nevada, Arizona, and Mexico.

The few united orders that were not producer cooperatives were patterned after the Brigham City united order (formerly the Brigham City Mercantile and Manufacturing Association), a joint-stock company with significant cooperative characteristics. The Brigham City–type united orders were intended to strengthen and reinforce existing cooperative arrangements. Such orders did not require consecration of all one's property and labor but operated much like a profit-sharing capitalist enterprise, issuing dividends on stock and hiring labor. There was no necessary connection between owning stock in the united order and working for the order, although workers were encouraged to take part of their wages in stock. Several Brigham City–type united orders were established in northern Utah and southern Idaho. Wards in larger cities in the territory used a modified Brigham City plan in which members pooled their capital to establish a needed cooperative or corporate enterprise. These enterprises were similar in many respects to stake welfare projects organized in the twentieth century as part of the Church welfare system.

Brigham Young believed that pooling capital and labor would not only promote unity and self-sufficiency but would also provide increased production, investment, and consumption through specialization, division of labor, and economies of scale. In spite of some notable successes, however, the united order movement was relatively short-lived. Most of the St. George–type orders never fully operated or operated only briefly. When President Young died in 1877, most of the united orders had already failed. Some, like those in Orderville and Brigham City, functioned successfully for a decade, and a very few continued in some form into the 1890s. At least one, a joint enterprise of the Logan Second and Third wards, survived into the twentieth century, selling out to private interests in 1909. Many factors combined to hamper the united order movement, including uncertainty as to operating rules, influx of immigrants with no capital to contribute, internal disputes, difficulties surrounding legal incorporation, and persecution and federal prosecution of united order leaders.

In spite of the short life of the movement, the united order was important to the development of LDS pioneer society and economy in several ways. First, the united order was an important vehicle for COLONIZATION of the inhospitable southern part of the Great Basin, where cooperation and organization were essential for survival. Second, the united order provided a mechanism through which Church leaders were able to promote economic self-sufficiency. The diversification of Utah's economy that resulted from this process helped Utah avoid the mineral-based economic colonialism experienced by other mountain states during the late nineteenth century. Finally, for Latter-day Saints of the time, the united order was a symbol of separateness from the world, a means of maintaining group identity in a hostile society, and a way of meeting their religious commitment to individual and group perfection. Today, the united order experience remains in Mormon historical consciousness as a symbol of the more perfect society that Latter-day Saints believe will one day be achieved.

BIBLIOGRAPHY

Arrington, Leonard J. *Great Basin Kingdom: An Economic History of the Latter-day Saints, 1830–1900*. Cambridge, Mass., 1958.

———, Feramorz Y. Fox, and Dean L. May. *Building the City of God: Community and Cooperation Among the Mormons*. Salt Lake City, 1976.

Israelsen, L. Dwight. "An Economic Analysis of the United Order." *BYU Studies* 18 (Summer 1978):536–62.

L. DWIGHT ISRAELSEN

UTAH EXPEDITION

The Utah War of 1857–1858 was the largest military operation in the United States between the times of the Mexican War and the Civil War. It pitted the Mormon militia, called the NAUVOO LEGION, against the army and government of the United States in a bloodless but costly confrontation that stemmed from the badly handled attempt by the administration of President James Buchanan to replace Brigham YOUNG as governor of UTAH TERRITORY. It delayed, but did not prevent, the installation of Governor Alfred Cumming, and it had a significant impact on the territory, its predominantly Latter-day Saint inhabitants, and the Church itself. Because the conflict resulted from misunderstandings that were distorted by time and distance, had the transcontinental telegraph been completed in 1857 instead of 1861, the expedition almost certainly would not have occurred.

The decision to replace Governor Young was inevitable, given the national reaction to the Church's 1852 announcement of PLURAL MARRIAGE and Republican charges in the campaign of 1856 that the Democrats favored the "twin relics of barbarism"—polygamy and slavery. The method chosen to implement that decision, however, is still puzzling. Apparently influenced by reports from Judge W. E. Drummond and other former territorial officials, Buchanan and his cabinet decided that the Latter-day Saints would reject a non-Mormon governor. So, without investigation, mail service to Utah was suspended and 2,500 troops led by Albert Sidney Johnston were ordered to accompany Cumming to Great Salt Lake City.

Remembering earlier difficulties with troops and perhaps swayed by the ardor of the recent reformation movement (*see* REFORMATION [LDS] of 1856–1857), Church leaders interpreted the army's unannounced coming as religious persecution and decided to resist. Brigham Young, still acting as governor, declared martial law and deployed the Nauvoo Legion to delay the troops with "scorched earth" tactics. Harassing actions, including burning three supply trains and capturing hundreds of government cattle, forced Johnston's expedition and the accompanying civil officials into winter quarters at Camp Scott and Eckelsville, near burned-out Fort Bridger, some 100 mountainous miles east of Salt Lake City.

During the winter both sides strengthened their forces. Congress, over almost unanimous Republican opposition, authorized two new volunteer regiments, and Buchanan, Secretary of War John B. Floyd, and Army Chief of Staff Winfield Scott assigned 3,000 additional regular troops to reinforce the Utah Expedition. Meanwhile, Utah communities were called upon to equip a thousand men for a spring campaign. Predictions of hostilities came from LDS pulpits, Camp Scott, and the national press.

There is persuasive evidence, however, that Brigham Young never intended to force a military showdown. He and other leaders often spoke of abandoning and burning their settlements rather than permitting their occupation by enemies, as had happened in Missouri and Illinois.

That Brigham Young hoped for a diplomatic solution is clear from his early appeal to Thomas L. KANE, the influential Pennsylvanian who had for ten years been a friend of the Mormons. Soon after Christmas, Kane received Buchanan's permission to go to Utah, via Panama and California, as an unofficial mediator. Reaching Salt Lake City late in February, he found Church leaders ready for peace but distrustful. When the first reports of Kane's contacts with General Johnston were discouraging, the apprehension was reinforced.

The "Move South" resulted. President Young announced on March 23, 1858, that all settlements in northern Utah must be abandoned and prepared for burning if the army came in. The evacuation started immediately. Though at first perceived as likely to be permanent, the Move South was transformed into a tactical and temporary maneuver soon after word came that Kane had persuaded Cumming to come to Salt Lake City without the army. Still, in numbers at least, it dwarfed the earlier Mormon flights from Missouri and Illinois: about 30,000 people moved fifty miles or more to Provo and other towns in central and southern Utah. There they remained in shared and improvised housing until the Utah War was over.

When Kane and Cumming arrived early in April, Young surrendered his political title and soon formed an amiable working relationship with his successor. However, the Move South continued, probably because the government representatives insisted that Johnston's troops must be admitted but were unable to guarantee that they would come in peacefully.

Meanwhile, President Buchanan responded to rising criticism by appointing Lazarus Powell and Ben McCulloch to carry an amnesty proclamation to Utah. Arriving early in June, they found Church leaders willing to accept Cumming and a permanent army garrison in exchange for peace and amnesty. Johnston's army marched through a largely deserted Salt Lake City on June 26, 1858, and went on to build Camp Floyd forty miles to the southwest. Soon the refugees returned home; the Utah War was over.

From this episode the Buchanan administration reaped an unbalanced defense budget and some political embarrassment. With a fair and impartial approach, Governor Cumming soon became more popular with the Latter-day Saints than with the military. Camp Floyd and the nearby civilian town of Fairfield represented the first sizable non-Mormon resident population in Utah. Though the troops left Utah at the outbreak of the Civil War, the presence for three years of thousands of troops and camp followers ended the Latter-day Saint dream of a Zion geographically separate and distant from the world of unbelievers.

As for the LDS community in Utah, the exertions and expenditures strained both capital and morale. Defense efforts terminated some of the Mormon outpost settlements in present-day California, Nevada, Wyoming, and Idaho, interrupted and weakened the missionary effort in Europe, curtailed immigration, and dissipated much of the enthusiasm and discipline generated by the Reformation of 1856. Unsympathetic, if not hostile, troops and camp followers influenced economics, politics, and lifestyles. The Move South won media sympathy, but it also disrupted Latter-day Saint community and religious life and did little to increase the toleration for Mormon differences from mainstream American ideas and institutions.

In spite of the posturing and bumbling of those involved, what seemed like an inevitable military confrontation was ultimately resolved peacefully. The tensions, differences, and misunderstandings that preceded the resolution, however, remained, and it would be nearly forty years before Utah would be accepted as a state (*see* UTAH STATEHOOD).

BIBLIOGRAPHY

Furniss, Norman F. *The Mormon Conflict, 1850–1859*. Westport, Conn., 1977.

Poll, Richard D. *Quixotic Mediator: Thomas L. Kane and the Utah War*. Ogden, Utah, 1985.

———. "The Move South." *BYU Studies* 29 (Fall 1989):65–88.

RICHARD D. POLL

UTAH STATEHOOD

By 1847, experience had clearly taught the Latter-day Saints the importance of obtaining more political autonomy and protection than was offered by a territorial government, whose federally appointed officials would have little sympathy for the LDS way of life. Therefore, from the time the Mormon pioneers arrived in the Great Basin, they fervently sought statehood and self-government. In 1850, 1856, 1862, 1867, 1872, and 1882, LDS representatives made appeals for statehood to the U.S. Congress, all to no avail. In fact, statehood seemed to become more elusive as time went on, because those opposed to Utah statehood could generate emotional opposition through the issue of PLURAL MARRIAGE. In 1865, Schuyler Colfax, Speaker of the U.S. House of Representatives, visited Utah and pointedly warned Brigham YOUNG that his territory could never become a state so long as the Church upheld polygamy. Latter-day Saints persisted in the practice, which for another generation blocked Utah's admission as a state.

After the U.S. Supreme Court ruled decisively against plural marriage in 1879 (*see* REYNOLDS V. UNITED STATES), federal officials began to enforce laws more firmly during what became known as the antipolygamy raid (*see* ANTIPOLYGAMY LEGISLATION). The Edmunds-Tucker Act of 1887, intended to bar polygamists from voting, was still pending in Congress when LDS agents secured approval from President Grover Cleveland's administration and from President of the Church John TAYLOR for a strategy of seeking statehood by accepting a Utah Constitution prohibiting plural marriage. President Taylor's belief in plural marriage remained unaltered, but he recognized that elected state officials would likely enforce marriage laws more leniently than appointed federal officials had done. In mid-1887 such a Constitution was framed and ratified in Utah. Despite these efforts, congressional Democrats balked at delivering statehood until the Church gave up polygamy.

Soon thereafter, the First Presidency of the Church, acting as a committee on statehood, began working with members of the Republican party. Some Republicans had been hostile to the Church and its marriage practices; others recognized the value of the Mormon vote throughout the West. With the assistance of friendly

Republican party leaders, George Q. Cannon, counselor in the First Presidency, and others thwarted a proposed law that would have disfranchised all LDS voters, not just the polygamists. Yet, the threat of such legislation persisted, along with the even more ominous peril that the four Utah temples stood in danger of being confiscated under provisions of the Edmunds-Tucker Act.

Church leaders early faced the irony that the statehood and home rule desired as an additional protection for the Church and its institutions could seemingly be obtained only by yielding a part of the religious life they wished to protect. With ever harsher legislation, they now faced the necessity of bending on less central matters in order to protect the core mission and essential ordinances of the Church. In these circumstances, Church President Wilford WOODRUFF fervently sought and received divine direction. Accordingly, he publicly announced in his 1890 MANIFESTO that he would no longer permit plural marriages in opposition to the laws of the United States, thus removing the main obstacle to Utah statehood and protecting the temples and other matters central to the faith.

Perhaps the most important remaining problem to be resolved before Utah could gain statehood was normalizing political affairs within the territory. Up to that time, non-LDS voters had mainly backed the so-called Liberal party, while Church members belonged to the People's party, primarily associated in national affairs with the Democrats. LDS leaders recognized the necessity of convincing party members in Congress that Utah voters were not irretrievably aligned with the Democrats. It was time for Utah politics to mirror the federal, with the Democratic and Republican parties both being strong. This took place with impressive dispatch through determined efforts by John Henry Smith, an apostle, and others. At their urging, local LDS leaders—and in some cases entire congregations—were divided along national party lines.

However, as Republican party members became more convinced that admission of Utah as a state might give them two more U.S. senators in the closely balanced upper house, Democratic lawmakers became less committed to the cause of statehood, necessitating complex and intense behind-the-scenes lobbying efforts. The chief agents in these negotiations were Bishop Hiram B. Clawson and his relative

Colonel Isaac Trumbo, a close friend of President Wilford Woodruff, whose effective lobbying with Republican lawmakers was of critical importance. Through a series of discussions and agreements, Trumbo and Clawson finally regained the cooperation of key Democratic leaders, partly by agreeing that actual admission of the state would not take place until 1896, after Democrats had an opportunity to complete their congressional agenda without the possible opposition of Republican senators from Utah.

The enabling act for admission was passed in July 1894, allowing a state constitutional convention to meet in early 1895. Once the Constitution was approved by the U.S. Congress, it was submitted to Utah citizens for ratification at the same time that they elected their first state officers. Finally, on January 4, 1896, President Grover Cleveland proclaimed Utah a state, the forty-fifth, and the new government went into effect two days later.

BIBLIOGRAPHY

Larson, Gustave O. *The "Americanization" of Utah for Statehood.* San Marino, Calif., 1971.

Lyman, Edward Leo. *Political Deliverance: The Mormon Quest for Utah Statehood.* Urbana, Ill., 1986.

Wolfinger, Henry J. "A Reexamination of the Woodruff Manifesto in the Light of Utah Constitutional History." *Utah Historical Quarterly* 39 (Fall 1971):328–49.

EDWARD LEO LYMAN

UTAH TERRITORY

The arrival of the Latter-day Saints in the SALT LAKE VALLEY in July 1847 preceded by only a few months the transfer of the Utah area and much more of the American Southwest from Mexico to the United States. The Treaty of Guadalupe Hidalgo was signed on February 2, 1848, making the transfer final. A petition requesting the United States to grant statehood to the Utah area was delivered in 1849, but statehood was not granted. Instead, Utah Territory was created as part of the national Compromise of 1850. The compromise admitted California into the Union as a free state and designated Utah and New Mexico as territories with the right to decide whether to permit slavery or not.

Beyond the complications of the slavery issue, the petition for statehood was weakened by several other factors. The first was the tremendous size of the proposed State of Deseret (*see* DESERET, STATE OF) with boundaries extending into southern California. In addition, the small population of Deseret (less than 12,000 in 1850 excluding Native Americans) was far short of the 60,000 required for statehood by the Northwest Ordinance of 1785. And anti-Mormon sentiment in Congress added further weight to these reasons for organizing Utah Territory rather than admitting Deseret into the Union as a state.

The act creating Utah Territory was signed by President Millard Fillmore on September 9, 1850. The boundaries of the territory were the forty-second parallel on the north, the thirty-seventh parallel on the south, the summits of the Rocky Mountains to the east, and the Sierra Nevada Mountains to the west. In 1861, Utah Territory was significantly reduced when Nevada was admitted to the Union (with a smaller population than Utah), the western slope of the Rockies became part of the Colorado Territory, and the northeastern corner of Utah Territory was included in Wyoming Territory.

The 1850 act provided for a territorial legislature and a delegate to Congress, and established the following major offices to carry out governmental activities: territorial governor, secretary of the territory, U.S. marshal, U.S. attorney, chief justice, associate justice, and superintendent of Indian affairs. The president of the United States filled these offices by appointment—a situation fraught with problems, for territorial residents were excluded from electing their own governing officials. Federal appointees were often considered incompetent and malicious.

The transition from an autonomous government under the direction of Church authorities to one administered under provisions of the territorial organic act was made easier by the appointment of Brigham YOUNG as the first territorial governor and the superintendent of Indian affairs. Difficulties arose, however, as Brigham Young's forceful methods and local popularity rankled non-Mormon carpetbag appointees—especially the chief justice and associate justices. For their part, some of these non-Mormon imports from the East acted in ways that offended local sensibilities.

Conflicts also developed between territorial judges and locally elected county officials—especially the probate judges, who, in Utah, had unusually broad jurisdiction. Elected by popular vote and often serving concurrently as local bishops, the probate judges also served as chairmen of the county court, which included three other selectmen, and oversaw timber and water resources. In addition, they supervised the establishment of districts for roads, schools, voting, and other purposes; the levying of taxes; the construction of public buildings; the care of orphans, the insane, and stray animals; and the election or appointment of lesser officials. They also exercised original jurisdiction in both civil and criminal cases.

In 1850 the territory consisted of only seven counties: Salt Lake, Davis, Weber, Tooele, Utah, Sanpete, and Iron. While these counties still existed in 1896, when statehood was granted, their size had been reduced. When Utah became a state, twenty-eight of the present twenty-nine counties were functioning.

The election of James Buchanan as U.S. president in 1856 and his decision to put down the alleged Mormon rebellion and appoint a new territorial governor in place of Brigham Young led to the UTAH EXPEDITION of 1857–1858. At its peaceful conclusion, federal troops established Camp Floyd, forty miles south of Salt Lake City, and Alfred Cumming became territorial governor. During the ensuing years, eleven individuals were appointed territorial governor, and five territorial secretaries served briefly as acting governor. Most of the appointed officials were sincere in their efforts, though a few appeared to be political scoundrels. All were challenged by the task of interpreting, administering, and enforcing federal laws that went against the beliefs and practices of Utah's majority population (*see* ANTIPOLYGAMY LEGISLATION).

The fundamental conflict was resolved and the way to statehood opened when Church President Wilford WOODRUFF issued the 1890 MANIFESTO ending the practice of PLURAL MARRIAGE. In July 1894 U.S. President Grover Cleveland signed an enabling act to permit the people of Utah to prepare a state government. On January 4, 1896, President Cleveland proclaimed UTAH STATEHOOD, formally ending Utah's territorial period.

BIBLIOGRAPHY

Cooley, Everett L. "Carpetbag Rule Territorial Government in Utah." *Utah Historical Quarterly* 26, no. 2 (Apr. 1958):107–129.

LaMar, Howard R. *The Far Southwest, 1846–1912: A Territorial History*. New Haven, Conn., 1966.
Larson, Gustive O. *The "Americanization" of Utah for Statehood*. San Marino, Calif., 1971.
Lyman, Edward Leo. *Political Deliverance: The Mormon Quest for Utah Statehood*. Urbana, Ill., 1986.

ALLAN KENT POWELL

V

VISIONS OF JOSEPH SMITH

Ancient prophets were typically called through a revelatory process—visions and/or revelations: "If there be a prophet among you, I the Lord will make myself known unto him in a vision, and will speak unto him in a dream" (Num. 12:6). The prophet Joel anticipated that visions would increase in the last days, saying, "Old men shall dream dreams, [and] young men shall see visions" (Joel 2:28–32).

The Prophet Joseph Smith had his first vision at the age of fourteen while praying in a grove of trees in western New York (*see* FIRST VISION). The appearance of the Lord to him, like that to Saul of Tarsus, was attended by a shining light from heaven (Acts 9:3). The Lord spoke face-to-face with Joseph and called him to service. This was the first of a series of visions Joseph SMITH received, many of which were shared with other persons. Blessed like John on the isle of Patmos and Paul who spoke of the third heaven, the Prophet Joseph Smith affirmed, "Could you gaze into heaven five minutes, you would know more than you would by reading all that ever was written on the subject" (*TPJS*, p. 324; cf. *HC* 6:50). He also declared that "the best way to obtain truth and wisdom is not to ask it from books, but to go to God in prayer, and obtain divine teaching" (*TPJS*, p. 191).

President John TAYLOR said that Joseph Smith had contact with prophets from every dispensation:

> Because he [Joseph] stood at the head of the dispensation of the fulness of times, which comprehends all the various dispensations that have existed upon the earth, and that as the Gods in the eternal worlds and the Priesthood that officiated in time and eternity had declared that it was time for the issuing forth of all these things, they all combined together to impart to him the keys of their several missions [*JD* 18:326].

A new dispensation requires the conferral of priesthood and keys, in accordance with the law of witnesses: "In the mouth of two or three witnesses shall every word be established" (2 Cor. 13:1). During the restoration sequence when priesthood and keys were conferred by angelic ministrants, the Prophet was accompanied by one or more witnesses. Oliver COWDERY was a principal figure in the fulfillment of this law of witnesses; others were David WHITMER, Martin HARRIS, and Sidney RIGDON. Distinguishing dreams from visions and associating visions and visitations, Joseph said, "An open vision will manifest that which is more important" (*TPJS*, p. 161). Crucial visions received by the Prophet Joseph Smith are the source of many cardinal doctrines and teachings of the Latter-day Saints.

THE FIRST VISION. Lucy Mack SMITH recalled that as the Joseph Smith, Sr., family worked their Manchester, New York, farm in the period of 1820, "there was a great revival in religion, which extended to all denominations of Christians in the surrounding country." Lucy and three of the children joined the Western Presbyterian Church in Palmyra, but Joseph remained "unchurched." He later wrote, "It was impossible . . . to come to any certain conclusion who was right and who was wrong" (JS—H 1:8). In answer to a biblical prompting that "if any of you lack wisdom, let him ask of God" (James 1:5), Joseph retired to the woods and uttered what he termed his "first vocal prayer." His prayer of faith was answered. Joseph recorded, "I saw two Personages, whose brightness and glory defy all description, standing above me in the air. One of them spake unto me, calling me by name and said, pointing to the other—*This is My Beloved Son. Hear Him!*" Responding to his inquiry concerning which church he should join, the Lord instructed Joseph to join none of them, saying that he must continue as he was "until further directed" (JS—H 1:17–19, 26). When Joseph left the grove, he possessed the knowledge that God and his Son were actual personages, that the Godhead was composed of separate individuals, and that God hears and answers prayers. He also knew that he must not affiliate with the existing denominations (Backman, 1971, pp. 206–208). This vision set in motion a train of visitations by angelic ministrants directing the young prophet in the process of restoring the gospel of Jesus Christ.

VISITATIONS OF MORONI. The Prophet continued to pursue his common vocations until September 21, 1823, while "suffering severe persecution at the hands of all classes of men," in part as a result of his claims concerning his first vision (JS—H 1:27). As he prayed that evening that he might know his standing before God, an angel appeared at his bedside, saying that he had been sent from the presence of God and that his name was Moroni. He explained "that God had a work for [Joseph] to do; and that [his] name should be had for good and evil among all nations" (JS—H 1:33). He instructed Joseph concerning a book that was written on gold plates, giving an account of the former inhabitants of the continent. The fulness of the everlasting gospel was contained in the record as delivered by the Savior to these people. Joseph was also shown a vision of a nearby hill and the place where the plates containing this record were deposited.

The next day, Joseph went to the hill, subsequently known by his followers as Cumorah, removed a stone covering, and viewed the contents of the box beneath, the plates, the Urim and Thummim, and a breastplate. The angel reappeared and informed him that the time for the removal of the plates had not arrived and that he was to meet him for further instruction at that same site over a succession of four years (JS—H 1:53). A further vision was opened to Joseph's view, and he saw the "prince of darkness, surrounded by his innumerable train of associates." The heavenly messenger said, "All this is shown, the good and the evil, the holy and impure, the glory of God and the power of darkness, that you may know hereafter the two powers and never be influenced or overcome by that wicked one" (*Messenger and Advocate* 2:198).

From 1824 to 1827, Joseph returned to the hill each year as specified. On September 22, 1827, he met the angel and received final instructions regarding the record. Moroni gave the record to the

Prophet to translate. Joseph said, "The same heavenly messenger delivered them up to me with this charge: that I should be responsible for them; that if I should let them go carelessly, or through any neglect of mine, I should be cut off; but that if I would use all my endeavors to preserve them, until he, the messenger, should call for them, they should be protected" (JS—H 1:59). The messenger did not limit his instruction solely to these annual meetings, but made contact with Joseph on numerous occasions (Peterson, pp. 119–20). In all, the angel Moroni visited Joseph Smith at least twenty times (*see* MORONI, VISITATIONS OF). Joseph informed associates that other Book of Mormon prophets also visited him, including Nephi, son of Lehi (Cheesman, pp. 38–60). Lucy Mack Smith recalled that her son Joseph was enabled from this tutoring to describe "with much ease" the ancient inhabitants of America, "their dress, mode of traveling, and the animals upon which they rode; their cities, their buildings, with every particular; their mode of warfare; and also their religious worship" (p. 83).

JOHN THE BAPTIST. While translating the Book of Mormon at Harmony, Pennsylvania, on May 15, 1829, Joseph Smith and Oliver COWDERY became concerned about baptism for the remission of sins as described in 3 Nephi 11. They went into the woods to pray for enlightenment. Both record that a messenger from heaven, identifying himself as John the Baptist, laid hands on them and ordained them to the Aaronic Priesthood, saying, "Upon you my fellow servants, in the name of Messiah, I confer the Priesthood of Aaron, which holds the keys of the ministering of angels, and of the gospel of repentance, and of baptism by immersion for the remission of sins; and this shall never be taken again from the earth until the sons of Levi do offer again an offering unto the Lord in righteousness" (JS—H 1:69; D&C 13; cf. *TPJS*, pp. 172–73).

PETER, JAMES, AND JOHN. John the Baptist also informed Joseph and Oliver that "this Aaronic Priesthood had not the power of laying on hands for the gift of the Holy Ghost, but that this should be conferred on us hereafter." John stated "that he acted under the direction of Peter, James and John, who held the keys of the Priesthood of Melchizedek, which Priesthood, he said, would in due time be conferred on us" (JS—H 1:70, 72).

This restoration occurred during the latter part of May or early June 1829, someplace between Harmony and Colesville on the Susquehanna River. Of this visitation, Joseph Smith later testified, "The Priesthood is everlasting. The Savior, Moses, & Elias—gave the Keys to Peter, James & John on the Mount when they were transfigured before him. . . . How have we come at the priesthood in the last days? It came down, down in regular succession. Peter, James & John had it given to them & they gave it up [to us]" (*WJS*, p. 9).

THREE WITNESSES OF THE BOOK OF MORMON. By revelation Oliver Cowdery, David Whitmer, and Martin Harris were selected to be witnesses of the plates and the authentic translation of the Book of Mormon (2 Ne. 11:3; 27:12; Ether 5:2–4; D&C 5:11–18; D&C 17). During the latter part of June 1829, in company with Joseph Smith, these three men went into the woods adjacent to the Whitmer home in Fayette, New York, and knelt in prayer. When the promised revelation was not immediately received, Martin Harris stated that he felt he might be the cause of their failure. After Martin Harris withdrew, the others knelt in prayer again. David Whitmer described the visitation of Moroni:

> The angel stood before us. He was dressed in white, and spoke and called me by name and said "Blessed is he that keepeth His commandments. . . ." A table was set before us and on it the Records of the Nephites, from which the Book of Mormon was translated, the breast plates [and also the Urim and Thummim], the Ball of Directors [Liahona], the Sword of Laban and other plates. While we were viewing them the voice of God spoke out of heaven saying that the Book was true and the translation correct [quoted in "Letter from Elder W. H. Kelley," *Saints' Herald* 29 (Mar. 1, 1882):68].

Afterward, Joseph found Martin Harris, and together they experienced a similar manifestation. The Three Witnesses later endorsed a statement describing their experience that has been appended to all copies of the Book of Mormon. They swore that they had seen the angel and the plates and that "we also know that they have been translated by the gift and power of God, for his voice hath declared it unto us." Subsequently, eight others were privileged to see and handle the plates, but without the presence of the angel or having heard the voice of God.

VISION OF GLORIES. While preparing the text of his translation of the Bible, Joseph Smith, with Sidney Rigdon, moved to the John Johnson home in Hiram, Ohio, on September 12, 1831. As the two men worked on the Gospel of John, it became apparent to them that many important points concerning the salvation of individuals had been lost from the Bible. Joseph wrote, "It appeared self-evident from what truths were left, that if God rewarded every one according to the deeds done in the body the term 'Heaven,' as intended for the Saints' eternal home must include more kingdoms than one" (*HC* 1:245). On February 16, 1832, in an upper room of the Johnson home, while he and Sidney Rigdon were examining the passage from John 5:29, they saw a multifaceted vision (D&C 76), commencing with a vision of the Father and the Son in the highest glory. This scene was followed by a series of visions, including Perdition and the sons of Perdition and then the celestial, terrestrial, and telestial kingdoms of glory. One witness, Philo Dibble, present in the room recalled that the two men sat motionless for about an hour. One would say, "What do I see," and describe it, and the other would say, "I see the same" (*Juvenile Instructor* 27 [May 15, 1892]:303–304).

It is apparent that the Prophet Joseph Smith did not impart all that he saw in vision, for he later said, "I could explain a hundred fold more than I ever have of the glories of the kingdoms manifested to me in the vision, were I permitted, and were the people prepared to receive them" (*TPJS*, p. 305).

KIRTLAND TEMPLE VISIONS. From January 21 to May 1, 1836, many of the Saints in Kirtland experienced an outpouring of the Spirit, a "Pentecostal season." On January 21, the Prophet assembled with others in the west schoolroom on the third story of the Kirtland Temple. Here Joseph beheld a vision of the celestial kingdom of God (D&C 137). He beheld the Father and the Son and several ancient worthies, including Adam, Abraham, and his own mother and father (both still living), and his brother Alvin, who had died in 1823 (verse 5). As Joseph marveled over Alvin's station in the celestial kingdom, the voice of the Lord declared, "All who have died without a knowledge of this gospel, who would have received it if they had been permitted to tarry, shall be heirs of the celestial kingdom of God" (verse 7). He was also instructed concerning the destiny of little children. The Prophet recorded, "I also beheld that all children who die before they arrive at the years of accountability are saved in the celestial kingdom of heaven" (verse 10).

During the dedication of the Kirtland Temple on March 27, 1836, many testified of the presence of angels. The Prophet specifically identified the ancient apostles Peter and John as present among them (Backman, *The Heavens Resound*, 1983, pp. 299–300; cf. *JD* 9:376).

One week later, on April 3, 1836, Joseph Smith and Oliver Cowdery had retired to the Melchizedek Priesthood pulpits on the west side of the first floor of the temple. The curtains were dropped around the pulpit area as the men prayed. "The veil was taken from our minds, and the eyes of our understanding were opened" (D&C 110:1). The Lord stood before them on the breastwork of the pulpit. "His eyes were as a flame of fire; the hair of his head was white like the pure snow; his countenance shone above the brightness of the sun; and his voice was as the sound of the rushing of great waters, even the voice of Jehovah" (D&C 110:3). The Savior accepted the newly completed structure and promised that his name and glory would be present and that thousands of persons would receive an outpouring of blessings because of the temple and the endowment received by his servants in that house (D&C 110:6–9).

Following the Savior's appearance, three other messengers presented themselves. Each bestowed specific priesthood keys on the two leaders. Moses came and "committed [to them] the keys of the gathering of Israel" (verse 11). As Moses departed, Elias, possessing the keys of "the gospel of Abraham," appeared and administered the keys of this dispensation, saying "that in us and our seed all generations after us should be blessed" (verse 12). Further priesthood keys were restored by Elijah, who declared, "Behold, the time has fully come, which was spoken of by the mouth of Malachi—testifying that he [Elijah] should be sent . . . to turn the hearts of the fathers to the children, and the children to the fathers" (verses 14–15).

OTHER HEAVENLY MANIFESTATIONS. A variety of accounts affirm that other persons also witnessed such appearances not only in association with the Kirtland Temple but in an earlier period during meetings in the log schoolhouse on the Isaac Morley farm and in the SCHOOL OF THE PROPHETS, held in the Newel K. WHITNEY STORE

(K. Anderson, pp. 107–113, 169–77; Backman, *The Heavens Resound*, 1983, pp. 240, 264–68, 284–309).

The visions discussed herein are but a few of the myriad manifestations that gave the Prophet direction. Joseph mentions having seen others in vision, including Michael, Gabriel, and Raphael, but does not detail their association (D&C 128:20–21). President John Taylor identified yet others who ministered to the Prophet, notably Adam, Seth, Enoch, Noah, Abraham, Isaac, and Jacob (*JD* 17:374; 18:325–26; 21:65, 94, 161; 23:48).

One writer has commented, "He had visions of the past as well as of the future. As a seer, he knew things about the past that are not part of our own scripture, but which he spoke of in discourse" (Madsen, p. 44). "I saw Adam in the valley of Adam-ondi-Ahman" (*TPJS*, p. 158). To Joseph Knight, Sr., the Prophet commented on the vistas opened to him through the Urim and Thummim, which he found deposited with the gold plates. Knight explained, "He seemed to think more of the glasses or Urim and Thummim . . . says he, "I can see anything; they are marvelous"" (Jessee, 1976, p. 33). Accordingly, after reading Foxe's *Book of the Martyrs*, Joseph remarked that he had "seen those martyrs, and they were honest, devoted followers of Christ, according to the light they possessed, and they will be saved" (Stevenson, p. 6). He saw in vision marchers in ZION'S CAMP who had perished from cholera in Clay County, Missouri. He related their condition, observing to the survivors, "Brethren, I have seen those men who died of the cholera in our camp; and the Lord knows, if I get a mansion as bright as theirs, I ask no more" (*HC* 2:181n). The organizations of the Quorum of the Twelve Apostles and the First Quorum of the Seventy were made known to him "by vision and by the Holy Spirit," and he established those priesthood offices in February 1835 (*HC* 2:182). In an earlier vision, he "saw the Twelve Apostles of the Lamb, who are now upon the earth, who hold the keys of this last ministry, in foreign lands, standing together in a circle, much fatigued, with their clothes tattered and feet swollen, with their eyes cast downward, and Jesus standing in their midst, and they did not behold Him. The Savior looked upon them and wept" (*HC* 2:381). He saw a vision enabling him to designate the "central place" in Independence, Missouri (*TPJS*, p. 79). Of a vision of the resurrection of the dead, he explained, "So plain was the vision, that

I actually saw men, before they had ascended from the tomb, as though they were getting up slowly" (*TPJS*, pp. 295–96). He also saw the Kirtland and Nauvoo temples in vision before their construction and gave detailed instructions to the architects, describing the windows and their illumination (*JD* 13:357; 14:273; *HC* 6:196–97). He foresaw the struggles of the Saints in crossing the plains, their establishment in the Rocky Mountains, and the future condition of the Saints (*HC* 5:85n–86n).

He remarked late in his life, "It is my meditation all the day & more than my meat & drink to know how I shall make the saints of God to comprehend the visions that roll like an overflowing surge, before my mind" (*WJS*, p. 196).

BIBLIOGRAPHY

Anderson, Karl Ricks. *Joseph Smith's Kirtland*. Salt Lake City, 1989.

Anderson, Richard Lloyd. *Investigating the Book of Mormon Witnesses*. Salt Lake City, 1981.

Andrus, Hyrum. *Joseph Smith, the Man and the Seer*. Salt Lake City, 1960.

Backman, Milton V., Jr. *Joseph Smith's First Vision*. Salt Lake City, 1971.

———. *Eyewitness Accounts of the Restoration*. Orem, Utah, 1983.

———. *The Heavens Resound*. Salt Lake City, 1983.

Bushman, Richard L. *Joseph Smith and the Beginnings of Mormonism*. Urbana, Ill., 1984.

Cheesman, Paul R. *The Keystone of Mormonism*. Provo, Utah, 1988.

Ehat, Andrew F., and Lyndon W. Cook. *The Words of Joseph Smith*. Salt Lake City, 1980.

Jessee, Dean C. "Joseph Knight's Recollection of Early Mormon History." *BYU Studies* 17 (Autumn 1976):29–39.

———. *The Papers of Joseph Smith*, Vol. 1. Salt Lake City, 1989.

Ludlow, Daniel H. *A Companion to Your Study of the Doctrine and Covenants*, Vol. 1. Salt Lake City, 1978.

Madsen, Truman G. *Joseph Smith the Prophet*. Salt Lake City, 1989.

Peterson, H. Donl. *Moroni, Ancient Prophet, Modern Messenger*. Bountiful, Utah, 1983.

Porter, Larry C. "Dating the Restoration of the Melchizedek Priesthood." *Ensign* 9 (June 1979):4–10.

———. "The Priesthood Restored." In *Studies in Scripture*, ed. R. Millet and K. Jackson, Vol. 2, pp. 389–409. Salt Lake City, 1985.

Smith, Lucy Mack. *History of Joseph Smith*, ed. Preston Nibley. Salt Lake City, 1958.

Sperry, Sidney B. *Doctrine and Covenants Compendium*. Salt Lake City, 1960.

Stevenson, Edward. *Reminiscences of Joseph, the Prophet*. Salt Lake City, 1893.

LARRY C. PORTER

W

WELLS, EMMELINE B.

Emmeline Blanche Woodward Wells (1828–1921) was a strong advocate for women's rights and advancement as editor of the *Woman's Exponent* for nearly four decades, as general president of the Relief Society for over a decade, as a national suffrage leader, and as a Utah political activist.

Born to David and Deiadama Hare Woodward on February 29, 1828, at Petersham, Massachusetts, Emmeline experienced early the extremes of private tragedy and public triumph that would recur throughout her life. The death of her father when she was four years old and the controversy in her community occasioned by her conversion to The Church of Jesus Christ of Latter-day Saints ten years later were harrowing to the young girl. Yet Emmeline had opportunities for education not widely available to girls of her time. While still in her early teens she started teaching, but her teaching career was cut short by her marriage on July 29, 1843, at age fifteen, to James H. Harris, only two months her senior, and their subsequent move the following spring with his parents and other Latter-day Saints to Nauvoo, Illinois. However, within sixteen months of their marriage, James's parents abandoned both the Church and Nauvoo after Joseph Smith's assassination; the young couple's son, Eugene Henri Harris, died shortly after birth; and James left Nauvoo to look for work, never to return. Many years later, Emmeline discovered he had died in a sailing accident in the Indian Ocean.

She found refuge by returning to teaching, and among her pupils were the children of Bishop Newel K. and Elizabeth Ann Whitney. In February 1845, Emmeline became a plural wife to Whitney, who was thirty-three years older than she. He died in 1850, two years after they had arrived in the Salt Lake Valley, leaving her with two young daughters.

Emmeline's third marriage in 1852 proved more enduring, but not always satisfying. Seeking protection and stability, she petitioned Whitney's friend and prominent Church leader Daniel H. Wells to marry her. He already had six other wives, and, because of numerous business and ecclesiastical obligations, he and Emmeline rarely saw each other. Although three daughters were born to the union (two of them died in young adulthood), only in the later years of their marriage did Emmeline find the love and companionship that she had so long desired, but had found so elusive.

Emmeline Wells turned to civic affairs for fulfillment and found her cause in the fight for suffrage and women's rights. "I desire," she proclaimed, "to do all in my power to help elevate the condition of my own people especially women" (Journals, January 4, 1878). Her writing talent blossomed as she submitted articles to the *Woman's Exponent*, a feminist Mormon publication established in 1872. In 1877 she became its editor, a position she held for thirty-seven years.

In 1879 Emmeline was appointed one of two representatives from Utah to the suffrage convention in Washington, D.C., the first of many such meetings she would attend and address. She soon became friends with national suffrage leaders Elizabeth Cady Stanton and Susan B. Anthony, who were impressed with her abilities. Election to several offices in the National Woman Suffrage Association, the National Council of Women, the International Council of Women, and as president of the Utah Woman Suffrage Association followed. In 1899 she was invited by the International Council of Women to speak at its London meeting as a representative from the United States.

Emmeline Wells was nearly eighty-three years old when she was called as general president of the Relief Society in 1910, an organization she had previously served for twenty years as general secretary and as head of its grain storage program in the 1870s. Her tenure proved, like her life, to be bittersweet. In 1912 she was awarded an honorary doctorate of literature from Brigham Young University, yet two years later she suspended publication of *Woman's Exponent*, upon which she had labored for almost half her life, when the Relief Society declined her proposal to make it the official organ of the Relief Society. In 1919 she was honored by a visit to her home by U.S. President Woodrow Wilson and his wife; the occasion commemorated the sale of over 205,000 bushels of Relief Society wheat to the U.S. government during World War I, and, ironically, the loss of the Relief Society's autonomy over its grain-storage program.

Finally, in 1921 at age ninety-three and suffering from serious illness, Emmeline was released as President of the Relief Society, the first since Emma Smith not to die in office. Upon hearing of her release, she suffered a stroke and then died three weeks later on April 25, 1921. In death, she continued to receive honors: a funeral in the TABERNACLE (the second woman to be so commemorated) and the installation of a marble bust in the Utah State Capitol from the women of Utah engraved, "A Fine Soul Who Served Us."

BIBLIOGRAPHY

Madsen, Carol Cornwall. "A Mormon Woman in Victorian America." Ph.D. diss., University of Utah, 1985.

———. "Emmeline B. Wells: Romantic Rebel." In *Supporting Saints: Life Stories of Nineteenth-Century Mormons*, ed. D. Cannon and D. Whittaker, pp. 305–341. Provo, Utah, 1985.

Wells, Emmeline B. Journals. Division of Archives and Manuscripts, Harold B. Lee Library, Brigham Young University, Provo, Utah.

CAROL CORNWALL MADSEN
MARY STOVALL RICHARDS

WELLS, JUNIUS F.

Junius Free Wells (1854–1930) was the organizer of the Young Men's Mutual Improvement Association (YMMIA, in 1977 Young Men). Born June 1, 1854, in Salt Lake City, a son of Daniel H. and Hannah C. Free Wells, Junius attended school at the Union Academy and graduated from the University of Deseret at the age of seventeen. He was known as an exceptionally intelligent young man. As a youth, he managed his father's lumberyard and was a sales clerk for Zion's Cooperative Mercantile Institution (ZCMI).

He was called to serve a mission to Great Britain (1872–1874), and in 1874 he accompanied Elders George A. Smith, Lorenzo SNOW, Relief Society President Eliza R. SNOW, and others to Palestine, where, on the Mount of Olives, near Jerusalem, they dedicated the land for the restoration of the gospel. Immediately upon his return, Wells was asked by President Brigham YOUNG to organize the first YMMIA in the Thirteenth Ward in Salt Lake City, which he did on June 10, 1875. Wells married Helena Middleton Fobes on June 17, 1879. They were the parents of two children.

The YMMIA, counterpart to the previously organized association for young women, was charged to help boys develop intellectually and spiritually and to enjoy recreation under proper supervision. A central committee was formed on December 6, 1876, with Wells as president, to coordinate all associations organized throughout the Church. He served as president of the board for four years. In October 1879 he founded the *Contributor*, a monthly magazine that served both the young men and young women groups. Its motto was The Glory of God Is Intelligence (D&C 93:36). The publication featured articles written by young LDS men and women on a variety of literary and gospel themes. Wells served for thirteen years as its editor and publisher. In October 1899 the magazine was replaced by the *Improvement Era*.

Wells served a mission in the United States, laboring in the Midwest and New England. In 1919–1921, he served as associate editor of the *Millennial Star*, a Church magazine published in Liverpool, England, and accompanied the European Mission president on visits to the Scandinavian, Swiss, and German missions.

Acting as agent for the Church, Junius purchased the Solomon Mack farm, the birthplace of the Prophet Joseph Smith. A Church-history enthusiast, Wells designed a hundred-ton granite monument, with a shaft 38.5 feet tall, commemorating the thirty-eight and a half years of the Prophet Joseph SMITH's life. Erected near Sharon and South Royalton, Vermont, near the site of Joseph Smith's birthplace, the monument was dedicated by President Joseph F. SMITH on December 23, 1905, the centennial of the Prophet's birth. In 1918

Wells made a smaller replica, which was erected in the Salt Lake Cemetery in honor of Hyrum SMITH, the Prophet's brother.

Sustained as an assistant Church historian in 1921, Wells collected and preserved paintings and photographs of persons and scenes connected with the early history of the Church. In 1928 he was instrumental in purchasing thirty thousand dry-plate negatives of Church history scenes taken by LDS photographer George Edward Anderson.

He died of a cerebral hemorrhage in Salt Lake City on April 15, 1930. At his funeral on Easter Sunday, he was memorialized as a kind and thoughtful man of dignity who made friends easily, "a polished gentleman, a fearless servant of God" (Smith, p. 15).

BIBLIOGRAPHY

Jenson, Andrew. *Latter-day Saint Biographical Encyclopedia*, Vol. 1, p. 714; Vol. 4, p. 249. Salt Lake City, 1901.

Smith, George A. *Funeral Services for Junius Free Wells*. Salt Lake City, 1930.

PAUL THOMAS SMITH

WENTWORTH LETTER

John Wentworth, editor of the *Chicago Democrat*, wrote Joseph SMITH in 1842 to request information about the Church for a friend who was writing a history of New Hampshire. The "Wentworth Letter" was written by the Prophet Joseph Smith in response to this inquiry.

The letter contains a brief history of the Church to 1842, including the key events in the restoration of the gospel. It states that the purpose of the Church is to take the gospel to every nation and prepare a people for the Millennium. The letter also describes concisely the origin, contents, and translation of the Book of Mormon. It concludes with thirteen doctrinal statements that have since become known as the Articles of Faith and are published in the Pearl of Great Price (*HC* 4:535–41).

The contents of this letter were published March 1, 1842, in the Nauvoo *Times and Seasons*. There is no evidence that Wentworth or his friend, George Barstow, ever published it. In response to other inquiries in 1844, Joseph Smith sent revised copies of this letter to several publishers of works about various churches and religious groups. It has been published several times over the years (for the complete text of the letter, *see* Appendix 2, "The Wentworth Letter").

BIBLIOGRAPHY
Jessee, Dean C., ed. "'Church History,' 1842." In *PJS* 1:427–37.

EDWARD J. BRANDT

WEST INDIES, THE CHURCH IN THE

The Church of Jesus Christ of Latter-day Saints took root in the West Indies as English-speaking members moved from the United States to Puerto Rico. Finding no organized group of the Church there, they organized a branch and shared the gospel message with the local population, some of whom joined the Church and later became leaders themselves. Membership in the West Indies grew from 104 members in 1960 to over 50,000 in 1990, with seven stakes and six missions. It grew fastest in Puerto Rico and the Dominican Republic, and Spanish quickly became the language of the Church. The first Caribbean district of the Church was organized in 1963, the first meetinghouse was dedicated in 1970, and the first stake was organized in Puerto Rico by Elder Ezra Taft BENSON on December 14, 1980, in Puerto Rico, with Herminio De Jesus as president. In 1990 Church units were functioning throughout the West Indies in such additional places as Antigua, the Bahamas, Barbados, Bermuda, the Cayman Islands, Cuba (Guantanomo U.S. Naval Base), Curaçao, Grenada, Haiti, Jamaica, Martinique, the Netherlands Antilles, and Trinidad.

PUERTO RICO. In the early 1950s, as a few LDS families moved to Puerto Rico on business and to work or to serve in the military at Ramey Air Force Base, they organized the first branch, which met in a member's home in Guajataca. A second branch was organized in San Juan, and the first Puerto Rican converts were baptized there in the early 1950s. Puerto Rico led the way for the Church in the West Indies, receiving the first district, meetinghouse, stake, and mission. In 1990 it had almost 13,000 members attending more than fifty wards and branches in four stakes and one mission.

DOMINICAN REPUBLIC. The Church began in the Dominican Republic in 1978, when the John Rappeley family from Utah and the Eddie Amparo family from New York met in the customs office in Santo Domingo and initiated regular Church meetings. Two months later, Rodolfo Bodden and his family became the first LDS baptisms in the country. In 1986, Brother Bodden was ordained the first stake patriarch of the new Santo Domingo Dominican Republic Stake. In 1990 there were almost twenty thousand members in over seventy Church units, including one stake and two missions.

HAITI. The first LDS missionaries went to Haiti in 1980 and organized a branch of the Church in Port-au-Prince. In 1984 the Haiti mission was established, and by 1990 there were 3,000 members in eighteen branches, and the Book of Mormon was being translated into Haitian.

JAMAICA. The Church sent missionaries to Jamaica in 1841, but they were soon recalled because the prejudice against them made their efforts futile. However, the Church was finally established there in 1970 when several LDS families went to Jamaica to work. Victor Nugent and his family became converts in Jamaica in 1974. Brother Nugent was called as president of the Kingston District when the Jamaica Kingston Mission was organized in 1985. The Church in Jamaica is primarily Jamaican, and it had almost 2,000 members in thirteen branches in 1990.

EDWIN O. HAROLDSEN

WESTWARD MIGRATION, PLANNING AND PROPHECY

For Brigham YOUNG and his associates, the 1846 exodus from NAUVOO, far from being a disaster imposed by enemies, was foretold and foreordained a key to understanding LDS history and a necessary prelude for greater things to come. From a later perspective, too, scholars of the Mormon experience have come to see the exodus and COLONIZATION of the Great Basin as the single most important influence in molding the Latter-day Saints into a distinctive people. Popular histories invariably attribute the Saints' exodus from Nauvoo to increasing violence, mob action, and persecution. This view, that the exodus was forced upon a people who had no choice, is simplistic and fails to account for more complex reasons for the exodus or to explain its importance in LDS belief.

From its beginnings and with each successive move, the Church was seemingly drawn toward the West. As early as 1832, LDS publications connected the destiny of the Church with the American Far West. An 1840 letter preserves Joseph SMITH's prophecy about "a place of safety preparing for [the Saints] away towards the Rocky Mountains" (Esplin, p. 90); and throughout the Nauvoo period the Prophet collected information and prepared for a latter-day Zion to be established in the tops of the Rocky Mountains (see Isa. 2:2–3). Several diaries record Joseph Smith's February 1844 instructions to the Quorum of the Twelve Apostles to lead an expedition to the West to locate a new home for the Saints.

Though the Prophet put the plan on hold and his murder three months later further delayed implementation, Brigham Young and his fellow apostles firmly believed that their responsibility was to lead the Church to the West once the NAUVOO TEMPLE was completed and the Saints had received the endowment ordinances therein. Therefore, even had there been no violence against the Church in Illinois, there still would have been an exodus, a western migration, and western colonization.

Though most of the Saints, comfortable in a prosperous Nauvoo and not anxious to leave, knew little about the plans or the prophecy, some outside the Church were aware. In 1845, Illinois Governor Thomas Ford, anxious to solve the "Mormon problem" by having the Saints leave, chided Brigham Young for remaining when Joseph Smith had spoken of going west. Committed though they were to the West, however, Church leaders would not consider departing until the Saints were endowed in the Nauvoo Temple. Not until late summer 1845, with temple construction nearly completed, did they quietly resume preparations for the West.

When violence broke out in September 1845, Brigham Young had already announced that ordinance work would begin in December. He therefore "capitulated" to mob pressures and proclaimed to the Saints and to the world that he and his people would leave for the West the following spring. That announcement bought a peaceful interlude for ordinance work and preparation, while the threat of violence if they did not leave "put the gathering spirit" in the Saints, in Brigham Young's words, encouraging the entire community to depart.

In meetings that fall, Brigham Young and the Twelve explained to the Saints the reasons for the exodus. They presented it as the will of God and as a God-given opportunity—a necessary step toward their destiny. They also saw the exodus as an unfolding of scriptural prophecy, including Isaiah's vision of the last days when "the mountain of the Lord's house shall be established in the top of the mountains, and shall be exalted above the hills; and all nations shall flow unto it" (Isa. 2:2). Orson PRATT pronounced the proposed movement "a direct and literal fulfillment of many prophecies, both ancient and modern" (*MS* 6 [Dec. 1, 1845]:192). His brother, Parley P. PRATT, agreed that it was the event that "ancient prophets have long since pointed out" (*T&S* 6 [Nov. 1, 1845]:1011).

Therefore, while the sermons reflected a sense of urgency, their tenor was clearly optimistic. If the Saints were being driven, it was to their destiny. President Young spoke of "a crisis of extraordinary and thrilling interest," and admonished the Saints to "wake up, wake up" and accept "the present glorious emergency" (*T&S* 6 [Nov. 1, 1845]:1019). Orson Pratt saw the approaching exodus as "long looked for, long prayed for, and long desired." They were on the threshold, he declared, of "one of the grandest and most glorious events yet witnessed" in the Church (*MS* 6 [Dec. 1, 1845]: 191–92).

Numerous extant sermons from Nauvoo also suggested additional reasons for the exodus. A move west would permit greater expansion and continued growth. In the western wilderness the Church could more easily fulfill a divine commitment to take the gospel to the Lamanites. The mass migration would be a test separating the wheat from the chaff, a purifying furnace bringing greater unity and strength to the Church.

Later, in the Rocky Mountains, pioneer Latter-day Saints came to see the exodus from Nauvoo as a key to who they were and what they could become.

[*See also* History of the Church: c. 1844–1877.]

BIBLIOGRAPHY

Christian, Lewis Clark. "Mormon Foreknowledge of the West." *BYU Studies* 21 (Fall 1981):403–415.

Esplin, Ronald K. "'A Place Prepared'": Joseph, Brigham and the Quest for Promised Refuge in the West." *Journal of Mormon History* 9 (1982):85–111.

Leonard, Glen M. "Westward the Saints: The Nineteenth-Century Mormon Migration." *Ensign* 10 (Jan. 1980):6–13.

REED C. DURHAM, JR.

WHITMER, DAVID

David Whitmer (1805–1888) was one of the Three Witnesses to the Book of Mormon whose testimony has been printed in all published copies of the book. Although Whitmer was excommunicated from the Church in 1838, he never repudiated his testimony of the Book of Mormon, reaffirming it thereafter on at least seventy recorded occasions.

David Whitmer was born to Peter Whitmer, Sr., and Mary Musselman Whitmer near Harrisburg, Pennsylvania, on January 7, 1805. In 1809 thc family moved to Fayette, New York, where they worked a large farm. He learned about the Book of Mormon from Oliver COWDERY, who was scribe for Joseph SMITH during the translation. When persecution grew severe in Harmony, Pennsylvania, where the two were working, Whitmer invited Joseph, Oliver, and Joseph's wife, Emma, to his family's house in Fayette. The translation of the Book of Mormon was completed there in June 1829.

In the same month, Joseph Smith told David Whitmer that he, along with Cowdery and Martin HARRIS, another supporter of the work, were to be witnesses of the Book of Mormon. In answer to their prayers, an angel appeared to them near the Whitmer house and showed them the gold plates from which the Book of Mormon was translated. An account of this experience comprises the Testimony of the Three Witnesses in the Book of Mormon. David's brothers, Christian, Jacob, John, and Peter, Jr., were four of the Eight Witnesses to whom Joseph Smith showed the plates without an angelic visitation and whose testimony also appears in the book.

In 1829, David, John, and Peter, Jr., received revelations through Joseph Smith calling them to missionary work (D&C 14:6; 15:6;

16:6). In April 1830 the Church was organized in Peter Whitmer, Sr.'s, house. However, David's close association with Joseph Smith did not prevent occasional chastisement. A revelation in 1830 warned Whitmer, "Your mind has been on the things of the earth more than on the things of me, your Maker, and the ministry whereunto you have been called; and you have not given heed unto my Spirit, and to those who were set over you, but have been persuaded by those whom I have not commanded" (D&C 30:2). In view of Whitmer's later separation from the Church, this statement seems prophetic.

When the Church moved from New York in 1831, the Whitmers went with the Saints to Kirtland, Ohio, and then to Jackson County, Missouri, which had been designated as Zion, a gathering place for the Saints. By July 1832, the Whitmers had settled along the Big Blue River in Kaw Township (now Kansas City). To their great disappointment, the hopes for Zion were short-lived. The differences between the Latter-day Saints and the local settlers erupted into open conflict. On one occasion, a mob threatened to kill Whitmer and other Church leaders if they did not admit that the Book of Mormon was a fraud. Whitmer absolutely refused.

Driven from Jackson County, the Whitmers settled in adjacent Clay County, Missouri, along with other Latter-day Saint refugees. As their numbers grew, a stake was organized and Whitmer became the stake president in July 1834, making him the leading figure in Church administration in the area. By October 1834, David and John Whitmer had moved back to Kirtland, Ohio, to prepare for the spiritual blessing promised to the Saints when the KIRTLAND TEMPLE was completed. In February 1835, in accord with an earlier commission received by revelation, David Whitmer with Oliver Cowdery and Martin Harris selected the twelve men who constituted the first Quorum of Twelve Apostles in the Church (D&C 18:37–38). Whitmer was also a member of the committee that drafted rules for the regulation of the temple. On the day of its dedication, March 27, 1836, he testified of an outpouring of the Spirit from on high, as the Lord had promised (*HC* 2:427).

In spite of all their great contributions to the work, by 1838 David and the remainder of the Whitmers had left the Church (Christian and Peter, Jr., had previously died in Clay County). The year 1837 was a time of disillusion and financial trial for the Saints in Kirtland. To help shore up the local economy, Joseph Smith and other leaders organized a banking society (*see* KIRTLAND ECONOMY). When it failed, many members who lost their savings were embittered. Brigham Young said it was a time when the "knees of many of the strongest men in the Church faltered" (Elden Jay Watson, ed., *Manuscript History of Brigham Young, 1801–1844*, Salt Lake City, 1968, p. 16). Even earlier, in February 1837, some dissenters wanted to depose Joseph Smith and replace him with David Whitmer. Whitmer, a proud and stubborn man, was still smarting from conflicts over his leadership in Missouri. In the disciplinary council that excommunicated Whitmer, on April 13, 1838, one of the main charges brought against him was "possessing the same spirit with the Dissenters" (Donald Q. Cannon and Lyndon W. Cook, eds., *Far West Record, Minutes of The Church of Jesus Christ of Latter-day Saints, 1830–1844*, Salt Lake City, 1983, p. 177).

After Whitmer left the Church, he moved to Richmond, Missouri, and opened a livery stable, which he ran until 1888. A respected citizen in the community, he served on fair boards, was a member of the city council, and was elected mayor. Over his lifetime, hundreds of visitors inquired about and heard his testimony of the Book of Mormon.

A year before his death Whitmer wrote a pamphlet, *An Address to All Believers in Christ* (1887), apparently to justify his separation from the Church. In the pamphlet, he again gave witness to the truth of the Book of Mormon, but claimed that Joseph Smith drifted into errors after completing the translation. Whitmer rejected many later developments in the Church, such as the offices of high priest and prophet, seer, and revelator; the Doctrine and Covenants; and the doctrines of gathering and of PLURAL MARRIAGE.

Shortly before his death, Whitmer repeated once more, for the *Richmond Conservator*, what he had written in the *Address*: "I have never at any time denied that testimony or any part thereof, which has so long since been published with that Book, as one of the three witnesses. Those who know me best, well know that I have always adhered to that testimony." He died in Richmond, Missouri, on January 25, 1888, bearing testimony again on his deathbed of the authenticity of the Book of Mormon.

BIBLIOGRAPHY

Anderson, Richard Lloyd. *Investigating the Book of Mormon Witnesses.* Salt Lake City, 1981.

Cook, Lyndon W., and Matthew K. Cook, eds. *David Whitmer Interviews: A Restoration Witness.* Orem, Utah, 1991.

Nibley, Preston, comp. *The Witnesses of the Book of Mormon.* Salt Lake City, 1973.

Perkins, Keith W. "True to the Book of Mormon: The Whitmers." *Ensign* 19 (Feb. 1989):34–42.

KEITH W. PERKINS

WHITNEY STORE

The Newel K. Whitney store played a major role in the history of the Latter-day Saints in KIRTLAND, OHIO, during the years 1831–1838. When the Prophet Joseph SMITH arrived in Kirtland on February 1, 1831, he strode up to the counter where Whitney was clerking and extended his hand: "Newel K. Whitney, . . . I am Joseph, the Prophet. . . . You've prayed me here; now what do you want of me?" (*HC* 1:146).

The Prophet later received a number of significant revelations in the Whitney store, including the Word of Wisdom (D&C 89) and two important revelations on priesthood (D&C 84, 88). Joseph Smith also worked on his translation of the Bible in an upstairs room.

The store started in a log cabin in 1823. The present frame structure was built in the flats of Kirtland, Ohio, by 1827. Operating the N. K. Whitney & Co. store as a mercantile establishment and as a post office, Whitney and his partner Sidney Gilbert maintained as large an inventory as any store in northeastern Ohio.

One of the first adult education programs in the United States, the SCHOOL OF THE PROPHETS, was held in the store during the winter of 1833 in accord with revelation (D&C 88:127–41). The school's purpose was to prepare missionaries to take the gospel to the world. Many people told of receiving visions in the store's upper room. The UNITED ORDER, the predecessor of the current welfare system of the Church, had its beginning in the store, which was also used as the bishop's storehouse (D&C 72:8–10; 78:3).

Today the building is owned by The Church of Jesus Christ of Latter-day Saints and has been restored to its 1830s form as a historical site for visitors. President Ronald Reagan awarded the restored store the President's Historic Preservation Award on November 18, 1988.

BIBLIOGRAPHY

Anderson, Karl Ricks. *Joseph Smith's Kirtland: Eyewitness Accounts*. Salt Lake City, 1989.

Backman, Milton V., Jr. *The Heavens Resound: A History of the Latter-day Saints in Ohio, 1830–1838*. Salt Lake City, 1983.

KEITH W. PERKINS

WILLIAMS, CLARISSA

Clarissa Smith Williams (1859–1930) served as the sixth general president of Relief Society from 1921 to 1928, a period in which the Relief Society focused on health care and other social issues. She began her Relief Society activity as a visiting teacher at age sixteen and later served as secretary and president of both the Salt Lake Seventeenth Ward and Salt Lake Stake Relief Societies. In 1901 she was appointed treasurer and a member of the general board. Ten years later she became first counselor to President Emmeline WELLS. In April 1921, President Heber J. GRANT appointed her general president of the Relief Society and editor of its magazine.

Clarissa was born April 21, 1859, in the residential wing of the Church Historian's Office in Salt Lake City, Utah. She was the first of five daughters born to George A. Smith, an apostle and Church historian, and his seventh and last wife, Susan Elizabeth West Smith. This family shared the residential apartment in the Historian's Office with the apostle's first wife, Bathsheba W. Smith, and her children. The polygamist wives and their families lived amicably in their comfortable pioneer residence.

Clarissa and her sisters received the best education available in the territory at that time. In 1875 she received a teaching certificate from the Normal Department of the University of Deseret (later the University of Utah).

Clarissa married William Newjent Williams on July 17, 1877, the day before he left on a mission to Wales. They had eleven children and lived to celebrate their fiftieth wedding anniversary.

William was a successful businessman, regent of the University of Utah, and state senator. In spite of their busy schedules, their family was always their first concern.

William supported Clarissa in her Relief Society activities. She later wrote: "After I was married and had seven children, I was asked to be secretary of the Seventeenth Ward Relief Society. I felt that I could not do this with all my little babies. But my husband said, 'My dear, you must do it; it is the very thing you need; you need to get away from the babies, and I will help you all I can, either by taking care of the children or making out your reports or copying your minutes, or any other thing I can do'" (*Relief Society Magazine* 15 [Dec. 1928]:668–69).

As general Relief Society president, Clarissa Williams concentrated on social problems. During her presidency, the Relief Society funded loans for training public health nurses, distributed free milk to infants, provided health examinations for preschool children, and operated summer camps for underprivileged children. She encouraged ward Relief Societies to prepare layettes for new mothers and distribute them according to need. In 1924 under her supervision the Relief Society established the Cottonwood Maternity Hospital, which continued in operation until 1963.

A member of the National Council of Women, Clarissa was one of nine U.S. delegates to the International Council of Women in Rome, Italy, in May 1914. She was appointed chairwoman of the Utah Women's Committee of the National Council of Defense during World War I. She died March 8, 1930, at her home in Salt Lake City.

BIBLIOGRAPHY

Lyman, Amy Brown. "Clarissa S. Williams." *Relief Society Magazine* 15 (Dec. 1928):639–43.

Peterson, Janet, and LaRene Gaunt. *Elect Ladies: Presidents of the Relief Society*. Salt Lake City, 1990.

EVALYN DARGER BENNETT

WINTER QUARTERS

Brigham YOUNG's original plan for the LDS exodus from NAUVOO, Illinois, envisioned a quick journey across Iowa in the spring of 1846 and, at least for some, a journey "over the mountains" by fall. That plan called for small winter camps in Iowa, at the Missouri River, and at Grand Island, whence later encampments could depart in the spring of 1847 for their mountain home. As the first wagons took over three months just to cross windblown and storm-drenched Iowa, this plan could not be carried out. By the time advance companies had reached the Missouri River, it was mid-June and too late for them or the 12,000 following to attempt a mountain crossing that season. A layover place had to be found.

The term "winter quarters," often used by trappers and explorers to describe a place of refuge from the hazards of winter, took on special significance in Mormon pioneer history. Built on Indian lands on the west bank of the Missouri River—now Florence, a suburb of Omaha, Nebraska—their Winter Quarters became a vital new center for planning, regrouping, preparing, and religious renewal. Surveyed in October 1846 and subsequently laid out in a grid with 14 streets, 38 blocks, and over 760 lots and stockyards, and with houses ranging from two-story brick homes to sod huts, Winter Quarters housed almost 4,000 Latter-day Saints by December 1846. For the next two years, the name was also loosely applied to scores of much smaller settlements on the river's east side, home for another 8,000 LDS immigrants.

After the establishment of SALT LAKE CITY in 1847 and upon orders from government officials concerned about settlement on Indian lands, the Saints vacated Winter Quarters in 1848 to go either to the Salt Lake Valley or back east across the river, where they created the city of Kanesville, Iowa (*see* COUNCIL BLUFFS [KANESVILLE], IOWA).

Winter Quarters was more than a resting spot on the way to the West: It became a place of implementation and experimentation in Church practice and government. It was there, for example, that the law of adoption and PLURAL MARRIAGE were first openly practiced, though they had been taught in Nauvoo. Also at Winter Quarters Brigham Young and the Quorum of the Twelve Apostles deliberated at length about leadership and Church government before reorganizing the First Presidency at Kanesville, December 1847. The role of bishop was also refined. Because of the needs created by the July 1846 departure of 500 able-bodied men to serve in the MORMON

BATTALION, Winter Quarters became the first community divided into small wards (congregations) of 300 to 500 people, with a bishop responsible for each.

Winter Quarters also represents the tragic side of Mormon history: Some 2,000 Latter-day Saints died there and across the river between June 1846 and October 1848. This high death rate is attributable to excessive fatigue, heavy spring storms, generally inadequate provisions, the malaria then common along the river lowlands, improvised shelters, and the weakened condition of the "poor camp" refugees driven out of Nauvoo in the fall of 1846.

Winter Quarters tested Brigham Young's remarkable leadership abilities and the faith of thousands who followed him through sickness and wilderness to their eventual mountain refuge. In Latter-day Saint chronicles, Winter Quarters will be forever remembered as a place of suffering and of faith.

BIBLIOGRAPHY

Bennett, Richard E. *Mormons at the Missouri, 1846–1852*. Norman, Okla., 1987.

Brooks, Juanita, ed. *On the Mormon Frontier: The Diary of Hosea Stout, 1844–1861*, 2 vols. Salt Lake City, 1964.

Bryson, Conrey. *Winter Quarters*. Salt Lake City, 1986.

Stegner, Wallace. *The Gathering of Zion: The Story of the Mormon Trail*. New York, 1964.

RICHARD E. BENNETT

WOODRUFF, WILFORD

Wilford Woodruff (1807–1898), the fourth President of the Church, is especially remembered for his 1890 MANIFESTO, which led to the discontinuance of PLURAL MARRIAGE among the Latter-day Saints and to the assimilation of Utah into the political and economic mainstream of America. Prior to that event he led a strenuous life, notable for his remarkable success as a missionary and his diligence as one of the Church's premier diarists.

Wilford was born in Farmington, Hartford County, Connecticut, on March 1, 1807. His father, a miller, worked hard to support a family of eight sons and one daughter. Wilford was fifteen months old when his mother died of spotted fever at age twenty-six. During his early years Wilford worked as a miller, attended school, fished with his brother Thompson, and engaged in the social life of the community. At an early age he became concerned about religion and looked for a denomination whose doctrines and practices agreed with biblical Christianity. He spent much of his leisure time in reading, meditation, and prayer. Not far from a mill where he worked was a tree-covered island in a stream of rapid water. "I spent many a midnight hour alone upon that island in prayer before the Lord," he recalled ("Autobiography of Wilford Woodruff," Ms., p. 13). His quest eventually led him to Richland, Oswego County, New York, where he was baptized by Latter-day Saint missionaries on December 31, 1833. In April of 1834 he arrived at Kirtland, Ohio, where he met the Prophet Joseph Smith for the first time.

A month later, Woodruff participated in the March of ZION'S CAMP, a military company organized to help the Saints who had been driven from their homes in Jackson County, Missouri. Soon afterward, he began missionary work for the Church in Arkansas, Tennessee, and Kentucky in 1835–1836 and on the Fox Islands, off the coast of Maine, in 1837. His mission there ended in 1838 when, at age thirty-one, he was called to the Church's Quorum of the Twelve Apostles. On his return from Maine to the new headquarters of the Church in Nauvoo, Illinois, he led a company of fifty-three converts in ten wagons nearly 2,000 miles. Brigham Young ordained him an apostle on April 26, 1839, at Far West, Missouri.

A short time later, he was among the missionaries sent to England. He traveled there twice, first with other members of the Twelve in 1839 (D&C 118) and then to take charge as president of the mission in 1844. During his first mission in England, some 1,800 people, including 200 ministers, were baptized under his direction.

After embracing the restored gospel, Woodruff found himself in touch with the heavenly powers he had sought as a youth. As a missionary in the southern states in 1835, he went into a small room to meditate one evening and was overwhelmed by the appearance of a heavenly messenger who unfolded a panorama of events that would transpire on the earth before the second coming of Christ. In London one night, as he contemplated teaching the people of that city, he was beset by an evil spirit that nearly choked him to death before he was freed from its power by "three personages dressed in white" ("Autobiography of Wilford Woodruff," 1883–1884, p. 302).

He was also beset with an unusual number of accidents during his life. He suffered broken bones in his arms and legs, split his foot with an ax, was bitten by a rabid dog, and was crushed and pinned by falling trees. He nearly lost his life from blood poisoning when he accidentally cut his arm while skinning an ox that had died of poison. He survived the wreck of a speeding train, nearly drowned, was frozen and scalded, and suffered several severe illnesses. Woodruff believed that the promptings of the Holy Spirit saved his life on several occasions. He explained his preservation as a divine approval of his record keeping. He had prayed to know why the force of evil harassed him all his life. "The only answer I could ever get . . . was: 'The devil knew you would write, if you lived'—and I guess he did" ("Address to YMMIA Officers," Apr. 8, 1883, HDC).

One of Woodruff's most enduring legacies is his diary, a meticulous multivolume work covering nearly the entire History of the Church in the nineteenth century: "I have been inspired and moved upon to keep a Journal and write the affairs of this Church as far as I can. . . . You may say that this is a great deal of trouble. Very well it has been. . . . It has occupied nearly every leisure moment of my time. . . . But what of it? I have never spent any of my time more profitably for the benefit of mankind than in my journal writing" ("Wilford Woodruff Diary," Mar. 17, 1857, HDC). His diary contains the only record of many events and speeches of Church leaders. Although he was not a polished writer, his dedication, candid observations, and accurate reporting of speeches established his reputation as a devoted chronicler and brought his colleagues to his door to seek his services. In 1852 Woodruff was appointed clerk and historian of the Quorum of the Twelve Apostles, and in 1856 he commenced thirty-three years of service as a church historian. In addition to his diary, he left an extensive autobiographical record and some 12,000 items of correspondence.

Following his appointment to the Quorum of the Twelve in 1839, Woodruff was engaged in a variety of ecclesiastical and secular labors. He assisted in publishing the *Times and Seasons* and *Nauvoo Neighbor* in Illinois and the *Millennial Star* and Doctrine and Covenants in England. He was a member of the Nauvoo City Council, chaplain of the Nauvoo Legion, and a member of the Council of Fifty. He was a member of the pioneer company of Latter-day Saints to arrive in the Great Basin on July 24, 1847. He served in the Utah territorial legislature for twenty-two years and the territorial council for twenty-one; served on the board of directors of Zion's Co-operative Mercantile Institution (ZCMI); and was foreman of a Salt Lake City grand jury, president of the Cooperative Stock Company Association, president of the Universal Scientific Society, and chairman of the territorial Medical Board of Examiners.

Despite responsibilities that often took him away from home, Woodruff cared for a large family. Living during the years when PLURAL MARRIAGE was an authorized practice among the Latter-day Saints, he married five women: Phoebe Whittemore Carter, Mary Ann Jackson, Emma Smoot Smith, Sarah Brown, and Sarah Delight Stocking. They bore him thirty-three children. He was not immune from the heartaches and frailties of domestic life. His marriage to Mary Ann Jackson ended in divorce, and another wife and thirteen children preceded him in death. His philosophy of family living is reflected in words he wrote to a daughter: "We are all expecting to live together forever after death. I think we all as parents and children ought to take all the pains we can to make each other happy as long as we live that we may have nothing to regret" (letter to Blanche Woodruff, Sept. 16, 1894).

In addition to his public and domestic labors, Woodruff was a devoted farmer. His Salt Lake City farm, consisting of a garden, an orchard, and herds of cattle and sheep, did more than sustain his family; he worked at farming as a calling and profession. For fourteen years he presided over the Deseret Agricultural and Manufacturing Society, which sponsored the annual territorial fair, and in 1855 was appointed president of the Utah Territorial Horticultural Society. He exchanged information and samples with horticulturists in the United States and Europe, seeking to improve a species of tree or crop, or to develop plants suited to the arid conditions of the Great Basin. Products from his land repeatedly won awards at the territorial fair. Not a large man (Woodruff weighed 135 pounds in his prime), he nevertheless had a reputation as a hard worker. He continued tilling the soil, when not away on Church assignments, until he was nearly ninety.

Among his few leisure pursuits, Woodruff was an avid outdoorsman. He enjoyed fishing and hunting from his Connecticut days until his later years in the Great Basin. In August 1892 he wrote to *Forest and Stream* magazine about a fishing and hunting trip on the Weber River in the Uinta Mountains, where in four hours he caught twenty trout, four of which weighed over four pounds, and noted that he lost a ten-pounder because the bank was too steep to land it.

At the death of Church President John TAYLOR in 1887, Wilford Woodruff first led the Church as President of the Quorum of the Twelve Apostles and was then sustained as President of the Church at the general conference in April 1889, at the age of eighty-two. He had not expected to outlive his predecessor, who was younger, and saw his appointment as a case of the Almighty choosing "the weak things of the world" to perform his work ("Wilford Woodruff Diary," July 25, 1887). One observer noted that "he was not so learned, nor so eloquent a man as President John Taylor, but there was an earnest, honest zeal about him that convinced his hearers" (Cowley).

Woodruff's ordination as President came at a crucial time in the Church's history. Like other leaders, he had gone into seclusion to avoid imprisonment under provisions of federal ANTIPOLYGAMY LEGISLATION before word came of President Taylor's death. By the summer of 1890, legislation had been enacted that dissolved the Church as a legal entity, confiscated much of its property, and drove many of its leaders into hiding or prison. Federal legislation against polygamy had almost totally destroyed the effectiveness of the Church. For weeks President Woodruff "wrestled mightily with the Lord," and then, on September 24, 1890, after seeing in vision the consequences of inaction, he issued his now-famous Manifesto of 1890, which announced the end of the official practice of plural marriage (D&C, Official Declaration—1). On September 25 he wrote in his diary, "I have arrived at a point in the history of my life as the president of the Church . . . where I am under the necessity of acting for the temporal salvation of the Church. . . . and after praying to the Lord and feeling inspired by his spirit I have issued the following Proclamation." He then declared his intention to submit to the laws of the land "and to use my influence with the members of the Church over which I preside to have them do likewise" ("Wilford Woodruff Diary," Sept. 25, 1890).

While this action opened the door to a resolution of the issues that divided the Church from the nation, it did not relieve the pressures on the aging Church president. The financial burden incurred by the antipolygamy crusade, the completion of the SALT LAKE TEMPLE, demands of Church education, increased welfare expenditures due to the 1893 depression, and costs of funding local industries created apparently insurmountable financial difficulties. In 1893 he wrote to a friend, "I never saw a day in my life when I was so overwhelmed in business care and responsibility as I am today" (letter to W. H. Atkins and family, Aug. 10, 1893). He did not live to see the financial relief he had hoped for. He died on September 2, 1898, at the age of ninety-one, in San Francisco, California, where he had occasionally gone to seek relief from the ailments of old age.

Although Woodruff's leadership was somewhat eclipsed by colleagues who were more articulate and astute in matters of finance and politics, his pen produced the instrument that led to UTAH STATEHOOD in 1896 and opened the door for the twentieth-century progress and growth of the Church. During his administration, other milestones were reached. In 1890 he inaugurated weekday religious education classes, a precursor to the later seminary and institute programs of the Church. He supervised the completion of the Salt Lake Temple and presided at its dedication in 1893. He placed temple recommends, which certify a Latter-day Saint's worthiness to enter the Church's temples, formerly issued only by the President of the Church, under the responsibility of bishops and stake presidents. Fast Day, formerly held on the first Thursday of each month, was changed to the first Sunday. In 1896 he signed a "political manifesto" that required all general Church officials, before they accepted any political position, to discuss the prospective appointment with presiding Church authorities.

A statement written while he was presiding over the Saints in England is a fitting epitaph to his life: "I am overwhelmed as it were in Mormonism for it is my life, meat, and drink and I do not expect to be anything else but a Mormon either in life or death. . . . It certainly looks like a marvelous work and a wonder that an obscure unlearned miller should stand . . . at the head of ten thousand saints" (letter to Aphek Woodruff, Apr. 18, 1845).

BIBLIOGRAPHY

Cowley, Matthias F. "President Wilford Woodruff." Address at University Branch, Chicago, Ill., Oct. 4, 1925, Ms., HDC.

Jessee, Dean C. "Wilford Woodruff." In *The Presidents of the Church*, ed. L. Arrington, pp. 117–43. Salt Lake City, 1986.

Woodruff, Wilford. "History of Wilford Woodruff." *Deseret News* 8 (July–Aug. 1858).

———. "The Autobiography of Wilford Woodruff." Ms., HDC.

———. "The Autobiography of Wilford Woodruff." *Tullidge's Quarterly Magazine* 3 (Oct. 1883–July 1884):1–25, 121–37, 302–311.

———. "Wilford Woodruff's Journal, 1833–1898," ed. Scott G. Kenny, typescript, 9 vols. Midvale, Utah, 1983–1984.

DEAN C. JESSEE

WYOMING, PIONEER SETTLEMENTS IN

Beginning in 1855, LDS settlements were located in western Wyoming on the eastern approach to Utah. Fort Bridger was purchased and Fort Supply was founded in part to control the Oregon-California Trail entrance into the Great Basin. The MORMON PIONEER TRAIL crossed the breadth of Wyoming from Fort Laramie on the east to Fort Bridger on the west. Across Wyoming the Oregon, California, and Mormon trails were one and the same, with the exception of Sublette's Cutoff, until they reached Fort Bridger, where the Mormon Trail turned southwest along the Hastings Cutoff.

Fort Bridger, near present-day Evanston, was founded in 1843 by mountainmen Jim Bridger and Louis Vasquez. Brigham Young and the original pioneers of 1847 stopped there en route to the Salt Lake Valley, and in 1855 the Church purchased the fort from Vasquez. Church leaders desired it as a supply station for the thousands of converts coming into the Great Basin and, because of its strategic location, as a base for missionary work among the Indians. When the men sent to occupy Fort Bridger encountered armed mountain men who refused to vacate, they established Fort Supply twelve miles to the southwest. Eventually Latter-day Saints took possession of Fort Bridger, but with the approach of the UTAH EXPEDITION in 1857, they abandoned and destroyed both forts.

Individual LDS families began to resettle in the vicinity of Fort Bridger beginning in 1890, and a branch of the Church was organized there in 1894, eventually becoming headquarters for a stake.

LDS settlements were also established in western Wyoming's Star Valley (1879) and in north central Wyoming's Big Horn basin (1893, 1900). The latter was one of the last colonizing efforts conducted under official Church auspices (*see* COLONIZATION).

BIBLIOGRAPHY

Campbell, Eugene E. "Brigham Young's Outer Cordon: A Reappraisal." *Utah Historical Quarterly* 41 (Summer 1973):221–53.

Gowans, Fred R., and Eugene E. Campbell. *Fort Bridger: Island in the Wilderness*. Provo, Utah, 1975.

———. *Fort Supply: Brigham Young's Green River Experiment*. Provo, Utah, 1976.

TED J. WARNER

Y

YOUNG, BRIGHAM

[*This entry consists of two articles:*

Brigham Young
Teachings of Brigham Young

Brigham Young *is a biography of the famed pioneer leader and second President of the Church;* Teachings of Brigham Young *provides a glimpse of the variety and significance of his teachings as preserved in his discourses. The overviews* History of the Church: c. 1831–1844 *and* c. 1844–1877 *review LDS history during Brigham Young's lifetime and the period of his presidency. He was a central figure in the subjects dealt with in* Westward Migration, Planning and Prophecy; Immigration and Emigration; *and* Colonization.]

BRIGHAM YOUNG

Colonizer, territorial governor, and President of The Church of Jesus Christ of Latter-day Saints, Brigham Young (1801–1877) was born in Whitingham, Vermont, on June 1, 1801, the ninth of eleven children born to John Young and Abigail (Nabby) Howe. Following service in the Revolutionary Army of George Washington, John Young settled on a farm in Hopkinton, Massachusetts. After sixteen years in Hopkinton, John and Nabby moved to southern Vermont, where Brigham was born. When Brigham was three the family moved to central New York state, and when he was ten, to Sherburne, in south-central New York. Brigham helped clear land for farming, trapped for fur animals, fished, built sheds and dug cellars, and helped with planting, cultivating, and harvesting crops. He also cared for his mother, who was seriously ill with tuberculosis.

Brigham's mother died in 1815, when he was fourteen. Not long after, in search for someone to look after his younger children, John Young married a widow, Hannah Brown, who brought her own children into the family. Brigham decided to leave home. Living for a period with a sister, he became an apprentice carpenter, painter, and glazier in nearby Auburn. Over the next five years he assisted in building in Auburn the first marketplace, the prison, the theological seminary, and the home of "Squire" William Brown (later occupied by William H. Seward, who served as governor of New York and Lincoln's secretary of state). As a master carpenter, Brigham built door fittings and louvered attic windows, and carved ornate mantelpieces for many homes. Many old homes in the region to this day have chairs, desks, staircases, doorways, and mantelpieces made by Brigham Young.

Brigham left Auburn in the spring of 1823 to work in Port Byron, New York, where he repaired furniture and painted canal boats. He developed a device for mixing paints, and turned out many chairs, tables, settees, cupboards, and doors. He also helped organize the local forensic and oratorical society. On October 5, 1824, at the age of twenty-three, Brigham married Miriam Works. They established a home in Aurelius township, where they joined the Methodist Church. Within a year their first child, Elizabeth, was born.

After four years in Port Byron, Brigham and Miriam moved to Oswego, a port on Lake Ontario, where he added to his reputation for good craftsmanship, trustworthiness, and industry. He joined a small group of religious seekers, offering fervent prayers and singing enlivening songs. An Oswego associate testified that his conduct was exemplary, humble, and contrite.

Near the end of 1828 Brigham took his family to Mendon, New York, forty miles from Port Byron, near his father and other relatives. At Mendon, Miriam gave birth to a second daughter, Vilate, but contracted chronic tuberculosis and became a semi-invalid. Brigham prepared the meals, dressed the children, cleaned the house, and carried Miriam to a rocking chair in front of the fireplace in the morning and back to bed in the evening. In Mendon he built a shop and mill, made and repaired furniture, and put in windowpanes, doorways, staircases, and fireplace mantels.

In the spring of 1830 Samuel Smith, brother of Joseph SMITH, passed through Mendon on a trip to distribute the Book of Mormon. He left a copy with Brigham's oldest brother, Phineas, an itinerant preacher. Phineas was favorably impressed with the book and lent it to his father, then to his sister Fanny, who gave it to Brigham. Though impressed, Brigham nevertheless counseled caution: "Wait a little while . . . I [want] to see whether good common sense [is] manifest" (*JD* 3:91; cf. 8:38). After nearly two years of investigation, Brigham, moved by the testimony of a Mormon elder, was baptized in the spring of 1832. All of Brigham's immediate family were also baptized, and they all remained loyal Latter-day Saints throughout their lives. Miriam, who also joined, lived only until September 1832.

One week after his baptism, Brigham gave his first sermon. He declared "[After I was baptized] I wanted to thunder and roar out the Gospel to the nations. It burned in my bones like fire pent up, so I [commenced] to preach. . . . Nothing would satisfy me but to cry abroad in the world, what the Lord was doing in the latter days" (*JD* 1:313). Brigham felt the impulse to "cry abroad" so strongly that he enlisted the assistance of Vilate and Heber C. KIMBALL to care for his daughters and abandoned his trade to devote himself wholeheartedly to building the "kingdom of god." That fall, after Miriam's death, he, Heber Kimball, and several relatives traveled to KIRTLAND, OHIO, where he first met the twenty-six-year-old Prophet Joseph Smith. Invited to evening prayer in the Smith home, Brigham was moved by the Spirit and spoke in tongues, the first speaking in tongues witnessed by the Prophet.

Brigham's subsequent missionary tours carried him north, east, west, and south of Mendon. He and his brother Joseph Young made several preaching trips into the New York and Ontario, Canada, countryside. In the summer of 1833 he traveled to Kirtland with several of his Canadian converts, where he heard Joseph Smith teach about the gathering, emphasizing that building the kingdom of God required more than just preaching. Thus instructed, Brigham returned to New York and, with the Kimballs, moved his household to Kirtland so he could participate in building a new society.

Among those whom Brigham met in Kirtland was Mary Ann Angell, a native of Seneca, Ontario County, New York, who had worked in a factory in Providence, Rhode Island, until her conversion to the Church and move to Kirtland. Brigham married her on February 18, 1834. She looked after Brigham's two daughters by Miriam and subsequently had six children of her own.

In 1834 Brigham and his brother Joseph served with ZION'S CAMP, a small army that walked from Ohio to Missouri in the summer of 1834 to assist those driven from their homes by hostile mobs. Brigham regarded the difficult trek, which was led by Joseph Smith, as superb education and later called it "the starting point of my knowing how to lead Israel" (Arrington, pp. 45–46).

Dedication and potential, more than accomplishments, qualified Brigham Young to be selected in February 1835 as a member of the Church's original Quorum of the Twelve Apostles. The Twelve were a "traveling high council" charged to take the gospel "to all the nations, kindreds, tongues, and people." They presided not "at home" but "abroad," where no local stakes were established. This group later became the leading quorum in the Church after the First Presidency.

Each summer Brigham undertook proselytizing missions in the East; each winter he cared for his family and helped build up Kirtland. He helped construct the KIRTLAND TEMPLE, attended the SCHOOL OF THE PROPHETS, participated in the Pentecostal outpouring that accompanied the dedication of the Kirtland Temple in the spring of 1836, and engaged in Church-related business activities assigned to him by Joseph Smith. When the Kirtland community became divided over Joseph Smith's leadership, Brigham Young's strong defense of the Prophet so enraged the critics that Brigham had to flee Kirtland for his safety.

By the summer of 1838 most of the Kirtland faithful, including Brigham and his family, had moved to Caldwell County, in northern Missouri. Growing numbers of Latter-day Saint arrivals rekindled antagonisms with old settlers, and violence erupted (*see* MISSOURI CONFLICT). Disarmed, violated, and robbed of most of their holdings, the Latter-day Saints were driven from the state. With Joseph Smith, his brother Hyrum, Sidney RIGDON, and other Church leaders imprisoned, Brigham Young, senior member of the Quorum of the

Twelve, directed the evacuation of the Saints to Quincy and other Illinois communities. To ensure that members without teams and wagons would not be left behind, he drew up the Missouri Covenant. All who signed it agreed to make their resources available to remove every person to safety.

In the spring of 1839 Joseph Smith designated Commerce (renamed NAUVOO), Illinois, the new central gathering place of the Saints. Brigham's family were hardly settled in the area when he and other members of the Twelve left to fulfill their calls to Great Britain as missionaries. Despite poverty and poor health all around, Brigham left his wife and children in September, determined to go to England or to die trying. He and his companions finally docked at Liverpool in April 1840 (*see* MISSIONS OF THE TWELVE TO THE BRITISH ISLES).

As quorum president, Brigham directed the work of his quorum in Britain during an astonishing year in which they baptized between 7,000 and 8,000 converts; printed and distributed 5,000 copies of the Book of Mormon, 3,000 hymn books, 1,500 volumes of the *Millennial Star,* and 50,000 tracts; and established a shipping agency and assisted nearly 1,000 to emigrate to Nauvoo. Brigham traveled to the principal cities in England and took time to visit Buckingham Palace, St. Paul's Cathedral, Westminster Abbey, the Lake district, factory towns, the Potteries, museums, art galleries, and, of course, the homes of converts, both rich and poor. In later years he often commented on what he had seen and learned in England.

Such striking success, the first such experience of a united quorum, prepared the Twelve for additional responsibilities. Back in Nauvoo, Brigham was given the assignment of directing the Twelve in their supervision of missionary work, the purchase of lands and settling of immigrants, and various construction projects. Along with others, Brigham was also taught the principle of PLURAL MARRIAGE; he accepted it after much reluctance and considerable thought and prayer. With Mary Ann's consent, he married Lucy Ann Decker Seeley in June 1842, and later other plural wives. He was among the first to receive the full temple endowment in 1842 and, later, with Mary Ann, participated with others who had received temple ordinances in sessions during which Joseph Smith gave additional instructions on gospel principles.

Because Brigham Young was now the president of the quorum,

which came second only to the First Presidency in authority and responsibility, he was highly prominent and influential in Nauvoo. Nonetheless, though he helped direct everything from the construction of the NAUVOO TEMPLE to missionary work abroad, he also continued the pattern established in Kirtland of personally undertaking preaching missions each summer. In February Joseph Smith further instructed Brigham Young and others of his quorum about a future move to the Rocky Mountains. In March 1844 Brigham participated in the creation of the COUNCIL OF FIFTY—an organization suggesting a pattern of government for a future theocratic society and the last such organizational pattern left by Joseph Smith. Soon after, as if in foreboding of his impending death, Joseph Smith gave Brigham and other members of the Twelve a dramatic charge to "bear off this kingdom," telling them that they now had all the keys and instruction needed to do so successfully (*CR* [Apr. 1898]:89; *MS* 5 [Mar. 1845]:151).

In May 1844, Brigham and other apostles left on summer missions. While they were gone, events in Nauvoo deteriorated. Joseph Smith was arrested and, on June 27, was killed with his brother Hyrum when a mob stormed the jail where they were being held (*see* CARTHAGE JAIL; MARTYRDOM OF JOSEPH AND HYRUM SMITH). Brigham was in the Boston area and did not hear definite word of the assassination until July 16. He and his companions immediately rushed back to Nauvoo, arriving August 6. After a dramatic confrontation with Sidney RIGDON on August 8, Brigham and the Twelve were sustained to lead the Church. Brigham remained the leader until his death in 1877.

Although privately committed to leaving Nauvoo, Brigham and his associates were determined to complete the Nauvoo Temple so that the Saints could receive their temple ordinances. Even as they labored to defend themselves and finish the temple, they held meetings to decide on when and where to move farther west. Soon after violence erupted in September 1845, they publicly announced their intention to leave by the following spring. By December the temple was ready for ordinance work, and by February nearly 6,000 members had received temple blessings therein. The Saints had also spent the fall and winter preparing for the exodus. Committees were appointed, and a Nauvoo Covenant was signed, helping to ensure that those with property would assist those without.

Partly because of concerns about governmental intervention, Brigham Young began the migration in the cold and snow of February 1846 rather than await spring. By hundreds, then by thousands, people, animals, and wagons crossed the Mississippi River and trudged across Iowa mud to a WINTER QUARTERS (now Florence, Nebraska) on the Missouri River. In late spring nearly 16,000 Saints were on the road.

Brigham personally directed this massive odyssey, which involved the allocation of foodstuffs, wagons, oxen, and Church property to organized companies setting out on the trail. The preparation and the move through Iowa took so long that none of the companies could reach the Rocky Mountains that year, as was hoped. This demanding Iowa experience taught Brigham Young valuable lessons about men and organization that he used throughout his years of leadership. He also learned anew that when human resources prove inadequate, one must turn in faith to God. That winter Brigham announced "The Word and Will of the Lord" (D&C 136) to help organize the Saints and prepare them for the westward trek.

Brigham Young set out with an advance group of 143 men, 3 women, and 2 children on April 5, 1847. Delayed by illness, he arrived in the SALT LAKE VALLEY on July 24, a few days behind the advance party. Once he saw the valley with his own eyes, he announced it as the right place for a new headquarters city and confirmed that the region would be the new gathering place. He also identified the exact spot for a temple. He directed the exploration of the region; helped survey and apportion the land for homes, gardens, and farming; named the new settlement "Great Salt Lake City, Great Basin, North America"; held meetings where he appointed John Smith religious leader of the new colony and agreed on basic policies of cooperative work and sharing. On August 26, Brigham joined the return party to Winter Quarters.

In Winter Quarters, in December 1847, Brigham and other members of the Twelve reorganized the First Presidency of the Church, with Brigham as president. The following April he, his family, and approximately 3,500 other Saints headed for the Salt Lake Valley. Brigham's activities in organizing companies, building bridges, repairing equipment, and training oxen developed abilities that would be in evidence the rest of his life.

A series of problems confronted Brigham, now forty-seven, as he established his permanent home in the Salt Lake Valley. The first problem was to provide housing for his family. On a lot adjoining City Creek in what is now the center of SALT LAKE CITY, he built a row of log houses for his wives and children that, collectively, were called Harmony House. To the south of this he later built the White House, a sun-dried adobe structure covered with white plaster. Still later, he built a large, two-story adobe house faced with cement that fronted on what came to be known as Brigham Street (now South Temple Street). Sporting a tower surmounted by a gilded beehive, this building was known as the Beehive House and was Brigham's official residence as governor and President of the Church. In 1856, Brigham added an impressive three-story adobe structure, which came to be called the Lion House from the statue of a crouching lion on the portico. Several of his families lived in this building, just west of the Beehive House. He later built homes in south Salt Lake City, Provo, and St. George. Brigham's homes were all well constructed and finely appointed.

A central public problem was finding places to accommodate the incoming Saints. Salt Lake City was divided into ten-acre blocks, and each family head was allotted by community drawing a one-and-one-fourth-acre lot on one of the blocks in the city. There people would keep their livestock, gardens, and other "home" properties (*see* CITY PLANNING). A ten-acre block just west of Brigham's was designated the Temple Block (*see* TEMPLE SQUARE), and on this were located the Bowery, a temporary shelter built of tree boughs, where the Saints first held religious services; the TABERNACLE; and various shops used in constructing public buildings. Construction of the SALT LAKE TEMPLE was begun in 1853.

Outside the city, five-acre and ten-acre plots were apportioned to those who wanted to farm. Under Brigham Young's direction, cooperative teams were assigned to dig ditches and canals to irrigate crops and to furnish water to homes. Other brigades fenced residential areas, built roads, cut timber, and set up shops. Other groups selected new locations for settlements and helped place people in the best areas. Still others were called on missions to proselytize in the United States, Europe, or the Pacific.

In the spring of 1849 Brigham Young organized Salt Lake City into nineteen wards; organized wards in other settlements; set up the state of Deseret with himself as governor; and established the PERPETUAL EMIGRATING FUND as a device for assisting with the emigration of Saints from Great Britain, Scandinavia, and continental Europe.

With thousands of Saints arriving from the eastern United States and Europe, COLONIZATION demanded Brigham Young's attention. Under his direction, four kinds of colonies were established: first, settlements intended to be temporary places of gathering and recruitment, such as Carson Valley in Nevada; second, colonies to serve as centers for production, such as iron at Cedar City, cotton at St. George, cattle in Cache Valley, and sheep in Spanish Fork, all in Utah; third, colonies to serve as centers for proselytizing and assisting Indians, as at Harmony in southern Utah, Las Vegas in southern Nevada, Lemhi in northern Idaho, and present-day Moab in eastern Utah; fourth, permanent colonies in Utah and nearby states and territories to provide homes and farms for the hundreds of new immigrants arriving each summer. Within ten years, nearly 100 colonies had been planted; by 1867, more than 200; and by the time of his death in 1877, nearly 400 colonies. Clearly, he was one of America's greatest colonizers.

As President of the Church, Brigham conducted regular Sunday services in Salt Lake City and each year visited as many outlying communities as possible. He appointed bishops for each ward and settlement and encouraged each ward to provide cultural opportunities for its members, such as dances, theater, music recitals, and, above all, schools. He listened to people with complaints, responded to myriad questions about personal and family affairs as well as religion, and dictated thousands of letters with instruction, counsel, friendly advice, and casual comment about Church and national affairs. He was a firm Latter-day Saint and a wise counselor.

Brigham gave some 500 sermons in pioneer Utah that were recorded word for word by a stenographer. These, all delivered without a prepared text, may have seemed rambling in organization, but they were well thought out and suggest remarkable mental power. They were well adapted to his audiences. His discourses were like "fireside chats," an informal "talking things over" with his audiences. Interweaving subjects as diverse as women's fashions, the atonement of Christ, recollections of Joseph Smith, and how to make good bread,

Brigham kept his audiences enthralled, amused, and in tears, sometimes for hours. He inspired, motivated, taught, and encouraged.

The Latter-day Saints had settled among various tribes of Native Americans. Intent upon helping them, converting them, and avoiding bloodshed, Brigham established Indian farms, took Indians into his own home, advocated a policy of "feeding them is cheaper than fighting them," and held periodic meetings with chiefs. His policies were not always successful, but he consistently sought peaceful solutions and firmly opposed the all-too-common frontier practice of shooting Indians for petty causes.

In 1851, Brigham was appointed governor and superintendent of Indian Affairs of UTAH TERRITORY by U.S. President Millard Fillmore. His principal problem as governor was dealing with the "outside" federal appointees, many of whom were, from any point of view, both unsympathetic to the Church and inexcusably incompetent. There were problems over the small federal expenditures, the failure of Saints to use federal judges in cases of civil disputes, the lack of tact of the federally appointed officials in discussing the Church, their opposition to the union of church and state, and their assumption that Latter-day Saints were immoral because of their tolerance of plural marriage. [For other events that occupied Brigham Young's attention in 1856 *see* HANDCART COMPANIES; REFORMATION (LDS) of 1856–1857.]

This continuing controversy eventually led to the decision of U.S. President James Buchanan in 1857 to replace Brigham Young with an "outside" governor, Alfred Cumming of Georgia. At the same time, President Buchanan, who had been (wrongly) informed that the Mormons were "in a state of substantial rebellion against the laws and authority of the United States," sent a major portion of the U.S. Army to Utah to install the new governor and to ensure the execution of U.S. laws (*see* UTAH EXPEDITION). Though Governor Young was not notified of this action, armed forces were observed secretly heading for Utah. Fearful of a repetition of the "mobocracy" of Missouri and Illinois, he called people home from outlying colonies and mobilized the Saints to defend their homes. Eventually, with the assistance of Thomas L. KANE, he arranged a peaceful settlement whereby the Army occupied Camp Floyd, a post some forty miles from Salt Lake City. The U.S. Army was an irritant, but not a hindrance, to continued Church expansion and development. President Young remained, as his colleagues boasted, governor of the people, while his replacements merely governed the territory. The Army left Utah in 1861 with the start of the Civil War.

A believer in adapting the newest technology to the advantage of LDS society, Brigham Young contracted in 1861 to build the transcontinental telegraph line from Nebraska to California, and then proceeded to erect the 1,200-mile Deseret Telegraph line from Franklin, Idaho, to northern Arizona. This connected nearly all Mormon villages with Salt Lake City and, through that connection, with the world. While the transcontinental railroad was under construction, he negotiated for contracts with Union Pacific and Central Pacific for LDS contractors to build the roadbeds east of Salt Lake City into part of Wyoming and west well into Nevada. He then organized the Utah Central, Utah Southern, and Utah Northern railroads to extend the line south from Ogden to Frisco in southern Utah and north to Franklin, Idaho, and eventually to Montana.

Aware that the completion of the railroad would imperil the independent social economy of his people, President Young inaugurated a protective movement that sought to preserve, as much as possible, their unique way of life. He organized cooperatives to handle local merchandising and manufacturing; initiated several new enterprises to develop local resources; promoted Relief Societies in each ward in order to provide opportunities for self-development, socialization, and compassionate service for women; opened the doors of the University of Deseret (later the University of Utah) for both young men and women; encouraged women to become professionally trained, especially in medicine; and gave women the vote. In 1875 he established Brigham Young Academy (later Brigham Young University), in 1877 Brigham Young College (Logan, Utah) and the Latter-day Saints College. In 1874 he also promoted the United Order movement in an effort to encourage cooperation and home production and consumption (*see* ECONOMIC HISTORY OF THE CHURCH).

Brigham Young remained vigorous until his death in August 1877. Just before his death, he dedicated the St. George Temple and launched there the full scope of LDS temple ordinances, something he had anticipated since Nauvoo; and he overhauled Church organization at every level, formalizing for the first time practices that would characterize the Church for nearly a century.

Brigham was a well-built, stout (in later years, portly) man of five feet, ten inches, somewhat taller than average for his day. His light brown hair, often described as "sandy," had very little gray. Visitors noticed his penetrating blue-gray eyes lined by thin eyebrows. Though he later wore a full beard, Brigham was clean-shaven until the 1850s, when he first sported chin whiskers. His mouth and chin were firm, bespeaking, visitors thought, his iron will. He was generally composed and quiet in manner, but he could thunder at the pulpit. Sometimes called the "Lion of the Lord," he could also roar when aroused.

Brigham Young's manner was pleasant and courteous. His dress, generally neat and plain, was often homespun. He combined vibrant energy and self-certainty with deference to the feelings of others and a complete lack of pretension. By the time of his death, Brigham Young had married twenty women, sixteen of whom bore him fifty-seven children. He died on August 29, 1877, of peritonitis, the result of a ruptured appendix.

Brigham's most obvious achievements were the product of his lifelong talent for practical decision making. He instituted patterns of Church government that persist to this day. In leading the Saints across Iowa, he issued detailed instructions that were followed by the hundreds of companies that crossed the plains to the Salt Lake Valley in succeeding years. In the Great Basin he directed the organization of several hundred LDS settlements; set up several hundred cooperative retail, wholesale, and manufacturing enterprises; and initiated the construction of meetinghouses, tabernacles, and temples. While doing all this, he carried on a running battle with the United States government to preserve the unique LDS way of life.

But for Brigham Young these were means, not ends. His overriding concern was to build on the foundation begun by Joseph Smith to establish a commonwealth in the desert where his people could live the gospel of Jesus Christ in peace, thereby improving their prospects in this life and in the next. He loved the Great Basin because its harshness and isolation made it an ideal place to "make Saints."

BIBLIOGRAPHY

Arrington, Leonard J. *Brigham Young: American Moses*. New York, 1985.

Bringhurst, Newell G. *Brigham Young and the Expanding American Frontier*. Boston, 1986.

Palmer, Richard F., and Karl D. Butler. *Brigham Young: The New York Years*. Provo, Utah, 1982.

Walker, Ronald W., and Ronald K. Esplin. "Brigham Himself: An Autobiographical Recollection." *Journal of Mormon History* 4 (1977):19–34.

LEONARD J. ARRINGTON

TEACHINGS OF BRIGHAM YOUNG

In leading the Latter-day Saints for over thirty years, Brigham Young wrote comparatively little, except for his letters, but he spoke frequently and on numerous subjects. He was constantly obliged to speak ex cathedra on many topics relative to life in this world and the next. His discourses were vigorous and forthright, filled with candid realism and common sense, and many of his speeches were recorded in shorthand by scribes. Along with his practical attainments and mechanical skills, he was one of the most discursive and lucid of men. Here was a man tested by fire (e.g., he was actually driven from his home five times) and who knew all the trials of life, from the corridors of power to the roughest frontiers. He sometimes made statements that surprised or even offended those who tended to accept his every utterance as doctrine, but with a New Englander's passion for teaching and learning, he plunged ahead.

All the commentators concede that Brigham Young was one of the ablest and most dynamic leaders in American history. He was one of the supremely practical men of his age, a hardheaded, even-keeled, no-nonsense realist who got things done. But, for him, all of that was incidental. The important thing was that the people should know what they were doing and why. His orders and recommendations came with full and persuasive explanations.

His teachings begin with faith in Jesus Christ: "My faith is placed upon the Lord Jesus Christ, and my knowledge I have received from him" (*JD* 3:155). "Jesus is our captain and leader; Jesus, the Savior of the world—the Christ we believe in" (*JD* 14:118). "Our faith is placed upon the son of God, and through him in the Father, and the Holy Ghost is their minister to bring truths to our remembrance" (*JD* 6:98).

Brigham Young gained much of his knowledge of Jesus Christ through his constant association with the Prophet Joseph SMITH: "What I have received from the Lord, I have received by Joseph Smith" (*JD* 6:279). To the end of his life, Young testified of the mission of Joseph Smith in restoring knowledge of Christ to earth. "I love his doctrine," he said. "I feel like shouting Hallelujah, all the time, when I think that I ever knew Joseph Smith, the Prophet whom the Lord raised up and ordained" (*JD* 13:216; 3:51). His dying words were "Joseph, Joseph, Joseph."

On this foundation, Brigham Young emphatically taught the law of eternal progression. This life is a part of eternity. Eternal knowledge and glory are to be obtained and promoted on this earth. Improvement, learning, training, building, and expanding are the joy of life: "We do not expect to cease learning while we live on earth; and when we pass through the veil, we expect still to continue to learn" (*JD* 6:286). And eternal progression leads to godhood: "The faithful will become gods, even the sons of God" (*JD* 6:275).

Brigham Young recognized that many people were not prepared to understand the mysteries of God and godhood. "I could tell you much more about this," he said, speaking of the role of Adam, but checked himself, recognizing that the world would probably misinterpret his teaching (*JD* 1:51).

All of the descendants of Adam (men, women, and children) must work. "What is this work?" Brigham asks. "The improvement of the condition of the human family. This work must continue until the people who live on this earth are prepared to receive our coming Lord" (*JD* 19:46).

For Brigham, improvement meant "to build in strength and stability, to beautify, to adorn, to embellish, to delight, and to cast fragrance over the House of the Lord; with sweet instruments of music and melody" (*MS* 10:86). More specifically, the one way man can leave his mark on the face of nature without damage is to plant. President Young ceaselessly counseled his people to do as Adam was commanded to do in the Garden of Eden when he dressed and tended the garden: Our work is "to beautify the face of the earth, until it shall become like the Garden of Eden" (*JD* 1:345).

In caring for the world, "every accomplishment, every polished grace, every useful attainment in mathematics, music, and in all science and art belongs to the Saints, and they should avail themselves as expeditiously as possible of the wealth of knowledge the sciences offer to every diligent and persevering scholar, and that's our duty. . . . It is the duty of the Latter-day Saints, according to the revelation, to give their children the best education that can be procured, both from the books of the world and the revelations of the Lord" (*JD* 10:224). "If an elder shall give a lecture on astronomy, chemistry, or geology, our religion embraces it all. It matters not what the subject be if it tends to improve the mind, exalt the feelings, and enlarge the capacity. The truth that is in all the arts and sciences forms part of our religion" (*JD* 2:93–94).

President Young's fascination with the things of the mind extended to mundane experience. The enjoyment of the senses, he said, is one of our notable privileges upon the earth and a wonderful source of enjoyment.

Although Brigham Young's destiny led him to the desert barrenness of the West, he sensed a spiritual beauty in that land. "You are here commencing anew," he told the people. "The soil, the air, the water are all pure and healthy. Do not suffer them to become polluted with wickedness. Strive to preserve the elements from being contaminated by the filthy wicked conduct of those who pervert the intelligence God has bestowed upon the human family" (*JD* 8:79). For Brigham, moral and physical cleanliness and pollution are no more to be separated than mind and body: "Keep your valley pure, keep our towns as pure as you possibly can, keep your hearts pure, and labor what you can consistently, but not so as to injure yourselves" (*JD* 8:80).

Brigham Young also had a Yankee passion for thrift, but it rested on a generous respect for the worth of material things, not on a mean desire simply to possess them. When he said, "I do not know that during thirty years past, I have worn a coat, hat, or garment of any kind, or owned a horse, carriage, &c, but what I have asked the Lord whether I deserved it or not—Shall I wear this? Is it mine to use or not?" (*JD* 8:343), he was expressing the highest degree of human concern and responsibility.

Brigham Young often spoke of Zion and of building up the kingdom of God. He used the name Zion to describe the intended state of affairs and constantly had Zion in his view: "There is not one thing wanting in all the works of God's hands to make a Zion upon the earth when the people conclude to make it" (*JD* 9:283). He recognized that the ideal of Zion stood in the face of contemporary economic values: "It is thought by many that the possession of gold and silver will produce for them happiness; . . . in this they are mistaken" (*JD* 11:15). "If, by industrious habits and honorable dealings, you obtain thousands or millions of dollars, little or much, it is your duty to use all that is put in your possession, as judiciously as you have knowledge, to build up the Kingdom of God on the earth" (*JD* 4:29).

Zion was to be established on the basis of cooperation: "The doctrine of uniting together in our temporal labors, and all working for the good of all is from the beginning, from everlasting, and it will be for ever and ever" (*JD* 17:117). In this there was no room for debate or contention, least of all rancor: "Cast all bitterness out of your own hearts—all anger, wrath, strife, covetousness, and lust, and sanctify the Lord God in your hearts, that you may enjoy the Holy Ghost" (*JD* 8:33).

The contrast between light and darkness was vivid to President Young: "Whence comes evil? It comes when we make an evil of good. Speaking of the elements in the creation of God, their nature is as pure as the heavens, and we destroy it. I wish you to understand that sin is not an attribute in the nature of man, but is an inversion of the attributes God has placed in him" (*JD* 10:251). He recognizes a conscious, active agent in the spreading of evil: "Satan never owned the earth; he never made a particle of it; his labor is not to create, but to destroy" (*JD* 10:320).

The true stature of Brigham Young emerges if one seeks to compose a list of his peers. He led a ragged and impoverished band, stripped of virtually all their earthly goods, into an unknown territory. His critics and biographers note that the man was unique among the leaders of modern history, for he alone, without any political and financial backing, established from scratch in the desert an ordered and industrious society, having no other authority than the priesthood and the spiritual strength with which he delivered his teachings. By constant exhortations and instructions, he drew his people together and inspired them in carrying out the divine mandate to build up the kingdom of God on earth.

BIBLIOGRAPHY

The *Journal of Discourses* contains more than 350 of Brigham Young's speeches. For a selection of passages organized topically, see John A. Widtsoe, comp., *Discourses of Brigham Young*, Salt Lake City, 1954.

Melville, J. Keith. "The Reflections of Brigham Young on the Nature of Man and the State." *BYU Studies* 4 (1962):255–67.

———. "Brigham Young's Ideal Society: The Kingdom of God." *BYU Studies* 5 (1962):3–18.

Nibley, Hugh W. "Educating the Saints—A Brigham Young Mosaic." *BYU Studies* 11 (Autumn 1970):61–87.

———. "Brigham Young on the Environment." In *To the Glory of God*, ed. T. Madsen and C. Tate, pp. 3–29. Salt Lake City, 1972.

Walker, Ronald W. "Brigham Young on the Social Order." *BYU Studies* 28 (Summer 1988):37–52.

HUGH W. NIBLEY

YOUNG, ZINA D. H.

Zina Diantha Huntington Young (1821–1901), third general president of the Relief Society, possessed great faith and compassion. Sometimes called "the heart of the women's work in Utah" (Susa Young Gates, *History of the Young Ladies' Mutual Improvement Association* [Salt Lake City, 1911], p. 21), "Aunt Zina" led the Relief Society from 1888 to 1901.

Born January 31, 1821, in Watertown, New York, Zina Diantha was the eighth of William and Zina Baker Huntington's ten children. Her father served in the War of 1812, and his father, William Huntington, Sr., in the Revolutionary War. Zina's great-great-uncle, Samuel Huntington, was a signer of the Declaration of Independence.

Zina spent her childhood on the family farm learning the skills taught girls of that time—spinning, weaving, soap making, candle dipping, and other household skills. She attended school intermittently and acquired a basic education.

When Zina was fourteen, LDS missionaries, including Hyrum SMITH and David WHITMER, visited the Huntington home in Watertown. The family listened, prayed, and believed, and all but the oldest son, Chauncey (Chancy), joined the Church.

Zina was a spiritually sensitive young woman. She later wrote that soon after her conversion, "the gift of tongues rested upon me with overwhelming force." Somewhat awed, she endeavored to repeat the experience but discovered that the gift had left her, and she feared she had offended the Holy Spirit. "One day while mother and I were spinning together, I took courage and told her of the gift . . . and how . . . I had lost it entirely. Mother appreciated my feelings, and told me to make it a matter of earnest prayer, that the gift might once more be given to me" (Young, pp. 318–19). Zina thereafter spoke in or interpreted unknown tongues on many occasions throughout her life.

Counseled by Joseph SMITH, Sr., father of the Prophet Joseph SMITH, to unite with the Latter-day Saints in KIRTLAND, OHIO, the Huntingtons sold their home and property in New York and moved to Ohio in October 1836. Their nineteen months in Kirtland were a period of great physical privation but rich spiritual experiences.

In May 1838 the Huntington family joined the Saints' migration to Far West, Missouri, arriving at the height of bitter mob persecution, which resulted in the infamous EXTERMINATION ORDER issued by Missouri governor Lilburn Boggs. Zina's father helped coordinate the Saints' evacuation. The family then settled with other Saints in NAUVOO, Illinois, where Zina's mother died of cholera in July 1839. Joseph and Emma SMITH cared for Zina and others of the sick in their home.

On March 7, 1841, Zina married Henry Bailey Jacobs. She later married Joseph Smith and, after Joseph's death, Brigham YOUNG. She had two sons, Zebulon William and Henry Chariton Jacobs, and one daughter, Zina Presendia (Prescindia, Precindia) Young.

Following the expulsion from Nauvoo, Zina migrated with the Saints to the West. In the 1850s she studied obstetrics and subsequently helped deliver the babies of many women, including those of some of the other plural wives of Brigham Young. At their request, she anointed and blessed many of these sisters prior to their deliveries. Other women in need of physical and emotional comfort also received blessings under her hands.

Zina helped establish DESERET HOSPITAL, built in Salt Lake City in 1872, and served as its vice-president. She also organized a nursing school and instructed in a school for obstetrics.

In 1876 the Deseret Silk Association was organized, and Zina was appointed president by her prophet-husband Brigham Young. She traveled extensively throughout the territory to promote this home industry.

In 1880 the general organization of Relief Society, encompassing all local Relief Societies, was formed. Eliza R. SNOW, the president, selected Zina as her first counselor. They were instrumental in the development of the Relief Society, the Young Ladies' Retrenchment Association, and the Primary Association for children.

In the winter of 1881–1882, the First Presidency sent Zina to the East to advocate women's suffrage and dispel misinformation about the Church. She attended the Women's Congress in Buffalo and the National Suffrage Association Convention in New York. She also addressed many temperance societies.

Following the death of Eliza R. Snow in 1887, President Wilford WOODRUFF appointed Zina general president of the Relief Society. She continued in that capacity until her death August 28, 1901.

In her later years she wrote of her hope to have accomplished some lasting good: "As the mantle of time is fast draping its folds around many of us [w]hen we go hence to our rest, after our sacrifices may it be . . . that many in the future may have reason to praise God for the noble Women of this generation" (Zina Card Brown family collection). Inscribed on her gravestone is the Relief Society motto: Charity Never Faileth.

BIBLIOGRAPHY

Beecher, Maurine Ursenbach, ed. "'All Things Move in Order in the City': The Nauvoo Diary of Zina Diantha Huntington Jacobs." *BYU Studies* 19 (Spring 1979):285–320.

Young, Zina D. H. "How I Gained My Testimony of the Truth." *Young Woman's Journal* 4 (Apr. 1893):317–19.

Zina Card Brown family collection, LDS Archives.

MARY FIRMAGE WOODWARD

Z

ZION'S CAMP

Zion's Camp was a Latter-day Saint expedition from Kirtland, Ohio, to Clay County, Missouri, during May and June 1834. The Mormon settlers in adjacent Jackson County, Missouri, had been driven out in the fall of 1833 by hostile non-Mormon elements, and the initial objective of Zion's Camp was to protect those settlers after the Missouri militia escorted them back to their homes. The camp was to bring money, supplies, and moral support to the destitute Saints.

A revelation to Joseph SMITH in July 1831 (D&C 57) designated Independence, Jackson County, Missouri, as the site of Zion, a gathering place for the Saints and the location for the New Jerusalem spoken of in the Bible and the Book of Mormon. By the summer of 1833, the Latter-day Saints numbered about one-third of the population in Jackson County. Their increasing numbers and distinctive beliefs troubled the other settlers, who shortly demanded that the Church members leave. When these demands were not immediately complied with, the Missourians attacked the settlements, compelling the Saints to flee. Most went north across the Missouri River to Clay County in November 1833.

Lyman Wight and Parley P. PRATT brought word of their plight to Joseph Smith and the main body of Saints in Kirtland, Ohio, on February 22, 1834. Wight and Pratt informed the Prophet that after their conversation with Governor Daniel Dunklin, Attorney General

Robert W. Wells of Missouri promised to supply a force to escort the exiles back to their homes. With this in mind, Joseph Smith saw the wisdom of sending a force to protect his people from further attacks once they were safely back in Jackson County.

A revelation on February 24, 1834 (D&C 103), commanded the Saints to send to Missouri a relief force consisting of at least 100 and as many as 500 volunteers. Eight Church leaders were told to recruit participants for the march, which later was called Zion's Camp. Four teams of two men each went east to obtain men, money, and supplies. A fifth pair, Lyman Wight and Joseph Smith's brother Hyrum SMITH, went to Michigan and Illinois. The northern group was to join the marchers from Kirtland at the house of James Allred, a Church member living on the Salt River in eastern Missouri about one hundred miles northwest of St. Louis.

An advance party of 20 left Kirtland on May 1, 1834, to prepare the first camp at New Portage, near present-day Akron, Ohio, and the main group of about 85 joined them on May 6. When Joseph and Hyrum's contingents rendezvoused at the Allred settlement, east of Paris, Monroe County, Missouri, there were approximately 200 men, 11 women, and 7 children. Included in these figures were the 20 men, women, and children comprising Hyrum's company from the Pontiac, Michigan, area.

The marchers were well armed, carrying muskets, pistols, swords, and knives, and they attempted to prevent the Missourians from knowing of the expedition. But Jackson County residents learned of their coming and burned down virtually all the remaining Mormon buildings. Lacking in military training, the members of Zion's Camp conducted military exercises and sham battles along the way of the 900-mile journey. They were organized into groups of ten and fifty, with a captain over each. After the rendezvous at the Salt River on June 8, Lyman Wight, a veteran of the War of 1812, was elected general of the camp, and William Cherry, a British dragoon for twenty years, was made drill master.

Contrary to the attempted military discipline, the men sometimes quarreled among themselves. On June 3, as the group approached the Mississippi, Joseph warned them that in consequence of their misconduct a scourge would strike the camp. His words proved prophetic when, at the conclusion of their journey on June 23 at

Rush Creek in Clay County, Missouri, cholera struck the camp. Some sixty-eight men were afflicted, and thirteen of them and one woman died of the disease. Earlier at Fishing River a band of about 300 armed Missourians threatened to invade the camp, but a fierce hailstorm drove them off and prevented a conflict.

In the meantime, negotiations were conducted between the Zion's Camp leaders, Missouri State officials, and the citizens of Jackson County. Joseph Smith learned that, contrary to expectations, Governor Dunklin would not provide troops to escort the Mormons into Jackson County, fearing a civil war if he did. The two sides exchanged proposals for buying out each other's property in Jackson County, but these efforts broke down.

On June 22, 1834, while still at Fishing River, the Prophet received a revelation that rebuked some members of the Church for not sufficiently supporting Zion's Camp, but accepted the sacrifice of the camp members. They were not to fight but to wait for the Lord to redeem Zion (D&C 105). The experience had been intended to test their faith. The revelation directed the Saints to build goodwill in the area in preparation for the time when Zion would be recovered by legal rather than military means. Since there was little more to be done to help the displaced Jackson County Saints, the remaining Zion's Camp supplies were distributed to the refugees, and the camp disbanded on June 30, 1834. Most of the troops soon returned to Ohio.

Zion's Camp failed to achieve its ostensible purpose of protecting the Jackson County Saints. In retrospect, however, Brigham Young and other participants felt that they learned valuable lessons. In subsequent migrations, the Mormons used the organizational experience gained in Zion's Camp. Most importantly, they had answered the Lord's call (D&C 103). Nine of the first twelve apostles and all of the first Quorum of Seventy (seven presidents and sixty-three members) were later called from the ranks of Camp members.

BIBLIOGRAPHY

Crawley, Peter, and Richard L. Anderson. "The Political and Social Realities of Zion's Camp." *BYU Studies* 14 (1974):406–20.

Launius, Roger D. *Zion's Camp*. Independence, Mo., 1984.

Talbot, Wilburn D. "Zion's Camp." Master's thesis, Brigham Young University, 1973.

LANCE D. CHASE

APPENDIX 1

A CHRONOLOGY OF CHURCH HISTORY

The following are significant events in the history of The Church of Jesus Christ of Latter-day Saints. Words in small capitals refer to articles in this volume of the *Encyclopedia.*

1771, July 12. Joseph SMITH, Sr. (1771–1840) b. Topsfield, Essex Co., MA.

1775, July 8. Lucy Mack SMITH (1775–1856) b. Gilsum, Cheshire Co., NH.

1796, January 24. Joseph SMITH, Sr., and Lucy Mack SMITH m. in Tunbridge, VT.

1801, June 1. Brigham YOUNG (1801–1877) b. Whitingham, Windham Co., VT.

1804, July 10. Emma Hale SMITH (1804–1879) b. to Isaac Hale and Elizabeth Lewis Hale, HARMONY, Susquehanna Co., PA.

1805, December 23. Joseph SMITH (1805–1844) b. to Joseph Smith, Sr., and Lucy Mack Smith, Sharon, Windsor Co., VT.

1807, March 1. Wilford WOODRUFF (1807–1898) b. Farmington, Hartford Co., CT.

1808, November 1. John TAYLOR (1808–1887) b. Milnthorpe, Westmoreland, England.

1814, April 3. Lorenzo SNOW (1814–1901) b. Mantua, Portage Co., OH.

1816. The "year without a summer." Crops failed throughout New England. Joseph SMITH, Sr., left Norwich, VT, settled his family in Palmyra, NY.

1820, Early spring. Joseph SMITH received FIRST VISION in a grove near his home in Palmyra, NY.

1823, September 21–22. Joseph SMITH visited by Angel Moroni and told of Book of Mormon record. Joseph viewed gold plates buried in nearby hill (Cumorah). [*See* Moroni, Visitations of.]

1825, October. Joseph SMITH hired by Josiah Stowell to work at HARMONY, PA. Boarded at Isaac Hale's and met Emma Hale.

1826, March 20. Joseph SMITH tried and acquitted on charge of being a disorderly person at SOUTH BAINBRIDGE, NY. [*See* Smith, Joseph: Legal Trials of Joseph Smith.]

1827, January 18. Joseph SMITH m. Emma Hale in SOUTH BAINBRIDGE, NY. [*See* Smith, Emma Hale.]

September 22. Joseph SMITH obtained gold plates from hill Cumorah.

December. Joseph and Emma SMITH moved to HARMONY, PA, where plates could be safely translated.

1828, February. Martin HARRIS took a transcript of characters from the gold plates to Charles Anthon in New York City.

April 12–June 14. First 116 translated manuscript pages stolen from the Harris home (June–July).

1829, April 7. Joseph SMITH resumed translation of the record assisted by Oliver COWDERY as scribe.

May 15. John the Baptist conferred Aaronic Priesthood on Joseph SMITH and Oliver COWDERY near HARMONY, PA.

May–June. Joseph SMITH and Oliver COWDERY received Melchizedek Priesthood from Peter, James, and John, near the Susquehanna River between HARMONY, PA, and COLESVILLE, NY.

June. Translation of Book of Mormon completed and copyright applied for (June 11). The Three Witnesses shown the plates and other Nephite artifacts by Moroni in FAYETTE, NY. The Eight Witnesses shown the gold plates by Joseph SMITH in Manchester, NY.

August. Egbert B. Grandin began printing the Book of Mormon at PALMYRA, NY. Martin HARRIS guaranteed payment.

1830, March 26. First copies of Book of Mormon available at Grandin Bookstore.

April 6. The "Church of Christ" organized, Fayette township, NY, and "Articles and Covenants of the Church" revealed (D&C 20). [See FAYETTE, NY.]

June. "Visions of Moses" received by Joseph SMITH as part of Bible translation (now chapter 1 of the book of Moses, Pearl of Great Price).

June 9. First conference of the Church held in Whitmer log home, FAYETTE, NY.

September–October. First missionaries called to preach to the Lamanites (Native Americans). [*See* Lamanite Mission.]

October–November. "Lamanite missionaries" converted some 130 non-Indians in KIRTLAND, OH, area en route to western border of Missouri.

December. Sidney RIGDON called as scribe to assist Joseph SMITH in Bible translation (D&C 35:20).

December. First revelation on gathering given. Command for Church to move to Ohio (D&C 37). Reiterated (D&C 38).

1831, **February 1.** Joseph SMITH arrived at Newel K. WHITNEY STORE in KIRTLAND, OH, and commenced ministry there.

February 4. Edward Partridge called and ordained first bishop of Church.

February 9. Revelation on Church government and law of consecration received (D&C 42).

May. Fayette, Colesville, and Manchester branches of Church in New York arrived in KIRTLAND-Thompson areas, OH.

June 3–6. Fourth general conference of Church held, Kirtland township. Brethren first ordained to the High Priesthood.

July 20. Site for city of Zion in Independence, MO, revealed to Joseph SMITH (D&C 57).

August 2. Saints laid first log for a schoolhouse as a foundation of Zion, Kaw Township, Jackson Co., MO. Sidney RIGDON consecrated land of Zion by prayer.

August 3. Temple site, Independence, MO, dedicated by Joseph SMITH.

November 1. Conference, at HIRAM, OH. Decision made to print revelations received by Joseph SMITH.

1832, **January 25.** Joseph SMITH sustained President of High Priesthood at conference, Amherst, OH.

February 16. Revelation known as "The Vision" (D&C 76) received by Joseph SMITH, HIRAM, OH. [*See* Visions of Joseph Smith.]

March 24. Joseph SMITH and Sidney RIGDON beaten, tarred, feathered by mob, HIRAM, OH.

June. First issue of *The Evening and the Morning Star*, Independence, MO.

December 25. Revelation and Prophecy on War (D&C 87) received by Joseph SMITH.

December 27. Revelation known as The Olive Leaf (D&C 88) received by Joseph SMITH, calling for building a temple in Kirtland and establishing SCHOOL OF THE PROPHETS.

1833, **February 27.** Revelation known as the Word of Wisdom (D&C 89) received by Joseph SMITH.

March 18. Sidney RIGDON and Frederick G. Williams set apart as Counselors in Presidency of the Church (D&C 81 headnote).

July 2. Joseph SMITH concluded first draft of Bible translation.

July 20. Mob at INDEPENDENCE demanded removal of Saints from Jackson Co. Printing office destroyed, halting printing of Book of Commandments.

July 23. Saints at INDEPENDENCE made treaty with mob to leave Jackson Co. KIRTLAND TEMPLE cornerstones laid.

November 7. Saints fled from Jackson Co. mobs across Missouri River into Clay Co. [*See* Missouri Conflict.]

December 18. Joseph SMITH, Sr., ordained first Church patriarch.

1834, **February 17.** First stake and high council of Church organized, KIRTLAND, OH.

May 5. Joseph SMITH left KIRTLAND for Missouri as leader of ZION'S CAMP to bring relief to Saints expelled from Jackson Co.

July 3. Presidency and high council organized, Clay Co., MO, David WHITMER, president.

October. First issue of *Messenger and Advocate* published, KIRTLAND, OH.

December 5. Oliver COWDERY made Assistant (Associate) President of Church.

1835, **February 14.** Quorum of the Twelve Apostles organized, Kirtland, OH.

February 28. First Council of the Seventy organized, KIRTLAND, OH.

March 28. Revelation on priesthood (D&C 107) given through Joseph SMITH.

July 3. Michael Chandler exhibited Egyptian mummies and papyrus, KIRTLAND, OH.

July 6. Mummies and papyrus purchased, and Joseph SMITH commenced translation.

August 17. Doctrine and Covenants adopted as standard work of the Church, KIRTLAND.

September. Doctrine and Covenants issued from press in KIRTLAND.

September 14. Emma SMITH appointed to select hymns according to previous revelation (D&C 25).

1836, **January 21.** In KIRTLAND TEMPLE, Joseph SMITH, received vision of celestial kingdom and revelation concerning salvation of the dead (D&C 137). [*See* Visions of Joseph Smith.]

March 27. KIRTLAND TEMPLE dedicated. Outpouring of Spirit of the Lord and presence of angels reported.

April 3. Jesus Christ appeared to Joseph SMITH and Oliver COWDERY, KIRTLAND TEMPLE. Moses, Elias, and Elijah appeared and conveyed priesthood keys (D&C 110).

November 2. Kirtland Safety Society Bank organized. [*See* Kirtland, Ohio: Economy.]

1837, **July 19.** Heber C. KIMBALL and others arrived in Liverpool, England, on first overseas mission. [*See* Missions of Twelve to British Isles.]

July 30. Nine persons baptized in river Ribble, Preston, England. First converts in BRITISH ISLES.

September. *A Voice of Warning* published, New York City, by Parley P. PRATT.

October. The *Elders' Journal* first published in KIRTLAND, OH.

1838, **March 14.** Joseph SMITH established headquarters of Church in FAR WEST, MO.

April 26. Name of the Church—The Church of Jesus Christ of Latter-day Saints—specified by revelation (D&C 115).

May 19. ADAM-ONDI-AHMAN selected as settlement site in Daviess Co., MO.

July 4. Temple cornerstones, FAR WEST, MO, laid. Sidney RIGDON delivered July 4 oration.

July 8. Revelation on tithing received (D&C 119).

August 6. Election-day fight, Gallatin, MO. [*See* Missouri Conflict.]

October 25. Battle of Crooked River, between Missouri State militia and Saints. David W. PATTEN, apostle, slain.

October 27. Missouri Governor Lilburn W. Boggs issued EXTERMINATION ORDER, Jefferson City, MO. (Rescinded June 25, 1976, by Governor Christopher S. Bond.)

October 30. HAUN'S MILL MASSACRE, Caldwell Co., MO.

October 31. Joseph SMITH and other leaders of the Church arrested by Missouri State militia, FAR WEST.

November 9. Joseph SMITH and fellow prisoners arrived at Richmond, MO, and put in chains. Joseph rebuked guards. [*See* Richmond Jail.]

November 13. Joseph F. SMITH (1838–1918) b. FAR WEST, Caldwell Co., MO.

December 1. Joseph SMITH and others imprisoned, LIBERTY JAIL, Liberty, Clay Co., MO.

1839, **February 23.** Many refugee Saints arrived at Quincy, IL, and local citizens adopted relief measures.

March 20–25. Joseph SMITH still imprisoned in LIBERTY JAIL, wrote epistle to Saints (D&C 121, 122, 123).

April 26. Apostles (at great personal risk) gathered at Far West Temple site, to fulfill revelation regarding second apostolic mission to BRITISH ISLES (D&C 118).

May 9–10. Joseph SMITH moved from Quincy to Commerce (later renamed NAUVOO), IL.

August 8. John TAYLOR and Wilford WOODRUFF, the first Apostles to leave Commerce on British mission.

October 29. Joseph SMITH left Commerce for Washington, D.C., to petition U.S. Government for redress of losses in Missouri.

November. First issue of *Times and Seasons* published, Commerce, IL.

1840, **May.** First number of *Millennial Star* published, Manchester, England.

August 15. Baptism for the dead publicly announced by Joseph SMITH.

September 14. Joseph SMITH, Sr., d. NAUVOO, age 69.

December 16. Nauvoo charter signed by Illinois Governor Thomas Carlin.

1841, January 19. Saints commanded to build NAUVOO TEMPLE and NAUVOO HOUSE (D&C 124).

April 6. NAUVOO TEMPLE cornerstones laid.

October 24. Orson HYDE dedicated Palestine for return of Jews.

1842, March 1. Publication of book of Abraham commenced in *Times and Seasons*.

March 1. WENTWORTH LETTER published in *Times and Seasons*. [*See* Appendix 2.]

March 17. Female Relief Society organized, Nauvoo, IL.

May 4. First endowment ordinances given, Red Brick Store, Nauvoo.

August 6. Joseph SMITH prophesied Saints would be driven to Rocky Mountains.

1843, July 12. Revelation on celestial marriage received (D&C 132).

1844, March 11. The General Council (COUNCIL OF FIFTY) organized in Nauvoo.

April 7. KING FOLLETT DISCOURSE delivered by Joseph SMITH.

June 7. NAUVOO EXPOSITOR, anti-Mormon newspaper, published.

June 10. NAUVOO EXPOSITOR declared public nuisance and destroyed.

June 27. Joseph SMITH and Hyrum SMITH martyred in Carthage Jail. [*See* Martyrdom of Joseph & Hyrum Smith.]

August 8. At Church meeting, Nauvoo, mantle of Prophet fell upon senior apostle, Brigham YOUNG. Apostles sustained by people to lead Church.

1845, April 6. The Twelve Apostles issue "Proclamation . . . To all the Kings of the World; To the President of the United States of America; To the Governors of the Several States, And to the Rulers and People of all Nations."

1846, February 4. Nauvoo Saints commenced crossing Mississippi river to move to the Great Basin.

February 4. Ship *Brooklyn* sailed from New York for California with 238 Saints, Samuel Brannan, leader.

May 1. NAUVOO TEMPLE publicly dedicated by Orson HYDE.

June 30. U.S. Army asked Church at COUNCIL BLUFFS, IA, to raise 500 volunteers to fight in war with Mexico.

July 16. MORMON BATTALION mustered into U.S. service.

September 10–17. Battle of Nauvoo fought between remaining Saints and Illinois mob.

1847, **January 14.** Brigham YOUNG received revelation concerning organization of Saints for move west (D&C 136).

April 5. First element of Brigham YOUNG's pioneer company left WINTER QUARTERS on the journey west.

July 21. Orson PRATT and Erastus Snow made first LDS reconnaissance of SALT LAKE VALLEY.

July 24. Brigham YOUNG entered SALT LAKE VALLEY.

July 28. SALT LAKE TEMPLE site selected by Brigham YOUNG.

December 5. Brigham YOUNG unanimously sustained as President of Church by council of Apostles, Kanesville, Pottawattamie Co., IA.

December 27. Conference of Church at Kanesville sustained Brigham YOUNG, Heber C. KIMBALL, Willard Richards as First Presidency.

1848, **June.** Crickets came from mountains into Salt Lake Valley, devastating crops. Fields saved as flocks of SEAGULLS devoured crickets.

1849, **Fall.** PERPETUAL EMIGRATING FUND company established.

December 9. Sunday School organized by Richard Ballantyne.

1850, **June 15.** *Deseret News* began publication in SALT LAKE CITY.

September 20. Brigham YOUNG appointed governor of UTAH TERRITORY by U.S. President Millard Fillmore.

1851, **July 11.** Pearl of Great Price first published, Liverpool, England.

November 1. First issue of *Journal of Discourses* published, Liverpool, England.

November 11. "University of Deseret" opened, SALT LAKE CITY, UTAH.

1852, **August 29.** Public announcement of PLURAL MARRIAGE made, SALT LAKE CITY.

1853, **February 14.** Temple Block consecrated and ground broken, SALT LAKE CITY. [*See* Temple Square.]

April 6. SALT LAKE TEMPLE cornerstones laid under direction of First Presidency.

1855, May 5. Endowment House on Temple Block dedicated at SALT LAKE CITY.

Fast day inaugurated as first Thursday of each month.

1856, May 14. Lucy Mack SMITH, mother of the Prophet Joseph SMITH, d. NAUVOO, age 81.

September 26. First two handcart companies arrived at SALT LAKE CITY, led by Edmund L. Ellsworth and Daniel D. McArthur.

October 28. HANDCART COMPANY of Captain Edward Martin detained by early snow storms. Found by members of rescue company from SALT LAKE VALLEY.

November 9. Captain James G. Willie's HANDCART COMPANY arrived in SALT LAKE CITY. Suffered 67 deaths of a company of 500.

November 22. Heber J. GRANT (1856–1945) b. SALT LAKE CITY.

November 30. Martin HANDCART COMPANY arrived, SALT LAKE CITY. Suffered between 135 and 150 deaths.

1856–1857. "Mormon Reformation." [*See* Reformation (LDS) of 1856–1857.]

1857, May 13. Elder Parley P. PRATT murdered near Van Buren, AK.

July 24. Word received of UTAH EXPEDITION.

August 5. Governor Brigham YOUNG placed UTAH TERRITORY under martial law and forbade U.S. troops to enter Salt Lake Valley.

September 7–11. Emigrating party led by John T. Baker and Alexander Fancher besieged by Indians at Mountain Meadows; killed by Indians and Mormon militia. [*See* Mountain Meadows Massacre.]

1858, May. "Move South" began evacuation of all northern Utah settlements in preparation for war with U.S. troops.

June 11. Peaceful settlement to "Utah War" negotiated through efforts of Brigham YOUNG, Governor Alfred Cumming, Thomas L. KANE, and government peace commissioners.

1862, July 8. Morrill antibigamy bill became law, designed to prevent practice of POLYGAMY IN U.S. Territories. [*See* Antipolygamy Legislation.]

1867, October 6. First general conference held in new Tabernacle, SALT LAKE CITY.

December 8. Relief Society program reemphasized by President Brigham YOUNG, under President Eliza R. SNOW.

1869, March 1. Zion's Cooperative Mercantile Institution (ZCMI), a cooperative business system, began in SALT LAKE CITY.

May 10. Great Pacific Railroad completed by junction of Union Pacific and Central Pacific Railroads, Promontory Summit, UT.

November 28. Young Ladies' Retrenchment Association organized by Brigham YOUNG, forerunner of modern Young Women organization.

1870, April 4. George Albert SMITH (1870–1951) b. SALT LAKE CITY.

August 30. Martin HARRIS (age 88) arrived in SALT LAKE CITY and bore testimony to truth of Book of Mormon at general conference.

1872, June. First issue of *Woman's Exponent* published, SALT LAKE CITY, UTAH.

1873, September 8. David O. MCKAY (1873–1970) b. Huntsville, UT.

1873–1874, Winter. UNITED ORDERS movement established under direction of President Brigham YOUNG.

1875, June 10. Young Men's Mutual Improvement Association organized, forerunner of Young Men Program.

July 10. Martin HARRIS, one of Three Witnesses to the Book of Mormon, d. Clarkston, Cache Co., UT, age 92.

October 16. Brigham Young Academy organized, Provo, UT, first Church academy.

1876, July 19. Joseph Fielding SMITH (1876–1972) b. SALT LAKE CITY.

1877, April 6. St. George Temple dedicated. President Brigham YOUNG received revelation to set in order the Church priesthood organization and stakes of Zion.

August 29. President Brigham YOUNG d. SALT LAKE CITY, age 76.

1878, August 25. Aurelia Spencer ROGERS founded Primary organization, Farmington, UT.

1879, January 6. U.S. Supreme Court upheld 1862 antibigamy law in George Reynolds case. [*See* Antipolygamy Legislation; Reynolds v. United States.]

April 30. Emma Hale SMITH Bidamon d. Nauvoo, IL, age 74.

1880, April 6. Fiftieth year since organization of Church declared Year of Jubilee.

October 10. John TAYLOR sustained President of Church. Pearl of Great Price accepted as standard work.

1882, March 22. Edmunds bill signed into law by President Chester A. Arthur. [*See* Antipolygamy Legislation.]

1887, March 3. Edmunds-Tucker bill became law without signature of President Grover Cleveland. [*See* Antipolygamy Legislation.]

July 25. President John TAYLOR d. in exile, Kaysville, Davis Co., UT.

1889, April 7. Wilford WOODRUFF sustained President of Church.

1890, September 24. President Wilford WOODRUFF received the vision which led to his issuance of the "MANIFESTO" stating PLURAL MARRIAGE officially discontinued in the Church.

October 6. "MANIFESTO" accepted in general conference.

1893, April 6. SALT LAKE TEMPLE, forty years in construction, dedicated by President Wilford WOODRUFF.

1894, April 5. President Wilford WOODRUFF presented to his counselors and quorum of the Twelve a revelation concerning endowments and adoptions.

November 13. Genealogical Society of Utah organized.

1895, March 28. Spencer W. KIMBALL (1895–1985) b. SALT LAKE CITY.

1896, January 4. Utah became U.S. 45th state, proclamation signed by President Grover Cleveland.

April 6. LDS "Political Manifesto" issued at general conference.

December 6. Fast Day changed from first Thursday of month to first Sunday.

1897, November. First issue of *Improvement Era* published.

1898. Publication of first serial *Conference Report.*

September 2. President Wilford WOODRUFF d. San Francisco, CA, age 91.

September 13. Lorenzo SNOW became President of Church.

1899, March 28. Harold B. LEE (1899–1973) b. Clifton, Oneida Co., ID.

May 17. President Lorenzo SNOW received revelation in St. George prompting him to emphasize tithing.

August 4. Ezra Taft BENSON (1899–1994) b. Whitney, Oneida Co., ID.

1901, October 10. President Lorenzo SNOW d. SALT LAKE CITY, age 87.

October 17. Joseph F. SMITH became President of Church.

1902, January. First issue of *Children's Friend* published.

1903, October 15. Brigham Young Academy became Brigham Young University.

1904, April 5. President Joseph F. SMITH issued "Second Manifesto."

1904–1906. U.S. Senate hearings regarding seating of Reed Smoot, an apostle, elected to Senate in 1902. [*See* Smoot Hearings.]

1909, November. First Presidency issued statement on "Origin of Man."

1911. Church adopted Boy Scout program.

1912, Fall. First LDS seminary opened at Granite High School, SALT LAKE CITY.

1915, January. *Relief Society Magazine* began publication.

1916, June 30. First Presidency and Quorum of the Twelve Apostles issued statement on "The Father and the Son."

1917, October 2. Church Administration Building completed.

1918, October 3. President Joseph F. SMITH received "Vision of the Redemption of the Dead" (D&C 138).

November 19. President Joseph F. SMITH d. SALT LAKE CITY, age 80.

November 23. Heber J. GRANT became President of Church.

1922, 6 May. Restored gospel taught by radio for first time as station KZN broadcast message from President Heber J. Grant.

1926, Fall. First institute of religion, Moscow, ID.

1929, July 15. Tabernacle Choir began weekly network radio broadcasts.

1930, April 6. Centennial of Church organization.

1931, April 4. *Church News* section of *Deseret News* began publication.

1936, April 7. Church Security Program instituted to assist poor during Great Depression; became Church Welfare Program.

1938. DESERET INDUSTRIES Program established.

Inauguration of microfilming of genealogical records by Genealogical Society.

1941, April 6. Assistants to the Twelve first called.

1945, May 14. President Heber J. GRANT d. SALT LAKE CITY, age 88.

May 21. George Albert SMITH became President of Church.

1946, February. Elder Ezra Taft BENSON left to administer to physical and spiritual needs of European Saints after World War II.

1947. Church membership reached 1 million.

July 24. Centennial of Pioneer entry into SALT LAKE VALLEY.

1951, April 4. President George Albert SMITH d. SALT LAKE CITY, age 81.

April 9. David O. MCKAY sustained President of Church.

1952, November 25. Elder Ezra Taft BENSON, apostle, appointed U.S. secretary of agriculture by President Dwight D. Eisenhower.

1955, February 12. President David O. MCKAY broke ground for Church College of Hawaii.

1961, October. All-Church Coordinating Council established to correlate curriculum and activities for children, youth, and adults.

1963. Church membership reached 2 million.

March 7. Stake Presidencies also became presidencies of stake high priests quorums.

1964, October. Observance of Family Home Evening reemphasized.

1965, January. Home Evening program manual placed in homes.

1966. Uniform Church Curriculum year inaugurated; all organizations begin curriculum year at same time.

1967, September 29. First Regional Representatives called, to begin January 1, 1968.

1969, August 3–8. First World Conference on Records held, SALT LAKE CITY.

1970, January 18. President David O. MCKAY d. SALT LAKE CITY, age 96.

January 23. Joseph Fielding SMITH became President of Church.

1971. Church membership reached 3 million.

January. New Church magazines, *Ensign, New Era,* and *Friend* commenced publication.

August 27–29. First Area Conference held, Manchester, England.

1972, July 2. President Joseph Fielding SMITH d. SALT LAKE CITY, age 95.

July 7. Harold B. LEE became president of the church.

1973, December 26. President Harold B. LEE d. SALT LAKE CITY, age 74.

December 30. Spencer W. KIMBALL became President of the Church.

1974. Church-owned hospitals divested.

1975, **July 24.** The 28-story Church Office Building dedicated, SALT LAKE CITY.

October 3. President Spencer W. KIMBALL announced organization of First Quorum of Seventy.

1976, **April 3.** Two revelations added to Pearl of Great Price. Later became D&C 137 and D&C 138, 1981.

October 1. Assistants to the Twelve made Seventies.

1978. Church membership reached 4 million.

June 8. First Presidency issued letter announcing revelation granting the priesthood to worthy men of all races.

September 16. First annual women's meeting held.

September 30. June 8 revelation on priesthood sustained by church; "emeritus" status announced for General Authorities other than First Presidency and Twelve.

1979, **February 18.** The 1,000th stake of the Church organized, Nauvoo, IL, by Ezra Taft BENSON, President of the Twelve.

August. LDS edition of King James Bible with study helps published.

1980, **March 2.** Consolidated ward meeting schedule inaugurated in Church units in U.S., Canada.

April 6. Church sesquicentennial general conference held, with commemorative activities.

1981. Announcement made of network of satellite receiving dishes or "downlink" antennas for stake centers outside Utah for receiving Church broadcasts.

September 26. New editions of Book of Mormon, Doctrine and Covenants, Pearl of Great Price published.

1982. Church membership reached 5 million.

1983. Stake welfare properties placed under general Church control.

1984, **April.** Genealogical management system for home computers, Personal Ancestral File, made available.

June. Area presidencies inaugurated, with members called from the Seventies.

April 4. Museum of Church History and Art dedicated, SALT LAKE CITY, UTAH.

October 28. The 1,500th Church stake organized, Ciudad Obregon Mexico Yaqui Stake.

1985, **August 2.** Revised LDS Hymnbook published.

October 23. The Family History Library dedicated.

November 5. President Spencer W. KIMBALL d. SALT LAKE CITY, age 90.

November 10. Ezra Taft BENSON became President of Church.

1986. Church membership reached 6 million.

October 4. Seventies quorums in stakes were discontinued.

1987, **February 15.** Tabernacle Choir performed 3,000th radio broadcast.

July 24–26. 150th anniversary of first missionary labors in Britain celebrated.

1989. Church membership reached 7 million.

April 1. Second Quorum of Seventy organized.

May 16. BYU Jerusalem Center dedicated by Howard W. Hunter, President of the Twelve.

1990, **September 13.** Registration of Leningrad Branch of Church approved by Soviet government.

December. Number of missionaries serving reached 43,651.

1991. Church membership exceeded 8 million members.

June. Mormon Tabernacle Choir toured Eastern Europe.

June 24. The Russian Republic, the largest republic in the Soviet Union, granted official recognition to the Church.

APPENDIX 2

The Wentworth Letter

The Prophet Joseph Smith explained the origin of the WENTWORTH LETTER as follows:

> At the request of Mr. John Wentworth, Editor and Proprietor of the *Chicago Democrat*, I have written the following sketch of the rise, progress, persecution, and faith of the Latter-day Saints, of which I have the honor, under God, of being the founder. Mr. Wentworth says that he wishes to furnish Mr. Bastow [Barstow?], a friend of his, who is writing the history of New Hampshire, with this document. As Mr. Bastow has taken the proper steps to obtain correct information, all that I shall ask at his hands, is, that he publish the account entire, ungarnished, and without misrepresentation. [*Times and Seasons*, III, 9, p. 706.]

Following is the complete text of the letter as published in the *Times and Seasons*, III, 9, 706–710, March 1, 1842, Nauvoo, Illinois. (Original spelling and punctuation are preserved; however, obvious errors are corrected in brackets.)

> I was born in the town of Sharon Windsor co., Vermont, on the 23d of December, A.D. 1805. When ten years old my parents removed to Palmyra New York, where we resided about four years, and from thence we removed to the town of Manchester.
>
> My father was a farmer and taught me the art of husbandry. When about fourteen years of age, I began to reflect upon the importance of being prepared for a future state, and upon inquiring the plan of salvation, I found that there was a great clash in religious sentiment; if I went to one society they referred me to one plan, and another to another; each one pointing to his own particular creed as the summum bonum of perfection: considering that all could not be right, and that God could not be the author of so much confusion I determined to investigate the sub-

ject more fully, believing that if God had a church it would not be split up into factions, and that if he taught one society to worship one way, and administer in one set of ordinances, he would not teach another, principles which were diametrically opposed. Believing the word of God I had confidence in the declaration of James; "If any man lack wisdom let him ask of God who giveth to all men liberally and upbraideth not and it shall be given him," I retired to a secret place in a grove and began to call upon the Lord, while fervently engaged in supplication my mind was taken away from the objects with which I was surrounded, and I was enwrapped in a heavenly vision, and saw two glorious personages, who exactly resembled each other in features and likeness, surrounded with a brilliant light which eclipsed the sun at noon-day. They told me that all religious denominations were believing in incorrect doctrines, and that none of them was acknowledged of God as his Church and kingdom. And I was expressly commanded to "go not after them," at the same time receiving a promise that the fulness of the Gospel should at some future time be made known unto me.

On the evening on the 21st of September, A.D. 1823, while I was praying unto God, and endeavoring to exercise faith in the precious promises of scripture on a sudden a light like that of day, only of a far purer and more glorious appearance and brightness burst into the room, indeed the first sight was as though the house was filled with consuming fire; the appearance produced a shock that affected the whole body; in a moment a personage stood before me surrounded with a glory yet greater than that with which I was already surrounded. This messenger proclaimed himself to be an angel of God, sent to bring the joyful tidings, that the covenant which God made with ancient Israel was at hand to be fulfilled, that the preparatory work for the second coming of the Messiah was speedily to commence; that the time was at hand for the gospel in all its fulness to be preached in power, unto all nations that a people might be prepared for the millennial reign.

I was informed that I was chosen to be an instrument in the hands of God to bring about some of his purposes in this glorious dispensation.

I was also informed concerning the aboriginal inhabitants of this country, and shown who they were, and from whence they came; a brief sketch of their origin, progress, civilization, laws, governments, of their righteousness and iniquity, and the blessings of God being finally withdrawn from them as a people, was made known unto me; I was also told where were deposited some plates on which were engraven an abridgment of the records of the ancient prophets that had existed on this continent. The angel appeared to me three times the same night and unfolded the same things. After having received many visits from the angels of God unfolding the majesty, and glory of the events that should transpire in the last days, on the morning of the 22d of September, A.D. 1827, the angel of the Lord delivered the records into my hands.

These records were engraven on plates which had the appearance of gold, each plate was six inches wide and eight inches long, and not quite so thick as common tin. They were filled with engravings, in Egyptian characters and bound together in a volume as the leaves of a book with three rings running through the whole. The volume was something near six inches in thickness, a part of which was sealed. The characters on the unsealed part were small, and beautifully engraved. The whole book exhibited many marks of antiquity in its construction and much skill in the art of engraving. With the records was found a curious instrument which the ancients called "Urim and Thummim," which consisted of two transparent stones set in the rim of a bow fastened to a breast plate.

Through the medium of the Urim and Thummim I translated the record by the gift and power of God.

In this important and interesting book the history of ancient America is unfolded, from its first settlement by a colony that came from the Tower of Babel, at the confusion of languages to the beginning of the fifth century of the Christian era. We are informed by these records that America in ancient times has been inhabited by two distinct races of people. The first were called Jaredites, and came directly from the tower of Babel. The second race came directly from the city of Jerusalem, about six hundred years before Christ. They were principally Israelites, of the descendants of Joseph. The Jaredites were destroyed about the time that the Israelites came from Jerusalem, who succeeded them in the inheritance of the country. The principal nation of the second race fell in battle towards the close of the fourth century. The remnant are the Indians that now inhabit this country. This book also tells us that our Saviour made his appearance upon this continent after his resurrection, that he planted the gospel here in all its fulness, and richness, and power, and blessing; that they had apostles, prophets, pastors, teachers, and evangelists; the same order, the same priesthood, the same ordinances, gifts, powers, and blessings, as was enjoyed on the eastern continent, that the people were cut off in consequence of their transgressions, that the last of their prophets who existed among them was commanded to write an abridgment of their prophecies, history, &c., and to hide it up in the earth, and that it should come forth and be united with the Bible for the accomplishment of the purposes of God in the last days. For a more particular account I would refer to the Book of Mormon, which can be purchased at Nauvoo, or from any of our traveling elders.

As soon as the news of this discovery was made known, false reports, misrepresentation and slander flew as on the wings of the wind, in every direction, the house was frequently beset by mobs, and evil designing persons, several times I was shot at, and very narrowly escaped, and every device was made use of to get the plates away from me, but the power and blessing of God attended me, and several began to believe my testimony.

On the 6th of April, 1830, the "Church of Jesus Christ of Latter-Day Saints," was first organized in the town of Manchester, Ontario co., [Fayette, Seneca County] state of New York. Some few were called and ordained by the Spirit of revelation, and prophecy, and began to preach as the spirit gave them utterance, and though weak, yet were they strengthened by the power of God, and many were brought to repentance, were immersed in the water, and were filled with the Holy Ghost by the laying on of hands. They saw visions and prophesied, devils were cast out, and the sick healed by the laying on of hands. From that time the work rolled forth with astonishing rapidity, and churches were soon formed in the states of New York, Pennsylvania, Ohio, Indiana, Illinois, and Missouri; in the last named state a considerable settlement was formed in Jackson co.; numbers joined the Church and we were increasing rapidly; we made large purchases of land, our farms teemed with plenty, and peace and happiness was enjoyed in our domestic circle and throughout our neighborhood; but as we could not associate with our neighbors who were, many of them, of the basest of men, and had fled from the face of civilized society, to the frontier country to escape the hand of justice, in their midnight revels, their sabbath breaking, horseracing and gambling; they commenced at first to ridicule, then to persecute and finally an organized mob assembled and burned our houses, tarred, and feathered, and whipped many of our brethren and finally drove them from their habitations; who, houseless, and homeless, contrary to law, justice and humanity, had to wander on the bleak prairies till the children left the tracks of their blood on the prairie, this took place in the month of November, and they had no other covering but the canopy of heaven, in this inclement season of the year; this proceeding was winked at by the government, and although we had warrantee deeds for our land, and had violated no law we could obtain no redress.

There were many sick, who were thus inhumanly driven from their houses, and had to endure all this abuse and to seek homes where they could be found. The result was, that a great many of them being deprived of the comforts of life, and the necessary attendances, died; many children were left orphans, wives, widows and husbands, widowers. Our farms were taken possession of by the mob, many thousands of cattle, sheep, horses and hogs were taken and our household goods, store goods, and printing press and type were broken, taken, or otherwise destroyed.

Many of our brethren removed to Clay where they continued until 1836, three years; there was no violence offered, but there were threatenings of violence. But in the summer of 1836 these threatenings began to assume a more serious form; from threats, public meetings were called, resolutions were passed, vengeance and destruction were threatened, and affairs again assumed a fearful attitude, Jackson County was a sufficient precedent, and as the authorities in that county did not interfere, they boasted that they would not in this, which on application to the authorities we found to be too true, and after much violence, privation and loss of property we were again driven from our homes.

We next settled in Caldwell, and Daviess counties, where we made large and extensive settlements, thinking to free ourselves from the power of oppression, by settling in new counties, with very few inhabitants in them; but here we were not allowed to live in peace, but in 1838 we were again attacked by mobs, an exterminating order was issued by Gov. Boggs, and under the sanction of law an organized banditti ranged through the country, robbed us of our cattle, sheep, hogs, &c., many of our people were murdered in cold blood, the chastity of our women was violated, and we were forced to sign away our property at the point of the sword, and after enduring every indignity that could be heaped upon us by an inhuman, ungodly band of marauders, from twelve to fifteen thousand souls, men, women, and children were driven from their own fire sides, and from lands that they had warrantee deeds of, houseless, friendless, and homeless (in the depths of winter,) to wander as exiles on the earth or to seek an asylum in a more genial clime, and among a less barbarous people.

Many sickened and died, in consequence of the cold, and hardships they had to endure; many wives were left widows, and children orphans, and destitute. It would take more time than is allotted me here to describe the injustice, the wrongs, the murders, the bloodshed, the theft, misery and woe that have been caused by the barbarous, inhuman, and lawless proceedings of the state of Missouri.

In the situation before alluded to we arrived in the state of Illinois in 1839, where we found a hospitable people and a friendly home; a people who were willing to be governed by the principles of law and humanity. We have commenced to build a city called "Nauvoo," in Hancock co., we number from six to eight thousand here, besides vast numbers in the county around and in almost every county of the state. We have a city charter granted us and charter for a legion the troops of which now number 1500. We have also a charter for a university, for an agricultural and manufacturing society, have our own laws and administrators, and possess all the privileges that other free and enlightened citizens enjoy.

Persecution has not stopped the progress of truth, but has only added fuel to the flame, it has spread with increasing rapidity, proud of the cause which they have espoused, and conscious of our innocence, and of the truth of their system, amidst calumny and reproach have the elders of this church gone forth, and planted the gospel in almost every state in the Union; it has penetrated our cities, it has spread over our villages, and has caused thousands of our intelligent, noble, and patriotic citizens to obey its divine mandates, and be governed by its sacred truths. It has also spread into England, Ireland, Scotland, and Wales: in the year of 1839 [and 1840] where a few of our missionaries were sent, and over five thousand joined the standard of truth; there are numbers now joining in every land.

Our missionaries are going forth to different nations, and in Germany, Palestine, New Holland, the East Indies, and other places, the standard of truth has been erected; no unhallowed hand can stop the work from progressing; persecutions may rage, mobs may combine, armies may assemble, calumny may defame, but the truth of God will go forth boldly, nobly, and independent, till it has penetrated every continent, visited every clime, swept every country, and sounded in every ear, till the purposes of God shall be accomplished and the great Jehovah shall say the work is done.

We believe in God the Eternal Father, and in his son Jesus Christ, and in the Holy Ghost.

We believe that men will be punished for their own sins and not for Adam's transgression.

We believe that through the atonement of Christ all mankind may be saved by obedience to the laws and ordinances of the Gospel.

We believe that these ordinances are: 1st, Faith in the Lord Jesus Christ; 2d, Repentance; 3d, Baptism by immersion for the remission of sins; 4th, Laying on of hands for the gift of the Holy Ghost.

We believe that a man must be called of God by "prophesy and by the laying on hands" by those who are in authority to preach the gospel and administer in the ordinances thereof.

We believe in the same organization that existed in the primitive Church, viz: apostles, prophets, pastors, teachers, evangelists &c.

We believe in the gift of tongues, prophecy, revelation, visions, healing, interpretation of tongues, &c.

We believe the Bible to be the word of God as far as it is translated correctly; we also believe the Book of Mormon to be the word of God.

We believe all that God has revealed, all that he does now reveal, and we believe that he will yet reveal many great and important things pertaining to the kingdom of God.

We believe in the literal gathering of Israel and in the restoration of the Ten Tribes. That Zion will be built upon this continent. That Christ will reign personally upon the earth, and that the earth will be renewed and receive its paradasaic glory.

We claim the privilege of worshiping Almighty God according to the dictates of our conscience, and allow all men the same privilege let them worship how, where, or what they may.

We believe in being subject to kings, presidents, rulers and magistrates, in obeying honoring, and sustaining the law.

We believe in being honest, true, chaste, benevolent, virtuous, and in doing good to *all men*; indeed we may say that we follow the admonition of Paul, "we believe all things, we hope all things," we have endured many things, and hope to be able to endure all things. If there is anything virtuous, lovely, or of good report, or praiseworthy, we seek after these things. Respectfully, &c.,

JOSEPH SMITH.

See also: Jessee, Dean C. (comp. and ed.). *The Personal Writings of Joseph Smith*, pp. 212–220, Salt Lake City, 1984. Jessee also includes other background information to the letter.

INDEX